STUDIES IN BIBLICAL INTERPRETATION

JPS דור דור
SCHOLAR ודורשיו
OF DISTINCTION
SERIES

NAHUM M. SARNA

STUDIES IN BIBLICAL INTERPRETATION

THE JEWISH PUBLICATION SOCIETY

Philadelphia   *2000 • 5760*

The Jewish Publication Society
2100 Arch Street, 2nd Floor
Philadelphia, PA 19103-1399
Composition by Varda Graphics, Inc.
Design by Adrianne Onderdonk Dudden
Manufactured in the United States of America

09 08 07 06 05 04 03 02 01 00 10 9 8 7 6 5 4 3 2 1

Publisher's Note:
With few exceptions, the articles in this anthology are as they appeared in their original. As a result, there are variations in spelling and language style from piece to piece.

Library of Congress Cataloging-in-Publication Data

Sarna, Nahum M.
Studies in biblical interpretation / Nahum M. Sarna.—1 st ed.
p. cm. — (JPS scholar of distinction series)
Includes bibliographical references and index.
ISBN 0-8276-0689-3
1. Bible. O.T.—Criticism, interpretation, etc. 2. Bible. O.T.—Criticism, interpretation, etc., Jewish—History. I. Title. II. Series.
BS1171.2 .S25 2000
221.6—dc21

To Helen

*The Jewish Publication Society wishes
to acknowledge the generosity of*

The Lucius N. Littauer Foundation

in support of the publication of this volume.

Contents

Foreword   ix
Preface   xxi
Acknowledgments   xxiii

ESSAYS ON BIBLICAL AND RELATED TOPICS

The Divine Title *'abhîr ya'ăqôbh*   3
Paganism and Biblical Judaism   13
The Biblical Sources for the History of the Monarchy   29
Ancient Libraries and the Ordering of the Biblical Books   53
The Authority and Interpretation of Scripture
    in Jewish Tradition   67
Hebrew and Bible Studies in Medieval Spain   81
Rashi the Commentator   127
Abraham Ibn Ezra as an Exegete   139
Abraham Geiger and Biblical Scholarship   161
Jewish Bible Scholarship and Translations
    in the United States   173

TORAH

The Anticipatory Use of Information
    as a Literary Feature of the Genesis Narratives   211
Genesis 21:33: A Study in the Development
    of a Biblical Text and Its Rabbinic Transformation   221
The Decalogue   229
Introduction to the Hilleli Manuscript   239
Writing a Commentary on the Torah   253

PROPHETS

Naboth's Vineyard Revisited (1 Kings 21)   271
The Abortive Insurrection in Zedekiah's Day (Jeremiah 27–29)   281
Zedekiah's Emancipation of Slaves and the Sabbatical Year   295
Ezekiel 8:17: A Fresh Examination   305

WRITINGS

Prolegomenon to the Psalms   313
The Psalm Superscriptions and the Guilds   335
Legal Terminology in Psalm 3:8   357
Psalm XIX and the Near Eastern Sun-God Literature   365
Psalm 89: A Study in Inner Biblical Exegesis   377
The Psalm for the Sabbath Day (Psalm 92)   395
Epic Substratum in the Prose of Job   411
The Mythological Background of Job 18   425

Bibliography of the Published Writings of Nahum M. Sarna   431
List of Biblical Passages Cited   437
Index   447

Foreword

I

The invitation to write a foreword to this collection of Nahum M. Sarna's studies was an occasion of delight for me. Ever since I studied with him at the Jewish Theological Seminary in the 1960s, I have found Prof. Sarna an inspiring model of *Torah 'im derekh 'eretz,* scholarship combined with *mentschlichkeit.* Rereading the studies that he selected for this volume was an opportunity to experience again the lucidity of his thought, the breadth and insight of his scholarship, his exegetical acumen, and his unsurpassed sensitivity to the ethical and spiritual dimensions of the Bible and its commentaries.

Nahum Sarna is a distinguished member of a small group of American and Israeli scholars who guided Jewish biblical scholarship to maturity in the second half of the twentieth century. As he notes in the preface to this volume, two of the major stimuli for the growth of modern Jewish biblical scholarship have been "research into the languages, literatures, history, religions, cultures, and archaeology of the ancient Near East" and creative research into the rich Jewish exegetical tradition. Sarna and his contemporaries united these two resources in a harmonious blend that is common, even if not universal, today. Yet, this was not always the case.

For reasons that Sarna discusses in "Abraham Geiger and Biblical Scholarship" (1975), when the Jüdische Wissenschaft movement inaugurated the academic study of Judaism in the nineteenth century, it avoided biblical studies altogether. When Jewish academic scholars did take up the study of the Bible at the end of that century and in the first half of the twentieth century, they were largely stimulated by archaeology and Semitic studies. Although there were exceptions, most made little use of postbiblical Jewish resources in their exposition of the Bible. It was Sarna and his contemporaries, thoroughly trained in postbiblical Judaica as well as ancient Near Eastern languages and literatures, who showed how illuminating this combination of fields can be. It is not only that postbiblical learning provides a valuable resource for understanding the Bible's original meaning, though that is a very important aspect of their methodology; it is a broader vision of what Jewish biblical scholarship should embrace. Citing Gershom Scholem's observation that "Commentary on Scripture became the characteristic expression of Jewish thinking about truth," Sarna spells out this vision in his prescription for a biblical commentary:

> commentary cannot be confined solely to elucidating the text by attempting to rescue the supposed "original meaning". . . through recourse to philological research and recovery of the contemporary cultural milieu in which the works were authored. This approach is without doubt indispensable. It is the *sine qua non* and starting point of any modern interpretive endeavor. But to believe that this alone is determinative is to commit what literary critics call the "intentional fallacy." Throughout the millennia Jewish interpretation of the Hebrew Bible was informed by the abiding consciousness that it was the major source for the national language, the font of all Jewish values, ideals and hopes, and the fountainhead of inspiration for the distinctive lifestyle of the Jew. . . . The literature of Biblical interpretation itself became an essential propaedeutic discipline for the cultivated Jew. This vast, inexhaustible store of exegetical material reinforced and enhanced the study of Tanakh [Bible] as a religious obligation, a spiritual exercise, a mode of worship, and a moral training. ("Writing a Commentary" [1990])

The study of the Bible as "a spiritual exercise. . . and a moral training" is a pervasive theme in Sarna's writings. Repeatedly he shows how God's morality is inherent in the monotheistic idea and how the corollary, that "there is an intimate, in fact, inextricable connection between the sociomoral condition of a people and its ultimate fate," underlies the biblical interpretation of history (*Understanding Genesis*, p. 146). These observations underlie many of Sarna's exegetical insights. In "The Decalogue" (1982) he notes that the Ten Commandments begin with "I am the Lord your God" and conclude with "your neighbor." This framing reflects the Decalogue's interweaving of religious and sociomoral duties. Alone in the ancient world, Israelite law is not strictly secular but treats life holistically: moral offenses against others are simultaneously religious offenses because all are infractions of the divine will. The Decalogue states its injunctions and prohibitions categorically, without specific penalties for violations, because the motivation for observing the law is not—or should not be—fear of punishment but the desire to conform to God's will. Since human society is not utopian, however, the coercive power of the state is indispensable, and elsewhere in the Torah laws with specific penalties are the general rule. In connection with the Psalms he notes that Psalm 1 was placed first in the Psalter, in part because it affirms that "the lives of human beings are ultimately governed by a divinely ordained, universal moral order," an affirmation "that constitutes the ideological basis for any meaningful appeal to God" (*Songs of the Heart*, p. 29). Psalm 92, which does not mention the Sabbath but is recited on that day, must have been selected for that purpose because it interweaves allusions to two central themes of the Sabbath: the creation of the world (vv. 5–9) and justice and righteousness (vv. 8–16), themes which Sarna shows are themselves connected elsewhere in the Bible ("The Psalm for the Sabbath Day" [1962]).

Sarna is a strong comparativist, using ancient Near Eastern studies in a variety of ways. This is evident in all of his books as well as the present volume. He clarifies countless passages in the Bible by reference to ancient Near Eastern literature. In "Epic Substratum in the Prose of Job" (1957) he shows that the prose narrative in the prologue and epilogue of the Book of Job shares so many stylistic, linguistic, and literary features with ancient Ugaritic poetry that it must have been based on an earlier epic poem about Job. By extensive comparison of Psalm 19 with Egyptian and Babylonian literature about the sun-god he shows that the two parts of the psalm use the standard terminology of ancient Near Eastern sun-god literature to praise God and the Torah. But Sarna insists that the point of comparing the Bible and ancient Near Eastern literature is not only to show the similarities but also the differences, which are at least as important an index of cultural configuration. Psalm 19, he argues, is an anti-sun-god polemic that reduces the sun to one of God's creations and shows that all of its attributes belong instead to God and His Torah ("Psalm XIX and the Near Eastern Sun-God Literature" [1967]). Such creative use of ancient Near Eastern motifs by the Bible is a theme that Sarna points out frequently: Scripture uses materials from ancient Israel's polytheistic neighbors willingly, but never slavishly, always adapting them to biblical beliefs and values. Frequently, as in the psalm, the Bible engages in subtle antipagan polemic, a theme explored in depth in "Paganism and Biblical Judaism" (1977). The Bible's departure from contemporary values is also reflected in its attitude toward the monarchy: Ahab's inability to simply confiscate Naboth's vineyard shows that crown rights in Israel were severely limited in comparison to those of neighboring states ("Naboth's Vineyard" [1997]), and biblical historiography criticizes the kings, rather than glorify them as did that of Egypt and Mesopotamia ("The Biblical Sources for the History of the Monarchy" [1979]). Sarna, following the Israeli scholar Yehezkel Kaufmann (see below) is convinced that, for all of its indebtedness to the ancient world, the Bible constituted a revolutionary break with its moral and spiritual values, and that therein lies its greatness and its impact on history.

Sarna's scholarship is characterized by a strong literary orientation, ferreting out the unifying compositional strategies, recurring motifs, and structure of the biblical text as he explicates it. These aims help explain his reservations about the usefulness of source criticism, the scholarly method that seeks to identify earlier literary sources used in the composition of biblical books. He has certainly recognized the validity of the method in principle. "In its general outlines, the nonunitary origin of the Pentateuch has survived as one of the finalities of biblical scholarship," and isolating the components is indispensable for appreciating the qualities produced when they were combined and harmonized. Nor does Sarna see this as a problem for religious faith. God can work through four documents as effectively as through one, unfolding His revelation in successive stages as well as in a single moment of time (he notes that even the most traditional Jew must admit that this happened in the case of the second division of the Bible, the Prophets, which developed over several centuries). Nevertheless he holds, like Franz Rosenzweig, that "source differentiation . . . alone is inadequate to the appreciation of the Bible as a religious document. . . . Things in combination possess properties and produce qualities neither carried by, nor inherent in, any of the components in isolation. . . . [T]he inspired genius at work behind the interweaving of the originally disparate elements is ultimately of greater significance," and it is only as an integrated whole that the Bible had its impact on Jewish history (*Understanding Genesis*, pp. xxiv f.; "The Bible and Judaic Studies" [1970]*, pp. 39f.). Sarna became increasingly convinced—apparently as he began writing his commentaries—that source criticism is in any case overly hypothetical and of limited value, and that what the final text says is more interesting than its history. Hence, his commentaries are not based on "dissecting a literary corpse," but are concerned with the Bible as "a living literature and a dynamic force in history" (*Genesis: The JPS Torah Commentary*, pp. xvii-xviii; Sarna applies the same approach in his articles on Psalms 19 and 89 [1967 and 1963]; see also "The Anticipatory Use of Information" [1981]).

A number of Sarna's studies, particularly in the "History" section of this volume, illustrate how the Bible functioned as a dynamic force, indeed "as a living organism that perpetually rejuvenates and transforms itself" ("Authority and Interpretation" [1987]). Building on the observation of Wilhelm Bacher, the great historian of Jewish biblical exegesis, that biblical exegesis is "the one indigenous science created and developed by Israel," Sarna shows that parts of the Bible, both legal and non-legal, were already reinterpreted during the pre-exilic period ("Psalm 89: A Study in Inner Biblical Exegesis" [1963], a seminal article in stimulating current scholarly interest in the subject; "Zedekiah's Emancipation" [1973]). The commentators of the talmudic and medieval periods continued the process. In a typical example, the midrash transforms the enigmatic account in Genesis 21:33 about Abraham planting a tree and worshiping God beside it into an account of how he established a hospice for providing wayfarers with food and shelter. In this way the rabbis made the account exemplify man's sociomoral duties and they elevated the provision of wayfarers into a mode of worshiping God ("Genesis 21:33" [1989]). As Sarna shows in "Authority and Interpretation" [1987]), the rabbis did not shy away from criticizing the morality of biblical heroes. Implicitly they seem to have felt that the written text is not the exclusive source of religious truth, but rather the foundation upon which the edifice of moral truth may be constructed. Or, as they might have preferred to put it: no single passage, but the biblical canon as a whole, functions as normative.

If the commentators appear to be assuming a stance outside of and over against the text, if they appear to leave room for the play of the intellect and the role of conscience and of moral sensibilities, then it must be appreciated that it is the Hebrew Bible itself *in its entirety* [emphasis added— J.H.T.], as a composite work, that developed and honed these faculties, and that sensitized men to the critical standards to which that same text is now being subjected. The claim is that the commentators are simply actualizing what is potentially there all along, but what is potential can be discerned only through a unitary, comprehensive, holistic approach.

Interestingly enough, medieval Jewish commentators often criticized midrashic exegesis, and some observed that the rabbis' interpretation of biblical laws did not accord with their plain meaning. These commentators were fully committed to the halakhic way of life and did not question the rabbis' rulings, only their exegetical derivation. They seemed to hold that the halakhah is an autonomous discipline, independent of exegesis, and the commentator is therefore free to investigate the Bible independently of dogmatic or traditional considerations. Their freedom and intellectual honesty point to a separation of scholarship from matters of faith and law, "a distinction that, alas, is often blurred today." In fact, says Sarna, we have no reason to assume that the medieval Jewish exegetes would necessarily have rejected the critical views of modern scholarship.

> The medieval scholars made the most of all the limited tools at their disposal. But they did not have access, naturally, to the modern sciences of literary and textual criticism and to the disciplines of sociology, anthropology, linguistics, and comparative religion. We simply do not know how they would have reacted had all this material been available to them. To assume a blind disregard of evidence on their part is as unwarranted as it is unfair. (*Understanding Genesis*, p. xxii; "Modern Study of the Bible" [1983]*, p. 27).

The pluralism of the Jewish exegetical tradition, its refusal to absolutize any single stance, is an important theme to Sarna. To him, one of the noblest expressions of rabbinic Judaism is the *Mikra'ot Gedolot*, the Great Rabbinic Bible in which

> [t]he Hebrew text is surrounded by a sea of commentaries of diverse authorship, provenance, dating and exegetical approaches, often mutually incompatible and contradictory. They coexist within the confines of a single page, all accommodated within the framework of a single tradition. ("Writing a Commentary" [1990]).

It would be impossible in the space available to call attention to the contents or highlights of all twenty-seven articles presented in this volume. Let me briefly call attention to a few more of my favorites. The first two papers in the "Psalms" section, surveying the history of research on the Psalms and identifying the groups of musicians who composed and preserved them, are important companion pieces to Sarna's magnificent *Songs of the Heart* (as is his *Encyclopaedia Judaica* article "Psalms" [1972]*). In "Ezekiel 8:17" (1964) Sarna proposes that the puzzling word *zemorah* refers to bands of thugs hired by the rich to dispossess the poor; this calls attention to a "Wild West" aspect of life in ancient Israel. Comments in "Biblical Sources" (1979) and elsewhere discuss the relationship between historicity and the message of the Bible (see also *Understanding Genesis*, p. 52 and, in connection with the fantastic life spans in Genesis, pp. 81–85). "Ancient Libraries and the Ordering of the Biblical Books" (1989), concerning the order prescribed in the Babylonian Talmud for the books of the Bible, discusses the meaning of order in a period when the books of the Bible were written on separate scrolls. "Authority and Interpretation" (1987), cited above, explains why Jewish Bibles place the Book of Chronicles last whereas Malachi comes last in the "Old Testament" of Christian Bibles. One of the most valuable articles is Sarna's magisterial study of "Hebrew and Bible Studies in Medieval Spain" (1971). It shows that even such basic facts as the triliteral character of Hebrew roots were not discovered until the Middle Ages. On the other hand, various linguistic and literary phenomena that were discovered by modern scholarship were already recognized by the medievals (see also "The Interchange of the Prepositions *Beth* and *Min*" [1959]*). The fascinating study "Jewish Bible Scholarship and Translations in the United States" (1988), co-authored with Sarna's son Jonathan, a distinguished historian of American Jewry, explains, among other things, why it was necessary for Jews to produce their own English translations of the Bible. And, finally, there is Sarna's retelling, at the end of the last chapter of this book, of Immanuel of Rome's visionary tour of Heaven and Hell and his discovery of the fate awaiting biblical scholars!

II

Prof. Sarna's approach to scholarship is a distillation of educational experiences that began as far back as he can remember. He was born in

London on March 27, 1923 (10 Nisan, 5683) to Jacob and Millie (née Horonzick) Sarna. His father, a learned Jewish book dealer who knew the German classics as well as Jewish literature, filled his home with books. Sarna was born there, fittingly, in a book-lined room and was taught Bible stories from a young age. His father was also a Zionist leader (Sarna's middle name, Mattityahu, the Hebrew equivalent of Theodor, was chosen in honor of Theodor Herzl). As a youngster Sarna met Jewish leaders and scholars, such as Chaim Weizmann, Vladimir Jabotinsky, Moses Gaster, and Benjamin Maisler (Mazar), who visited his home.

While in elementary school Sarna also attended an intensive Talmud Torah (after-hours Hebrew school) for some thirteen hours a week. He later attended London's all-day Jewish Secondary School which taught both Jewish and secular studies, and he spent an additional two hours a day studying Talmud at a yeshiva. At age sixteen he matriculated at the University of London, having already learned Latin and the English classics and read Edward Gibbon's *The Decline and Fall of the Roman Empire*. At the University he studied Rabbinics and Semitics, Bible at Jews' College (London's rabbinical seminary, then a part of the University), general studies at University College, and medieval Hebrew and Arabic in the School of Oriental and African Studies. He received his B.A. with first class honors in 1944, his M.A. in Rabbinic Literature and Languages from the University of London in 1946, and his ordination from Jews' College in 1947. His teachers included Isidore Epstein, Arthur Marmorstein, and Cecil Roth. It was in those years that he discovered Yehezkel Kaufmann, whose writings he found in his father's library after hearing about them from an Orthodox rabbi (though Kaufmann's views are decidedly un-Orthodox). Reading Kaufmann's *Toledot ha-Emunah ha-Yisre'elit (The History of Israelite Religion* opened Sarna's eyes to modern biblical scholarship and exercised a profound influence on him (see "From Wellhausen to Kaufmann" [1961]* and "Ruminations" [1988]*).

Nineteen forty-seven was also the year Sarna married Helen Horowitz, whom he met when the two were teenagers in a religious Zionist youth movement. He was her first Hebrew teacher, and she went on to become a learned Hebraist and Judaica librarian and to maintain an active involvement in all of Sarna's work. The Sarnas' sons David and Jonathan were born, respectively, in 1949 and 1955.

During his student years Sarna's main field was rabbinic literature, and he had a particular interest in the Geonic literature of the post-talmudic period. But after receiving his B.A. and being appointed Instructor (later Lecturer) of Hebrew and Bible at University College, he began to realize that one could not do justice to the Bible without a firsthand knowledge of the literatures and cultures of biblical Israel's ancient Near Eastern neighbors. Hoping to study these subjects, he went to Israel in 1949, but conditions at the Hebrew University immediately after the War of Independence made this impossible. Eventually, in 1951, he came to the United States to continue his studies at Philadelphia's Dropsie College. There he studied Bible and Semitic languages, primarily under the tutelage of Cyrus H. Gordon, who was then in the heyday of his work on Ugaritic, a Semitic language rediscovered in 1929 that shed much light on biblical Hebrew. Sarna wrote his doctoral thesis on "Studies in the Language of Job" and received his Ph.D. in 1955. Several of his early publications, particularly "Epic Substratum in the Prose of Job" (1957), grew out of his doctoral studies.

III

While studying at Dropsie, Sarna taught at Philadelphia's Gratz College and also became the first of several distinguished Scholars-in-Residence at Har Zion Temple. In 1957 his broad knowledge of Jewish literature led to his simultaneous appointments as a member of the Bible Department and as librarian at the Jewish Theological Seminary of America in New York, where he was associated with such giants as H. L. Ginsberg and Saul Lieberman. In 1965 he accepted an appointment at Brandeis University, where he served as the Dora Golding Professor of Bible until his retirement in 1985. Over the years he also served as a visiting professor at Columbia University, Andover-Newton Theological School, Dropsie College, and Yale University. After his retirement he served for several years as the academic consultant of The Jewish Publication Society. Following a move to Boca Raton, Florida, both Sarnas were called out of retirement to help develop Florida Atlantic University's Judaic Studies Program, he as professor and acting director of the program and she as manager of the Judaica collections at the university's library.

Throughout his teaching career Sarna stimulated and inspired students, and many leading scholars of Judaica today, in the United States and Israel, were his pupils. His classes were characterized by pedagogically sophisticated syllabi as well as the qualities one finds in his publications: lucidity, careful organization, breadth of knowledge, and insights based on newly recognized evidence or new angles of vision. All of this was seasoned with wit and humor. Notwithstanding his imposing learning, Sarna was always ready to discuss students' own ideas and would frequently credit particular students by name for insights offered in class in previous years. Students remember him with great affection as a stimulating and caring mentor.**

Ever the pedagogue, one of the most important aspects of Sarna's scholarly career has been his devotion to scholarly projects that serve Jewish communal needs. All of his books have been written with lay as well as scholarly readers in mind. *Understanding Genesis* (1966), originally published by the Jewish Theological Seminary's Melton Research Center for Jewish Education, was written to inform Bible teachers about modern scholarship on Genesis. Its appeal turned out to be much broader, leading to its republication by Schocken and setting the pattern for *Exploring Exodus* (1986) and the more recent *Songs of the Heart: An Introduction to the Book of Psalms* (1993; reprinted as *On the Book of Psalms* [1995]). From 1966 to 1981 Sarna served, along with Moshe Greenberg, and Jonas C. Greenfield, on the committee that translated the Writings (*Ketuvim*) for The Jewish Publication Society's *Tanakh: The Holy Scriptures* (1982). In 1973, Sarna and Chaim Potok initiated the JPS Bible commentary project, the first stage of which culminated in the five volume *JPS Torah Commentary* (1989–96) for which Sarna served as the scholarly editor and author of the commentaries on Genesis and Exodus. It is a fitting twist of history that this series succeeds the venerable *Pentateuch and Haftorahs* (1929–36), edited by Joseph H. Hertz. Sarna was brought up on Hertz's commentary, and Hertz was the chief rabbi of the British Empire and president of Jews College when Sarna was a student there. (An abridged version of the Torah commentary is soon to be published as part of the Conservative movement's one-volume Torah commentary that will replace Hertz's in synagogue pews.) No scholar has done as much as Sarna to educate English-speaking Jewry about the Bible, and he has done so in the conviction that intelligent readers prefer serious scholarship lucidly presented over popularizing simplifications. The response to his books has proven him correct.

Notwithstanding his commitment to inform American Jews, Sarna's scholarship is far from parochial. Biblical scholarship today is largely an interfaith enterprise in which Jews, Christians, and secular scholars participate with the shared goal of advancing knowledge. Sarna has been active in the major scholarly societies and publishes many of his articles in nondenominational journals. One of the reasons his work is so widely appreciated in those contexts is his expertise in Jewish exegetical resources in which non-Jewish scholars are generally not schooled.

Sarna has been honored in many ways for his contributions to scholarship. *Understanding Genesis* won the 1967 Jewish Book Council Award for the best book on Jewish Thought. He has received a senior fellowship from the American Council of Learned Societies and was a fellow at the Institute for Advanced Studies at the Hebrew University in Jerusalem. He was elected a fellow of the American Academy for Jewish Research and of the Royal Asiatic Society, and was president of the Association for Jewish Studies. He has received honorary doctorates from Gratz College, Hebrew Union College-Jewish Institute of Religion, Boston Hebrew College, and Baltimore Hebrew University, and was named a Moses Aaron Dropsie fellow by the University of Pennsylvania's Center for Judaic Studies, the successor to Dropsie College. In 1988 he received the interdenominational Layman's National Bible Association Citation of Appreciation for his life of service as an educator, writer, and editor, particularly for his role in the *JPS Torah Commentary*. In 1994 he received the National Foundation for Jewish Culture's Scholarship Award for Literary Studies.

IV

Much of what Nahum Sarna values in biblical scholarship he finds already precedented in medieval Sephardic biblical exegesis:

> Jewish biblical studies reached their apogee in Moslem Spain. . . . The Spanish-Jewish achievement . . . had about it a uniqueness and originality, a vitality and pioneering quality that set it apart from anything that came before or after. It was in biblical studies, in all their ramifications, that the intellectual history of Spanish Jewry found its most fundamental and concrete articulation. . . . Unlike the experience of the Jews of Christian Europe, the study of the Scriptures in Spain did not become the consolidation of past learning. To be sure, antiquity and authority were cherished sufficiently to warrant preservation and transmission. But to the Spanish Jews, tradition was revered in not so rigid and inordinate a manner as to become static and decadent. An element of contention and controversy was allowed to penetrate, and a considerable admixture of critical independence and intellectual daring imparted a quality of excitement to biblical

studies. The diversity and multiplicity of approach, the acute sensitivity to difficulties, the forging of the essential tools of scholarship, and the extraordinary degree of sophistication—all these characterized the Sephardi contribution to biblical scholarship and led to a remarkable and unparalleled efflorescence in this field. ("Hebrew and Bible Studies in Medieval Spain" [1971])

Jewish biblical scholarship is enjoying a similar efflorescence today, and Nahum Sarna occupies an honored place among those who brought it about.

Jeffrey H. Tigay
Erev Hanukkah, 5760

*Articles marked by an asterisk and, of course, Prof. Sarna's books, are not reprinted here; see bibliography for full information.

**Prof. Sarna's advice and assistance were indispensable to me when I was his student at the Jewish Theological Seminary. The Sarnas' warm family life and their devotion to learning also set a meaningful example. Helen Sarna was studying at the Seminary and Columbia while their sons were still young (I met her when we both took a course with Columbia's formidable professor of ancient history Morton Smith), and their sons were learning Mishnah by heart and reciting it for the Seminary's great Talmudist Saul Lieberman. I still remember vividly what a sense of loss I felt the day I heard that the Sarnas were leaving for Brandeis, and I was very gratified when the *JPS Torah Commentary* later provided the opportunity to renew our close contact.

Preface

Times have changed greatly since the advent of the movement of the *Wissenschaft des Jüdentums* in the second decade of the nineteenth century when its founding father and architect, Leopold Zunz, published his path-breaking pamphlet *Etwas über die rabbinische Literatur* (1818). The very title excluded, not unintentionally, biblical studies. With few exceptions, the first generation of scholars in the field of Judaic studies avoided the subject. Was it considered to be too sensitive to deal with, too controversial in the light of the newly developing critical approaches of German academicians with their "documentary hypotheses," and as a result, regarded as being too hazardous to the spiritual health of their co-religionists? At any rate, it was also felt that whereas biblical studies were being well taken care of by Christian scholars, the rich lode of rabbinic texts remained largely unknown, unorganized, and inchoate, as far as the world of learning was concerned, and was deplorably neglected. In fact, such has continued to be the case down to the present time in the yeshiva world in which disregard of the study of the biblical text and ancillary subjects is well-nigh total.

With the establishment of the Hebrew University in Jerusalem, and subsequently of similar institutions in the State of Israel, this lamentable situation has undergone a radical change. The serious inclusion of biblical studies into the curriculum of universities, as well as instruction and research into the languages, literatures, history, religions, cultures, and archaeology of the ancient Near East, the faculty appointments of outstanding scholars of the highest excellence--all this has reclaimed the field for Jews. Not only in Israel but in the United States too, mostly under the influence of developments in Israel, Jewish biblical scholarship has flourished. Moreover, in both countries, the thousands of years of an accumulated rich mine of Jewish exegesis of the Hebrew Bible has begun to be creatively, imaginatively, and profitably quarried. Whoever possesses familiarity with rabbinic sources or is able to handle them can both extend and expand the field of vision, can often discover and extract a fresh dimension of interpretation, can obtain new and deeper insight into the purpose and meaning of a text.

Unfortunately, it is in the nature of the enterprise that a scholar's life-work is mostly dispersed in learned journals and is, in the main, not accessible to the intelligent and interested non-scholar. The present author is extremely grateful to The Jewish Publication Society, and is heartily appreciative of the efforts of its Editor-in-Chief, Dr. Ellen Frankel, and her staff in including my work in this series. He also wishes to express his gratitude to Florida Atlantic University Fund and to its president, Dr. Anthony J. Catanese, who kindly enabled this volume to be published.

Nahum M. Sarna

Acknowlegments

We are grateful to the following publishers for their kind permission to reprint the articles included here.

"The Divine Title '*abhîr ya 'ăqôbh.*" Reprinted from *Essays on the Occasion of the 70th Anniversary of the Dropsie University* (Philadelphia: Center for Judaic Studies, Philadelphia, 1979.)

"Paganism and Biblical Judaism." Reprinted from *Great Confrontations in Jewish History: The J. M. Goodstein Lecture Series on Judaica, 1975,* edited by Stanley M. Wagner and Allen D. Breck (Denver: University of Denver, Department of History, 1977/5737).

"The Biblical Sources for the History of the Monarchy." Reprinted from *The World History of the Jewish People* (Jerusalem: Massada Press, Ltd.).

"Ancient Libraries and the Ordering of the Biblical Books." Reprinted from a lecture presented at the Library of Congress, Center for the Book, 6 March 1989.

"The Authority and Interpretation of Scripture in Jewish Tradition." Reprinted by permission of Paulist Press Inc. from *Understanding Scripture,* edited by Clemens Thoma and Michael Wyschograd (© 1987 by Stimulus Foundation).

"Hebrew and Bible Studies in Medieval Spain." Reprinted by permission from R. D. Barnett (ed.), *The Sephardi Heritage, Vol. 1* published by Vallentine, Mitchell & Company, 900 Eastern Avenue, Ilford, Essex, England. Copyright Vallentine, Mitchell & Company, Ltd.

"Rashi the Commentator." Reprinted from a lecture presented at the Smithsonian Institution, circa 1990.

"Abraham Ibn Ezra as an Exegete." Reprinted from *Rabbi Abraham Ibn Ezra: Studies in the Writings of a Twelfth-century Jewish Polymath*, edited by I. Twersky and J. M. Harris (Cambridge: Center for Jewish Studies, Harvard University, 1993).

"Abraham Geiger and Biblical Scholarship." Reprinted from *New Perspectives on Abraham Geiger*, edited by J. J. Petuchowski (Hebrew Union College–Jewish Institute of Religion, 1975).

"Jewish Bible Scholarship and Translations in the United States." Reprinted from *The Bible and Bibles in America*, edited by Ernest S. Frerichs (Atlanta: Scholars Press, 1988). This article was written jointly by Jonathan D. Sarna and Nahum M. Sarna.

"The Anticipatory Use of Information as a Literary Feature of the Genesis Narratives." Reprinted from *The Creation of Sacred Literature*, edited by R. E. Friedman (University of California Press, copyright 1981 by The Regents of the University of California).

"Genesis 21:33: A Study in the Development of a Biblical Text and Its Rabbinic Transformation." Reprinted from *From Ancient Israel to Modern Judaism: Intellect in Quest of Understanding; Essays in Honor of Marvin Fox*, Volume 1, edited by Jacob Neusner, Ernest S. Frerichs, and Nahum M. Sarna; Managing Editor, Joshua Bell (Atlanta: Scholars Press, 1989).

"The Decalogue." Reprinted from *The Solomon Goldman Lectures: Perspectives in Jewish Learning, Volume 3*, edited by Nathaniel Stampfer (Chicago: The Spertus College of Judaica Press, 1982).

"Introduction to [the Hilleli Manuscript]." Reprinted from *The Pentateuch: Early Spanish Manuscript (Codex Hilleli) from the Collection of the Jewish Theological Seminary, New York* (Jerusalem: Makor Publishing, Ltd., 1974).

"Writing a Commentary on the Torah." Reprinted from The Thirteenth Annual Rabbi Louis Feinberg Memorial Lecture in Judaic Studies, Judaic Studies Program, University of Cincinnati, 6 March 1990.

"Naboth's Vineyard Revisited (1 Kings 21)." Reprinted from *Tehillah le-Moshe: Biblical and Judaic Studies in Honor of Moshe Greenberg,* edited by Mordechai Cogan, Barry L. Eichler, and Jeffrey H. Tigay (Winona Lake, IN: Eisenbrauns, 1997).

"The Abortive Insurrection in Zedekiah's Day (Jer. 27–29)." Reprinted from *Eretz-Israel: Archaeological, Historical and Geographical Studies,* Vol. 14 (Jerusalem: The Israel Exploration Society, 1978).

"Zedekiah's Emancipation of Slaves and the Sabbatical Year." Reprinted from *Orient and Occident: Essays Presented to Cyrus H. Gordon on the Occasion of His Sixty-fifth Birthday,* edited by Harry A. Hoffner, Jr. (Verlag Butzon & Bercker Kevelaer, Neukirchener Verlag Neukirchen-Vluyn, 1973).

"Ezekiel 8:17: A Fresh Examination." Reprinted by permission from *Harvard Theological Review* 57:4, October 1964 (copyright 1999 by the President and Fellows of Harvard College).

"Prolegomenon to an Edition of the Psalms." Reprinted from *The Psalms: Chronologically Treated with a New Translation,* by Moses Buttenwieser (New York: Ktav Publishing House, Inc., 1969).

"The Psalm Superscriptions and the Guilds." Reprinted from *Studies in Jewish Religious and Intellectual History,* edited by Siegfried Stein and Raphael Loewe (London: The Institute of Jewish Studies, in association with The University of Alabama Press, 1979).

"Legal Terminology in Psalm 3:8." Reprinted from *Sha'arei Talmon: Studies in the Bible, Qumran, and the Ancient Near East,* edited by Michael Fishbane and Emmanuel Tov with the assistance of Weston W. Fields (Winona Lake, IN: Eisenbrauns, 1992).

"Psalm XIX and the Near Eastern Sun-God Literature." Reprinted from the *Proceedings of the Fourth World Congress of Jewish Studies* (Jerusalem: World Union of Jewish Studies, 1967).

"Psalm 89: A Study in Inner Biblical Exegesis." Reprinted by permission of the publisher from *Biblical and Other Studies,* edited by Alexander Altmann (Cambridge, Mass.: Harvard University Press, Copyright © 1963 by the President and Fellows of Harvard College).

"The Psalm for the Sabbath Day (Psalm 92)." Reprinted from *Journal of Biblical Literature,* Volume LXXXI, Part II, 1962.

"Epic Substratum in the Prose of Job." Reprinted from *Journal of Biblical Literature,* Volume LXXVI, Part I, 1957.

"The Mythological Background of Job 18." Reprinted from *Journal of Biblical Literature,* Volume LXXXII, Part III, 1963.

STUDIES IN BIBLICAL
INTERPRETATION

ESSAYS ON BIBLICAL AND RELATED TOPICS

The Divine Title *'abhîr ya'ăqôbh*

One of the distinguishing characteristics of the Book of Genesis is the high concentration of rare or unique divine titles to be found there. One such is אֲבִיר יעקב (Gen. 49:24) which is exceptional in that it appears in a poetic text and again occurs elsewhere four times (Isa. 49:26; 60:16; Ps. 132:2, 5).[1] It further shows up in the variant form אֲבִיר ישראל (Isa. 1:24).[2] Two problems present themselves, one morphological, the other semantic. The first relates to the fact that אֲבִיר is invariably found in the *status constructus* and that another form אָבִיר exists as well, so that the relationship between the variants has to be established; the second involves the interpretation of the epithet itself.

The attempts to reconstruct the putative absolute singular form have yielded three defensible suggestions, each of which has its proponent(s).

The first possibility is אֲבִיר*. As a *qĕṭîl* form, it would follow the pattern of such nouns as בְּסִיל (Num. 31:22), גְּבִיר (Gen. 27:29), כְּסִיל (Ps. 49:11), כְּפִיר (Judg. 14:5), and, with initial guttural, חֲזִיר (Lev. 11:7), חֲנִית (I Sam. 13:19) and חֲסִין (Ps. 89:9). This is the understanding of Judah ibn Balʿam (d.c. 1090)[3] and is given as a possible alternative explanation by Jonah ibn Janakh (c. 985–c. 1040).[4] Ben-Yehuda lists אֲבִיר as a separate entry in his *Thesaurus*, though not without some hesitation.[5]

Another option is אָבִיר*. This would follow the well attested *qāṭîl* pattern which yields the construct form *qeṭîl* such as appears in קְצִיר (Gen. 30:14) < קָצִיר (Gen. 8:22) < בְּצִיר < (Judg. 8:2), בָּצִיר (Lev. 26:5), < פְּקִיד (Neh. 11:14) < פָּקִיד (II Kings 25:19), and with initial guttural[6] חֲצִיר (II Kings 19:26) < חָצִיר (I Kings 18:5). This suggestion has enjoyed wide popularity. Jonah ibn Janakh,[7] followed apparently by Solomon ibn

Parchon,[8] embraced it, and modern lexicographers have by and large concurred.[9]

The third explanation derives אָבִיר from an original אַבִּיר, a *qaṭṭîl* form, by analogy with the sing. constr. form פְּרִיץ (Isa. 35:9) פָּרִיץ = *parrîṣ* (Ezek. 18:10; Ps. 17:9), the absolute form being determined by פָּרִיצִים = *parrîṣîm* (Jer. 7:11; Ezek. 7:22) פָּרִיצֵי *parrîṣê* (Dan. 11:14). This theory was advanced by J. Barth,[10] but found no support and is explicitly rejected by some lexica.[11]

Whatever be the hypothetical absolute form of אָבִיר, there exists well-nigh[12] scholarly unanimity that the received vocalization is artificial, the product of a later pietistic, dogmatic alteration of an original אַבִּיר made for the purpose of distinguishing the sacred usage of the word as a divine epithet from its secular meaning.[13] The authors of this "emendation" have variously been identified as "the Soferim,"[14] "the Rabbis"[15] and "the Massoretes,"[16] although most scholars have been content merely to record the phenomenon without specifying its initiators.

As to the motivation for the separation of the sacred and secular usages, a wide consensus maintains that it is because אַבִּיר means "a bull." Opinion is divided, however, as to whether the divine epithet denoted the actual representation of YHWH as a bull, or whether it simply employed the bull image as a literary figure, or whether it was merely the connotative theriomorphism that supposedly evoked the opposition of pietists.

The father of the literalist school was K. Budde[17] who was convinced that YHWH was pictured as a bull-god in the Hebrew Bible. If it be asserted that bull-worship, where attested, is designated by עגל,[18] and not אַבִּיר, the answer is, according to this scholar, that the latter term carried a more noble sound than the former which was redolent of scorn and derision.[19] To the anticipated challenge that the biblical use of אביר as an appellative of God is surprisingly sparse in contrast to the allegedly widespread cult of the bull, Budde responded that the received Hebrew text had been tampered with and the originally more frequent usages excised or emended. He thereupon cavalierly proceeded to "restore" אביר in many places where the present text has אפוד[20] or ארון.[21]

Budde's singular methodology did not find much support, but the notion that the epithet אביר יעקב testifies to the one-time existence of bull-worship in Israel, or that it conjured up bovine attributes, persisted. Thus Skinner, while not certain as to whether the epithet is really a survival of the bull-worship of Bethel and Dan, is nevertheless sure that אֲבִי is intended to avoid an association of ideas with אַבִּיר "bull," the idolatrous emblem of YHWH in Northern Israel.[22] Gunkel translates the phrase in question *Stier Jacobs* which, he says, is *"ein Nachklang des Stiersymbols."*[23] This is based on the view of G. Hoffmann.[24] B. Luther asserted that, *"Der 'Stier Jakobs' ist der Stier der Jakob gehört, das Kultobject, in dem der Gott Jakob verehrt wird. . . ."*[25] On the other hand, Alt has scoffed at "the mania amongst modern scholars for seeing bulls everywhere" which "has led several of them to suggest without very convincing reasons" a meaning "the Bull(-god) of Jacob."[26] Kapelrud appears to share Alt's view, but he attributes the non-dagheshed form אביר to the Massoretes who "clearly heard in the word *'abyr* (*sic!*) the idea of 'bull,' and who possibly had in mind I Kings 12:25–33." He says that it cannot be determined "whether they also were thinking of the Canaanite Bull cult, but probably they were not."[27] Kapelrud does not inform us how the Massoretes, who labored between the 6th–8th centuries C.E., might have obtained a knowledge of ancient Canaanite religion. Be that as it may, it is largely under the influence of Ugaritic literature that the association of YHWH with a bull has been revived.

The Canaanite supreme god El frequently bears the designation "bull." This symbol has been taken by M. Pope to signify his procreative powers.[28] Albright has noted that the title carries the idea of precedence and strength,[29] an aspect of the epithet that has also been stressed by Eissfeldt.[30] P. D. Miller has effectively demonstrated that El in Ugarit is not a fertility god and that the primary characteristic of bull imagery is strength and belligerence whether in Ugaritic or in Hebrew.[31]

Now the equation: Ug. "El the bull" = Heb אֲבִיר יעקב is taken for granted by many scholars, and the earlier interpretation of Gen. 49:24 as "Bull of Jacob" seems, at first sight, to be reinforced by the Ugaritic texts, though opinion differs as to whether the Hebrew title is a carry-over from Canaan or is indigenous to Israel and belongs to the original patriarchal El cult.[32] The problem is, however, that the Ugaritic term in question is not *'ibr* but *tr* which corresponds to Heb. שׁוֹר, "ox." It is this that is the title of El and it remains to be explained—which it never has—why Israel should not have carried over the Canaanite epithet intact. The question is the more pertinent since שׁוֹר is a frequent Hebrew word and one actually used in connection with the wilderness calf worship in Ps. 106:20,

"They exchanged their glory
for the image of a bull (שׁוֹר) that
feeds on grass."

The Hebrew equivalent of Ug. *ṭr il* should have been שׁוֹר אֵל a phrase that N. H. Tur-Sinai[33] brilliantly postulated to be embedded in the consonantal text of Hos. 8:6 מִי שֹׁר אֵל = מישׂראל. This reading seems to have been adopted by *NEB*. "For what sort of a god is this bull?" Tur-Sinai[34] himself categorically rejected the association of אביר with a bull and tried to show that, in fact, none of its usages need be so understood.

Conscious, perhaps, of the weakness of connecting El with the Hebrew appellative, some scholars have claimed that the prototype was Baal who, it is asserted, is connected with Ug. *ibr*, the equivalent of Heb. אביר. Thus, Mowinckel tells us that "Baal is called the 'bull,' *ibr* in the Ugaritic texts, the hump-backed bull, the bison."[35] Vawter writes that "Ugar. *ibr*, which always means 'bull,'[36] is associated in 75:I:32; :II:55 f.; 76:III:21 with Baal and his offspring."[37] What is the evidence? Ug. text 75:I:30–33 reads:

(30) *bhm qrnm* (31) *km. ṭrm. wgbtt* (32) *km. ibrm*
(33) *wbhm. pn. bᶜl*

The reference is to the birth of gods who have "on them horns like bulls and humps like buffaloes and on them is the face of Baal." The text actually tells us nothing about the bull character of Baal. Ug. text 75:II:55 f. merely informs us that "Baal fell like a bull *(ṭr)*, Hadd collapsed like a buffalo *(ibr)*." The precise context is obscure because the text is broken, but the image again tells us nothing about Baal's nature or representation, only about the manner in which he collapsed. Text 76:III:21 (36 f.) indeed informs us that Baal sired a "buffalo" *(ibr)*, "a wild bull" *(rʾum)*, but once again, the context is unknown due to the fragmentary state of the text. If there is evidence for Baal having the character of a bull, it can hardly rest on the literary evidence.[38] There is certainly no basis for the claim that Baal actually bears the title *ibr*.

How is 'BR used in Semitic languages? Albright has noted that *'a-bi-ir-ya* (= *'abîr*) was borrowed from Canaanite by the Egyptians of the New Empire as a word for "stallion."[39] This is the precise meaning of Heb. אַבִּירִים in Judg. 5:22 and Jer. 8:16. In both texts the term appears in synonymous parallelism with סוּסִים "horses." The same meaning certainly applies also in Jer. 47:3 and seems to be most appropriate in Jer.

50:11 as well. Hence, אָבִיר can hardly be said unequivocally to signify "bull." Furthermore, in several passages the term is used of humans, certainly in Ps. 76:6 where אַבִּירֵי־לֵב "stout-hearted," is synonymous with אַנְשֵׁי־חַיִל "warriors," and in Lam. 1:15 where אַבִּירַי parallels בַּחוּרַי "young men." The same is most likely true also in Ps. 78:25 לחם אבירים,[40] I Sam. 21:8 אביר הרעים[41] and Isa. 46:12 אבירי לב.[42] In only a minority of cases[43] does אַבִּיר unambiguously refer to animals, probably "bulls." Isa. 34:7; Ps. 22:13; 50:13; 68:31 and apparently also in Jer. 46:15.[44]

Now it is possible, of course, that in those texts in which אביר is applied to humans we may be witnessing a phenomenon attested in Ugaritic, the use of animal names as designations for warriors, high officials or dignitaries.[45] Even if this be the case it would only prove that אביר had early become metaphorically stereotyped and that, therefore, when used of God, could hardly have had cultic associations.[46]

Turning to the use of the term in Akkadian, we find the noun *abāru*,[47] "strength," applied to kings and gods. Sargon is described as *gamir dunni u abāri* "consummate in power and strength." The title *bēl abāri*, "endowed with strength," is an epithet of the gods Nergal, Tammuz and Ninurta.[48] This has particular relevance for the Hebrew divine appellative אֲבִיר יעקב. One wonders why this cannot simply mean "The strong One of Jacob," which is exactly the way it is rendered in the ancient versions.

Thus, the Targumim have תקיפ(א) for all occurrences. The Greek has δυνάστου in Gen. 49:24, ἰσχύοντες in Isa. 1:24, ἰσχύος in Isa. 49:26; similarly, Vulg. has *potentis* in Gen. 49:24 and *fortis* in the Isaiah passages.[49] It is worth noting that the Hebrew of Ben Sira uses אביר as "mighty one"[50] and in Rabbinic Hebrew there is the phrase אביר שבאבירים, "the mostly highly esteemed,"[51] as opposed to קל שבקלים "the least esteemed," as well as, remarkably, even a verbal form אִיבֵּר[52] "to strengthen," "harden."

To sum up, the primary meaning of אביר is "strong one," whether applied to humans or animals. There is no warranty for the widespread belief that the dagheshed form ever conjured up in Hebrew the specific image of a bull in all its bovine qualities much less as a cultic object. For this reason the non-dagheshed form is not an artificial dogmatic creation.

The implausibility of the emendation theory is further strengthened by the employment of the divine epithet on the part of First and Second Isaiah. The earlier prophet lived at a time when, supposedly, the so-called "bull" association of אביר was still part of the living language and when the influence of paganism on Israel was still strong. It is hardly conceivable that he would have used an appellative redolent of the grossest pagan associations.[53] Equally incomprehensible would be the two-fold use by Second Isaiah whose uncompromising monotheism and anti-pagan rhetoric rule out any possibility of insensitivity to אביר if that term invoked bull-cult imagery.

For all the afore-going reasons, the distinction between the sacred epithet אֲבִיר יעקב and the secular dagheshed form cannot be the artificial product of late pietism. Rather, the two forms existed side by side from the beginning.

NOTES

1. H-J. Kraus, *Psalmen* [Biblischer Kommentar Altes Testament XV /2] (1960), p. 884, mistakenly includes Ps. 78:25; *cf.* his comment to that passage, I, p. 545.

2. IQIsa.ᵃ has a lacuna after צבאות, but the reading ישראל is found also in the Greek, Vulg. and Pesh. A. Alt, "Der Gott der Väter," *Kleine Schriften*, I (Munich, 1953), pp. 19 ff. (=*Essays in Old Testament History and Religion*, translated by R. A. Wilson, New York, 1968, p. 32), simply explains the variant as due to the later identification of Jacob with Israel. On the other hand, G. B. Gray, *Isaiah* [I.C.C.], Edinburgh, 1912, p. 34, notes approvingly that Budde and Marti omit the epithet here as a later insertion (see on this further below, n. 53). A. B. Ehrlich, *Randglossen zur Hebräischen Bible*, Leipzig, 1908, I, p. 251, merely remarks on the rarity of the combination. S. Mowinckel, *The Psalms in Israel's Worship* (translated by D. R. Ap-Thomas), Oxford, 1962, I, p. 100, n. 57, strangely cites "'*abbîr yiśra'el*" (sic!) as occurring in Ps. 132:2, 5. L. F. Hartman in *Encyclopaedia Judaica* (1971), vol. 7, col. 681, suggests that בורא ישראל in Isa. 43:15 should be read אביר ישראל. The fact of the matter is that ישראל in Isa. 1:24 is conditioned by the fossilized epithet ה' צבאות אלהי ישראל (*cf.* Isa 21:10; 37:16) which never appears with a יעקב variant. Therefore, it is doubtful that an independent epithet אביר ישראל ever existed.

3. Commentary to Isa. 1:24, reprinted in *Commentaries on the Book of Isaiah*, Jerusalem, 5731/1971. II, p. 21.

4. *Sefer HaShorashim*, ed. W. Bacher, Berlin, 1896, p. 11.

5. E. Ben Yehuda, *Thesaurus*, I, p. 23 and n. 1.

6. No *qāṭîl* noun with 'aleph exists in both sing. abs. and const. forms, but clearly belonging to this class are אָסִיר (Ps. 79:11), pl. אֲסִירִים, אֲסִירֵי (Gen. 39:22, 20); אֲצִילֵי, *אָצִיל* (Exod. 24:11) and אֲפִיק*, אָפִיק (Job 6:15; *cf.* 12:21; II Sam. 22:16).

7. *Op. cit.*, p. 11.

8. *Makbereth he-Arukh*, ed. S. G. Stern, Pressburg, 1844, s. v. אבר.

9. So the biblical Hebrew dictionaries of Brown, Driver and Briggs, Gesenius-Buhl (1962) and Baumgartner-Koehler (1967). B. Luther, *ZAW*, 21 (1901), p. 72, states that "*Im massoretischen Text wird punktiert* אָבִיר" (sic!). S. R. Driver, *The Book of Genesis*, 1904, p. 409; W. F. Albright, *The Vocalization of the Egyptian Syllabic Orthography* [American Oriental Series 5], New Haven, 1934, p. 33, III A.1; A. S. Kapelrud in *Theologisches Wörterbuch zum Alten Testament*, eds. G. J. Botterweck u. H. Ringgren, Stuttgart, 1970, I, p. 43 (=*Theological Dictionary of the Old Testament*, translated by J. T. Willis, Grand Rapids, 1974, I, p. 42), all presuppose אָבִיר*.

10. Nominalbildung in dem Semitischen Sprachen, Leipzig, 1889, pp. 51 f. §35.

11. E. g., Gesenius-Buhl; *cf.* Gesenius' Hebrew Grammar, ed. Kautzsch-Cowley, Oxford, 1910, p. 234, § 84ᵇ, f. 25.

12. As far as I can ascertain, only M. Haran in *Oz leDavid* [Hebrew], Jerusalem, 1964, p. 59, n. 39 among modern scholars has suggested that the received vocalization may well be original.

13. In addition to the authors cited in n. 9 above, this view has been espoused by T. K. Cheyne, *The Prophecies of Isaiah*, New York, 1886, II, p. 136; A. B. Ehrlich, *Die Psalmen*, Berlin, 1905, p. 344; C. A. Briggs, *Psalms* [ICC], Edinburgh, 1907, II, p. 473; J. Skinner, *Genesis* [ICC], 2nd ed., Edinburgh, 1930, p, 531; H. Gunkel, *Genesis*, 3rd. ed., Göttingen, 1910 [reprint, 1964], p. 486. Strangely confused is Th. J. Meek, *Hebrew Origins*, New York, 1960, p. 138, n. 60, to whom "the vocalization *'abbîr* (sic!), 'mighty one,' is clearly an artificial one for *'ābîr*, 'bull.'" The same theory is repeated on p. 140 which mentions "the term *'abîr*, 'bull' (later vocalized *'abbîr*, "mighty one," when the bull cult fell into disrepute), as an appellative of deity."

14. Ben Yehuda, *op. cit.*, I, p. 23, s. v., אֲבִיר.

15. Gunkel, *op. cit.*, p. 486.

16. So Ehrlich, Briggs, Skinner, *op. cit.*, n. 13 above, Kapelrud, *op. cit.*, n. 9 above.

17. ZAW, 39 (1921), pp. 1–42. L. Waterman, *AJSL*, XXXI (1915), 229–255, without mentioning אביר יעקב had expressed his conviction that the bull-cult of YHWH in Israel "was widespread and deep-seated, and the most prominent interpreter" of YHWH throughout the period from the Judges to the eighth century prophets.

18. So Exod. ch. 32; Deut. 9:16, 21; I Kings 12:28, 32; II Kings 10:29; 17:16; Hos. 8:5 f.; 10:5; 13:2; Ps. 106:19; II Chron. 11:15; 13:8. It should be noted that the syncretistic pr. n. עגליו in the Samaria Ostraca No. 41, further proves that it is עגל, not אביר that is redolent of the bull cult.

19. Budde, *op. cit.*, p. 38. Of course, there is no warranty for this notion. Heb. עגל is "a bullock of two or three years, just at the prime of life" (W. F. Albright, *From the Stone Age to Christianity*, 2nd. ed., New York, 1957, p. 300), and as such was particularly desirable for sacrifice.

20. Viz., Judg. 8:27; 17:5; 18:14; I Sam. 14:3; 21:10; 23:9.

21. E. g., I. Sam. 14:18.

22. *Op. cit.*

23. *Op. cit. Cf.* E. Meyer, *Die Israeliten und Ihre Nachbarstämme*, Halle, 1906, pp. 283–285.

24. ZAW, 3 (1883), 124.

25. *Op. cit.*, pp. 72 f. Skinner, *op. cit.*, p. 531, note, finds the idea that Jacob was the deity originally worshipped in the bull to be "perhaps too adventurous."

26. *Op. cit.*

27. *Op. cit.*

28. *El in the Ugaritic Texts*, Leiden, 1955 [Suppl VT II], pp. 35–42. *Cf.* A. S. Kapelrud, *Baal in the Ras Shamra Texts*, Copenhagen, 1952, pp. 21, 68, 97.

29. W. F. Albright, *Archaeology and the Religion of Israel*, 5th ed., New York, 1968, p. 145; *Yahweh and the Gods of Canaan*, New York, 1968, p. 120.

30. O. Eissfeldt, *El im Ugaritischen Pantheon*, Berlin, 1951, p. 56; *Kleine Schriften*, Tübingen, 1966, III, pp. 481–485; IV, p. 85. *Cf.* Mowinckel, *op. cit.*; B. Vawter, *CBQ*, 17 (1955), p. 11; M. Dahood, *Biblica*. 40² (1959), p. 1006; N. C. Habel, *Yahweh v. Baal*, New York, 1964, p. 48, n. 11; U. Oldenburg, *The Conflict between El and Baal in Canaanite Religion*, Leiden, 1969, p. 174.

31. HTR, 60 (1967), pp. 411–431, esp. pp. 418–422.

32. *Cf.* F. M. Cross, *Canaanite Myth and Hebrew Epic*, Cambridge, 1973, pp. 4 (n. 6), 15, 244.

33. *Halashon VeHaSefer*, III, Jerusalem, 1955, p. 47; *'Encyclopedia Miqra'ith*, I, col. 31. Pope, *op. cit.*, p. 35, is dubious about this reading, but Miller, *op. cit.*, p. 422, n. 46 seems to endorse it.

34. *ZAW*, 39 (1921), 296–300; *HaLashon VeHaSefer*, *op. cit.*, pp. 39–47. Tur-Sinai based his philological argument on the suggestion of S. D. Luzzato, *Commentary to Isaiah* [Hebrew], Padua, 1867, p. 40, deriving the term from אֶבְרָה "a wing." Whereas Luzzato saw in the latter the idea of protection (*Cf.* Ps. 91:4), Tur-Sinai understood the underlying idea to be "elevation, exaltation."

35. *Op. cit.*, p. 100, n. 57. Incidentally, *'abbîr* is there cited in place of the correct *'ăbhîr*. A. S. Kapelrud, *The Ras Shamra Discoveries and the O. T.*, translated by G. W. Anderson, 1963, p. 39, also claims that Baal is referred to as a bull.

36. *Cf.* J. Gray, *The Krt Text in the Literature of Ras Shamra*, Leiden, 1964, p. 49. It should be noted that H. L. Ginsberg, *The Legend of King Keret*, New Haven, 1946, pp. 16, 39, prefers to render *ibr* in KRT, 1. 120, "stallion;" so *ANET*, p. 144. Actually, the word is not common in Ugaritic. In text 51:7:55 f. it is more likely the equivalent of Heb. אַבָּר "wing" (*cf. ANET*, p. 135).

37. Vawter, *op. cit.*

38. *Cf.* P. W. Miller, *HTR*, *op. cit.*, p. 419; A. S. Kapelrud, *Baal*, *op. cit.*, pp. 20 f. 52, 62 f., 93. T. H. Gaster, *Thespis*, 2nd. ed., New York, 1961, p. 172, notes that S. Arabian inscriptions record the title *Ṯ-r-bᶜl*, "Bull Baal." Significantly, it is *ṯr*, not *'br*, that is used.

39. *The Vocalization*, *op. cit.*, p. 33, III.A.1; p. 52, X1.B1; *BASOR*, 62 (1936), p. 30.

40. *Cf. NJPS*, "a hero's meal:" *RSV* and *NEB* render, "bread of angels," based on G. Αρτον ἀγγέλων; so Rashi, *cf.* Targ. Certain it is that אַבִּירִים here has no connotation of bulls or any other theriomorphic association.

41. This is the only non-poetic usage of אַבִּיר. C. D. Ginsburg, *The Massorah*, London, 1905 [Ktav reprint: New York, 1975], IV, p. 24, § 69, points out that in some mss. the punctuation is אֲבִיר followed in the *editio princeps* of Soncino, 1488. The Aleppo Codex reads אַבִּיר (courtesy of Prof. M. Goshen-Gottstein). The Greek reads νέμων τὰς ἡμιόνους, "herdsman of the mules," apparently based on a Hebrew *Vorlage* / רועה הפרדים העירים. S. R. Driver, *Notes on the Hebrew Text. . . Samuel*, 2nd. ed., Oxford, 1913, p. 176 retains אביר, but favors the emendation of Graetz רָצִים for רצים. This is rejected by M. H. Segal, *Sifrê Shemuel*, Jerusalem, 1956, *ad loc.*, on the grounds that Doeg was not a runner as is clear from the narrative in I Sam. 22:17 ff. He suggests that אֲבִיר in this context may be an Edomite title. A. B. Ehrlich, *Randglossen*, III, p. 243, emends אֲבִיר to אַדִּיר (*cf.* Judg. 5:25). P. D. Miller, *Ugarit-Forschungen*, 2 (1970), p. 180 and n. 18, recognizes here the phenomenon of animal name designation for high officials. N. H. Tur-Sinai, *ZAW*, 39 (1921), p. 300, also finds no difficulty in the phrase. He takes אֲבִיר in the sense of "officer," drawing attention to the parallel אביר – רעה in Gen. 49:24 and the epithet with, האדון in Isa. 1:24. The same point is made by M. Haran, *op. cit.*, who also suggests that I Sam. 21:8 should be vocalized אֲבִיר, a reading which, indeed, enjoys some support, as noted above.

42. Behind the Greek οἱ ἀπολωλεκόντες τήν καρδίαν seems to be אֹבְדֵי לב a reading adopted by J. L. McKenzie, *Second Isaiah* [Anchor Bible], New York, 1968, p. 86. 1QIsaᵃ=MT.

43. Isa. 10:13; Job 24:22; 34:20 are all obscure.

44. Heb. מדוע נסחף אבירך is rendered by *NJPS*, "Why are stalwarts swept away?" The translators give no alternate translation, not even their "emendation yields" footnote. *NEB*, so J. Bright, *Jeremiah* [Anchor Bible], New York, 1965, p. 303, accepts the Greek which bisects נסחף, taking the second syllable as "Apis," the sacred bull of the Egyptians and reading אבירך sing., the latter supported by several Heb. mss.

45. P. D. Miller, *Ugarit-Forschungen*, *op. cit.*, pp. 177–186, esp. p. 180.

46. Incidentally, the figurative use of animal imagery with God in poetic texts is not necessarily objectionable. Witness II Sam. 22:3 = Ps. 18:3 ישעי קרן, lit., "the horn of my salvation," clearly deriving from bull imagery. Similarly, God roars like a lion (Jer. 25:30; Joel 4:16; Amos 1:2).

47. *CAD, A/1*, p. 38.

48. *Ibid.* K. Tallqvist, *Akkadische Götterepitheta*, Helsingfors, 1938, pp. 40, 395, 427.

49. In Isa. 60:16; Ps. 132:2, 5, G. has simply θεός; Vulg. has *Deus* in the latter passage.

50. Ed. M. H. Segal, Jerusalem, 1953, p. 288; *cf.* R. H. Charles, *The Apocrypha and Pseudepigrapha*, Oxford, 1913, I, p. 474, and notes m-m.

51. Rosh Hashanah 25[b]; Yer. Rosh Hashanah II:9, 58[b]; Koheleth Rabbah I:8 (to 1:4)

52. Sanhedrin 109[b] שאיבר עצמו; var. שאיבר לבו.

53. Budde (*op. cit.*, n. 2 above) regarded the presence of the divine appellative in Isa. 1:24 as a late intrusion. Is it because it interfered with his theory?

Paganism and Biblical Judaism

The people of Israel appeared on the scene of history exceedingly late. By the time they managed to establish an independent political entity in their own national homeland, the great civilizations of the Tigris-Euphrates and Nile valleys were long past their prime. Their great architectural and cultural achievements were already behind them; the period of their greatest vigor and literary creativity was largely over.

By their own testimony, the Israelites originated in Mesopotamia, wandered through Canaan, settled in Egypt for a prolonged sojourn, then again pushed into that narrow strip of land lying between the Mediterranean Sea and the desert, where they long struggled against and lived side by side with the existing Canaanite population before they were finally able to found a secure state of their own. The term "Canaanite," it should be pointed out, is a rather loose usage that defies precise definition, because "Canaan" is employed in the biblical and extra-biblical sources in a variety of ways. The term is used in this study in its widest possible sense, embracing the Land of Israel and its non-Israelite peoples and cultures in pre-exilic times, i.e. before the year 586 B.C.E.

THE FACTOR OF GEOGRAPHY

In order to understand the nature of the problem we are dealing with— the interaction of paganism with biblical Judaism—we must reflect for a moment on the geography of the country and assess the impact it had on Israelite history. The strategic location of Canaan, as the land bridge between the continents of Asia and Africa, inevitably ensured that the land was open to all kinds of influences. Conquering armies from Egypt and from the lands of Asia Minor and Assyria and Babylonia recurrently traversed the country, sometimes occupying it for shorter or longer periods. Migrant peoples passed along the arteries of communication. Nomads intruded from the East, crossing the boundary line between the desert and the sown; and Mediterranean peoples, especially from the Aegean area, invaded from the Sea. In addition, the extraordinary heterogeneity of topographical features concentrated within a very narrow land area induced fragmentation and centrifugalism. The Book of Genesis refers to a surprisingly large number of ethnic groups inhabiting the country and at the time of Joshua's conquest no fewer than 31 separate petty kingdoms were recorded. In fact, throughout the long history of this land, no single people was ever able to impose a unity on it from within—no people, that is, with the sole and remarkable exception of the people of Israel.

The land that Israel came to possess thus constituted the crossroads of the ancient world. It lay wide open to a multitude of diverse ethnic, cultural and religious cross-currents. An interpenetration and cross-fertilization of cultures took place unceasingly, although, admittedly, this was less true of the mountainous areas within which the earliest stage of the Israelite conquest concentrated. Lying somewhat beyond the major trunk roads, this region was not so highly receptive to foreign influences, and it afforded a measure of insulation.

THE AVERSION TO CANAANITES

What impact did Canaanite culture have on the Israelites? According to the narratives in the Book of Genesis, the local inhabitants of the country were not highly esteemed. The strong Israelite aversion to them recorded by the biblical writers is already implicit in the story of Noah's drunkenness (Gen. 9:20–27). Here, the father of the Canaanites is cursed for some unspecified, clearly indecent act. The "sin of the Amorite" (the latter being but a generic term for the pre-Israelite inhabitants of the land) is central to the theophany of the covenant ceremony carried out between God and Abraham. (Gen. 15:16) and the depravity of the men of Sodom is overwhelming (Gen. 19). The patriarch himself does not expect to find the "fear of God" among the people of Gerar (Gen. 20:11). In fact, intermarriage with the local girls is strongly discouraged. In the legal portions of the Pentateuch, the interdict prohibiting fraternization with the Canaanites is frequently featured and so is the call for the destruction of their cultic objects. It is abundantly apparent that, to the Scriptural authors, the religion and culture of Canaan were an abomination.

THE HISTORICAL PROBLEM

On the other hand, there is no lack of evidence to show that these same cults seem to have had a considerable fascination for the Israelite masses. The narratives of the Book of Kings are replete with reports of popular idolatry and sometimes record royal tolerance or even patronage of them. The classical prophets from Amos to Jeremiah and Ezekiel unceasingly denounced Israel's unfaithfulness to the covenant and they imply a condition of national apostasy. Indeed, there are scholars who contend that during the period of the First Temple, the people of Israel were little different from the Canaanites and that it became truly monotheistic only during the exile and Second Temple period. This picture is in such sharp contrast to the other that emerges from the Pentateuchal sources that further consideration is called for.

During the past hundred years archaeologists and Semitists have been able to demonstrate through monumental and documentary finds that the entire area of the ancient Near East—what has become known as the Fertile Crescent—constituted, more or less, a cultural continuum. The people of Israel came into being within this culture area and were naturally heir to its common patrimony. Comparative studies, particularly those conducted in the course of the past forty years, have provided us with a plethora of detailed parallels between the literary sources of the ancient Near East and the biblical text. These researches leave no doubt whatsoever as to Israel's indebtedness to its forebears and neighbors in the realms of literary genres, religious imagery and theological vocabulary, cultic institutions, forms and terminology, legal structures and codifications. Does not this intricate and complex commonality of cultural heritage serve to substantiate the claim that until a late period the differences between Israel and its neighbors were hardly significant?

In relationship to this picture is another one that relates to the phenomenon of Israel in exile. The northern tribes suffered a series of deportations at the hands of the Assyrian rulers Tiglath-Pileser III (744–727) and his sons and successors Shalmaneser V (727–722) and Sargon II (722–705) who destroyed the Kingdom of Israel in 722 B.C.E. (2 Kings chs. 17–18). Yet, well over a century later Jeremiah could issue a call to repentance to these tribes and could repeatedly predict their return to the Land of Israel and their reunification with their Judean brethren (Jeremiah 3:11; 30:3, 31:1–19, 26, 30; 33:7, 14, 24–26). In the Babylonian exile, the prophet Ezekiel also promised the return of the northern Israelites and their reincorporation within the body politic of a united nation (Ezekiel 16:33 ff; 37:15–28). In reality, however, the northerners could entertain no hopes of reoccupying their ancestral lands, since the Assyrians had transplanted there a foreign population from distant regions of the empire (2 Kings 17:24). There is good reason to believe that the Israelites were not persecuted or especially maltreated in the exile. This means, of course, that assimilation into the dominant Assyrian culture could not have been too difficult, and must certainly have been pursued by many. Nevertheless, it is clear from the post-exilic biblical sources that the Israelites survived for hundreds of years and, in fact, that a sizeable element left its Mesopotamian homeland to return with the Judeans to the Land of Israel and to settle in Jerusalem and its environs. If the tribes of the North were as thoroughly paganized as the biblical sources seem to imply and as some modern scholars confidently claim, whence did they derive the spiritual and cultural resources to withstand total absorption into Mesopotamian society? What motivated them to preserve their identity and distinctiveness for such a long period of time in their Assyrian domicile?

The same question arises, and with even greater force, in respect to the southern Kingdom of Judah. The Babylonian exile was obviously the great testing time of the Judean religion. Here was a people, militarily defeated, deprived of the organs of statecraft, bereft of its central shrine, unable to practice its traditional cult, forcibly removed from its land, and existing as a tiny minority amidst a vastly superior, overwhelmingly victorious civilization possessed of a hoary antiquity. Nonetheless, it managed to maintain its national identity on alien soil, and it succeeded in resisting the seductive pressures of the mightiest state on earth. We know that powerful forces of assimilation were at work. We are certain that the Jews adopted the Aramaic language and script, exchanged their native calendar for that of Babylon, and appropriated Babylonian personal names. Yet they retained a consciousness of exile and fostered a yearning to return to Zion.

How are we to explain this astonishing and, as far as we know, unique phenomenon? Still more intriguing; how are we to account for a supposedly half-pagan people managing, in the midst of a pagan exile, to purge itself of idolatry, to assert an aggressive monotheism, to project a universalistic vision of a world free of paganism turning to the one

God whose (now ruined) Temple in Jerusalem was to be a house of prayer for all peoples? Here in Babylon the Jews collected and edited their national literature. How are we to account for the intellectual vigor and spiritual vitality of this community in exile? What nourished its self-conscious, its self assertive distinctiveness?

Surely, an acute polarity exists between the reality behind the events of the exilic period and the image of the people of Israel that seems to emerge, at first sight, from the literary sources. The reality is wholly inexplicable on the assumption of a paganized or syncretized Israel, at least in the late monarchy period. The struggle, therefore, between monotheism and polytheism must have been fought out and decisively settled before the exile took place.

It should be pointed out that, in actual fact, irrespective of what date one assigns to the biblical documents, or the period of the struggle and the victory, the mystery of the phenomenon remains. There is absolutely no parallel in the ancient Near East for a people resisting the current universal religious thought patterns, challenging the prevailing world views and producing a national religion and literature that in its fundamentals goes against the stream of the entire existing tradition of which historically, culturally and geographically it is a constituent part. The phenomenon defies all attempts at rational explanation, for a linear, evolutionary development of monotheism from polytheism is not otherwise attested. Furthermore, to ascribe it to "national intuition" is merely to substitute one enigma for another.

CONCEPTIONS OF GOD

If we are unable to account for the religio-cultural mutation, we can, at least, delineate in considerable detail the major areas of confrontation between the official religion of Israel, as presented in the biblical sources, and the religion of the pagans. We must start, of course, with the respective understandings of the nature of God, for herein lies the fundamental difference. The basic characteristic of polytheism is that its gods have no absolute freedom. The discriminating essence of Israelite monotheism is that God's will is absolute and sovereign.

The freedom of the pagan gods is circumscribed by the twin factors of their natural qualities and their multiplicity. Being creatures of nature, they are subject to powers beyond themselves. They participate in all the life processes: they require a means of subsistence; they possess sex and sexuality, and they reproduce; they experience development, aging, decline, even death. Because nature manifests itself in a variety of modes and powers, each individualized and personalized, multiplicity and variety must be inherent in the world of the gods, so that a plurality of wills must inevitably characterize the pantheon. Now a plurality of wills inescapably engenders a clash of wills, which means that no single will can possibly be eternally sovereign.

The Israelite conception of God is the antithesis of the pagan notion. God is not immanent in nature because nature is His creation and, for that reason, a reflection of His greatness. Removed from all corporeality, He cannot be subject to its limitations. His utter uniqueness yields Him absolute freedom; His will is sovereign: His ethical integrity is unqualified.

This state of divine freedom constitutes the quintessence of Israelite monotheism. All else flows from it. Everything that is characteristically and uniquely Israelite has its origin in this basic conviction. The absolute freedom of God became the conceptual framework that determined the configuration of the national religion and that shaped its struggle with paganism. It constituted a kind of ideological filter through which much of pagan culture could be received into Israel, permitting what was appropriated to be purified of its polytheistic dross.

Every educated man knows that the first eleven chapters of Genesis contain numerous and detailed parallels with Mesopotamian literature; that Israelite law has its origins in ancient Near Eastern legal traditions; that Psalms literature is replete with Near Eastern analogies; and that biblical Wisdom texts have a remarkable number of correspondences with Egyptian and Mesopotamian counterparts. In every one of these areas we can discern an underlying history of careful selectivity and a process of transmutation. The struggle with polytheism was, thus, in a very real sense, a matter of continuing interaction, of selective and creative acculturation, rather than of outright, indiscriminate rejection of an entire culture. A wholly new Israelite monotheistic culture was indeed created, but much of it was erected by reusing many of the building blocks of the old. Always, however, the overriding issue and the selective criterion was the compatability or incompatability with God's absolute freedom. It was this principle, embodied in an amalgam of ideas, practices and institutions, that enabled the people of Israel to survive the threat of being swamped by the indigenous and competing cultures.

THE ANTI-PAGAN POLEMIC

One of the most effective weapons employed against paganism by the writers of Israel's national literature was an ongoing polemic with myth. The personalization of the powers of nature that is at the root of polytheism meant that mythology, or the tales about the deeds of the gods, was an integral part of religion and, therefore, the ancient Near East produced a rich mythological literature. Strangely, the Bible does not openly acknowledge the existence of this mythology. No one would know from the Israelite sources that the names of the great gods and goddesses were associated with a fertile, colorful and variegated mythology. Nevertheless, the early chapters of Genesis are replete with terms and motifs that resound with clear echoes of this same mythological literature. They are employed, in fact, in contexts that serve to refute or transmute them so that they become, ever so obliquely and subtly, weapons in an anti-pagan polemic. A few examples will serve to illustrate the point.

Mesopotamian and other accounts of cosmology generally commence with vivid descriptions of a titanic struggle that takes place between opposing forces of creativity and aridity. It is the victory of the former that makes possible the subsequent cosmogony. This entire notion is nullified, imperceptibly but decisively, through the biblical account of Creation. The divine fiat, "Let there be" (Gen. 1:3–6) expresses the sovereign will of God, ineluctable, irrevocable, not subject to effective challenge by opposing force. Moreover, the emphasis on the fact that "God created the great sea monsters" (Gen. 1:21) simply reinforces the same idea, for it is these beings that in pagan mythology constitute the embodiment of the contesting polar forces. To assert that the "great sea monsters" are simply creatures of God is to deprive them at once of their divine or demonic nature.

Another seemingly innocent description of Creation is the statement that God made humans as male and female and that he blessed them, as well as the animal world, with fertility (Gen. 1:22, 28; 5:2). However, in a mythopoeic culture, one in which man's thinking about the origin and nature of the world finds expression in mythological phraseology, the biblical assertions about sex and fertility take on extraordinary meaning. Polytheism, especially in the ancient Near East, envisaged cosmogony largely in terms of sexuality. Sex is a pre-creation force engendered in the mingling of the sweet-water and salt-water oceans, identified respectively as a male and female monster, which initiated the generative process. The gods are creatures of sex, and the fertility of humankind and the animal world is personified as a divine being. The Canaanite religion, in particular, was given to fertility cults, and sexual promiscuity is a standard feature of its mythology. It is no coincidence that the Pentateuch repeatedly emphasizes the sexual depravity of the Canaanites in both narrative and legal texts, and it is not to be wondered that this moral blemish is regarded as the primary cause of their downfall. By emphasizing that sexuality is a divine creation and that fertility is a gift of God, not a god, the Genesis account again unobtrusively and firmly refutes pagan notions and excises all fertility cults from the religion of Israel.

The subtlety of the biblical anti-pagan polemic achieves a degree of high sophistication when it deals with the origins of the arts of civilization. As is well known, the gods are always closely associated with magic, with wisdom and with the arts and crafts, and divine culture heroes are familiar features of the mythological landscape. The Bible, in contrast, has no myths dealing with such matters. The arts of civilization are, instead, assigned human origins and are presented as historical developments that occurred in the seventh generation of natural born man (Gen. 4:20–22). It has become increasingly clear in recent years that the Scriptural selection of sheeprearing, of music and of metalwork as the three basic arts of civilization is a faithful reflection of the early semi-nomadic society of the ancient Near East. The ascription of their origins to the three sons of Lamech quietly cuts at the roots of the mythological approach to the historical process.

The anti-pagan polemic of the universal history of man in the first eleven chapters of Genesis reaches its fullest and most sustained form in two narratives, both of which have the closest contacts with Mesopotamia. The first is the flood story (Gen. 6:5–9:17) which, in structure, theme and detail, exhibits such remarkable parallels with cuneiform literature. The second is the narrative about the Tower of Babel (Gen. 11:1–9) which, as a unit, yields no Mesopotamian counterpart, but which, in its numerous details, is dependent on Babylonian sources.

The story of Noah and the Flood provides the classic example of the Israelite transformation of mythic material. Here we see the unambiguous contrast between the inherent limitations of the pagan gods, who cannot control the destructive processes they have set in motion, and the absolute freedom of the God of Israel whose sovereign and purposeful will prevails at all times. The seemingly insignificant change from the Babylonian "boat" to the Israelite "ark" as the instrument of salvation neatly illustrates the point, for Noah's ark, unlike its Babylonian counterpoint, had neither rudder nor helmsman and was wholly at the mercy of the devastating floodwaters—except for the providence of God. Similarly indicative of the conscious monotheistic metamorphosis that the flood story underwent at the hands of the biblical writers is the closing scene of the epic. Utnapishtim, the Mesopotamian hero, is blessed by the gods after the flood, is deified and granted immortality, while he is removed from the world of humans. Noah, on the other hand, is not to withdraw from society, but is to be fruitful and to multiply, to replenish the earth and to father a regenerated human family.

The narrative about the building of the Tower of Babel completes the first part of the Book of Genesis. With this episode, the universal history of humankind narrows its focus and concentrates thereafter on the patriarchs of Israel. It is just at this point that the anti-pagan literary polemic reaches its highest and most sweeping expression. Here we find an entire narrative that actually constitutes a satirical negation of polytheistic beliefs. The founding of the city of Babylon, center of a mighty civilization, and the creation of its great temple tower, sacred to the supreme god Marduk, are portrayed as an offense to God. Mesopotamian theological propaganda that described the building of Babylon as the work of the gods at creation is tacitly refuted and the popular pagan notion that the ziqqurat was the navel of the earth, the channel of physical communication between heaven and earth, is subject to scorn and derision. *Babel,* taken to mean "the gate of god" by the Semites of Mesopotamia, is, by an Israelite play on words, construed as "confusion," and the confutation of mythological paganism is completed.

HISTORICIZATION

Biblical religion comprises a phenomenon unique in the annals of the ancient faiths. If, as has been pointed out, Israel rejected the mythological matrix in which other religions of the ancient Near East were embedded, what did it put in its place?

Any one who reads the biblical narrative can discern at once that the Israelite religion is cradled in the historical experience. Its verities are communicated through the norms of history and not only is the historical narrative one of the major modes of theological exposition, but the religious message cannot, in fact, be separated from its historical framework. This circumstance explains the strikingly contrasting roles that cosmogony plays in the pagan and Israelite religions. In Mesopotamia it is the theme of the great national epic; in Scripture it appears in a relatively minor key, having been replaced in prominence and influence by the Exodus from Egypt. Witness how the Sabbath institution, grounded in the creation of the world and so described in the first recording of the Decalogue (Exod. 20:8–11), has become wholly reinterpreted in terms of the redemption from Egyptian slavery in the second recounting of this great document (Deut. 5:12–15). The three major pilgrim festivals, Passover, Pentecost and Tabernacles, were undoubtedly, in origin, agricultural celebrations bound up with the life of the soil. In Israel they likewise underwent a process of historicization to be reinterpreted in terms of the national liberation at the Exodus.

Less obvious, but perhaps even more crucial to the struggle with paganism is the application of the process to the problem of evil. As a matter of fact, the existence of evil did not really present a major theological problem to polytheism, for the gods were capricious and could hardly be expected to act according to any set of rational principles that the worshipper might comprehend. Evil was perceived as a constituent of the cosmic order, an autonomous force that found effective expression through the activities of demons and spirits. In other words, evil was a metaphysical phenomenon.

Israelite monotheism entirely rejected this idea and, in so doing, created for itself a theological problem. The existence of evil seemed to compromise God's integrity as being incompatible either with His absolute goodness, or with His Omnipotence. Israelite monotheism proclaimed that God has ethical integrity, that the world is essentially good, and that society rests on a divinely ordained order of justice.

The Genesis narratives grapple with the theological problem of evil and seek a solution to it on the moral plane in place of the metaphysical. The phenomenon of evil is seen as the corruption of the moral order resulting from man's exercise of his God-given freedom. Adam and Eve, Cain, the generation of the Flood, the builders of Babel, the inhabitants of Sodom and Gomorrah—all exemplify the claim that evil is a human production. In other words, the problem was historicized.

An unusual opportunity to watch this process at work on the literary level is afforded by a text from the city of Ugarit. An epic struggle for power takes place between Baal, the god of fertility, and Yam, the personification of watery chaos. In the course of the contest, the divine craftsman, called *Ktr - w - Ḥss,* encourages Baal with these words:

Lo, your enemy, O Baal,
Lo, your enemy, O Baal,
Lo, your adversary will you smite.

Now this formula is remarkably parallel to a passage in the Book of Psalms (Ps. 92:10):

Lo, your enemies, O Lord
Lo, your enemies will perish
All evildoers will be scattered.

Here, however, the scene is not a mythical conflict between opposing forces of fertility and primeval chaos in which the outcome may be in doubt, but one in which God decisively punishes the evil deeds of the historical wicked. The language of mythology has been borrowed and transformed into a statement asserting the inevitable defeat of evil men.

THE COVENANT

The interplay between the two world views of polytheism and Israelite monotheism gave rise to yet another distinguishing feature of biblical religion, one that came to dominate all subsequent developments: the unique covenant concept. The notion that there existed a binding and exclusive relationship between God and an entire people is the most imperious and demanding factor in the evolution of the national faith and its institutions. It provided one of the most potent weapons in the struggle against paganism, for the covenant meant the divine election of Israel and it fostered a consciousness of difference and created a sense of national destiny. The community of Israel became a corporate personality, a politico-moral entity.

The practical effect of the covenant idea is immediately apparent in the novel direction taken by Israelite law. Whoever takes the trouble to compare the half-dozen law-collections that have survived from the ancient Near East will see at once that a common legal culture existed throughout the area. The collections exhibit a shared terminology, style, content and spirit. If we then compare the legislation of Israel with these earlier codes, we cannot fail to admit that Israel partook of this common legal tradition. The parallels are so striking and so numerous as to leave not a shadow of a doubt that such is the case. Nevertheless, as in all other spheres of Israelite-polytheistic relationships, the Biblical material does not slavishly transmit what it received from the past but creatively transformed its legal tradition so that it became something new and original.

It is here that the covenant consciousness comes into play, for the law is conceived as the expression of the will of God. It has its source in, and derives its sanction from Him alone. In sharp contrast to pagan practice which made the legislator the king, prince or sage who is inspired by the gods to promulgate law, no law in Israel is ever ascribed to prophet, sage or monarch. Moses, himself, is never the author of legislation, only its mediator. The consequence of this is that Israelite legal tradition ended up running counter to its Near Eastern analogues. Law, uniquely, was bound up with religion. It became an expression of man's relationship to God, so that crime is simultaneously also sin. No longer is law a matter solely of the individual concern. Society has a collective responsibility since the national covenant concept had turned the community of Israel into a corporate politico-moral entity. The welfare of all Israel was regarded as being inextricably intertwined with and conditional upon obedience to the law, and not, as elsewhere, dependent upon the life of the king and the performance of magical rituals.

The covenant idea permeated every facet of national life and proved to be a most powerful instrument of self-preservation that enabled Israel to resist the all but overwhelming pressures for assimilation to the dominant pagan culture. Already in the period of the patriarchs the narrative has Abraham carefully avoiding the possibility of intermarriage between his son Isaac and the local inhabitants. The same precautions preoccupy Rebekah and Isaac in respect of their son Jacob. Undoubtedly, the institution of marriage as an instrument for ensuring group survival is given clear recognition in these early traditions. Later, the prohibition of intermarriage finds explicit formulation as an expression of the covenant. The motivation is the maintenance of the religious integrity of Israel. We do not know the extent to which the prohibition was actually observed by the masses, but we have positive evidence in the covenant texts of a conscious attempt to fashion an ideal, religiously self-contained society fortified against the onslaught of paganism.

THE TERRITORIAL COMPONENT

One further salient and distinguishing characteristic of Israelite religion is its territorial component. The promise of nationhood, first made to Abraham and thereafter repeated successively to his descendants, is invariably coupled with the pledge of a national territory (Gen. 12:1–4;

15:16–18; Deut. 1:8). This land becomes the special and ideal arena of God's relationships with His people. It is not that God is looked upon as a territorial deity. He is not, for all the earth is His. But just as he selected (Exod. 4:22) Israel from among the nations, His creatures, to be His "first-born son," so the land of Israel is cherished by Him above all lands of his possession. It is described as the one on "which the LORD your God always keeps His eye from year's beginning to year's end" (Deut. 11:10–12). Israel and its land were both chosen by God to play crucial and central roles in the fulfillment of His plan of history. This elevation of the land to the status of a religious value-concept is peculiarly Israelite and has grave practical consequences, for the biblical idea of holiness carries with it decidedly moral implications. The sacred quality of the land of Israel imposes on its inhabitants imperious demands. The Torah declares that pre-Israelite peoples dwelling there had "defiled the land" and so forfeited their right to it. The land had "spewed them out," and would do so likewise to Israel should it be unfaithful to the covenant. The prophet Hosea surveys the degeneracy of the people of his time and concludes,

> Therefore the land shall mourn,
> and all who live in it shall languish.
> (Hos. 4: 1–3)

In the same vein, his contemporary Isaiah pronounces judgement on his generation,

> For the earth has become defiled under its
> inhabitants, because they have transgressed
> teachings, have violated law, have broken
> the ancient covenant. That is why a curse
> consumes the earth, and its inhabitants pay
> the penalty. That is why earth's dwellers
> have dwindled and but few men are left.
> (Isa. 24:5–6)

Statements like these give vivid expression to the intimate connection between the sacred land and the life and destiny of Israel. It is true that love of ancestral soil may be a feature of other ancient literatures, but it has to be remembered that the biblical account does not place the origins of Israel in the land of Canaan. This territory becomes Israel's homeland and acquires sanctity solely because it was chosen by God, and for no other reason. This is a phenomenon totally without analogy. It lent to the misfortune of exile an added dimension of horror, and it made the yearning for the return all the more intense. The exiles in Babylon cannot sing the songs of the Lord on alien soil (Ps. 137:4–6). They swear fearful oaths never to forget Jerusalem, and when the opportunity arises many prefer the perils of returning and rebuilding their ruined land to the comforts of exile. It is obvious that a religion in which the sacredness of the national land played a central role and in which that land is inextricably interwoven with the moral quality of the life of the people—such a religion is far from paganism and in confrontation with it.

THE NATIONAL AND THE UNIVERSAL

The covenantal and territorial bases on which the religion of Israel rests must, of necessity, generate a certain degree of tension in the immediacy of its monotheistic foundation, for monotheism implies universality. If the utterly unique Creator is the sovereign of all lands and all peoples, then monotheism should be inherently universalistic. Indeed, it perceives all human history as constituting a unity. It is no accident that the Bible, unprecedentedly, conceives of a family of man, so that Adam and Eve provide a common parentage for all humanity. It was inevitable that the Scriptural Flood story should radically depart from its Mesopotamian counterparts in that only a single family is saved which becomes, once again, the progenitor of a renewed humankind. The Bible begins with universal history. It tacitly presumes that all the world was monotheistic until it degenerated into polytheism. It presupposes that a universal moral code existed from the beginning of time and that all peoples are responsible for its observance and are called to account by God for its infraction. That is why the generation of the Flood, the men of Sodom and Gomorrah and the peoples of Canaan were all punished. There is not the faintest hint that their culpability lay in their idolatry, only that they violated the moral code.

How then do the national elements in the religion of Israel harmonize with the universal matrix? The answer is that the one complemented the other and the tension generated light. The innate universalism of ethical monotheism was given its most articulate and eloquent expression in the rhetoric of the prophets. These men held a vision of the universal recognition of the one God:

And the LORD will become king over all
the earth; on that day the LORD will be
one and His name one.
(Zech. 14:9)

This was the prophecy of a man who lived and worked in Jerusalem
after the return from exile. At a time when the tiny community was
struggling for its very existence, Zechariah could see the day when,

Many people and strong nations shall come to
Jerusalem to entreat the favor of the LORD.
(Zech. 8:22)

He was echoing the words of an earlier prophet who foresaw the day
when universal harmony and peace would prevail among nations who,
by virtue of their recognition of the God of Israel would establish their
relationships, one with the other, on principles of international morality:

And the many peoples shall go and shall say:
Come, let us go up to the Mount of the
LORD, to the House of the God of Jacob:
That he may instruct us in His ways,
And that we may walk in His paths.
For instruction shall come forth from Zion,
The word of the LORD from Jerusalem.
Thus He will judge among the nations
And arbitrate for the many peoples,
And they shall beat their swords into
plowshares
And their spears into pruning hooks:
Nation shall not take up sword against nation:
They shall never again know war.
(Isa. 2:3–4)

In every one of these lofty visions the national Israelite element is an
indispensable ingredient. Messianism never involves the effacement of
national identity. The land of Israel and the people of Israel always
retain their central and crucial roles. Never is there a nation of a purely
religious entity to which international dispersion is a normal and desirable state for the realization of its destiny. The consciousness of exile is
always present in prophetic literature and the reconstitution of the
political—ethnic—religious center is invariably an ideal.

With the prophetic national universalism, the struggle of Israelite monotheism against paganism turned full cycle. Rising above the polytheistic world to which it owed much, Israel succeeded in fashioning a wholly new religion. The initial, defensive anti-pagan polemic became a vision of universal monotheism. The national and universal elements became so interblended that they reacted upon each other in a way that the omission of either would distort the whole and deprive the messianic ideal of all meaning.

The Biblical Sources for the History of the Monarchy

A. THE PAUCITY OF THE SOURCES

The somewhat less than half a millennium when there was a Monarchy in Israel is only meagerly documented. This period, so rich in national and international experience, so fertile in literary creativity, so strikingly original in the life of the spirit, so momentous and clamorous in the expression of its social conscience, so imperious in its demands upon the future, has not disclosed its history to a degree commensurate with its time-span and importance.

The corpus of canonical sources dealing directly with the period of the Monarchy comprises no more than one hundred and fifty chapters in the books of Samuel[1] (I Sam. 9–31; II Sam.), Kings[2], and Chronicles[3] (I Chron. 10–29; II Chron.), supplemented by narrative appendages in Isaiah, chaps. 36–39 and Jeremiah, chap. 51. Much additional information can be culled from the literary prophets in whose reactions to contemporary events solid historical data are presumably embedded. All in all, however, the biblical sources available for detailed reconstruction of the period of the Monarchy are not bulky and, as will be seen, are limited in scope, due to their particular nature.

B. CONTENTS OF THE BIBLICAL SOURCES

The material about the Monarchy in the book of Samuel begins with the election of Saul (c. 1020 B.C.E.) and closes with events in the life of

David, a period of about sixty years. It divides naturally into four groupings:

I Sam. 8–15 deal with the demand for monarchic government and the fortunes of Saul from his election as king, his military campaigns, and his rejection by the prophet Samuel after the war with Amalekites.

I Sam. 16–II:1 cover the rise of David and his checkered relationship with Saul until the disastrous defeat of Israel by the Philistines at Gilboa, where Saul and three of his sons met their deaths.

II Sam. 2–8 treat David's succession to the throne of Judah and Israel, the consolidation of his kingdom, the capture of Jerusalem and its conversion into the religious and political center of the nation, and Nathan's oracle to David promising an eternal Davidic dynasty.

II Sam. 9–24 describe events at the court of David, the rebellion against him, and some of his wars of conquest. The last four chapters are only appendixes with varied contents.

The book of Kings opens with the last days of David (c. 960 B.C.E.) and closes with the release of King Jehoiachin from prison on the accession of Evil-merodach to the throne of Babylonia in 561 B.C.E., thus covering about 400 years in the history of the nation. This work, too, falls into several natural divisions.

I Kings 1–11 is the story of Solomon's forty-year reign from the struggle for succession until his death. His efforts to consolidate his power, organize his empire, erect great buildings, and cope with the growing internal and external problems are recorded at length. The narrative is interspersed with popular material illustrating the wealth and grandeur of Solomon's court and his reputation for shrewdness and wisdom.

I Kings 12–II Kings 17 is an interlocking, synchronized account of the Divided Monarchy, the vicissitudes of the kingdoms of Judah and Israel until the destruction of the latter in 722 B.C.E. It presents first the events precipitating the secession of the north and then the affairs of its first king, Jeroboam. From here the narrative returns to Rehoboam of Judah and continues with the kings of the south contemporaneous with Jeroboam. When Asa, the last of these, dies, the account once again turns to the northern kings, including the successors of Jeroboam who had been contemporaneous with Asa. Returning to Judah, the story progresses in this fashion back and forth. Besides information about the kings, much popular prophetic tradition, especially about Elijah and Elisha, is recounted.

II Kings 18–25 concentrate exclusively on the fortunes of the Judean kingdom from the accession of Hezekiah in 715 B.C.E., especially upon the reform of the cult, Sennacherib's invasion of Judah, and the king's illness. The personality of Isaiah is interwoven into these two latter events. After recording the abominations of Manasseh and the great reforms of Josiah, the narrator tells of the decline and fall of the kingdom in the succeeding forty years and concludes with the murder of Gedaliah, the Babylonian-appointed governor of Judah after the destruction of 587 B.C.E. The last four verses are really an appendix to supply a note of hope.

The third biblical source is of quite a different nature. While Samuel and Kings form a continuous history, Chronicles is a parallel presentation of the two with numerous passages duplicated exactly or with minor variants relating to matters of orthography, grammar, syntax, or vocabulary.[4] But it is much more than this, both adding and subtracting material and occasionally even contradicting the book of Kings.[5] Because of its own special emphases and distinctive approach, Chronicles really constitutes an independent historical work.

The history of the Monarchy commences with I Chron. 10 and continues to the end. Its main divisions are as follows:

I Chron. 10–29 retells the history of David after he ascends the throne. Its interest lies mainly in the organization of the kingdom, about which it is remarkably detailed, and in the preparations for building the Temple and establishing the cult.

II Chron. 1–9 contains the history of Solomon, focusing especially on the Temple.

II Chron. 10–36 is a history of the Kings of Judah with little about the northern monarchs and no synchronisms. By way of contrast, the Chronicler often reports expansively on the Kings of Judah and adds a great deal about their military, political, and economic activities that appear in no other biblical sources. An appendix tells how Cyrus permitted the exiles to return to Jerusalem to rebuild the Temple.

C. THEIR COMPOSITION

1. THE BIBLICAL SOURCES AND MODERN RESEARCH

The complex known as the Former Prophets is a continuous expansion of the Pentateuchal narratives from the beginnings of the conquest through the settlement until the Destruction of the Temple and the

Exile. The entire work is clearly animated by a single spirit, and events are treated with a uniformity that makes it possible to speak of a unified body of historical material covering Joshua, Judges, Samuel, and Kings; the latter two are roughly three-fifths of the whole. The Greek Bible indicates that the present division of Samuel and Kings into separate books is a secondary development, and the fact that I Kings 1–2 is the sequel to II Sam. 9–20 further supports this conclusion.

Modern scholarship has increasingly focused on isolating the various literary types *(Gattungen)* embedded in the compositions, on distinguishing the blocs of material at the disposal of the editors or compilers, and on examining the literary techniques to learn how the works achieved their extant form. Research has made it clear that Samuel-Kings (and to a lesser extent, Joshua-Judges) bear the characteristic imprints of the Deuteronomic school, and that reference to Deuteronomistic compilers or editors is therefore appropriate.[6]

The initial clue comes, of course, from the extraordinary amount of space accorded the story of the discovery of the Book of the Law and Josiah's reform of the cult (II Kings 22:3–23:24). Beyond this, the two specific references to the "Book of the Law of Moses" really identify with Deuteronomy (I Kings 2:3; cf. Deut. 6:1 f.; II Kings 14:6; cf. Deut. 24:16), and the distinctive phraseology of the work saturates the language of Samuel and especially Kings.[7] The narratives of these two books, moreover, are embellished with prophetic sermons and discourses (e.g., I Kings 11:31–39; 14:7–11, 13–16) and with historical summaries of a reflective nature (e.g. I Sam. 12; II Kings 17:7–23; 21:10–16; 22:15–20), clearly patterned after the book of Deuteronomy, itself constituting the moralistic and exhortatory speeches of Moses' farewell address.[8] Finally, and above all, it is in their leading and recurrent themes that the Deuteronomic influence is overwhelmingly manifest. The emphasis on the divine election of the city of Jerusalem and the Temple (I Kings 8:16, 44, 48; 11:13, 32, 36; 14:21; II Kings 21:7; 23:27) only expands upon the "place that God will choose" concept of the earlier work (cf. Deut. 12, *passim*; 14:23–25; 15:20; 16, *passim*; 17:8, 10; 18:6; 26:2; 31:11) which also is the ideological inspiration for the pervasive doctrine of centralization of worship, while the notion of destruction and exile as punishment for the national sin of idolatry (e.g. II Kings 17:23; 21:2–15; 22:16 f.; 23:26 f.; 24:3) is drawn directly from Deut. 4:25–27; 28: 15–69.

If the extant historiography of the Monarchy is part of a larger, continuous, Deuteronomistic history, some fundamental issues concerning its composition must be raised. How was the previous material utilized by the writers? Did they correlate an unorganized collection of individual facts and compose a literary work, or did they reshape earlier narrative blocs? If the latter, what did the older history include and how did it relate to the Pentateuchal sources?

No scholarly unanimity exists. Some regard the Former Prophets as a Deuteronomistic redaction of the JE narratives extended beyond the Pentateuch, although opinion differs as to whether Kings belongs in this category.[9] Those who accept the three-source theory are similarly uncertain, adding a L(ay) document to JE and thus considering that the historical compositions combine three parallel strands.[10] The most widely held view sees (Joshua-) Samuel-Kings, not as parallel sources interwoven, but as originally independent sagas juxtaposed chronologically by the compilers and supplied with connectives and an ideological framework.[11]

2. THE SOURCE MATERIALS

Is it possible to isolate and delineate the blocs of tradition the writers used? The relative sparseness of the biblical historiographic material cannot be charged to a paucity of sources, for the books themselves disclose rich documentation to which the reader is referred for further information. The frequency of these source citations decreases dramatically with the antiquity of the books.

The book of Samuel ascribes David's lament over Saul and Jonathan to a presumably poetic work known as the "Book of Jashar"[12] (II Sam. 1:18; cf. Josh. 10:13), but does not again mention any other source. The book of Kings states that Solomon's history is supplemented by the "Book of the Acts of Solomon"[13] (I Kings 11:41), and that the deeds of seventeen of the nineteen monarchs of Israel are described at greater length in the "Book of the Chronicles of the Kings of Israel"[14] (*ibid.*, 14:19; 15:31 etc.). The "Book of the Chronicles of the Kings of Judah" offers additional information about all but four of the Judean kings[15] (*ibid.*, 14:29; 15:7 etc.).

The contents of these two chronicles upon which the biblical historian relied cannot be reconstructed, but they must have been far more extensive than our canonical works since they described at length military affairs (*ibid.*, 14:19; 15:23 etc.), political events (*ibid.*, 16:20; II Kings 15:5), royal building projects (I Kings 22:39), and engineering feats (II Kings 22:20). Probably, however, they were not primary sources like royal memoirs or contemporary annals, because they are always described as well-known writings, easily accessible to the public for whom the book of Kings was aimed; that is, the generation after the destruction of the kingdom of Judah. It is hardly feasible that original palace or Temple archives either survived the Babylonian destruction or, if they did, were widely known and readily available. Furthermore, the numerous dynasties in northern Israel which violently succeeded each other must have been inimical to the continuous production of a connected court history from Jeroboam to the fall of Samaria, especially in view of the source-formula citation even for reigns of such brief duration as Zechariah's six months (*ibid.*, 15:11), Shallum's one month (*ibid.*, v. 15), and Zimri's seven days (I Kings 16:20). It is far more plausible to assume that the two chronicles were historiographical developments from original sources. That of the kings of Israel was probably written soon after the destruction of the northern kingdom, was circulated among the Judeans and the exiles, and inspired a parallel chronicle for the southern monarchy. Both documents must have at one time been popular enough for the author of Kings to consult them and suggest that his readers do so as well.

By far the most varied and extensive series of source citations is in the post-exilic canonical book of Chronicles. It is uncertain whether the so-called "Book of the Kings of Israel and Judah" (I Chron. 9:1; II Chron. 27:7; 35:26; 36:8) or the "Book of the Kings of Judah and Israel" (*ibid.*, 16:11; 25:26; 28:26; 32:32) or the "Book of the Kings of Israel" (*ibid.*, 20:34) or simply the "[midrash of] the Book of the Kings" (*ibid.*, 24:27) refer to a single work or to several books which may or may not be identical with the sources cited under somewhat different titles in the book of Kings. Why does the nomenclature vary and why is the phrase, *dibrei ha-yāmīm*, frequently employed in Kings, replaced with other phrases in Chronicles? Why again, despite the reference to "Israel" in these titles, is every citation concerned only with a Judean king?

The Chronicler's other source has the same characteristic. The prophetic historic compositions of Samuel, Nathan, and Gad deal with the United Kingdoms of David and Solomon (I Chron. 29:29; II Chron. 9:29). Beyond this, however, the focus of interest is exclusively Judah. Ahijah, Iddo, and Shemaiah are cited for the period of the division of the kingdom (*ibid.*, 9:29; 12:15; 13:22), and Jehu son of Hanani for the reign of Jehoshaphat (*ibid.*, 20:34). A work by Isaiah is given as the source for information about Uzziah and Hezekiah (*ibid.*, 26:22; 32:32). Whether all these compositions had been previously available to the compilers of the Former Prophets is unknown, but certainly the biblical references could not have exhausted the literary treasury available to the historiographers, who must have had access to a vast amount of material neither explicitly nor independently mentioned in the Bible.

First, and most obvious, would have been various archival records, whose existence is assumed not only on the basis of contemporary Near Eastern customs, but by certain grammatical, syntactical, and stylistic eccentricities in our narratives which betray the direct use of archival data.[16] The lists of high officials in the administrations of David and Solomon (II Sam. 8:16–18; 20:23–26; I Kings 4:1–6) clearly derive from archives, although integrated into the narratives, just as the relatively extensive treatment of Temple themes can be traced to Temple annals. Details about construction, furnishings, and dedication (*ibid.*, 6; 7:13–51; 8), its despoiled treasury in the days of Rehoboam (*ibid.*, 14:26–28), Asa (15:18), Jehoash (II Kings 12:19), Amaziah (14:14), Hezekiah (18:16), Jehoiachin (24:13), and Zedekiah (25:13–17), the Temple repairs initiated by Jehoash (12:5–16) and Josiah (22:3–7), and the innovations of Ahaz (16:10–18) can probably all be assigned to Temple priests or scribal schools. Throughout the Near East, such temple-affiliated scribes were responsible for temple records and annals.[17]

Two long self-contained compositions, widely accepted as having been incorporated more or less in their entirety into Samuel-Kings, tell of the rise of the Monarchy and the problem of David's succession. The latter would have comprised all the incidents preceding the central theme (cf. I Kings 1:20) and the final formula asserting Solomon's unchallenged supremacy (*ibid.*, 2:46).[18]

The conspicuous and pervasive role of the prophet in the book of Kings makes it clear that the historiographers used cycles of prophetic legends. Not only is he intensively involved in state affairs, delivering the word of God as an active force in history at critical moments in the life of the nation,[19] but he becomes part of the folkloristic embellishment. The stories about Ahijah of Shiloh (*ibid.*, 11:29–39; 14:1–18), Shemaiah (*ibid.*, 12:22–24), and the anonymous "man of God" at Bethel (*ibid.*, 12:32–13:32) all seem to be self-contained units, as do the tales of Elijah (*ibid.*, 17–19; 21; II Kings 1) and Elisha (*ibid.*, 2–13), which originated in northern Israel.[20] An independent Judean collection of legends about Isaiah similarly draws upon and is integrated into the history of Hezekiah[21] (*ibid.*, 18:13–20:19). It can also be postulated that an ancient collection of songs, mentioned not in the Hebrew Bible but in the Greek translation,[22] was the source for the several poetic compositions in the prose narration.[23]

3. DATE OF COMPOSITION

It is certain that the historiography of the monarchic period was finally redacted in the Babylonian Exile. The last event recorded is the release of King Jehoiachin from prison in 561 B.C.E. when Evil-merodach ascended the throne of Babylonia (*ibid.*, 25:27–30). Since there is not another word about the life of the Jews in exile, this epilogue can only be interpreted as a desire to conclude optimistically. The absence of any reference to the downfall of Babylon and to the actions of Cyrus means, therefore, that Kings was edited well before 538 B.C.E, probably not long after 560 B.C.E.

It is difficult to go beyond this, however, with any degree of certainly because the materials are composite and the issues involved complex. The view that the entire Former Prophets is a historical continuum written about the middle of the sixth century B.C.E., seems less plausible than that there were multiple editions, the bulk pre-exilic, from the period not long after Josiah's great reform of the cult.[24]

Whether a comprehensive pre-Deuteronomistic history was utilized and transformed is debatable, as is the amount of expansion and redaction made in the exile to bring it up to date and achieve a retrospective examination of the monarchic period that would vindicate divine justice after the great national catastrophe.[25]

D. HISTORY AND FAITH

The historiographers, then, had many sources at their disposal, thus raising a question about the relatively sparse biblical documentation of the half a millennium between Saul and Zedekiah. Scrutiny of the works of the scriptural writers may explain the fact.

This leads to one of the most extraordinary features of biblical religion: that its verities are communicated through the forms of history. The historical writings are actually documents of faith. Their theocentricity, however, lies less in interest in God's essence than in concern for His activities among men. If the historical framework of biblical literature is inseparable from its religious message, this demands considerable caution, and severely limits the use to which biblical historiography can be put as a means for recovering the past.

The fact is that the biblical writer was not interested simply in preserving for posterity a record of the past, nor with an objective, dispassionate, comprehensive, and integrated delineation of human affairs. He was in fact not detached from but completely involved in the events he described. He had little use for the pursuit of objectivity because he was committed to a particular point of view. He laid no claim to comprehensiveness, but was thoroughly and consciously selective. He was dedicated to the proposition of using historic events to demonstrate, objectify, and transmit truths to which he was passionately committed.[26]

E. THE PROBLEMS OF BALANCE

How the foregoing affects the understanding of the biblical sources as history becomes apparent if the documentation is examined in relation to the three divisions into which the period of the Monarchy naturally falls.

The 100-year United Kingdom under Saul, David, and Solomon is covered in eighty-seven chapters of scriptural historiography. The divided kingdoms of Judah and Israel, which lasted for just over two centuries until the fall of Samaria, are given forty-seven chapters, and Judah alone between 722 B.C.E. and 587 B.C.E. sixteen. This is surely remarkably uneven; well over half of the source material is devoted to less than one quarter of the time involved. Clearly, the United Monarchy holds pride of place for the historiographers, as it does for the prophets, whose messianic vision featured the reunification of Judah and Israel.

Imbalance as a didactic aspect of the scriptural history is most striking in the treatment of David's forty-year reign. Since there are sixty biographical chapters, 40% of the material is devoted to less than 10% of the period. Once again, prophetic themes also suggest themselves. The personality of David, the royal ideal, the dynastic symbol and embodiment of messianic prophetic aspiration, seems to dominate biblical historiography.[27]

Consistently uneven treatment is exhibited throughout, as a few striking examples from the book of Kings amply illustrate. Several of the nineteen Judean monarchs were blessed with extraordinary longevity. Asa reigned forty-one years (I Kings 15:10), but is given only seventeen verses (*ibid.*, 15:9–25), Jehoshaphat for twenty-five years (*ibid.*, 22:42) and is given fifty-one verses (*ibid.*, 22:1–51), Jehoash for forty years (II Kings 12:2) and receives twenty-two verses (*ibid.*, 12:1–22), Uzziah for fifty-two years (*ibid.*, 15:2) and gets seven verses (*ibid.*, 15:1–7), and Manasseh for fifty-five years and merits eighteen verses (*ibid.*, 21:1–18). The Bible says nothing about this, and only from Assyrian sources do we know that Azariah (Uzziah) led a Syrian coalition against Tiglath-pileser III.[28] When we turn to the monarchs of the kingdom of Israel, we discover that eight verses suffice for Baasha's twenty-four years (I Kings 15:3 f.; 16:1–6), seven for the forty-one years of Jeroboam II (II Kings 14:23–29), and five for Pekah's twenty (*ibid.*, 15:27–31).

Imbalance persists not only in the space devoted to a reign, but in the data presented. A case in point is Omri king of Israel, whose only achievement, blandly recorded and not evaluated, was the transfer of the capital of his kingdom to Samaria, newly built for the purpose, and who is otherwise condemned as an evil idolater, whose twelve-year reign is dismissed in six scriptural verses (I Kings 16:23–28). Yet he was undoubtedly one of the greatest and most competent of the Israelite monarchs and left his mark on the international scene. Founder of the first dynasty in the north, three of his descendants sat on the throne in Samaria. The inscription of Mesha king of Moab makes clear that Omri conquered Moab as well as much territory north of the River Arnon in Transjordania. Shalmaneser III (858–824 B.C.E.) of Assyria even called Jehu, who destroyed the dynasty, an "Omride." During the following century Assyrian records customarily referred to the kingdom of northern Israel as "Omri-land." The biblical record, however, gives no inkling of Omri's stature and importance in the contemporary world.[29]

Similar is the scriptural treatment of Ahab. During his twenty-two-year rule he pursued his political, commercial, and military policies with such daring, imagination, and farsightedness that his kingdom became one of the most important in the area. Assyrian records show that Ahab was a leader of a coalition of western monarchs who, in the climactic battle of Qarqar against Shalmaneser III in 853 B.C.E., upset the Assyrian advance on the west.[30] Not a word of this is mentioned in the biblical sources. The verdict about Ahab is unqualifiedly negative and attention is focused almost exclusively on his tolerance of idolatry and his immoral and murderous expropriation of the ancestral vineyard of one of his subjects, thus, in the eyes of the writer, disqualifying the entire house of Ahab and dooming it to perdition (*ibid.*, 21).

The technique of highlighting those episodes that suit the theological purposes of the scriptural writers is exemplified by the story of Josiah. Of the numerous events in his thirty-one-year rule, attention is expressly called to his eighteenth year when his religious reforms reached their climax, although incidental intelligence, now supported by archaeological evidence, reveals Josiah's bold political maneuvers and important military activities.[31]

F. INDIFFERENCE TO INTERNATIONAL AFFAIRS

From the viewpoint of the modern historian, it is curious that biblical historiography disregards the impact of the world situation upon the Land of Israel. Only from external sources do we know, for instance, that the mighty empire of David and Solomon was expedited by successfully exploiting a unique international situation, the power vacuum then prevailing in the Near East.[32]

This, and the international situation behind the truncation of the empire, is ignored by the biblical historiographer. Not by chance did the contraction coincide with the resurgence of Egyptian power and the reawakening of interest in Palestine among the XXIInd Dynasty kings. This is clearly the reason why a number of facts are recorded incidentally and disconnectedly: Solomon's marriage alliance with the Egyptian royal house (*ibid.*, 3:1), Pharaoh's mysterious invasion of Philistia and his presentation of Gezer to Solomon as a dowry (*ibid.*, 9:15–16), the harboring and sponsoring of Solomon's political enemies by the Egyptian court (*ibid.*, 11:14–22, 26–28, 40), and Shishak's invasion of Palestine and his plundering of the Temple in the fifth year of Rehoboam[33] (*ibid.*, 14:25–26; II Chron. 12:2–9).

This lack of international perspective and the introverted, theological presentation of events sometimes suggest that episodes are separate from each other and they sometimes turn integrated and coordinated actions into diffuse ones. An example of the former is the assassination of Sennacherib, which appears to follow his return to his land after his Judean fiasco (II Kings 19:36–37). In actual fact, it happened twenty years later. An instance of diffusion is the story of Hezekiah's neutralization of Philistine and other hostile military potential (*ibid.*, 18:8; I Chron. 4:41–43), his measures to secure Jerusalem's water supply in event of siege (II Kings 20:20; II Chron. 2:30), his bolstering of the city's defenses (Isa. 22:8–11), the reinforcement and provisioning of cities in central Judah (II Chron. 32:28), and the survey of national resources (I Chron. 4:38–41). All these precautions certainly anticipated an Assyrian invasion, which gave rise to the diplomatic activities described in II Kings 20:12–13 (Isa. 39:1–2), but the biblical writers have reported his activities in many sources as disconnected incidents. Similarly, nothing is said of Hezekiah's political activities that provoked Sennacherib's invasion in 701 B.C.E., nor is his reform of the national cult (II Chron. 29–31) equated with the world situation as it undoubtedly must be.[34] By contrast, the story of Hezekiah's illness and his treatment by Isaiah with a fig-plaster is featured at length (II Kings 20:1–11; Isa. 38).

The handling of Josiah's thirty-one-year reign, already mentioned, further exemplifies disregard for the international background to internal Judean affairs. Egypt and Assyria are briefly mentioned, but merely to describe how Josiah met his death (II Kings 23:29; II Chron. 35:20–21). The biblical historiographer does not suggest that Josiah's sweeping reform of the cult (II Kings 22–23; II Chron. 34–35) might be understood in the light of the decline of Assyrian power in the west and evaluated better in terms of cultural developments in Egypt, Phoenicia, and Mesopotamia.[35]

G. CHRONOLOGICAL DATA

The scriptural authors were nonetheless aware of the historic truths they were dealing with and that they were rooted in a specific time and place. This is especially evident in their concern, for the first time in biblical historiography, with precise chronological information, and the data given is rich and varied. The lengths of the reigns of the kings are carefully recorded and throughout the divided kingdom the initial year of each king is coordinated with that of his rival. His age at accession is noted and sometimes the year of a particular episode. One event is occasionally dated by another or by the time between incidents. There are even synchronisms with the reigns of neighboring kings.

All this information, however, presents serious problems for the modern historian, since the different data and chronological systems do not interlock and, in fact, seem inconsistent.[36] Nor do they always accord with established Assyrian chronology, thus making it difficult to reconstruct history by using the biblical sources. Possibly we are dealing with a late, artificial, and perhaps schematized chronological system imposed by the editors, although it seems unlikely. The synchronistic method of dating can now be shown to have been a feature of Assyrian-Babylonian king lists as early as the twelfth century B.C.E., and it may well have been an attribute of the royal annals utilized by the author of Kings.[37] Moreover, even though there were 480 regnal years between the building of the Temple and the Cyrus Declaration and the same number between the Exodus and the Temple (I Kings 6:1), this must nevertheless be regarded as coincidence and not the result of the deliberated schematizing of a late Deuteronomistic redactor. Such a possibility is negated by the absence of references to the Restoration in the book of Kings, and by the inconsistencies themselves, which are incompatible with an artificially constructed system.

We can resolve the chronological problems in the biblical sources only by establishing certain facts, presently unknown. Until definitive answers to the problems are forthcoming, the chronological information in our biblical sources cannot be said to have yielded its mysteries and its value as history must remain limited.

H. THE THREE MOTIFS

Biblical historiography about the Monarchy is characterized by three dominant motifs—the divine election of Israel, the Davidic Dynasty, and Jerusalem and its Temple—all of which illustrate the high degree of selectivity.

1. THE ELECTION OF ISRAEL

The first, basic to the Torah and the Prophets, is expressed by the multitudinous references to Israel as God's people, and the explicit assertion that God redeemed Israel, a singular nation which He took as His very own for all eternity (II Sam. 7:23–24) to be His chosen people (I Kings 3:8). This is also the reason for the frequent references to the Exodus.[38]

The divine election of Israel affects the presentation of historical data, for the historiographers were less interested in recording the past than in demonstrating how Israel, by virtue of its special relationship with God, became responsible for its own history, its fate being determined by its fealty or disloyalty to demands of that relationship.

2. THE ELECTION OF DAVID

The second pillar upon which scriptural historiography rests is the symbol of David. The texts stress his divine election (II Sam. 6:2; I Kings 8:16, 11–34) and elevate to the level of doctrine the unchallengeable and exclusive right of the Davidic line to the throne of Judah for all eternity (II Sam. 7:11–16, 25; I Kings 2:33, 45; 8:25; 9:5). David becomes the dynastic symbol and the ideal model of kingship for all subsequent monarchs.[39] For this reason, as we have said, David is allotted space entirely disproportionate to the length of his reign.

3. THE ELECTION OF JERUSALEM AND THE TEMPLE

Woven into the previous motifs and their most tangible expression is the divine election of Jerusalem and its Temple. The motif originated with David's conquest of Jerusalem, establishing it as his capital (II Sam. 5:6–11), and reinforcing and validating its political role by transferring there the Ark of the Covenant (*ibid.*, 6). David's desire to build the Temple is strongly emphasized even though Solomon carried out the project (*ibid.*, 7; I Kings 5:7; 8:17–18). Jerusalem and its Temple as God's chosen place, to the exclusion of all others, is repeatedly eulogized (*ibid.*, 8:16, 44, 48 etc.). Like the preceding themes, this is a major selective and evaluative criterion. The impact of the three themes upon the material becomes clear upon examination of several of the narratives.

a. The Treatment of Saul

From a factual standpoint, the biography of Saul, first king of Israel, is so brief that it is difficult to evaluate his place in Israelite history. We do not even know how long he reigned (cf. I Sam. 13:1). It is the failures that arrest the attention of the writer because they pave the way for the Davidic succession. Similarly, the narratives focus so heavily upon the rivalry between Saul and David that it encompasses three-quarters of the book of Samuel, although it involves no more than one-third of his reign. The Chronicler even omits Saul's biography, except his death, which is attributed to his sins (I Chron. 10:2–14). Only bare and scattered hints supply an image of Saul as a strong ruler of military, administrative, political, and religious importance.[40] For the biblical writers, the towering personality and symbolic role of David has obscured Saul in biblical historiography.

b. The Treatment of Solomon[41]

Solomon's glittering reign undoubtedly marks the golden age of the Monarchy, and the frequent occurrence of his name in Hebrew Scripture—nearly 300 times—is an index of the mark he made on tradition. Although he ruled Israel for forty years, nearly half of what is written, however, deals with his Temple project (I Kings 5:16–32; 6; 7:12–51; 8). That the Temple enterprise largely fired the historian's imagination is consistent with the circumscribed interests and didactic purposes of the book of Kings and illustrates and exemplifies once again the principle of selectivity.

c. Jerusalem and the Cult

Narrative after narrative is overwhelmingly preoccupied with Jerusalem, the Temple, and the cult. Jeroboam's motivation for the introduction of novel forms of worship and for the establishment of new cultic centers in northern Israel is portrayed as grounded in his fears of the attractiveness of Jerusalem (*ibid.*, 12:26–33). These acts constitute the cardinal sin of that kingdom, and their perpetuation stigmatizes practically every one of its monarchs. In fact, this is often all that the writer has to report about them.

The numerous occasions on which the Temple was plundered are carefully recorded; the cultic innovations of Ahaz occupy nine of the eighteen verses devoted to the sixteen years of his reign (II Kings 16:2–19); renovations of the Temple and reforms of the cult receive special prominence, as do Manasseh's cultic aberrations and their consequences (II Kings 21:21; 23:26; 24:3f). The fate that befell the Temple, its appurtenances, and its officers constitutes a major part of the story of the Babylonian destruction of Jerusalem (II Kings 25:9–18).

I. THE JUDGMENTS ON THE KINGS

Perhaps the most eloquent testimony to the historiographer's preoccupation with cultic matters is in the judgments passed on the rulers of the two kingdoms.

Israelite historiography is unusual in that it generally does not glorify the kings, but criticizes a majority of them. This strongly contrasts with the adulatory tone of documents from Egypt and Mesopotamia. Of nineteen Judean monarchs, eleven are called by the author of the book of Kings "evil in the eyes of the Lord." Only two, Hezekiah (II Kings 18:3–6) and Josiah (*ibid.*, 22:2), are adjudged wholly virtuous, while the other six merit qualified approval. Israel's nineteen monarchs predictably fare worse. Not one is wholeheartedly endorsed. Jehu, the most fully accepted, is criticized for tolerating the "sins of Jeroboam" (*ibid.*, 10:29–31). Some meager virtue is detected in Jehoram (*ibid.*, 3:2), but the rest are dismissed as unregenerate reprobates.

To what extent do these estimates conform to historic reality? The stereotypic nature of the condemnatory formulae is immediately suspect. Zimri, for instance, is said to have died because he sinfully followed the path of Jeroboam (I Kings 16:19), but his reign lasted only seven days. The criteria for judgment are definitely not those of the modern historian. Native intelligence, statesmanship, political wisdom and administrative skill, military prowess, and material contribution to the nation are not taken into account. Such virtues and achievements are not belittled but found wanting from the historiographer's viewpoint of eternity. Censure or approval of the kings is generally given on the basis of fidelity or infidelity to the demands of the Covenant and thus is expressed in term of the purity of the national cult and its exclusive concentration in the Jerusalem Temple.

This extraordinary feature of the scriptural sources offers further proof that the aim of the historiographer was not to produce a history of the Monarchy, but to provide an explanation for the disasters that befell the nation in the form of the original division of the kingdom, the destruction of the northern state, and the downfall of Judah. The final editor of Kings did his work in the Babylonian Exile and, as has been pointed out, it constitutes a retrospective criticism, in the spirit of the Deuteronomic revolution, of the period of Hezekiah to Josiah. To this extent, the judgments on the kings are really based on standards that were not yet operative in the days of most of them, for it cannot be accidental that Hezekiah was the first monarch to remove the *bamoth* (II Kings 18:3–4, 22) and that no fewer than six of his predecessors are characterized as virtuous and one or two even reformistic, although they did not act against this particular cultic practice.[42] On the one hand, the judgments on the Judean kings provide valuable historical raw material for reconstructing the history of the *bāmāh* institution:[43] on the other, they constitute important evidence for determining the historiosophic nature of the book of Kings.

J. THE ATTITUDE TO THE NORTHERN KINGDOM

The Judean origin of the scriptural historiographer is sufficient to account for the fact that none of the northern monarchs is regarded as truly virtuous and that the kingdom is considered sinful from its inception because of the illegitimacy of its cult (I Kings 13:33–34). Destruction and exile are, in fact, inevitable (*ibid.*, 14:15–16) because of the cumulative cultic sin (II Kings 17).

Nevertheless, practically all our information about the northern kingdom springs from the book of Kings which, surprisingly, devotes more space to its affairs than to the history of the south. That it does not regard the kingdom of Israel itself as illegitimate is clear from the royal synchronisms which give the kings of the north all but equal status with those of the Davidic dynasty.[44] Most of the prophetic narratives in Kings focus upon the north, and a prophet never pleads for reunification or asserts the exclusive political and religious hegemony of Jerusalem while the kingdoms are separate. The prophets, who spoke in the name of the Lord were, after all, often involved in anointing, selecting, or destroying the northern king. After Ahijah of Shiloh appointed Jeroboam (I Kings 11:29–31), he apprised him of the destruction of his dynasty (*ibid.*, 14:1–16); Jehu son of Hanani foretold the downfall of Baasha (*ibid.*, 16:1–7, 12) as did Elijah the house of Ahab (*ibid.*, 21:17–24); Elisha actually had another prophet seditiously anoint Jehu king of Israel (II Kings 9:1–10).

All this must mean that the Judean writer of Kings saw the people of Israel as one in spite of the schism, and looked upon northern history no less than southern as the unfolding of the word of God.

K. PROPHECY AND HISTORY

It is this aspect of biblical historiography that provides its prophetic flavor. The writers admittedly drew upon prophetic source material, and emphasized the decisive role of the prophets in the fortunes of Israel by repeatedly showing how God's will, expressed through His appointed agents, was exactly fulfilled. So important to them is the prophetic ingredient that predictions later modified or withdrawn are recorded in their original form.[45]

This is not to say that scriptural historiography derives from prophetic circles. The prophet is restricted to the northern kingdom, appearing in Judah only after the fall of Samaria.[46] In any case it is not the literary but the popular type of prophet who is the center of attention. There is, besides, a great difference between the historiographic and the classical-prophetic evaluation of the national-historic sin, the former blaming cultic corruption for Israel's misfortunes, the latter, Israel's infidelity to the Covenant on the socio-moral plane.

L. THE WORK OF THE CHRONICLER

The ideology and selectiveness of Samuel-Kings are heightened in Chronicles, where the arguments for the late composition are incontrovertible. Both the report of the "Declaration of Cyrus" of 538 B.C.E. (II Chron. 36:22 f.) and linguistic considerations point to the Persian period, and since the genealogy of the Davidic dynasty is recorded to the seventh generation from Jehoiachin (I Chron. 3:10–26), a date around 400 B.C.E. is reasonable. Nothing warrants a connection with Hellenistic times.[47]

In Chronicles the data relating to the Monarch have been thoroughly reworked. Over half the narrative is devoted to the United Kingdom. Of Saul's reign only his last battle and his death are reported (I Chron. 10:1–4). Although there is no word about David's long struggle for the throne, the divine right of his rule (*ibid.*, 11:3, 10; 12:24) and its national, pan-tribal nature (*ibid.*, 11:1, 3, 4; 12:38) are stressed. Anything disparaging to David's reputation is omitted, while detailed information, not found elsewhere, about his administrative and military organization is added (*ibid.*, 27). David is unequivocally called the initiator of the Temple project, the one who made all the preparations and was responsible for fixing the Temple service in its priestly and levitical framework (*ibid.*, 21–26, 28–29:9). Solomon is presented as the natural and, by implication, the sole possible heir to David. Nothing that might reflect adversely on this is recorded and Solomon's accession is depicted as the fulfillment by David of divine decree. Whatever might be denigrating to Solomon is disregarded.[48]

Especially in respect to the northern kingdom is the Chronicler's editorializing apparent. His sweeping negation of Ephraim, on the grounds of God's own rejection (II Chron. 25:7), sets the tone for omitting all prophecies relating to the schism, all Judean-Israelite synchronisms, and all mention of northern kings except when it is essential to the story of a Judean monarch. Even the destruction of Samaria is ignored, and the Exile of the Israelite tribes only incidentally included in genealogical lists (I Chron. 5:25–26). Similarly unrecorded are the activities of northern prophets, but not those in Judah.[49]

Since the Chronicler wants to show that the promise of eternity to the Davidic line (II Sam. 7:15; I Chron. 17:16) was fulfilled despite the schism, he refers to the northern kingdom in order to tell about the Judean recovery of northern Israelite cities in the days of Jeroboam II (II Chron. 13:2–20) and the southward migration of the legitimate priests of the north (*ibid.*, 11:13–15), and emphasizes that the Temple served all Israel, and that the reforms of Hezekiah and Josiah embraced the north. The frequent use of "Israel" as an epithet for Judah speaks for itself.[50]

But the Chronicler's overwhelming concern with Jerusalem and the cult most fully reveals his ideology. He interweaves God's choice of Jerusalem with that of the Davidic line and expands upon the relationship of David and Solomon to the Temple which was begun because of divine revelation and which sanctified the city once it was built. The detailed descriptions of the Temple service and administration, the genealogies of the High Priests and Levites, the full accounts of the various reforms of the cult and of violations of the Temple precincts, and the interest shown in royal-priestly relationships all testify to the Chronicler's fascination with cultic matters. These are the signposts by which the historical value of the book of Chronicles for the period of the Monarchy must be charted.

SUMMARY

The books of Samuel, Kings, and Chronicles constitute almost our sole means for reconstructing the history of the Monarchy, even though the period was once rich in contemporary documentation. The disproportion between the available and the transmitted material results not from lack of availability but from deliberate and selective editing. There are no royal autobiographical annals, no law codes or documents, no royal decrees. The inner life of the nation, its military, political, diplomatic, social, economic, and intellectual history, and the mechanics of government can just barely be glimpsed.

The material has been selected according to the didactic purposes of the writers, who sought to demonstrate that the life of the people of Israel was equated with the unfolding of God's purpose. History is thus divine self-revelation.

Biblical historiography is largely retrospection, after the Destruction, about the contrast between the golden age of the United Monarchy and the subsequent disasters. Because of their subjectivity, the authors idealized the United Monarchy and considered what followed to be, in effect, a theodicy, a divine punishment for national sin. The scriptural material is therefore interpretive, defining events in terms of their religious significance, thus lending coherence to otherwise discrete incidents and thereby setting off the Israelite historiographical achievement from that of its Near Eastern contemporaries. Archives and annals yielded to a quest for meaning, which, when discovered, was meant to be disseminated and internalized and thus to influence the heart, mind, and future of the people of Israel. The ingredients of objective history nevertheless do exist in the vast number of facts preserved in the biblical texts, whose reliability has been repeatedly and impressively verified in recent years by archaeological and epigraphic finds.[51]

NOTES

1. See the commentaries on Samuel by H. P. Smith, *International Critical Commentary*, Edinburgh, 1899; A. F. Kirkpatrick, *Cambridge Bible*, 1930; M. H. Segal (Hebrew), Jerusalem, 1956; H. W. Hertzberg (German), Göttingen 1968[4], (English, London, 1964); J. Mauchline, London, 1971; P. R. Ackroyd, Cambridge, 1971.

2. See the commentaries of R. Kittel, Göttingen, 1900; J. A. Montgomery and H. S. Gehman, Edinburgh, 1951; J. Gray, London, 1963 (2nd ed. 1971); M. Noth, Neukirchen, 1968.

3. See the commentaries of R. Kittel, Göttingen, 1902; E. L. Curtis and A. A. Madsen, Edinburgh, 1910; J. W. Rothstein and J. Hänel, Leipzig, 1927; K. Galling, *Die Bücher der Chronik, Ezra–Nehemia*, Göttingen, 1954; W. Rudolph, Tübingen, 1955; J. M. Myers, Garden City, N.Y., 1965.

4. On the nature of these variants, see A. Kropat, *Die Syntax des Autors der Chronik*, Berlin, 1909 (= BZAW, 16); M. Rehm, *Textkritische Untersuchungen zu den Parallelstellen der Samuel–Königstücher und der Chronik*, 1937; F. Zimmerman, *JQR*, 42 (1951/52), 265–282, 387–412; S. Japhet, *Leshonenu*, 31 (1967), 165–179, 262–279; *idem, VT*, 18 (1968), 330–371; A. Ben–David, *Biblical Hebrew, and Mishnaic Hebrew*, I, Tel Aviv, 1967, pp. 66–72 (Hebrew).

5. Cf, e.g., II Kings 9:27 f., according to which Ahaziah of Judah fled to Megiddo and died there of the wounds inflicted by Jehu's henchmen. In II Chron. 22:8–9, however, the king is said to have fled to Samaria.

6. Such has been the practice ever since the appearance of M. Noth's *Überlieferungsgeschichtliche Studien*, Stuttgart, 1943, 1966[3].

7. For an exhaustive and classified listing of the distinctive stylistic features of the Deuteronomist, see M. Weinfeld, *Deuteronomy and the Deuteronomic School*, Oxford, 1972, esp. Appendix A, pp. 320–380; cf. also S. R. Driver, *Introduction to the Literature of the Old Testament*[9], Edinburgh, 1913, pp. 200–202.

8. Noth, *op. cit.*, pp. 5 ff., 14.

9. K. Budde, *Richter und Samuel*, 1890, pp. 167–276; G. Hölscher, "Das Buch der Könige, seine Quelle und seine Redaktion," *Gunkel Eucharisterion*, I, Göttingen, 1923, pp. 158–213; *idem.*, *Geschichtschreibung in Israel*, Lund, 1952, pp. 7 f.; R. H. Pfeiffer, *Introduction to the Old Testament*,[2] New York, 1949, p. 380.

10. R. Smend, "JE in den geschichtlichen Büchern des Alten Testament", *ZAW*, 39 (1921), 181–217; O. Eissfeldt, *Die Komposition der Samuelsbücher*, 1931; *idem, The Old Testament, An Introduction*, Oxford, 1965, pp. 271–281, 297–300.

11. This is the view of M. Noth, *op. cit.*, esp. pp. 87–100.

12. It should be noted that the Greek of I Kings 8:13 (= G.v. 53) contains an addition ascribing the source for Solomon's prayer to a "Book of the Song" in the Greek version, which title would correspond to a Hebrew *sefer ha-šîr*. This may be a corruption of *sefer ha-yāšār*, but since the Solomonic prayer differs in style from the other material drawn from that work, the possibility of a genuine source behind I Kings 8:13 cannot be ruled out. See St. J. Thackeray, "New Light on the Book of Jashar," *JTS*, II (1910), 518–532; Eissfeldt, *op. cit.*, pp. 132 f.

13. See J. Liver, "The Book of the Acts of Solomon," *Biblica*, 48 (1967), 75–100.

14. The formula is omitted for Jehoram and Hoshea.

15. The formula is omitted for Ahaziah, Jehoahaz, Jehoiachin, and Zedekiah.

16. J. A. Montgomery, "Archival Data in the Book of Kings," *JBL*, 53 (1934), 46–52. It is possible that the high royal administrative office of *mazkir* may have been responsible for the archives. It is mentioned in II Sam. 8:16; 20:24; I Kings 4:3; II Kings 18:18, 37; Isa. 36:3, 22; I Chron. 18:15; II Chron. 34:8. The Targumim and the Greek consistently understand the Hebrew term in the sense of "archivist." For a contrary view, see

J. Begrich, ZAW, 58 (1940/41), 1–25, and R. de Vaux, *Ancient Israel*, London, 1961, p. 132; cf. T. N. D. Mettinger, *Solomonic State Officials*, Lund, 1971, p. 61.

17. On this subject, see M. Weitmyer, *Libri*, 6 (1955/56), 217–238; A. L. Oppenheim, *Ancient Mesopotamia*, Chicago, 1964, pp. 14 f., 17–20, 240 f.; E. Posner, *Archives in the Ancient World*, Cambridge, Mass., 1972. The discovery of the archive at the temple in Arad proves that Israel followed the practice of the ancient world; see Y. Aharoni, *BAR*, 31 (1968), 1–32; idem, *New Directions in Biblical Archaeology*, (ed. D. N. Freedman and J. C. Greenfield), Garden City, N.Y., 1969, pp. 25–39; idem., *Arad Inscriptions*, Jerusalem, 1975 (Hebrew).

18. See L. Rost, "Die Überlieferung von der Thronnachfolge Davids," *BWANT*, III, 6, 1926, who identifies the units as II Sam. 9–20 + I Kings 1–2. His position has been basically adopted by G. von Rad, "Der Anfang der Geschichtsschreibung in Alten Israel," *Gesammelte Studien zutn Alten Testament*, III, München, 1958, pp. 148–188; and M. Noth, "Zur Geschichtsauffasung des Deuteronomisten," *Proceedings XXII Conqress of Orientalists*, II, 1958, pp. 558–566, and others, although opinion varies as to whether the unit begins at ch. 9, 10, or 13. See also R. N. Whybray, *The Succession Narrative*; A Study of I Sam. 9–20 and I Kings 1–2, London, 1968.

19. G. von Rad, *Studies in Deuteronomy*, London, 1953, pp. 78–81; Weinfeld, *op. cit.*, pp. 15–27.

20. Apart from the general northern Israelite ambience of these stories, a remark like "Beer–sheba that is in Judah" (I Kings 19:3) could not have been included in a southern document.

21. It should be pointed out that Kings completely ignores the existence of the canonical prophetic books. Of the literary prophets, only Isaiah is mentioned and solely in the role of prognosticator and miracle worker; see Y. Kaufmann, *Toledot*, II, pp. 277, 298. For a study of the two versions of the Isaiah–Hezekiah narrative, see H. M. Orlinsky, "The Kings–Isaiah Recensions of the Hezekiah Story," *JQR*, 30 (1939/40), 33–49.

22. See above, n. 12.

23. So I Sam. 2: 1–10; II Sam. 1:17–27; 3:33–34; 22; 23:1–7; I Kings 8:12–13; II Kings 19:21–28.

24. See M. Noth, *op. cit.*, p. 12. A. M. Brunet, "Le Chroniste et ses sources," *RB*, 60 (1953), 481–508; 61 (1954), 349–386.

25. A. Jepsen, *Die Quellen des Königsbuches*, Halle (Saale), 1956[2], recognizes three stages of redaction, the first immediately after the fall of Samaria, the second immediately after the fall of Jerusalem, and the last during the exile. Kaufmann, *op. cit.*, pp. 360–365, would limit the Deuteronomistic editing to certain sections of the book. He especially excludes those parts drawn from northern sources and rejects the idea of a unified authorship. Eissfeldt, *op. cit.*, pp. 297–301, likewise argues for a pre-Deuteronomic edition, later reworked. F. M. Cross, *Canaanite Myth and Hebrew Epic*, Cambridge, Mass., 1974, pp. 274–289, makes a strong case for a pre-exilic edition intended to serve the cause of Josiah's reform and imperial program, and an exilic edition executed c. 550 B.C.E., in which minor modifications brought the original up to date and transformed it into a theodicy.

26. On the historiosophic nature of biblical historiography, see C. R. North, *The Old Testament Interpretation of History*, London, 1946; O. Eissfeldt, *Geschichtsschreibung im Alten Testament*, Berlin, 1948; F. V. Filson, "Method in Studying Biblical History," *JBL*, 69 (1950), 1–18; R. H. Pfeiffer, "Facts and Faith in Biblical History," *JBL*, 70 (1951), 1–14; B. Maisler (Mazar), "Ancient Israelite Historiography," *IEJ*, 2 (1952), 82–88; A. Malamat, "Doctrines of Causality in Hittite and Hebrew Historiography," *VT*, 5 (1955), 1–12; M. Burrows, in *The Idea of History in the Ancient Near East* (ed. R. C. Dentan), New Haven, 1955, pp. 101–131; J. Liver, "History and Historiography in Chronicles", *A. Biram Volume*, Jerusalem, 1956, pp. 152–161 (Hebrew); D. N. Freed-

man, "The Chronicler's Purpose," *CBQ*, 23 (1961), 436–442; R. McKenzie, *Faith and History in the Old Testament*, Minneapolis, 1963; G. von Rad, "The Beginnings of Historical Writing in Ancient Israel. The Deuteronomistic Theology of History in I and II Kings," *The Problems of the Hexateuch and other Essays*, Edinburgh, 1966, pp. 166–221; E. A. Speiser, "The Biblical Idea of History in its Common Near Eastern Setting," *IEJ*, 7 (1957), 201–216.

27. B-Z. Dinur, *The Kingdoms of Israel and Judah* (ed. A. Malamat), Jerusalem, 1961, pp. 9–23 (Hebrew).

28. The text is to be found in *ANET*, p. 282, on which see H. Tadmor, "Azriyau of Yaudi," *Scripta Hierosolymitana*, 8 (1961), 231–271.

29. The inscriptional material on Omri is to be found in *ANET*, pp. 280, 281, 284, 285, 320, on which see A. J. Thompson, "Extra Biblical Data and the Omri Dynasty," *Australian Biblical Review*, 3 (1953), 25–40; A. H. van Zyl, *The Moabites*, Leiden, 1960, pp. 137 f.

30. See *ANET*, p. 279; cf. C. F. Whitley, "The Deuteronomic Presentation of the House of Omri," *VT*, 2 (1952), 137–152, on which see Gray, *op. cit.*, pp. 369–372.

31. Y. Yadin, *Yediot*, 15 (1950), pp. 86–98; A. Malamat, *The Military History of the Land of Israel in Biblical Times* (ed. J. Liver), Tel Aviv, 1964, pp. 296–299 (Hebrew).

32. On this subject, see Y. Aharoni, *The Land of the Bible*, London, 1967, pp. 258–280; A. Malamat, "Aspects of the Foreign Policies of David and Solomon," *JNES*, 22 (1963), 1–17.

33. On the expedition of Shishak (Sheshonk I), see *ANET*, pp. 263 f., and B. Mazar, "The Campaign of the Pharaoh Sheshonk to Palestine," *VTS*, 4 (1957), 57–66.

34. Aharoni, *op. cit.*, pp. 330–346; H. H. Rowley, "Hezekiah's Reform and Rebellion," *BJRL*, 44 (1962), 395–432.

35. F. M. Cross and D. N. Freedman, "Josiah's Revolt Against Assyria," *JNES*, 12 (1953), 56–58, on which see the comments of J. M. Meyers, *II Chronicles*, Garden City, N.Y., 1965, pp. 205 f.; W. F. Albright, *From the Stone Age to Christianity*[2], Garden City, N.Y., 1957, pp. 314–321; Aharoni, *op. cit.*, pp. 347–350. See also M. Cogan *Imperialism and Religion*, Missoula, Mont., 1974.

36. The complex chronological problems of the book of Kings are treated at length in Chap. III of this volume.

37. Montgomery, *op. cit.*, p. 55.

38. The theme of Israel as God's people appears nearly fifty times in Samuel-Kings, while the Exodus is cited nearly twenty times.

39. I Kings 3:14; 9:4; 11:4, 6, 38; 15:3, 5, 11; II Kings 14:3; 16:2; 18:3; 22:2; so even Jeroboam of Israel (I Kings 14:8).

40. O. Eissfeldt, *Cambridge Ancient History*, fasc. 32, 1965, pp. 34–44, esp. p. 41; Dinur, *op. cit.*, pp. 12 f.; Z. Kallai, *The Military History of the Land of Israel in Biblical Times*, (ed. J. Liver), Tel Aviv, 1961, pp. 132–145; Aharoni, *op. cit.*, pp. 254–258.

41. For the literary structure of the narrative, see B. Porten, *HUCA*, 38 (1967), 93–128.

42. The kings in question are Asa (I Kings 15:11 f.), Jehoshaphat (22:43 f.), Jehoash (II Kings 12:3 f.), Amaziah (14:3 f., cf. 15:3), Amaziah (15:3 f.) and Jotham (15:34 f.).

43. J. Wellhausen, *Prolegomena to the History of Ancient Israel*, New York, 1957, pp. 17–51; Kaufmann, *op. cit.*, I, pp. 81–104, 114–116; II, see index, *bamot;* N. Raban in *A Biram Volume*, Jerusalem, 1956, pp. 228–255 (Hebrew); Albright, *VTS*, 4 (1957), 242–258; B. Uffenheimer, *Tarbiz*, 28 (1959) 138–153 (Hebrew).

44. See above, n. 19.

45. Weinfeld, *op. cit.*, pp. 18–20.

46. It should be noted that God communicates directly with Solomon and not through a prophet (cf. I Kings 3:5–15; 9:2–9; 11:11–13).

47. Noth, *op. cit.*, pp. 150–155, dates the authorship of Chronicles to between 300 B.C.E. and 200 B.C.E., so Pfeiffer, *op. cit.* pp. 811 f. M. Z. Segal, *Mevo ha-Miqra*, III, Jerusalem, 1955, p. 801 opts for between 475 B.C.E. to 429 B.C.E. W. F. Albright, *Alexander Marx Jubilee Volume* (English Section), New York, 1950, pp. 69–74, strongly argues for the Persian period early in the fourth century B.C.E. Rothstein and Hänel, *op. cit.*, place the core of the book around 430 B.C.E. and the final redaction about 400 B.C.E, a position largely followed by Rudolph, *op. cit.*; Eissfeldt, *op. cit.*, p. 540; Myers, *op. cit.*, pp. lxxxvii ff. and B. Mazar, "The Book of Chronicles", *Enc. Miqr.*, II, col. 604.

48. Thus Solomon is portrayed as the natural and undisputed heir of David; cf. I Chron. 22:7–10; 23:1; 28:1–7; the narratives of II Sam. 13:15–18; I Kings 1–2; 11:1–13 are omitted. See R. L. Braun, "Solomonic Apologetic in Chronicles," *JBL*, 92 (1973), 503–516.

49. Cf. II Chron. 21:12–19, associating Elijah with Judah. On this letter, see Rudolph, *op.cit.*, p. 264; Meyers, *op. cit.*, pp. 121 f.; J. D. Shenkel, *Chronology and Recensional Development in the Greek Text of Kings*, Cambridge, Mass., 1968, pp. 101 f.

50. M. Gil, "Israel in Chronicles," *Beth Mikra*, 32 (1967), pp. 105–115 (Hebrew).

51. See Albright, *op. cit.*, esp. pp. 64 ff.; H. N. Richardson, "The Historical Reliability of Chronicles," *JBR*, 26 (1958), 9–12.

Ancient Libraries and the Ordering of the Biblical Books

The law establishing the Center for the Book in 1977 gave the center a broad mandate: "to provide a program for the investigation of the transmission of human knowledge and to heighten public interest in the role of books and printing in the diffusion of this knowledge." Lectures from eminent scholars such as Nahum Sarna have proven to be an effective way of stimulating public interest in books and reading while simultaneously encouraging the study of books. In this clear and insightful paper, presented at the Library of Congress on March 6, 1989, Dr. Sarna examines the reality behind Talmudic language concerning the ordering of the biblical books, drawing on his wide-ranging knowledge of ancient archives and libraries.

For help in arranging this lecture, the center is grateful for the cooperation of The Foundation for Jewish Studies and the assistance of Michael Grunberger, head of the Hebraic Section of the Library of Congress.

The Center for the Book's reading promotion projects, lectures, symposia, exhibitions, and publications are supported primarily by tax-deductible contributions from individuals and corporations. For further information, please write the Center for the Book, Library of Congress, Washington, D.C. 20540.

John Y. Cole
Director, Center for the Book.

The Center for the Book offers a most appropriate forum for the topic I have chosen, for one of the center's principal goals is to promote the study of the history of books, and I propose to deal with the Book of Books or, at least, with one small facet of its history.

King Solomon, notwithstanding his marital follies, recorded in I Kings 11:1–6, managed to earn the sobriquet "the wisest of men" (I Kings 3:9–12; 5:9–14). He once observed that "of the making of many books there is no end." Concerning the problems of storage, preservation, organization, and retrieval of this limitless literary output, however, he offered no advice. He did note that "much study is a wearying of the flesh," but as an author himself, he probably deemed it to be the better part of discretion to pass over in silence the fact that the librarian's task too may be a wearying of the flesh, and a vexation of the spirit to boot.

Let me now set forth directly the issue on which I intend to elaborate:[1]

From some time before the year 200 C.E. there appear anonymous statements recorded in the Babylonian Talmud, tractate Bava Bathra 14[b], listing the proper order of the books in the biblical prophetical corpus and in the Hagiographa, the third division of the Hebrew Scriptures. These statements read as follows:

> Our Rabbis taught: the order of the Prophets is Joshua, Judges, Samuel and Kings, Jeremiah and Ezekiel, Isaiah and the Twelve.

> The Order of the Hagiographa is Ruth, the Book of Psalms, and Job and Proverbs, Ecclesiastes, Canticles, and Lamentations, Daniel, the Scroll of Esther, Ezra, and Chronicles.

It is of no relevance to my topic that the sequence of the books given here diverges in many respects from that found in medieval manuscripts and the printed editions of the Hebrew Bible. Rather, my interest lies in the phenomenon that though the Amoraim, the teachers listed in the Talmud who stem from the beginning of the third century C.E. on, after the close of the Mishnah, query some of the more unusual features of these lists and attempt to rationalize them, they do not cavil against the concept of a fixed, standardized arrangement for the biblical books.

Of course, in the light of the venerable traditions of both Synagogue and Church, it may be difficult to comprehend why this should be a source of wonderment. At first glance, it might be supposed that the above-cited Talmudic statements reflect or legislate scribal practice in copying the Scriptures onto a scroll, book after book. In such a case the proper and uniform order of books would, of course, be important.

Attractively simple though it may seem, however, this hypothesis must be firmly rejected. There is abundant evidence to prove that in the period under review, the entire Talmudic era, which came to an end around the year 500 C.E., it was not normative practice for scribes to copy the Hebrew Scriptures onto a single scroll. This was for obvious, practical reasons, for such a gigantic roll would have been thoroughly unwieldy, if not wholly unusable. The books of the Bible were intensely studied, and utilitarian considerations would have been decisive in their production, that is, in determining the length of the scrolls. Note that the Torah, the Pentateuch, was canonized as a single work, yet it was divided into five books for ease of handling.

Papyrologists have noted that both in ancient Egypt and in classical Greece, usage imposed similar limitations on the length of the papyrus scroll. Throughout Egyptian history, until the Arab conquest, the maximum number of papyrus sheets contained in a scroll was twenty. The width of the individual sheets would vary between 14.5 inches and 16.5 inches during the Middle Kingdom (2000–1780 B.C.E.) and between 6 inches and 7.5 inches during the New Kingdom (1575–1087 B.C.E.). These dimensions dictated that the average length of a papyrus scroll varied between 25 feet and 27.5 feet in the earlier period, and between 10 feet and 13 feet in the later one. True, there are exceptions. The Harris Papyrus from the time of Rameses III in the twelfth century B.C.E. measures 133 feet by 17 inches. But this anomaly and a few like it arose because the lengthy scrolls were not meant to be read. They were often placed in coffins for the entertainment of the dead in the next world.[2]

Greek papyrus scrolls were generally much shorter than their Egyptian counterparts. A literary scroll rarely exceeded 35 feet in length. When rolled up, a Greek scroll would be only 2.5 inches thick, and thus easily carried in the hand.[3]

The history of Homer's *Iliad* and *Odyssey* provides an excellent example of this tendency to limit the size of scrolls to dimensions consistent with usability. Zenodotus, the first chief librarian of the library at Alexandria in the third century B.C.E., divided both works into twenty-four books so that each book should contain under one thousand verses and could therefore be comfortably transcribed onto a manageable roll.

The hoard of manuscripts found at Qumran by the shores of the Dead Sea tell a similar story. The Great Isaiah Scroll (I Q Isaᵃ), containing the sixty-six chapters of the Hebrew, measures 24.5 feet in length, smaller than the average Greek scroll. What is preserved of the great Psalms scroll from Cave 11, written on leather, now measures about 13.5 feet, but it too is estimated originally to have been about 24 feet long. With the single exception of the so-called Twelve Minor Prophets discussed below, all biblical books found at Qumran are inscribed on separate scrolls. As far as I know, no other scroll so far discovered contains more than one biblical book.[4]

No fewer than eight copies of the Twelve Minor Prophets have turned up in the manuscript collection at Qumran; in each case, all twelve are inscribed on a single scroll. This accords with the rabbinic tradition cited above that the Minor Prophets are simply called "the Twelve." The practice of clustering these books together was already known to Ben Sira (Sirach), the sage of the second century B.C.E. who wrote the wisdom book that bears his name (also called Ecclesiasticus). He cites all the great biblical worthies by name, mentioning Isaiah, Jeremiah, and Ezekiel but not the names of the Minor Prophets. These he simply refers to as "The Twelve Prophets" (49:10). The Jewish historian of the Second Temple period, Josephus, must also have had the same tradition, for he registers thirteen books of the biblical prophetic corpus, a figure that can be sustained only if all the Minor Prophets are reckoned as one book, and they would have been regarded as such only if they all appeared on one scroll.[5] Further proof of this scribal convention comes from the pseudepigraphical work known as the Fourth Book of Ezra (14:45), a late first century C.E. production. The author is apparently the earliest witness to the widespread Jewish custom of counting twenty-four books in the Hebrew Bible. Here again this number presupposes treating the twelve Minor Prophets as one.

The exceptional nature of the handling of the Twelve Minor Prophets serves to emphasize the fact that in late antiquity each biblical book was regularly written by Jewish scribes on a single scroll. True, we do possess records of some discussions among the Sages of the Talmud from before the year 200 C.E. about the status of mixed biblical scrolls. The Palestinian Talmud reports a dispute on this topic between the Sages and Rabbi Meir, who, incidentally, was a professional scribe. But the difference of opinion and the language used indicate that the conjoining of individual books was not the usual practice, and that it was discouraged.[6]

This conclusion inevitably raises a question about the reality behind the language of the Talmud laying out "the order of the Prophets" and "the order of the Hagiographa." From a practical standpoint, what was the significance of establishing "order" for the biblical books and how did the "ordering" express itself? By these questions I do not refer to the considerations that led to the classification of the literature or to the specifics of the sequential order. What we need to understand is the very concept of *order* itself, as the term was used by the authors of the Talmudic statements I have cited above.

At this point it might be objected that given that the use of large scrolls was impractical, would not the references to the order of the biblical books pertain to the use of the codex? As is well known, the codex is a manuscript arranged by leaves sewn together in the form of a modern book. The codex enjoyed an enormous advantage over the scroll. It eliminated the awkwardness in the handling of the scroll, which required a cumbersome shifting backward and forward, and it enabled the reader easily to open up to a desired passage. Further, since both sides of its pages could be written on, the codex could contain more script than a scroll, and it weighed less. Once a scribe wrote out the biblical texts in a codex, the question of the proper sequence of the component books would inevitably arise. An authoritative ruling governing scribal practice would therefore be called for. So perhaps this codex form supplies the answer to our original question. Perhaps the prescribed rabbinic order of the biblical books refers to the codex.

Unfortunately, this solution must be abandoned for the simple reason that the codex was not used by Jews until long after the close of the Talmudic period.

The codex is never mentioned in rabbinic literature and there was no technical term for it in Hebrew. The term eventually adopted, *mishaf,* is borrowed from the Arabic usage *mushaf,* itself derived from *sahafa-ashafa*—"to bind sheets together." *Mishaf* first appears in Hebrew in the eighth century C.E. in Geonic texts in which it is decoded that the religious obligation to read the book of Esther on the festival of Purim is not fulfilled if a codex is used. Only a scroll is normative for such a purpose.[7]

There does appear in rabbinic-tannaitic literature the word *pinkas,* which is the Greek *pinaks* (pl. *pinakes*). This is a term for writing tablets hinged together and used for notes or quotations. Only a very small book could have been written in this manner.[8] The pinkas form has a Near Eastern origin. In 1953, ivory and wooden rectangular writing boards hinged together were found in the northwest palace at Nimrud (Calah). These derive from the eighth century B.C.E. As many as sixteen such boards were apparently hinged together. These polyptychs, as they are called, may well have had widespread use in the Aramaic speaking world, and it seems that civilization has been deprived of an entire literature, lost through scribal use of such a device.[9]

The history of the codex has now been thoroughly documented.[10] It has been shown that, even in the pagan world, the form had not really established itself before the fourth century C.E. About this time it was embraced by the Christians for the New Testament, and their use of the codex remained one of the distinguishing characteristics of Christian communities that marked them off from their Jewish neighbors. It appears to have been an innovation of the Egyptian churches, which gradually spread to others. The Jews, however, stubbornly adhered to the scroll for their Sacred Scriptures, and the Hebrew Bible in codex form did not appear until long after the close of the Talmudic age.

In sum, the rabbinic statements concerning the order of the biblical books cannot refer to the codex form. A different solution to the meaning of "the order of the books" must be sought. And now we turn for an explanation to the cataloging and storage systems of the ancient world.

The *Encyclopaedia Britannica* begins its article on "Bureaucracy" by observing that "in everyday usage the term bureaucracy connotes the 'red tape' and inefficiency that one often experiences in dealing with large-scale organizations, especially with a state administration."[11] But disregarding such popular illusions, we may safely credit the bureaucrats of the Mesopotamian states with the establishment of archives and with originating and developing an efficient system by which documents could be stored, classified, and recovered without undue complication.

At first, such establishments were attached to the royal palace, the locus of state administration, and later to temples as well. They contained such records as would be needed for the administration of the realm and of the organized institutions of religion. As affairs became more complex and ever more ramified, the archives responded to new demands.[12]

The discoveries at the ancient Sumerian city of Ur in southern Mesopotamia, perhaps the birthplace of the patriarch Abraham, exemplify these developments. By the period of its greatest prosperity, in the course of the twenty-third dynasty, that is, around 2100 B.C.E., records—on cuneiform tablets—were already classified by topic and stored in especially made clay boxes called *šaduppu*. Each container received an identifying clay tag on which was noted the number of tablets inside and the subject classification.[13]

In the ancient city of Mari (Tel Hariri) in Syria, high up on the Euphrates, twenty thousand clay tablets were uncovered in the three-hundred-roomed palace of King Zimrilim. These archives, written in the Babylonian language, demonstrate how the expansion of the state administration generated a highly developed system of classification. The tablets were arranged to correspond to the division of labor and reflected the increased decentralization and specialization within the bureaucracy. There were concentrations of political-diplomatic records, records pertaining to the maintenance of the palace, to commercial transactions, to legal matters, and so forth—each subject carefully distinguished.[14]

At first, archives and libraries may not have been differentiated, but this changed later on as men wakened to a heightened consciousness of the past and cultivated an enthusiasm for its literary productions.

The ancient religious capital of Assyria was the city-state of Ashur, the site of the present-day Qalat Sharqat. Located on the west bank of the Tigris River about one hundred kilometers south of modern Mosul in northern Iraq, it lent its name to the entire country. Altogether some fifty archives and libraries, some official, some private, were unearthed in the course of the German excavations conducted there in the first decade of this century. One library in this city, possibly founded by the great imperialist conqueror Tiglath-Pileser I (ca. 1115–1077 B.C.E.), yielded the famous legal collection now known as the Middle Assyrian Laws as well as copies of some celebrated literary texts. Of particular pertinence to our present topic are the clay tablets that constitute the catalogs for various categories of texts. One such, for instance, is a catalog of incantation texts. Another interesting feature of the library is the arrangement in series of certain tablets that share a theme in common.[15]

The high point of archival and library assemblage in ancient Mesopotamia was, of course, the great collection, originally numbering some twenty-five thousand tablets, that Ashurbanipal (668–627 B.C.E.), the last effective king of Assyria, established at Nineveh. This city, situated on the east bank of the Tigris River across from the modern city of Mosul, became the royal residence and main capital of the Assyrian empire in the days of Sennacherib (ca. 700 B.C.E.). This is the place to which the Hebrew prophet Jonah was sent. Its destruction in the year 612 is celebrated in the biblical book of the prophet Nahum.

The library was excavated by Sir Austen Henry Layard in 1849. Ashurbanipal himself was a highly educated man, thoroughly at home in the accumulated learning of his day. There is plenty of evidence to show that he personally supervised the systematic collection of the great classical texts of Mesopotamia. He had his scribes scour the temples throughout the extent of his vast realm. They brought to Nineveh, or diligently copied, texts in all the various branches of traditional learning and in all genres of literature.

One extremely important aspect of this activity was the fact that the texts were carefully studied, collated, and edited with a view to establishing an authoritative recension. The scribes were conscious of the authority of tradition behind the texts they copied. They made efforts to locate the archetype, and consulted a variety of text traditions, in order to be able to hew as closely as possible to the earliest recension they could obtain. They even counted the number of lines, and recorded the total in the colophons. Sometimes, the scribe mentions that he checked the copy he made against the original. Here are examples of colophons found at the end of some texts:[16]

> Eighth tablet of the series Antagal = *šaqu* (which) Ashurbanipal wrote, checked, collated and placed in the library of the temple of Nabu his lord, which is in Nineveh.

Another colophon reads:

> I wrote on the tablets the wisdom of Ea, the craft of the temple-singers, the secret of the master, checked and collated (it) and deposited it in the library of Ezida, the chapel of Nabû my lord, which is in Nineveh. O Nabû, my lord, look with favor upon this library.

Every librarian will appreciate this one:

> May Ishtar look with favor upon the scholar who does not change a line and deposits (the tablet) in the library.

The activities of Ashurbanipal's scribes encompassed all genres of literature—omens, incantations, medical treatises, astrology, lexical texts, literary classics, wisdom compositions, and hymns. It has been convincingly demonstrated in recent years that a canon of Mesopotamian classical texts finally emerged, arranged in a standard order in which they were to be read or studied. Excavations at numerous sites have produced evidence that suggests a very limited edition of the complete literary texts in spite of their wide geographical and chronological attestation. This conclusion is reinforced by the discovery of catalogs of titles and incipits.[17]

All this had direct implications for the librarian or archivist. Tablets would be grouped together by series *(iškaru)* and often by subseries *(pirsu)*, each being properly numbered. They were equipped with informative, identifying colophons, or were indexed at the rims. They were topically arranged in series, tablets from each series being stored together either in built-in bookcases or in buckets. The bundles were frequently tied together with string, with tags or dockets attached to indicate the contents. Of special interest for assessing the establishment and significance of fixed sequence is the frequently encountered scribal practice of including the first line of the next tablet or series at the end of the preceding item.

The existence of catalogs is further proof of the fixation of order within a given collection. These catalogs contain the serial catch-lines and they have been found in duplicate copies. The concept of a standardized order of classical works became part of the Mesopotamian scribal-bibliographic tradition. This tradition was nurtured both by archival and library needs and by pedagogic considerations answering the requirements of the curriculum of the scribal schools.

We know little about archives and libraries and the way they were organized in pre-Hellenistic Egypt, though we do know that such institutions existed, for some of the catalogs have been found. We know also that the ancient Egyptians took the office of librarian very seriously. The head librarian of the palace was an ex officio member of the pharaoh's privy council. The common technical term for a library was "the hall of books," and schools were located there. Papyrus rolls were stored in wooden chests or in jars, and sometimes in niches. Librarians had a patron god—Thot—who was scribe and secretary of the gods. He had the title "Lord of Books" and to him was ascribed the invention of writing, among other things. It is no reflection on librarians that Thot, their patron, was variously represented pictorially as an ibis and a baboon. To the contrary, he was closely associated with Maat, goddess of divine order, truth, and justice. The consort of Thot was Seshet, a minor deity, who had the title "Mistress of the Hall of Books."

A paragraph from a work by Ernest Cushing Richardson called *Some Old Egyptian Librarians,* published in New York in 1911, commented: "Those therefore who take alarm at the rapid feminisation of libraries and might feel badly to think that the patron divinity of libraries was a goddess, may take comfort in the fact that the great god of libraries was in truth masculine and Seshait only his better half" (p. 13–14).

Both private and state archive libraries have been found in the Mediterranean port city of Ras Shamra-Ugarit in Syria, which flourished in the second millenium B.C.E. but was destroyed by the Sea Peoples ca.

1180 B.C.E. The excavation of the house of the chief priest *(rb khnm)* yielded a large and rich library of mythological and religious texts, as well as schoolboy exercises, vocabularies, and syllabuses. Apparently, the chief priest held a school for priestly scribes in his own house. Five distinct archives were found in the royal palace of Ugarit. These were found to have been arranged very carefully, based on a system of administrative departmentalization.[18]

Libraries, private and public, existed in the classical Greek world from early times. The palace of Nestor at Pylos in Messenia, Greece, dates from ca. 1300 B.C.E. It was excavated from 1952 on. The archive room housed hundreds of clay tablets written in the now famous Linear B script. Many tablets were discovered still standing upright in bundles and wrapped around with string. Others were found in wicker baskets, and still others clearly had once been held in wooden boxes with hinged lids. The important thing for our purposes is the use of clay tags to identify the contents, just as had been the practice in Mesopotamia.[19]

There is no doubt that the archival and library techniques that had developed over a long period of time in Mesopotamia, that found their consummate expression in Ashurbanipal's library at Nineveh, exerted a profound influence throughout the Near Eastern and Mediterranean world. It is known that the Persians borrowed the system and that Alexander the Great was so profoundly influenced by the Persians that he imitated their organizational system in arranging his own archives.

The crowning achievement of the Hellenistic spirit with which Alexander infused the Near East was the Museum Library in the city named after him in Egypt. Originally planned by Ptolemy I Soter who died in 283 B.C.E., this monumental institution was brought to completion by his son Ptolemy II Philadelphus (308–246 B.C.E.) with the collaboration of his adviser Demetrius of Phalerum (in Attica, Greece). Appropriately situated in the temple of the Muses, which as everyone knows enriched the English language with the word *museum*, it was undoubtedly the greatest of all libraries of antiquity. For a long while it remained unsurpassed in the size and scope of its collections.[20]

The founders of the library, if not directly inspired by the example of Ashurbanipal in Nineveh, had the same purpose as he did: to assemble the entire corpus of classical literature, in this case Greek, in the best available copies, arranged in systematic order. In addition, this enterprise would provide the basis of published commentaries.

By the time the Alexandrian library celebrated the first half-century of its existence, its main collection could boast 400,000 "mixed rolls," that is, scrolls containing more than one composition, in addition to 90,000 "unmixed scrolls" or single works, as well as another 42,800 single scrolls in its outer or subsidiary library, making 432,000 scrolls in all. By the year 41 B.C.E., when Marc Antony succeeded to Caesar's authority, the museum-library with its by now 700,000 holdings had achieved a well deserved reputation as *the* center of all branches of human learning. According to Plutarch, though the historicity of the story has been challenged, Marc Antony (ca. 82–30 B.C.E.) added still another 200,000 volumes that he stole from the other famous library of antiquity, that of the city of Pergamum in the district of Mysla in northwestern Asia Minor. That great collection had been started by its king Eumenes III (197–159 B.C.E.). It was here that the use of parchment as writing material was developed. This was the city's response to the interruption in the supply of papyrus from Egypt, occasioned by the invasion of that country by Antiochus Epiphanes, and not, as has been often claimed, by any embargo of the Ptolemies.

I do not know how typical of the acquisitions policy of the Alexandrian library was Marc Antony's action, but it may have enjoyed a venerable tradition by his day, for Ptolemy III Euergertes ("the benefactor") (246–221 B.C.E.) is said to have borrowed from the Metröon of Athens the works of Aeschylus, Sophocles, and Euripides in order to have them copied by the scholars of his library. He is said to have paid a security deposit of fifteen talents of silver, which he then forfeited by returning the copies and retaining the originals.

Incidentally, this Metröon was the sanctuary of the Great Mother goddess Rhea, and had become the official repository of the city archives of Athens.[21] One of its rules was that entry was barred to anyone who had partaken of garlic. Whether the restriction was meant to protect the delicate olfactory organ of its patron goddess or of the library staff and users is difficult to decide today.

To return to Alexandria. The librarians faced a challenging organizational problem. How does one prevent one large work credited to a single author or several compositions that belong to the same genre from becoming dispersed, given the thirty-five-foot limit placed upon the size of a Greek scroll? Apparently, librarians and scribes decided that the only effective method of avoiding chaos was to adopt and adapt the devices used by their Mesopotamian counterparts. The scribes inscribed the informative colophons at the end of the rolls, and as an additional precaution book boxes or buckets were used in which to store related scrolls. Further, they would attach an identifying tag to each roll, and they compiled a checklist of the contents of each container.

The immense size of the collection necessitated the introduction of innovative measures on a grand scale if the entire library of hundreds of thousands of scrolls was not to degenerate into an unusable, disordered collection. Accordingly, an ingenious strategem was designed. The Greeks had already conceived of differentiating ten major categories or departments of knowledge. Accordingly, ten great halls were constructed to house the library, each hall representing one of the divisions of Hellenic learning. The manuscripts were then distributed by genre throughout the various sections of the building. The walls of the halls were lined with the *Armaria*, or book-lockers, in which the scrolls were deposited. The key to retrieving the volumes was the great classification system and the 120-volume catalog. This was the famed *pinakes* developed by Callimachus (ca. 305–240 B.C.E.), the great poet, literary critic, and grammarian, himself credited with the authorship of some eight hundred books. The emergence of the "Alexandrian Canon" was one of the most significant results of the labors of this great bibliographer and of the "grammarians," as the scholar-fellows of the library were called. This was the authoritative, standardized corpus of the great Greek classics, arranged according to certain principles of order.

The influence of the Alexandrian school radiated far beyond the confines of the museum-library, and it had an impact upon Jewish culture in Palestine during the period of the Second Temple, an impact that was multifaceted and profound. After all, Palestine was the crossroads and point of convergence of Near Eastern and Hellenistic traditions, and the largest Jewish community in the world at the time existed in Alexandria itself. It is not to be wondered at that the work of the Alexandrian grammarians, their professional practices, and even their technical terminology, influenced the Jewish scholars of Palestine, although this phenomenon has only been explored and documented in detail fairly recently.[22] It must surely be taken for granted that in the libraries of the Jerusalem Temple and of the schools and synagogues throughout Palestine in that era, the established, time-tested, and efficient library techniques and bibliographic practices of the Mesopotamian and Hellenistic worlds were fully operative.

This brings us back to the starting point of this study. We have shown that the biblical books were generally copied onto single scrolls, that mixed scrolls were exceedingly rare, and that biblical Hebrew codices were nonexistent. The tannaitic discussions about the "order" of the

Scriptural books that we cited at the outset must be seen against the Mesopotamian-Hellenistic traditions just described.

The Hebrew Bible, as is well known, has always had a tripartite division: the Torah (Pentateuch), the Prophets (Hebrew *Nevi'im*), and the Hagiographa, or Writings (Hebrew *Kethuvim*); hence, the common Hebrew acronym *TaNaKh* as a designation for the Scriptures. These three corpora would have been stored in the libraries, each in its proper section. The individual scrolls that made up each corpus, or series, would have been placed in the *Armaria*, or book-lockers, in their appropriately assigned order, and shelflisted accordingly. The tannaitic lists for the Prophets and Hagiographa constitute, in effect, the shelflistings of the libraries and schools of Jewish Palestine in the second century C.E. What the criteria were that determined the particular order within each corpus must remain the subject of a different study.

NOTES

1. A preliminary study of the present topic appeared in *Studies in Jewish Bibliography, History, and Literature in Honor of I. Edward Kiev*, edited by Charles Berlin (New York: Ktav, 1971), pp. 407–13.

2. I. Cerny, *Paper and Books in Ancient Egypt* (London: University College, 1947).

3. Frederic G. Kenyon, *Books and Readers in Ancient Greece and Rome*, 2d ed. (Oxford: Clarendon Press, 1951), especially pp. 53f.

4. Frank M. Cross, Jr., *The Ancient Library of Qumran* (Garden City, N.Y.: Doubleday, 1961), pp. 43–44.

5. *Contra Apion* 1.8, 34–42 = Loeb Classical Library I, p. 179; cf. *Antiquities* 10.2.1, 35 = Loeb 6, p. 177.

6. P. Megillah 3:1 (73[b]): cf. Bava Bathra 13[b].

7. *Halakhot Pesukot* (Laws of Megillah), attributed to Yehudai Gaon of Sura, Babylon, 757–61 C.E.

8. Saul Lieberman, *Hellenism in Jewish Palestine* (New York: Jewish Theological Seminary, 1962), pp. 203–8.

9. A. L. Oppenheim, *Ancient Mesopotamia* (Chicago: University of Chicago Press, 1964), p. 242; Colin H. Roberts and T. C. Skeat, *The Birth of the Codex* (London: British Academy, 1987), pp. 11–14.

10. Roberts and Skeat, *Birth of the Codex*.

11. Fifteenth edition, vol. 3, p. 484.

12. M. Weitmyer, "Archive and Library Technique in Ancient Mesopotamia," *Libri* 6.3 (1955–56), 217–38.

13. Ernst Posner, *Archives in the Ancient World* (Cambridge: Harvard University Press, 1972), pp. 46, 59, 61.

14. Ibid., pp. 29–31, 62–64.

15. O. Pedersén, *Libraries and Archives in the City of Assur:* vols. 1 and 2 (Uppsala: University Press, 1985–86).

16. These citations are culled from *The Assyrian Dictionary*, vol. 5, (Chicago: The Oriental Institute, 1956), pp. 86–88, s.v. *girginakku*.

17. This subject has been investigated by W. W. Hallo, "Viewpoints on Cuneiform Literature," *Israel Exploration Journal* 12 (1962), 13–26, "On the Antiquity of Sumerian Literature," *Journal of the American Oriental Society* (*JAOS*) 83 (1963), 167–76; "Individual Prayer in Sumerian: The Continuity of a Tradition," *JAOS* 88 (1968), 71–89.

18. Margaret S. Drower in *The Cambridge Ancient History*, vol. 2, pt. 2 (Cambridge: University Press, 1975), p. 151; B. R. Widbin, "The East Archives in Le Palais Royal d'Ugarit: A Structural and Economic Analysis" (Ph.D. diss., Brandeis University, 1985).

19. Posner, *Archives*, pp. 42–44.

20. Edward A. Parsons, *The Alexandrian Library, Glory of the Hellenic World* (Amsterdam and New York: Elsevier, 1952; 2d ed., 1967).

21. Posner, *Archives*, pp. 102–14.

22. Lieberman, *Hellenism in Jewish Palestine;* idem, *Greek in Jewish Palestine* (New York: Jewish Theological Seminary, 1942).

The Authority and Interpretation of Scripture in Jewish Tradition

1. THE ROLE OF SCRIPTURE IN JEWISH CIVILIZATION

"The Holy Scriptures may not be read but may be studied, and lectures on them given. . . ."[1]

Although this tannaitic statement is a halakhic ruling within the context of the Sabbath laws, yet, if disengaged from its immediate reference, and taken as an abstract formulation, it expresses a profound truth. For the Bible cannot be read; it can only be studied and expounded.

This none-too-obvious, yet incontrovertible, fact is to be accounted for partly as a product of a particular historical circumstance. The floodtides of Hellenism engulfed the ancient Near Eastern world and transformed its civilization, so that the cultural environment that produced the Hebrew Bible was no longer familiar to the reader. Thereafter, the traditional metaphors of biblical thought ceased to be immediately intelligible, and the biblical text ceased to be instantly readable; it could only be studied and expounded.

But there is much more to it than this. The very fact that the Hebrew Scriptures, the canonized, definitively fixed body of sacred literature, became the focus, long the exclusive focus, of Jewish cultural activity, and constituted the very protoplasm of Jewish existence, the matrix out of which emerged all subsequent development—this fact inevitably predetermined the approach to the text. The interpretation thereof was informed by the ever-abiding consciousness that it was the major source for the national language, the well-spring of the peculiar life-style of the Jew, the font of Jewish values, ideals and hopes. These were matters of transcendent seriousness that demanded not surface reading but deep study and interpretation, and interpretation itself became a propaedeutic discipline indispensable to the training of the cultivated Jew. As Gershom Scholem pointed out, commentary on Scripture became "the characteristic expression of Jewish thinking about truth."[2] The unbelievably rich hermeneutical literature subsumed generically under the rubric of *parshanut ha-Miqra'*, the exposition of the Scriptures, supplies all the essential ingredients of Jewish intellectual and spiritual history. A product of over two millennia of intensive intellectual activity, it is characterized by infinitely variegated attitudes and approaches—with a refusal to absolutize any single stance.[3]

Rabbinic exegesis is firmly grounded in the cardinal principle that embedded in the sacred text is a multiplicity of meanings, the full richness of which cannot be expressed through a single body of doctrine or by any monolithic system that is logically self-consistent. To the contrary, the intrinsic, endless variety of interpretation, even if, or perhaps especially because, it may be internally contradictory and replete with antinomies, reinforced the reality of the divine inspiration behind the text. The sages of the Talmud vividly expressed the matter this way: The prophet Jeremiah proclaimed: "'Behold, My word is like fire—declares the Lord—and like a hammer that shatters rock' (Jer. 23:29). Just as a hammer shatters rock into numerous splinters, so may a single biblical verse yield a multiplicity of meanings."[4] This same concept is expressed in several ways, whether as: "There are seventy facets to the Torah,"[5] the number, of course, being typological and communicating comprehensiveness, or whether as, in the words of the tanna Ben Bag-Bag, "Turn it over, turn it over, for everything is in it."[6]

All this means, of course, that for more than two thousand years the Hebrew Bible has been accepted and studied by Jews as the seminal body of religious literature, which has been filtered through a continuous process of rabbinic interpretation and reinterpretation within the community of practice and faith whence its immediate authority derived.

2. RABBINIC EXEGESIS

Already in the year 553 C.E., the emperor Justinian took note of this fact in his *novella constitutio* concerning the Jews to whom he granted permission to read their sacred Scriptures in Greek, Latin or any other language. He stipulated, however, that they should "read the holy words themselves, rejecting the commentaries" by which he clearly meant rabbinic exegesis. As Justinian put it, "the so-called second tradition *(deuterosis)* we prohibit entirely, for it is not part of the sacred books nor is it handed down by divine inspiration through the prophets, but the handiwork of men, speaking only of earthly things and having nothing of the divine in it."[7]

Justinian's motives and purposes are irrelevant to the present theme, for they belong within the category of medieval Jewish-Christian polemics. But this specified restriction does illustrate an historic fact of cardinal importance that differentiates the Jewish study of the Scriptures from the Christian approach which, of course, has its own venerable tradition of theological reinterpretation of the Bible of the Jews. The literate, committed Jew, to whom the study of the Bible is at one and the same time a religious obligation, a spiritual exercise, a mode of worship, and a moral as well as an intellectual discipline, is confronted with a vast array of texts which are not in themselves authoritative, yet which command attention, concentrated thought, and study. Jewish scriptural exegesis is a literature that has become endowed with a life and energy of its own, and in its independent existence the light of the Hebrew Bible has become refracted through a thousand prisms. To my mind, the most noble expression of rabbinic Judaism is the Great Rabbinic Bible exemplified by Jacob b. Hayyim's edition of 1524/25.[8] What I mean is that the Hebrew text is surrounded by a sea of commentaries of diverse authorship, provenance, dating and exegetical approaches, often mutually incompatible, all of which coexist peacefully within the confines of a single page, all accommodated within the framework of a single tradition. To use rabbinic parlance, "The one and the other alike are the words of the living God."[9]

3. INNER BIBLICAL EXEGESIS

At this point, I wish to advance the thesis that the traditional Jewish approach to the text as a living organism that perpetually rejuvenates and transforms itself was not a rabbinic innovation but a continuation of an established process that was contemporaneous with the formation of biblical literature itself. Recent studies in the concept of "Canon" have focused attention upon a hitherto neglected aspect of the subject. There is "Canon" as the formal expression of religio-legal decision-making on the part of some ecclesiastical body—about which, incidentally, we know next to nothing. But there is also "canon" as a dynamic process whereby a text, once it is recognized as being Scripture, necessarily and spontaneously generates interpretation and adaptation so that often the original text is transformed into a new and expanded text.[10] Thus is created inner-biblical exegesis.[11] As a matter of fact, it may be noted that even the Canon in the traditional, formal, sense of the word as a delimited, definitive and authoritative body of literature is ultimately a product of exegetical activity as is even more so the internal, final arrangement of the books in both Jewish and Christian traditions. The conclusion of the Hebrew Scriptures with Chronicles makes a statement that the consummation of history involves the ideal of the return of the Jewish people to its land, of the restoration of Jewish sovereignty and of spiritual renewal.[12] The arrangement of what Christians call the "Old Testament" so that it closes with the words of the prophet Malachi interprets the coming of Elijah and the "great and awesome day of the Lord" in 3:23 as proleptic of the New Testament in which the role of John the Baptist and the advent of the Christian Messiah is pivotal.

It seems to me that an excellent example of the process of inner-biblical exegesis being discernible within the Scriptures themselves, and being continued in rabbinic and medieval exegesis, is to be found in Gen. 21:33 which informs us that Abraham "planted a tamarisk (*'eshel*) at Beer-sheba and invoked there the name of the LORD, the everlasting God." Now this passage is extraordinary in that the action of the patriarch appears to be in contradiction to the strict prohibition in the Torah on the cultic use of trees[13] and on the planting of a tree near the altar of God.[14] The phenomenon of the sacred tree, particularly one associated with a hallowed site, is well known in a variety of cultures. Sometimes the tree is a medium of oracles and divination, to which names like *'elon moreh,* "the terebinth of the oracle-giver" in Gen. 12:6, and *'elon me'onenim,* "the terebinth of the soothsayers" in Judg. 9:37, are witness. Sometimes fertility cults flourished in connection with these trees, a form of paganism that seems to have been very attractive to many Israelites.[15] In light of all this, it is remarkable that the tradition about Abraham planting a tamarisk and invoking there the name of the Lord should appear in the Abrahamic biography, and not have been expunged.

A close look at the text reveals that the narrative already exhibits a sensitivity to the problem. Firstly, the descriptive title of God is given as *'el 'olam.* This epithet appears nowhere else in the Bible, but *'olam* is known to be one of the Canaanite divine titles.[16] Yet the God whom

Abraham worshiped is explicitly named YHWH, using the tetragrammaton, the exclusive name for the God of Israel. Secondly, unlike the other instances of the use of the formula, "He invoked the name of the LORD,"[17] the usual concomitant of altar building is, tellingly, here omitted. A subtle process of inner-biblical exegesis is at work in order to disengage Abraham's act from the Canaanite cults.

4. RABBINIC TRANSFORMATIONS

How has this passage fared at the hands of rabbinic commentators? At first glance, the exegesis appears to be so naive as to be worthy of immediate dismissal. In T.B. Sotah 10a[18] we read that R. Nehemiah interpreted *'eshel* not as a tamarisk but as a hospice.[19] Abraham, he said, received wayfarers there, providing them with food and shelter, and bringing them closer to God. To add force to this interpretation, *'eshel* is even taken as an acronym from *'akhilah, šetiyah, linah,* "eating, drinking and lodging the night."[20] All this, of course, is fanciful exegesis but what is seminal is that rabbinic and medieval commentary have extended the process of inner-biblical exegesis, thereby reinterpreting Abraham's cultic act to endow it with profound pedagogic value. An incident belonging to the realm of man's individual personal approach to God in a ritual ambience has been so transformed that it now exemplifies God's demands on man in a socio-moral context. The provision of wayfarers is itself elevated to being a mode of divine worship.

At times, rabbinic and medieval Jewish exegesis give every appearance of constituting critiques of biblical morality. The story of Noah is a case in point. The text of Gen. 6:9 declares him to be a perfectly righteous man. Nevertheless, the silence of Noah, and his seeming unconcern for the fate of his fellow human beings, contrast strikingly with Abraham's vocal and passionate plea for the lives of his contemporaries in Sodom and Gomorrah. Rabbinic sensitivity to what appears to be a moral flaw in his character expresses itself in two ways. On the one hand, *Genesis Rabba* 30:7 has Noah building the ark for no less than one hundred and twenty years,[21] all the while preaching to his compatriots and calling on them to repent of their evil ways;[22] on the other hand, some sages did not hesitate to characterize Noah as being among those of little faith, and to relativize his righteous state. They were careful to note that the text itself appears to qualify its verdict on Noah's moral condition by the careful formulation "He was righteous *in his generation*"; had he lived in the days of Abraham, he would not have been significant.[23]

Another example of this type of critical approach may be found in the treatment of the story of the kidnapping of Sarai, as told in Gen. 12:11–20. Abram is fearful of the evil of which human beings are capable. In order to save his own life, he appears to place the honor of his wife in jeopardy through misrepresentation of their relationship. Sarai's collusion may be looked upon as an act of self-sacrifice on behalf of her husband, but how is Abram's conduct to be judged? It is instructive to compare the reactions of some modern commentators with that of their medieval counterparts.

S.R. Driver remarks: "Untruthfulness and dissimulation are extremely common faults in the east; and it would be manifestly unjust to measure Abram by Christian standards."[24]

H.E. Ryle tells us: "It is repellent to our sense of honor, chivalry and purity. . . . This story doubtless would not have appeared so sordid to the ancient Israelites as it does to us. Perhaps the cunning, the deception and the increase of wealth may have commended the story to the Israelites of old times. . . the moral of the story does not satisfy any Christian standard in its representation of either Jehovah or of the patriarch."[25]

J. Skinner notes: "There is no suggestion that either the untruthfulness or the selfish cowardice of the request was severely reprobated by the ethical code to which the narrative appealed. . . ."[26]

Now let us turn to the treatment of the problem as presented in the commentaries of Naḥmanides (RaMBaN, 1194–1270) and David Kimḥi (?1160–1235?). The former unequivocally declares:

"Know that our father Abraham inadvertently committed a great offense in that he placed his virtuous wife in jeopardy of sin because of his fear of being killed. He should have trusted in God to save him, his wife and all he had, for God has the power to help and to save. . . . On account of this act, his descendants were doomed to suffer the Egyptian exile at the hand of Pharaoh" *(ad loc.)*.

David Kimḥi first observes that had Abraham been aware of the ugliness of the Egyptians and of their being steeped in immorality he would never have gone to Egypt in the first place, but would rather have suffered famine than jeopardize his wife. In the circumstances, however, in which the patriarch now finds himself, says Kimḥi, in effect, he is confronted with a moral dilemma and forced to make a choice between two evils: should he disclose the truth, he would assuredly be killed, and Sarai, beautiful and unprotected in an alien society of low moral standards, would certainly be condemned to life-long shame and degradation. If, however, he resorts to subterfuge, she might be violated by some Egyptian, but at least husband and wife would both survive. It would not have been proper, adds Kimhi, to have relied on a miracle as an excuse for inaction.

Whatever be the shortcomings of Kimhi's interpretation, it is clear that, unlike modern commentators, he sees the patriarch faced with a very real moral problem. Abraham's decision involved a conflict between human life and human dignity and their respective positions within a hierarchy of values. Unlike the above-cited moderns, he does not confuse chivalry with morality. What is of significance is that both Nahmanides and Kimhi are sensitive to a problem of biblical morality.

One final example is the thoroughly repellent folk-narrative, preserved in 2 Kings 2:23–24, about the prophet Elisha. Following his miraculous curing of the polluted waters of Jericho, the prophet made his way to Bethel. Some little children poked fun at his baldheadedness. Elisha pronounced a curse upon them in the name of the Lord, whereupon two bears came out of the woods and mangled forty-two children.

What did the rabbis do with this story? By the time they were through with it, nothing means what it appears to mean on the surface.[27] The "children" are not minors but of the age of moral responsibility. Note that the text initially describes the offenders as *ne'arim*, which in biblical Hebrew is an indeterminate noun that can cover a three month baby, as in Exod. 2:6, and a grown man, as in 2 Chron. 13:7. Moreover, a play on the verbal form of the word suggests that these people were *meno'arim min ha-mitsvot*, "they had divested themselves of the *mitsvot*." The reference to their being "little" (*qetannim*) actually refers, not to their physical stature, but to their spiritual condition. They were men of little faith. These people, say the rabbis, were the water carriers of Jericho who had been deprived of their livelihood by Elisha's miracle that made their local brackish water potable.[28] They had no confidence in God's providence, that He would provide them with alternative means of subsistence. They did not call the prophet "baldhead" (*qereah*) in reference to his shiny pate, but they said to him, "You have made this place bare for us," that is, "Through you, we lost our means of making a living." In the end, the rabbis make Elisha the guilty one, and he is punished by God for stirring up the bears against the children.

Obviously, this fanciful explanation cannot be defended, but by their wholesale reinterpretation of the narrative, the rabbis of the Talmud actually seem to be passing critical judgment on a particular aspect of biblical morality as reflected in this folk narrative. As Kimḥi noted in his comment to 2 Kings 2:24: "They had difficulty in understanding how he (i.e., Elisha) caused their death (i.e., of the children) for such a thing."

A modern scholar might formulate the underlying issue thus: The Hebrew Bible is not a single, uniform, self-consistent system, but is a stratified work, layers of which sometimes represent the imperfect human understanding of the nature of God and His demands on man. That is to say, the written text is not the exclusive source of religious truth, but is, in general, the foundation upon which the edifice of moral truth may be constructed. Such a scholar, depending on his personal commitment, might even say, "the indispensable foundation." However, it is not clear that this formulation would have been acceptable to the rabbis or to the traditional exegetes. Still, rabbinic reinterpretation, or rewriting, of the narratives as described above, raises questions about the authority of the text, the legitimacy of the exegesis, and the relationship between tradition and text.

5. THE HOLISTIC APPROACH

It seems to me that the rabbis, had they been challenged, might have defended their approach on the following grounds: It is the biblical canon in its definitive form that functions as normative. The sacred Scriptures are cumulative in their effect and impact. If the commentators appear to be assuming a stance outside of and over against the text, if they appear to leave room for the play of the intellect and the role of conscience and of moral sensibilities, then it must be appreciated that it is the Hebrew Bible itself in its entirety, as a composite work, that developed and honed these faculties, and that sensitized men to the critical standards to which that same text is now being subjected. The claim is that the commentators are simply actualizing what is potentially there all along, but what is potential can be discerned only through a unitary, comprehensive, holistic approach. This, in fact, is what is partially meant by the rabbinic dictum: "Whatever a mature student may expound in the future, was already told to Moses on Sinai,"[29] which, incidentally, affords an interesting contrast with the axiom of Pope Stephen I: *Nihil innovetur nisi quod traditum est.*

To return to our point. The classicist, M. I. Finley, noted that the world of the Iliad is saturated with blood because that represented archaic Greek values.[30] We may point out that the Hebrew Scriptures are not saturated with blood and, unlike Homer's role in the world of the Greeks, their morally problematic texts did not, despite constant repetition, promote an inferior code of values. The reason is that the teaching of the text was always accompanied by traditional exegesis which succeeded in transforming that which is time-bound into that which is eternally relevant, and in translating the timelessness of the text into that which is supremely timely. The chronological and cultural gap between the reader and the text was effectively bridged, and the text could and was utilized to mold the mind and to shape the moral character of the Jew.

6. THE PROBLEM OF *PESHAṬ*

As we have noted, what we have just discussed raises the question of the literal sense of Scripture and its place in the hierarchy of interpretation. There is an interesting exchange on the subject in the works of Maimonides (1135–1204) and Naḥmanides (1194–1270) relative to the Talmudic rule of Shab. 63[a] *et al.* that the text of Scripture may not depart from its straightforward meaning *(peshaṭ)*. In his *Sefer Ha-Mitsvot*,[31] Maimonides states that "there is no Scripture except according to its literal sense" *(peshaṭ)*, to which Naḥmanides retorted that the rabbis "did not say that the Bible only has its straightforward meaning, but we have its Midrashic meaning side by side with its straightforward meaning, and the text departs from neither. It can encompass both, and both are the truth; that is to say, the homiletic *(derash)* does not neutralize the literal sense *(peshaṭ)*. Both are substantive."[32]

As R. Loewe and others have shown, what the rabbis meant by *peshaṭ* is less straightforward than meets the eye.[33] What interests me at the moment, however, is the oft-stated proposition that the true and sole task of the biblical scholar is to discover what the contemporary audience understood when the writer wrote what he did, and that such meaning, when recovered, is the one true meaning of the text. Granted, of course, that sound historical research must be the foundation of all biblical scholarship, and that every commentator must commence his exegetical work at that level; but is the interpretation of a text necessarily exhausted by the results of historical investigation, however well based? (In asking this question, I ignore the undeniable fact that there can hardly be a branch of human learning more strewn with the debris of discarded theories than biblical scholarship.)

It seems to me that the rabbis would have held the view that this thesis, taken to its extreme, is of doubtful validity because it is predicated on the presupposition that the biblical writers consciously wrote only for their contemporaries. The rabbis would have said that the internal biblical evidence refutes such a notion and points in the opposite direction, namely that the biblical writers were fully conscious of writing for, and thereby influencing, future generations. Apart from such oft-repeated passages like, "When your son shall ask you in the future, 'What means. . . ?'"[34] and other explicit documentation,[35] the very transmission and survival of the biblical corpus, no less than its astonishing and sustained impact on vast segments of the human race for over two and one half millennia, would be difficult to explain unless the text was very early understood to be proleptic in nature. In other words, the rabbis would have claimed that embedded in the text and context is a deliberate equivocality, the full implication(s) and meaning(s) of which are valid subjects of study by the biblical exegete.

7. MEDIEVAL CRITIQUES OF RABBINIC EXEGESIS

Of course, I am not suggesting that biblical self-understanding always coincides with rabbinic understanding. In fact, as I have elsewhere shown, medieval Jewish exegesis frequently criticizes rabbinic exegesis. Its literature is replete with observations of the most daring kind, much of which well anticipates aspects of modern higher and lower criticism.[36] In fact, the commentators not only may interpret legal or ritual texts not in accord with halakhic ruling, but are quite aware of what they are doing, and sometimes even criticize the rabbinic authorities for divesting the text of its plain meaning. This critical approach constitutes an important element in medieval Jewish exegesis, particularly but not exclusively in the Spanish school, and is not to be viewed as exotic or eccentric though admittedly some of its most extreme expression is both. I should like to emphasize that these scholars were men who were fully committed to the halakhic way of life, and did not question the authority of the rabbis in their legal rulings, only the exegesis by which such were derived from the text. It is almost as though they held— though as far as I know no one has ever articulated it quite this way— that the halakhah enjoys its own autonomous existence and authority, so that the biblical exegete is free to investigate the text independently of dogmatic or traditional considerations.

By way of illustration, I might point to Rashi's rejection of the tannaitic exegesis of Exod. 23:2. There Scripture states: "You shall not side with the mighty to do wrong—you shall not give perverse testimony in a dispute so as to pervert it in favor of the mighty." The Mishnah understands this verse to require a simple majority of judges for an acquittal but a majority of two for a conviction in capital cases.[37] On this Rashi comments, "There are interpretations of this verse by the sages of Israel, but the language of the text cannot accommodate them." Rashi's grandson, known as RashBaM (ca. 1080–1158), in discussing the rabbinic exposition of Lev. 7:18 as found in M. Zev 2:2–4, T.B. Zev 29[b], asserts that "The sages have wrested it from its plain meaning." Perhaps the most forthright expression of the independence of medieval Jewish exegesis from tradition is to be found in an observation by Samuel b. Hofni, Gaon of Sura (d. 1030), cited by David Kimḥi in his comment to 1 Sam. 28:24: "Even though the words of the sages in the Talmud imply that the woman (the witch of Endor) really did revive Samuel, yet insofar as human reason rejects this, they cannot be accepted."

In the same strain, we may cite the comments of Isaac Abravanel (1437–1508) in connection with the narrative of 2 Sam. 11–12. In the Talmud,[38] it is related that the 3rd–4th century C.E. Palestinian Amora R. Samuel ben Nahman, citing R. Jonathan ben Eleazar (3rd century C.E.) as his source, exonerated David from any sin. This is achieved by means of contortive exegesis in plain defiance of the straightforward intent of the text, the Prophet Nathan's severe castigation of David's shameful conduct, David's self-confession of his guilt, and the tradition reflected in Ps. 51. Although most of the medieval commentators follow the talmudic rationale, Abravanel launches into a blistering indictment of David, probingly analyzing the multiple sins that the king committed. He does this in full and open consciousness of his contradiction of the talmudic exegesis which he describes as being contrary to "the simple truth."

The kind of freedom and intellectual honesty that such comments, and many more like them, display clearly points to a separation of matters of faith and law from matters of scholarship on the part of these medievals, a distinction that, alas, is often blurred today. Put another way, these traditional Jewish exegetes are really operating according to rabbinic doctrine that the oral Torah, the *torah she-be'al peh*, codified as Halakhah, is one of the two modes of God's self-revelation to Israel, and the process of continuous reinterpretation and adaptation of the Halakhah to new and everchanging conditions is affected by the indwelling of the Divine Presence in those whose piety, learning and acknowledged authority are such as to give normative force to their halakhic decisions. Where the exegetes assert their intellectual independence is, first, in respect of the humanly wrought exegetical process by which the oral Torah is interlaced with the written Torah, *torah she-bikhtav*, and, second, in the exposition of the non-halakhic sections of the Bible.

NOTES

1. Tosef. Shab. 13:1.
2. Gershom Scholem, *The Messianic Idea in Judaism* (New York, 1971), p. 290.
3. See S. Rawidowicz. "On Interpretation" in *Studies in Jewish Thought*, Philadelphia, 1974, pp. 45–80.
4. TB *Sanh.* 34[a], cf. *Shab.* 88[b].
5. Num.R. *Naso'*, 13:15.
6. M. *A vot* 5:26.
7. See A. I. Baumgarten, "Justinian and the Jews" in *Rabbi Joseph H. Lookstein Memorial Volume*, ed. Leo Landman (New York, 1980), pp. 37–44.
8. On Ben Hayyim's Rabbinic Bible, see now Jordan S. Penkover, *Jacob ben Hayyim and the Rise of the Biblia Rabbinica* [Hebrew], Hebrew University Doctoral Dissertation, Jerusalem, 1982.
9. TB *Erubin* 13[b].
10. See J. A. Sanders, *Torah and Canon* (Philadelphia, 1972); *idem*, "Available for Life: The Nature and Function of Canon" in *Magnalia Dei: Essays on the Bible and Archaeology in Memory of G. Ernest Wright* (New York, 1976), pp. 531–60; B. S. Childs, *The Introduction to the Old Testament as Scripture* (Philadelphia, 1979); J. Barr, *Holy Scripture: Canon, Authority, Criticism* (Philadelphia, 1983); M. Fishbane, *Biblical Interpretation in Ancient Israel* (Oxford, 1984).
11. Cf. N. M. Sarna, "Ps. 89: A Study in Inner Biblical Exegesis," in *Biblical and Other Studies*, ed. A. Altmann, Philip W. Lown Institute of Advanced Judaic Studies, Brandeis University, Studies and Texts, Vol. I (Cambridge, 1963), pp. 29–46.
12. 2 Chron. 36:23.
13. Exod. 34:13; Deut. 12:2–3.
14. Deut. 16:21.
15. Cf. 1 Kings 14:23; Jet. 2:20; Ezek. 6:13.
16. Cf. *špš 'lm* in U. T. 2008:7 and *rpu mlk 'lm* in U. T. 52.1 on which see M. Pope, *BASOR*, 251 (1983), p. 68; cf. F. M. Cross, *Canaanite Myth and Hebrew Epic* (Cambridge, 1973), pp. 17, n. 29; 18 and n. 33.
17. Cf. Gen. 12:8; 13:4; 26:25.
18. So *Gen. R.* 54.7.
19. *pundok* = Gr. *Pandocheion*.
20. Rashi to TB *Sotah* 10[a] interprets ". . . *leviyah*" "escorting."
21. Cf. Gen. 6:3.
22. TB *Sanh.* 108[a-b].
23. *Gen. R.* 32:9.
24. S. R. Driver, *Genesis*, Westminster Commentaries (London, 1904), *ad loc.*
25. H. E. Ryle, *The Book of Genesis*, Cambridge Bible (Cambridge, 1921), *ad loc.*

26. J. Skinner, *Genesis*, International Critical Commentary (Edinburgh, 1910), *ad loc.*

27. TB *Sotah* 46ᵃ–47ᵇ.

28. 2 Kings 2:19–25.

29. P. *Peah* 2:4 *et al.* See A. J. Heschel, *Torah Min Ha-Shamayim* (London-New York, 1965), Vol. 2, p. 23 and n. 10.

30. *The World of Odysseus* (New York, 1959), p. 127.

31. ed. Ch. Heller, Vol. II (Jerusalem-New York, 1976), pp. 7–8.

32. *Hassagot Ha-RaMBaN* 11, p. 27.

33. See R. Loewe, *Papers of the Institute of Jewish Studies* I, ed. J. G. Weiss (Jerusalem, 1964), pp. 140–185; cf. B. S. Childs, "The Sensus Literalis of Scripture: An Ancient and Modern Problem," in *Beiträge zur Alttestamentlichen Theologie, Festschrift für Walther Zimmerli zum 70 Geburtstag* (Göttingen, 1977), pp. 80–93; M. Schneiders, "Faith, Hermeneutics and the Literal Sense of Scripture," in *Theological Studies*, 39 (1978), pp. 719–736.

34. Exod. 13:14, cf. v. 8; Deut. 6:8; Josh. 4:6, 21; 22:27–28, cf. v. 24.

35. Cf. Isa. 30:8; Jer. 30:2–3; 36:28–29; Hab. 2:2–3; Dan. 12:4.

36. "Hebrew and Biblical Studies in Medieval Spain," in *The Sephardi Heritage*, ed. R. Barnett (London, 1971), pp. 344–394; "Unusual Aspects of Medieval Biblical Exegesis" [Hebrew] in *Thought and Action: Essays in Memory of Simon Rawidowicz on the Twenty-fifth Anniversary of His Death*, ed. A. A. Greenbaum and A. L. Ivry (Tel Aviv, 1983), pp. 35–42; "The Modern Study of the Bible in the Framework of Jewish Studies," in *Proceedings of the Eighth World Congress of Jewish Studies: Bible and Hebrew Language* (Jerusalem, 1983), pp. 19–27.

37. M. *Sanh.* 1:6.

38. TB *Shab.* 56ᵃ.

Hebrew and Bible Studies in Medieval Spain

INTRODUCTORY

Jewish biblical studies reached their apogee in Moslem Spain. Throughout the centuries of exile the Hebrew Scriptures were naturally studied
as the revealed word of God. Occupying a central place in the Jewish
tradition, they were looked upon as the faithful witness to the national
past, the main source for the knowledge and use of the national language, the font of truth, wisdom, law and morality, the embodiment of
the hopes and dreams of a glorious future. In short, as the animating
force of Jewish existence, biblical words saturated the mind, the spirit
and the literature of all medieval Jewry.

The Spanish-Jewish achievement was not simply the highest and
most intense expression of this phenomenon. It had about it a uniqueness and originality, a vitality and pioneering quality that set it apart
from anything that came before or after. It was in biblical studies, in all
their ramifications, that the intellectual history of Spanish Jewry found
its most fundamental and concrete articulation. In fact, the Bible, the
Book *par excellence*, constituted the very protoplasm of its tradition.

Unlike the experience of the Jews of Christian Europe, the study of
the Scriptures in Spain did not become the consolidation of past learning. To be sure, antiquity and authority were cherished sufficiently to
warrant preservation and transmission. But to the Spanish Jews, tradition
was revered in not so rigid and inordinate a manner as to become static
and decadent. An element of contention and controversy was allowed to
penetrate, and a considerable admixture of critical independence and

intellectual daring imparted a quality of excitement to biblical studies. The diversity and multiplicity of approach, the acute sensitivity to difficulties, the forging of the essential tools of scholarship, and the extraordinary degree of sophistication—all these characterized the Sephardi contribution to biblical scholarship and led to a remarkable and unparalleled efflorescence in this field.[1]

Strangely, however, the beginnings were humble enough and not in the least auspicious. The Jewish community of Spain could certainly claim to have existed since Roman times, even if it could not validate its boast to descent from the biblical tribe of Judah.[2] Yet before the Arab conquest, and for quite a while after, it gave no evidence of any contribution to Jewish culture, much less of any predilection for, or even particular interest in Scriptural or linguistic studies.[3] This situation is well illustrated through the correspondence of the Babylonian Geonim. Although *responsa* to enquiries on biblical matters are addressed to other Jewish communities, none such, surprisingly, appear in connection with the Jews of Spain.[4] Moreover, it was not until the tenth century was far advanced that Spanish Jewry could boast of having produced a native-born Bible commentator or grammarian.

The astonishing upsurge of intellectual activity which distinguished later Spanish Jewry and which found such glorious expression in the biblical and Hebraic fields, cannot be said to have been the result of a slow process of internal growth and development. The Sephardim absorbed a rich and variegated legacy and the main river of their scholarship was fed by many literary streams and sustained by numerous cultural tributaries.

On the one hand, the Arab conquests of the seventh and eighth centuries, which imposed the unity of Islamic-Arabic culture upon a far-flung empire, brought Sephardi Jewry out of its isolation to give it free access to the great Jewish centres from which it had formerly been cut off. On the other hand, the mass immigration to Spain that came in successive waves following the victory of Tariq ibn Ziyad in 711, brought Jews from Morocco, Tunis and Egypt, as well as from the remoter lands of Palestine and Syria, and even far-away Babylon. The established community found itself immeasurably enriched by the commingling of diverse influences and the inter-penetration and cross-fertilization of varying traditions and intellectual trends.

THE INFLUENCE OF BABYLON

The most powerful influence upon Spain in the earlier period was that of the Babylonian academies. From them was received a mature and well-ordered tradition of talmudic study, and for a long time the Jewish community was culturally and religiously subservient to the Babylonian Gaonate. This state of affairs adequately explains the exclusive concentration of Spanish scholars upon Halakhah until the tenth century. An indication of how far the decline in biblical studies had gone in Babylon is the fact that the Gaon Natronai (853–56) felt impelled to explain away the contemporary flagrant contravention of the Talmudic prescription that one third of the curriculum of studies be devoted to the Bible.[5] In these circumstances, the contribution of Babylonian scholars to Sephardi biblical and linguistic achievements was minimal, despite the fact that the twin centres of Jewish spiritual life, Sura and Pumbedita, were both within close proximity to Baghdad, an important seat of Arabic philological studies. True, the Gaon Semah ben Paltoi (872–90) compiled the first talmudic lexicon, and Hai Gaon (998–1038) wrote a dictionary in Arabic covering biblical, Mishnaic and Aramaic words; true also, that Saᶜadiah (882–942) and Samuel ben Hofni (997–1013) had a tremendous impact on Sephardi scholarship, while the great Spanish Hebraist, grammarian and poet, Dunash ibn Labrat (c. 920–c. 990), had studied in Babylon. But it remains a fact, nevertheless, that philological accomplishments were atypical of Babylonian learning. Moreover, the lexica of Semah and Hai were not really based on sound scientific principles; Saᶜadiah acquired his learning outside of Babylon, and Dunash, in all likelihood, was attracted to the place only by the fame of Saᶜadiah.[6]

By the middle of the tenth century, the hegemony of the Babylonian academies over Jewry had declined disastrously and the installation of R. Moses ben Hanokh as head of the academy at Cordova (c. 960) really signalized a final gesture of independence on the part of the Spanish community.[7] It is no accident that it is precisely at this point that the hitherto exclusive concentration upon talmudic studies gave way to broader interests.

THE INFLUENCE OF PALESTINE

Among the influences at work here must be mentioned that of Palestinian Jewry. Generally speaking, its spiritual and cultural impact upon

Spain was very small indeed. The mainstream of Sephardi tradition issued from Babylon, so that even the Jerusalem Talmud did not find acceptance in Spain. Yet the renewed contacts with Palestine that followed the Arab conquest led to very beneficial results for Sephardi culture in the fields of Hebrew language and Bible study.

The widespread popularity of the Palestinian esoteric work, *Sefer Yeṣirah* which contained the first known phonetic classification of the letters of the Hebrew alphabet, stimulated an interest in the phonology of the Hebrew language.[8] Similarly propaedeutic to linguistic and biblical studies were the activities of the Palestinian Masoretes, the undisputed leaders in the field, whose invention of a great mnemotechnic apparatus designed to guard the biblical text from error won authoritative acceptance, just as did the Tiberian system of vocalization and accentuation.[9]

Spanish indebtedness to Palestine in these matters was gratefully acknowledged in all periods. The pupils of Menaḥem ben Saruq (910–970) rely upon the authority of Palestine for the correct reading and accents.[10] Jonah ibn Janaḥ (985–1040) speaks of "the men of Tiberias who excel all others in the clarity of their Hebrew speech."[11] He rightly saw in the work of the Palestinian Masoretes the origins of systematic research into the Hebrew language,[12] and it was a Palestinian Bible codex and Masoretic lists and notes from the same source that he used as the most reliable texts on which to base his grammatical researches.[13] Spanish Jewish pilgrims to the Holy Land apparently served as the medium of transmission for these materials. Ibn Janaḥ cites the work of a Jerusalem grammarian brought back by "Jacob the pilgrim of Leon."[14] Abraham ibn 'Ezra (1092–1167) who, incidentally, also pays tribute to the Tiberians, was likewise familiar with the works of the Palestinians.[15] He mentions an anonymous "sage of Jerusalem" who authored no less than eight books on Hebrew grammar.[16] In the light of all this, it will be readily understood why the Sephardim, despite their subservience to Babylon, adopted the order of the Books of the Bible as current in Palestine.[17]

This situation, however, must not be exaggerated. Palestine hardly produced grammarians of stature, and its biblical exegetical tradition, with its homiletic bias, was rejected outright by the Spanish scholars.[18]

THE ARAB IMPACT

The imposition of Arabic culture upon a far-flung empire left its impact upon Jewry in numerous subtle ways.[19] Internally, Karaite sectarianism, which owed not a little to the inspiration of Moslem schismatic movements, stimulated the study of the Scriptures through its vigorous anti-Rabbanite polemics.[20] Furthermore, the spirit of criticism fostered by the spread of rationalism soon found expression in a skeptical approach to the Bible. Ḥivi ha-Balkhi's two hundred arguments and queries (c. 880) purporting to demonstrate the internal contradictions of the text and the unlikelihood of miracles achieved very wide circulation.[21] Externally, Moslem anti-Jewish polemics frequently involved attacks on the sacred Book of the Jews and inevitably engendered apologetics and counter-polemics, all of which served as a goad to the re-examination of Scripture.[22]

Somewhat paradoxically, the displacement of Aramaic by Arabic as the spoken language of a very large segment of Jewry brought in its wake a great renascence of Hebrew learning. It meant that the educated Jew had at his disposal an astonishingly varied linguistic equipment comprising the Hebrew of the Bible and the Tannaim, Aramaic in its biblical, targumic and talmudic dialects, and now Arabic. This alone must have served to sharpen a sensitivity to philological matters. Further, the meticulous regard of the Arabs for their language and the great attention they paid to proper grammatical and stylistic usage, could not but have developed among Jews a high degree of linguistic consciousness and aesthetic appreciation that was bound to carry over into their approach to Hebrew. The Moslem conviction, ceaselessly propagated, that the Arabic of the Qur'an represented linguistic purity and literary elegance in its most exalted form, must certainly have stimulated a countervailing movement among Jews to promote the Hebrew Bible as the yardstick of literary excellence—an idea that was in any case accepted as being self-evident.[23]

The impact of all these factors at work among the Jews of Spain was reinforced by the policies of 'Abd ar-Raḥman III (912–61) and his son 'Al-Ḥakam II (961–76), Caliphs of Cordova. As a result of their active cultivation of linguistic studies through the import and patronage of scholars, the glittering city had become, by the second half of the tenth century, a most important centre of Arabic philological research. The foremost scholars of the age succeeded in gathering about them coteries of students instilled with pride in the beauty of their language and inspired with enthusiasm for its systematic study.[24] Spurred by the example of the Moslem ruling classes, the Jewish aristocracy followed suit. Ḥisdai ibn Shapruṭ (940–66), cultured, scholarly, wealthy and powerful, became the leading patron of Hebrew studies in Cordova which was soon to become the Mecca of Jewish scholars who could be assured of a hospitable welcome from Jewish courtiers and men of means.[25]

One final factor, decisive for the Hebrew renascence in Spain, must be mentioned. The expansive Moslem culture broadened the intellectual horizons and altered the cultural perspective of the Jews beyond all previous experience. For the first time they became acquainted with a wealth of Greek and Islamic philosophical analysis and speculation, scientific lore, Arabic philological research and poetic achievement of a high order. New, challenging, unconventional ideas, topics and literary forms suddenly confronted them. The need to give adequate Hebrew expression to this new-found learning and sophistication strained to the limits the existing linguistic resources.

THE INADEQUACY OF HEBREW

The adaptation of the language to this purpose proved, however, to be a herculean task. Biblical Hebrew, as the medium of revelation, was the obvious norm by which excellence of style could be measured. But instead of regarding it as the foundation upon which a linguistic superstructure might be erected, the Spanish enthusiasts looked upon it as ideally self-sufficient. The result was the disappointing discovery that biblical Hebrew was woefully inadequate to the cultural needs of the times.[26]

This situation was further aggravated by the current philosophy of language.[27] The Spanish Hebraists had no understanding of evolutionary development and, with few exceptions,[28] did not realise that Mishnaic Hebrew might be a legitimate lineal descendant of the same language in which the Bible was written. Thus, the first Spanish grammarian of stature, Menaḥem ben Saruq, made a clear distinction between the "language of the Bible" which alone was the "holy tongue," and the language of the Tannaim.[29]

To be sure, the inadequacy of the biblical language was easily rationalized. Menaḥem, himself, provided the explanation that was to be repeated time and again by later writers. The Books of the Bible represent but a small fragment of the lost literary productions of ancient Israel. Hence, the biblical vocabulary is bound to be severely limited. If only the lost works might be recovered, the language would prove itself more than satisfactory to modern needs.[30]

Later scholars appended to this apologia the further observation that the loss of national independence and the tribulations of exile had contributed greatly to the impoverishment of the holy tongue.[31]

THE DIFFUSION OF HEBREW

It is difficult to assess the true extent of Hebrew learning among Spanish Jews on the basis of existing sources. From the tenth to the fifteenth century, poets and grammarians bewailed the ignorance and neglect of the national language. The historian Abraham ibn Daud (1110–80) actually goes so far as to say that it "had become forgotten throughout the Diaspora."[32] His contemporary Solomon ibn Parhon (c. 1160) reports that, whereas the Jews of the Arabic-speaking countries did not converse in Hebrew, the diversity of tongues that characterized Christendom was a powerful stimulant to the use of Hebrew as the one common language of communication for Jews.[33] A century earlier, Moses ibn Chiquitilla (c. 1080) had stated that the Jews of Catalonia and Provence were devoted to Hebrew and accustomed to speak it.[34] Jonah ibn Janah, for his part, found it necessary to launch a tirade against the scholars, especially the Talmudists who, he said, trifled with the laws of the Hebrew language and did not even read the Bible accurately.[35] The fact of the matter is that between the tenth and the twelfth centuries the Jews of Moslem Spain, in contrast to their coreligionists in Christian lands, used Arabic, not Hebrew, as the primary vehicle of literary expression.[36]

On the other hand, it is known that the Spanish syllabus of studies required intensive application to the biblical text and extensive rote learning from a tender age.[37] The contrast in this respect between Franco-German and Spanish Jews is well illustrated by the ethical will of Judah ben Asher (d. 1349), Rabbi of Toledo, who had migrated from Germany. Writing at a time when Spanish Jewry was already well past its prime, he admonished his son to set aside regular times for the study of the Bible, grammar and exegesis. He, himself, he confessed, had neglected these subjects in his youth, for such was the German-Jewish custom. As a result he had found himself unable to teach the Bible in Toledo.[38]

The primacy of Bible in the traditional education of the Spanish community inevitably equipped the Jew with a rich store of Hebrew learning. Testimony to this is the fact that in their Arabic writings the Jewish scholars always cited the biblical text solely in the original. Further evidence is supplied by the honored position in Jewish society enjoyed by a relatively large number of Hebrew poets who succeeded in deriving a livelihood from the practice of their art.[39] Such was possible only on the assumption of the existence of a fairly wide, appreciative and apperceptive audience.

THE EXPANSION OF THE LANGUAGE

The deeply-rooted commitment to the biblical model as the ideal and exclusive standard predetermined the direction of development in meeting the challenge posed by the confrontation with Islamic society. The Hebraists made a conscious, sincere and brave effort both to improve the literary style and to mould the limited material at their disposal into a more flexible and practical cultural instrument.

By the end of the eleventh century, the systematic study of biblical Hebrew, its vocabulary, grammar, syntax and style, had become fundamental to the education of every enlightened Jew.[40] Judah Ḥayyuj (c. 950–c. 1000), whose spectacular discoveries revolutionized the scientific study of Hebrew grammar and lexicography, had as one of his expressed purposes the satisfaction of the needs of Hebrew writers.[41] Jonah ibn Jonah, the greatest of all the classical Jewish grammarians, declared the cultivation of a more elegant Hebrew style among contemporary writers to be one of the prime motivating aims of his researches.[42] Similar affirmations may be found in the writings of Solomon ibn Gabirol (1021–1069)[43] Abraham ibn ʿEzra,[44] and others.

In their strivings to achieve linguistic expansion, the Spanish Hebraists, by virtue of their self-imposed terms of reference, hewed closely to the form and substance of classical Hebrew, and eschewed the radical innovations so dear to the *payytanim* of Palestine.[45] The results were little short of miraculous.

Biblical vocables found but once or rarely, usually of uncertain meaning, were resuscitated and pressed into common usage, first in poetry, then in prose, through the endowment of specific significance. Conventional words often took on fresh nuances under the influences of Talmudic or Arabic usage. Nouns appearing only in the singular form were given their normative plurals, and singulars were derived from those found only in the plural. A biblical noun might serve as the basis of a new denominative verb, and a noun be freshly coined from a verb.

The technical terminology of poetry and philosophy could be produced by the combination of biblical words and phrases by analogy with Arabic prototypes.[46]

The remarkable success of this experiment, in itself an achievement of no mean order, is immediately apparent if one considers that the Spanish writers preserved the biblical quality of their secular poetry up to the thirteenth century, notwithstanding the great variety and unconventionality—from the Jewish point of view—of the themes they cultivated. It was not until the time of Meshullam ben Solomon da Piera (d. c. 1260), who was one of the first to introduce the language of Halakhah and Agadah into secular Hebrew poetry,[47] that the attachment to pure biblical style began to weaken. Yet the degree of loyalty to the Hebrew language and the earnest desire to avoid, as far as possible, foreign importations, may be measured by the surprising calculation that, of approximately three thousand philosophic terms in use in original Hebrew works or employed in translations from Arabic, only about eighty are actually loan words.[48]

Finally, it says much for the deep and well-nigh universal attachment of Spanish Jews to Hebrew that, although there was opposition to the introduction of secular themes into poetry, we do not find throughout the period under discussion any protest based on the argument of the impropriety of the use of Scriptural quotation for a purely secular and divertive literature.[49]

THE POETIC MEDIUM

A distinction between the language of social intercourse and the language of literature was well established among both Moslems and Christians in Spain. It was thus not unnatural for the Jewish community to follow suit. But that the Hebrew renascence should have found its purest and most profound expression dressed in poetic vestment, rather than in prose garb, is indeed a strange phenomenon that is to be adequately explained only on several grounds.

First and foremost was the influence of a venerable tradition of liturgical poetry in Hebrew which was powerful enough to overcome the initial Arabic secular inspiration. Moreover, the very existence of this tradition naturally made the poetic medium the most effective, because the most readily acceptable, literary vehicle for the resuscitation of the language. The high prestige enjoyed by the poet in upper-class Moslem society also helped not a little. At the same time, the competitive spirit with Arabic proved to be a further stimulus, for to the Arabs poetry was supposed to exemplify the unrivalled beauty of the sacred Qur'an. The Jews, therefore, would tend to shun versification in the Arab tongue and would be prone to use, instead, the language of their own sacred Scriptures.[50]

POETRY, PHILOLOGY AND BIBLE STUDIES

It is obvious that the expansion of Hebrew on the basis of the biblical prototype could not have been pursued without the indispensable precondition of intensive research in the fields of grammar, lexicography and interpretation of the sacred text. Of necessity, therefore, the course of the Hebrew rebirth and efflorescence in Spain proceeded in three distinct directions—poetic composition, linguistic studies and biblical exegesis.

In actual fact, however, it is not always possible to separate the disciplines since all three were often inextricably intertwined, and they reacted one upon the other. The ability to write Hebrew poetry, where Hebrew was not the vernacular, required a thorough mastery of the biblical text, a keen sensitivity to the distinctive peculiarities of biblical prose and poetry, and a fine perception of the meaning of words and the subtleties of their use. A poet had either himself to be a philologist or an exegete, or at least to be thoroughly familiar with the results of philological and exegetical scholarship. No biblical interpretation could be convincing if it ignored sound philology. The Spanish-Jewish grammarians carefully studied the Bible to extract from it the laws of the language. Once having formulated them, they reapplied them for the deeper understanding and interpretation of the text.

The close connection between poetry and philology was maintained from the beginning to the end of the Spanish period. The very first generation of grammarians, Menaḥem ben Saruq and Dunash ibn Labraṭ, set the pattern and left an indelible imprint on Hebrew poetry. Levi al-Tabban (11th cent.),[51] a respected philologist, is known to have authored no less than seventy poems, and his poetic ability was highly praised. Moses ibn Chiquitilla, Bible exegete and illustrious grammarian, was "distinguished for his poetry."[52] This tribute, coming from the usually vitriolic pen[53] of Judah ibn Bal'am (d. c. 1090), may be taken as praise indeed. Ibn Bal'am, himself, was another great grammarian who was also a poet of merit. Admittedly, the greatest of all Hebrew grammarians left behind not a line of poetry; but such was the spirit of the age that Jonah ibn Janaḥ apparently felt compelled to lay claim to poetic accomplishment, maintaining that his compositions had erroneously been circulated under the authorship of another.[54] The first of the real giants of Spanish-Hebrew poetry, Samuel ibn Nagrela (993–1056), is reported to have composed twenty-two treatises on philological topics.[55] Solomon ibn Gabirol, "the nightingale," wrote a poem entitled 'Anaq (Necklace) comprising four-hundred double-verses summarizing the important laws of Hebrew grammar.[56] The celebrated exegete and grammarian Abraham ibn 'Ezra, whose work marks a turning-point in Spanish-Jewish intellectual activity, was a prolific and versatile poet of high calibre. Even as the curtain fell on the last generation of Spanish Jews, the traditional association of the disciplines was still being maintained. Saʿadiah ben Maimun ibn Danan, who left Spain in 1492, wrote a comprehensive grammar of Hebrew, a dictionary, a commentary on part of Isaiah and an analysis of Hebrew prosody, as well as some Hebrew poetry.[57]

The Spanish poets who drew on the Bible for their inspiration themselves, in turn, left biblical studies greatly in their debt. Not only did their writing stimulate and promote the closer study of Scripture, but their poetry, secular and religious, is an important, though still largely untapped, source of biblical scholarship. The assigning of particular meaning to *hapax legomena,* rare words or difficult phrases, was neither arbitrary nor gratuitous. It was mostly a reflection of an exegetical tradition, the recovery of which is invaluable for the history of biblical exegesis. The Hebrew poetry of the period may also be of great service in textual criticism since its biblical quotations often vary from our received text. Even if due and proper allowance be made for the vagaries of human memory, the considerable license exercised by poets, and the carelessness of later scribes, there yet remains a respectable residue of biblical citations which contains textual variants worthy of serious scholarly examination.[58] Finally, it should not be forgotten that the Spanish-Hebrew poetry contains much original, if incidental, exegesis if only for the reason that the poets were frequently scholars who left the impress of their learning and originality in the manner in which they put Scripture to the service of the Muse.

MENAHEM BEN SARUQ

The work of the poets was immeasurably facilitated by the compilation of dictionaries. Sa°adiah had initiated the process in compiling his *Agron* specifically for the benefit of poets.

To Menaḥem den Saruq (910–970) must be credited the distinction of having been the first Spanish-Jewish scholar to write a dictionary. His work, popularly known as *Maḥberet*,[59] was the first attempt to classify the entire biblical thesaurus on the basis of characteristic consonants, and to group together roots according to the varying meanings they can bear, as illustrated by scriptural citations. The *Maḥberet* can also boast the added virtue of having been the first complete dictionary written in the Hebrew language.

The lexicon was prefaced by an introductory survey of Hebrew grammar analysing some of the outstanding features of the form and structure of the holy tongue. These notes really explain the principles upon which Menaḥem operated in his lexicographical work. His overriding aim was to clarify the distinction between "radicals" and "auxiliaries." By the former he meant those consonants that consistently maintain their identity. By the latter he understood those consonants that serve as infixed, prefixed or suffixed elements. This distinction is reflected in the arrangement of the dictionary.

Other data included in the introduction or scattered throughout the lexicon comprise observations on the use of the *dagesh,* the vowel system, homonyms and impossible combinations and sequences of consonants as radicals. Some problems of Hebrew syntax, particularly the phenomena of ellipsis and pleonasm, also receive attention. Menaḥem believed these latter to be the basic features of the language. He also paid heed to parallelism as the outstanding characteristic of biblical poetry.

The *Maḥberet* of Menaḥem ben Saruq was a pioneering work. It managed to combine an exhibition of deep feeling for, and keen sensitivity to, linguistic subtleties with a lack of systematic and comprehensive understanding of the structure of the language. His criterion for distinguishing the root-form led him to postulate the existence of uni-, bi-, tri-, quadri- and quinque-consonantal radicals. In failing to grasp the nature of weak consonants he was led into serious confusion of etymologies. His grammatical treatment was rudimentary, unsystematic, selective, and far from exhaustive even in the topics discussed. Another serious fault is the absence of paradigms of the inflections of nouns and verbs.

Compared with the work of his non-Spanish predecessors Saᶜadiah and Judah ibn Quraish (born c. 900) with which he was familiar, Menahem not only showed little progress in the science of language, but was actually retrogressive in many respects. Thus, he deliberately refrained from utilizing Arabic cognates to elucidate Hebrew words, and even Aramaic and Mishnaic Hebrew he used but rarely. As a result, he was forced to rely solely upon the nexus of thought to elicit meaning from *hapax legomena* and other unusual words. This, of course, is a highly subjective method of very limited value. Also retrogressive was his opposition to the idea of consonantal interchange and metathesis, phenomena of language already well recognized by his day.

On the other hand, all these drawbacks, serious as they are, must not be allowed to obscure the undoubted fact that Menahem b. Saruq occupies a place of historic importance in the annals of the study and development of the Hebrew language. It is of little consequence that this is due less to the intrinsic merit of his work than to the rule it played in precipitating a new movement.

In restricting himself, for whatever reasons, to the language of Scripture, he turned biblical Hebrew philology into an independent discipline. By insisting upon writing in Hebrew, instead of Arabic, he succeeded in raising the national language to the status of a value-concept that triggered a revival of Hebrew consciousness. In eschewing Arabic technical terminology he set the pattern for the coinage of a complete Hebrew grammatical nomenclature. By the use that he made of his non-Spanish predecessors in the field, he introduced the Spanish community to the scientific work of scholars abroad, including that of the Karaites, thereby helping to discard the earlier midrashic philological tradition and to inaugurate new methods of research.[60]

Menahem ben Saruq's *Mahberet* was soon superseded by superior works of other Spanish scholars and scant attention was paid to it by later generations in his own homeland. However, since it was written in Hebrew, it enjoyed an extensive popularity among the Jews of Christian Europe who had no access to Arabic. It exerted a profound influence upon Rashi (1040–1105) and, through him, upon Franco-German biblical exegesis in general. Rashi's grandson, Jacob ben Meir Tam of Rameru (d. 1171), greatly favoured it.[61] Menahem ben Solomon in Italy based his own dictionary, the *'Eben Bohan* (c. 1140), on that of his namesake,[62] and R. Abraham ben ʿAzriel was still making much use of it in Bohemia in 1234, nearly three centuries after its publication.[63]

DUNASH IBN LABRAṬ

The scientific study of the Hebrew language initiated by Menaḥem in Spain took a further step forward with the criticisms to which his contemporary Dunash ibn Labraṭ (c. 920–c. 990) mercilessly subjected his work. In his *Teshubot* (Responsa) he assailed the *Maḥberet* on one hundred and sixty counts.[64]

Dunash was possessed of a highly developed critical faculty and a biting tongue, both of which attributes he employed to the full in pinpointing, and then exploiting, the flaws and imperfections in Menaḥem's work. Yet his own positive contributions to Hebrew linguistics, as distinct from poetry, were hardly revolutionary. Very often, in fact, he differed from his rival only in matters of detail and judgment. He did not write a grammar, and his strictures are really a collection of notes in no systematic order. But in the introduction to his polemical work he knew to outline the problems and tasks confronting the Hebrew grammarian.[65]

In another critical study, this time directed against Saʿadiah, Dunash displayed considerable progress in the maturation of his philological observations. This second work was apparently written at a much later period in his life, for in his diatribe against Menaḥem he had defended Saʿadiah against his opponent's strictures.[66]

In the field of grammatical analysis, Dunash has the distinction of being the first to differentiate transitive from intransitive verbs, the first to classify verbs according to the letters of the root *paʿal*, and the first to divide the verbal conjugations into "light" and "heavy" groupings. He introduced considerable refinement into Menaḥem's system of "radicals" and "auxiliaries" by recognizing the function of "weak" letters. In this way, several of his rival's uni- and bi-consonantals became bi- and tri-letter roots, with important consequences for lexicography. Following Menaḥem's precedent, Dunash also enriched Hebrew grammatical terminology by the coinage of new words.

Of particular interest is his criticism of Menaḥem's deliberate neglect of Arabic cognates in the elucidation of difficult Hebrew words. In contrast, he lauded the value of Arabic for such purposes and listed one hundred and sixty-seven vocables common to the two languages.

Dunash, like his literary opponent, did not write biblical commentaries. But like him too, he helped provide the tools for the exegete, and included an abundance of exegetical material scattered throughout his notes. Whether sincerely, or merely to press advantage, it is no longer possible to say, Dunash accused Menahem of heretical, especially Karaite, tendencies. He was not satisfied simply to correct misinterpretations of Scripture which might result from lexicographical errors, but paid special attention to renderings that might be misleading in matters of Halakhah and faith.

THE GRAND DEBATE

The intemperate attack of Dunash upon Menahem proved to be the opening shots in a grand debate. Isaac ben Chiquitilla, Ephraim ibn Kafron and Judah ben David rallied to the defence of their master.[67] They forcefully rejected the imputations of heresy, and, in turn, made much of Dunash's use of Arabic and Aramaic as an aid to the interpretation of the sacred literature. In addition, they directed their barbs against the imposition of Arabic metre onto Hebrew poetry, a revolutionary innovation for which Dunash had been responsible. They rightly claimed that such adaptation did violence to the rules of grammar, particularly in regard to accentuation, syllable division and vowel quantity. They also made detailed replies to fifty-five of the one hundred and sixty strictures of Dunash, pointed out his own errors, and expanded many of their remarks into excursuses which constituted valuable and original studies into grammatical problems. For instance, the first systematic attempt to deal with nominal formations and their declensions are to be found among these rejoinders. Dunash, personally, made no response to the counter-attack of the pupils of Menahem, but one of his students, Yehudi ben Sheshet, took up the cudgels on his behalf.[68]

Despite the sterile aspects of the debate which was conducted in an acrimonious atmosphere and generated considerable heat, the long term effects were decidedly favourable to the growth of the scientific study of the Hebrew language. The polemics stimulated wide interest in the subject in general, focused attention upon and clarified numerous specific problems, and greatly advanced the cause of biblical Hebrew grammar as an independent discipline. Best of all, they helped produce the man who was to overthrow completely one of the most basic assumptions of both Menahem and Dunash.

JUDAH BEN DAVID ḤAYYUJ

If there be any doubt about the identity of this individual with the pupil of Menaḥem,[69] there is certainly unanimous agreement on the role of Judah ben David Ḥayyuj (c. 950–c. 1000) as the real founder of Hebrew grammar as we know it today.[70]

Taking full advantage of the opportunities offered by Cordova as a centre of Moslem scholarship, he steeped himself in the works of the Arab grammarians and applied their achievements, insofar as they were relevant, to the solution of the problems of Hebrew grammar. Hitherto, no one had succeeded in clarifying the basic rules governing the interchange and assimilation of the weak consonants. This lacuna had hindered the proper understanding of the verbal system. Moreover, the belief in the existence of uni- and bi-consonantal verbal stems, despite the modifications of Dunash, caused utter lexicographical confusion. Already two centuries earlier, the basic triconsonantal nature of the verbal stem had been discovered by the Arab grammarians. Ḥayyuj was the first to realize its equal applicability to Hebrew, thereby inaugurating a new era in Hebrew philology. With a single stroke he put the phonology of the language on a scientific basis, made possible the construction of a consistent, comprehensive, methodologically sound system of Hebrew grammar, and opened up entirely new vistas for the lexicographer.

All this Ḥayyuj embodied in works dealing with the weak consonants, the geminated verbs, and the vowel system.[71] He also adapted many Arabic technical terms to Hebrew grammatical nomenclature.[72] Very strangely, although he arrived at his conclusions via his Arabic studies, and although he wrote his works in Arabic and not Hebrew, yet he avoided the use of Arabic cognates to explain Hebrew words. However, his grammars had a tremendous impact upon Hebrew writers in Spain, and more than any other person he helped to make biblical Hebrew the accepted style.

JONAH IBN JANAḤ

The grammatical break-through achieved by Ḥayyuj quickly bore fruit. Basing himself on the master's discoveries, a younger contemporary, a scholar of true genius, soon outstripped all others in the field. With Jonah ibn Janaḥ (Abu'l Walid ibn Merwan, c. 985–c. 1040), biblical Hebrew studies in Spain soared to a pinnacle of attainment unequalled subsequently until the nineteenth century.

His first work, *Kitab 'Al-Mustalḥaq,* consisted simply of critical observations upon Ḥayyuj's researches into the weak and geminated verbs which he supplemented with a list of fifty such roots omitted therefrom. Further small tracts resulted from a polemic with Samuel ibn Nagrela that erupted over these remarks, a polemic that served the good purpose of disseminating the discoveries of Ḥayyuj, thereby improving the general level of grammatical knowledge.[73] All this, however, was merely preparatory to his *magnum opus,* a two-part work comprising a grammar, known as the *Kitab 'Al-Luma'* "Book of Coloured Flower-beds,"[74] and a dictionary, *Kitab 'al-Uṣul* "Book of Roots".[75] This work, written in Arabic like all his others, is a veritable mine of information of great historic and scientific value. The grammar is detailed and comprehensive, except for the treatment of the vowel system. The lexicon carefully differentiates the sundry meanings of the individual roots which are illustrated by appropriate biblical citations. A novel feature is the principle that where the context alone is inadequate to the explanation of a word or phrase, recourse may be had to rabbinic Hebrew and Aramaic and, if still necessary, to Arabic cognates. The most revolutionary and enduring part of the work is the methodical analysis of biblical syntax in relation to sentence structure and, especially, stylistic peculiarities. This aspect will be later discussed in greater detail. Suffice it to mention here that Ibn Janaḥ was the most outstanding representative of this type of study, antedating by about eight centuries many of the findings of modern critical scholarship.[76]

SAMUEL IBN NAGRELA

As has been stated, Ibn Janaḥ's critique of Ḥayyuj involved him in a literary feud with the statesman, poet and talmudist, Samuel ibn Nagrela (Ha-Nagid, 993–1056). The, latter, together with others, composed the *Epistles of the Companions* as well as another grammatical work rejecting the rejoinder it had evoked. Although a pupil of Ḥayyuj, Ibn Nagrela still adhered to the biconsonantalism of verbal stems. Nevertheless, he was a grammarian and lexicographer of note. According to Abraham ibn 'Ezra, he authored no less than twenty-two philological treatises,[77] all now lost except for some fragments of the *Kitab 'al-Istighna* "Book of Amplitude."[78] If these be fairly representative of the entire original, then the work must have been a comprehensive dictionary of considerable dimensions. Its loss is doubly tragic since it seems to have contained many features unique in both arrangement and content. The entry for each root included a listing of the varying definitions and per-mutations of the root found in biblical Hebrew supplemented, most remarkably for the times, by a wealth of related exegetical and lexico-graphical matter culled from a host of sources, some of which are other-wise quite unknown.

MOSES IBN CHIQUITILLA

It will have been observed that the successors of Menaḥem and Dunash wrote their scientific works in Arabic, reserving Hebrew for purposes of poetry. The popularity enjoyed abroad by Menaḥem's *Maḥberet* on account of the employment of the sacred language as its medium illus-trates a wide-spread interest in the field of philology. Now that Ḥayyuj had revolutionized the study of Hebrew grammar there was an impera-tive need for his works to be made available to a wider circle of Hebrew readers, especially in Christian Europe. The task of translation was suc-cessfully undertaken by Moses ibn Chiquitilla (d. c. 1080) who rendered the works on the weak and geminated verbs into a free-flowing Hebrew style.[79] He thus became the first Spanish Jew to translate a scientific work from Arabic into Hebrew.

But Ibn Chiquitilla was also a grammarian in his own right.[80] Some of his independent observations he had actually incorporated inconspic-uously into his translations. He hardly earned the encomium "the great-est of grammarians" bestowed upon him by Abraham ibn 'Ezra[81]; nor, probably, did he deserve to be placed alongside of Ḥayyuj and Ibn Janaḥ, as Abraham ibn Daud thought.[82] He did, however, compose an important monograph, now fragmentary, entitled *Kitab 'al Tadhkir w'al-Ta'anith*, which was a kind of detailed dictionary of "masculine and fem-inine nouns" arranged alphabetically, and not by root. It discussed the grammatical implications of gender differentiation and listed nouns with erratic plural forms.[83]

Ibn Chiquitilla also included much original philological material in his extraordinary commentaries to the Bible. Of these also we shall have more to say later on.

JUDAH BEN SAMUEL IBN BAL'AM

Another exegete of great distinction who made original and important contributions to biblical philology was Judah ben Samuel ibn Bal'am (d. c. 1090). Basing himself on Ḥayyuj and his own teacher Ibn Janaḥ, he wrote a text-book of grammar and Hebrew language that drew high praise from Moses ibn 'Ezra (c. 1070–1139).[84] For the benefit of poets and biblical expositors, he composed the *Tajnis*,[85] a work on Hebrew homonyms that achieved wide circulation. The external arrangement is alphabetic, but the order of words subsumed under each letter is haphazard. A peculiarity of the work is its restriction to nouns to the disregard of verbs. In setting forth the different meanings which words of identical consonantal spellings can bear, Ibn Bal'am occasionally resorted to Arabic cognates. There is also apparent an emphasis on interpretations with an anti-Karaite bias.

Other grammatical compositions by the same author include a treatment of Hebrew particles and a work on the denominative verbs. A lectionary guide to the accentuation of the books of Psalms, Proverbs and Job has also been attributed to him.[86]

ABRAHAM IBN 'EZRA

These scholars, whose grammatical and lexicographical work has been reviewed here, were the most illustrious representatives of the Spanish school. But the list is by no means exhaustive. The Arabic medium which the Jews of Moslem Spain employed was destined to consign to oblivion much of the results of their research. A man like the exegete Isaac ibn Yashush (982–1057), whom Moses ibn 'Ezra classed with Ibn Janah as one of "the two greatest scholars in the Hebrew language,"[87] must surely have deserved such acclaim for more than the single treatise on the Hebrew conjugations now known to us only by name *(Sefer ha-Serufim)*.[88]

We have no way of evaluating the *Sefer ha-Melakhim* of David ibn Hagar of Granada,[89] anymore than we can know at present whether Abraham ben Meir ibn Kamnial of Saragossa (11th cent.) had any greater claim to fame than the invention of a mnemotechnic device for the eleven letters of the alphabet used as auxiliaries.[90] Unfortunately we know practically nothing, too, of the *Sefer ha-Mafteah* of Levi (Abu'l-Fahm) ibn al-Tabban of Saragossa (11th cent.), nor of any other grammatical work he might have written. Yet he was the teacher of the outstanding comparative philologist, Ibn Baron, whose work we shall presently discuss.[91]

If more of the work of the Spanish school has not been lost, it is in no small measure due to the efforts of Abraham ibn 'Ezra (1092–1167). There may have been much justice in the observation of Profiat Duran

(14th–15th cents.) that this scholar contributed little new to the store of philological knowledge.[92] But just because his forte lay in his thorough familiarity with the entire field of grammatical, lexicographical and exegetical scholarship from Saᶜadiah to his own day, including that of the Karaites, and precisely because he was an anthologist and synthesizer, rather than an innovator, Ibn 'Ezra had the great merit of salvaging for future generations much of what would otherwise have certainly disappeared beyond reclaim.

He lived at a time when the Jewish communities of Andalusia were disintegrating under the pressure, first of the persecutions of the fanatical Almohades, and then of the ever-increasing Christian encroachments upon large areas under Moslem rule. By the middle of the thirteenth century Spanish Jewry lived almost entirely under Christian sway, and the enlightened, sophisticated and aristocratic culture of the Golden Age gave way to one simpler, more popular and more circumscribed in its intellectual horizons.[93] Abraham ibn 'Ezra's life thus marked the transition from one era to another in the fortunes of the Jews of Spain. It was most fitting, therefore, that his literary activity should have been characterized more by the consolidation of the achievements of the past than by the creation of new knowledge.

The significance of ibn 'Ezra's role in Jewish history was enhanced by his consistent use of Hebrew. He not only preserved, in summarized form, the results of Jewish philological research written in Arabic, but he mediated these, through the agency of the Hebrew language, to the non-Arabic speaking Jews of Christian countries. He personally translated the most important works of Ḥayyuj.[94] In this way, the Jews of Provence, Italy, Germany and England became acquainted with the scientific study of grammar, the discovery of the triconsonantal root, the elements of Hebrew prosody, and the closeness of Arabic and Aramaic to Hebrew.[95]

Apart from his commentaries to the Bible, in which much attention is paid to philological matters, Ibn 'Ezra's main works included the *Sefer Mo'znayim* "The Book of Scales"[96] which deals mainly with the grammatical nomenclature, but which actually comprises a complete outline of grammar and contains an invaluable historical preface; the *Sefat Yeter* "The Preferred Language,"[97] a defense of Saᶜadiah against the criticisms of Dunash; the *Yesod Diqduq* "The Elements of Grammar"[98]; the *Sefer Ṣaḥut* "The Book of Clarity,"[99] a more complete grammar that has a lengthy discussion of the vowel system, a classification of the consonants and an outline of Hebrew prosody; the *Yesod Mora'*,[100] a philosophical-ethical work with much grammatical information; the *Safah Berurah* "Pure Language"[101] which, despite its title, is among the least lucid of Ibn 'Ezra's grammatical works. In it he deals with sundry topics, defends the antiquity of the Hebrew language and affirms the view that Arabic and Aramaic are derivatives of it.

COMPARATIVE STUDIES

The views of Ibn 'Ezra on the inter-relationships of what are today called the Semitic languages were, of course, extremely naive; but they were widely shared throughout the period of Moslem domination. As a matter of fact, since it appeared to be self-evident from Scripture that Hebrew was the original tongue of mankind, no other conclusion was really possible. Yet the important thing is that the Spanish scholars generally were conscious of the relationships between Hebrew, Aramaic and Arabic and made great efforts to use the recognized affiliations to the advantage of biblical Hebrew studies. This was a distinct advance over Moslem scholarship. The Arabic grammarians and lexicographers perforce restricted themselves to the Arabic language, having neither the linguistic equipment available to their Jewish counterparts, nor any natural interest in the field.

The Spanish Jews did not originate this kind of research. Already in talmudic times the rabbis had explained several biblical words according to Arabic roots.[102] Sa'adiah had used Aramaic and Arabic, together with the Hebrew of the Mishnah and Talmud, to explain biblical *hapax legomena*.[103] Dunash (Adonim) ibn Tamim of Kairuwan (c. 895–c. 960) had authored a work on comparative Hebrew-Arabic-Aramaic philology,[104] and Hai Gaon at the opposite extremity of the Jewish world had likewise used comparative material in his dictionary.[105] Among the Karaites, the great lexicographer David ben Abraham Al-Fasi[106] (10th cent.) had even made use of Persian. All this, however, was unsystematic. It was left to another North African, Judah ibn Quraish[107] (b. c. 900), to put the study of comparative Semitic linguistics on a methodical, organized basis. He may be regarded as the real founder of the science and he went so far as to utilize Berber dialects and even Greek and Latin to elucidate otherwise intractable biblical words.

The Spanish-Jewish scholars thus inherited a well-established tradition in the use of cognate languages for biblical exegesis. But in their hands this tradition took on two distinctive nuances. One characteristic is an evident and decided hesitancy and self-consciousness on their part not to be found elsewhere.[108] Another is their use of the comparative material at their disposal far more sophisticatedly and to far greater profit, due to the tremendous advances they were able to make in the science of Hebrew grammar. Menaḥem ben Saruq, who fully conceded the limited nature of biblical Hebrew, apparently regarded it as irreverent to use the language of Ishmael in the service of the holy tongue. He did not mind Aramaic so much, but he criticized both Saᶜadiah and Ibn Quraish for their employment of Arabic cognates. Dunash ibn Labraṭ, on the other hand, lauded the value of Arabic in solving Hebrew lexicographical problems, and he pointed to over eight score words common to both languages. Menaḥem's disciples, in turn, claimed that Arabic and Hebrew were not comparable, and they actually criticized even Dunash's use of Aramaic.

Even Ḥayyuj, the founder of scientific Hebrew grammar who was steeped in the works of Arabic grammarians and who drew his inspiration from them, did not avail himself of Arabic to elucidate Hebrew. His pupil Ibn Janaḥ, however, enunciated clearly his guiding principles in the use of comparative linguistics. Alluding to those exegetes who expounded Holy Writ by reference to "Greek, Persian, Arabic, African and other languages besides," he explains that he himself, when biblical Hebrew is inadequate, will have recourse: first, to the lingo of the rabbis; then, to Aramaic and finally, failing these, to Arabic. Yet Ibn Janah is highly conscious of the opposition to this comparative methodology and feels compelled to justify it by reference to the authority of Saᶜadiah and other Geonim.[109] Ibn Balᶜam, too, made use of Arabic cognates to explain Hebrew words, but is thoroughly apologetic about it and also evokes the precedents of Saᶜadiah and Hai Gaon.[110]

Outstanding on the Spanish scene was Isaac (Abu Ibrahim ben Joseph ibn Benveniste) ibn Baron (d. before 1128). His *Kitab 'al Muwazana* "Book of Comparison"[111] was a bold attempt to continue the work of Ibn Quraish. It is a two-part systematic presentation of the grammatical and lexicographical correspondence between Hebrew and Arabic. Apart from his citations from the works of his Jewish predecessors, his frequent quotations from the Qur'an and Arabic poetry exhibit considerable daring as well as broad-minded learning. Far less significant, but nonetheless interesting, is Judah Ha-levi's attention to the "problem" of the "origin" of Hebrew, Aramaic and Arabic relationships, in his great philosophical work, the *Kuzari*. He explains their similarity to each other "in their vocabulary, grammatical rules and formations," by the fact that Abraham, deriving from Ur of the Chaldeans, employed

Aramaic for every-day use, but Hebrew for sacred purposes. It was Ishmael, Abraham's son, who mediated Hebrew to the Arab peoples."[112]

Such explanations indicated the embarrassment engendered by comparative Semitic studies. This reaction was caused as much by the need to emphasize the pre-eminence and unrivalled antiquity of Hebrew in answer to Arab polemicists, as by the opposition of the unenlightened pietists in the Jewish community to the humanist movement.

THE APPROACH TO THE TEXT

The science of textual, or so-called "lower", criticism, in the modern understanding of the term, was unknown in the Golden Age. Nowhere do we find expressed in so many words any awareness of the possibility that our received text of the Bible might have had a long history behind it and that it might not be free from scribal corruption; nor do we encounter attempts to solve textual difficulties on the basis of the ancient versions. Speculation along these lines generally appears to have been beyond the horizon of medieval Jewish thinking or, at least, it transcended the bounds of literary freedom.[113]

Nevertheless, the Spanish-Jewish grammarians and exegetes displayed an unrivalled and sophisticated sensitivity to textual problems. They successfully developed a peculiar approach to the subject which delicately avoided any and all philosophic implications while simultaneously yielding results frequently acceptable to the least inhibited of the modern practitioners of textual anaplasty.

This kind of sensitivity to the text manifested itself, first of all, in a general concern for the possession of correct manuscripts. Spanish Talmud texts achieved an enviable reputation for reliability.[114] This may be traced to the fact that, since Aramaic was at no time native to Iberian Jewry, carelessly copied manuscripts compounded the difficulties inherent in talmudic studies. The demand for accurate Talmud texts was thus, from the beginning, dictated by practical pedagogic considerations which, in turn, played a major role in establishing scribal traditions in general. At the same time, the Spanish-Jewish devotion to linguistic studies would, in any case, have generated a natural attention to detail and an obvious interest in the minutiae of spelling, vocalization, accentuation and Masoretic notation. It is not to be wondered at, therefore, that Spanish biblical texts became famous for their accuracy.

In the earliest period books were imported from abroad, and Babylonian manuscripts appeared in Spain as early as the ninth century. At the beginning of the sixteenth century, the three converted Jews who worked on the Complutensian Polyglot could still make use of four-hundred year old Babylonian manuscripts.[115] Yet there is no doubt that Palestine was the main source of supply; the superiority of its Masoretic schools was unchallenged. Palestinian manuscripts were copied with such great care that even tenth century sources could already speak of "accurate and ancient Spanish-Tiberian Bibles."[116] A German-Jewish commentator on the Code of Maimonides refers to the "excellent and exact books of Spain,"[117] and the records tell of Jews travelling from Germany to Toledo for the sole purpose of acquiring model Torah codices.[118] The pre-eminence of the Spanish Bibles was attested by the great grammarian and Masoretic scholar, Elijah Levita (1468–1549),[119] and it was a Toledo manuscript of 1277, and mainly Spanish notes, that served Jedidiah Solomon Norzi (1560–1626)[120] for his great text-critical and Masoretic commentary.

So much for the well-deserved reputation for exactitude earned by the Spanish-Jewish scribes. What of the approach of the grammarians and exegetes to the obscurities of the Hebrew text? Already Saᶜadiah had accepted the principle that the meaning required by the nexus of thought was the paramount exegetical criterion.[121] This rule was accepted wholeheartedly by the Spanish school. But it could mean only one thing: the text as written was not always decisive for the extraction of sense and the construction of interpretation. Such a notion, however, clashed head-on with the theory of the inviolability of the received text. An ingenious system was therefore developed by which all apparent textual aberrations were actually explained as being inherent characteristics of biblical Hebrew style.

This technique of rationalization had found its first formulation among the thirty-two exegetical rules commonly ascribed to R. Eliezer ben Yose ha-Galili, but actually authored by the Gaon Samuel ben Hofni who found them grounded in Saᶜadiah's commentaries.[122] They were made use of by the first native Spanish-Jewish grammarian who accepted the phenomenon of ellipsis as a feature of the thought process of biblical man. According to Menahem ben Saruq, particles and entire words might be omitted from the written text since the deficiency was intended to be supplied by the imagination of the reader.[123] Subsequent scholars continued to utilize the system to the full, and in this way the Spanish-Jewish exegetes practically covered the entire range of what modern scholars refer to as "textual corruptions."

With Jonah ibn Jonaḥ, this type of textual exegesis approached perfection. He laid great stress upon the accuracy of manuscripts as the essential precondition for grammatical research. More than anyone else, he realized that to establish the precise meaning of a passage, the wider context, not just the import of the words, has to be taken into account. The application of this principle might easily have led Ibn Janaḥ far afield into many a perilous situation, for the pages of Scripture are strewn with numerous contradictions between text and context. He, therefore, systematized these difficulties and formulated on the basis of them what he claimed to be the syntactical laws of biblical Hebrew.[124]

The long-recognized phenomenon of ellipsis,[125] for example, was employed by Ibn Janaḥ to cover numerous instances of haplography and other omissions of letters and words. Thus,

sharshot (Exod. 28: 22) stands for *sharsharot;*

bat-'ayin (Ps. 17:8) is really *babat-'ayin* (cf. Zech. 2:12);

shalman (Hos. 10:14) is a contraction of *Shalmaneser* (2 Kings 17:2);

just as

Noṣrim (Jer. 4:16) is abbreviated from *Nebukhadneṣṣar.*

Transposition of letter and word-sequence[126] is another characteristic of the language emphasized by Ibn Jonaḥ. Thus, for instance, the present word sequence of Lev. 14:3 requires a translation,

". . . the leprous disease be healed in the leper."

However, by inverting the word order, a superior translation is obtained, thus,

". . . the leper has been healed of the leprous disease."[127]

Similarly, in Ps. 104:6 the literal translation is:

"The waters stood above the mountains."

Ibn Janaḥ preferred to understand

"The mountains stood above the waters."

He was not averse to the idea that even whole sentences might not be in their proper sequence, as is proved by, for example, Exod. 21.11 which refers to vv. 8f. and not to v. 10 and by the concluding phrase of Deut. 15:17 which is an extension of v. 14. In the same way, I Sam. 4:1 belongs with 3:20 rather than with the immediately preceding verse.

The most daring of all the contributions of Ibn Janaḥ is the phenomenon of "substitution."[128] This assumes that the biblical writer "intended one thing, but wrote another." It devolved upon the exegete to penetrate the mind of the writer in order to restore the true meaning of the text. In practice, "substitution" actually encompasses the vast majority of textual difficulties. A few examples will serve to convey the extent and significance of this technique.

In Exod. 19:23 Moses is told to "set bounds about the mountain and sanctify it." However, vv. 10, 12 show clearly that not the mount, but the *people* are the target of the restrictions. Hence, we must conclude that the text wrote mount but intended *people*.

In Jud. 14:15 the *seventh* day, in the light of vv. 17, 18, must be the *second* day; that is, the written text must be ignored in exegesis.[129]

The same applies to the irrelevant reference to *forefathers* in I Sam, 12:15. Since they could not possibly be the object of punishment, *king* is clearly preferable.[130]

In II Sam. 21:8, *Merab*,[131] *not Michal*, must be intended in the light of the clear statements of I Sam. 18:19 and II Sam. 6:23. In II Sam. 21:19[132] the writer must have had in mind the *brother* of Goliath, as is proven by I Chron. 20:5, in the same way as he meant *Solomon*, although he wrote *Absalom*, in I Kings 2:28.

All in all, Ibn Janaḥ produced what, in effect, constitute over two hundred textual emendations.[133] The question may well be raised as to whether he and the other Spanish scholars who used this system were aware of the fact. In other words, did they really believe in the inviolability of the received Hebrew text of the Bible? Were they communicating, albeit esoterically,[134] the idea that sound exegesis frequently may require the restoration of a defective text?

No certain answers can be given to these questions for the simple reason that nowhere do we find any explicit statement casting doubt, in general, upon the integrity of the text.[135] Furthermore, there is even a good deal of ambiguity concerning the sanctity of the vocalization. Dunash attacked Saᶜadiah for interpreting a passage in such a way as to necessitate a change of vowels[136] but he, himself, occasionally felt impelled to emend the traditional vocalization.[137] Abraham ibn 'Ezra ascribed the invention of the vowel system to the Tiberians and found "all vowels to be interchangeable;" but he also indicated that the system is very ancient.[138] Judah Ha-levi,[139] contrary to the opinion of Natronai Gaon,[140] even believed that the vowels, syllable divisions and accents go back to Mosaic times. Naḥmanides (1194–1270)[141] and Joseph Albo (1340–1444)[142] were aware of the fact that our present Hebrew script is not that in which the biblical books were originally written, and the former even knew that the text was once set forth *scriptio continua*, without the benefit of gaps or other indication of division between the words.[143] Yet there is not the slightest suggestion in the works of these scholars that the changes in script and format might have engendered textual errors. Abraham son of Maimonides (1186–1237) most likely represented the prevailing view that regarded textual eccentricities as impenetrable mysteries handed down by tradition.[144]

On the other hand, Isaac ibn Yashush (982–1057) actually seems to have emended the text of Gen. 36:33, reading *Job* in place of *Jobab*.[145] For this he was soundly castigated by Abraham ibn 'Ezra who also vigorously objected to the idea that in Ps. 77:3 "my eye" would be preferable to the MT "my hand." In this latter instance, his comments are highly suggestive. He speaks of "a great scholar who composed an important book" which, however, is marred by "mistakes," this being one of them. Ibn 'Ezra then goes on to observe that "no intelligent person, let alone the Scriptures, speaks this way (substituting one word for another) even in *obiter dicta*."[146] Whatever Ibn 'Ezra really meant by these remarks, it suggests that Ibn Janah's theory of "substitution" was understood in some quarters, at least, as textual emendation and hence objectionable. Yet in a comment to Exod. 25:29 Ibn 'Ezra himself actually maintains that there is a mistake in I Chron. 28:17, to which observation Nahmanides caustically took exception.[147]

HISTORICAL AND LITERARY APPROACH

Whatever may have been the views of the Spanish scholars about the doctrine of the inerrancy of the received biblical text, there can be no doubt of their interest in critical problems of the most sensitive kind. If the scraps of information preserved largely in quotation—the greater part of the Spanish-Jewish exegetical productions having been lost—be indicative of the trend and spirit of the times, then the Spanish school may be truly regarded as the forerunner of the modern historical approach to the Scriptures.

We have no evidence that among these Jews anyone openly challenged the divine origin and Mosaic authorship of the Pentateuch. Nevertheless, Nahmanides felt it necessary to commence his commentary to Genesis with a lengthy excursus reiterating the fact that the entire Torah, from its first to its last word, was written by Moses at the dictation of God. Judah ben Barzillai of Barcelona (c. 1070–1130) reported[148] that "many of the biblical scholars" of his day came perilously "close to being heretics." It certainly comes as a surprise to learn from Abraham ibn 'Ezra that "many people" were of the opinion that Num. 21:1–3 were written by Joshua. Even more astounding is the assertion of Isaac ibn Yashush that Gen. 36:31ff. is an interpolation from the time of Jehoshaphat, king of Judah.[149]

Thoroughly intriguing are Ibn 'Ezra's own views. In the first place, one wonders why he so frequently cited the "heresies" of others when the effect was to give wide circulation to the very ideas he so vehemently denounced and would, presumably, have preferred to suppress. Furthermore, the virulence of his attacks creates the impression that he protests too much and that he is writing with greater circumspection than real conviction. Admittedly, this is a subjective judgment, but its persuasiveness is enhanced by the fact that not only does he frequently not refute the objectionable opinions, but even when he buttresses invective by reasoned argument the latter is usually far less satisfying than the original "heresy." Finally, Ibn 'Ezra, himself, listed six pentateuchal passages which seem to be post-Mosaic interpolations.[150] True, he does not explicitly say so, but his placing of these examples in juxtaposition and the esoteric language he employs, not to mention the plain implication of each text cited, would appear to make other conclusions less plausible.[151]

Moses ibn Chiquitilla[152] seems to have restricted his commentary to the Pentateuch to philological, rather than historical observations. However, he introduced some revolutionary ideas into his treatment of the Prophets and the Book of Psalms. He shows a clear tendency to naturalize miracles and his rationalistic explanation of Josh. 10:12 earned him the severe condemnation of Judah ibn Bal'am. He broke away from traditional eschatological exegesis in interpreting the prophetic books as historical documents rooted in time and place.

The Book of Isaiah provided fertile soil for the pioneering scientific approach of Ibn Chiquitilla. In 11:1 he saw a reference to Hezekiah, and he explained chapters 24, 26 f, 30 and 34 against the background of the Assyrian invasion of Western Asia. Anticipating modern critics, he challenged the very unity of the book by noting the different historical situation pre-supposed by chapters 40ff., a conclusion which seems to have won the covert support of Ibn 'Ezra.

The Minor Prophets fared no less well, eschatologically speaking, at the hands of Ibn Chiquitilla. He assigned the Book of Joel to the days of Jehoshaphat, and Obadiah to Hezekiah's time, while the messianic prophecies of Micah and Zephaniah he related to the period of the Second Commonwealth. The fact that this interpretation does violence to the traditional exegesis of these two books is both a measure of his courage and intellectual daring and a witness to the prevailing climate in

Spanish-Jewish biblical scholarship. The same conclusion may be drawn from Ibn Chiquitilla's defiance of the accepted belief in the Davidic authorship of the Psalter by his ascription of Psalms 42, 47, 102 and 106 to the Babylonian exile and his conjecture that Ps. 51:20f. constituted a pietistic addendum from the same period.

The rationalistic humanistic spirit that produced so sophisticated an approach to the historical and literary problems of the Bible found an outlet of a different kind in the work of Moses ibn Ezra (c. 1070–1139). His *Kitab 'al-Muhadharah w'al-Mudhakarah* "Book of Discussion and Remembrance"[153] contains an investigation of the style and poetry of the Bible from an aesthetic point of view. It is highly significant that this unique work on the *ars poetica* subjects the language of Scripture to the same kind of analysis as it does medieval Hebrew and Arabic versification. The poetry of the Bible is not viewed as being *sui generis*, as a supernatural creation, but is treated as the natural, artistic, expression of the human spirit.[154] It is clear that in Spain of the Golden Age, the line between heresy and orthodoxy was far less sharply drawn than in any other Jewish community throughout the Middle Ages.[155]

TYPES OF EXEGESIS[156]

PHILOLOGICAL

The pioneers of Hebrew and biblical scholarship in Spain did not compose systematic commentaries to Scripture. Rather, they forged the essential tools of scholarship and created the materials from which commentaries could be later produced. Yet it must not be forgotten that they incorporated an enormous amount of first-rate and original biblical exegesis into their grammars and lexica. In the case of Ibn Janah,[157] for instance, it has been possible to extract and reconstruct from his writings a verse by verse commentary to the entire Bible; and the same could be done for many another Spanish Hebraist.

The first systematic exposition of a scriptural book to appear in Spain, that of Joseph ibn Abitur (ibn Satanas, 10th–11th cent.),[158] seems to have been midrashic in character and wholly untouched by the new learning. Yet very soon, the impact of the philological studies and their offspring was to make itself felt in the radical exegesis of an Isaac ibn Yashush. If the surviving fragments of Samuel ibn Nagrela's dictionary be indicative of his exegetical approach, then his now lost biblical commentaries[159] must occupy an honoured place in the history of the philological school. Of even greater importance were the works of Moses ibn Chiquitilla and Judah ibn Balʿam, already discussed. The former based his Arabic commentaries to a large part of the Bible on the linguistic researches of Ḥayyuj and Ibn Janaḥ, supplementing these by his own original rationalistic and historic approach. The commentaries of Ibn Balʿam to the entire Bible likewise made full use of the philological achievements of his predecessors.[160] They were described by a younger contemporary as being "excellent, containing not a superfluous word."[161] Their historic importance lies in the combination of linguistic and scientific precision with faithfulness to Halakhic tradition. In this, as well as in his opposition to Ibn Chiquitilla's rationalization of miracles and interpretation of prophecies, he showed himself highly sensitive to the suspicions of the talmudists about biblical studies.

PHILOSOPHIC—ALLEGORIC

Among the influences of Arab learning upon the Jews few were more enduring and more profound than philosophic speculation. In truth, this subject lies far beyond the purview of our study, constituting as it does a separate discipline. The Jewish philosophers of Spain, however, as indeed those of other lands, were constantly exercised by two problems. They needed to anchor their philosophic predilections to the scriptural text since they professed to believe that the latter really expressed the former, though in different language. At the same time, the system demanded the harmonization of any apparent divergencies between the teachings of revelation and those of reason. The inevitable result was the rise of a species of philosophic allegoric exegesis, the record of which must find a niche, however small, in the annals of biblical studies.[162]

The first representative of this school in Spain was Solomon ibn Gabirol (1021–69)[163] who is counted among the Neoplatonists. Remarkably, he completely avoided the citation of Scripture in his *magnum opus,* the *Fons Vitae* "Fountain of Life". His allegorical exposition of the Bible has survived through the work of Abraham ibn ʿEzra and through Gabirol's ethical work, *Tiqqun Middot ha-Nefesh* "Improvement of the Qualities of the Soul." Typical of his system is his interpretation of the verse, "The Lord God planted a garden in Eden" (Gen. 2:8). The place-name is not really that, but an esoteric reference to the supra-sensory realm, whereas the "garden" symbolized to him the mundane world. In the same vein, Ibn Gabirol regarded the ladder of Jacob's dream (Gen. 28:12) as signifying the rational soul, while the angels denoted intellectual activities. There is also a rationalistic strain in Ibn Gabirol's exegesis, for he explained away the miraculous speech of the serpent to Eve (Gen. 3:1) and of Balaam's ass (Num. 22:28).

Two followers of Ibn Gabirol's Neoplatonistic exegesis were Bahya ibn Paqudah (ca. 1040–1100) in his *Hobot ha-Lebabot* "Duties of the Heart,"[164] and Abraham bar Hiyya (Savasorda, ca. 1065–1136), the first Jewish philosopher to write in Hebrew, in his *Sefer Hegyon ha-Nefesh*.[165] The latter, however, was not an out-and-out Platonist, for he incorporated many Aristotelian and other notions into his system. Both these philosophers devoted much of their works to the exegesis of biblical texts into which they read their metaphysical and ethical ideas. Another philosopher who belonged to the Neoplatonist trend was Joseph ibn Saddiq (d. 1149), author of *Sefer ha-ʿOlam ha-Qatan* "Microcosm".[166] Like his predecessors to whom he was greatly indebted, he too, identified theology with biblical exegesis.[167]

It was not long before these attempts to reconcile philosophy with Scripture met with spirited resistance. Judah Ha-levi (1086–1141)[168] took up the cudgels in his *Kuzari*, subtitled "Book of Argument and Proof in Defence of the Despised Faith," which became one of the great classics of Jewish philosophy. He challenged the claims of philosophy by denying its adequacy as a tool for the attainment of truth. For Ha-levi, biblical revelation was the exclusive source of religious truth. The *Kuzari* does not contain a great amount of exegesis, though its views on the history and form of Scripture are not without interest since it deals with such matters as the vocalization of Hebrew and the Masoretic notations, as well as the divine names, appellations and attributes.

Ha-levi's assault on reason was directed primarily against Aristotelianism which had been gaining ground steadily. Within half a century of Ha-levi's death it achieved it highest expression in Jewish circles in the *Guide for the Perplexed* of Moses Maimonides (1135–1204).[169] This work represented the high-water mark of biblical philosophic-allegoric exegesis in the reconciliation of reason with Scripture, in the achievement of a true synthesis of Aristotelianism with biblical revelation. Maimonides sought to demonstrate the degree of identity underlying the apparent diversity between the two.

How far one could proceed upon this prescribed course depended upon the proper understanding, i.e. interpretation, of Scripture. It was, therefore, necessary to postulate the theory of the dual sense of Scripture, the metaphoric-esoteric alongside the literal-exoteric.

Hence, the *Guide* commences with, and devotes no less than forty-seven chapters to, a lengthy lexicographical investigation. The multiple meanings of the verbs and nouns employed in biblical Hebrew are examined in the light of philosophical concepts, the grammatical laws as formulated by Ḥayyuj and Ibn Janaḥ, and the requirements of style and rhetoric.

This linguistic analysis received its most immediate application in the elucidation of the doctrine of negative divine attributes. By his homonymic principle, Maimonides was able to show that the Scriptural passages ascribing to God positive and anthropomorphic qualities did not really clash with the proven impossibility of possessing knowledge of God. Abraham ibn Daud (1110–80)[170] had actually preceded the *Guide* in the use of the homonymic principle, but this had not been central to his system and he had not exploited its potentialities.

Two other biblical problems to which Maimonides addressed himself were miracles and the phenomenon of prophecy. In both instances he displayed his rationalistic approach, reinterpreting many of the former allegorically and the latter psychologically without, however, emptying either of its religious content.

The enormous authority of the author, and the wide circulation achieved for the *Guide* through its Hebrew translation, proved to be a tremendous stimulus to the school of philosophic allegorization of Scripture. The system, of course, was highly artificial and became nothing more than a new form of Midrash dressed in philosophic garb, and removed even more so from the plain sense of the text which was subordinated to a particular trend of philosophic speculation. In essence, it was the antithesis of philological exegesis for it had no controls. Yet strangely enough, both schools encountered violent opposition and for similar reasons. Ibn Bal'am had tried hard to remove the suspicions of the talmudists about the heretical tendencies of the grammarians. He had especially taken exception to Ibn Chiquitilla's rationalistic views on miracles and prophecy, pointing to their deleterious effects on faith and their social consequences. Those who treated the Bible allegorically were subjected to the same kind of attack and likewise branded—with more serious results—with the stigma of heresy.

From the extant records of the great controversy which erupted at the end of the thirteenth century,[171] it would appear that the allegorical school of exegesis gained wide popularity, became completely arbitrary in its interpretations of the sacred text, and denied the historicity of the biblical narratives, It was even accused of tampering with the laws of the

Torah, A few instances of this extreme exegesis will demonstrate at once its menacing nature: Abraham and Sarah were regarded as the symbolization of form and matter; the twelve sons of Jacob represented the twelve constellations; Lot and his ill-fated wife denoted intellect and matter.[172] Yet it is not entirely certain that the indictment of the traditionalists was fully merited, that the allegorists did, in fact, preclude the literal meaning of the text by their symbolization. The latter, to them, may well have been supplementary to, rather than exclusive of, the former. Moreover, there is good reason to believe that the severity of the reaction was conditioned more by the broader conflict between religion and rationalism than by the immediate exegetical issues involved.[173]

MYSTICAL

Side by side with philosophical exegesis, and not dissimilar to it in its basic pre-suppositions, occurred a movement towards mysticism which penetrated northern Spain from Languedoc in the thirteenth century. This trend gained added impetus from the Maimonidean controversy and the retreat from rationalism.

At the same time, the shift of the centres of Jewish life from Moslem to Christian hegemony had brought with it a corresponding constriction of cultural horizons, so that by the end of the thirteenth century, Spanish-Jewish intellectual life had begun to stagnate. The conception of biblical studies changed radically to become more and more spiritual and less and less scientific. Biblical learning became, almost exclusively, a devotional, spiritual, experience, devoid of intellectual exercise. The principle of the dual meaning of the text pursued by the allegorists was taken over by the Kabbalists, except that the esoteric sense was now mystical instead of philosophical, and the mystical meaning was looked upon as representing the most sublime stage of biblical understanding.[174]

THE BLENDING OF EXEGETICAL TRENDS

The varying exegetical approaches which evolved in the Middle Ages gradually crystallized into four distinct trends, subsumed conveniently, under the Hebrew mnemonic *PaRDeS*.[175] The letters of the word stood for *Peshat* (literal), *Remez* (allegorical), *Derash* (tropological, moral homilies) and *Sod* (anagogical, mystical). It was inevitable that the various schools would, in time, tend to merge into a new type of synthesized exegesis, combining several, or all, of the characteristics of each.

First and foremost among the synthesizers was Abraham ibn 'Ezra[176] whose work in the fields of grammar, lexicography and historical criticism has already been surveyed. He was not, however, a mere eclectic, for his commentaries bear the unmistakable imprint of his own personality. They are distinguished by originality of treatment, clarity of style, pungent humor, depth of learning and an astonishing breadth of erudition, embracing philosophy, mathematics, poetry, astronomy and astrology. Ibn 'Ezra was thoroughly familiar with the exegetical work of his predecessors and contemporaries, including the Geonim and Karaites, and in his introduction to his commentaries he critically assayed their different approaches. He even showed an acquaintanceship with the Christian allegorists. His sophistication ensured for him an enduring place in Jewish intellectual circles.

Second in popularity only to Ibn 'Ezra's commentary are those of Moses Ben Naḥman (1194–1270).[177] This scholar was the first to introduce the new esoteric exegesis into his systematic expositions of the Bible. A native of northern Christian Spain, he absorbed the learning of the French rabbis which he harmoniously blended with the secular scholarship characteristic of Spanish Jewry. He thus displayed a balanced combination of a deeply pietistic and mystical approach, traditional rabbinic interpretation and attention to contextual, philologic and scientific matters.

Naḥmanides was fully conscious of the existence of varying levels of exegesis and his hierarchy of values in this respect is established by practical, rather than doctrinal considerations. He did not automatically accord pride of place to the mystical sense. He also endeavoured, when necessary, to reconcile rabbinic comments with the plain sense of the text. He frequently quoted, and often disagreed with, both the French exegete Rashi and his own Spanish confrère Abraham ibn 'Ezra. He objected to the homiletic tendency of the former and assailed the rationalism of the latter. But his respectful and usually delicate criticism of Rashi contrasts strongly with his harsh treatment of Ibn 'Ezra. Here we may discern both the influence of his own rabbinic training and predilections, and the impact of the reaction to philosophic allegorism and the rationalist movement. This latter factor is further visible in his own rejection of many of Maimonides' views and interpretations. Yet Naḥmanides was well aware of the fact that the philosophers were trying to find solutions to very real problems. It is to his credit that he did not ignore these issues, but did his best to provide his own answers to such topics as the nature of the miraculous, the phenomenon of prophecy, and the rationale of the laws and precepts of the Torah. In doing so, however, his commentary often became verbose and digressive.

The introduction of the mystical element into biblical exposition soon found an enthusiastic adherent in Baḥya ben Asher (d. 1340).[178] He elevated the Kabbalah to a position of importance far greater than that accorded it by Naḥmanides. With him it became the fourth exegetical arm, next to the literal, midrashic and philosophic-allegorical modes. The latter, Baḥya used but sparingly, and then mainly following Maimonides, but avoiding all problems of conflict between revelation and reason. He utilized it only where it could be unqualifiedly subservient to, and in confirmation of, tradition. In reality, Baḥya was a very imperfect synthesizer, being obviously an eclectic whose originality lay mainly in his mystical interpretations. Yet, because of his extensive use of medieval exegetical sources and his vast erudition in the field of midrashic literature, his work has special value. Another interesting feature of his commentary is his frequent use of Arabic, Spanish and French equivalents of Hebrew words.[179]

The ever-increasing use of the mystical approach to Scripture during the last two centuries of Spanish-Jewish existence is the measure of the sad deterioration in biblical and linguistic scholarship that beset the community. Jacob ben Asher (1280–1340), known as the *Ba'al ha-Turim*,[180] pursued the esoteric principle to such an extent that he was able to derive homilies from the equation of totally unrelated words and passages through the sum of the numerical value of the individual consonants.

Spanish Jewry produced only one more Bible commentator of note before the lights of one of the most glorious eras in the history of the Jewish creative genius were extinguished forever. Don Isaac Abrabanel[181] (1437–1508), heir to the millennial-long tradition of biblical exegesis in all its varied trends, was still able to make some novel contributions in this field. He may be credited with making a start in the direction of the science of biblical propaedeutics. Others had prefaced their commentaries by preliminary remarks. Abrabanel expanded his so that they became veritable introductions. Rather than give verse by verse explanations, he divided the biblical books on which he commented into contextual units, prefacing each with questions, the answers to which he intended to supply in the subsequent exposition. His comments thus partook of the nature of long excursuses dealing with such matters as the general character of the passage discussed, the date of composition and historical problems. Most unusual is the attention he paid to the realia of biblical life. As a statesman, he was particularly interested in the political and administrative system of ancient Israel, and he drew analogies between contemporary European social and political patterns and those of the Bible, as he understood them. He even discussed the advantages of a republic over a monarchy.

Abrabanel was an outspoken opponent of the rationalistic tendencies of Maimonides and of the French scholar Levi ben Gershon (1288–1344). He was also against the philosophic-allegorical school of exegesis. This, however, did not prevent him from indulging in his own, very superficial, brand of philosophic speculation. He eschewed Kabbalistic interpretations, and where he cited rabbinic homilies, he was well aware that they do not represent the straightforward meaning of the text. He also engaged in polemics with Catholic exegetes. On the whole, his commentaries are not of the highest calibre, and his avoidance of philological and grammatical observations, together with his prolixity, greatly limit their exegetical worth.

(*Completed August 1964*)

KEY TO THE NOTES

A   ASTHOR, A., *Qorot Ha-Yehudim Bi-Sefarad Ha-Muslemit*, I, Jerusalem, 1960.

ADN   Abraham IBN DAUD, *Sefer Ha-Qabbalah*, in A. NEU-BAUER, *Medieval Jewish Chronicles and Chronological Notes*, I, Oxford, 1887.

AEW   ABRAHAMS, I., *Hebrew Ethical Wills*, Phila., 1948.

AG   ASAF, S., *Tequfat Ha-Geonim Ve-Sifrutah*, Jerusalem, 1955.

AI   ALBO, Joseph, *Sefer Ha-'Iqqarim*, ed. I. Husik, Phila., 1930.

AM   ASAF, S. *Meqorot u Mehqarim Be-Toledot Yisrael*, Jerusalem, 1946.

AR   Abraham b. HaRaMBaM, *Responsa*, ed. A. H. Freimann, Jerusalem, 1957.

B   BAER, Y., *A History of the Jews in Christian Spain*, I, Phila., 1961.

BA   BACHER, W., "Die Anfänge der hebräischen Grammatik," *ZDMG*, XLIX (1895), 1–62, 335–392.

BAE   ____, *Abraham ibn Esra als Grammatiker*, Strassburg, 1882.

BB   ____, "Die Bibelexegese vom Anfange des 10-ten bis zum Ende des 15-ten Jahrhunderts," in J. WINTER u. A. WÜN-SCHE, *Die Jüdische Literatur*, II, Trier, 1894. 239–339.

BG   ____, *Die grammatische Terminologie des Jehuda ben D. Hajjug*, Vienna, 1882.

BH   ____, *Die hebräische Sprachwissenschaft vom 10 bis zum 16 Jahrhundert*, Trier, 1892.

BHA   ____, *Die hebräisch-arabische Sprachvergleichung des Abulwalid Merwan ibn Ganah*, Vienna, 1884.

BHN   ____, *Die hebräisch-neuhebräische* u. *hebräisch-aramäische Sprachvergleichung des Abulwalid Merwan ibn Ganah*, Vienna, 1885.

BIE   ____, *Ibn Esra's Einleitung zum Pentateuchkommentar*, Vienna, 1876.

BL   ____, *Leben u. Werke des Abulwalid Merwan ibn Ganah*, Budapest, 1885.

BM   ____, *Die Bibelexegese Moses Maimunis*, Budapest, 1869.

BMR   ____, *Ha-RaMBaM Parshan Ha-Miqra'*, Tel Aviv, 1932 (=BM translated by A. Z. Rabinowitz).

BN   ____, *Niṣṣaney Ha-Diqduq*, Tel Aviv, 1927 (=BA translated by A. Z. Rabinowitz).

BR   ____, *Die Bibelexegese der jüdische Religions-philosophen des Mittelalters vor Maimuni*, Budapest, 1892.

BS   ____, ed. *Sefer Ha-Shorashim* by Jonah ibn Janaḥ, Berlin, 1896.

BSA   ____, *Aus der Schrifterklärung des Abulwalid Merwan ibn Ganah*, Budapest, 1889.

D   DINUR, B., *Toledot Yisrael: Yisrael Ba-Golah*, IV, Tel Aviv, 1961.

DL   DERENBOURG, J., *Le Livre des Parterres Fleuris (Kitab'al-Luma')*, Paris, 1886.

DO   DERENBOURG, J. and H., *Opuscules et Traités d'Abou'l-Walid Merwan ibn Djanah de Cordoue*, Paris, 1880.

DSI   DOZY, R., *Spanish Islam* (translated by F. G. STOKES), London, 1913.

E   YEHUDAH b. ELIJAH HADASSl, *Eshkol Ha-Kofer*, Kozlov, 1836.

FIE   FRIEDLAENDER, M., *Ibn Ezra Literature*, London, 1877.

FPP   FRIEDLANDER, I., *Past and Present*, New York, 1919.

FR BRÜLL, A., Fremdsprachliche Redensarten. . . , Leipzig, 1869.

G GOITEIN, S. D., *Sidrey Ḥinnukh*, Jerusalem, 1962.

GBT GORDIS, R., *The Biblical Text in the Making*, Phila., 1937.

GJA GOITEIN, S. D., *Jews and Arabs: Their Contacts Through the Ages*, New York, 1964.

GK *Studies in Memory of A. Gulak and S. Klein*, Jerusalem, 1942.

GLG GUNKEL, H., *The Legends of Genesis*, New York, 1964.

GP GUTTMANN, J., *Philosophies of Judaism* (translated by D. W. SILVERMAN), Phila., 1964.

HA Joseph ibn AQNIN, *Hitgalut Ha-Sodot*. . . , (Commentary to Canticles), ed. A. S. HALKIN, Jerusalem, 1964.

HB HALKIN, A. S., in *Biblical and Other Studies*, ed. A. ALTMANN, Cambridge, 1963, 232–248.

HJ ____, in *The Jews*, ed. L. FINKELSTEIN, New York, 1960, 1116–1148.

HL HIRSCHFELD, H., *Literary History of Hebrew Grammarians and Lexicographers*, London, 1926.

HP HESCHEL, A. J., *The Prophets*, New York, 1962.

HT ____, *Torah Min Ha-Shamayim*. . . , London-New York, 1962.

HY *Henoch Yalon Jubilee Volume* (Hebrew), ed. S. LIEBERMAN *et al.*, Jerusalem, 1963.

IEM ABRAHAM IBN 'EZRA, *Sefer M'oznayim*, ed. W. Heidenheim, Offenbach, 1791.

IES ____, *Sefer Saḥut*, ed. G. LIPPMANN, Furth, 1827.

IESY ____, *Sefat Yeter*, ed. G. LIPPMANN, Frankfort A. M., 1843.

IEY ____, *Yesod Mora'*, Hamburg, 1860.

JB JUDAH B. BARZILLAI, *Commentary to Sefer Yeṣirah*, ed. S. J. Halberstam, Berlin, 1885.

JBS ____, *Sefer Ha-'Ittim*, ed. J. SCHOR, Cracow, 1903.

JQ JUDAH IBN QURAISH, *Risala*, ed. J. J. L. BARGÈS and D. B. GOLDBERG, Paris, 1857.

JQK ____, ____, ed. M. KATZ. Tel Aviv, 1952.

K KLAR, B., *Meḥqarim Ve-'Iyyunim*, Tel Aviv, 1954.

KCG KAHLE, P. E., *The Cairo Genizah*, New York, 1959.

KM KAUFMANN, D., *Meḥqarim Ba-Sifrut Ha-'Ivrit* (translated by I. ELDAD), Jerusalem, 1962.

KP   KOKOWZOW, P., *K istorii sredneviekovoy yevreiskoy filologii i yevreiskoy-arabskoy literaturi*, I, St. Petersburg, 1893; II, Petrograd, 1916.

LM   LEVY, K., *Zur Masoretischen Grammatik*, Stuttgart, 1936.

M   *Mahberet Menahem b. Saruq*, ed. H. FILIPOWSKY, London, 1854.

MHH   MARGALIOTH, M., *Hilkhot Hannagid*, Jerusalem, 1962.

MR   MANDEL, N. M., *RaMBaM 'Al Ha-Torah*, I, Tel Aviv, 1964.

MSB   MARGOLIS, M. L., *The Story of Bible Translations*, Phila., 1943.

MV   *Mahzor Vitry*, ed. S. HURWITZ, Nuremberg, 1923.

N   NEUMAN, A. A., *The Jews in Spain*, 2 vols. Phila., 1948.

NA   NETANYAHU, B., *Don Isaac Abravanel*, Phila., 1953.

NC   *Commentary of Nahmanides to the Torah*, (Hebrew), ed. Ch. CHAVEL, 2 vols., Jerusalem, 1959–63.

NH   NUTT, J. W., *Two Treatises etc. by R. Jehuda Hayug of Fez*, London and Berlin, 1870.

NK   JONAH IBN JANAH, *Kitab 'AI-Usul* (Book of Hebrew Roots), ed. A. NEUBAUER, Oxford, 1873–75.

NN   NEWMAN, J., *Nahmanides Commentary on Genesis Chapters 1–8*, Leiden, 1960.

P   POZNANSKI, S., *Mose b. Samuel Hakkohen ibn Chiquitilla*, Leipzig, 1895.

PD   PROFIAT Duran, *Sefer Ma'seh Efod*, ed. J. FRIEDLANDER and J. KOHN, Vienna, 1865.

PG   PRIJS L., *Die grammatikalische Terminologie des Abraham ibn Esra*, Basel, 1950.

PK   POZNANSKI, S., *The Karaite Literary Opponents of Saadiah Gaon*, London, 1908.

Q   DAVID QIMHI, *Sefer Mikhlol*, ed. I. RITTENBERG, Lyck, 1872.

R   JONAH IBN JANAH *Sefer Ha-Riqmah*, ed. M. WILENSKY Berlin, 1930.

RP   RABINOWITZ, A. Z., *Perush Le-Kitvey Ha-Qodesh Le-R. Jonah ibn Janah*, Tel Aviv, 1936.

S   SCHIRMANN, J., *Ha-Shirah Ha-'Ivrit Bi-Sefarad Ubi-Provence*, 2 vols., Jerusalem, 1954–60.

SA   STEINSCHNEIDER, M., *Die arabische Literatur der Juden*, Frankfurt a.M., 1902.

SB   SMALLEY, B., *The Study of the Bible in the Middle Ages*, Oxford, 1941.

SIG   *Shirey Shelomoh b. Yehudah ibn Gabirol*, ed. Bialik-Ravnitzky, Berlin, 1924.

SJ   SPIEGEL, in *The Jews*, ed. L. Finkelstein, New York, 1960, 854–892.

SKD   SCHRÖTER, A., *Sefer Teshubot Dunash Halevi b. Labrat 'al R. Saadia Gaon*, Breslau, 1866.

SKF   DAVID B. ABRAHAM 'Al-FAZI, *Kitab Jami' 'Al-Aflaz*, ed. S. L. SKOSS, 2 vols. New Haven, 1936–45.

SM   SOLOMON IBN PARHON, *Maḥberet He-'Arukh*, ed S. G. STERN, Pressburg, 1844.

SMT   SCHOLEM, G. G., *Major Trends in Jewish Mysticism*, New York, 1941.

SP   SEGAL, M. H., *Parshanut Ha-Miqra'*, Jerusalem, 1952.

SPA   STEINSCHNEIDER, M., *Polemische u. apologetische Literatur in arabischer Sprache*, Leipzig, 1877.

SPW   STRAUSS, L., *Persecution and the Art of Writing*, Glencoe-Illinois, 1952.

SRH   BARON, S., *A Social and Religious History of the Jews*, Phila., 1952–1960.

SRT   SOLOVEITCHIK, M., and RUBASHEFF, S. *Toledot Biqqoret Ha-Miqra'*, Berlin, 1925.

SSZ   STRAUSS, A., in *Sefer Zikkaron Le-Bet Ha-Midrash Le-Rabbanim Be-Vinah*, Jerusalem, 1946.

ST   *Teshubot Talmidey Menaḥem Le-Dunash*, ed. S. G. STERN. Vienna, 1870.

SY   MOSES IBN EZRA, *Shirat Yisrael* (Hebrew Translation by B. HALPER,), Leipzig, 1924.

SYA   SHEMUELI, E. *Don Yiṣhaq Abrabanel*, Jerusalem, 1963.

TD   *Teshubot Dunash ibn Labrat*, ed. H. FILIPOWSKI, London, 1855.

TG   *Teshubot Ha-Geonim*, Lyck, 1864.

UAB   URBACH, E. E., *Sefer 'Arugat Ha-Bosem*, IV, Jerusalem, 1963.

UBT   ____, *Ba'aley Ha-Tosafot*, Jerusalem, 1955.

UN   UNA, M., *R. Moshe b. Nahman*, Jerusalem, 1952.

WB   WECHTER, P., *Ibn Barun's Arabic Works on Hebrew Grammar and Lexicography*, Phila., 1964.

WDB   WEISS, I. H., *Dor Dor Ve-Dorshav*, New York-Berlin, 1924.

Y   YELLIN, D., *Toledot Hitpaṭhut Ha-Diqduq Ha-'Ivri*, Jerusalem, 1945.

Z   ZIMMELS, H. J., *Ashkenazim and Sepharadim*, London, 1958.

ZS   ZUCKER, M., *Rav Saadya Gaon's Translation of the Torah* (Hebrew), New York, 1959.

NOTES

1. See HT LOX for the possibility that the school of R. Yishmael may have been the ultimate inspiration of the rationalistic trend in biblical exegesis.

2. Cf. SY 62. On this tradition, see B 15 f., 381 n. 1a.

3. S, I, intro., 24.

4. A 90.

5. TG 28^b, para. 90.

6. A 165.

7. *Ibid.*, 152 ff., esp. 155. On the entire episode, see COHEN, G. D., *PAAJR*, XXIX (1960–61), 55–131.

8. BA 20–23; BN 24–27.

9. BA 7–20; BN 11–24; LM.

10. ST 67 f.

11. R 39.

12. *Ibid.* 15 f.

13. R 253; Cf. Q 164^b.

14. R 338; see AG 92 f; AM 103–113.

15. IES 3b, 7a.

16. IEM 1^b. On his identity, see W. BACHER, *REJ*, XXX (1895), 232–56; S. POZNANSKI, *ibid.*, XXXIII (1896), 24–39, 197–218; LVI (1908), 42–69; H. HIRSCHFELD, *JQR*, XIII (1922–23), 1–9.

17. Cf. Z 139.

18. S. ASAF, *Ha-Shiloah*, 35 (1928–29), 514.

19. See SA. For general surveys, see HJ; GSA, G 15 ff.

20. On Karaites in Spain, see B 50 f., 77, 95. For their biblical scholarship see SRH V, 159, 278 f; VI, 242–46, 275–77; PK.

21. SRH VI, 298–306, 478 f. nn. 88–100.

22. SPA, esp. 244–388; SSZ; J. M. ROSENTHAL, *Perakim*, III (New York, 1963), 85–95; M. PERLMANN, *PAAJR*, XXXII (1964) 18–24. For a Zoroastrian critique of Genesis, see J. NEUSNER, *JAOS*, LXXXIII (1963), 283–294.

23. HB 234 f.

24. DSI 454 f.

25. A 248 ff.

26. Cf. the remarks of Judah ibn Tibbon in his introduction to his translation of Bahya ibn Paqudah's *Hobot Ha-Lebabot*.

27. SRH VII, 56 f.

28. Cf. SY 60 f.

29. N. ALLONY, *Oṣar Yehudey Sefarad*, V (1962), 22–26.

30. H 12 (Hebrew section), s.v. *'abh*.

31. Cf. Ibn Chiquitilla's introductory words to his translation of Ḥayyuj's treatise on the feeble and double letters, NH 1; HB 239.

32. ADN, I, 81.
33. SM 75.
34. NH 2.
35. R 11 f.
36. N, II, 81–98; S, I, intro., 25; HB 234 ff.
37. N, II, 70; S, I. intro., 32; G 19 f.
38. AEW II, 174; Z 145. Cf. UAB 139.
39. SJ 878.
40. G 159.
41. NH 4.
42. R 11.
43. SIG, I, 173 f., 176.
44. *Safah Berurah*, ed. LIPPMANN (see n. 101), 15ª f.
45. SRH VII, 104, 270 n. 57.
46. S, I, intro., 29 f.
47. SJ 879.
48. K 31–41.
49. S, I, intro., 33.
50. *Ibid.*, 26; A 250; HB 234.
51. D. PAGIS, *Leshonenu*, 25 (1962–63), 49 f; S, I, 329 ff. see also *infra*, n. 91.
52. Cited by W. BACHER JE, V, 666.
53. Cf. SY 73.
54. *Ibid.*, 111 f.
55. IEY 5a.
56. SIG 173–80. On his grammatical achievements, see HL 49 f.
57. S, II, 665.
58. K 117 ff., 120–24, 174–19; A. MIRSKY, *Textus*, III (1963), 159–162; Cf. M. WALLENSTEIN, *BJRL*, XXXIV (1951/2), 474–6.
59. M; supplemented by D. KAUFMANN, *ZDMG* XL (1886), 367–409.
60. For evaluations of Menahem's works, see HL 24 ff.; BA 342–367; BH 23–27; BN 73–98; A 161–64; Y 63–66; SRH VII, 20 f.
61. TD; H. ENGLANDER, *HUCA*, XV (1940), 485–95; UBT 92 f.
62. HL 68 f.
63. UAB 140; UBT 92 f.
64. TD.
65. On Dunash's contributions to Hebrew grammar, see BA 367–86; BN 99–118; BH 27–33; HL 26–29; Y 67–93 supplemented by GK 105–14 and *Leshonenu*, XI (1941–2), 202–15; N. ALLONY, *Leshonenu*, XV (1947–8), 161–72 and *JQR*, XXXVI (1945), 141–46; A 164–68; SRH VII, 21 f.
66. SKD. See, however, A 254 and esp. 310, n. 55 for the possibility that this work may have been mistakenly ascribed to Dunash ibn Labraṭ.
67. ST; BH 33–39; HL 29–31; Y 94–106; SRH VII, 22 f; A 168–70.
68. Y 107–112.
69. SRH VII, 23, 228 f. n. 23; A 309, n. 52.
70. BH 39–48; HL 34–40; S. POZNANSKI, *JQR*, XVI (1926), 245–66; Y 113 f; SRH VII, 42 ff; A 251–54.
71. M. JASTROW published the Arabic text of *Kitab 'al-'Af 'al Dhawat Huruf al-Lin* as, *The Weak and Geminative Verbs in Hebrew*, Leiden, 1897. J. W. NUTT published Moses Chiquitilla's Hebrew translation, together with Abraham ibn 'Ezra's rendering of the *Kitab 'al-Tanqit* and his own English translation of both, as *Two Treatises...*, London-Berlin, 1870. Fragments of Ḥayyuj's philological notes to individual passages in

the prophetical books were published by KP II, 1–58, 191–204. See also Y 154–165 and N. ALLONY, *Beth Miqra'* 7 (16), (1963), 90–105.

72. BG.
73. For the minor works of Ibn Janah, in Arabic with French translation, see DO.
74. For the Arabic edition, see DL. For Judah ibn Tibbon's Hebrew translation, see R.
75. For the Arabic edition, see NK. For Judah ibn Tibbon's Hebrew translation, see BS.
76. On Ibn Janah's life and work, see BL; BSA; BH 48–58; HL 40–47; M. WILEN-SKY, *Tarbiz*, IV (1932), 97–103; SRH VII, 24 ff., 44 ff.
77. See note 55, *supra*.
78. KP II, 74–194, 205–24, 235 f., HL 48 f., SRH VII, 26.
79. See note 71, *supra*.
80. HL 54–57; P 20–23, 39–44; SRH VII, 48 f.
81. IEM 13^b, cf. 41^b and Ibn 'Ezra's comment to Deut. 8: 13.
82. ADN 81.
83. KP II, 59–66. It was highly praised by Moses ibn 'Ezra, SY 156.
84. SY 110.
85. See S. ABRAMSON in HY 51–149; N. ALLONY, *Beth Mikra'*, 20–21 (1964), 87–122.
86. In addition to the sources cited in the previous note, see HL 58–61; BACHER *MGWJ*, XXXIV (1885), 468–80, 497–504; SRH VII, 49.
87. SY 111 f.
88. HL 57 f.
89. IEM 2a.
90. A. KAMINKA, *JE* VII, 431.
91. IEM 2a; HL 61; D. PAGIS, *Leshonenu*, 26 (1962–63), 49–57.
92. PD 44.
93. B 186–159.
94. See *supra*, n. 71.
95. On Abraham ibn 'Ezra's work in the field of grammar, see HL 71–75; BH 62–69; BAE; PG; SRH VII, 50 ff.
96. IEM.
97. IESY.
98. N. ALLONY. *Sefarad*, XI (1951), 91–99.
99. IES.
100. IEY esp. chap. ix.
101. Ed. G. LIPPMANN, Fürth, 1839, supplemented by M. WILENSKY, *Debir*, II (1923), 274–302; N. BEN MENAHEM, *Sinai*, IV (1941), 43–53.
102. FR; A. COHEN, *JQR*, III (1912–13), 221–33; S. KRAUSS, *ZDMG*, LXX (1916), 338–49.
103. Cf. HA 494 f.
104. IEM 1^b; HL 20; SRH VII, 16 f.; 225, n. 16; A 171.
105. On the *Kitab 'al-Hawi*, see B. M. LEVIN, *Ginzey Qedem*, III (1925), 69–71; M. STEINSCHNEIDER, *ZDMG*, LV (1901), 129–134; S. POSNANSKI, *ibid.*, 597–604.
106. SKF.
107. For Arabic, see JQ. For Hebrew translation, see JQK. On his work, see HL 17–20; BA 335–342; Y 41–48; SRH VII, 11 f.
108. See S.D. GOITEIN, *Zion*, 2 (1937), 2 ff.; HB 241 ff., esp. nn. 43–45; cf. HA 491 ff.
109. R 16–19; BHA; NHN.
110. S. POZNANSKI, *ZDMG*, LXX (1916), 449–76; LXXI (1917), 270; S. ABRAMSON, HY 59.
111. WB.

112. KUZARI II, 68.
113. See, however, *infra.*, n. 135.
114. Z 136, 138; A 83.
115. KCG 73 f., 124, 128; cf. AM 182–85.
116. ST 67 f.
117. MEIR HA-KOHEN, *Haggahot Maimuniyyot to Mishneh Torah*, " Hilkhot Sefer Torah," VIII (2).
118. Z 138.
119. *Ibid.*
120. KCG 130, 140.
121. Y 39.
122. M. ZUCKER, *PAAJR*, XXIII (1954), Hebrew Section 1–39; ZS 229–66.
123. Y 60.
124. SP 45–48; SRH VI, 291–94.
125. R 263–93.
126. R 352–68.
127. Cf. NJPS *ad loc.*
128. R 307–35.
129. Cf. Greek, Syriac *ad loc.*
130. So Greek; cf. ReDaQ *ad loc.*
131. Cf. Targum, Rashi, ReDaQ *ad loc.*
132. Cf. Targum and commentaries *ad loc.*
133. SRT 33.
134. On esoteric communication in the Middle Ages, see SPW esp. p. 17.
135. SRH VI, 292 f. The entire question of the medieval Jewish attitude to the text needs thorough elucidation. Was the Karaite Isma'il 'al-'Ukbari (mid. 9th cent.) alone in suggesting that our MT may be frequently corrupt and should be emended on the basis of the Septuagint and Samaritan versions (E para 97, p 41[b]; SRH V, 195)? Cf., to cite but a few examples at random, Tanhum Yerushalmi's observations on biblical numerology (SP 93), Rashi to Job 15: 24b and I Kings 20:33—on which latter see Targum and ReDaQ—, and Abraham ibn 'Ezra's comment to Exod. 25:29. See, also, GBT 12 for Abrabanel's view of Kethib-Qere.
136. SRH VI, 270.
137. SRT 32.
138. IESY 4[b]; cf. MSB 127 with regard to Ibn 'Ezra's contradictory views on the accents.
139. *Kuzari* III, 27 ff., esp. 31.
140. MV 91, No. 120.
141. NC II, 507.
142. AI III, 144.
143. NC I, 7.
144. AR 31, no. 16.
145. See the comment of Ibn 'Ezra *ad loc.*, cf. the appendix at the end of the Greek Job.
146. Cf. IES 72[a]. *Safah Berurah*, ed. LIPPMANN (see n. 101), 9[b]-10.
147. FIE iv, 155 f., n. 3, is not convincing.
148. JB 5.
149. On the basis of I Kings 11:19; I Chron. 1:5; see Ibn 'Ezra *ad loc.*
150. Viz., Gen. 12:6; 22:14; Deut. 1:1: 3:11; 31:9; Chap. 34. see his comment to Deut. 1:2.
151. Cf. FIE iv. 60–67.
152. P 13–20, 26–38, 95–195; S. POZNANSKI, *JQR*, XV (1924), 2; SP 48 f.; SRH VI, 310 ff.

153. Arabic partly published by P. KOKOWZOW, St. Petersburg, 1895; Hebrew rendering SY; see SRH VII, 198 ff.

154. SP 50 f.; see also HP 369–71.

155. Interesting in this connection is the report in JBS 267, II. 12 f.

156. I have here followed the convenient classification of SP.

157. Cf. the remarks of S. POZNANSKI, *JQR*, XV (1924), 1; see RP.

158. A 233–36.

159. Cf. MHH 55, n. 26.

160. On Ibn Bal'am see S. POZNANSKI, *op. cit. supra*, n. 156, pp. 1–53, esp. 2 ff; SP 50; SRH VI, 311, 485 f.; VII, 201.

161. SY 73.

162. BR; SP 51 f.

163. BR 45–55; SP 52–54; GP 89–103; KM 126–35.

164. BR. 56–81; SP 54; GP 104–110.

165. BR 82–93; SP 54 f.; GP 112f.

166. BR 99–105; GP 114–18.

167. For a similar trend among the Christian exegetes see SB 54.

168. BR. 106–36; SP 55 f.; GP120–133; KM 206.

169. BM; BMR; FPP 193–216; I. HUSIK, *JAOS*, LV (1935), Suppl., 22–40; SP 57–60; MR.

170. BR. 137–55; GP 143–52; SP 56 f.

171. N II, 117–45; B 240 f. 289–305.

172. On allegory and symbolism, see SMT 25–28. For an interesting modern revival of the astral myth theory, see GLG 121, n. 1.

173. See the study on this subject by A. S. HALKIN, *Jewish Mediaeval and Renaissance Studies*, to appear in a forthcoming volume of the Brandeis University *Studies and Texts* series. I am grateful to Professor Halkin for making it available to me in advance of publication.

174. B 243–50, 261–80; BB 319–26; SMT.

175. Based on B. Hagigah 14[b].

176. FIE; BB 289–306; BIE; SP 79–86.

177. SP 96–102; UN; NC; NN.

178. B. BERNSTEIN, *MWJ* XVIII (1891), 27–47, 85–118, 165–196.

179. *Ibid.*, 114–118.

180. WDV, V, 118–123.

181. M. H. SEGAL, *Tarbiz*, 8 (1937), 260–99; SP 105–8; GP 253–56; NA esp. 95–257; SYA esp., 71–88.

Rashi the Commentator

It is well known that the name Rashi is an acronym formed by the initial consonants of "Rabbi Shelomo (Solomon) Yitshaki (son of Isaac)." Another explanation was attached to it, once he became famous: "Rabban shel Yisrael" (Master Teacher of Israel). His tombstone was discovered at the end of the nineteenth century, but by then the year of his death was no longer legible. However, several sources record that it occurred on the twenty-ninth day of the Hebrew month of Tammuz in the year 4865 Anno Mundi, which corresponds to the third day of July 1105, of this era. When was he born? Most traditions place it in 1040. This happens to coincide with the year of the demise of one of the greatest Jewish luminaries of the Middle Ages, Rabbenu Gershom. People later cited in this connection the verse from Ecclesiastes 1: 5, "The sun rises and the sun sets," which was reinterpreted to mean "The sun rises *as* the sun sets," referring to the sun of Rashi rising as that of Rabbenu Gershom set.

In the course of his sixty-five years of life, from 1040 to 1105, he was a contemporary of three great scholars of the "Golden Age" of Spanish Jewry: the poet-philosophers Solomon ibn Gabirol, who died in 1070, and Judah Halevi, who passed on in 1083, and the polymath Abraham ibn Ezra, who entered this life in 1092. When Rashi was twelve years of age, he might have heard that the building of Westminster Abbey had begun under King Edward the Confessor in 1052 and later, at age twenty-five, he might have been told that it had been completed. He could have heard that the Normans had invaded England in 1066, and that the cleavage between the Roman and Eastern churches had become permanent in 1054. Rashi was probably well aware of his contemporaries, the great Christian scholars Peter Abelard (d. 1142) and

Bernard of Clairvaux, and he certainly knew of the start of the First Crusade in 1096, and the capture of Jerusalem in 1099. He was thus born into a world in ferment.

As we noted, Rashi died in the year 1105. Within a century of his death, his Hebrew Commentaries on the Bible and Talmud had spread from the communities of France and Germany to Spain and Africa, to Asia and Babylon. Considering the enormous expense and the mighty energies entailed in the production of hand-copied books, the high cost of paper and parchment, and the great difficulties and obstacles encountered in their distribution in the eleventh and twelve centuries, the early popularity of Rashi, and the wide and unprecedented dissemination that his commentaries on the Bible achieved, are nothing short of remarkable.

The first dated Hebrew printed book comes form Reggio di Calabria in Italy in 1475, and it is Rashi's commentary on the Torah. The first Hebrew printed book from the Iberian Peninsula was the same, deriving from Guadalajara in 1476. Again, the first Hebrew text of the Pentateuch, printed in 1482, was accompanied by Rashi's commentary. It may quite safely be asserted that, in the entire history of the written, let alone printed, word, no other commentary on the Hebrew Scriptures in any language had ever attained comparable recognition, acceptance, and sustained popularity or similar wide geographic distribution, or ever equaled it in its profound impact on human lives. It literally shaped the education, character, and behavior of every generation of Jews since its first appearance, at least until fairly recent times.

A commentary on a text must, by definition, be a secondary production, ancillary to the master text that it seeks to illuminate. Yet Rashi's commentary to the Torah practically became an independent work in its own right. It acquired an integrity of its own, and an absolute indispensability quite apart from the function it was originally intended to fulfill. It is worth nothing that it has engendered to date over two hundred super-commentaries.

Who was this person who assembled such a remarkable record? We know nothing about his parents, but tradition has it that he was a descendant of King David. We do know that Troyes, the capital of the Duchy of Champagne in northeastern France, was the place of his birth. Legend surrounds his entry into this world. It is said that his father owned a precious jewel, which was greatly desired by the local authorities in order to adorn what he regarded as an idol. His father refused to sell it for such a purpose, no matter how high the offer. As a result, he was entrapped to board a ship and was then badgered to sell the precious stone. Thereupon, Rashi's father threw it overboard. A heavenly voice was heard to proclaim: "You have lost a brilliant jewel that the Name of Heaven may not be profaned; you shall have a son who will illumine the eyes of all Israel in the Torah, and the Name of Heaven will be sanctified through him."

Little is know of Rashi's life. He is said to have started school at the age of five on the festival of Shavuot (Pentecost), traditionally the festival celebrating the receipt of the Torah on Mount Sinai, as well as the birth and death of King David. He records in his Responsa, written later in life, that he married while still a student and pursued his studies in Troyes in great poverty. When he had exhausted the intellectual resources of his local teachers in Bible and Talmud, he left for the Rhineland, and entered the great Jewish academies of Mayence and Worms. In the year 1070, or a little before, he returned to Troyes where he established his own academy. Students flocked to him from all over. I should add that in those days, rabbis were not paid for their services, but engaged in various occupations. Rashi never held any formal position in the community. Tradition has it that earned a living from growing vines and from making and selling wine.

When we contemplate the phenomenon that is Rashi, our spontaneous reaction is wonderment. We stand almost incredulous at the sheer magnitude of his intellectual and literary achievements. In an age of limited sources of night-time illumination, of inefficient means of indoor heating, devoid of the typewriter, fountain pens or ball-point, without means of mechanical copying, unsupported by governmental funding or any institutional financial aid, and at the same time engaged in his scholarly writing only at odd hours stolen from earning a living, he managed to produce his commentaries to practically the entire Hebrew Bible as well as to the Babylonian Talmud. No one before or since can lay claim to a comparable achievement. What shall we say when this vast bulk, produced under these inherently adverse conditions, also features unmatched qualitative excellence in both content and style? We can only marvel at the phenomenon, bow our heads in reverence, and in all humility profess our boundless admiration for the man.

Then again, in weighing and assessing Rashi's achievement from a historical perspective, we are overwhelmed by the realization that this scholar single-handedly, and without in anyway so intending, actually fashioned the classical Jewish educational curriculum that was to last nearly one thousand years. The study of his commentaries to the Torah introduced the masses at an early age to the characteristic phraseology, vocabulary, technical terminology, style and thought processes, themes and contents of rabbinic literature. Through him, the language, law, and lore of the rabbis inextricably entered into the warp and woof of the fabric of Jewish culture. We must not forget that fully three quarters of his comments on the Torah are drawn from rabbinic sources. He transformed and immeasurably enriched the vocabulary of Jewish life.

The celebrated contemporary of Rashi, Abraham ibn Ezra (1092–1167), renowned grammarian, poet, and biblical scholar, humorously bestowed on our hero the title "parshandatha." This word appears once in the Bible as the name of the eldest son of the wicked Haman who was killed after his father's downfall, as related in the Book of Esther 9:7. The name is Persian and has actually turned up on an Aramaic cylinder seal from the Achaemenid period. Scholars are divided as to its true meaning, whether it conveys "created for war," "one given to questions," or "born multicolored." However, Ibn Ezra took it as a hybrid of Hebrew and Aramaic indicating "Expounder of the Law," which he applied to Rashi in a laudatory poem: "An awesome commentary he affixed to the Torah, therefore he is dubbed Parshan Datha." This epithet, taken up by subsequent generations, was doubly apt because it had been noted that it was Rashi himself who originally coined the Hebrew word *parshan* for "exegete." It is not to be found anywhere earlier than Rashi's commentary to tractate Keritot 4a.

This brings me to another insufficiently appreciated aspect of Rashi's accomplishments. He was one of the pioneers of the revival of literary Hebrew in the Middle Ages. At that time, Hebrew had been a non-spoken language for hundreds of years. The superb contributions to the revival of Hebrew on the part of the Spanish Hebraists have been generously and rightfully acknowledged. Those of Rashi have barely been recognized. No less a master of Hebrew style than the modern national Jewish poet laureate, Chaim Nachman Bialik, expressed his admiration for the marvelous elasticity and flexibility of Rashi's Hebrew. Bialik pronounced his unambiguous verdict that the commentator "produced a wonderful linguistic achievement."

That poet actually placed Rashi on a par with the great liturgical poet Eliezer Kalir and with Moses Maimonides in that respect. He urged that a dictionary of Rashi's Hebrew be made. Yitshak Avinery took Bialik's advice seriously and produced his *Dictionary of Rashi's Commentaries to the Bible and Talmud* (Hebrew, Tel Aviv, 1949) recently expanded and revised in the magnificent second volume of his *Hekhal*

Rashi (Hebrew, Jerusalem, 1985). This important work is indispensable for a proper assessment of Rashi's enormous contribution to the development of the Hebrew language. By means of Avinery's work, it is calculated that our hero may be credited with about thirteen hundred neologisms. Large numbers of now every-day, common Hebrew words are all found for the first time in his writings. Thus, the terms for "jester," "erudition," "support," "ambition," "agreement," "success," and for "Judaism," to mention but a very few, appear there initially. Moreover, we are only just beginning to appreciate fully the great variety, richness, and noble simplicity of Rashi's Hebrew style, the naturalness of his harmonious and smooth blending of biblical and rabbinic Hebrew.

Another aspect of Rashi's commentaries is his extraordinary penchant, almost unique for the Middle Ages, for attempting to explain the realia of life in biblical and talmudic times. He was a very keen observer of nature and of human activities. His innate intellectual curiosity was fueled by the cosmopolitan atmosphere that pervaded the regions of Troyes and Worms. The commercial fairs in the Champagne region in his days attracted merchants from all over Europe. Worms was a port city on the left bank of the Rhine and an expanding commercial center. So Rashi learned an enormous amount from observing and conversing with the visitors to these cities. Leopold Zunz compiled a register of the items of every-day life that Rashi dealt with. The variety of data is astonishing. The list includes methods of wine-making, animal husbandry, agriculture, the manufacture of cloth, the treatment of leather, differing currencies and standards, banking practices, metal soldering, engraving, procedures at fairs, shipbuilding, seafaring, and a host of other items. Of course, most of this abundance of information from eleventh-century Europe can hardly be relevant to biblical or talmudic culture. But Rashi's historical approach, his attempt to understand and illuminate the every-day life and customs of Israel in biblical and talmudic times, as a contribution to the understanding of the texts, was hundreds of years before its time and marks him a forerunner of modern exegetes in that respect. As a matter of fact, it is known that in his original manuscript, he sometimes included drawings to illustrate his explanations. This is clear from medieval manuscripts in which the copyist left a blank space after writing "like this." The early printers omitted the phrase and left no space.

In a similar modernistic spirit, he made ample use of his French vernacular to interpret obscure or difficult words in the Hebrew and

Aramaic texts. The local Jews of his day spoke French as the language of every-day discourse, and Rashi often transliterated the appropriate French rendering into Hebrew script. In his commentaries he made use of some eleven hundred French glosses, and a vocabulary of about three thousand different words appear in his works. Occasionally, he combines his observations on realia with glosses in Old French. Thus, in describing, the ephod in Exodus 28:4, one of the priestly garments, he comments that "it is like a kind of apron which is called *'poinceint'* in French, which women of rank tie on when they ride horseback." In describing the ordination of Aaron and his sons, as reported in Exodus 28:41, he explains the phrase "you shall fill their hands" as follows: "When someone is appointed to take charge of anything the ruler places a leather glove in his hand. They call it *'gant'* in French, and by this means he empowers him. They term that transmission of the glove *'revestir'* in French." These glosses are indispensable for the study of Old French, of which, I understand, not much had survived. The late professor of French at Columbia University, David Blondheim, collected and analyzed them. Rashi's unintended, significant, and enduring contribution to the history of the French language has been increasingly recognized and appreciated by scholars in recent years.

Some other distinguishing features, characteristic of Rashi's work deserve special emphasis. One is the innate modesty and singular humility of the man. When the resources at his disposal left him unsatisfied as to the true meaning of a word or phrase, he was not ashamed to admit ignorance. His writings are spiced with such comments as "I am unable to explain it" or "I do not know what it teaches us" or simply, "I do not know" (e.g. Gen. 28:5; 35:13; 43:11; Exod. 22:28; Lev. 8:11; 13; 4; 27:3; Num. 21:11; 26:13 etc.). Moreover, he showed no vested interest in his exegesis. He was quite prepared to revise his work in the light of new scholarly research, which came to hand. We possess the unambiguous testimony of his grandson, the eminent Rabbi Samuel ben Meir (b.ca. 1085-ca. 1174) to that effect in the latter's commentary to Genesis 37:2 in which he states: "Our master Solomon, father of my mother, who illumined the eyes of the exile, who expounded the Torah, the prophets, and the Hagiographa, was bent on explaining the *sensus literalis* of Scripture. I, Samuel ben Meir (his grandson), argued with him face-to-face, and he admitted to me that, had he the time, he would need to produce other commentaries, based on the innovative meanings that appear daily." Not only so, but Rashi was quite prepared to admit to having erred in making a certain comment. Thus, in a letter found in the collection of his Responsa he freely states in regard to Ezekiel 40:17: "I erred in that comment." Such confessions are practically unparalleled among the great medieval Jewish exegetes and, I might add, are virtually nonexistent among modern scholars. Moreover, Rashi was not only a non-dogmatic seeker of the truth, but he displayed intellectual honesty and scholarly integrity.

It is quite certain that his goal was not simply to write a commentary, but rather to expound the text in accord with rabbinic sources. He had in mind to create a running commentary drawn from the vast, variegated and sometimes mutually exclusive rabbinic observations. However, he is not an anthologist. His material is highly selective, carefully winnowed, and meticulously reworked rabbinic source material based upon the problematics of the text, its language and its context. But he is no slavish copier. Intellectual daring and independence of mind are strikingly original features of his work. There are some three hundred instances in his comments on the Hebrew Bible when he does not accept an interpretation of the rabbinic sages and says so. It is not that Rashi rejects in principle the midrashic or homiletic interpretation of a biblical text. On the contrary, he certainly agreed with the cardinal rabbinic, exegetical, rule that there may be several layers of meaning embedded in a verse. This doctrine of the multiple sense of Scripture is clearly and specifically enunciated in the Talmud in two statements: the first is "One text may yield several meanings" (that is, simultaneously), an observation that accompanies a proof-text citation of Ps, 62:12: "One thing God has spoken, two things have I heard." The other exegetical rule is "A biblical text may not depart from its straightforward meaning." This principle occurs three times in the Talmud (Shab. 63a; Yebam. 11.bB; 24a). Rashi combined both of them. In his introduction to Canticles he declares that "a single biblical text may yield several meanings, but (in the long run) the text may not depart from the *sensus literalis,* ('the plain, straightforward meaning')." This statement is another way of saying that the latter must take preference over all other interpretations. To state this specifically in connection with Canticles seems to me to be especially significant. These two modes of exegesis have come to be known in Hebrew as *peshaṭ* and *derash.* I point out, however, that Rashi himself, never uses these terms. As far as I know, they appear for the first time in the commentary of his grandson, the Rashbam. How important the *sensus literalis* was to Rashi may be gauged by the fact that he emphasizes it more than forty times in his commentary to Genesis alone, even though it is cited only three times in the Talmud. Rashi was also the first Jewish commentator we know of to have left a commentary on most of the Bible that exhibits as its distinguishing feature a conscious attempt to explain the Hebrew text according to its linguistic characteristics and its context as an independent level of meaning to which he gave the descriptive term *peshuṭo shel miqra'* (the straightforward meaning of Scripture, e.g. Gen. 3:8).

Is it credible that Rashi, a Jewish exegete, who lived and taught in Troyes in the eleventh century, and who wrote in Hebrew, could have had any influence on the King James Version produced in English in 1611? Yet the sober and prestigious John Rylands Library in England once published a serious monograph entitled *Rashi and the English Bible*. Behind this phenomenon hangs a long tale.

It is little appreciated that prior to the First Crusade of 1096, Jews in many communities in Europe were fairly well integrated into the societies in whose midst they resided. They were generally indistinguishable from their non-Jewish neighbors in language, dress, and in most of the occupations in which they engaged, except, of course, in religious beliefs and observance. In general, between the seventh and eleventh centuries, fairly cordial relationships prevailed between Jews and Christians. It has been demonstrated that many Jewish scholars, especially of the school of Rashi, such as Joseph Kara (ca. 1050) and Rashi's own grandson, the Rashbam, were familiar with Latin and with the Latin Bible and with contemporary Christian exegesis. The reverse situation was also true. Latin scholars would approach Jews for guidance in the study of Hebrew and to be informed about traditional rabbinic exposition of the text.

In the case of Rashi, it was the priority he claimed to give to the *sensus literalis,* the plain sense of Scripture as he understood it, that primarily attracted Christians to his works. In addition, it was also his clear Hebrew style, his uncomplicated exposition, the avoidance of issues of faith, and its wide popularity among Jews, which also meant its ready availability, that were all factors which made Rashi's works especially accessible and appealing to Christian scholars.

Hugh of the Abby of St. Victor in Paris (d.1141), like the Church Father Jerome before him (347–419/20), not only emphasized the superiority of the Hebrew text over the Greek and Latin translations, but also insisted on the primary importance of the literal understanding of the Hebrew text as the basis of the exposition of Scripture. Hugh of St. Victor was quite familiar with Rashi's comments, and sometimes translated them word-for-word even though he does not cite his source by name, to the best of my knowledge. He does, however, employ such phrases as *Hebraei dicunt* (the Hebrews say) and *Judaei dicunt* (the Jews say).

Another important Christian Hebraist and biblical commentator who exhibited considerable knowledge of Rashi's exegesis was Andrew of St. Victor, who died in 1175. More remarkable is the fact that Rashi's works had become well-known in England among Christian scholars in less than a century after his death. Herbert of Bosham, who died in 1190, a superb Hebraist, made abundant use of them in his own writings. Another erudite scholar, Raymundus Martini, whose *Pugio Fidei* (Dagger of Faith) appeared in 1278, cites freqently from Rashi in Latin translation.

The dissemination and careful study of Rashi's commentaries among Christian Hebraists eventually exerted a profound influence upon vernacular translations of the Bible. One individual more than any other was responsible for this development. It is most curious that the first dated Hebrew printed books from both Italy and Spain were Rashi's commentaries to the Pentateuch, and the first printed Christian commentary to the Bible in Latin was a work that drew heavily on those same masterpieces and which cited them on every page. I refer to the commentaries of the great Christian Hebraist and biblical exegete, Nicholas of Lyra (1270–1349). He was a Franciscan monk, who came to head the Franciscan Order, and was a member of the Faculty of Theology at the University of Paris. He authored the *Postillae,* marginal notes, actually a continuous commentary on the entire Hebrew Bible and New Testament, first published in Rome in 1471–72. This work of vast erudition in fifty volumes became the most widely used and most influential of all medieval Latin commentaries on the Bible.

Nicholas of Lyra mastered biblical Hebrew. He made an intensive and close study of Rashi's commentaries, and was quite captivated by them. He wrote in the Introduction to his Postillae: ". . . I intend, for making clear the literal sense, to introduce, not only the statements of the Catholic doctors, but also of the Hebrews, especially of Rabbi Solomon who, among the Hebrew doctors, has spoken most reasonably."

Indeed, Nicholas of Lyra frequently cities Rashi word for word. He often uses the phrase, *"dicit Rabbi Solomon. . ."* According to Herman Hailperin, in his extremely important study entitled *Rashi and the Christian Scholars* (1963), there is hardly a page on which Rashi is not cited by name.

This profuse utilization of Rashi, the Jew, disturbed some people. A professor of Hebrew called Jean Mercier of the Royal College at Paris in 1550 dubbed Nicholas of Lyra *simius salomonis*, "the ape of (Rabbi) Solomon." Especially angry was a person named Pablo de Santa Maria (ca.1350–1435), an apostate Jew, originally Salomon Halevi, better known as Paul, Bishop of Burgos, Spain. This bishop penned a work entitled *Additiones ad Postillium Magistri Nicolai Lyra.* It severely attacked Nicholas of Lyra's profuse citations from the Jewish commentator. The great German humanist, Johannes Reuchlin, wrote that not many pages would remain if one were to cut out Rashi from Nicholas of Lyra's *Postillae.* Reuchlin himself knew the work of Rashi first-hand. His *De Rudimentis Hebraicis* (1506) drew heavily on Rashi as well as on Kimhi's *Book of Roots* (printed 1480).

As early as ca. 1388 the first comprehensive English translation of the Bible, the so-called Lollard Bible, produced by the Wycliffite movement, acknowledged in the Preface its indebtedness to the Postillae of Nicholas of Lyra. In this way, that scholar served as the intermediary through whom Rashi indirectly influenced the English Bible. This influence was reinforced and extended by Martin Luther who relied heavily on Nicholas of Lyra and incorporated Rashi's interpretations into his own version. Again, the four new Latin translations that appeared in the sixteenth century, those of Pagninus (1528), Leo Juda of Zurich (1545), Sebastian Munster (1534), and Tremellius (1579), all utilized Rashi. Pagninus, in particular, often cited Rashi in his Hebrew glosses (published in Lyons 1529; Antwerp 1570). No wonder then that the translators of the classic English rendering known as the King James Version made abundant use of Rashi directly from the original Hebrew, indirectly from Latin versions, and from the earlier Christian Hebraists.

To return to Rashi himself. His commentary on the Talmud breaks off in tractate Makkot 19b on the Hebrew word *tahor* (pure). His grandson, the Rashbam, added a note at that point: "Our master, pure of body—his soul departed in purity." In his comment to Psalm 49:11: "For one sees that the wise die, that the foolish and ignorant alike perish," Rashi takes note of the variant verbs used here for the demise of the wise and for that of the foolish and ignorant. He appropriately observes that in respect of the wise, only their bodies expire in this world, but in respect of the foolish and ignorant both body and soul perish. We may confidently assert that Rashi's body alone died in this world, but that his soul went marching on throughout the ages. Rabbi Isaac Halevi of the academy at Worms, Rashi's teacher, once wrote to his outstanding student, perhaps having in mind the horrors of the Crusades: "The generation in which you are present is by no means orphaned. May the likes of you increase in Israel." The first part of this encomium was true, the second not, for the likes of Rashi never again arose. He was *sui generis*.

Abraham Ibn Ezra as an Exegete

It can hardly be contested that in the entire star-studded galaxy of medieval Jewish Bible commentators not one can compare with Abraham ben Meir ibn Ezra (1092–1167) in respect of vast erudition, broad range of disciplines, subtle sophistication, intellectual daring, and sensitivity to linguistic and stylistic phenomena in all their manifestations. Grammar, syntax, lexicography, literary strategies, elements of style, sparkling witticisms, and felicitous use of the Hebrew language—mastery of all these accord him a unique place in the history of Jewish exegesis.

We may pay whole-hearted tribute to his undoubted copious natural talents; yet it is quite uncertain that they would have germinated and flourished had not several external factors converged to cultivate and develop them to maturity, and to direct them upon the path they finally took. On account of the adversity which dogged his way through life, and the poverty which was his perpetual lot, by dint of his restless temperament and extensive wanderings, and because of the particularly tragic times in which he lived, he was able to leave an indelible mark on the history of Jewish literature, and to gain lasting fame as an unusual scholar of first rank, an ironic twist of fate which Ibn Ezra himself would have appreciated.

His ill-fortune is registered in a short poem which he composed. In it he concludes that the moment of his birth happened to coincide with a deviation of the celestial bodies from their fixed paths. As a result, however much he struggles, he can never succeed. Were he perchance a candle maker, the sun would never set; if he dealt in shrouds, no one would die as long as he lives.[1] In another poem, he laments with sardonic humor his tattered, threadbare cloak.[2]

One major consequence of this ne'er-do-well's unvarying state of penury was that he perforce became directly dependent for economic support and facilities upon individual sponsors. There is much evidence to show that many of his grammatical and exegetical works were commissioned by his patrons or were produced for the benefit of his students who were often their sons. These circumstances help to explain certain peculiar features which his works exhibit. The system of patronage in the Middle Ages was notoriously unreliable, just like the government support of the arts and humanities in our own day. Ibn Ezra vividly illustrates his predicament in another poem in which he reports that whatever the time he calls upon his patron it proves to be inopportune, and he laments, "woe to the poor man, born to ill fortune."[3]

The uncertainties and limitations inherent in patronage, and the frustrations which it generated, meant that periodically Ibn Ezra needed to be in search of fresh sponsors. This, in turn, led him to find them wherever he could, a reality which spurred his peregrinations. The incidental beneficial effect was the exposure to diverse cultures, the enrichment of his life's experiences, and encounters with scholars and their works in many fields of human endeavor. All this added immeasurably to his store of knowledge and enhanced his versatility. The results are abundantly evident in his biblical commentaries. To cap it all, his wanderings took him from Moslem Spain to Christian countries, so that instead of Arabic he was forced to employ Hebrew as his linguistic medium. His works were therefore largely saved from oblivion, a fate which overtook much of Jewish literature written in Arabic. On the other hand, the life of an itinerant left its mark on his work. It frequently meant lack of access to book collections, even to his own compositions. He often had to rely on his memory, and his citations are not always dependable. Also, his work is characterized by a certain lack of ordered arrangement and by much duplication, and often gives the impression of having been hastily written.

Nothing is known for certain of any attempt by Ibn Ezra to write works on Hebrew grammar or to compose commentaries to the books of the Bible during the first fifty years of his life, which were spent in Spain. At age fifty, he abandoned his native land, never to return, and he made his way to Rome where he arrived in 1140. This traumatic episode apparently stimulated introspection and self-judgment. A poem by Ibn Ezra on the ages of man may well carry an autobiographical echo of his state of mind at this time of life, for he writes:

At fifty, one takes note of one's days of futility, grieves that the days of mourning approach, scorns the precious things of this world, fearful that one's time has come.[4]

It was only in the course of his last twenty-four years that he undertook the serious pursuit of systematic biblical exegesis, on which his reputation and claim to lasting fame have rested. Surprisingly, it took another crisis in his life to stimulate his commenting systematically on the five books of the Torah. An oath taken during a severe illness proved to be the incentive experience. The author twice refers to this critical stimulus, once in a poem, and again in his introduction to Genesis. In the former, entitled "May the Lord be Blessed," which was dedicated to a patron, Rabbi Moses ben Meir, he states, "In my illness, I made a vow to God to expound the Law given on Mount Sinai";[5] in the latter, he promises to explain some of the mysteries of the text "if God will help me pay my vow."[6]

Why Ibn Ezra delayed so long—until age sixty-four—to compose his commentary to the Torah, is unclear. Whether he first wished to hone his exegetical skills by expounding other biblical books before tackling the Pentateuch, or whether he underwent some psychological restraint in applying his gifted though somewhat spirited pen to the exposition of the Torah, can no longer be determined. Possibly, accusations of heresy, which had been hurled against him in Rome, were a contributory factor.[7] At any rate, his dire sickness alerted him to the peril of further procrastination.

Ibn Ezra did not manage to complete commentaries to the entire Bible. What are extant are those to the Torah, Isaiah, the Twelve Minor Prophets, Psalms, Job, the Five Megillot, and Daniel. This corpus in itself would be an astonishing scholarly achievement within a span of just twenty-five years. In addition, we have the author's own testimony to having compiled commentaries to many other books. He mentions Joshua,[8] Judges,[9] Samuel,[10] Kings,[11] Jeremiah,[12] Ezekiel,[13] Proverbs,[14] Ezra-Nehemiah,[15] and Chronicles.[16] None of these has survived, and they must have disappeared quite early, for the supercommentaries on Ibn Ezra's works do not mention them.

In attempting to evaluate Ibn Ezra's exegetical work, the loss of so many of his productions must be taken into account. So must another factor in dealing with the commentaries, namely, the often problematical state of their texts. No autograph exists. Apart from corruptions in medieval manuscripts, and later in the printed editions, not to mention tampering by Church censors, there are clear indications of copyist initiatives. In some cases, the scribe openly inserted into his manuscript what he claimed to be oral interpretations from Ibn Ezra himself.[17] Thus, at one point, the fragmentary commentary to Genesis carries this preliminary note:

> I, Joseph son of Jacob of Moreil,[18] heard this interpretation of the section in London, and I recorded it in my own language.[19]

Another note by this same scribe appears at the end of a manuscript of Ibn Ezra's commentary to the Twelve Minor Prophets:

> I, Joseph son of Jacob of Moreil, copied from the author's manuscript; I also added a brief explanation to his text (just) as he had explained [it] to me while he was composing.[20]

He adds that he had indicated such glosses by means of colons. These, however, have long disappeared in the printed editions. There are also clear indications of unacknowledged scribal interpolations of explanatory glosses on the part of later scribes.[21]

There can be no doubt that Ibn Ezra knew exactly what he was about when he undertook to compose systematic commentaries to the biblical books. In his introduction to the Torah he critically surveyed four different approaches which characterized previous exegetical endeavors.[22] The first is that pursued by the Geonim; their commentaries, he says, are diffuse and contain an excess of extraneous matter drawn from the secular sciences. The second approach is that of the heretical Karaites who reject the tradition and authority of the oral law and arbitrarily interpret the Torah. The third is the "benighted way" of the Christians to whom the biblical text is wholly esoteric and who interpret it subjectively and allegorically. Here Ibn Ezra observes that "the Torah was not given to the unintelligent; the intellect must be the intermediary between man and his God." The fourth type of commentary is that of the Jewish exegetes in the lands of Christendom. They erroneously take literally the homiletics of the Sages of the Talmud, who themselves had had no such intentions, and they pay no heed to the requirements of grammar. This review is capped by Ibn Ezra's own system. To him, the plain, straightforward meaning of the text, as determined by grammatical, philological, and contextual research, is decisive. However, in regard to the legal portions of the Torah, the expositions of the Rabbis are authoritative.

How seriously Ibn Ezra viewed his mission may be seen from the prefatory poem to the introduction to Genesis in which he effectively, if succinctly, epitomizes his basic approach. It rests, he explains, on the twin foundations of grammatical analysis and intellectual acceptability. It is no wonder then that one of the most unusual features of the commentaries, unmatched by any other in the field, is the attention to grammatical detail. Our author had a passion for the Hebrew language, which he calls, "the sacred tongue" or even "our language," although Arabic was his native tongue. He was the first Spanish Jewish Bible commentator to compose his works solely in Hebrew, forced to do so, as we have pointed out, by his sojourning in the lands of Christendom, where the Jews were ignorant of Arabic. It is not easy to gauge the extent of their Hebrew learning, for the sources are contradictory. The chronicler, Abraham ibn Daud (1110–1180), goes so far as to say that Hebrew had become forgotten throughout the Diaspora,[23] but Solomon ibn Parhon (c. 1160) asserts that the diversity of tongues characteristic of Christian lands stimulated Jews to use Hebrew as the one common language of communication.[24] At any rate, Abraham ibn Ezra's pioneering role in the transmission of the Jewish scholarship of Moslem Spain to Christian lands cannot be gainsaid. This was recognized by Judah ibn Tibbon (c. 1120–c. 1190), the great translator, who testified that "the exiles in France and throughout Christian lands do not know Arabic so that these [Arabic] works were a sealed book to them, inaccessible, unless translated into the sacred tongue. . . until the sage Rabbi Abraham ibn Ezra arrived in their lands and aided them with short compositions."[25] What Ibn Tibbon is referring to is that Ibn Ezra influenced the intellectual lives of the Jewish communities of both the Moslem and Christian worlds. He personally translated from Arabic into Hebrew the three basic grammatical works of Judah ben David Hayyuj (c. 950–c. 1000), the real founder of the scientific study of biblical Hebrew whose researches inaugurated a new era in Hebrew scholarship.

Ibn Ezra also compiled his own grammar books in Hebrew. It may be true, as Prophiat Duran (d. 1414) noted, that these contributed little new to the accumulated store of Hebrew grammatical knowledge;[26] nevertheless, this does not diminish his achievement in educating generations of Jews in Christian lands in the basics of scientific Hebrew grammar and philology and in sensitizing them to the importance of these studies for the proper understanding of the biblical text, and for the advancement of the Hebrew language in general.

The agenda of Ibn Ezra is quite clear. As noted above, the prefatory short poem to the introduction to the commentary on Genesis clearly states that his work "is bound with cords of grammar." In the body of the introduction, in which he classifies the different approaches to biblical exegesis, his own system, he says, is first to explain the grammatical form of each difficult word before expounding the text as a whole. He kept to his plan for Genesis, but abandoned it for Exodus, perhaps because it was too innovative and not favorably received. He still injected a considerable amount of grammatical information into his verse by verse commentary, but integrated it into the broader exposition. His reliance on the productions of his predecessors, and his thorough familiarity with the field, are illustrated by the authorities he cites. In the historical preface to his *Sefer Mo'znayim*[27] he listed the "doyens of the holy tongue" from Saadiah (882–942) to his own day, sixteen in all.[28] Of these, all but one are cited,[29] with varying frequency, in his commentaries, whether favorably or critically. This meticulous regard for the correct understanding of the rules of Hebrew grammar led him, occasionally, to use his commentaries for wider instructional purposes. Thus, in his exposition of Ecclesiastes 5:1, he takes the opportunity to excoriate the liturgical poetry of the *paytanim*. The most prominent target of his verbal arrows is the renowned Eleazer Kallir (7th cent.?) whom he accuses of introducing egregious errors into Hebrew.[30]

It is clear that grammatical and philological research must rest upon manuscripts of undoubted accuracy, and Spanish Bible texts and Talmud editions early acquired enviable reputations for exactitude. By the tenth century, scholars could refer to the "accurate and ancient Spanish-Tiberian Bibles."[31] In the thirteenth century, the German-Jewish talmudist, Meir Ha-Kohen, in his commentary on the *Mishneh Torah* of Maimonides, spoke of the "excellent and exact books of Spain."[32] Jews would travel from Germany to Toledo just to acquire model Torah codices.[33] The great grammarian and masoretic scholar, Elijah Levita (1468–1549), at the very close of Spanish Jewish history, attested to the pre-eminence of Spanish Bibles,[34] and Jedidiah Solomon Norzi (1560–1626) used the Toledo Bible manuscript of 1277 for his great critical masoretic commentary.

The foregoing quotations illustrate the tradition in which Ibn Ezra was reared—the meticulous attention to every detail of the revered Hebrew text of Scripture. An excellent example is his note to Exodus 25:31:

I have seen copies which the scholars of Tiberias examined, and fifteen of their elders swore that they thrice inspected every word and dot, every *plene* and defective [spelling], and lo, the word *tey'aseh* is written with a *yodh;* but I have not found the like in the books of Spain, France, and England (lit. "beyond the sea.").

Despite such careful precautions, it must be stated that, on account of his wanderings, Ibn Ezra did not always appear to have had access to the best codices since his commentaries contain erroneous spellings and vowels in biblical quotations.[35] Nevertheless, to him it was axiomatic that the masoretic vocalization and cantillation notes constituted the authoritative guide to the understanding of the text. In one of his early grammars, he admonishes the reader to follow the accentuation signs and to reject any interpretation not in accord with them.[36] This principle is reiterated several times, although he, himself, occasionally departs from it.[37] Surprisingly, he attaches no exegetical significance to the *plene* and defective spellings, even though the orthography plays an important role in both halakhic and midrashic interpretation. At the same time, he daringly asserts that there is a scribal error in the text of I Chronicles 28:17.[38] On the other hand, in taking note of such variants as *Dodanim* and *Rodanim* in Genesis 10:4 and I Chronicles 1:7, and of *Deuel* and *Reuel* in Numbers 1:14 and 2:4, Ibn Ezra rejects out of hand the suggestion that the graphic similarity of the consonants *resh* and *daleth* was a cause of confusion.[39] He prefers a midrashic harmonization that each of the individuals concerned possessed two names. On contextual grounds, he also prefers the masoretic text of Lamentations 4:18 over a proposed emendation based on assumed scribal inaccuracy in respect of the same two letters, and apparently supported by Proverbs 4:12.[40] His reverence for the received Hebrew text is so great that he even dismisses the notion of "scribal corrections" *(tiqqunei soferim)* mentioned in several rabbinic sources.[41]

In this connection, Ibn Ezra's reaction to the "substitution theory" of Jonah ibn Janah (Abul Walid ibn Merwan, c.985–c.1040) is most instructive. This scholar had emphasized that the meaning of a given text must be established by the larger context in which it is set, and not simply by the import of the individual words. Barring textual emendation, contradictions between text and context could be resolved by the presumption that the biblical writers "had in mind one thing but wrote another," not mistakenly, but deliberately.[42] This "substitution theory" could take care of a large number of textual difficulties. Ibn Ezra refers to this theory, derogatively, several times: "Take special care not to believe the words of the grammarian who, in his book, mentions more than one hundred[43] terms, all of which, he says, are in need of substitution—perish the thought! This would not be correct in secular speech, let alone regarding the words of the living God. His book deserves to be burnt."[44] Again, in another of his grammatical works, he cites several examples of Ibn Janaḥ's substitutions, and concludes, "It is not as the blabberer says, and his book deserves to be burnt."[45] In his comment on Psalm 77:3, once more referring to Ibn Janaḥ's substitution to explain this verse, Ibn Ezra writes, "A great scholar authored an important book, but it contains errors," and he goes on to observe, "No intelligent person speaks in this manner even in everyday speech let alone in the sacred books."

What is intriguing about these responses is that Ibn Ezra attacks the substitution theory on rational, not dogmatic grounds. He does not explain why Ibn Janaḥ's book should be consigned to the flames. After all, no emendations of the text were suggested, nor does he accuse that author of heresy. But he must have sensed that the theory, precisely on account of its implausibility, would be interpreted as camouflage for recognition of textual corruption and the need for emendation. And Ibn Ezra would have no part of it.[46]

No other commentator on the Bible pays as much attention to matters of usage, style and rhetoric as does Abraham ibn Ezra, and in this too he was far ahead of his time. His favorite hermeneutical tool is ellipsis.[47] He advises: "Know that there are places in the Bible which lack a word; I cannot count them because they are more numerous than locusts." By this he does not mean that the text is in need of correction, but that it is a characteristic of Hebrew style to use an economy of words, that is, to omit a word or a phrase when such can easily be inferred by the reader. One example is in Exodus 6:3: "I appeared to Abraham, Isaac, and Jacob as El Shaddai, but I did not make Myself known to them [by] My name YHVH." Another is the extension of the negative particle in the first clause of a compound sentence to the second clause without needing to repeat it, as in Deuteronomy 33:6: "May Reuben live and not die, and may his numbers [not] be few." This type of stylistic concision may cause an entire word or phrase to be left to the imagination of the reader. For instance, Ibn Ezra understands Genesis 24:67 to be, "Isaac brought her to the tent, [the tent of] Sarah his mother." He applies this rule of ellipsis to explain many varieties of textual difficulties.[48]

Another feature of biblical style, according to Ibn Ezra, is transposition, whether of the natural or rational order of words, verses or even of pericopes. He cites the talmudic rule that "there is neither anteriority nor posteriority in the Torah,"[49] and he repeats it verbatim[50] and in his own variant formulations, such as, "There are many verses in the Torah which more fittingly belong earlier,"[51] or "This is the way of the Torah—to pre-position or to postpone."[52] By these observations he means that the present sequence is not necessarily a governing factor in the interpretation of a passage. On other occasions he uses the term "inverted" or "invert!" in regard to the present word order.[53] He also notes that chronologically Genesis 11:29 and 12:1 are in reverse order, and similarly, that the report of the arrival of Jethro at the "mountain of God," as told in Exodus 18:1–12, is not in its proper time sequence within the larger pericope.

Notwithstanding the foregoing rule, Ibn Ezra also, selectively, adheres to the idea that the juxtaposition of verses or pericopes is meaningful and exegetically significant. Here, again, he could fall back on talmudic precedent.[54] Yet he is cautious in its application. He writes, "Before I begin to expound, I will articulate a rule: each norm and each commandment stands on its own; but if we can find a reason as to why this norm is juxtaposed to that, and this commandment to that, we shall [explain] the association as best we can. However, should we be unable to do so, we shall reckon that the deficiency is due to our own intellectual shortcoming."[55] This would seem to mean that Ibn Ezra fully accepts the notion that there is always an underlying reason for the immediate interconnections of the biblical passages and, indeed, he employs this principle as an exegetical tool many times.[56] In Deuteronomy 16:18 he goes as far as to say that even though each commandment stands by itself, their juxtaposition is meaningful even if the explanation is redolent of homiletics. Quite inconsistently, however, he vehemently attacks the Karaites for using the same interpretive device,[57] and he rejects Saadiah's attempt to explain the sequence of the psalms by means of the same principle.[58]

Chiasmus is another rhetorical figure which Ibn Ezra often highlights. This device was implicitly recognized in the Talmud in a passage explaining the structure of a mishnah.[59] Our author observes that "it is a rule in Hebrew that when two items are mentioned, the second is mentioned first," when repeated.[60] Ingeniously, he also applies this principle to explain the reversal of sequence in the repetition of an entire pericope.[61]

Resumptive repetition following an interval or interruption, the importance of which has only recently been properly recognized in biblical scholarship, is also a literary feature to which Ibn Ezra draws attention. For instance, Exodus 14:8 tells that Pharaoh gave chase to the Israelites, but verse 9 repeats that the Egyptians gave chase to them. Ibn Ezra comments that such is "the habit of the language." To reinforce this assertion, he cites Exodus 20:15 that "the people stood at a distance" and the repetition of the phrase in verse 18. Similarly, when the Gaddites and Reubenites petitioned Moses for land beyond the Jordan, the text in Numbers 32:2 and 5 twice has "they said." Ibn Ezra observes that this is due to the length of the intervening data.[62]

In light of Ibn Ezra's independence of mind and intellectual integrity, his attitude to rabbinic exegesis is of particular interest. As we saw, in the introduction to his commentary on Genesis, he sets forth his position quite unambiguously. He excoriates the Karaites and other sectarians "who do not believe in the words of the transmitters [of the tradition]" and who arbitrarily interpret the biblical text.[63] He tries to show the absurdity of attempting to understand and fulfill numerous biblical commandments without the oral tradition.[64] In describing his own approach, he admits that the Torah can bear multiple levels of meaning, but with regard to the halakhic material he plainly states, "If we determine two possible explanations [of a biblical passage], one of them being as the Rabbis expounded, we shall firmly rely on their true [understanding]. . . for our ancestors were true, and all their words are the truth. . . ."[65] In the introduction to his shorter commentary on Genesis he states, "with regard to the commandments and laws, I shall rely on our ancient [Sages]."

Ibn Ezra repeats these convictions many times in the course of his commentaries which are laced with statements such as these: "Unless one relies on the words of the oral law, a cultured person is powerless properly to understand one commandment in the Torah. . . . All the commandments require the traditional explanation of our ancestors;"[66] "We cannot fully explain a commandment in the Torah unless we rely on the words of our Sages, for when we received the Torah from our ancestors we similarly received the oral law; there is no difference between them;"[67] "In a matter about which we find no tradition there is no point to our theorizing;"[68] "We shall rely on the received tradition and not depend on our deficient intellect;"[69] "The truth is as our Sages handed down;"[70] "We rely on the received tradition of our ancestors;"[71] "We believe solely in the words of our ancient [Sages]."[72] A particularly instructive observation is to be found in Ibn Ezra's comment to Exodus 21:20–21. This passage legislates that the slave who has been irreparably injured by his master must go free. The ethnic identity of the slave is not specified, and Ibn Ezra notes that the Karaites apply the law to an Israelite slave, contrary to rabbinic interpretation. He then comments, "If two interpretations are equally possible, the received tradition will determine the truth."

There is no reason to doubt the sincerity of Ibn Ezra in expressing these sentiments even though they often occur in the context of anti-Karaite polemic. There is abundant, independent evidence to show that he was a deeply religious man, thoroughly committed to the binding authority of rabbinic halakhah. His works on theological subjects, his *Iggeret ha-Shabbat* in defense of the traditional rabbinic interpretation of when the day begins, not to mention his religious poetry,[73] all eloquently confirm this judgment.

At the same time, Ibn Ezra's reverential attitude to the rabbinic Sages does not lead him to accept their interpretations uncritically when matters of halakhah are not involved, and sometimes even when they are. He makes a distinction between transmitted tradition *(qabbalah)* and what the Sages derived from the text by means of the exercise of logic and argumentation *(sevarah)*.[74] In the fourth exegetical approach, as set forth in his introduction to Genesis, he deals at length with midrashic interpretations of various kinds which are mistakenly taken literally. In his theological work *Yesod Mora'* he states, "He who has a mind is able to recognize when they (the Rabbis) speak homiletically and when they say the straightforward meaning."[75] Thus, in reference to rabbinic interpretations, he notes that their citations of biblical passages may merely be to find scriptural support *('asmakhta)*[76] and is not the real source of their exegesis.

Revealingly, he may imply that a traditional interpretation cannot be reconciled with the *sensus literalis* as he sees it. Thus, on Exodus 12:24 he comments that "were it not for the decisive, authentic tradition," reason would indicate that the daubing of the blood on the doorpost on the eve of Passover was intended to be an annual rite. Similarly, on Exodus 15:22 he states, "In my opinion," which he then conveys, such is the case, but if what the rabbinic sages understood is tradition then "we shall abandon our own logical conclusion and rely on tradition." In presenting his own views in contrast to that of the Sages, it is difficult to avoid the inference that he is critical of the latter, and that in passages such as these his acknowledgment of tradition is more a matter of form than conviction.[77]

There are instances of outright rejection of a well known rabbinic interpretation, but with no mention of its source. An example of this is the midrashic rendering of Genesis 28:11 which tells that when Jacob fled before his brother Esau, "he came upon a certain place." The Rabbis reinterpreted this phrase to mean, "he entreated the Omnipresent,"[78] based upon a varying signification of the verb[79] and a rabbinic epithet for God.[80] Ibn Ezra dismisses this midrash on the ground that "place" as designation for God is never found in the Bible. Another instance is his denial that "house" is ever used as a figurative for a "wife" although this is explicitly stated in Mishnah *Yoma* 1:1, citing Leviticus 16:6 in support.[81] In connection with Exodus 33:18–23, which tells that Moses asked to see God's Presence, and God replied, "You shall see My back but My face must not be seen," the Sages interpreted the "back" to refer to "the knot of the *tephillin*."[82] On this midrash, our commentator observes, "Their words are correct, but not literally, as contemporary scholars [take it], for it is a deep mystery."

Ibn Ezra's clearest statement on his attitude to rabbinic homiletical exegesis is to be found in the *Safah Berurah*.[83] He writes as follows:

> You, my son, be mindful that our ancient [Sages], transmitters of the commandments, by themselves expounded pericopes, verses, even words and consonants by the method of homiletics, whether in the Mishnah, the Talmud or the *baraithot*. Without doubt, they knew the straightforward path as it is. Hence, they framed the rule that (the scriptural verse may not depart from its straightforward meaning.'[84] The homiletical explanation imparts an additional meaning. But subsequent generations made the homiletical paramount. . . .

In sharp contrast to his deferential respect for the classical Sages, Ibn Ezra often exhibits irreverent detachment from the post-Talmudic exegetes. In his introduction to Genesis he asserted, "The Lord alone do I fear, and I show no partiality in [interpreting] the Torah."[85] It was precisely this mettlesome quality that appealed to the author of the apparently spurious letter supposedly sent by Moses Maimonides (1135–1204) to his son, recommending that he concentrate exclusively on the commentaries of Ibn Ezra, among the virtues of which he cited the latter's dauntless independence: "For the aforementioned scholar fears no man and shows no partiality to anyone."[86]

This bold stance of our exegete expresses itself in diverse ways, not least in caustic comments about those with whom he disagrees. This is immediately apparent in his introduction to Genesis where he casts a scornful eye upon the modes of scriptural interpretation pursued by his predecessors. He had familiarized himself with the works of a vast array of earlier scholars in the field, had subjected them to critical scrutiny and had formed very definite opinions about them. No previous or subsequent commentator on the Bible throughout the Middle Ages cited the works of so many authorities.[87] Often he does so without mentioning a name, simply referring to the views of "a scholar" or "scholars," to "a great Spanish scholar"[88] or "one of the scholars of Spain,"[89] to "a scholar in Rome,"[90] or "one of the scholars in Egypt,"[91] to "the scholars of Israel in the land of Greece"[92] or "the books of the scholars in France."[93] More often, he cites them by name, about forty authorities in all, including several Karaites.[94] The entire roster covers an astonishingly wide range of geographic origins: Persia, Iraq, Tiberias, Egypt, Kairouan, France, Italy and Spain.

The interpretations of such luminaries as Saadiah,[95] Jonah ibn Janah[96] and Samuel b. Hofni,[97] although greatly admired, are rejected at times. The illustrious Rashi is mercilessly criticized: "He expounded the Torah homiletically believing such to be the literal meaning, whereas his books do not contain it except once in a thousand [instances]."[98] About other prominent French exegetes, like Samuel ben Meir[99] (RaShBaM 1085–1160) and Joseph ben Simon Kara (b. c.1160–70), both of whom belonged to the school of literal exegesis (*peshat*), Ibn Ezra has nothing to say although it is certain that his *Iggeret ha-Shabbat*[100] was composed in response to RaShBaM's interpretation of Genesis 1:5, 8. Apparently he did not value their exegetical contributions.

Throughout his commentaries, and even in his grammars, he habitually injects derisive epithets about other exegetes, describing them as "intellectually deficient,"[101] "mindless,"[102] "lacking in faith,"[103] "purblind,"[104] "empty-headed."[105] This polemical strain finds particularly harsh expression in his dismissal of heterodox and Karaite interpretations. He cites "a certain heretic, may his bones be ground to dust."[106] The same malediction is attached to the notorious freethinker, Hiwi Al-Balkhi (9th cent.), who is referred to by word-play as *ha-kalbi*, "the dog," with the additional imprecation "may his name rot."[107] A certain Yitshaqi is ridiculed with the question, "Was he given the name Yitshaqi so that all who hear [his comment] will laugh at him?"[108] He is also given the epithet "the blabberer."[109] Karaites are called "Sadducees" and also "the deniers."[110]

It may be asked why Ibn Ezra wanted to circulate, through his polemics and gibes, the names of commentators and their—in his opinion—misguided views and interpretations rather than consign them to oblivion by disregarding them. It may be supposed that he had in mind when citing them the educated elite segment of his readership among whom those writings had presumably gained currency. As a pedagogue, he felt it his duty to combat them. One may also speculate whether an additional motivation was not at work. He had to endure hostility and charges of heresy while in Italy, so that his overdrawn demurrers and overstated criticisms of others may have served as a device for deflecting such accusations.

This brings us to the matter of Ibn Ezra's involvement in historical criticism, an issue made prominent through Spinoza's interpretations, in his *Tractatus Theologico-Politicus*[111] (1670), of some of his comments on passages that give the appearance of being anachronisms in the Torah, and so later interpolations. On Deuteronomy 1:2 Ibn Ezra cryptically comments, "If you understand the deep meaning of the twelve, and also 'That day Moses wrote down this poem,' 'The Canaanites were then in the land,' 'In the mountain of the Lord it will be seen,' 'His bedstead is an iron bedstead,' you will recognize the truth."

"The twelve" refers to the closing chapter of Deuteronomy; unlike the body of the book, which is couched in autobiographical style, these twelve verses speak of Moses in the third person, indicating that they were not written by him. In fact, on Deuteronomy 34:1 our commentator explicitly says, "In my opinion, Joshua wrote from this verse on, for once Moses ascended the summit of Pisgah, (where he died), he wrote no more; or he wrote prophetically (about himself)."[112]

Having stated his own considered opinion about the last chapter of the Torah, Ibn Ezra gives a list of the other passages he must also have taken to be later interpolations. He includes Deuteronomy 31:22, which also refers to Moses in the third person, and Genesis 12:6 (cf. 13:7) which verse implies that the Canaanites were no longer in the land at the time of the writer. On this last verse, Ibn Ezra comments, "Possibly, Canaan (grandson of Noah) seized the land of Canaan from someone else, but if it is not so, then I have a deep meaning, and the prudent one will keep silent." Genesis 22:14 records that in consequence of Abraham's naming the site of the binding of Isaac, Adonai-yireh, there arose a saying, "on the mountain of the Lord there is vision." But such an appellation would be applicable only subsequent to Solomon's Temple building. The reference to the iron casket of the king of Bashan, Deuteronomy 3:11, mentions that the relic survived in Rabbah of the Ammonites. The Israelites would not have placed it there after defeating the monarch. Hence the archaeological note suggests that it was written from the perspective of a later age, and is an interpolation.

In the light of his acceptance of the existence of anachronisms within the Torah, albeit an admission expressed cautiously and allusively, it is surprising that Ibn Ezra preferred a forced interpretation for another crux. Numbers 21:1–3 mentions the "king of Arad" who waged war on Israel, was soundly defeated, and his city utterly destroyed. Ibn Ezra points out that the "king of Arad" is included in the list of Joshua's captive kings given in Joshua 12:14, and he comments, "Many have said that this section (in Numbers) was written by Joshua. . . but the truth is that there were two sites (bearing the same name)." In another comment, this one to Genesis 36:31–39, which lists "the kings who reigned in the land of Edom before any king reigned over the Israelites," he severely condemns the unidentified Yitshaqi. He writes, "There are those who maintain that this section was written prophetically. Yitshaqi said in his book that this section was written in the days of (king) Jehoshaphat (of Judah). . . Perish the thought. . . His book deserves to be burnt."

It is hard to establish the criterion by which Ibn Ezra differentiated acceptable from inadmissible anachronisms unless it be that his own esoteric mode of expression was directed to the cognoscenti who would know to separate matters of faith from matters of scholarship, whereas the explicit, unrestrained formulations of others who lacked the same sensitivity were felt to pose a threat to the common reader who would surely confuse the two.

Ibn Ezra engages in historical criticism in commenting on the Book of Isaiah. Here he was obviously influenced by Moses ha-Kohen ibn Chiquitilla (d. c. 1080) in attributing the second part of the book, chapter 40 on, not to the eighth century B.C.E. prophet Isaiah, but to an anonymous prophet who lived centuries later, at the end of the period of the Babylonian exile when Cyrus of Persia was overthrowing the Babylonian empire and would soon liberate the Jewish captives and allow them to return to their homeland.[113]

The influence of Ibn Chiquitilla[114] also shows itself in Ibn Ezra's commentary to the Book of Psalms.[115] That scholar had assigned several of the compositions to the exilic period, and although Ibn Ezra does not accept all his interpretations, he, himself, cautiously explains Psalms 69 (verse 10), 85, 120, 137 as pertaining to the Babylonian exile.

It must be pointed out that Ibn Ezra is not always consistent in keeping to the strict limitations that he set for himself. He is often guilty of the very things which he regards as defects in the works of others. For instance, in his comment to Genesis 14:14 he rejects outright as homiletical the notion expressed in Talmud and Midrash, that the "318 retainers" of Abram were really one individual, his servant Eliezer, the "proof" of which is that the numerical value of the Hebrew consonants of that name add up to 318.[116] He explicitly maintains that "Scripture does not speak in (terms of) *gematria.*" A remark of a similar kind is made in his comment to Exodus (short commentary). Yet in a long excursus to Exodus 33:21, the same author utilizes this very device in connection with the tetragrammaton, and again in his comments to Isaiah 21:8 and Zechariah 3:8. As to his criticism of the Geonim for introducing extraneous information from the secular sciences, he does the same thing by inserting digressions on such subjects as the Hebrew calendar,[117] the sacred divine names,[118] mathematics,[119] astronomy,[120] and astrology,[121] as well as some personal reminiscences.[122] Nevertheless, these discursive comments testify to a conviction that the Bible cannot be properly understood without recourse to a wide spectrum of varied branches of human knowledge. In this, too, he was quite ahead of his time. Furthermore, as was customary among the medievals, he made use of his commentaries as vehicles for the expression of his philosophic ideas. He did not author any systematic work on philosophy. He did compose a few booklets of minor significance on some specific theological matters.[123] However, numerous observations of a philosophic nature are scattered throughout his commentaries. When collected and collated,[124] these discursions demonstrate that he was essentially a Neoplatonist much influenced by Solomon ibn Gabirol whose allegorical expositions he cites,[125] even though in his introduction he discounts allegorical and symbolic interpretations. Apart from this, Ibn Ezra designates a biblical passage by the Hebrew term *sod* which conveys that it carries an esoteric meaning.[126] What that may be is generally unexplained, and the language that he uses is so veiled and succinct as to leave in doubt any interpretation placed upon it.

Of course, all this makes Ibn Ezra's commentaries that much more intriguing. He left plenty of room for supercommentary.[127] Abraham ibn Ezra died in 1167. By mid-fourteenth century Judah Leon ben Moses Moskoni from Ocrida, Bulgaria, was able to report having inspected about thirty such supercommentaries, and in the first half of the seventeenth century Joseph Solomon Delmedigo (1591–1655) testified that he had seen twenty-four in Constantinople. The most important of all is the *Safenat Pa'neah* authored by Joseph ben Eliezer Bonfils in Damascus (second half of the fourteenth century).[128]

NOTES

1. The text of this poem has been published several times: D. Kahana, *Rabbi Abraham ibn Ezra* [Hebrew], Warsaw, 1894, vol. I, no. 2, pp. 9f.; H. Schirman, *Ha-Shirah ha-'Ivrit bi-Sfarad u-vi-Provence*, Jerusalem, 1961, vol. I, 2, pp. 575–576; T. Carmi, *The Penguin Book of Hebrew Verse*, New York, 1981, p. 353 [with English translation]; I. Levin, *Yalkut Abraham ibn Ezra*, New York-Tel Aviv, 1986, Nos. 39–40, p. 108, and notes, pp. 199–200.

2. Kahana *op cit.*, No. 4, pp. 10–11; Schirman, *op. cit.*, p. 576; Carmi, *op. cit.*, pp. 353–354; Levin, *op. cit.*, No. 44, p. 111, and notes, p. 209.

3. Kahana, *op. cit.*, No. 3, p. 10; Schirman, *op. cit.*, p. 575; Canal, *op. cit.*, p. 353; Levin, *op. cit.*, No. 41, p. 109, and notes, pp. 201–202.

4. Schirman, *op. cit.*, p. 589.

5. Levin, *op. cit.*, No. 46, pp. 69–70.

6. See Ibn Ezra's "third approach," ed. A. Weiser, *Ibn Ezra's Commentary to the Torah* [Hebrew], Jerusalem, 1976, p. 139.

7. See the poem *Nedod hesir 'oni* in D. Rosin, *Reime und Gedichte des Abraham Ibn Esras*, Breslau, 1885–1894, I, No. 58, pp. 87–98, esp. lines 117–120; Kahana *op. cit.*, No. 14, p. 26. See U. Simon *in Proceedings of the Ninth World Congress of Jewish Studies: Bible and Ancient Near East*, Jerusalem, 1985 [Hebrew section], p. 25.

8. Deut. 32:4.

9. Deut. 29:19; cf. Nahmanides' comment on Lev. 27:24.

10. Exod. 27:21; Ps. 51:2, and David Kimhi's comment to I Sam. 27:10.

11. Deut. 21:17.

12. Lev. 20:20.

13. See short commentary to Exod. 28:41.

14. Exod. 31:3. S. R. Driver, *A Commentary on the Book of Proverbs Attributed to Abraham ibn Ezra*, [reprint] Jerusalem, 1962, who notes that it was really authored by Moses Kimhi.

15. Deut. 23:2

16. Lev. 26:34; cf. David Kimhi to 2 Chron. 30:18.

17. E.g. on Ps. 69:19; 80:16; 116:16; 119:103; Mal. 1:11. See U. Simon, *Abraham Ibn Ezra's Two Commentaries on the Minor Prophets* [Hebrew], Ramat-Gan, 1989, I, p. 30, n. 48 (on Hos. 1:6); p. 36, n. 34 (on Hos. 2:9); p. 38, n. 46 (on Hos. 2:13); p. 46, n. 10 (on Hos. 3:2); p. 52, n. 12 (on Hos. 4:6); p. 59, n. 50 (on Hos. 4:15).

18. The printed texts read here Modvil, which has been variously interpreted as Monteville in Normandy, and Marvil or Morvil in England; see E. Z. Melammed, *Bible Commentators* [Hebrew], Jerusalem, 1975, p. 520, n. 9. However, C. Roth, *The History of the Jews in England*, Oxford, 1941, p. 126, identifies this glossator as Joseph de Moreil.

19. Weiser, *op. cit.*, p. 194.

20. Melammed, *op. cit.*, p. 520.

21. E.g. Exod. 12:9; Mal. 1:11.

22. See Weiser, *op. cit.*, I, p. 1 of text. The order of the four approaches differs somewhat in the second introduction, ibid., pp. 137–146; see U. Simon, *op. cit.*, n. 7, pp. 23–42.

23. *Sefer Ha-Qabbalah*, ed. G. Cohen, Philadelphia, 1967, p. 73 [Hebrew], pp. 101–102 [English].

24. *Mahberet He-'Arukh*, ed. S. G. Stern, Pressburg, 1844, p. 75.

25. See *Sefer Ha-Riqmah*, ed. M. Wilensky (Introduction of Ibn Tibbon), Jerusalem, 1964, pp. 4–5.

26. *Ma'aseh Efod*, eds. J. Friedlaender and J. Kohn, Vienna, 1865, p. 44.

27. Ed. W. Heidenheim, Offenbach, 1791, introduction.

28. See W. Bacher, *Abraham ibn Esra als Grammatiker*, Budapest, 1891, pp. 173–187; Hebrew translation by A. Z. Rabinovitz, [reprint] Jerusalem, 1970, pp. 127–140.

29. The sole exception is David ibn Hajjar of Granada (12th century).

30. A. M. Haberman, *Toledot Ha-Piyyut Ve-ha-Shirah*, Ramat-Gan, 1970, I, pp. 47, 48, 74, 198, points out that in his criticism of Kallir, Ibn Ezra speaks as a grammarian and lexicographer, not as a *paytan*, for in his own religious poetry he perpetrated the same offenses that he criticized.

31. *Teshubot Talmidei Menahem Le-Dunash*, ed. S. G. Stern, Vienna, 1870, pp. 67–68.

32. *Hagahot Maimoniyot to Mishneh Torah*, Hilkhot Sefer Torah 8(2).

33. H. J. Zimmels, *Ashkenazim and Sephardim*, London, 1958, p. 13.

34. Ibid.

35. Friedlaender, *Essays on the Writings of Abraham Ibn Ezra*, London, 1877, pp. 140–141.

36. Cited by Weiser, *op. cit.*, p. 17. See Ibn Ezra to Gen. 3:22; Isa. 1:9; Ps. 20:10; contrast, e.g., RaShBaM to Gen. 49:9, Kimhi to Hos. 12:12; Friedlaender, *op. cit.*, p. 128.

37. E.g. Eccl. 10:6. Friedlaender, *op. cit.*, p. 129, n. 1, posits that Ibn Ezra's copy of the Bible may have contained different accentuation.

38. So in his comment on Exod. 25:29, on which see Nahmanides' commentary *ad. loc.*

39. On this problem, see Fr. Delitzsch, *Die Lese- and Schreibfehler im Alten Testament*, Berlin, 1920, section 104 a-c, pp. 105–107.

40. Cf. the masoretic note to Lam. 4:18 and Kuzari III, 27.

41. See Ibn Ezra's introduction to Genesis, "fifth approach," his *Sefer Sahot*, ed. G. Lippmann, Fürth, 1827, p.74, and his comments to Num. 11:15; 12:12; Job 7:20; 32:3. He mostly ignores the traditions about "corrections of the scribes" (I Sam. 3:13; I Kings 12:15; Jer. 2:11; Ezek. 8:17; Hab. 1:12; Zech. 2:12; Mal. 1:13; Psalms 106:20). On the "corrections," see S. Lieberman, *Hellenism in Jewish Palestine*, New York, 1962, pp. 28–37.

42. *Sefer Ha-Riqmah*, *op. cit.*, 307–335; see N. M. Sarna, "Hebrew and Biblical Studies in Medieval Spain," *The Sephardi Heritage*, ed. R. D. Barnett London, 1971, pp. 338–339, 344–349.

43. M. Soloveitchik and Z. Rubashov, *Toledot Biqqoret Ha-Miqra'*, Berlin, 1925, p. 33, estimate that Ibn Janah's "substitutions" encompassed about two-hundred emendations.

44. *Sefer Sahot*, *op. cit.*, p. 72a.

45. *Sefer Berurah*, ed. G. Lippmann, Fürth, 1839, pp. 9a-b.

46. On Ibn Ezra's attitude to the biblical Hebrew text, see U. Simon, *Bar Ilan* 6 (1968), pp. 191–236.

47. See Friedlaender, *op. cit.*, pp. 131–134; Melammed, *op. cit.*, pp. 568–572.

48. Exod. 9:30; 18:25; 24:10; Lev. 5:1; Num. 23:7; Deut. 20:19; 31:16; Amos 9:13; Ob. 13; Ps. 15:2; 80:5; 84:9; see Melammed. *op. cit.*, pp. 561–568.

49. On this rule, see *Talmudic Encyclopedia* [Hebrew], Jerusalem, 1948, I, cols. 302–303. This rule is the last of the "Thirty-Two Rules" of aggadic exegesis attributed to R. Yose ha-Galilee, but actually authored by the Gaon Samuel ben Ḥofni who based himself on Saadiah's commentaries; see M. Zucker, *PAAJR* 23 (1950), pp. 1–39.

50. Gen 6:3; Exod. 16:15; Lev. 25:1.

51. Exod. 19:19; cf. 16:32.

52. Eccl. 12:2.

53. Gen. 51:57; Lev. 4:22; Hos. 7:4; Amos 9:12; Ps. 112:5.

54. *Ber.* 23a; *Sotah* 2a; *Yev.* 4a; *Taan.* 26b; *MQ* 28a; *Zev.* 88b; *Arakh.* 16a.

55. Exod. 21:2.

56. Exod. 22:4, 5 , 6, 14; Lev. 19:27–28; Num. 15:1; Isa. 40:1; see Melammed, *op. cit.*, pp. 538–539.

57. Deut. 24:6.

58. U. Simon, *Four Approaches to the Book of Psalm*, Ramat-Gan, 1982, pp. 197, 241.

59. *Ber.* 2a.

60. See his comment to Exod. 17:7 where he cites, in addition, Josh. 24:4; Joel 3:3; Ps. 74:16; Ruth 1:3.

61. Exod. 25:22 and 35:11.

62. He makes the same remark to Lev. 16:11 and Deut. 29:22.

63. Introduction to Genesis, the "second approach."

64. *Yesod Mora'*, Jerusalem, 1955, p. l, third paragraph.

65. Introduction to Genesis, "third approach."

66. *Yesod Mora'*, *op. cit.*

67. Exod. 21:24.

68. Exod. 32:15.

69. Lev. 22:22.

70. Num. 6:21.

71. Deut. 14:28.

72. Deut. 22:12.

73. I. Levin, *The Sacred Poetry of Abraham Ibn Ezra* [Hebrew], vols. I–II, Jerusalem, 1976–1980.

74. Gen. 22:4; Exod. 9:10; 25:5; cf. the question of Abbaye to R. Joseph in *Eruv.* 60a (cf. 3a), but contrast Ibn Ezra's comments to Exod. 12:24; 15:22; Amos 5:25.

75. *Yesod Mora'*, *op. cit.*, section 6, p. 9.

76. Gen. 1:26; 16:3; 18:28; Exod. 20:21; 21:7; Lev. 19:20; 22:7.

77. Gen. 3:23; 25:1; 37:15; Exod. 1:8; 9:10.

78. *Ber.* 26a; *Gen. R.* 68, 9. Ibn Ezra reiterates this in his introduction to Esth. 4:14.

79. Gen. 23:8; Isa. 47:3; Jer. 7:16; 27:18; Ruth 1:16.

80. See A. Marmorstein, *The Old Rabbinic Doctrine of God*, London, 1927, I, pp. 92–93.

81. Cf. *Shab.* 118b; *Git.* 52a.

82. *Ber.* 7a.

83. *Op. cit.*, pp. 4b–5a.

84. *Shab.* 63a; *Yev.* 11b, 24a.

85. "Fifth approach," ed. Weiser, *op. cit.*, p. 142, second introduction.

86. Kahana, *op. cit.*, II, pp. 82–86 maintains the authenticity of this letter, but see now I. Shailat, *Letters and Essays of Moses Maimonides* [Hebrew], Maaleh Adumim, 1988, II, pp. 697–698. I owe this reference to Professor Marvin Fox. For an English rendering, see L. D. Stitskin, *Letters of Maimonides*, New York, 1977, p. 156.

87. See Weiser, *op. cit.*, pp. 59–71; Melammed, *op. cit.*, pp. 669– 678.
88. Gen. 1:14.
89. Ps. 51:20.
90. Lev. 23:11.
91. Ps. 106:47.
92. Jonah 1:2.
93. Introduction to Zechariah.
94. Melammed, *op. cit.*, pp. 676–678.
95. Introduction to Genesis, "first approach"; Gen. 1:2; Exod. 2:9; Lev. 23:11.
96. Gen. 20:2; Exod. 19:12. On Dan. 1:1 Ibn Ezra cites several examples of supposed substitutions, and says of him, "Who says thus may be reckoned among the crazies."
97. Introduction to Genesis, "first approach"; cf. Gen. 28:11.
98. *Safah Berurah, op. cit.*, p. 5a; cf. Gen. 32:9; Exod. 9:30; 12:6; 15:2; 16:15; 18:26; 19:2; 23:19; 26:18, 31; 28:6, 36. Ibn Ezra did not always cite Rashi accurately; see Melammed, *op. cit.*, pp. 672–673. His authorship of the poem in praise of Rashi (Kahana, No. 34, p. 59) is discounted entirely by Simon, *op. cit.*, (above, n. 7), p. 41, nn. 62, 63.
99. See, however, A. Margaliot, "The Relationship Between Rashbam's Commentary and Ibn Ezra's Commentary" [Hebrew], *Sfer Asaf,* Jerusalem, 1953, pp. 357–369.
100. On this issue, see U. Simon, *Bar Ilan* 3 (1965), pp. 130–138.
101. Gen. 32:33.
102. Gen. 15:13; cf. 20:19.
103. Deut. 33:2. On the identity of the "mindless," see Simon, *Bar Ilan* 3, *op. cit.*, pp. 100–111.
104. Gen. 25:34.
105. Gen. 31:18.
106. Exod. 20:21.
107. Exod. 14:27; 16:13; 34:29.
108. A play on Gen. 21:6.
109. Heb. *ha-mahabil*; cf. Gen. 36:31–32; Job 42:16.
110. Introduction to Genesis, "second approach"; cf. Lev. 7:20; 19:20.
111. Chapter 8.
112. Here, Ibn Ezra has circumspectly combined two different views given in *BB* 15a, *Men.* 30a, *Sifre Deut.* 34, para. 357, 15, ed. Horovitz-Finkelstein, p. 427.
113. See to Isa. 40:1; 41:4, 23; 42:1, 8; 49:7; 55:6; U. Simon, "Ibn Ezra Between Medievalism and Modernism: The Case of Isa. 40–66," *VTS* 36 (1985), pp. 257–271.
114. On Ibn Chiquitilla's commentary on Psalms, see U. Simon, *op. cit.*, (*supra*, in n. 58), pp. 96–119.
115. Ibid., pp. 121–248.
116. Ned. 32a; *Gen. R.* 43:2.
117. Ibn Ezra authored *Sefer Ha-'Ibbur*, ed. S. H. Halberstam, Lyck, 1874, on intercalation. See his lengthy comments to Exod. 12:2; Lev. 23:3. See also N. Ben-Menahem, *Tarbiz* 27 (1958), p. 103; A. A. Akavia, "Sefer Ha-'Ibbur Le'R. Abraham ibn Ezra," *Tarbiz* 26 (1957), pp. 304–316.
118. Ibn Ezra authored *Sefer Ha-Shem*, ed. G. H. Lippmann, Fürth, 1834; see Weiser, *op. cit.*, pp. 30–36.
119. Ibn Ezra composed *Sefer Ha-'Ehad* (on the numbers 1–9), eds. S. Pinsker and M. A. Goldhart, Odessa, 1867, and *Sefer Ha-Mispar* (on arithmetic), ed. M. Silberberg, Frankfurt A.M., 1895.
120. See I. M. Millas, "The Work of Abraham ibn Ezra in Astronomy" [Hebrew], *Tarbiz* 9 (1938), pp. 306–322. He also published a work on the subject entitled *Ta'amei*

Ha-Luhot, and another on the astrolabe, called *Kli Nehoshet*, Koenigsberg, 1845. Ibn Ezra includes astronomical notes in his comments to Gen. 1:14; Lev. 25:9; Isa. 14:12; Amos 5:8; Job 9:9; 38:31; Eccl. 1:3, 5. He refers to the Alexandrian astronomer and mathematician Ptolemaeus and his system in Lev. 25:9 *et al.*

121. See R. Levy, *The Astrological Works of Abraham Ibn Ezra*, Baltimore, 1927.

122. E.g. Exod. 1:7; 10:22; 15:13; Ruth 2:17.

123. *Sefer Ha-Shem, op. cit., Yesod Mora', op. cit.*

124. This was done by N. Krochmal, in *The Writings of Nachman Krochmal* [Hebrew], ed. S. Rawidowicz, second enlarged edition, London-Waltham, 1961, pp. 285–394; D. Rosin, "Die Religionsphilosophie Abraham ibn Esra's," MGWJ 42 (1898); 43 (1899); I. Husik, *History of Medieval Philosophy,* Philadelphia 1944, pp. 187–196; J. Guttmann, *Philosophies of Judaism*, transl. D. W. Silverman, Philadelphia, 1964, pp. 118–120. See also R. Jospe, *Bible Exegesis as a Philosophic Literary Genre: Abraham ibn Ezra and Moses Mendelssohn*, [prepublication copy] Jerusalem, 1991.

125. E.g. Gen. 3:1; 28:12; Num. 22:28; Isa. 43:7; Ps. 16:2; 143:10; 150:6. The source of these citations is unknown.

126. Gen. 3:24; Exod. 15:2; 16:28; Lev. 19:19; Ps. 11:7; Job 23:13.

127. See N. Ben Menahem, *'Areshet 3* (1961), pp. 71–92.

128. Ed. D. Herzog, Cracow-Heidelberg-Berlin, 1912–1930.

Abraham Geiger and Biblical Scholarship

Abraham Geiger as a biblical scholar. How can we appraise his role except within the general context of his contemporary biblical scholarship? How can one form a balanced judgment without consideration of the attitudes of nineteenth-century Jüdische Wissenschaft to the discipline? How can we achieve a proper understanding of his investigations into the biblical text unless we probe the animating forces that imparted meaning and motivation to the "Science of Judaism" in his day?

By the time Geiger had reached the age of religious maturity in the eyes of the Jewish people, biblical criticism had already achieved respectability in Protestant university circles. Even the term "higher criticism," borrowed from classical scholarship, had gained currency by this time.[1] The Introduction to the Bible of Johann Gottfried Eichorn (1752–1827), which was largely responsible for bringing this about, had run through three editions, and the fourth was just beginning to appear.[2] The results of previous scholarship, summarized and systematized, were readily accessible to anyone who wished to be informed on the source-critical dissection of the Pentateuch and the theological stance of each document. Wilhelm M. L. De Wette (1780–1849) had eight years earlier published his revolutionary dissertation on Deuteronomy, which he had isolated as a distinct document within the Pentateuchal complex and had assigned to the time of King Josiah of Judah in the seventh century B.C.E.[3]

The formative years of Geiger's life, his student days at the universities of Heidelberg and Bonn between 1829 and 1832, and his first decades in the rabbinate, thus coincided with an era of intense productivity in biblical studies, and the most illustrious personalities in the field were his contemporaries. What a galaxy of scholars he could have known! K. D. Ilgen (1763–1834), Heinrich Ewald (1803–1875), Ferdinand Hitzig (1807–1875), E. W. Hengstenberg (1802–1869), Wilhelm Vatke (1806–1882), Franz Delitzsch (1813–1890), August Dillman (1823–1894), Eduard Reuss (1804–1891), Paul de Lagarde (1827–1890), Abraham Kuenen (1828–1891) and K. H. Graf (1815–1869)—all these founders of the science of biblical criticism taught and wrote and disseminated their latest theories in his day.[4] Only Julius Wellhausen (1844–1918) is missing from the list of worthies in that he did not publish his magnum opus until two years after Geiger's demise.[5]

To how much of all this was Geiger really exposed? We learn that he began to read Hebrew at the age of three, and that his half-brother, Salomon, had early in his youth introduced him to the study of the Bible—along traditional lines, of course.[6] When he first tasted of the forbidden fruit of the new learning is uncertain, but he lists as his "early guides through the realm of the Bible" none other than Johann Gottfried Herder (1744–1803) and Eichorn himself, and he admits that he did not find them altogether satisfying, although they did succeed in "broadening his perspective."[7] We shall later return in greater detail to Geiger's own views. Revolutionary that he was, he was yet a child of his times, and it is highly instructive to observe him against the background of nineteenth-century Jewish scholarship.

Moses Mendelssohn (1729–1786) himself had been familiar with the recently developed school of critical biblical scholarship, but he never allowed the critical theories to intrude upon his *Biur,* and he was careful to avoid anything that might cast doubt on the traditional viewpoint.[8] Leopold Zunz (1794–1886) had been a student of De Wette,[9] yet his epoch-making essay containing a plea for the recognition of Jewish scholarship as a discipline (1818) concentrated on rabbinic literature.[10] His self-justification for this was that since biblical literature was also the property of Christians, much effort had been devoted to it. Rabbinic literature on the other hand, being an exclusively Jewish domain, had therefore been neglected.[11] This rationalization for the disregard of biblical studies in the program of Jüdische Wissenschaft implies an identification and satisfaction on the part of Zunz with the biblical scholarship then current. Nevertheless, when Zunz edited a new German translation of the Hebrew Bible (1837–38) it was largely dependent on Mendelssohn and entirely faithful to tradition. His great work on the history of the liturgical addresses of the Jews[12] commences with the postexilic books. Not until the age of seventy-three did Zunz seriously take up critical biblical studies, and here he openly subscribed to contemporary source-critical theories. It is highly significant that he did not publish his researches in his own journal or in any other Jewish periodical.[13] It is true that Moses Moser, at the opening of the *Verein für Kultur und Wissenschaft des Judentums*, called for a thorough study of the Bible, but his was a lone voice and went unheeded.[14] The movement of the "Science of Judaism" produced practically nothing original in this field, and those Jews who did trespass upon it mainly confined themselves to problems of canonization, the ancient versions, the Masorah, and the like innocuous subjects.[15]

Jewish historiographers fared no better when it came to the history of the preexilic period. Writing in the Jewish Encyclopaedia at the turn of the century, Joseph Jacobs observed: "As regards the historical treatment of the Biblical phases of Jewish history, this has become part of general Biblical exegesis, and does not call for treatment in this place, especially as scarcely any Jewish writers have produced works of importance on this subject. . . ."[16]

Isaac Marcus Jost (1793–1860), who in nine volumes produced the first comprehensive history of the Jewish people, really began his story with the Maccabees.[17] The first Jewish economic historian, Levi Herzfeld (1810–1884), commenced his major work with the fall of Jerusalem, although he had separately published some studies on biblical problems and had lamented the neglect of biblical studies by Jews.[18] The great Heinrich Graetz (1817–1891) began his publication schedule in 1853 with volume 4 of his history, dealing with the Talmudic period.[19] He tarried twenty years before producing the two volumes on the biblical era. His professed reason was that he needed a measure of first-hand authority about the background and could not attain this until he had the opportunity to visit the Holy Land. Some scholars, however, believe that Graetz was actually long afraid to deal with the subject of biblical history.[20] Actually, from 1871 Graetz concentrated on biblical research and pursued a very radical approach in his work on the Prophets and Hagiographa, freely indulging in both higher and lower criticism. Nevertheless, he refused to apply the same to the Pentateuch, and he insisted on the unity and preexilic origin of the entire Torah.[21] Moritz Steinschneider (1816–1909) reviewed Jewish literary creativity, but he began with Ezra, and he had little to report on the achievements of biblical historiography.[22]

To sum up: the Jewish scholarship of Geiger's time generally avoided biblical studies. Scholars who did happen to venture into those perilous waters steered clear of the Pentateuch. By and large, they simply had no conception of any possibility of a specifically Jewish contribution to the field.

This highly disappointing, thoroughly ambivalent, and deliberately self-restrictive approach to biblical scholarship contrasts sharply with the brilliant efflorescence of the same in that earlier golden age of Jewish scholarship in Spain.[23] The explanation must largely be sought in the soterial role that nineteenth-century scholars had assigned to Jüdische Wissenschaft. Given the dual crises in which Jews and Judaism found themselves in that period, scientific scholarship was supposed to be the instrument for the achievement of Nirvana—the successful emancipation of Western Jewry. Zunz had made this clear in no uncertain terms in his pioneering, programmatic vision of 1818.[24] Jewish literature was to be exploited, honestly exploited, for political ends. Wissenschaft would gain non-Jewish recognition for postbiblical Jewish intellectual creativity as an academic discipline for its own sake. This, in turn, would perforce effectuate the civic equality of the Jews, which was the ultimate eschatological goal.[25] Eduard Gans (1798–1839), one of the cofounders of the *Verein,* had echoed the same sentiments. Jüdische Wissenschaft was to be a contrivance by means of which the Jews might be integrated into European society.[26] It is true that Immanuel Wolf, another co-founder, did demand that the scientific pursuit of Jewish culture must be thoroughly objective and free of tendentiousness, but he was out of tune with the times.[27]

It is in the light of this pervasive soterial intent that nineteenth-century Jüdische Wissenschaft, and particularly its meager biblical ingredient, must be viewed. The strongly held, if naively mistaken, belief that the dissemination of the knowledge of Judaism would inevitably cause prejudice to dissolve and the barriers to emancipation to disintegrate[28] simply could not fit the Bible into its scheme of things. Moreover, by concentrating on postbiblical literature, Jewish scholars could avoid uncomfortable and delicate issues of faith, such as the problem of divine inspiration. They could also, by the simple device of benign neglect, de-emphasize the Pentateuch, which symbolized to them Jewish halakhah-bound particularism and national and ethnic identity, both of which were regarded as undesirable qualities. It was the theological and political nature of Jüdische Wissenschaft that largely determined its attitude and direction in the field of biblical studies.

This verdict is decisive when it comes to evaluating Geiger's place in the movement of the "Science of Judaism." Being the supreme activist, he, more than all the others, subordinated scholarship to practical ends, and in so doing he promoted the proposition that the transfiguration of Judaism was indispensable to the achievement and security of emancipation. Thus, in 1841 he expressed the fear that "the more profound minds who are active within Judaism. . . may withdraw into the field of scholarship and be utterly lost for all the practical ends of Judaism."[29] He freely admitted that the "scientific foundation" of Judaism had "a practical purpose."[30] He wanted to justify his reforms in worship and Jewish law on the basis of historical research. Nothing is more instructive than his observation that the era of Moses Mendelssohn, while highly beneficial for the individual, had shaken the foundations of Judaism without replacing it with something new and vigorous.[31]

It was this urge to create a new Judaism and so a new Jew, this largely practical aim, which scholarship had to serve, that led Geiger to biblical studies but also circumscribed his field of interests. In both respects he was a highly original figure in the hall of fame of Jewish scholarship in the last century.

What was Geiger's attitude to biblical criticism? We have already cited his admission that he had been early influenced by Herder and Eichhorn, although they did not entirely satisfy him. Again, in his famous *Open Letter* to Holtzmann, dated 1865, he expressed dissatisfaction with the present state of scholarship in relation to the origin and completion of the Pentateuch, and he promised to make his own contributions to the subject.[32] As early as 1836 he had very strongly lamented what he termed the "deceit" of presenting to the public as historical events of a supernatural nature what were clearly to be regarded as nothing but legends,[33] and he gave vent to his conviction that what he felt to be the true spirit of Judaism does not shine forth with sufficient clarity from the Pentateuch.[34] On another occasion and in a popular work, he quite matter-of-factly expressed the view that the first four books of the Pentateuch reflect the thinking of the Northern Kingdom.[35]

There can thus be no doubt of Geiger's commitment to the radical biblical scholarship of his day. He was the first Jewish scholar to incorporate the modern systematic study of the biblical books within the program of Jüdische Wissenschaft, and he was the first to introduce this into the curriculum of a rabbinical seminary.[36] How are we to account for Geiger's departure from the contemporary pattern of Jewish scholarship in respect of the Bible? It was not simply a matter of his personal courage or intellectual daring, although, doubtless, these were factors. Rather, we must look for an explanation to the pragmatism we have already discussed. In order to find the historical basis for his reforms, he had to adopt the conception of Judaism as a religion that had been steadily evolving from its inception to his own day. He wanted to prove that his reformism did not constitute a sundering of the past, a rupturing of tradition, but simply the latest stage in a process of natural growth entirely consistent with the long history of Jews and Judaism. He therefore felt constrained to construct an imposing, comprehensive, scientific system in which intellectual honesty and the broader purpose demanded that no valid distinction could be made between the Bible and the Talmud in respect of critical judgment.[37]

So far so good. But the inherent weakness in a scholarship designed to serve an ideological and practical purpose extrinsic to itself lies in its inevitable selectivity and eisegesis, and both are transparently present in Geiger's biblical studies. Take, for example, his attitude to the Pentateuch. It was no different from that of the Protestant theologians, and he had little original to add to the literary criticism it had produced. However, while other Jewish scholars felt uncomfortable with the heterogeneity and declared lateness of the Pentateuch, Geiger obviously saw these views as scientific support for his own intuitive early dissatisfaction with the Pentateuch as a religious document. If we wonder, then, why Geiger neglected the study of the Pentateuch, the answer is not embarrassment or cowardice, but that Protestant scholars had already largely preempted the field and had produced the conclusions he needed. The presumed scientific demotion of the Pentateuch served to de-emphasize the authority behind its laws and made easier the assault on the national and particularistic aspects of its religion. It enabled Geiger to emphasize and magnify the ethical monotheism of the Prophets, which to him constituted the true Jewish universalism, and provided a natural meeting-ground between Jews and Christians.[38]

In this respect, it is a fascinating exercise to examine the inconsistency to which Geiger the Jew was driven in his views on the development of biblical religion. On the one hand, he is critical of the conception of God found in the Pentateuch and is apologetic about certain aspects of biblical Judaism, such as the sacrificial system and the existence of a priesthood.[39] He accepts the critical view of Israelite paganism. Yet at the same time, in his division of the historical development of Judaism into four periods, he can designate the first, which ends with the canonization of the Bible, "the period of revelation."[40] Of this period, Geiger can actually write:

> Nor does Judaism claim to be the work of individuals but that of the whole people. It does not speak of the God of Moses or of the God of the prophets, but of the God of Abraham, Isaac and Jacob, of the God of the whole race, of all the patriarchs who were equally endowed with the gift of the prophetic vision, the genius of revelation which was latent in the whole people and found concentration and expression in individuals. . . .
>
> Judaism arose within the people of revelation . . . an illumination proceeding from a higher mind and spirit which cannot be explained; which is not a compound produced by a process of development even if it is further developed afterwards; which all at once appears in existence as a whole, like every new creation proceeding from the Original Spirit. . . .[41]

Geiger even invokes Yehuda HaLevi, who, he says, "emphatically designated revelation as a disposition that was present in the whole people."[42] Moreover, Geiger asks the crucial question:

> How did it happen that such a people, a mere tribe surrounded by so many mightier nations, which had no opportunity of having an unobstructed view of the great events in the world, which had to fight many battles for its bare existence, which was confined within a limited territory and had to employ all its resources to defend itself against its powerful enemies—how did it happen that such a people rose to those sublime conceptions? It is an enigma in the world's history. Who will give us a complete solution?[43]

It is amazing that Geiger here parts company with his contemporary Christian scholars, who saw in the biblical descriptions of idolatry in Israel the true national religion, and in the concept of Israel's infidelity the fruit of later retrospection. Several scholars have independently noted the striking similarity between Geiger's idea of the original, intuitive, spontaneous, and national character of Israelite monotheism and the basic premise of the great *History of the Religion of Israel* by Yehezkel Kaufmann.[44] Unfortunately, Geiger did not develop his remarkable insight and did not seem to realize its shattering implications for the contemporary source-critical reconstruction of the religion of Israel. He had the distinction of being the first to include biblical studies within the scope of Jüdische Wissenschaft, but he missed the opportunity to make a truly Jewish contribution to the subject.

Nevertheless, it is true to say that without the insight about the inextricable relationship between the Bible and the people, Geiger could not have given birth to his *magnum opus,* the *Urschrift,* published in 1857.[45] At the root of that great work lies the basic presupposition that the history of the biblical text is interwoven with the history of the people, that the text itself, being a response to life, constantly adapted itself to the needs of the people so that it is possible to reconstruct the inner history of Israel's faith from the external history of the biblical text.[46] In other words, Geiger believed that what the process of midrash and exegesis accomplished in a later age, was achieved through textual manipulation in the period before the final stabilization of the biblical text.

In support of his thesis about the onetime fluidity of the biblical text, Geiger could point to the variants between our received text and the Septuagint, the Targumim, and the Samaritan Pentateuch. He could also show that in some instances the interpretation of a biblical passage in older halakhic sources presupposes a reading different from ours. Of course, none of these observations was original to him. Zecharias Frankel and Samuel David Luzzatto had addressed themselves to the same problems. But only Geiger constructed a coherent thesis that assumed a different Hebrew *Vorlage* behind the translations and versions rather than a simple ascription to copyist errors and imperfections and mere tendentiousness on the part of the translators. Geiger penetrated even deeper to devise an explanation as to how the variants arose in the original Hebrew texts he believed the versions to reflect. He concluded that the social, political, and religious conditions and intellectual cross-currents of the period of the Second Temple—more specifically, the challenge of Hellenism and the Maccabean revolt and the subsequent struggles between the Pharisees and the Sadducees—were the prime causes.[47] It was only after the destruction of the Temple, with the final victory of the Pharisees, that the pristine text was gradually recovered to achieve final fixation in the time of Rabbi Akiba.

Geiger's *Urschrift* predictably aroused great controversy,[48] but Theodore Nöldeke called it an "epoch-making work,"[49] and Moritz Steinschneider praised it highly,[50] while the otherwise critical Solomon Schechter admitted it to be "monumental."[51] If, after the passage of a century, it can still merit scholarly appreciation and evaluation—this in itself is tribute indeed, irrespective of the results of our investigation and quite apart from the original ideological motives of the author. The immense erudition, the astonishing command of a vast scholarly apparatus, and the author's wide catholicity of interests cannot fail to arouse our admiration and more. But how much remains of his general presuppositions and conclusions?

There can now be no doubt as to the correctness of Geiger's insight into the fluid state of the text in early times, for the Dead Sea Scrolls have abundantly confirmed the existence of a multiplicity of text-types in the period between 300 B.C.E. and the first century C.E.[52] These same documents further prove that Geiger was absolutely right—at least for the historical books—in contending that the Septuagint accurately reflects a Hebrew *Vorlage* current in the third and second centuries B.C.E., and that its divergences from the received Hebrew text are in the main not due to the idiosyncrasies of the translators.[53] Geiger has been proven correct, once again, in his evaluation of the Samaritan Pentateuch. He challenged the prevailing view, which had the great prestige of W. Gesenius behind it, that the Samaritan text was a corrupt and relatively late recension of an inferior Jewish version, and thus a useless witness to the Hebrew. Geiger boldly and, as it now turns out, correctly insisted that the Samaritan Pentateuch represented a very ancient textual tradition which is indeed a valuable tool for reconstructing the history of the biblical text.[54] His instinct was once again unerring in detecting the direct link between the Sadducees and the Karaites.[55] Here, too, the Dead Sea Scrolls have amply illustrated the truth of the point.[56]

Still, the Qumran and other finds have also exposed the great complexity of the issues involved, far beyond what Geiger could possibly have imagined. There is absolutely no evidence that the textual diversity can be attributable to the Sadducean-Pharisaic rivalries. The mere fact that the sectarian community at Qumran could embrace a variety of manuscripts of the same biblical book, diverging one from the other in respect of orthography and readings, proves that the explanation for textual diversity must be sought elsewhere than where Geiger located it. This argument is strengthened by the fact that although this sect pursued its own halakhic tradition, which was certainly close to that of the Sadducees, the Masoretic text-type still figures prominently in its library. Furthermore, there is nothing to warrant the notion of sectarian manipulation of the text to give expression to certain ideas. To accomplish this purpose, the men of Qumran made use of the *pesher*, or quasi-midrashic exegesis, leaving the scriptural citation intact.

Finally, it is worth mentioning one other point of interest that arises from Geiger's biblical studies, and this is the repeatedly positive evaluation of our received Hebrew text. True, he does not think it is free of error,[57] but he has a high estimation of its authenticity, and of its "closeness to the original" and its superiority over the Septuagint and the

Samaritan Pentateuch.[58] This view is quite surprising, given the reckless emendation of Scripture indulged in by Geiger's contemporaries, but it is consonant with his own cautious approach to textual emendation, as is evident from his Hebrew philological studies. In one of these[59] he explicitly warns against the facile tampering with the text in order to explain away difficulties.[60] The history of the biblical text certainly has not turned out to be as Geiger imagined, but it is of great interest to note that the position of biblical scholarship in the latter half of this century is far closer to Geiger's view than to that of his contemporaries.

In summation: any evaluation of Geiger as a biblical scholar must take account of the fact that his scholarship was incidental to his practical and ideological goals. He wrote no commentaries and did not deal with preexilic biblical history. His supreme interest was the history of the Halakhah. He was not afraid to investigate issues of biblical research that intimidated others. If his broader theories have not stood the test of time, he was possessed of brilliant and original insights in several areas that modern discoveries have confirmed. Perhaps his greatest achievement in the field was to reclaim biblical studies as the legitimate concern of Jewish scholarship.

NOTES

1. See A. T. Chapman, *An Introduction to the Pentateuch* (Cambridge, 1911), p. 19.
2. *Einleitung in das Alte Testament*, 3 vols. (Leipzig, 1780–83; 4th ed. in 5 vols., 1823–26).
3. His celebrated *Dissertatio* was published in 1805, and his two-volume *Beiträge zur Einleitung in das Alte Testament* appeared in 1806–7.
4. On these, see T. K. Cheyne, *Founders of Old Testament Criticism* (1893; reprint ed., 1971).
5. "Die Composition des Hexateuchs" first appeared as a series of articles 1876–77.
6. See *Abraham Geiger's Nachgelassene Schriften* (hereafter cited as *NS*), ed. L. Geiger, I (1875), 301 f.; *idem, Abraham Geiger: Leben und Lebens-werk* (1910), p. 10; cf. E. Schreiber, *Abraham Geiger als Reformator des Judenthums* (1879), p. 1.
7. *NS* I, 302; M. Wiener, *Abraham Geiger and Liberal Judaism* (hereafter cited as *Abr. G.*) (1962), p. 142.
8. See A. Altmann, *Moses Mendelssohn: A Biographical Study* (1973), p. 376.
9. See F. Bamberger, *Proceedings of the American Academy for Jewish Research*, XI (1941), 5; H. Albeck, introduction to the Hebrew ed. of Zunz's *Die Gottesdienstliche Vorträge der Juden [HaDerashot BeYisrael]* (1947), p. 12, n. 6.
10. "Etwas über die rabbinische Literatur," reprinted in *Gesammelte Schriften* (1875), I, 1–31.
11. Ibid., p. 4; see M. A. Meyer, *The Origins of the Modern Jew* (1967), p. 160.
12. *Die Gottesdienstlichen Vorträge der Juden Historisch Entwickelt* (1832; 2nd ed. 1892; Hebrew trans., M. A. Zack, ed. H. Albeck, 1947).

13. They appeared in the *ZfDMG.*, XXVII (1873), 669–89, and were reprinted, together with unpublished studies, in his *Gesammelte Schriften* (1875), I, 217–70. On Zunz's biblical criticism, see M. Soloveitchik and S. Rubasheff, *Toledot Biqqoret HaMiqra* (1925), pp. 136–38.

14. See M. A. Meyer, *op. cit.*, p. 165.

15. Cf. the observations of M. Z. Segal in *Parshanut HaMiqra* (1952), pp. 125 f., and of N. N. Glatzer in *Studies in Nineteenth Century Jewish Intellectual History*, ed. A. Altmann (Philip Lown Institute of Advanced Jewish Studies, Brandeis University Studies and Texts, II, 1964), p. 32.

16. *Jewish Encyclopedia* (1904), VI, 425.

17. The title is instructive: *Geschichte d. Israeliten seit der Zeit der Maccabäer bis auf unsere Tage*, 1820–28.

18. See Salo W. Baron, *History and Jewish Historians* (1964), pp. 326 f., 337, 339, 341.

19. *Ibid.*, p. 264.

20. See I. Abrahams, *Jewish Quarterly Review*, IV (1892), 185 f.

21. On Graetz's biblical criticism, see Soloveitchik and Rubasheff, *op. cit.*, pp. 139–41; M. Wiener, *Jüdische Religion in Zeitalter der Emanzipation* (1933), pp. 231–36 (Hebrew ed. [1974], pp. 258–62).

22. See Baron, *op. cit.*, pp. 306 f.

23. See "Hebrew and Bible Studies in Medieval Spain," in *The Sephardi Heritage*, ed. R. D. Barnett (1971), pp. 323–66.

24. See above n. 10, "Etwas. . . ," pp. 4 f., 30 f.

25. See N. Rotenstreich, *HaMahashavah HaYehudit Ba'et HaHadashah* (1966), pp. 35–38; Glatzer, *op. cit.*, p. 39.

26. See S. Federbusch, *Hokhmat Yisrael BeMa'arab Eiropah* (1958), I, 10. Gans converted to Christianity in 1825.

27. *Ibid.*, II, 9.

28. See S. B. Freehof in D. Philipson, *The Reform Movement in Judaism* (2nd ed., 1967), p. XV.

29. Wiener, *Abr. G.*, p. 93.

30. See Philipson, *op. cit.*, p. 46.

31. Wiener, *Abr. G.*, p. 89.

32. English translation in A. Geiger, *Judaism and Its History*, trans. Ch. Newburgh (2nd ed., 1911), p. 404.

33. Wiener, *Abr. G.*, p. 86. It is of interest to note that thirty-three years later the Leipzig Synod discussed and rejected the inclusion of the critical study of the Bible in the curriculum of the religious schools; see Philipson, *op. cit.*, 299.

34. Wiener, *Abr. G.*, p. 84.

35. *NS*, II, 77; Wiener, *Abr. G.*, p. 159.

36. See his "Einleitung in die biblischen Schriften," *NS* (1876), IV, 1–279.

37. See H. Liebeschütz in *Essays Presented to Leo Baeck on the Occasion of His Eightieth Birthday* (1954), pp. 75–93.

38. Contrast Ahad Ha'Am's nationalistic interpretation of the same prophetic material; see A. Gottschalk, in *Studies in Jewish Bibliography, History and Literature in Honor of I. Edward Kiev* (ed. Ch. Berlin, 1971), pp. 133–44, esp. 141 f.

39. *Das Judentum u. seine Geschichte* (1910), pp. 50–65; English trans. pp. 60–67.

40. *Das Judentum*, pp. 28–37; English trans., pp. 39–48; *NS* II, 63, 65 ff.; Wiener, *Abr. G.*, p. 156.

41. *Das Judentum*, pp. 36 f.; English, p. 47.

42. *Das Judentum*, pp. 37 f.; English, p. 48.

43. *Das Judentum*, pp. 27 f.; English, p. 38.

44. *Toledot Ha'Emunah HaYisre'elit*, 8 vols. (1937–57), esp. Vol. I, 1–22; English abridged translation by M. Greenberg (1960). The similarity to Kaufmann's views has been noted by J. B. Agus, *Modern Philosophies of Judaism* (1941), p. 7, n. 3; J. Klausner, introduction to the Hebrew edition of Geiger's *Urschrift* (see next note), p. 43, n. 1. Kaufmann, I, 12, n. 12, acknowledges his affinity with Krochmal, but does not refer to Geiger.

45. *Urschrift und Übersetzungen der Bibel in ihrer Abhängigkeit von der innern Entwicklung des Judenthums* (1st ed. 1857, 2nd ed. 1928; Hebr. Trans. J. L. Baruch with introduction by J. Klausner, *HaMiqra WeTargumaw*, 1949). See L. Geiger, *op. cit.*, pp. 316–27.

46. *Urschrift*, pp. 19, 432; Hebrew, pp. 9, 277.

47. *Urschrift*, pp. 170–99; Hebrew, pp. 110–27.

48. See, e.g., S. L. J. Rapoport, *Naḥalat Yehudah* (Or Torah) (1868); H. M. Pineles, *Darkah shel Torah* (1861), secs. 144–66.

49. *ZdDMG*, XX (1866), 457.

50. See Baron, *op. cit.*, pp. 297 f. Steinschneider also criticized the work; ibid., p. 307.

51. *Studies in Judaism* (1924), III, 51; cf. also Klausner's verdict, *op. cit.*, pp. 35, 44.

52. For a summary of the present state of scholarship on these issues, see *Encyclopaedia Judaica*, IV, cols. 832–36.

53. See F. M. Cross, *The Ancient Library of Qumran* (1961), pp. 168–87, esp. 181. On the proper use of the LXX as witness to the Hebrew, see H. M. Orlinsky, *Biblical Archaeologist*, IX (1946), 21–42, esp. 24, 32 f.

54. *NS*, III (1876), 255–66, 283–321; IV (1876), 54–68; see J. D. Purvis, *The Samaritan Pentateuch and the Origin of the Samaritan Text* (1968), pp. 59, 75–80.

55. *Das Judentum*, pp. 227–33; English trans., pp. 362–69.

56. See N. Wieder, *The Judean Scrolls and Karaism* (1962).

57. Cf., e.g., *Abraham Geiger's Gesammelte Abhandlungen in hebräischer Sprache* [Hebrew: *Kebuṣat Ma'amarim*], ed., S. Poznanski (1910), pp. 25–33.

58. *Urschrift*, pp. 17–100, 159–60, 433; Hebrew pp. 64–66, 103, 276.

59. *Kebuṣat Ma'amarim*, p. 17.

60. Mendelssohn had similarly adopted a negative attitude to textual criticism; see Altmann, *op. cit.*, pp. 286 f.

Jewish Bible Scholarship and Translations in the United States*

For two thousand years, the Hebrew Bible has been studied by Jews not simply as a self-contained, sacred work on its own terms, but largely as a body of religious literature that has been filtered through a continuous process of rabbinic interpretation and reinterpretation within the community of practice and faith from which its immediate authority derived. Already in 553 C.E., the emperor Justinian (527–565 C.E.) took note of this fact in his *novella constitutio* concerning the Jews to whom he granted permission to read their sacred scriptures in Greek, Latin, or any other language. He stipulated, however, that they should "read the holy words themselves, rejecting the commentaries," by which he clearly meant rabbinic exegesis. As he put it, "the so-called second tradition *(deuterosis)* we prohibit entirely, for it is not part of the sacred books nor is it handed down by divine inspiration through the prophets, but the handiwork of men, speaking only of earthly things and having nothing of the divine in it" (Baumgarten: 37).

Justinian's motives and intentions are irrelevant to the present theme, for they belong within the category of medieval Jewish-Christian polemics. But his specified restriction has illustrated a historic fact of cardinal importance that differentiates the Jewish study of the Scriptures from the Christian approach, which, of course, has its own venerable tradition of theological reinterpretation of the Bible of the Jews. The educated, committed Jew to whom study of the Bible is at one and the same time a religious obligation, a spiritual exercise, a mode of worship, and a moral as well as an intellectual discipline, is confronted with a vast array of texts which, if not of equal authority, and most have no authority at all, yet command his attention, his concentrated thought and study. It is a literature that has long been endowed with a life and energy of its own, and in its independent existence the light of the Hebrew Bible has become refracted through a thousand prisms. In discussing the role of the Bible in any Jewish community, this circumstance must be taken into account.

Another factor that requires recognition is the term "American Judaism." It is an appellation that well-nigh defies meaningful definition. The variable, restless, frequently chaotic, and always kaleidoscopic configurations of American Jewish life do not easily yield to procrustean generalizations. American Judaism is not, strictly speaking, simply a peer group of the Protestant and Catholic faith communities, for it encompasses a considerable number of individuals who possess no affiliation with religious institutions but whose sense of Jewish self-identity is strong and for whom "Judaism" carries with it a humanistic, secular nuance and/or nationalistic orientation. Nevertheless, it appears to be an incontrovertible fact that the ultra-Orthodox and the ultra-Reform, as well as those who represent the variegated shadings of religiosity between these poles, together with the secular Jew, all accept the Hebrew Scriptures as the bedrock of Jewish civilization, and all share a common recognition and conviction that the Hebrew Bible is a living force within the community of self-identifying Jews from which the structure of values to which Judaism subscribes ultimately derives. That this *consensus omnium* may also be accompanied by a commonality of ignorance of the biblical text itself is beside the point. What is pertinent is that the peculiar makeup of American Judaism distinguishes it from Protestantism and Catholicism in a very significant way.

Still another, no less important, singularity is that the received Hebrew text forever remains the sole authentic and valid basis for Jewish study and interpretation. Translations of the Bible have no authority for Jews. Particular English versions, like those of Isaac Leeser and of the Jewish Publication Society of 1917, achieved universal acceptance by English-speaking Jews, as will doubtless the new JPS translation. However, in no instance was the version initiated, sponsored, authorized or sanctioned by any official Jewish ecclesiastical body. In each case, the English version was a decidedly lay production even though learned rabbis representative of the three organized wings of American Judaism actively participated in the work.

THE LEESER TRANSLATION

American Jewish Bible translations date back to the foremost Jewish religious leader in early America: Isaac Leeser (1806–1868). Born in Westphalia and orphaned as a child, Leeser studied both at the gymnasium in Muenster and with Rabbi Abraham Sutro (Grossman). He arrived in this country in 1824 to work with his uncle, Zalma Rehine, a storekeeper in Richmond, Virginia. There he learned English, assisted on a volunteer basis at Congregation Beth Shalome, studied with Richmond's three most learned Jews, and in 1829 undertook to defend Judaism in print against the strictures of a British critic. Shortly thereafter, Congregation Mikveh Israel called him to Philadelphia to serve as its *hazan*. He spent the rest of his life in Philadelphia, first at Mikveh Israel, later on his own, and still later at Congregation Beth El Emeth. He never married and never made much money. His time, energy, and resources went exclusively to the congregation and the Jewish community, which he served faithfully as spiritual leader, writer, organizer, translator, and publisher. The magnitude of his achievements defies easy summary. Merely to read Bertram Korn's list of Leeser's "firsts," however, is to gain some appreciation of his formative role in American Judaism:

> The first volumes of sermons delivered and published by an American Jewish religious teacher (1837); the first complete American translation of the Sephardic prayer book (1837); the first Hebrew primer for children (1838); the first Jewish communal religious school (1839); the first successful American Jewish magazine-news journal (1843); the first American Jewish publication society (1845); the first Hebrew-English Torah to be edited and translated by an American Jew (1845); the first complete English translation of the Ashkenazic prayer book (1848); the first Hebrew "high school" (1849); the first English translation of the entire Bible by an American Jew (1853); the first Jewish defense organization—the Board of Delegates of American Israelites (1859); the first American Jewish theological seminary—Maimonides College (1867). Practically every form of Jewish activity which supports American Jewish life today was either established or envisaged by this one man. Almost every kind of publication which is essential to Jewish survival was written, translated, or fostered by him. (1967: 133)

Leeser's scholarly equipment was somewhat limited. The more learned and often more religiously radical Jewish religious leaders who followed him to America's shores had no trouble confounding him with intricate Talmudic arguments. Leeser's energy, however, was boundless, and likewise boundless was his desire to strengthen the Jewish community against assimilation and protestantization. Reanimating Jews' "almost expiring desire for critical inquiry into the sacred text" formed part of Leeser's program for stimulating Jewish revival (Leeser, 1856: vii). His other activities—educational, religious, philanthrophic and political ones—similarly related to his broad mission, that of preserving Jewish identity in the face of Christian conversionism and Jewish apathy.

While Isaac Leeser's decision to translate the Bible largely stemmed from these domestic concerns, it was also partly influenced by Moses Mendelssohn's translation of the Pentateuch from Hebrew to German (1780–1783), an epoch-making event whose reverberations spread throughout post-Emancipation Jewry (Weinberg; Billingheimer; Altmann). Mendelssohn served as one of Leeser's early role models, and when he first contemplated a Bible translation, the young *hazan* may have wanted to carry forward the master's work in a new language. But by the time he actually began his work in 1838, Leeser was less enamored with Mendelssohn, and he had a better conception of his own community's needs. Mendelssohn had translated the Bible as part of his program to enlighten the Jews of his day. Leeser's translation, by contrast, aimed to fight too much enlightenment; it sought to help Jews preserve their own identity intact.

The average American Jew in Leeser's day did not read Hebrew and, therefore, studied the Bible, if at all, from the venerable King James Version obtained cheaply or at no charge either from missionaries or from the American Bible Society. These Bibles contained the Hebrew Scriptures and New Testament bound together, in one volume according to the Christian canon, and in a thoroughly Christological format. Every page and every chapter of the Bible society's Bible bore a brief summary heading, many of which read Christian interpretations into the text. Jews who used these Bibles often condemned, as Leeser did, the "unfairness" of those who chose such headings as "the Prediction of Christ" (Psalm 110), "A Description of Christ" (Song of Solomon 5), and "Christ's Birth and Kingdom" (Isaiah 9) (1867: 41). Innocent Jews seeing these headings had, Leeser feared, "no means of knowing what is Scriptural and what is not" (1867: 42)

Format aside, the King James Bible translated many verses in a manner that Jews found thoroughly objectionable. As Leeser saw it, (*Occident*, 1851: 480) "wherever it was possible for the translators to introduce Christianity in the Scriptures, they have uniformly done so," in order, he said on another occasion, (1853: iii), "to assail Israel's hope and faith." He found particularly galling what he called the "perversions" introduced into the standard English text of the Prophets and the Psalms.

Leeser was not alone in his wrath. English Jews, as early as David Levi, had penned critiques of the Authorized Version, while Selig Newman's *Emendations of the Authorized Version of the Old Testament* (1839) filled seventy-two closely-printed pages with examples of where "the translators were either decidedly wrong, or. . . have not given the happiest rendering" (iv). Particularly troubling from a Jewish point of view were such readings as "virgin" for the Hebrew *'almâ* (Gen 24:43, Isa 7:14), or young woman; repeated capitalization of the word "saviour," and the like.

Had Leeser's objections to the King James Version only been confined to these kinds of Christological biases, he might have composed a Jewish revision without undue difficulty, simply by deleting the headings, repairing offensive verses, and rearranging the order of the books to conform with Jewish tradition. Just as the Ferrara Bible of 1553 appeared in a Christian edition where *'almâ* in Isa 7:14 was translated "virgin," and a Jewish edition where the same word was rendered "young woman" or transliterated as "la alma" (Margolis, 1917: 62), so there could have been Jewish and Christian editions of King James. But a Judaized version of a Christian translation would not have satisfied Leeser. To his mind, Jews were the guardians of Scripture, bearers of a long interpretive tradition of their own. They had no reason to defer, as subordinates, to a translation authorized by, as he put it, "a deceased king of England who certainly was no prophet" (1856: v). Nor did he agree that the Authorized Version created the standard from which all subsequent revisions derived. He rather staked Jews' claims on the Bible in the original; that was their source of legitimacy. By publishing a translation "made by one of themselves," he placed Jews on an equal footing with Protestants. To the extent that his translation could claim to be a better approximation of the original, he could even insist that Jews were more than equals.

Leeser was not alone in seeking independent legitimacy through a Bible translation. His Philadelphia contemporary, Bishop Francis P. Kenrick, was making a new Catholic translation of the Bible at roughly the same time (1849–1860), though whether the two men knew each other is not clear. Kenrick's translation principles, of course, differed from Leeser's, since the Catholic translator, though informed by the

Hebrew, "did not always feel at liberty to render closely where it would imply a departure from the Vulgate" (Fogarty: 171). But the two translators shared a common desire: to translate the Bible into an English version that was both visibly different from, and arguably better than, the Authorized (Protestant) Version that the majority of Americans held dear.

The translation that Leeser finally produced in 1853, after fifteen years of work, derived from the original Hebrew, and depended, according to the preface, only on traditional Jewish commentators and "the studies of modern German Israelites" (including that of the German Reform leader, Ludwig Philipson). Leeser avoided making use of Christian or English language scholarship, boasting with only slight exaggeration that "not an English book has been consulted except Bagster's Bible" (even this exception was deleted in a later preface.) Although he was more familiar with Christian works than he admitted, he wanted to stress that his was a *Jewish* translation. When he was done, he pridefully pointed to the many differences which distinguished his version from the authorized one. His only concession to the King James was to follow its old English style, which, he felt, "for simplicity cannot be surpassed," and to conform to many of its spellings (Sussman, 1985).

Leeser strove to render the Hebrew text into English "as literally as possible," even at the expense of stylistic beauty (1856: vi). This immediately set his translation apart from the flowery King James, and simultaneously ensured that it would face criticism on literary grounds, criticism that was frequently deserved. Leeser provoked Israel Abrahams's scorn (1920: 254–59) by abandoning the standard translation of Ps 23:2: "He maketh me to lie down in green pastures," for the awkward, if slightly more literal "in pastures of tender grass he causeth me to lie down." "The heavens relate the glory of God; and the expanse telleth of the work of his hands" (Ps 19:1) rang similarly awkward, especially when contrasted with "the heavens declare the glory of God; and the firmament sheweth his handiwork," the King James reading. Leeser did carry over the standard and to his mind literal "until Shiloh come" for his translation of the controversial passage in Gen 49:10, which Christians have interpreted as foreshadowing Jesus. (The new Jewish Publication Society translation, by contrast, reads "So that tribute shall come to him," following the Midrash.) Rather than deviating from the plain meaning as he saw it, he appended a long explanatory footnote, which concludes by asserting that "the pious and intelligent reader will have enough to satisfy all doubts."

Matitiahu Tsevat (1958) has pointed out that in his quest for literalism "Leeser wanted the impossible." Translation by its very nature involves interpretation. Furthermore, all Bible translators are heir to interpretive traditions which, consciously or not, shape their scriptural understanding. Calls for "literalism," or movements "back to the Bible," Tsevat shows, really seek to cloak with legitimacy efforts aimed at replacing one mode of interpretation with another.

In Leeser's case, literalism usually meant resorting to rabbinic exegesis. Thus, in Exod 21:6, dealing with the laws for servants; the King James translation reads straightforwardly "his master shall bore his ear through with an awl; and he shall serve him for ever." Leeser, influenced by rabbinic interpretation of Lev 25:10 and, likely as not a raging American debate over the relationship between the biblical form of slavery and the Southern one,[1] translated the last clause "and he shall serve him till the jubilee"—which, of course, is not what the verse literally says. It must be admitted that this is an unusual instance. It was more often the case that Leeser encased his interpolations in parentheses. Instead of halving Samuel "lying down in the temple of the Lord," for example, he more demurely had him sleep "in (the hall of) the temple of the Lord" (1 Sam 3:3)—a bow to decorum that the commentators endorsed, but that literalists assuredly would not.

Isaac Leeser labored initially under the assumption that Jews alone would be interested in his translation. In 1845, when his Hebrew-English edition of the Pentateuch appeared, he presented the volume only to his "Jewish friends," explaining that "I speak of my Jewish friends in particular, for however much a revised translation may be desired by all believers in the word of God, there is no probability that the gentiles will encourage any publication of this nature emanating from a Jewish writer" (1845: iii). Leeser, however, was mistaken. By the time his full Bible with notes appeared in 1853, he himself realized that those "who are of a different persuasion" might indeed find the work valuable "as exhibiting. . . the progress of biblical criticism among ancient and modern Israelites" (iv). When Rev. Charles Hodge, a leading Presbyterian theologian at Princeton Theological Seminary, recommended his (Leeser's) translation in the *Princeton Review*, and called for "a work on a similar plan from a competent Christian scholar," Leeser happily reprinted the review in the *Occident* (1854: 360), the Jewish monthly that he founded and edited.

Christian interest in Leeser's work reflects yet another aspect of the Jewish-Christian relationship that deserves attention. More than it is generally recognized, American Protestants in the nineteenth century sought out and respected Jewish expositions of the Hebrew Scriptures. The roots of this interest, of course, lay in Europe, where Christian scholars had overtly or covertly been studying the Bible with Jews for centuries. They knew, as did their nineteenth-century successors, that Jewish religious leaders understood Hebrew, read the Bible in the original, and studied traditional Jewish commentators—or at least claimed to. But beyond this, especially in America, many Protestants saw Jews as lineal descendants of the biblical figures they read and heard about. According to the Richmond *Constitutional Whig* in 1829:

> When we see one of these people, and remember that we have been told by good authority, that he is an exact copy of the Jew who worshipped in the Second Temple two thousand years ago—that his physiognomy and religious opinions—that the usages and customs of his tribe are still the same, we feel that profound respect which antiquity inspires. (Ezekiel and Lichtenstein: 56)

Protestants who adhered to this view naturally assumed that Jews preserved special knowledge of the biblical world that others did not share. Acting on that basis, they often turned to Jews when Hebrew or Old Testament questions arose.

Two early American Jews, Jonathan (Jonas) Horwitz and Solomon Jackson received non-Jewish encouragement when they sought to publish Hebrew texts of the Bible—a much needed task considering that in 1812, by Horwitz's estimate, fewer than a dozen Hebrew Bibles were available for purchase in the whole United States. Horwitz, a scholarly European immigrant who brought Hebrew type with him when he came to Philadelphia, collected recommendations from twelve Christian clergymen and numerous subscriptions for his work, but eventually transferred his rights to the edition to Thomas Dobson who completed the task based on the text of van der Hooght's Hebrew Bible that Horwitz had prepared. The Dobson Bible (1814) is the first independently produced edition of the Hebrew Bible in the United States (Vaxer; Wolf and Whiteman: 308–311; Fein: 75–76).

Jackson, better known as editor of *The Jew*, an antimissionary periodical and the first Jewish magazine in America, planned an even more ambitious undertaking: a Hebrew-English linear Bible. His earlier vituperative attacks on leading Protestants notwithstanding, three clergymen, including the Episcopal Bishop of New York, John Henry Hobart, joined six leading Jews in recommending him and urging support for his work. One of the clergymen specifically praised the fact that the "author and editor belong to the *literal* family of Abraham," suggesting that this improved the proposed volume's credibility (Jackson). Apparently, the recommendation did not help, for the book never appeared.

Americans also looked to Jews from time to time to defend the Bible against "infidels." *Letters of Certain Jews to Monsieur Voltaire* (1795), a French work defending both Jews and the integrity of Scripture, appeared in two American editions, as did England's David Levi's *A Defence of the Old Testament in a Series of Letters Addressed to Thomas Paine* (1797). Thomas Jefferson, who read Levi's earlier *Letters to Dr. Priestly*, noted in 1816 that Levi "avails himself all his advantage over his adversaries by his superior knowledge of the Hebrew, speaking in the very language of divine communication, while they can only fumble on with conflicting and disputed translations" (Lipscomb: 469–70; Abrahams and Miles). Three decades later, when the Bible was "threatened" by new discoveries in geology, Jonathan Horwitz, who since the appearance of the Dobson Bible had become a medical doctor, published *A Defence of the Cosmogony of Moses* (1839), a "vindication" of the Bible "from the attacks of geologists," based on a close reading of the Hebrew text (which, he lamented, was so little known), a cursory reading of geological theory, and a firm conviction that "not the slightest foundation is to be seen in the Holy Record for any interpretation lengthening the age of the world beyond 6,000 years" (29). Later still, Rabbi Isaac Mayer Wise, the leading figure in American Reform Judaism, attempted to defend tradition against what he called the theory of "homo-brutalism," as expounded by Charles Darwin (1876: 47–69).

More commonly, Americans looked to Jews to teach them the language of the Bible: Hebrew and Hebrew grammar. Many of the Hebrew grammars used by Americans were composed by Jews or Jewish converts to Christianity, and numerous Jews taught Hebrew to Christian students (Chomsky; Fellman). Isaac Nordheimer, the most notable early American Hebrew grammarian, wrote the highly original *Critical Grammar of the Hebrew Language* (1835–1841) and was the first Jew to teach Hebrew at New York University (Pool; Neill). Joshua Seixas, son of the famous Shearith Israel minister and also the author of a Hebrew grammar (1833, 1834), taught Hebrew at various colleges in Ohio. His best known student was Joseph Smith, the Mormon prophet, who held Seixas in high regard (Davis, 1970: 347–54). Jews continued to be associated with Hebrew and Hebrew studies later on in the century, in a few cases at the university level.

The fact that these Jews were exceptional—most American Jews could not understand Hebrew—detracted not at all from the image of all Jews as biblical experts. McGuffey's *Eclectic Third Reader* taught school children to "consider the Jews as the keepers of the Old Testament. It was their own sacred volume, which contained the most extraordinary predictions concerning the infidelity of their nation, and the rise, progress, and extensive prevalence of Christianity" (Westerhoff: 139). Seeing Jews in this light, Christians periodically called on Jews to offer biblical views on questions of the day. Jewish leaders presented widely publicized testimony regarding "The Biblical View of Slavery" (the question divided Jews as much as it did non-Jews), the biblical view of temperance, the biblical view of capital punishment, and even on the biblical view of baptism (Kalisch: 37). Biblical magazines, particularly late nineteenth-century ones like *The Old Testament Student,* welcomed Jewish participation. Jewish lectures and books on biblical subjects received respectful Christian attention. Even those who considered Jews misguided and doomed recognized that Jews preserved important traditions and could be valuable assets in the battle against infidelity. Not surprisingly, therefore, Leeser's Jewish Bible translation met with considerable approbation.

THE RISE OF JEWISH BIBLE SCHOLARSHIP IN THE UNITED STATES

The decades following the publication of Isaac Leeser's translation saw the first flickering of Jewish biblical scholarship on American shores. Harry Orlinsky, in his valuable survey (1974), highlights the pioneering efforts in this area of Isidor Kalisch, Adolph Huebsch, Isaac Mayer Wise, Michael Heilprin, and Benjamin Szold. All of these men were trained in Europe, all but Heilprin were active rabbis, and all immigrated with the great wave of central European Jews that swelled America's Jewish population from less than 15,000 in 1840 to about 250,000 just forty years later. A desire to strengthen the hands of the faithful against missionaries and biblical critics motivated some of these men, notably Kalisch in his *Wegweiser für rationelle Forschungen in den biblischen Schriften* (1853), and Wise in his *Pronaos to Holy Writ* (Kalisch, 1891: 14–18; Wise, 1954: 180; Sandmel). Others, especially Michael Heilprin, best known as an editor for *Appleton's Cyclopaedia,* "accepted, not grudgingly, but with enthusiasm and delight, those views of the Old Testament which have been defended by Graf and Kuenen and Wellhausen and Reuss" (Pollak: 9). Indeed, Heilprin's articles about biblical criticism in the *Nation* helped familiarize Americans with what these European scholars were doing, and his magnum opus, *The Historical Poetry of the Ancient Hebrews Translated and Critically Examined* (1879–1880), carried critical scholarship forward and won considerable academic acclaim.

The lonely efforts of these scholarly pioneers contrast with the widespread neglect of biblical studies on the part of the mass of American Jews. Heavily engaged as most were in mercantile pursuits, they found little time for any kind of study; critical scholarship was certainly beyond them. Immigrants did sometimes send their intellectually gifted youngsters back to Germany for advanced degrees, a practice that continued down to World War I. Once there, however, few American Jews took the opportunity to gain mastery in biblical scholarship—and for good reasons.

First of all, they found the subject of the Bible heavily freighted with Christian theology, if not anti-Judaism, and particularly with the dogma of the Hebrew Scriptures as *praeparatio* for the New Testament. Second, they learned that the Jewish renaissance movement known as *Das Wissenschaft des Judentums* generally excluded biblical studies from its purview. It concentrated instead on rabbinic literature, which had been sorely neglected and stood in dire need of redemption for scientific research. Leopold Zunz, programmatic founder of the Wissenschaft movement, was content to leave biblical scholarship in Christian hands. Many American Jews followed suit, believing that the Bible was, as Max Margolis put it, "a non-Jewish subject" (Gordis: 2). Finally, American Jews knew that biblical studies held open to them almost no promise of gainful employment. Positions in biblical studies at major American universities remained generally the preserve of Protestants, many of them ministers. Jews—witness the case of Arnold Ehrlich or Israel Eitan— found themselves excluded, even if their contributions did win recognition elsewhere. This may help explain why no Jews numbered among the founders of the Society of Biblical Literature (SBL), and only a mere handful (notably the father and son teams of Rabbi Marcus Jastrow and Prof. Morris Jastrow and Rabbi Gustav Gottheil and Prof. Richard J. H Gottheil) took out membership during its first decade, even though the regulations of the society explicitly specified that conditions of membership were to disregard what it termed "ecclesiastical affiliation." By the semicentennial meeting, the roster of members included at least forty-three Jews, of whom, it would seem, seventeen bore the title "Rabbi," and twenty were professional Jewish scholars. Whether the proportionately large number of rabbis may be taken as indicative of broader intellectual horizons and deeper scholarly interests on the part of the Jewish clergy of two generations ago than is the case with their modern successors or whether it means that a relatively large number of would-be Jewish biblical scholars turned to the rabbinate as the outlet for their thwarted aspirations in an era of complete lack of opportunity of academic employment is hard to say. What is worthy of more than the mere passing mention possible here, is that a half-century ago Jewish scholars in Talmudics and the traditional branches of medieval learning maintained an abiding and serious interest in biblical studies, something apparently made all but impossible today due to the unprecedented explosion of scholarship and research, pursued with ever-increasing degrees of specialization. We refer to the presence on the 1930 membership rolls of such illustrious names as Cyrus Adler, Salo Baron, Israel Davidson, Alexander Marx, Ralph Marcus, Chaim Tchernowitz, Harry Wolfson and Solomon Zeitlin (*Journal of Biblical Literature*, ii, xvii, xx, lii).

Theoretically, of course, Jews and Christians could join together on a scientific basis to study the Bible. Rabbi Bernhard Felsenthal made this clear in 1884 when, in an article in *The Old Testament Student,* he declared that "a Bible scholar should free his mind from all misleading preconceptions, from all sectarian bias;—truth, nothing but the truth, should be his aim." In fact, however, this proved easier said than done. William Rainey Harper, although agreeing with Felsenthal's *"principle . . .* that, whether Jews or Christian, we are to seek the truth" nevertheless reminded the rabbi that "Our paths diverge. Our conceptions of the Old Testament must, of necessity, be largely molded by what we find in the New."

American Jewish scholars found themselves more easily welcomed as fellows in the broader realm of Semitic studies, a field which was from a theological point of view far safer than biblical studies, yet did nevertheless still bear on the biblical text and history. Cyrus Adler (1926), in his cursory survey of "The Beginnings of Semitic Studies in America," mentions several very early American Jewish contributions to the subject, most of them dealing with language and grammar, as well as the valuable if amateurish pre-Civil War work of Mendes I. Cohen who brought to America a large collection of Egyptian antiquities, later deposited at Johns Hopkins University. More rigorous works of scholarship began to appear only in the last quarter of the nineteenth century, when, as part of a larger movement to upgrade American higher education, Semitics programs were initiated, first at the graduate level at Johns Hopkins, and later at other major universities. At Hopkins, under the direction of Paul Haupt, brought over from Göttingen in 1883, such Jewish students of Semitics as Cyrus Adler, William Rosenau, and Aaron Ember embarked on their first serious scholarly endeavors. At the same time, Maurice Bloomfield, already a professor at Hopkins, was beginning his pioneering studies of Sanskrit, which also held important implications for students of Semitics. Other Jewish Semitists of this period included Richard J. H. Gottheil, who became chairman of the Semitics Department at Columbia University; Morris Jastrow, who became Professor of Semitic Studies at the University of Pennsylvania; and Max L. Margolis, of whom more below, who from 1909 until his death occupied the chair in biblical philology at Dropsie College. Gottheil, Jastrow, and Margolis all served terms as president of the Society of Biblical Literature: Gottheil as its first Jewish president, in 1903, and the other two, respectively, in 1916 and 1923.

That so many Jews found a home in Semitic studies is not accidental. Jews, particularly the great Jewish philanthropist Jacob Schiff supported Semitic studies with liberal endowments in the belief that Jews were, in Schiff's words, "the modern representatives of the Semitic people." To combat "social prejudice and ostracism" against Jews, Schiff felt that "opportunities should be created for a more thorough study and a better knowledge of Semitic history and civilization, so that the world shall better understand and acknowledge the debt it owes to the Semitic people" (Adler, 1929: 21). To this end, Schiff supported archeological acquisitions and excavations in the Near East, built the Harvard Semitics Museum, and founded the Semitic and Hebrew departments of the New York Public Library and the Library of Congress. Other Jews supported Semitic studies at Yale and the University of Chicago (Chiel; Fever: 433). Although for the time being biblical studies remained a separate domain, outside the realm of Semitic studies, in fact, albeit through the backdoor and under the guise of a more acceptable rubric, the groundwork for Jewish Bible scholarship in America had been laid. A new era was about to begin.

THE FIRST JEWISH PUBLICATION SOCIETY TRANSLATION

As biblical and Semitic studies developed in Jewish scholarly circles, popular pressure mounted within the American Jewish community for a new Bible translation to replace Isaac Leeser's. The late nineteenth century witnessed a great upsurge of general interest in the study of the Bible. In Jewish circles, as also in Christian ones, the demand for Bibles that embodied "the Jewish point of view" reached unprecedented levels. A Jewish cultural revival took place—a fact that the onrush of East European Jewish immigration during this period usually overshadows—and during one stunning decade the Jewish Publication Society, the American Jewish Historical Society, the National Council of Jewish Women, and the Jewish Chautauqua Society all came into being, while at the same time preparations began for publication of the *Jewish Encyclopedia*. Except for the American Jewish Historical Society every one of the above had as one of its aims the furthering of biblical scholarship or the encouraging of Bible study by the laity. "There has been, during the past ten years, a great awakening among our people," Daniel P. Hays correctly noted in 1901. He considered the change "a realization that the Jew has not become great by his material achievements, but by his contribution toward the higher ideals of life and by his endeavors toward the uplifting of the race" (*American Jewish Year Book*, 1902: 216).

Christian interest in Jewish work on the Bible also reached new heights during this period. Rabbis, notably Emil G. Hirsch, Bernhard Felsenthal, and Gustav Gottheil received invitations to teach the Bible to Christian audiences, while Rabbi Moses Gries in Cleveland reported having "many requests from non-Jews who wish to secure a translation accepted by Jewish scholars" (*JPS Annual Reports*, 1897: 24).

In the face of all this popular interest in Jewish biblical exegesis, the Leeser Bible, although it had become the standard Anglo-Jewish Bible, nevertheless proved totally inadequate. First of all, it was too expensive. The smallest edition cost one dollar, much more than the equivalent Protestant edition, and more also than many people were apparently willing to pay. Over and over Jews called for "a cheap edition of the English Bible." The Central Conference of American Rabbis, in 1909, thought that a fifty-cent Bible was all that the market could bear (*CCAR Year Book*, 1895: 25; 1909: 155).

Even had the price been right, however, the Leeser Bible would still have proved unsatisfactory. Its English style was embarrassing and in some cases unintelligible. Its "literal" approach to the Bible along with Isaac Leeser's professed belief "in the Scriptures as they have been handed down to us, as also in the truth and authenticity of prophecies and their ultimate literal fulfillment" (1856: v) found fewer and fewer adherents. It was also antiquated; biblical scholarship had advanced enormously since Leeser's day, permitting new translations of formerly obscure passages. Most important of all, a new Protestant translation of the Bible had appeared, the (Anglican) English Revised Version (1885), which was produced by some of the greatest Christian scholars of the day, and from the point of view of biblical studies was relatively up-to-date. Leeser's translation paled by comparison.

It did not follow, however, that a whole new Jewish translation had to be produced from scratch. As had been true with the King James, so too with the English Revised Version Jews could simply have issued a "Jewish revised version," repairing offensive renderings (the ERV continued such Christological King James readings as "virgin" for Isa 7:14), and putting the biblical books into a traditional Jewish order and format. The Jewish Religious Education Board in London made the task of composing a Jewish revision easier by publishing sixteen pages of corrections titled *Appendix to the Revised Version* (1896). In 1907, the Central Conference of American Rabbis (CCAR) resolved to carry out the project:

> Be it resolved, that in view of the immediate need of a cheap edition of the English Bible in the best available translation, the C.C.A.R. enter into negotiations with the publishers of the Revised version for an issue of the Old Testament exclusively (*CCAR Year Book*, 1907: 35).

Negotiations proceeded, and before long, Oxford University Press agreed to issue a special edition of its translation, complete with a sixteen-page appendix prepared by the CCAR, containing "corrections and emendations of the text necessary from the Jewish standpoint" (*CCAR Year Book*, 1908: 149).

Rabbi Samuel Schulman of Temple Beth El in New York rejoiced at the "implied recognition of a Jewish body by the Christian world, in so important a matter as changes in a widespread version of the Bible." But at the last minute, the CCAR backed out of the undertaking. Instead, it accepted an invitation from the Jewish Publication Society to cooperate in "issuing an English translation of the Bible under Jewish auspices" (JPS Publication Committee Minutes, 5 April 1908).

Whatever benefits cooperation with Oxford University Press might have promised faded before the renewed possibility of a translation produced by Jews independently.

The Jewish Publication Society (JPS) had been talking about a new Jewish Bible translation since 1892. Three years later, in the very midst of the heady revival already described, it proudly announced that a new translation was underway. Specialization and division of labor, concepts much discussed at the time, seem to have left their impact on the JPS, for it decided to produce its translation as a series of independent volumes, each one by a different person—mostly rabbis with European training. Marcus Jastrow, who had immigrated to America in 1866 and become one of American Jewry's leading luminaries (author of a Hebrew-Aramaic-English dictionary that is still in print) was appointed general editor. He was aided by Kaufmann Kohler and Frederick de Sola Mendes: both rabbis, both trained abroad. Rhapsodic reports of progress—descriptions of editors "busily pursuing the work of revising and editing the books of the Bible as they came to them from the hands of the translators"—had to be tempered annually by tedious reminders that "the work is necessarily slow, and. . . a considerable time must elapse before the entire Bible can be ready for publication" (*JPS Annual Reports*, 1899: 17). By the time Jastrow died in 1903, only Kaufmann Kohler's translation of Psalms, revised by the editors, had actually been published. Although work on a few other books had proceeded, a new translation of the whole Bible seemed more distant than ever.

Solomon Schechter, freshly arrived from Cambridge University and viewed in his day as America's preeminent Judaic scholar, replaced Jastrow as translation chairman, but he soon wearied of the task. The endlessly complex and hopelessly disorganized manner in which the translation was being pursued and a chronic scarcity of funds led him to submit his resignation in mid-1907. But just as the project seemed in danger of collapse, the CCAR overture to Oxford University Press became public. At first, Judge Mayer Sulzberger (1843–1923), chairman of the JPS Publication Committee and a lay scholar in his own right (Davis, 1965: 362–65), considered the CCAR scheme a good one, and wrote to Rabbi David Philipson that "it might be well for the Publication Society to consider the question of joining the Central Conference in its project of disseminating the Revised Version as widely as possible." A few months of reflection, however, convinced him that "official recognition" by Jews of the English Revised Version could be inappropriate (Philipson Papers). Since Philipson was coming around to the same view, Cyrus Adler, long the power behind the throne at JPS, stepped in and hammered out an agreement that both the JPS and the CCAR accepted.

Both sides agreed on "the desirability of issuing an English version of the Bible under Jewish auspices," and both sides agreed on the need to produce the new Bible as quickly as possible ("two years would be an outside limit"). Secretly, both sides also agreed that the only way to accomplish this feat was "that the text of the Revised Version be used as the basis, and that the revision of it. . . be primarily of such a nature that it will remove all un-Jewish and anti-Jewish phrases, expressions, renderings and usages" (JPS Publication Committee Minutes, 5 April 1908). The new Bible, in short, would conform to the latest Protestant fashion but would still be distinctive enough to bear a separate Jewish label.

Although it is likely that nobody noticed the fact at the time, the discussions between Adler, Sulzberger, and Philipson evidenced the growing Americanization of Jewish scholarship in the New World. All three of the men were products of the American educational system (Sulzberger, though born abroad, immigrated with his parents as a young boy) and had obtained the bulk of their Jewish knowledge in the United States. Perhaps it is not surprising that the man selected to be the new editor-in-chief of the Bible translation was also, at least in part, American trained: Max L. Margolis. Born in Russia, Margolis immigrated to America from Berlin in 1889 at the age of twenty-three, and two years later under Richard Gottheil received the first Ph. D. in oriental studies ever awarded by Columbia University. His subject was "an attempt to improve the damaged text of the Talmud through reference to variant readings in Rashi's Commentary on the Talmud, demonstrated through the tractate Erubhin," and Margolis wrote the thesis in Latin. But given the difficulty of obtaining rabbinic sources in the United States, he then shifted his focus to Semitics, and quickly gained scholarly recognition. The depth and breadth of his learning, coupled with his fine command of the English language, made him the ideal person to head up the translation effort (Gordis; Orlinsky, 1974: 305–10).

As editor-in-chief, Margolis singlehandedly prepared all of the first drafts of the Bible translation "with the aid of previous versions and with constant consultation of Jewish authorities." More than anyone originally expected, he also proceeded to deviate from the English Revised Version, sometimes on scholarly, not just religious, grounds. Only when he was done did he submit his drafts to an editorial committee consisting of six scholars, perfectly balanced so as to span both the Jewish academic world (two each from the Jewish Theological Seminary, Hebrew Union College, and Dropsie College) and the spectrum of Jewish observance. Cyrus Adler, well known for his administrative capabilities, chaired the translation committee, thereby ensuring that the work progressed and that the deliberations remained at least relatively peaceful.

Viewed retrospectively, the Bible translation committee, aside from Margolis himself, represented much less than the best that Jewish Bible scholarship in America had to offer. Morris Jastrow, Casper Levias, William Rosenau, Moses Buttenwieser, Julian Morgenstern, Jacob Hoschander, and, the most talented of all, Arnold Bogumil Ehrlich (Kabokoff), although recognized by their peers as qualified biblical and Semitic scholars, were conspicuously absent (several had contributed to the abortive 1895 JPS translation effort). Scholarly rabbis representing the CCAR (Samuel Schulman, David Philipson, and Hebrew Union College President Kaufmann Kohler), and wide-ranging Jewish scholars (Solomon Schechter, Joseph Jacobs, and Cyrus Adler) representing the JPS were deemed more suitable for the task. Religious politics, personality factors, facility in the English language, and, above all, the desire to move ahead expeditiously without becoming bogged down in scholarly fine points may explain this decision; evidence is lacking. Still, and despite all good intentions, unforeseen, highly delicate problems continually cropped up.

To cite just one example, at the very end of the translation process, a fierce and quite revealing dispute broke out over how best to render Isa 9:5 (9:6 in Christian texts). The King James translation exuded Christology:

> For unto us a child is born, unto us a son, is given: and the government shall be upon his shoulder: and his name shall be called Wonderful, Counsellor, The Mighty God, The Everlasting Father, The Prince of Peace.

The English Revised Version followed suit, with only minor modifications in style. Jewish translators properly insisted that nothing in Isaiah's original referred to the future (Leeser's text read "government is placed on his shoulders and his name is called. . ."), but they had trouble with the translation of "*śar šālôm.*" Leeser employed the phrase "prince of peace," using the lower case to avoid (presumably) misinterpretation. Samuel Schulman of the JPS translation committee urged his colleagues to follow the same practice, since "it calls attention to the fact, that we wish to avoid any possible Christological interpretation of the phrase." Max L. Margolis and Cyrus Adler, by contrast, insisted that using the lower case would imply that the "prince of peace" was a human being, "exactly the thing we wished to avoid." Strongly worded letters flew back and forth. The final translation, clearly influenced more by the desire to instruct Christians and defend Jews than by considerations of scholarship, banished "prince of peace" altogether:

> For a child is born unto us,
> A son is given unto us;
> And the government is upon his shoulder;
> And his name is called
> [a] Pele-joez-el-gibbor-Abi-ad-sar-shalom
> That is, Wonderful in counsel is God the Mighty, the
> everlasting father, the Ruler of peace.[2]

Many similar compromises had to be hammered out by the committee before it could, as a group, pronounce itself satisfied.

Seven years after it was promised, The Holy Scriptures finally appeared in print in 1917. The event received considerable publicity and this was fitting, since the Bible would sell more copies than any other JPS volume: over one million to date. The impact of the new Bible, however, went much further. As Abraham Neuman put it retrospectively:

> It was a Bible translation to which American Jews could point with pride as the creation of the Jewish consciousness on a par with similar products of the Catholic and Protestant churches. It was a peace-offering to the Jewish and the non-Jewish world. To the Jews it presented a Bible which combined the spirit of Jewish tradition with the results of biblical scholarship, ancient, mediaeval and modern. To non-Jews it opened the gateway of Jewish tradition in the interpretation of the Word of God. (156)

Neuman's comment encapsulates the major reasons why Jews felt that the enormous expenditure of time, energy, and money that the Bible translation represented had in the end been thoroughly justified. Having a Bible they could proudly call their own, the product of their community's scholars, in some cases native born and native trained, American Jews felt better both about themselves and about their relations with non-Jewish neighbors. The new Bible translation served, in a sense, like a rite of passage. With its completion, Jews looked forward hopefully toward a coming new era.

With respect to non-Jews, the community proved with its new Bible that it could successfully compete. The fact that Jews actually formed only three percent of the population made no difference. They acted as if they held complete parity with Protestants and Catholics. The others had long had official English Bibles; now Jews had an "official" Bible too. It took only a few more decades for this myth of the "triple melting pot"—Protestant-Catholic-Jew, all three equivalent—to gain acceptance on a broad level, a development of enormous importance in American and American Jewish history (Herberg).

The new Bible translation also allowed Jews to compete with Christians on the level of religious scholarship. The scholarly trappings of the English Revised Version had formerly given its Christological renderings an air of authority, which Leeser's "old fashioned" Bible could not pierce. In the formidable scholarship behind the new Jewish version, however, the English Revised Version met its match. Indeed, the Jewish translators, by boasting in their preface that they "took into account the existing English versions," as well as "the standard commentaries, ancient and modern, the translations already made for the Jewish Publication Society of America, the divergent renderings from the Revised Version prepared for the Jews of England, the marginal notes of the Revised Version, . . . the changes of the American Committee of Revisers, . . . the ancient versions," "Talmudic and midrashic allusions, . . . all available Jewish commentators, [and] all the important non-Jewish commentators," implied that their translation was even better than the Christian version. This triumphalist magniloquence was somewhat tempered by the pluralistic expression of gratitude, also found in the preface, "for the work of our non-Jewish predecessors, such as the Authorized Version with its admirable diction, which can never be surpassed, as well as for the Revised Version with its ample learning." But it still remained distant indeed from the near syncretism propounded by those who had earlier advocated that a modified version of the authorized Anglican revision be given a Jewish imprimatur.

Beyond competition lay the matter of internal Jewish pride. Solomon Schechter had long insisted that the Jew needs "his own Bible, not one mortgaged by the King James version" (*American Jewish Year Book*, 1914: 173). Though he was dead by the time that the JPS Bible appeared, its preface echoed his sentiments: "The Jew cannot afford to have his Bible translation prepared for him by others. He cannot have it as a gift, even as he cannot borrow his soul from others" (vii). More clearly than before, Jews stressed here their belief in a special, deeply spiritual Jewish relationship with the *Tanakh*, one that set Jewish and Christian readers of the Bible apart from one another. Since, as we have seen, American Christians had long before accepted the notion that the Old Testament was the Jews' "own sacred volume," for Jews to defend their separateness on this basis was thoroughly acceptable. Separateness, of course, did not imply strict exclusiveness. Indeed, the new Bible translation's preface specifically hoped that "the non-Jewish world" would "welcome" the translation. Instead, the Jewish Publication Society's Bible translation, like Leeser's before it, reflected the ambivalent nature of Jewish-Christian relations in America, the countervailing forces that on the one hand pushed Jews and Christians together and on the other hand kept them separate and distinct.

As a symbol, the new Bible also went further. It boldly announced the American Jewish community's emergence on the world stage as a center of Jewish life and creativity. "The historical necessity for translation was repeated with all the great changes in Israel's career," the new Bible's preface significantly declared. Then, with growing exuberance, it proclaimed that "the greatest change in the life of Israel during the last two generations" had taken place in the New World:

We have grown under providence both in numbers and in importance, so that we constitute now the greatest section of Israel living in a single country outside of Russia. We are only following in the footsteps of our greatest predecessors when, with the growth of our numbers, we have applied ourselves to the sacred task of preparing a new translation of the Bible into the English language, which, unless all signs fail, is to become the current speech of the majority of the children of Israel (vi).

The "sacred task" alluded to, akin to the biblical injunction that a king write for himself a copy of the law (Deut 17:18), signified legitimacy, seeming confirmation of American Jewry's momentous destiny. Along with the publication of *Jewish Encyclopedia* completed in 1906, the founding of the American Jewish Committee in the same year, and other developments in the years immediately before and after World War I, the new Bible translation reflected American Jewry's changing self-image, its growing cultural independence, its quest for preeminence. The community had arrived and was seeking the recognition that it thought it deserved.

THE NEW JEWISH PUBLICATION SOCIETY TRANSLATION

The years that followed the publication of the JPS translation confirmed the prescience of those who had predicted that a new era in American Jewish scholarship was aborning. The development of great Jewish libraries in the United States, the availability of positions in Jewish studies at American Jewish institutions of higher learning, particularly Hebrew Union College, the Jewish Theological Seminary, Dropsie College, Yeshiva University, the Jewish Institute of Religion, and Hebrew Theological College, and the mass migration of Jewish scholars from Europe to America's shores, particularly in the 1930s, adumbrated America's emergence as the center of Jewish scholarship in the diaspora even before the destruction of European centers of Jewish scholarship in World War II. After Hitler had wreaked his terrible toll, the only question remaining was how well American Jewry would measure up.

In terms of biblical scholarship, the answer was quite well. As early as 1930, Jews comprised some nine percent of SBL members (by contrast, they formed three and one-half percent of the population), and as indicated above, these were about evenly divided between professional Jewish scholars and scholarly-inclined rabbis. To be sure, few of these scholars actually held positions in biblical studies. Most were either Semitists or scholars of later periods of Jewish life, who nevertheless maintained an abiding and serious interest in biblical studies. Still, biblical studies had acquired a greatly elevated status among American Jews, far outstripping Talmud and rabbinics, which had held pride of place among traditional Jews in Europe. Indeed, the first full set of the Talmud was not printed in America until 1944 (Eidelberg), and not a single native-born professor of Talmud could be found in this country until recently. By comparison, Bible scholarship fared well.

At least three factors account for this interest in biblical studies among American Jews. First, Reform Judaism laid heavy stress on the Bible, particularly the prophetic writings, which were held up as ethical exemplars to contemporary Jews and non-Jews alike. Having declared themselves independent of rabbinic legislation, Reform Jews sought legitimacy in the Bible, frequently using it in proof-text fashion against conversionists on the one hand and traditional Jews on the other. This, of course, sometimes made for tendentious scholarship, but it did at least direct greater Jewish attention to the Bible than had hitherto been the case (Plaut: 224–31; Agus: 282–33).

The Zionist movement was the second factor that lay behind the revival of biblical studies among American Jews. Although Zionists tended to stress different chapters from the Bible than did Reform Jews, they too turned to the Bible for inspiration and ideological justification. The Bible legitimated the Jewish claim to a homeland. Biblical archaeology linked the Jewish past and the Jewish present. Spoken Hebrew, revived by the Zionist movement, was modeled on biblical Hebrew, not rabbinic Hebrew. Secular Zionists may have disdained works of Jewish law and scorned theology, but they respected the Bible. They also respected biblical scholars.

Finally, the interfaith movement led to greater Jewish attention to the Bible. As it emerged in the post-World War I era, the interfaith movement stressed elements common to Jews and Christians, particularly the Hebrew Bible. Not only did the Bible serve to legitimate efforts aimed at promoting "better understanding," it also frequently provided the central themes for dialogue groups and clergy institutes. Bible study led Jews and Christians to better appreciate the roots of what was termed "Judeo-Christian civilization." Indirectly, it also stimulated Jews to deepen their own knowledge of what the Bible was all about (Sussman).

Notwithstanding American Jews' growing interest in the Bible, Jewish Bible scholarship still remained largely the preserve of those born and trained abroad. There were already some important exceptions to this rule, among them Julian Morgenstern, Sheldon Blank, H. L. Ginsberg, and Harry M. Orlinsky (the last two were born in Canada, and all but Orlinsky received their advanced degrees abroad), but as late as 1948 only six of twenty-five prominent American Jewish scholars in the field of Bible, as enumerated by Ralph Marcus, could actually be termed both native-born and native-trained—the last time this would be true. The growth of academic opportunities in the postwar period, coupled with the coming-of-age of American-born children of immigrants soon resulted in a preponderance of locally produced scholars. Of thirty-one Jewish contributors to the *Interpreter's Dictionary of the Bible* (1962), for example, all but four were Americans. In the *Encyclopaedia Judaica*, published in Jerusalem in 1972, the divisional editor, associate divisional editor, and half of the departmental editors in Bible were all American Jews, and the other half was Israelis—an accurate reflection of the two mutually interacting centers of Jewish Bible scholarship in the world today.

   This latter point deserves more notice than it is usually given. There exists today a huge and ever-increasing body of high caliber scholarly literature in the Hebrew language produced by Israeli-trained scholars, mainly native born, who think and express themselves naturally in Hebrew, and whose researches appear in a variety of Hebrew scholarly journals, in the various annuals of the five universities, in the multivolumed *Encyclopaedia Biblica Hebraica,* in a large number of doctoral dissertations, and in the numerous volumes turned out annually by Israeli publishing houses. The Israelis are in daily contact with the land, its geography, topography, and geology, its climatic conditions, the nature of its soil, its flora and fauna, its natural resources. Archaeology of the biblical period is a national Israeli pastime. Inevitably, all this must leave, and it surely does, its impress on the direction and coloration of biblical scholarship in Israel. The history of the Hebrew language, the history of the land (especially geopolitical conditions), biblical history, military history, the realia of biblical life, the literary artistry of the narrative, masoretic studies—all these topics are fruitfully pursued with a vigor and a passion that is characteristic of those exploring their own civilization on their and its native soil.

   American Jewish scholars take it for granted that a knowledge of modern Hebrew is today as essential a tool of scholarship as is the ability to handle French and German. They are in continuous communication with their Israeli colleagues on social, intellectual, and scholarly levels. They send their students to study in Israel. There is frequent intercontinental travel in both directions. There is no doubt about the powerful impact that Israeli biblical scholarship will increasingly have on its American Jewish counterpart. The point may be illustrated by random reference to one aspect of research that is a specifically and typically Jewish contribution to the field, namely, the study of the biblical cult.

   That nineteenth-century German Protestant theological presuppositions colored the study of this subject and predetermined the parameters and approach of research everywhere is hardly deniable. Since Yehezkel Kaufmann reopened the topic, Menahem Haran in Israel and Baruch Levine and Jacob Milgrom in the United States have powerfully challenged the prevailing theories and reconstructions. They have shown how the sacrificial system, the laws of purity and impurity, and the notions of sin and atonement must all be understood within a broad framework of religious ideas, inside a structure of biblical theology and law. They have demonstrated that the pure and the impure are complementary to the moral and the immoral and are not in opposition to them, and they have been progressively uncovering the ethical supports upon which the sacrificial system was raised. Furthermore, very constructive use has been made of rabbinic sources in the exploration of these themes. In short, Jewish scholars would emphasize that biblical theology is not just story and prophecy but is equally law and cult.

Another development that needs to be recounted is that Jewish Bible scholarship in America is no longer restricted to those who teach at Jewish-sponsored institutions of higher learning. A large percentage of those presently engaged in Jewish studies generally, and biblical studies in particular, now teach at secular institutions—a function of the proliferation of Jewish studies during the 1960s and 1970s. Over ninety North American colleges and universities currently offer undergraduate concentrations in Jewish studies and almost fifty sponsor programs of graduate study. The Association for Jewish Studies, the professional organization devoted to the advancement of the academic standing and scope of Judaic studies, boasts one thousand members (1982), including emeriti, associate members, and students. Many of these members specialize in the Bible, as evidenced both by the large number of sessions devoted to biblical subjects at the association's annual meetings and by a survey of the fourteen largest graduate programs in Jewish studies in North America (1980), which found that "Bible and Ancient Near East" was the most popular of all fields of specialization for Ph.D. candidates. Harry M. Orlinsky (1974: 331), who has monitored the state of the field for many years, summarized succinctly the situation as he found it in the early seventies, and his words hold equally true a decade later: "Jewish biblical scholarship. . . is currently flourishing in America-Canada as never before."

The Jewish Publication Society's new translation of the Bible, completed in 1982, stands as one of the great achievements of modern American Jewish Bible scholarship.[3] Appearing as it did in the very midst of the Jewish cultural efflorescence already described, a burgeoning Jewish religious revival (Sarna, 1982), and heightened nationwide interest in the Bible and its teachings, it seemed a most natural development, one almost to have been expected. In fact, however, the Bible translation was planned long before any of these developments were envisaged.

Although the full history of the New Jewish Publication Society's translation cannot be recounted here, we need look no further than Harry Orlinsky's famous 1953 address at the annual meeting of the Jewish Publication Society—"Wanted: A New English Translation of the

Bible" (Orlinsky 1974: 345–62)—to see that the original call for a new Jewish translation of Scripture stemmed from many of the same motivations that had precipitated earlier undertakings. For one thing, the 1917 translation had become, in Orlinsky's words, "no longer as intelligible as it should be." Old-fashioned King James English had lost the last of its appeal; what was needed, Orlinsky said, was a "simplified and modernized" style and vocabulary, "without undue loss of majesty and dignity." In addition, Orlinsky pointed to "the increased knowledge which archaeology and refined methodology have made available." New discoveries had cleared up old mysteries; the 1917 translation no longer reflected the best scholarship available. Finally, and perhaps what was most important, a new Protestant translation had appeared, the Revised Standard Version (1952), and a new Catholic translation (published as the New American Bible) had been announced. Just as the 1885 English Revised Version stimulated Jews to prove that they could do as well or better, so too did these new revisions. The new Protestant Bible still contained Christological elements (a capital "S" in "spirit," for example), and it still remained Christian in origin. "The Jew," Orlinsky said, echoing Max Margolis before him, "cannot afford to have his Bible translation prepared for him by others" (361).

In retrospect, Orlinsky has admitted (1970: 10) that there was "strong sentiment among several important members of the Jewish Publication Society's Board of Trustees" for the society to issue only a "modest revision of. . . the Revised Standard Version of 1952" (1970: 10). It was predictable, however, that those sentiments went unheeded. Most American Jews, in the 1950s as before, used the Bible to demonstrate their apartness, their insistence on a Jewish identity separate from Protestants and Catholics. Consequently, in 1955, after years of discussion, the Jewish Publication Society finally set up a committee of seven—three scholars, three rabbis (one representing each of the major wings of American Judaism), and the editor of the JPS translation, Solomon Grayzel—and mandated it to translate the Bible afresh from a Jewish point of view.

The composition of the new translation committee is instructive. Two of its three scholars, Harry Orlinsky (editor-in-chief for the Pentateuch) and H. L. Ginsberg, were born in North America, and the third, Ephraim A. Speiser, immigrated to the United States in his teens. Orlinsky and Ginsberg, who taught respectively at Hebrew Union College-Jewish Institute of Religion and the Jewish Theological Seminary, both in New York, held chairs in Bible. Speiser, who taught at the

University of Pennsylvania, was Professor of Semitic Languages and Literatures. All three of the rabbis on the committee (Max Arzt, Bernard Bamberger, and Harry Freedman) trained in the United States. Grayzel, an accomplished historian, immigrated to the United States at the age of twelve and received all his degrees in this country. The contrast with the earlier translation committee, which had a much larger number of immigrants and only one biblical scholar, Margolis himself, is striking indeed.

The mechanics of producing the Torah translation also were quite different from what they had been in Margolis's day. Harry Orlinsky has described the process in a recent interview (1982: 39–40):

(W)e would work one day, usually a Thursday, usually in my office at the Jewish Institute of Religion in Manhattan. . . . I prepared the draft of the entire *Chumash*. I hardly ever would prepare more than two or three chapters ahead of the committee so that I would be able to benefit from the decisions that the committee members reached. Unlike the Revised Standard Version, I would prepare a draft of a chapter or part of a chapter with a tremendous amount of commentary culled from the readings and translations from sources going back to the ancient Near East, the Septuagint, Targum, Vulgate, Syriac translation, Talmud, the medieval commentators, medieval grammarians, Sa'adia's translation, the rationalist Protestant translation of the 16th century, the Catholic, and of course, the modern translations. So that, for example, when I handed in the draft of the first five verses of Genesis, the first day of creation—and believe me I worked much harder than God did, the first day anyway—I had a half a page of the text and about 12 or 13 pages of all kinds of notes for my other six colleagues to consult. So that they didn't have to, unless they wanted to, go and examine these things. I would send that off to the JPS where it would be run off and sent out to my colleagues. They, in turn, would react, verse by verse or word by word, with counter suggestions. They would type that up and send that into JPS where, again, it would be run off and sent out, so that when we got together to do Genesis, and then all the way through, we would have the draft, we would have the comments of each of the committee members, as many as had reacted. We had it all before us, and we could all study it before we came. On the other hand, however, once we got together, the argument and the discussion pro and con would go far beyond what anybody had on any sheet of paper. We were very stimulated by the oral arguments back and forth. Not infrequently what came out as our final draft was something that none of us had envisaged to begin with. It was often quite different. Maybe not always necessarily better, but different. More than once, I was convinced that my draft was not as good as I had thought originally—but my committee colleagues would disagree with me and out-vote me in favor of my draft. Not infrequently, it was the other way around. No one is every fully satisfied with a translation because no one ever gets all his ideas accepted. It is a compromise translation.

Two principles underlay every facet of this translation process. First, the translators insisted on basing their work strictly on the original Hebrew Masoretic text. Although they consulted other versions, translations, and commentaries, they refused to see themselves as "revisers" of any previous translation, not even the previous Jewish one. In this they openly distinguished their effort from that of the Revised Standard Version, which *was* a revision in name and in fact.

Second, the translators insisted on rendering their text into English idiomatically, rather than mechanically and literally. Convinced that word-for-word translation did violence to the spirit of the Hebrew original, the translators permitted themselves wider latitude than their English language predecessors ever had. They spoke of their fidelity to the deeper meaning of the biblical text, in contradistinction to the surface meaning, which they in some cases felt free to ignore.

In 1962 the new translation of the Torah appeared, after seven years of unstinting labor. (A revised version appeared in 1967, and to date over 350,000 copies have been sold.) The preface paid ritualistic tribute to "the work of previous translators," and praised earlier scholars. But having done that, the editors insisted that this translation—*The Torah: A New Translation of the Holy Scriptures According to the Masoretic Text*—was not only different but better. In an article in the *Journal of Biblical Literature*, for example, Harry Orlinsky argued that the new translation's rendering of the initial verses in Genesis was the first "correct rendering": "We are now, finally, in a position to understand exactly what the writer of the first three verses of the Bible meant to convey to his readers" (1974: 402).

Orlinsky also boasted, both in his article and in his published *Notes on the New Translation of the Torah*, that the new translation's policy on textual criticism ("translate the Hebrew text directly, and offer in a footnote the proposed emendation and its translation") was "best," and that its manner of translating Hebrew particles improved upon all that preceded it. To his mind, the New Jewish Version marked "a complete break with the past history of Bible translation." He compared it to Spinoza's philosophical revolution in that it "set out to discard" a 2,200 year tradition "of literal, mechanical translation," in order to capture the text's original meaning. Speaking in the name of the entire translation committee, he hoped that this "break with the past" would "set a new pattern which authorized Protestant and Catholic translations of the future will tend to follow" (1970: 12–14).

The trailblazing image that Orlinsky's comments conjured up found no parallel in earlier American Jewish versions. Expressions of pride and distinctiveness, claims of superiority, evocations of destiny, and hopes for Christian approval had, as we have seen, all been heard before, but in no previous translation had American Jews so triumphantly expressed the belief that Protestants and Catholics might follow their lead. That, as Orlinsky himself realized reflected American Jewry's heightened self-confidence, its "verve, growing maturity, and optimism," "its new status. . . unprecedented in the two and one-half millennia of Jewish Diaspora life" (1970: 11, 14). Whereas the 1917 translation announced American Jews' cultural emergence, the new translation displayed heady awareness of their cultural influence and impact, their capacity as innovators and leaders on the national and religious scenes. The Prophets translation, published in 1978 by the same committee with H. L. Ginsberg as senior editor, though E. A. Speiser was no longer alive, carried forward this mood of self-confidence in its very language. It then went further, boldly proposing in footnotes a host of possible emendations designed to render texts judged to be corrupt more intelligible than they had ever been before.

Having monitored the pace of the Bible translation for a full decade, the trustees of the Jewish Publication Society realized, in 1965, that the undertaking would be both more arduous and more time-consuming than anyone had originally envisaged. Determined that the translation should nevertheless appear within "a reasonable time," they decided to create a new committee, charged with the task of translating the third division of the Bible, known as the Kethubim (the Writings), with the exception of the five Megilloth, which had already been translated by the original committee.

In 1966, the new committee, younger by a full generation than the earlier one, and overwhelmingly American trained, came into being. Like the earlier committee, it consisted of three scholars (Moshe Greenberg, Jonas C. Greenfield, and Nahum M. Sarna), three rabbis, one representing each major wing of American Judaism (Saul Leeman, Martin Rozenberg, and David Shapiro), and the editor of the Jewish Publication Society, later better-known as a bestselling novelist, Chaim Potok. It is revealing that all of the scholars selected taught at secular universities, a fact that reflected both the growing acceptance of Jewish studies as a legitimate academic discipline and the increased willingness on the part of universities to permit biblical studies to be taught by Jews. It is also revealing that two of the three scholars on the committee (Greenberg and Greenfield) eventually assumed positions at the Hebrew University in Jerusalem. This illustrates the point made above that American Jewish Bible scholarship has in the last three decades been in close touch with its Israeli counterpart on social, intellectual, and scholarly levels. The fact that the new committee met in Jerusalem on numerous occasions both symbolized and reinforced this spirit of harmony.

In its procedures, the Kethubim translation committee generally adhered to the practices established for the translation of the Torah and Prophets. Each professional scholar undertook the preparation of an annotated draft, which was circulated to all concerned, and everyone then had an opportunity to criticize the rendering and to offer detailed suggestions at the regular, periodic gatherings of the committee. In its style, however, the new committee struck a decidedly more cautious and conservative stance. Unlike the older committee, it stressed (in the preface) the inherent difficulties in translating the Hebrew, and the "as yet imperfect understanding of the language of the Bible." It refused to hazard emendations, and its favorite footnote read "meaning of Heb. uncertain." Instead of exuding confidence, it admitted right from the beginning that its translation had "not conveyed the fullness of the Hebrew, with its ambiguities, its overtones, and the richness that it carries from centuries of use." It made no triumphalistic claims.

From a broader perspective, the scholarly caution expressed in the translation of the Writings may be more in harmony with the new mood that overtook Americans generally in the 1970s and 1980s, a mood at once both more hesitant and less self-confident. Americans seemed less self-assured in 1982, when the translation of the Writings appeared, than two decades earlier, at the time of the publication of the Torah. The translation of the Writings seems to have reflected this fact, even if those involved may not have realized it.

In light of past experience this should not prove surprising. As we have seen, a Bible translation is much more than just a scholarly effort to render a sacred text into a form easier for all to understand. Since it is created by human beings, a translation is also a child of history, a product of its times. It cannot escape the impact of contemporary concerns.[4]

NOTES

* This article was coauthored with Jonathan D. Sarna.

1. Leeser, like Rabbi Morris Raphall, believed that the Bible sanctioned slavery but mandated better treatment of the slave than was practiced in the South (*Occident*, 1861: 267–68, 274; Korn, 1970: 15–55; D. Davis, 1975: 523–56).

2. The New Jewish Publication Society translation reads, "For a child has been born to us, /A son has been given us. /And authority has settled on his shoulders. /He has been named /"The Mighty God is planning grace; /The Eternal Father, a peaceable ruler."

3. The Yehoash translation of the Bible into Yiddish, by Solomon Bloomgarden, first published in 1937, is a tribute to Yiddish scholarship in the United States, but stands outside the scope of this essay; see Orlinsky (1974: 418–22).

4. Part of the research for this essay was supported by the American Council of Learned Societies and the Memorial Foundation for Jewish Culture.

WORKS CONSULTED

Abrahams, Harold J. and Miles, Wynham D.
1961   "The Priestley-Levi Debate." *Transactions of the Unitarian Historical Society in London* 12:1–19.
Abrahams, Israel
1920   *By-Paths in Hebraic Bookland.* Philadelphia: Jewish Publication Society.
Adler, Cyrus
1914   "The Bible Translation." *American Jewish Year Book* 15:101–21.
1926   "The Beginnings of Semitic Studies in America." *Oriental Studies Dedicated to Paul Haupt*, eds. Cyrus Adler and Aaron Ember (317–28). Baltimore: Johns Hopkins Press.
1941   *1 Have Considered the Days.* Philadelphia: Jewish Publication Society.
Altmann, Alexander
1973   *Moses Mendelssohn.* Philadelphia: Jewish Publication Society.
American Jewish Year Book
1899–1920   Philadelphia: Jewish Publication Society.
Agus, Jacob M.
1978   *Jewish Identity in an Age of Ideologies.* New York: Frederick Ungar.
Baumgarten, A. I.
1980   "Justinian and the Jews." *Rabbi Joseph H. Lookstein Memorial Volume*, ed., Leo Landman (37). New York.
Billigheimer, S.
1968   "On Jewish Translations of the Bible in Germany." *Abr-Nahrain* 7:1–34.
Central Conference of American Rabbis
1895–1917   *Year Books.*

Chiel, Arthur A.
1978 "The Kohut Collection at Yale." *Jews in New Haven*, ed. Jonathan D. Sarna (80–94). New Haven: Jewish Historical Society of New Haven.
Chomsky, William
1958 "Hebrew Grammar and Textbook Writing in Early Nineteenth-Century America. *Essays in American Jewish History*, (123–45). Cincinnati: American Jewish Archives.
Davis, David Brion
1975 *The Problem of Slavery in the Age of Revolution*. Ithaca, NY: Cornell University Press.
Davis, Moshe
1965 *The Emergence of Conservative Judaism*. Philadelphia: Jewish Publication Society.
1970 *Beit Yisrael Be-Amerikah*. Jerusalem: Jewish Theological Seminary.
Eidelberg, Shlomo
1978 "The Story of the Shulsinger Press and Its Publications." *Kovetz Massad*, ed., Meir Havatzelet (44–56). New York: Massad Camps.
Elbogen, Ismar
1943 "American Jewish Scholarship: A Survey." *American Jewish Year Book* 45:47–65.
Englander, Henry
1918 "Isaac Leeser." *Central Conference of American Rabbis Year-Book* 28:213–52.
Ezekiel, Herbert T. and Lichtenstein, Gaston
1917 *The History of the Jews of Richmond from 1769 to 1917*. Richmond: Ezekiel.
Fein, Isaac M.
1917 *The Making of an American Jewish Community*. Philadelphia: Jewish Publication Society.
Fellman, Jack
"Notes Concerning Two Nineteenth-Century Hebrew Text-books." *American Jewish Archives* 32:73–77.
Felsenthal, Bernhard
1884 "Bible Interpretation: How and How Not." *The Old Testament Student* 4:114–19.
Feuer, Lewis S.
1982 "The Stages in the Social History of Jewish Professors in American Colleges and Universities." *American Jewish History* 71:432–65.
Fogarty, Gerald P.
1982 "The Quest for a Catholic Vernacular Bible in America." *The Bible in America*, eds., Nathan A. Hatch and Mark A. Noll (163–80). New York: Oxford.
Gordis, Robert, ed.
1952 *Max Leopold Margolis: Scholar and Teacher*. Philadelphia: Dropsie College.

Grossman, Lawrence
1980 "Isaac Leeser's Mentor: Rabbi Abraham Sutro, 1784–1869." *Rabbi Joseph H. Lookstein Memorial Volume*, ed., Leo Landman (151–62). New York: Ktav.
Harper, William R.
1884 "The Jewish Attitude." *The Old Testament Student* 4:187.
Hatch, Nathan O. and Noll, Mark A., eds.
1982 *The Bible in America*. New York: Oxford.
Herberg, Will
1955 *Protestant-Catholic-Jew*. Garden City, NY: Doubleday.
Horwitz, Jonathan
1812 *Prospectus*. Philadelphia (copy in Hebrew, Cincinnati: Union College Library).
1839 *A Defence of the Cosmogony of* Moses. Baltimore: Matchett.
Jackson, Solomon
1826 *Prospectus*. New York (Lyons Collection, Scrapbook I, American Jewish Historical Society, Waltham, MA).
Jewish Publication Society
n. d.   Papers. Philadelphia: Philadelphia Jewish Archives.
1888–1899 *Reports of the Jewish Publication Society*. Philadelphia: Jewish Publication Society.
Jick, Leon A.
1976 *The Americanization of the Synagogue*. Hanover, NH: Brandeis University Press.
Journal of Biblical Literature
1931
Kabakoff, Jacob
1984 "New Light on Arnold Bogomil Ehrlich." *American Jewish Archives* 36: 202–224.
Kalisch, Isidor
1928 *Studies in Ancient and Modern Judaism*. New York: George Dobsevage.
Karff, Samuel E., ed.
1976 *Hebrew Union College-Jewish Institute of Religion at One Hundred Years*. Cincinnati: Hebrew Union College Press.
Korn, Bertram W.
1967 "Isaac Leeser: Centennial Reflections." *American Jewish Archives* 19:127–41.
1970 *American Jewry and the Civil War*. Philadelphia: Atheneum.
Kraut, Benny
1983 "Judaism Triumphant: Isaac Mayer Wise on Unitarianism and Liberal Christianity." *AJS Review* 7.
Leeser, Isaac
1853 *The Twenty-Four Books of the Holy Scriptures*. Philadelphia: L. Johnson.
1856 *The Twenty-Four Books of the Holy* Scriptures. Philadelphia: C. Sherman.

1867 *Discourses on the Jewish Religion*, vol. 5. Philadelphia: Sherman.
1868 *Discourses on the Jewish Religion*, vol. 10. Philadelphia: Sherman.

Lipscomb, Andrew A., ed.
1904 *The Writings of Thomas Jefferson*, vol. 14. Washington, DC.

Marcus, Ralph
1948 "American Jewish Scholarship Today." *Chicago Jewish Forum* 6/4 (Summer): 264–68.

Margolis, Max L.
1917 *The Story of Bible Translations*. Philadelphia: Jewish Publication Society.
1918 "The New English Translation of the Bible." *American Jewish Year Book* 19:161–93.

Marx, Alexander
1947 *Essays in Jewish Biography*. Philadelphia: Jewish Publication Society.

Neill, H.
1874 "Reminiscences of I. Nordheimer." *New Englander and Yale Review* 33:506–12.

Neuman, Abraham A.
1942 *Cyrus Adler*. New York: American Jewish Committee.

Newman, Selig
1839 *Emendations of the Authorized Version of the Old Testament*. London.

Occident
1844–1864

Orlinsky, Harry M.
1965 "Old Testament Studies." *Religion*, ed., Paul Ramsey 51–109. Englewood Cliffs, NJ: Prentice Hall.
1970 *Notes on the New Translation of the Torah*. Philadelphia: Jewish Publication Society.
1974 *Essays in Biblical Culture and Bible Translation*. New York: Ktav.
1982 "Telling It Like It Was." *Moment* 8/11 (December):37–44.

Philipson, David
n.d. Papers. Cincinnati: American Jewish Archives.
1941 "Cyrus Adler and the Bible Translation." *American Jewish Year Book* 42:693–91.

Plaut, W. Gunther
1965 *The Growth of Reform Judaism*. New York: World Union for Progressive Judaism.

Pollak, Gustav
1912 *Michael Heilprin and His Sons*. New York: Dodd, Mead.

Pool, David de Sola
1934 "Nordheimer, Isaac." *Dictionary of American Biography*, 13:547–48.

Sandmel Samuel
    1976 "Isaac Mayer Wise's *Pronaos to Holy Writ.*" *A Bicentennial Festschrift for Jacob Rader Marcus*, ed., Bertram W. Korn (517–27). New York: Ktav.
Sarna, Jonathan D.
    1982 "The Great American Jewish Awakening." *Midstream* 28/8 (October):30–34.
Sarna, Nahum M.
    1974 "Bible: Old Testament, Canon, Texts and Versions." *Encyclopaedia Brittanica, Macropaedia*, 2:881–92. Chicago.
Saunders, Ernest W.
    1982 *Searching the Scriptures.* Chico, CA: Scholars Press.
Sussman, Lance J.
    1982 "'Toward Better Understanding': The Rise of the Interfaith Movement in America and the Role of Rabbi Isaac Landman." *American Jewish Archives* 34:35–51.
    1985 "Another Look at Isaac Leeser and the First Jewish Translation of the Bible in the United States." *Modern Judaism* 51:159–190.
Tsevat, Matitiahu
    1958 "A Retrospective View of Isaac Leeser's Biblical Work." *Essays in American Jewish History* (295–313). Cincinnati: American Jewish Archives.
Vaxer, M.
    1940 "The First Hebrew Bible Printed in America." *Jewish Journal of Bibliography* 1:20–26.
Weinberg, Werner
    1982 "Moses Mendelssohn's 'Biur' 200 Years Later." *Jewish Book Annual* 40:97–104.
Westerhoff, John H.
    1978 *McGuffey and His Readers.* Nashville.
Whiteman, Maxwell
    1959 "Isaac Leeser and the Jews of Philadelphia." *Publications of the American Jewish Historical Society* 48:207–44.
Wise, Isaac M.
    1876 *The Cosmic God.* Cincinnati: American Israelite.
    1891 *Pronaos to Holy Writ.* Cincinnati: Robert Clarke.
    1954 "The World of My Books." Translated and edited by Albert H. Friedlander. *American Jewish Archives* 6:107–48.
Wolf, Edwin 2nd and Whiteman, Maxwell
    1956 *The History of the Jews of Philadelphia from Colonial Times to the Age of Jackson.* Philadelphia: Jewish Publication Society.

TORAH

The Anticipatory Use of Information as a Literary Feature of the Genesis Narratives

The subject of this paper relates to one particular aspect of the process by which the collection of individual narratives in the Book of Genesis achieved their final form as a unified whole. Specifically, I refer to a little-noted phenomenon that recurs with a fair degree of frequency, namely, the sudden introduction into a text of certain information which is extraneous to the immediate context but which is later seen to be crucial to the understanding of a subsequent episode or theme.

As far as I know, the first to draw attention to this was Rashi's grandson, the renowned exegete Rabbi Samuel b. Meir, known by the acronym RaShBaM (Rashbam, c. 1080–c. 1175 C.E.). In his comment to Gen 1:1 he writes, "It is a characteristic of the Scriptures anticipatively to present an irrelevant item for the sake of the subsequent context."[1] He then goes on to illustrate his point by citing, among others, the case of Gen 9:18: "The sons of Noah who came out of the ark were Shem, Ham and Japheth—Ham being the father of Canaan." Now Noah's sons have previously been thrice listed[2] without the additional remark, which is quite beside the point in a context dealing solely with the three sons who emerged from the ark after the Flood, and through whom the earth was repopulated. The information about Canaan's relationship to Ham is repeated in v 22, again without immediate relevancy.

It is obvious that mention of Canaan in these two passages is connected with the succeeding narrative about Noah's drunkenness and the accompanying shameful act perpetrated by Ham, as a consequence of which Noah lays a curse upon Canaan. Modern commentators mostly take it for granted that the note about Ham being the father of Canaan is a gloss introduced into the text by a compiler or editor for the purpose of smoothing the transition from vv 18f. to 20ff. At first glance, Rashbam appears to give the same explanation, in that he takes the note to be a necessary clarification of the identity of Canaan, who is about to be cursed. Without it, the reader would not know who this Canaan is or what he had to do with Ham, who was the guilty party. Yet there is a fundamental difference between the perception of the Rashbam and the views of modern commentators. Whereas the latter relate to the note solely in terms of its immediately limited function within the specific pericope, Rashbam treats it from a broader perspective. To him it is one instance among several of an original, characteristic feature of the Narrator's literary technique, not a harmonizing gloss linking P and J materials.

It seems to me that there are some arguments that can be brought in favor of Rashbam's general observation. Admittedly, the story of the curse upon Canaan is replete with difficulties. We are left uncertain as to the precise nature of Ham's offense, whether v 22 is to be taken literally as a euphemism for some act of gross immorality.[3] We do not know why Ham is described here as "the youngest son" (v 24) when, in fact, all the lists uniformly make him Noah's second son. And, most difficult of all, we are not told why Noah cursed Canaan, Ham's son, rather than Ham himself.[4] One thing is certain: whatever happened to Noah, the biblical account of the experience has been thoroughly emasculated. Even as Shem and Japheth virtuously covered the nakedness of their father, so the narrator piously concealed from posterity the sordid details of the shameful incident, leaving us only a very truncated version and thus causing the insuperable difficulties of the present narrative. Incidentally, the same reticence and the same concision characterize the story of Reuben's sexual transgression.[5]

Be all this as it may, the fact of Canaan's Hamite paternity clearly had great significance for the narrator or redactor; otherwise it would not have been reiterated within the short space of five verses. Moreover, one may rightly wonder why the entire episode is told in the first place.[6] What role does it play within the wider story of Noah or, indeed, within the complex of pre-Abrahamic narratives? The answer is that it introduces one of the major themes of the Pentateuch, one which is repeated in one form or another several times in Genesis.

The Table of Nations, which appears in the following chapter, presents both Egypt and Canaan as sons of Ham (10:6). In other texts, Egypt is equated with Ham. Such is the case in Ps 78:51, which describes the last of the plagues:

> He struck every firstborn of Egypt,
> the first fruits of their vigor in the land of Ham.

In Pss 105:23, 27; 106:22 the identity is even more specific, Egypt being designated "the land of Ham." The close association between Ham/Egypt and Canaan undoubtedly has an historical basis. It harks back to that period when Canaan was a province of Egypt, i.e., in the course of the Late Kingdom, under the 18th and 19th dynasties (c. 1550–1200 B.C.E.).[7] The expression of political relationships in terms of genealogies constructed along familial lines is, of course, a well-recognized and recurring feature of Genesis. "Canaan" in 9:18, 22 is representative of the population group, at this time under Egyptian suzerainty. The curse of Canaan, invoked in response to an act of moral depravity, is the first intimation of the theme of the corruption of the Canaanites, which is given as the justification for their being dispossessed of their land and for the transfer of that land to the descendants of Abraham. This reason is explicitly stated in Lev 20:23f. following a list of sexual abominations:

> You shall not follow the practices of the nation that I am driving out before you. For it is because they did all these things that I abhorred them and said to you: You shall possess their land. . . .

A similar reason is given in 18:24f. This verdict concludes another long list of prohibitions dealing with sexual relations which, significantly, begins as follows (v 3): "You shall not copy the practices of the land of Egypt where you dwelt, of the land of Canaan to which I am taking you." Egypt and Canaan are coupled together as being equally guilty of moral perversion. This self-same theme is behind several episodes in the Book of Genesis: Pharaoh's treatment of Sarah (12:10–20), Abimelech's dealings with her (ch. 20), the sexual immorality of the Sodomites (19:5–8), Dina's experience with the Canaanite prince of Shechem (ch. 34), the sexual offenses of Er and Onan, sons of Judah's Canaanite wife (ch. 35), and, finally, Potiphar's wife's attempted seduction of Joseph in Egypt (ch. 39).

In light of all the above, it is pertinent to raise the question as to whether the contextually irrelevant remark in 9:18, 22 as to Ham's paternity of Canaan is simply a gloss, or whether it is a literary device deliberately introduced into the text in order to insinuate, first, the identity of the Canaan who is about to be cursed—a true son of Ham— Egypt!,[8] and, second, the Canaanites in general, a people whose depravity is a major theme of Genesis because it provides the moral justification for their displacement by the descendants of the patriarchs. The answer to this question will depend upon the cumulative effect of the frequency with which this anticipatory device is found in the Genesis narratives. Let us therefore consider some more examples.

The genealogy of Shem is listed in Gen 11:10–32, where it serves to close the gap between Noah and Abraham. The individual generations are given, all in identical formulaic language, until one arrives at v 26, when the pattern is suddenly varied. Hitherto, only the chief descendant has been noted, while other children are anonymously dismissed with the prosaic observation that the aforementioned "begot sons and daughters." In Terah's case, all three sons are named. This departure from the norm clearly indicates that a turning point in history has been reached, and this impression is reinforced by the introduction of the *'elleh tôledōt* formula in v 27 and the repetition of the information of v 26, except that this time we are supplied with the additional intelligence that "Haran begot Lot" and that he died young, before the exodus from Ur of the Chaldeans (v 28).

It cannot be accidental that every one of these facts is essential to the understanding of subsequent developments in the biographies of Abraham and his offspring. Nahor need be mentioned because his name recurs repeatedly in connection with Isaac's marriage and Jacob's flight from Esau. Abraham's servant travels to "the city of Nahor" (24:10), where he meets Rebekah, who is of the family of "Abraham's brother Nahor" (v 15), and the girl identifies herself as "the daughter of Bethuel son of Milcah whom she bore to Nahor" (v 24), a fact repeated by the servant later on (v 47). Jacob flees Esau's wrath to find shelter with "Laban the son of Nahor" (29:5), and "the god of Nahor" appears in the treaty concluded between him and his uncle (31:53). Lot has to be introduced because he is soon to be reported as traveling with Abraham (11:31; 12:5), and his being orphaned explains in advance why this happened.[9] In other words, all the data contained in 11:27–28 is anticipatory and integral to the drama yet to unfold.

But this is not all. There are other anomalous aspects of the genealogy of Terah. The names of the wives of Abram and Nahor are recorded

(11:29), but not that of Haran; Sarai is indisputably the more important of the two women, yet, most strangely, her parentage is omitted while Milcah's is given; Sarai is described as being "barren" (v 30), but not so Milcah, even though she too has no children. Here again, every item can be seen to be crucial to the subsequent narratives. Haran's wife is ignored because she plays no role in the patriarchal lives, while Milcah will be encountered again by virtue of her being Rebekah's grand-mother.[10] The preclusion of any information about the matriarch's fore-bears is so extraordinary that it must be deliberate and purposeful. It seems to me that this phenomenon can be satisfactorily explained only on the presumption of a foreknowledge of the encounter with Abimelech, as told in ch. 20. On that occasion, Abraham made the self-justifying claim that Sarah was truly his sister, i.e., his father's daughter, though not his mother's (20:12).[11] In the earlier confrontation with Pha-raoh, Abraham did not respond to the king's query, "Why did you say, 'She is my sister'?" because he is summarily expelled from the realm. In this instance, Abimelech insists on an answer (20:9), and the reader wonders how Abraham will extricate himself from his embarrassing pre-dicament. Had Sarah's parentage been disclosed in the genealogy of ch. 11, the story of ch. 20 would have been divested of its suspense, with its literary qualities and effect being gravely impaired as a result. Finally, the designation of the matriarch as "barren" is intended, as von Rad has noted, "not only to prepare the reader for the event that is conditioned by this fact, but, above all, to make him conscious of the paradox of God's initial speech to Abraham."[12] How can God's promises be fulfilled if the patriarch's wife is barren?[13] Of course, barrenness is a major motif of the patriarchal narrative cycles, one expression of the still larger *Leit-motif*, the interplay between divine promise and frustrating reality. In sum, the genealogy must be seen as being inseparable from the narra-tives.

Still another example of the literary technique of introducing a par-enthetic note not immediately germane to the subject at hand, but whose significance later becomes apparent, is to be found in ch. 13 in connection with the separation of Lot from Abraham. In selecting for himself choice grazing land, Lot observed that the whole plain of the Jordan was well watered "all the way to Zoar, like the garden of the LORD, like the land of Egypt" (13:10). The sequence of the thought, however, is interrupted by the remark, "this was before the LORD destroyed Sodom and Gomorrah." At the end of the narrative another note has been appended, to the effect that "the inhabitants of Sodom were very wicked sinners against the LORD" (v 13). It hardly requires much imagination to see that both observations are preparatory to the events of chs. 18 and 19. The question is, however, whether they are nothing more than the interpolations of a glossator or whether they are an integral, functional part of the narration. Taken in isolation, the phenomenon can certainly be more easily explained as belonging to the former category. If treated in conjunction with several analogous instances, the alternative hypothesis would be favored.[14]

In Gen 22:20–24 a genealogy appears wedged between two momentous events, the Akedah and the purchase of the Cave of Machpelah. It seems to have absolutely no connection with either, and certainly it does not forge a link between them. Yet a close look reveals several instructive features. The genealogy presumes a knowledge of 11:29, which mentions Milcah together with Sarai. The phrase "Milcah too has borne children to your brother Nahor" (22:20) is intelligible only in light of that passage and of the birth of Isaac. At the same time, it explains why Milcah was not described as barren in the earlier listing even though no offspring of hers was recorded there. Whoever inserted the genealogy of 11:29 deliberately withheld the list of her children because it has a special function in 22:20ff. The remarks relating to "Kemuel the father of Aram" and "Bethuel being the father of Rebekah" are clues to the function of the genealogy and point to the reason for its presence here. The previous pericope closed with divine blessings, and for these to be fulfilled Isaac must marry and found a family. The list therefore mentions Rebekah, Bethuel, Milcah, Nahor, and Aram as an intimation of Isaac's forthcoming marriage to Rebekah daughter of Bethuel son of Milcah of the city of Nahor in Aram-naharaim. In this way, its presence after the Akedah is purposeful, anticipating the events of ch. 24.

That chapter, too, contains elements that exemplify this narrative technique of slipping in seemingly innocent phrases that are portentous of later developments. The opening sentence reads as follows: "Abraham was now old, advanced in years, and the LORD has blessed Abraham in all things." This final clause appears to have no particular relevance to the matter at hand, which is the finding of a wife for the forty-year-old bachelor Isaac. Since it is the patriarch's extreme old age that lends urgency to the quest, the note about God's blessing of Abraham actually disturbs the smooth flow of the narration. It soon becomes clear, however, that Abraham's material wealth is crucial to the matchmaking procedure. The servant sets out with an entourage of ten camels carrying "all the bounty of his master" (v 10). He presents the girl who waters his beasts with expensive gold jewelry (v 22), and she and her family receive gifts of silver and gold, of garments and other things, once the negotiations are brought to a successful conclusion (v 53). Furthermore, the servant cleverly stresses his master's great wealth in his address to the bride's family: "The LORD has greatly blessed my master, and he has given him sheep and cattle, silver and gold, male and female slaves, camels and asses" (v 35). All this is critical to the softening-up process for the difficult task of persuading the girl and her family to consent to the marriage and to agree to her leaving home for travel to a distant land. The ultimate inducement is, of course, the servant's declaration that Isaac is Abraham's sole heir (v 36). Seen in the light of all these facts, the apparently intrusive opening remark about God having "blessed Abraham in all things" becomes endowed with literary importance and latent meaning. The same applies to the statement that "Rebekah had a brother whose name was Laban" and that when he saw the golden nose-ring and bracelets he "ran out to the man at the spring" (vv 29–30). Can it be doubted that here is an insight into Laban's character intended to prepare the reader for the developments of chs. 29–31?

The story of the birth of Rebekah's twins, Esau and Jacob, and of their rivalry for the birthright is replete with anticipatory data. We are informed of the elder son's red complexion[15] and hirsute body (25:25). Nether detail is again mentioned in the immediately ensuing narrative. It is clear, however, that the two descriptions provide etiologies for the names Edom and Seir, with both of which Esau is explicitly identified later in Genesis.[16] At the same time, the hairiness of Esau turns out to be crucial to the events of the next episode.[17] The same is true of Esau's being "a skillful hunter" (v 27) and of Isaac's fondness for game, a weakness that led him to favor Esau over Jacob (v 28). Every one of these facts is indispensable to the understanding of how Jacob succeeded in extracting the birthright blessing from his father by means of trickery (ch. 27).

Chapter 26 is the one section wholly concerned with Isaac. All other traditions relating to this patriarch are integrated into the biographies of Abraham or Jacob. In the account of the sundry adventures preserved in this chapter, there is not a hint of Isaac's being a family man. The two sons do not figure in any way in the various incidents, which, in fact, may well have taken place before their birth.[18] Yet, suddenly, the chapter ends with a remark about Esau's Hittite wives, who are a source of bitterness and vexation to his parents (vv 34–35). This extraordinary addendum, totally unrelated to what precedes, must either be a clumsy interpolation or else, on the contrary, its very discontinuity and irregularity belong to the rhetorical strategies of a gifted writer and constitute an important element of the creative process. Now, the perceptive reader will doubtless observe at once that the intrusive nature of Esau's marital affairs recalls the place and role of the genealogies of 11:10–32 and 22:20–24, both of which appear to be contextually extraneous but turn out to afford essential data preparatory to subsequent narrative developments. In like manner, the remarks presently under discussion make Rebekah's complaint to her husband in 27:46 intelligible. Having been apprised of Esau's murderous threat against Jacob, she realizes that, for his own safety, her younger son must be sent away (42–48). But she cannot disclose to her husband the true reason for Jacob's impending departure, and so she hits upon the pretext that it is time for the boy to marry. "'I am disgusted with my life because of the Hittite women,'" she says to Isaac. "'If Jacob marries a Hittite woman like these, from among the native women, what good will life be to me?'" The persuasiveness of this argument is decisive because, as 26:34–35 have already informed us, Esau's union with the local women has already turned out to be an intolerable torment to Isaac, and so he readily grants his consent (28:1–2).

My last example of the sort of device that I am illustrating here is 35:22. We are told that "While Israel stayed in that land, Reuben went and lay with Bilhah, his father's concubine; and Israel found out." The disagreeable details that form the background to this strange interlude have obviously been suppressed,[19] but a little light on this truncated story is shed by the Chronicler:

> The sons of Reuben the firstborn of Israel—for he was the firstborn; but when he disgraced his father's bed, his rank of firstborn was given to the sons of Joseph son of Israel, so he is not reckoned as firstborn in the genealogy. (1 Chron 5:1)

The Chronicler was certainly aware of much more than tradition had transmitted in Gen 35:22. What is particularly puzzling about the latter passage is the final phrase, which literally means "and Jacob heard," for the sentence is complete without it. Possessing no direct object, and indicating no reaction on Jacob's part, it juts out as a literary *membrum suspensum*, and one wonders why it is there. The most plausible solution is that suggested by Rashbam, who refers to Gen 49:3f. In his deathbed testament, Jacob condemns Reuben for his immoral act: "For when you mounted your father's bed, you brought disgrace." Because of it, Reuben forfeited his birthright. Brief and obscure though it be, the note of 35:22, which tells of the incident and informs us that Jacob heard about it even though he did not witness it, saves the poetic passage of 49:3f. from unintelligibility.

Gehard von Rad has rightly pointed out that, in dealing with the individual units of the Book of Genesis, "one must not lose sight of the great unit of which they are but parts," and that in its present form, it is "the narrative as a whole and the contexts into which all the individual parts fit and from which they are to be understood"[20] that must be kept in mind. The literary feature demonstrated above crosses all conventional source-critical divisions.[21] For this reason, it deserves to be taken seriously in any examination of the literary structure and ultimate unity of the Book of Genesis.

NOTES

1. D. Rosin, ed. (Breslau, 1882: reprinted New York, 1949), pp. 3f., commentary to Gen 1:1.
2. 5:32; 6:10; 7:13.
3. Whether Ham was guilty of castrating his father or of practicing sodomy upon him is discussed in Sanh. 70a. On the basis of Lev 20:11, S. Gevirtz, "A Father's Curse," *Mosaic* 2/3 (1969): 56–61, believes that Ham violated his father's wife. However, what is described in Gen 9:22–23 would be hard to reconcile with such an explanation.
4. Saadiah (882–942 C.E.) takes "Canaan" in vv 25, 26 as though it read "father of Canaan." This is followed by Jonah ibn Janah, *Sefer Ha-Riqmah*, ed. M. Wilensky (Berlin, 1930), I, p. 265, line 8, and by Prophiat Duran in his *Maase Efod*, ed. J. Friedländler and J. Kohn (Vienna, 1865), p. 150.
5. 35:22; on which, see below.
6. For an historical explanation, see D. Neiman, "The Date and Circumstances of the Cursing of Canaan," in *Biblical Motifs*, ed. A. Altmann, *Brandeis University Texts and Studies*, Vol. III (Cambridge, Massachusetts, 1966), pp. 113–34; A. Van Selms, "Judge Shamgar," *VT*, XIV (1964): 294–309.
7. See R. de Vaux, *The Early History of Israel*, trans. David Smith (Philadelphia, 1978), pp. 82–123.
8. So noted by Abraham ibn Ezra in his comment to Gen 9:18.
9. M. Noth, *A History of Pentateuchal Traditions* (Englewood Cliffs, New Jersey, 1972), trans. Bernhard W. Anderson, p. 13 and n. 28, observes that in 12:4a, which he assigns to J (p. 28), Lot appears suddenly with no introduction. The narrative is thus regarded as being fragmentary. He postulates that Gen 11:28–30 was inserted into the appendix of 1:27, 31, 32 [P] in order to provide certain specific details. It would appear to be simpler to explain the absence of an explanatory note about Lot in 12:4 as being unnecessary in light of the information already given in 11:27–31.
10. Gen 22:20, 23; 24:15, 24, 47.
11. This claim must be taken seriously. It is hardly likely to be the invention of a writer who was sensitive to the idea of Abraham resorting to falsehood even though in self-defense. The later the authorship of the passage, the less the likelihood of a writer inventing a tale ascribing to the patriarch a practice abhorrent to the sexual morality of Israel as expressed in the legal codes (Lev 18:9, 11; 20:17; Deut 27:22; cf. Ezek 22:11). Furthermore, to invent a claim of Sarah being a half-sister in order to save Abraham from telling a lie is to accept the preposterous conclusion that an incestuous marriage is

a lesser offense, something of which no biblical writer could have been guilty. As a matter of fact, the veracity of the claim of 20:12 is reinforced by the independently attested preference of the Terahites for endogamy. Thus, Nahor marries his niece (10:24); Isaac marries the granddaughter of Abraham's brother (11:29); the ostensible reason for sending Jacob to Paddan-aram is to find a wife among Rebekah's family (28:1f.), and the man indeed marries two cousins, something that Laban finds desirable (29:19).

12. G. von Rad, *Genesis*, O.T.L., trans. John H. Marks (Philadelphia, 1961), p. 154.

13. Cf. Gen 15:2.

14. Cf. J. Skinner, *Genesis*, International Critical Commentary, 2nd ed. (New York, 1930): "This notice of the sinfulness of Sodom is another anticipation of ch. 19."

15. *Contra* Th. H. Gaster, *Myth, Legend and Custom in the O.T.* (New York, 1975), 1, pp. 164f., this is more likely to be the meaning of *'dmwny* than is "redheadedness," if only for the reason that the latter's folkloristic association with the sinister and the dangerous is inappropriate to David, who is also, and approvingly, described as being *'dmwny* (1 Sam 16:12; 17:14). For a possible explanation of the ruddy complexion, see C. H. Gordon, *The Ancient Near East*, 3rd. rev. ed. (New York, 1965), p. 125 n. 26.

16. Esau is identified with Edom in 36:1, 8, 19; cf. vv 9, 43. Seir is the homeland of Esau in 33:14, 16; 36:8f., 21; Deut 2:4, 5, 8, 12, 22, 29; Josh 24:4.

17. Gen 27:11, 16, 23.

18. H. Hupfeld, *Die Quellen der Genesis* (Berlin, 1853), p. 155; cf. S. D. Luzzatto, *Commentary to the Pentateuch*, ed. P. Schlesinger (Tel-Aviv, 1965), p. 107.

19. In the received Hebrew text, a *pisqa' be'emṣac pasuq* appears after *yiśrā'el*, indicating some anomaly. For a comprehensive review of the research on this scribal phenomenon, see P. Sandler, in *D. Neiger Volume* (Jerusalem, 1959), pp. 222–48, to which should be added Sh. Talmon, *Textus*, V (1966), pp. 14–20.

20. *Genesis*, p. 13.

21. Thus, 9:18, 22 are assigned to J,. but 10:6 to P; 11:10–26 are ascribed to P, vv 27–32 to P and J, vv 28–30 to J, 28b to JE, and 12:1–8 to Jh, but ch. 24 goes to J, 29:5 to J or JE, 31–53 to E or JE, and 20:12 to E: 13:10, 14, and chs. 18 and 19 are attributed to J, with a dash of P in 19; 11:29; 22:20–24, and ch. 24 are all credited to J; 25:15 is linked to P, but vv 27, 28 to J, while ch. 27 is accounted to J or JE: 26:34f. 27:46, and 28:1–2 are all consistently assigned to P; finally, 35:22 is ascribed to J, but 45:3–4 are regarded as problematical.

Genesis 21:33: A Study in the Development of a Biblical Text and Its Rabbinic Transformation

Following the account of the pact that Abraham and King Abimelech concluded, as told in Genesis 21:32, it is recorded that the patriarch "planted a tamarisk at Beer-sheba, and invoked there the name of the Lord, the Everlasting God"[1] (v. 33). The Hebrew text reads as follows:
ויטע אשל בבאר־שבע ויקרא־שם בשם ה' אל עולם.

This notice, brief to the point of obscurity, contains several unusual features and raises numerous questions.[2]

First, there is the syntactical difficulty that the immediate antecedents in the plural—Abimelech and Pichol—cannot possibly be the subjects of the verbs in the singulars found in this verse. Only the remote "Abraham" can govern the verbs ויטע and ויקרא. For the sake of clarity, the Samaritan recension and the ancient versions, the Septuagint, Peshitta and Vulgate, all felt constrained to insert [Abraham] into the text, and the English translations, including the Jewish ones, have traditionally followed this practice.

The syntactical anomaly gives the appearance of thematic disjunction between the present verse and the preceding narrative. Some medieval Jewish commentators attempted to sustain the organic unity of the entire chapter. Thus, Bekhor Shor (12th cent.) for instance, understood the purpose of the tree-planting to be commemorative of the aforementioned pact.[3] David Kimchi (1060?–1135?) supposes that the aborcultic act adjacent to the well at Beer-sheba was intended to exhibit undisputed assumption of sovereign possession of the facility.[4] In modern times, Benno Jacob's[5] explanation is similar to that of Bekhor Shor, while E. A. Speiser, despite the vagueness of his formulation, also seems to connect the tree-planting with the pact-making.[6]

The difficulty with these interpretations is that no analogous practice within a legal context is again to be found in the Bible, nor does anyone else plant a tree simply to memorialize some experience. Moreover, were Abraham's deed really the sequel to the preceding narrative, it might have been expected to have occurred before, not after, the departure of the two Philistines. Some explicit indication of the connection would surely have been forthcoming in the text. There seems no way of avoiding the conclusion that Genesis 21:33 belonged to an independent narrative, now thoroughly truncated,[7] that dealt with Abraham's tamarisk at Beer-sheba. This irresistible inference itself raises two problems: Why has the original story been so radically abridged? And why was the notice about the tree preserved at all? The answers to these questions are dependent upon a third one: What is the connection between the two parts of verse 33—the act of tree-planting and the act of worshiping? This last issue must be addressed first since it provides the key to the understanding of the entire passage.

The straightforward implication of the text is that there exists an inextricable interconnection between the two clauses of the verse. That is to say, Abraham's planting of the tree is directly associated with his act of worship. Now it is well known that throughout the ancient Near East from Mesopotamia to Egypt, as well as in the Aegean and Minoan areas, the phenomenon of the sacred tree existed—not necessarily as an object of worship in itself, so much as the locus of a numinous presence. It was, therefore, an ideal place for theophany and worship. The tree served as a medium of oracles and revelation.[8]

Several biblical toponyms testify to the presence of many such sacred, arbored sites in Canaan. Genesis 12:6 records that "Abram passed through the land as far as the site of Shechem at the terebinth of Moreh." The term for "site" in Hebrew is *maqōm*: its combination with a city-name is unique in the Bible so that in the verse quoted it most likely carries the special meaning of "sacred site," just like Arabic *maqām*, as it does numerous times in biblical texts.[9] The name given to the terebinth is *'elon moreh* [plural in Deut. 11:30], which means "the terebinth of the teacher/oracle-giver." It was at this site that Abraham experienced a theophany and built an altar (v. 7). According to Joshua

24:26, the great military leader made a covenant with the people of Shechem, and "He took a great stone and set it up at the foot of the oak (Hebrew *'elah*) in the sacred precinct of the Lord." In the Book of Judges it is said that Abimelech was proclaimed king at "the terebinth (*'elon*) of the pillar at Shechem," and doubtless in the vicinity stood the "Diviners' Oak" (*'elon me'onenim*, 9:6, 37).[10] Earlier, Jacob had buried the pagan religious symbols possessed by the members of his entourage "under the terebinth (*'elah*) that was near Shechem" (Gen. 35:4). Hebron too had its sacred trees, for Abraham had pitched his tent "at the terebinths of Mamre (*'elonei mamre*), which are in Hebron," and had "built an altar there to the Lord" (Gen. 13:18). It is quite probable that it was beneath one of these special trees that the patriarch entertained his three unexpected visitors, for the text repeatedly mentions "the tree," the definite article seeming to indicate one well known (*ibid.* 18:4, 8). "The Oak of Weeping" (*'allon bakhut*) was where Rebekah's nurse Deborah was laid to rest (*ibid.* 35:8), while the later prophetess of the same name "used to sit under the palm of Deborah" to issue judicial decisions (Judg. 4:5), perhaps by oracular means. "The Terebinth of Tabor" and "The Valley of the Oak" (I Sam. 10:3; 17:2) are two more sites bearing arboreal names that appear to indicate the presence of sacred trees. Finally, it is not without significance that it was from "under the terebinth at Ophrah" that Gideon experienced a theophany (Judg. 6:10–21).

The association of sacred trees with pagan cults, especially with fertility cults, made them anathema to the official religion of Israel. Canaanite cult sites established "under any luxuriant tree" were to be utterly destroyed and were not to be imitated even in the worship of the God of Israel (Deut. 12:2–4). The planting of "any kind of tree" beside the altar of the Lord was unequivocally proscribed (*ibid.* 16:21), and no wonder, for male prostitutes who were active in Judea in the days of Rehoboam son of Solomon were apparently connected with shrines built "under every leafy tree" (1 Kings 14:23–24). Hosea testifies to the practice of prostitution in the northern kingdom at shrines erected "under oaks, poplars, and terebinths" (4:13–14).[11]

In light of all the above, it is extraordinary that tradition should have recorded an association of Abraham with a tree in a cultic context. This in itself constitutes eloquent testimony to the great antiquity of that tradition, to its reliability, popularity, and persistence. It was not expunged from the Torah's record.

Further evidence for the antiquity of the tradition behind Genesis 21:33 lies in the divine epithet *'el 'olam*. This title never recurs in the Bible, although it has turned up in a fifteenth century B.C.E. inscription found at Serabit el-Khadem in Sinai. There it appears in the form of '*l d 'lm* ('*l du 'olam*).[12] Further, *'lm* as an epithet of a deity occurs in Ugaritic[13] text 2008:7, *špš 'lm*; in text 68:10, *mlk 'lm*;[14] and in text 52:1 *rpu mlk 'lm*. It also shows up in the eighth century B.C.E. Phoenician inscription from Karatepe as *šmš 'lm*.[15] Once again, the retention of the unique Hebrew divine title *'el 'olam* in Genesis 21:33 means that it must have belonged to the original, pre-pentateuchal form of the narrative. It is of great significance, however, that in the present narrative the divinity whom Abraham invoked has been carefully dissociated from any pagan deity by identifying *'el 'olam* with YHWH. This development is particularly meaningful because the other unusual divine titles compounded with *'el* in Genesis are not generally so identified. *'El Shadday* appears five times and is not once particularized as YHWH.[16] *'El 'Elyon* is invoked four times in Chapter 14, but is connected with YHWH only when it issues from the mouth of Abraham in addressing a non-Hebrew (v. 22). That text and ours in 21:33, therefore, may be said to exhibit special sensitivity to the possibility of mistaken identification of an exceptional divine title.

Further clue to the pre-history of the text may be recognized in another curious anomaly that, it seems to me, has not been sufficiently evaluated. The phrase *va-yiqra' be-shem* YHWH occurs thrice more in the patriarchal narratives: 12:8, 13:4, and 26:25. In each instance, it is accompanied by or associated with mention of an altar. The present citation constitutes the exception. The reverse situation is found: that is, mention of altar-building without the invocation of God—12:7; 13:18; 33:20; 35:7—but not the invocation of God without reference to an altar. The solitary omission of the altar in Genesis 21:33 would therefore appear to be deliberate. It must flow from a sensitivity to the association of Abraham with the planting of a tree and his act of worship at that spot.

The specific plant favored by the patriarch is designated an *'eshel*. James Barr has persuasively illustrated that already within the formative period of the Hebrew Bible this term occasioned embarrassment. Such is reflected in the Chronicler's change of *'eshel* in 1 Samuel 31:13 to *'elah* in the parallel passage in 1 Chronicles 10:12 in the story about the burial of King Saul and his sons "under the tamarisk tree in Jabesh." Barr has also pointed to the great variety of interpretation of this term *'eshel* exhibited by the ancient versions of Genesis 21:33, a phenomenon engendered, as he puts it, by "a name unpleasantly similar to that of the notorious idolatrous symbol, the *Asherah*."[17]

Abraham's *'eshel* at Beer-sheba is not again mentioned in the Bible. However, it is to be noted that Isaac traveled to Beer-sheba, received a theophany, built an altar, and "invoked the name of the Lord" (Gen. 26:23–25). The narrative does not identify the site with that of Abraham's *'eshel*, but it is to be noted that the theophany twice refers to Abraham by name. Jacob too visited Beer-sheba, on his way down to Egypt, offered sacrifices to "the God of Isaac his father," and also experienced a theophany at that site (*ibid.* 46:1–4). It is reasonable to assume that all three traditions relate to the same sacred locale.[18] Such a conclusion provides a convincing explanation for Judahite Beer-sheba remaining an attractive and popular cultic site even for the citizens of the northern kingdom long after the division of the country following the death of Solomon. The prophet Amos found it necessary to condemn the custom of northerners traveling to the cult-site at Beer-sheba (Amos 5:5; cf. 8:14).

In sum, it would be difficult to find a better explanation for the preservation of the statement about Abraham's activities found in Genesis 21:33 than that it is excerpted from an originally larger narrative describing the origins and founding of the famous cult-center at Beer-sheba. In consequence of the great popularity of that shrine as a place of pilgrimage, the story had become a classic, and reference to it could not be entirely omitted. Due to the obnoxious nature of the tree-cult in the folk religion, and to the possibility of mistakenly finding legitimacy for it through the patriarch's venture, only the skeleton outline of the ancient narrative was retained. The careful editing is evidenced by the exceptional absence of altar-building, and the identification of the unique epithet *'el 'olam* with YHWH, as well as by the exclusion of any mention of a theophany.

The sensitivity to the presence of the *'eshel* persisted beyond the period of the early Bible translations into the rabbinic age. A discussion about the term is reported in B. Sotah 10a, and in several midrashic sources.[19] R. Judah, followed by Resh Lakish, maintained that it meant an orchard (*pardes*). The popularity of this rendering is attested by its acceptance on the part of the Psuedo-Jonathan, the Yerushalmi, the Neofiti, and the Samaritan targums. According to R. Nehemiah, however, the *'eshel* was not something arboreal, but a "hospice" (*pundaq*, Greek *pandocheion*). Abraham is credited with providing wayfarers with food and shelter, thereby bringing them close to the true God. To add force to this transformational interpretation, *'eshel* is even taken to be an acronym formed from the initial letters of three words, *'akhilah, shetiyah, levayah,* "eating, drinking, and accompanying on the way."[20]

Rabbinic exegesis has emptied the verse of its cultic content. An incident belonging to the realm of personal piety in a ritual context has been transformed so that it now exemplifies God's demands on man in a socio-moral context. At the same time, the provision of wayfarers and of the homeless has itself been elevated by the Rabbis to the status of a mode of divine worship. As the Talmud records in the name of Rab Judah who cited it in the name of Rab: "Hospitality to wayfarers is greater than welcoming the presence of the Shekhinah" (Shab. 127a).[21]

NOTES

1. Translations of biblical texts follow those of the new Jewish Publication Society's version *(TANAKH)*.

2. The documentary source attribution of v. 33 is quite irrelevant to the issues here discussed. In any event, modern commentators show no unanimity in assigning this particular verse.

3. Ed. J. Gad, Jerusalem, 1956 *ad loc.* His comment is: אילן גדול להיות לזכרון על הברית.

4. Ed. M. Kamelhaar, Jerusalem, Mosad Harav Kook, 1970, *ad loc.* His comment is: נטע שם נטיעה סמוך לבאר שתהיה לעדות כי נשארה הבאר בידו.

5. B. Jacob, *Das Erste Buch der Tora*, Berlin, Schocken, Verlag, 1934, (Reprint, Ktav, New York, s.d.), p. 489.

6. E. A. Speiser, *Genesis* (Anchor Bible), Garden City, New York, 1964, p. 159.

7. For examples of similarly truncated biblical narratives, cf. Gen. 9:20–27; 10:9–10 (cf. Micha 5:5); 35:22 (cf. 1 Chron. 5:1–2); Exod. 4:24–26.

8. R. de Vaux, *Ancient Israel: Its Life and Institutions*, Translated by J. McHugh, New York, McGraw Hill, 1961, pp. 278f; C. L. Meyers, *The Tabernacle Menorah: A Synthetic Study of a Symbol from the Biblical Cult*, ASOR Dissertation Series 2, Missoula, MT. Scholars Press, 1976, pp. 95, 133–156; cf. F. Matz in *The Cambridge Ancient History*, 3rd edition, II, 1. Cambridge, Cambridge University Press, 1978, p. 161.

9. For *maqōm* as "sacred space," cf. Gen. 28:11, 17, 19; 35:7; Exod. 20:24; Deut. Ch. 12 *passim*; 14:23 ff; 15:20; Ch. 16 *passim*; 17:8, 10; 18:6; 23:17; 26:2; 31:11. In 1 Sam. 7:16 the term is used of the shrines of Bethel, Gilgal, and Mizpah; other examples are 1 Kings 8:6; Isa. 17:7; 26:21; 66:1; Jer. 7:12; Ezek. 3:12; 43:7; Micah 1:2–3; Ps. 24:3; 26:8; 104:8; 132:5. In 1 Chron. 16:27 *maqōm* appears in place of *miqdash* in the parallel text in Ps. 96:6. Hebrew *maqōm* should probably also have the meaning of "sacred space" in Gen. 22:4, 9, 14: Num. 18:31; 23:27, and in Ezek. 3:12, a doxology parallel to that in Ps. 135:21 ("Zion").

10. The meaning of the problematical *muṣṣab* here is immaterial to the issue at hand. A. B. Ehrlich, *Mikra' Ki-Pheshuto*, Berlin, M. Poppelauer, 1899, p. 59, points out that in 1 Sam. 22:6, as in 31:13, the definite article also indicates the special sacred character of the tree.

11. Cf. 2 Kings 16:4; 17:10: Isa. 57:5; Jer. 2:20; 3:6, 13; 17:2; Ezek. 6:13. On Hos. 4:13–14, see M. Weinfeld, *Deuteronomy and the Deuteronomic School*, Oxford, Clarendon Press, 1972, pp. 322, 336.

12. F. M. Cross, Jr., "Yahweh and the God of the Patriarchs," *HTR*, 55 (1962), 225–59, esp. 233, n. 31; 238ff; *idem, Canaanite Myth and Hebrew Epic*, Cambridge, MA, Harvard University Press, 1973, pp. 17–22, 47–50.

13. Cyrus H. Gordon, *Ugaritic Textbook*, Rome, Pontifical Biblical Institute, 1965.

14. Cf. Jer. 10:10.

15. H. Donner-W. Röllig, *Kanaanäische u. Aramäische Inschriften*, Wiesbaden, Otto Harrassowitz, 1962, I, No. 26, p. 6, III, 19. The title *špš 'lm* is equivalent to *Šamaš dārītum* in El Amarna 155.6, 47. It should be noted that the term *'lt 'lm* in the Arslan Tash inscription, translated by Albright as "goddess of eternity," *BASOR*, 76 (1939), 8, is now to be rendered "an eternal bond;" see Franz Rosenthal, *The Ancient Near East: Supplementary Texts*, ed. J. B. Pritchard, Princeton, New Jersey, 1969, p. 658; cf. E. Lipinski, *Near Eastern Religious Text Relating to the Old Testament*, Ed. W. Beyerlin, Philadelphia, Westminster Press, 1987, p. 248.

16. Gen. 17:1; 28:3; 35:11; 43:14; 48:3.

17. J. Barr, "Seeing the Word for the Trees? An Enigmatic Ancient Translation," *JSS* 13 (1968), 11–20, esp. p. 14. On the Asherah, see J. Day, "Asherah in the Hebrew Bible and Northwest Semitic Literature," *JBL*, 105 (1986), 385–408.

18. See M. Haran, *Temples and Temple Service in Ancient Israel*, Oxford, Clarendon Press, 1978, p. 54ff.

19. The midrash appears in various forms in Genesis R. 54:5, ed. J. Theodor and Ch. Albeck, [Reprint] Jerusalem, Wahrmann Books, 1965, p. 583; Midrash Tehillim, ed. S. Buber, Vilna, 1891, to Ps. 37:1 (p. 253); Ps. 110:1 (p. 465); cf. Yalkut Shimoni, para 95; Midrash Lekah Tov, ed. S. Buber, Lemberg, 1884, p. 96.

20. Midrash Tehillim, *op. cit.*, to Ps. 37:1 (p. 253). See also the comment of Bahya ben Asher to Genesis 21:33, ed. C.B, Chavel, Jerusalem, 1962, p. 191, nn. 31–32.

21. ‫גדולה הכנסת אורחין מהקבלת פני שכינה‬.

The Decalogue

I

The observation of Moses Maimonides (1135–1204 C.E.) that the Decalogue constitutes the very essence of religion[1] would probably be shared wholeheartedly by the votaries of all major religions. From earliest times this document has occupied a pivotal position in the Jewish religious consciousness.[2] Philo of Alexandria (born circa 20 B.C.E.) devoted a special treatise to the subject, in which he declared the Decalogue to be the summation *(Kephálaia)* of all the particular and special laws recorded in the Scriptures.[3] Rabbinic midrash similarly emphasized that the Decalogue contained the essential Torah from which all else is derived.[4] Little wonder that it achieved a position of such paramount importance that the daily morning service in the Second Temple once began with its recitation preceded by a blessing[5] and that it was at one time part of the contents of tefillin.[6]

It is taken for granted that the Decalogue comprises the minimal moral imperatives essential to the maintenance of an ordered and wholesome society, and that it is the great Jewish contribution to the world. But what was the state of affairs before Sinai? Was the world steeped in savagery and barbarism? The Bible itself assumes the existence of a moral code from the beginning of the appearance of human life on this planet.[7] Otherwise, how could Cain have been guilty of murder? For what "lawlessness" could God have brought the great flood, and for what "evil" would the inhabitants of Sodom and Gomorrah and their allied cities have been brought to account? The rabbinic notion of a "Noahide code," obligatory upon the human race, is itself a recognition of pre-Sinaitic norms of law and order.[8] Anyone with even an elementary knowledge of ancient history is aware that the people of Israel arrived very late on the world scene. By then the great civilizations of the Fertile Crescent had all passed their prime and were already heirs to ancient traditions and cultures. Obviously, these great civilizations could not have come about without a "social contract," a commitment to enforceable criteria of right and wrong that covered most of the principles enshrined in the Decalogue. This elementary presupposition is, in fact, well illustrated by the discovery of no less than six collections of laws from the ancient Near East, from the third millennium B.C.E. down.[9]

There are the laws of Ur-Nammu, king of the Sumerian city of Ur (circa 2050 B.C.E.); those of Bilalama, king of the Amorite city of Eshnunna (circa 1925 B.C.E.); the law of Lipit-Ishtar, ruler of Isin (circa 1860 B.C.E.); the collection of Hammurabi of Babylon (circa 1700 B.C.E.); the Hittite code (circa fifteenth century B.C.E.); and the Assyrian laws from the city of Assur (circa 1350 B.C.E.). In addition to these, we have the wisdom and didactic literature of Egypt[10] and Mesopotamia,[11] which is replete with most of the injunctions found in the Decalogue, while magical texts, some of them from the Old Babylonian period (circa 1800 B.C.E.), often assume that sickness results from the violation of a taboo, and contain lists of wrongs committed, many of an ethical and moral nature.[12] Perhaps the most instructive text of all is the so-called *Book of the Dead* with its "negative confession."[13] This is a declaration or protestation of ignorance or innocence to be recited by the dead as a prior condition to entry into the next world. The negative formulation testifies to the reality of positive moral ideals, widely accepted as the indispensable imperatives of an ordered society. In the presence of Osiris and his court, convened in the "Hall of Two Truths," the dead man professed, among other items, "I have not committed evil among men, . . . I have not blasphemed a god, . . . I have not done violence to a poor man, . . . I have not killed, . . . I have not stolen, . . . I have not been covetous, . . . I have not robbed, . . . I have not told lies, . . . I have not committed adultery."

Clearly, the prohibitions of theft, murder, adultery, false witness, and so forth, were hardly novel at the time of the Exodus. Rather, they had long been accepted as the elementary standards of civilized, organized life. The fundamental question therefore arises: Wherein lay the uniqueness of Israel's contribution in giving the world the Decalogue?

II

One of the fundamental principles of rabbinic exegesis of the Bible is that the Scriptures employed contemporary forms and modes of speech in order to convey their message in an intelligible manner: "The Torah speaks in human language."[14] One of the major concerns of modern biblical scholars is to recover the "human language," the original life-setting of a scriptural passage, to discover why a text is expressed in the way it is and in the form it has assumed. Is there correlation between content and literary form? In other words, does an analysis of the typical structure of a biblical passage throw light on the context?

The only way such questions might be answered is by turning to the vast literature of the ancient Near East, which has preserved the "human language," the patterns of speech and the literary structures which were contemporaneous with the literary creativity of Israel or which were part of Israel's cultural baggage. Not always are the solutions forthcoming, but often they are, and in the case of the Decalogue comparative studies are particularly helpful.[15]

Now the term used in the Bible for the divine-Israelite encounter at Sinai is *berit*.[16] Hebrew makes no distinction in terminology between a covenant with God and a treaty drawn up between kings or between two individuals.[17] All are termed *berit*. This fact provides a clue to the true significance of the Decalogue. The conventional Near Eastern treaty served as the conceptual model for the national experience at Sinai. In the ancient world of the Fertile Crescent, the covenant treaty was the recognized instrument by which desired relationships were effectuated and regulated. Many examples of such treaties have survived the ravages of time. They divide themselves roughly into three general groupings. There are the Hittite treaties from the second half of the second millennium B.C.E., Aramaic treaties from the ninth century B.C.E. from the Syro-Palestine sphere, and treaties from the Assyrian Empire from the ninth to the seventh centuries B.C.E.

It is the oldest group, the Hittite treaties, that are of particular interest in connection with the present topic. It has been noted that these conform to a more or less fixed basic literary pattern. In general, legal terminology and documentary patterns exhibit a remarkable tenacity and consistency in the ancient Near East. The training of scribes, of course, had a lot to do with it, as is proved by extant Mesopotamian formularies and vocabulary lists for scribes who specialized in legal phraseology.[18] Scribes and diplomats who drafted treaties in the Hittite Empire generally hewed closely to a basic prototypal structure covering six sections. First comes the "Preamble." The author of the treaty is identified by name, and his titles, attributes, and genealogy are listed. Next comes the "Historical Prologue," or introduction, which surveys the historical relationships between the contracting parties. In this section are detailed the past benefactions bestowed upon the vassal by the suzerain king, which are the basis for the vassal's present gratitude and future allegiance. Then follow, in turn, the "Stipulations," which are the core of the treaty; the call for the "Deposition" of a copy of the treaty in the vassal's sanctuary, with provision for its periodic public reading; and a long list of gods who act as "Witnesses" to the terms of the document. Finally, the "Curses and Blessings" complete the covenant, the former describing the dire consequences of the vassal's infraction of the treaty terms, the latter pointing to the beneficial results of faithful adherence to them.[19]

III

Turning now to the Covenant at Sinai, one may detect at once the striking similarities between it and the Hittite treaty forms just described. The Decalogue opens with a preamble identifying the author of the Covenant: "I am the Lord your God."[20] Then comes the historical prologue, a retrospect of the benefactions that God has wrought for Israel: "who brought you out of the land of Egypt, the house of bondage."[21] This is the overriding, pivotal event, the dominant theme in Israelite history that cemented the relations between God and Israel, and that remained the cause for Israel's eternal gratitude and the basis of the obligations it owed Him. The third section, the "Thou shalt" and "Thou shalt not," comprises the stipulations,[22] the principles on which the future relations of Israel to God are to be based. The other three elements that characterize the Hittite treaties are not included in the Decalogue itself, but they are present elsewhere in the account of the Sinaitic revelation. A copy of the Covenant is required to be deposited in the sanctuary,[23] and provision is made for the periodic public reading of the text.[24] Of course, there is no room for gods as witnesses in Israel's monotheistic religion, but their place is taken by "heaven and earth,"[25] or by memorial stones,[26] and the curses and blessings—in reverse order—are very much alive in the great "Reproofs," or *Tokhahot*.[27]

IV

What significance attaches to the fact that the ancient Near Eastern treaty pattern became the model for the expression of the division of the divine-human encounter at Sinai? First and foremost it must be stressed with every emphasis at one's command that in using the term *berit*, "Covenant," the Bible is not resorting to a mere figure of speech, but is describing a living reality, an actual legal circumstance, nothing less than the assertion of an actual, eternally binding pact between God and His people.[28] Just as the ancient treaties served to regularize and control relationships between one individual and another and between one state and another, so the Covenant at Sinai aimed to delineate the proper relationships between God and Israel. But there is also one fundamental difference. The Near Eastern treaties are political documents that usually affect only the foreign policies of states. They do not infringe upon internal affairs except insofar as these impinge upon the interests of the suzerain state. The Sinai Covenant, on the other hand, projects a revolutionary expansion of the original concept, first by including each and every aspect of life within the treaty stipulations, and then by making God and an entire people the parties to the Covenant. These two features of the biblical exemplar are absolutely unique. There is no parallel in history for such concepts, no analogy to Israel's claim to have undergone a national religious experience, no conceptual prototype for that claim.

No less revolutionary than the innovations themselves are the consequences that flow from them. The entire nation of Israel is conceived as being a corporate entity, a "psychic totality." The obligation to keep the law is national, societal, and communal. Evil is a breach of the Covenant that undermines society. The welfare of society, the integrity of its fabric, is contingent upon the observance of the law.[29] No wonder that the conventional treaty provision requiring periodic public reading of the treaty's stipulations was expanded in Israel and transformed into a wholly new dimension—the obligation, oft-repeated, to disseminate the law among the masses, the universal duty of continuous self-education.[30]

In the ancient Near East the opposite was the case. Hammurabi, it is true, wrote the laws—so he said—so that a plaintiff or defendant might know what they were.[31] But this was largely a fiction, since mass illiteracy was the rule, and interest in the law was aroused only after the inception of a case, and was restricted to the details of the particular paragraph of the code that applied in the circumstances. More in common with the spirit of Mesopotamian society was the injunction forbidding the dissemination of the details of the temple service for the New Year festival.[32] One is reminded of the fact that until Draco (circa 621 B.C.E.) codified the laws of Athens, these remained the exclusive knowledge of the nobility, and their publication among the masses was forbidden. Diametrically opposed to such a notion is the biblical outlook. In Judaism the mass dissemination of the law in all its details is a major priority. The reason is obvious. Law is not simply an intellectual exercise, but a moral discipline through whose instrumentality the entire society is shaped.

V

A further crucial distinction between the Decalogue and ancient Near Eastern codes lies in the source and sanction of law. No biblical law is ever attributed to Moses himself or to any prophet personally. The narratives know nothing of a lawgiver-sage or a lawgiver-king. The great empire builders and organizers, David and Solomon, have no connection with law codes. The great reformers Jehoshaphat,[33] Hezekiah,[34] and Josiah[35] reorganize the judiciary and the cult, but they do so only to implement the ancient law of God. They make no claim to innovation. The only name exclusively connected with law is that of Moses, and he is a prophet who mediates the divine communication to Israel.

This picture is in striking contrast to the situation in the ancient world, where the legislators are kings, princes, and sages. The king and the state constitute the source of law, its sanction, and the authority behind it.[36] It is perfectly true that the polytheistic gods themselves did not behave according to moral norms, but they did, nevertheless, desire that mankind be in possession of just laws. They wanted the king to establish justice in the land. Some gods, such as Shamash, the sun-god, were looked upon as the custodians of justice and equity. Thus, Hammurabi invokes the gods in the prologue to his laws, and the stela on which they are inscribed is decorated with a relief depicting Shamash presiding over their promulgation.[37] The text, however, leaves no doubt that Hammurabi ascribes the laws to himself: "I established law and justice in the language of the land."[38] "The laws of justice which Hammurabi, the efficient king, set up."[39] "I am the king who is preeminent among the kings; my words are choice; my ability has no equal. By the order of Shamash, the great judge of heaven and earth, may my justice prevail in the land; by the word of Marduk, my lord, may my statutes have no one to rescind them."[40] It is very much Hammurabi who is the author of the laws, not the gods. The role of the god in law is to serve as the source of wisdom, as the one who implants in man the faculty of discernment and truth and the perception of justice. This is what enables kings to make righteous laws. But the actual origin and source of law lie in human wisdom, not in the revealed will of the gods. The biblical claim that the law, in fact, constitutes the revealed will of God remains unparalleled.

VI

There is no biblical tradition to indicate how the Decalogue was distributed over the tablets of stone.[41] The Pentateuch invariably refers to tablets, in the plural,[42] and usually mentions two specifically,[43] but what was written on each is not clarified. The Tannaitic midrash on Exodus—the Mekhilta—assumes that there were five on each tablet,[44] and Jewish art has fossilized this interpretation. In the Talmud of Palestine, however, another tradition is evident, to the effect that the Ten Commandments were written *in toto* on each stone separately.[45] Both traditions reflect an acute perception of the essential nature of Torah legislation, namely, that the covenant idea suffuses every aspect of life.

The Decalogue, indeed, falls more or less naturally into two divisions. The first four "Words" indubitably relate to the divine-human sphere; the last five clearly govern interpersonal relationships; and the fifth acts as a kind of bridge between the two parts, for the Bible uses the same vocabulary for revering parents as for revering God.

This balance between what we would call the "religious" and the "social" is well illustrated by the opening and closing words: "God . . . fellowman." Each of the first five declarations contains the phrase "the Lord your God," which does not appear in the last five. The "religious" demands precede the "sociomoral" because only a sense of responsibility to God provides the ultimate guarantee of the observance of our duties toward our fellow beings;[46] conversely, professed belief in God, and the observance of the outward forms of religious expression, are well-nigh worthless unless they profoundly affect human relationships. This interweaving of the spiritual, the cultic, the moral, and the legal, this lack of differentiation between "religious" matters, matters of interpersonal relationships, and matters of social and sexual morality—this is the quintessential differentiating characteristic of biblical law. All other systems in the ancient world display an atomistic approach to life. Civil obligations belong to the domain of law, moral demands to the domain of wisdom literature, cultic responsibilities to the domain of priestly handbooks. Law is strictly secular in content. In Israel, however, life is treated holistically. It is not compartmentalized. Crime is also sin. An offense against sexual morality, against business morality, against social morality, is simultaneously a "religious" offense because one and all they are infractions of the divine will.

VII

It will surely have been noted that the Decalogue is distinguished by the total absence of specific individual penalties for the violation of the injunctions and prohibitions. We find only "Thou shalt" or "Thou shalt not." These apodictic formulations have no definitions, no limitations, no punishments—they are unqualified, absolute declarations.[47] This is no coincidence. The phenomenon goes to the very heart of the meaning and significance of the Decalogue.

What the apodictic formulation asserts is that there are certain God-given values and behavioral norms which are absolute and not self-originating; morality is the expression of the divine will, and the motivation for observing the law is not fear of punishment but the desire to conform to the will of God. The Decalogue is a self-enforcing code that appeals to the conscience, the spiritual discipline, and the moral fiber of the individual, not to the threat of penalty that can be imposed by the external coercive power of the state. Of course, we do not live in a utopian society, and, as the Mishnah expresses it, "were it not for the fear of government, people would devour each other alive."[48] So elsewhere in the Torah the casuistic pattern of law with its specific penalties is the general rule.

The Decalogue is obviously not meant to provide an alternative to the coercive power of the state. But the dismal record of the modern state in providing for its citizens' quality of life suggests that without the value system of the Decalogue, society is unlikely to make much progress in solving its chronic ills.

NOTES

1. *Commentary to Mishnah,* Tamid 5:1.

2. The Decalogical tradition is already evident in biblical literature; cf. Jer. 7:9; Hos. 4:2, 12:10, 13:4; Ps. 81:10.

3. *De Decalogo, Philo Judaeus,* Loeb Classical Library, trans. F. H. Colson (London-Cambridge, 1937), 7:82–83, sec. 154.

4. Canticles Rabba 5:12; cf. Numbers Rabba 13:15. For an exhaustive list of the specific laws derived from each of the Ten Commandments, see *Ozar Yisrael,* ed. J. D. Eisenstein (New York, 1951), 8:154–68.

5. Mishnah Tamid 5:1; cf. B. Berakhot 11b–12a; P. Berakhot 1:8 (3c). On this subject, see L. Blau, "Origine et histoire de la lecture du schema," *Revue des Études Juives* 31 (1895): 179–201; V. Aptowitzer, "L'Usage de la lecture quotidienne du Décalogue à la synagogue et l'explication de Mathieu 19:16–19 et 22:35–40," *Revue des Études Juives* 88 (1929): 167–70; and G. Vennes, "The Decalogue and the Minim," *In Memoriam: Paul Kahle*, ed. M. Black and G. Fohrer (Berlin, 1968), pp. 232–40.

6. Mishnah Sanhedrin 11:3 mentions the possibility of five passages in the tefillin, but without specifying the Decalogue. *Sifre Deuteronomy*, ed. M. Friedmann (Vienna, 1864), 74b, sec. 35, makes clear that this is the issue. The church father Jerome (340–420 C.E.) reports that he actually saw tefillin containing the Decalogue. On this entire subject, see J. Mann, "Changes in the Divine Service of the Synagogue due to Religious Persecutions," *Hebrew Union College Annual* 4 (1927): 241–310. The finding of such tefillin at Qumran has fully vindicated Mann's position; see Y. Yadin, *Tefillin from Qumran (XQ Phyl. 1–4)* (Jerusalem, 1969), especially pp. 27–29, 34 f., 40.

7. Y. Kaufmann, *Toledoth HaEmunah HaYisreelith* (Tel-Aviv, 1952–56), has repeatedly made this point; cf. 1:185, 2:76 f.

8. There is no rabbinic unanimity as to the content of the "Noahide commandments." The list that enjoys the widest consensus is as follows: the prohibition of idolatry, blasphemy, bloodshed, incest, and robbery; the injunction to establish courts of law; and the proscription of eating from the body of a living animal (Tosefta Abodah Zarah 9[8]:4; B. Sanhedrin 56a; Maimonides, *Yad Hazakah*, Melakhim 9:1). On Maimonides' view, see Marvin Fox, *Diné Israel* (Tel Aviv University, 1972), 3:v–xxxvi.

9. J. B. Pritchard, *Ancient Near Eastern Texts Relating to the Old Testament* (hereinafter referred to as ANET), 2d ed. (Princeton, 1955), pp. 159–98; and *Supplementary Texts* (Princeton, 1969), p. 528.

10. ANET, pp. 412–25.

11. ANET, pp. 425–30; and W. G. Lambert, *Babylonian Wisdom Literature* (Oxford, 1960).

12. The reference is to the so-called atonement magic of the Shurpu series; see S. H. Hooke, *Babylonian and Assyrian Religion* (London, 1962), p. 96 f.

13. E. Wallis Budge, *The Book of the Dead*, reprint (New York, 1960), p. 568 ff.; *The Egyptian Book of the Dead*, trans. Th. G. Allen (Chicago, 1974), pp. 97–99; and ANET, p. 34 ff.

14. Cf. B. Berakhoth 31b; Yebamoth 71a; Kethuboth 67b.

15. S. Goldman, *The Ten Commandments*, ed. Maurice Samuel (Chicago, 1956); J. J. Stamm and M. E. Andrew, *The Ten Commandments in Recent Research* (Naperville, Ill., 1967); and E. Nielsen, *The Ten Commandments in New Perspective* (Naperville, Ill., 1968).

16. Exod. 34:10, 27; Deut. 5:2.

17. E.g., Gen. 14:3: 21:27, 32; and 31:44.

18. Cf. the Old Babylonian compendium called *ana ittishu*, published by B. Landsberger, *Materialien zum sumerischen Lexikon*, vol. 1 (Rome, 1937).

19. G. E. Mendenhall, *Law and Covenant in Israel and the Ancient Near East* (Pittsburgh, 1955), has thoroughly examined the relevant material. See also K. Baltzer, *The Covenant Formulary* (Oxford, 1971); D. J. McCarthy, *Treaty and Covenant* (Rome, 1963); D. R. Hillers, *Covenant: The History of A Biblical Idea* (Baltimore, 1969); K. A. Kitchen, *Ancient Orient and Old Testament* (Chicago, 1973), pp. 90–102; and B. Uffenheimer, *HaNebuah HaQedumah BeYisrael* (Jerusalem, 1973), pp. 70–94.

20. Exod 20:2; Deut. 5:6. This same self-identifying, introductory form of address is characteristic of Canaanite-Phoenician royal proclamations. So in those of Mesha of Moab (ANET, p. 320), Yehawmilk of Byblos (ANET, p. 502), Kilamuwa of Ya'udi (Sam'al; ANET, p. 500), Zakir of Hamath and Lu'ath (ANET, p. 501), Azitawadda of Adana (ANET, p. 499), and Bar-Rakab of Ya'udi (ANET, p. 501).

21. Exod. 20:2; Deut. 5:6.

22. Exod. 20:3–17; Deut. 5:7–18. Maimonides, *Sefer HaMadda'* 1:6, interpreted verse 2, "I am the LORD your God," to be a positive commandment of belief in one God, and the traditional Jewish order lists this as the first commandment. It should be pointed out that the biblical texts (Exod. 34:28; Deut. 4:3, 10:6) speak of "ten words/ declarations" (Hebrew *'aseret ha-debarim*. The postbiblical title *'aseret ha-dibbrot* derives from a singular *dibber* (Jer. 5:13), not *dibbrah*. For the feminine plural form of a masculine singular, cf. *kissé-kisseot, maqqel-maqqlot*.

23. Exod. 25:16; Deut. 10:5, 31:9, 24–26; cf. 1 Kings 8:9 = 2 Chron. 5:10.

24. Deut. 31:10–13.

25. Deut. 4:26, 30:19, 32:1.

26. Exod. 24:4; cf. Josh. 24:27.

27. Lev., chap. 26: Deut., chap. 28; cf. Josh. 24:19–20.

28. W. Eichrodt, *Theology of the Old Testament*, vol. 1 (Philadelphia, 1961), has emphasized this point.

29. Cf. Lev. 18:24–30, 26:3–13; Deut. 11:13–15, 22–32; 28:1–14.

30. Cf. Exod. 21:1; Deut. 31:1, 10–13; Neh. 8:1–8.

31. ANET, p. 178; C. H. rev., xxv:3–19.

32. ANET, p. 331; cf. p. 334.

33. Chron. 19:5–11, on which see W. F. Albright, "The Judicial Reform of Jehoshaphat," in *Alexander Marx Jubilee Volume*, ed. Saul Lieberman (New York, 1950), pp. 61–82.

34. 2 Chron., chaps 29–31.

35. 2 Kings, chaps. 22–23; 2 Chron., chaps. 34–35.

36. This point has been well made by Kaufmann, *Toledoth*, 2:587 f.

37. J. B. Pritchard, *The Ancient Near East in Pictures* (Princeton, 1954), # 515.

38. ANET, p. 165, prologue, v, 20.

39. ANET, p. 177, epilogue, reverse, xxiv, 1.

40. ANET, p. 178, epilogue, reverse, xxiv, 80.

41. On this subject, see Sh. HaKohen Weingarten, "'Aséret ha-dibbrot vehaluqa-tan," *Beth Mikra* 59 (1974): 549–71; and Th. Radai, "'Od 'al 'aséret ha-dibbrot ve-halu-qatan," *Beth Mikra* 62 (1975): 404 f.

42. Exod. 24:12; 32:16, 19; 34:28; Deut. 9:9; 10:2, 4, 5.

43. Exod. 31:18; 32:15; 34:4, 29; Deut. 4:13; 5:19; 9:9–11, 15, 17; 10:1, 3; 1 Kings 9:8 = 2 Chron. 5:10.

44. J. Z. Lauterbach, *Mekhilta de-Rabbi Ishmael* (Philadelphia, 1949), 2:262.

45. P. Sheqalim 6:1.

46. This is the implication of Lev. 19:18.

47. On apodictic and casuistic law, see Kitchen, *Ancient Orient*, p. 147 f.

48. Mishnah Abot 3:2.

Introduction to the Hilleli Manuscript

THE CODEX FORM

The extremities of the Fertile Crescent produced two distinct media of writing. The papyrus scroll was characteristic of Egypt; the tablet was the distinguishing mark of Mesopotamian literacy. Between them the scroll and the tablet constituted the oldest and the most persistent writing format in the ancient world.

Both types were in vogue in Israel. The Decalogue was, of course, inscribed on tablets of stone (Ex. 24:12; 31:18; 34:1, 4; Deut. 4:13, 5:19; 9:9–11; 10:1, 3; II Kings 8:9) and prophetic utterances were also recorded on tablets, though probably of wood (Isa. 30:8; Hab. 2:2). The wide-spread use of this format is attested by such figurative phases as "the tablet of the heart" (Jer. 17:1; Prov. 3:3; 7:3). The medium was, however, ill-suited to literary compositions or lengthy documents. For such purposes the "book-scroll" (Jer. 36:2, 4; Ezek. 2:9; Ps. 40:8), whether of papyrus or of animal hides, was the dominant form, so that a "book" *per se* could readily suggest a rolling-up action (Isa. 34:4). The scroll remained the standard form of the book throughout the lands of the Mediterranean zone until well into late Roman times and this was particularly true among the Jews.

The Letter of Aristeas[1] clearly informs us that in the third century BCE the High Priest in Jerusalem sent a Torah scroll form to King

Ptolemy II Philadelphus in Alexandria and the Greek translation thereof was likewise written on scrolls.[2] About a century later, at a prayer-service called together at Mizpeh by Judah Maccabeus, a book of the Law was "spread out" in the presence of the congregation (I Macc. 3:48), again proving that the scroll form had not been displaced.

If the tablet form was a less convenient literary device than the scroll, it was nonetheless destined ultimately to serve as the inspiration for a revolutionary development in the history of book-making. We have in mind the invention of the tablet-book, the hinging together of wax-covered wood or ivory writing boards. Sets of sixteen such, all attached end to end by means of a gold pin or leather straps and folding up like a screen, have turned up at Calah (Nimrud) in Assyria dating from the beginning of the eighth century BCE.[3] The format is believed to have originated much earlier and to have been widely employed in the writing of Aramaic.[4]

Throughout the Mediterranean world, in Roman times, *tabellae* were extensively used for notes, letters and documents, and several were often bound in book form (*polyptychon*), just as in Mesopotamia. It was inevitable that sooner or later the wooden book would be imitated in a more flexible material, and the parchment notebook appeared in Roman Italy. When it first did so cannot be positively determined, but the format is referred to by the Latin poet Martial[5] (c. 85 CE), and some scholars believe that the *Gallic Wars* of Julius Caesar (d. 44 BCE) was written on parchment codices.[6]

In Egypt, the papyrus scroll did not beget the papyrus notebook. For technical reasons involving problems of stress and strain that developed at the creases and caused cracking, it had not proved satisfactory to fold over papyrus and the scroll remained the sole mode of keeping a papyrus strip of any length.[7]

In Eretz-Yisrael in Tannaitic and Amoraic times it was customary to record Halakoth on *pinakes*[8] which were multileaved[9] and which could be made of papyrus,[10] but these codices were restricted to private use and never employed for public purposes. The codex form made no headway among Jews until comparatively late times.[11] The situation, however, was quite different among the early Christians who adopted the codex from the very beginnings of the Church. Following the accepted Jewish practice in Eretz-Yisrael, the disciples of Jesus would record their master's sayings in note-book form.[12] Thus, the Christian Scriptures initially and naturally came into being in codex form and the discovery of its numerous and diverse advantages ensured its retention. Its convenient portability contrasted with the unwieldiness that attached to large scrolls and was particularly attractive to itinerant missionaries who could also conceal it more readily if need be. It made for easier and quicker reference use, especially in the consultation of specific passages like proof texts, and it did not require the utilization of both hands as did the scroll. It was more economical in that both sides of the page could be written on and it permitted the composition of larger works than did the scroll with its normal length of about 35 ft. Indeed, its average content would be about six times that of its competing format and it no longer became necessary to divide works into more than one unit with the accompanying danger of misplaced volumes. Finally, it enabled more than one book to be encompassed within the confines of a single volume.[13]

The statistics drawn from the extant literary remains from Egypt between the second and fourth centuries CE tell their own story about the Christian adoption of the codex. Whereas less than 3% of the 690 pagan literary papyri deriving from the 2nd and the beginning of the 3rd centuries CE are in codex form, all known Christian papyri of the New Testament and the Jewish Scriptures from this period are so. From the three centuries being surveyed, 62 manuscripts of the latter and 49 of the former have survived, and only 12 of these are in scroll form, some of which are certainly of Jewish origin. By the 4th century, the parchment codex was supreme among the Christians of Egypt. This state of affairs bears elements of irony for though it was initially imitation of Jewish practice that led the Christians to utilize the codex for their own sacred works, it soon became the distinguishing mark of the independence of the Church from the Jewish community and its severance from Jewish traditions and practice. This is emphasized by the fact that already in the 2nd century the Jewish Bible had been transcribed by Christians from scroll to codex form, a process that could only have been the result of deliberate and tendentious choice.[14]

By the end of the 4th century, the codex had made rapid progress also in the pagan Egyptian community. No less than 74% of its extant literary manuscripts have come down to us in this format. It is all the more remarkable, therefore, that the Jews stubbornly resisted the tide of scribal innovation and stuck to the scroll form for the Hebrew Scriptures. The rich collection of the Dead Sea Scrolls contains not a single codex[15] and there is abundant evidence to prove that in the times of the Tannaim and Amoraim the scribes did not write the Bible continuously as a single scroll.[16] Of course, it would have been well nigh impossible to handle such a gigantic document for liturgical purposes and its usefulness for study or reference would have been extremely limited.[17] Rabbinic debate about the "writing" or "fastening together" of individual biblical books or corpora makes it perfectly clear that such attempts were discouraged by the religious authorities and were rare phenomena.[18] It is not accidental that all these discussions are predicated on the assumption of the scroll-form as the natural medium for the transcription of the Bible and that there are no controversies relating to possible halakhic implications of the employment of the codex.[19] In fact, the first unambiguous notice in Jewish literature of the scriptural codex, in contradistinction to the scroll, appears only in the 8th century,[20] though it cannot be doubted that the Hebrew Bible had already been reduced to the book form some centuries earlier.

One or two external sources also bear witness to the tardiness of Jews in adopting the new, more convenient format. In the last quarter of the 4th cent. Optatus of Mileum still made a clear distinction in terminology when referring to Jewish and Christian modes of writing the Scriptures.[21] Whereas for the latter he uses *membranae* ("parchment codices") or *codices* itself, he employs *volumen* ("scroll") for the Jewish type. His contemporary Hieronymous, it is true, in speaking of the sacred books of the Jews variously speaks of *volumina* or *codices*, but no conclusions can be drawn from this since, as has been shown, the two terms are used synonymously by this author.[22] More significant is the statement of Theodoret, bishop of Cyrrhus (d.c. 458), that in his time the use of the scroll was current among Jews.[23]

MODEL TEXTS

The scribal art in ancient times was the possession of an elitist group of specialists and the opportunities for its acquisition were restricted to a limited number of self-perpetuating schools that were highly conservative by nature. For these reasons, the training of a scribe would leave little room for innovation and would assuredly foster a profound respect for textual exactitude. Already by the end of the second millenium BCE, authoritative, standardized versions of the classical texts of Mesopotamia had emerged and the scribes were highly conscious of the importance of transmitting faithful copies of the parent-texts. The striving for accuracy often found expression in the colophons. Wherever possible the scribes did their best to copy from the original work or at least from the earliest recension they could find.[24] In like manner, the desire for a definitive text that would serve as a model for scribes is well exemplified in the history of the Greek classics. The Athenian tyrant Pisistratus (c. 535 BCE) ordered a body of scholars to establish definitive editions of the Iliad and the Odyssey of Homer. This, in turn, served as the basis of the text-critical work of the scholars at the Alexandrian Library three centuries later who produced the model texts for all subsequent editions.[25]

In the case of the sacred Scriptures of Israel, put to public liturgical use and employed as the curriculum of the schools, it is obvious that the natural scribal attitude of reverence for the classical text would have been greatly heightened. Care and accuracy in the transmission of a canonized text would be an elementary expectation, and the existence of model books must be taken for granted. The very fact that so few textual families can be discerned in the biblical scrolls from the Judean desert area gives added credence to this assumption.[26] In this connection it is of great significance that when the Jews of Alexandria in the third century BCE wanted to have the Torah translated into Greek, they displayed keen awareness of the fact that carelessly written texts were in circulation and they sent to the High Priest in Jerusalem to secure an exact copy.[27] Centuries later, soon after the destruction of the Temple, Josephus could boast of a long tradition of scrupulous accuracy that had characterized the textual transmission of the Jewish Scriptures.[28] All this again presupposes the existence of official, authoritative texts that served as models for scribes.

The extant literary sources indeed confirm that at least from late Second Temple times and into the Talmudic period such was the case. Witness the report of "the three Books" in the Temple court found to contain textual variants, and of the attempt on the part of the religious authorities to establish a unified text.[29] We are expressly informed that a scroll deposited in the Temple court served as the model for the correction of other copies[30] and there existed a class of "book-correctors" in Jerusalem who drew their salaries from the Temple treasury.[31] In the period of the Bar Kokhba revolt (c. 135 CE), Rabbi Akiva warned Rabbi Simeon bar Yochai against teaching from "uncorrected" books[32] and toward the end of the 3rd century CE, the Palestinian Amora Rabbi Ammi admonished against retention in the home for more than thirty days of "uncorrected" books.[33]

Unfortunately, no model texts of Scripture have survived from Talmudic times or, at least, none has hitherto been discovered. It is not until the Middle Ages were well advanced that the model codex appears embodying the final crystallization of the Hebrew consonantal text accompanied by its vowel symbols and its liturgical diacritical notations and equipped with the great Masoretic mnemotechnic apparatus designed to guard the Biblical text from error.[34]

SPANISH CODICES

At quite an early stage in its intellectual and cultural development, Spanish Jewry exhibited an unusual sensitivity to textual accuracy which won renown for the reliability of its Talmudic manuscripts. This particular acumen, coupled with a passion for biblical Hebrew linguistic studies, cultivated an attention to detail and textual minutiae which found an outlet in the production of Bible codices that gained fame for their excellence and exactitude.[35] Tenth century sources already refer to the "accurate and ancient Spanish and Tiberian Bibles"[36] and Jonah ibn Janah (c. 985–c. 1040) stressed the indispensable importance of exact manuscripts as tools for grammatical research.[37]

The reputation of Spanish codices spread far and wide, beyond the confines of Spain and into Germany. The famed glossator of the Code of Maimonides, Rabbi Meir ha-Kohen of Rothenberg, (end 13th cent.), mentions that he had examined the "superior and exact Books of Spain" which were famous for their high quality."[38] Jews in the Middle Ages would make the journey from Germany to Toledo for the sole purpose of acquiring model Spanish Torah codices.[39] The scribal schools of Toledo were the most prolific in the production of Hebrew manuscript Bibles and it is from that city that issue the oldest, most sumptuous and most reliable extant codices. That these lost nothing of their popularity with the passage of time is evidenced by the testimony to their superiority lavished by Elijah Levita (1468–1549) who came from Germany,[40] and Jedidiah Solomon Norzi who made use of a Toledo codex of 1277 and of Spanish notes for the great text-critical and masoretic commentary, the *Minhat Shai*, which he completed in Italy in 1626.[41]

THE CODEX HILLELI

The most famous of all Spanish Bibles is that known as the Codex Hilleli. A celebrated report by the astronomer-chronicler R. Abraham b. Samuel Zacuto, written c. 1504, provides practically everything that is known about the codex:

"In the year 4956 AM, on the 28th day of the month of Ab, a severe persecution (of Jews) occurred in the Kingdom of Leon at the hand of two kings who attacked them in a certain citadel. They carried away the Hebrew Scriptures written about 600 years earlier by R. Moses b. Hillel after whom it was called 'Hilleli.' They were exact, and all Bibles were corrected in accord with them. I myself saw two parts, the Former and the Latter Prophets written in bold and precise characters, which had been brought from Portugal at the expulsion and sold in Bugia, Africa, where they currently are, 900 years after their transcription. In his Grammar, David Kimhi, in connection with the verse 'that you may remember' (Num. 15:40), wrote that the Hilleli Pentateuch was in Toledo."[42]

Zacuto's narrative refers to the sufferings of the Jews in the campaign of the combined armies of Castile and Aragon against the fanatical Almohades in 1197.[43] Although the model Hilleli codex was among the spoils taken from Leon, it must very soon have been rescued in some manner and installed in Toledo, for Zacuto cites the testimony of David Kimhi, a contemporary of these events, to the presence of the Pentateuch section in that city in his day.[44] Actually, Kimhi also refers to the Kethubim section as having been there too,[45] while Zacuto himself reports the Prophets to have been in Jewish hands in Portugal in his own times, 300 years later. They may well have been taken to Portugal by exiles from Toledo. The Pentateuch herewith reproduced was completed in that city in 1241 and was corrected according to the Hilleli model. A complete Bible executed in Toledo in 1246 notes the absence of two verses in Josh. 21 (vv. 36, 37) "from the codex which is called Hilleli,"[46] while another Toledo Bible of 1280 adduces variations from the Hilleli in its Masoretic notes to Isaiah, Jeremiah and Ezekiel.[47] It is of further interest that the Hilleli is also cited in a codex completed in Lisbon, Portugal, in 1483.[48] It is quite possible that the copyist of this Bible actually consulted the codex in his native town whither it had been brought from Toledo and from which two parts, at least, were taken to Bugia, Africa, by the exiles of 1497. However, a note of caution must be injected here, since in 1487 the Hilleli is still cited in another Bible from Toledo.[49]

Zacuto's statement, taken in conjunction with the information that may be culled from Kimhi, indicates that the Hilleli was bound in four volumes. What happened to the rest of it or, indeed, even to the two prophetical sections, is a complete blank. As has been mentioned, it was present in Toledo in the days of Kimhi, although it is not correct, as Jacob Saphir asserts, that the grammarian claims to have seen it with his own eyes.[50] Kimhi adduces the codex in the name of his contemporary Jacob b. Eleazar, the poet, grammarian and philosopher of Toledo, in whose possession the Hilleli seems to have been at that time.[51] How hazardous it is to assume that a direct citation implies first-hand evidence may be demonstrated by a comparison of Kimhi's comment of Ps. 109:10 with the parallel note in his *Sefer Ha-Shorashim*.[52] In the former, the Hilleli is quoted directly, while in the latter the identical information is given in the name of Jacob b. Eleazar.

What is the date and origin of this famous codex? The only "information" at our disposal is the assertion of Zacuto that the manuscript was 600 years old in 1197. This would place its composition about 600 C.E. Were this to be historic fact, it would take us back to the period soon after the close of the Babylonian Talmud. This was precisely the time of the introduction of the codex Bible form among Jews and, even more significantly, the age when the invention and development of the system of vowel and accentuation signs took place. For these reasons, Zacuto's report cannot be accepted at its face value. If the Hilleli did indeed constitute the contemporary embodiment of two such revolutionary innovations, it would be inexplicable that tradition would not have preserved this momentous fact, especially when the codex became so famous as an exemplary model for scribes.

This brings us to the problem of the name and author of the codex. The confusion and uncertainty attending these issues is exemplified by the remark of Elijah Bahur Asher Ha-Levi (Levita) in the 16th century:

". . . I had thought that the codex was called after its author whose name was Hillel, but I discovered that in some recensions it is written *Hilali* הלאלי with an *aleph* between the two *lameds*. . . I also saw that in the *Mikhlol* printed in Constantinople they vocalized *Helali*, with *sere* under the *he*, and so I do not know what is what."[53]

The variety of spellings is indeed bewildering[54] and includes הילל, הללי, היללי, הלאלי, הלליה, הללייא, הילליא and even הלולים. These variants have generated a diversity of suggestions. The most popular is Levita's original conclusion deriving the title from the name of the copyist.[55] However, the exact name and identification is far from certain for some texts have simply "Hillel," while others have "Moses b. Hillel" and "Hillel b. Moses b. Hillel."[56] At any rate, all attempts to connect this name with a known historical personage have foundered. Menahem Ha-Meiri,[57] and after him Joseph Sambari,[58] believed him to have been Hillel the Elder; S. J. L. Rapoport[59] identified him with the Palestinian Patriarch Hillel II; S. H. Halberstam[60] wanted to recognize in him "Moses Ha-Naqdan" ("the Punctuator"), the supposititious inventor of the Masoretic system of the vowel and accentuation signs—according to a spurious document of Firkowitz.[61]

A different approach to the origin of the appellation is that first espoused by J. Fürst[62] and adopted by H. Graetz,[63] A. Jellinek[64] and C. D. Ginsburg,[65] namely, that "Hilleli" is derived from a locale, the town of Hilla on the Euphrates not far from the ruins of ancient Babylon. Even Halberstam,[66] who does not believe that such an insignificant place could have produced such an important model codex, yet concedes that the scribe, supposedly "Moses (The Punctuator)," came from Ḥilla and so was called "a son of Ḥilla (ben Ḥilla)" or "Hilleli". However, as A. A. Harkavy[67] pointed out, the form *Hilla* could not possibly have yielded an adjectival form *Hilleli*. Even more serious is the objection that the initial consonant of the town's name is a *ḥeth* not a *he*, so that the names cannot be interconnected. What is decisive is the fact that the town of Ḥilla was not founded until 1102.[68] If it were indeed the locale of the codex or the birthplace of its scribe, then the Hilleli would obviously have had to have been written well after this date.

All in all, notwithstanding the variety of spellings, it is simplest to accept "Hillel" as the given name or cognomen of the scribe.[69] After all, Hilleli is the most frequently found form and the variant Hillali is but its Arabized equivalent.[70] Some medieval manuscripts bear the inscription "from the codex of Hillel(i) the scribe"[71] and a Bible from Chufut-Kale (cod. 44) dated 994 CE is attributed to Moses ben Hillel. H. L. Strack, who examined it, pronounced the epigraph to be genuine and to have emanated from the writer of the manuscript himself.[72] The famed Codex Hilleli may well have been his work or that of his father. It would have thus originated in the 10th century. Leon may well have been its provenance or, at least, it must certainly have resided in Leon for a considerable period of time. There is no reason to doubt Zacuto's account of its removal from that city in 1197 and despite its attested presence in Toledo for so long, it could still be referred to as "The Hilleli of Leon" in a Spanish Bible completed in 1448 CE,[73] as well as by Jedidiah Solomon Norzi in the 17th century.[74] The association with Leon must have been very powerful to have preserved this kind of tradition.

The practice of using the Hilleli as a standard exemplar for the needs of scribes naturally gave rise to the compilation of independent lists detailing its orthographic singularities, especially in respect of *plene* and defective readings. Such lists seems to have enjoyed wide circulation in the Middle Ages and for this reason, marginal references to the Hilleli found in the Masoretic codices need not necessarily imply that the exemplar was consulted first hand. The scribe may simply have utilized one or other copy of these registers. Some have, in fact, survived until modern times.[75] Thus, the references to the Hilleli readings to be found in the work of Moses B. Isaac Botarel[76] (d. beg. 15th cent.), Menahem b. Judah b. Menahem de Lonzano[77] (d. beg. 16th cent.), Jedidiah Solomon Norzi[78] (1560–1616), Joseph b. Isaac Sambari[79] (1640–1703) and others,[80] may variously refer either to such lists or to marginal notes in Bible manuscripts or to codices directly copied from and modeled after the original Hilleli. The same would apply to the Torah with Haphtaroth and Five Megilloth printed in Guadalajara in 1475 and which laid claim to have been "corrected according to the Hilleli."[81] At any rate, all these citations and assertions attest to the unrivalled and sustained reputation of the Hilleli over a period of hundreds of years. Its present whereabouts is, alas, unknown.

The facsimile herewith presented is that of the codex housed in the library of the Jewish Theological Seminary.[82] Written on vellum in Spanish square characters, it is the work of the scribe Israel b. Isaac b. Israel who completed its execution in Toledo in the month of Sivan, 5001/1241 for Abraham b. Solomon Abidarham (sic.). The patron was doubtless a member of the wealthy and distinguished Abudarham family of Toledo. The scribe's name is known also as the copyist of an Oxford manuscript of the Latter Prophets, dated 1222.[83] He is also referred to by Menahem Ha-Meiri as having testified to the correct collation of a Pentateuch in Toledo.[84] He may well be identified with the scribe called "Rabbi Israel" to whose pen Isaac Abravanel attributed "the exact Scriptures we have with us in Spain."[85] The work originally encompassed the entire Hebrew Bible, but the Nebi'im and Kethubim have vanished. The Torah, practically complete, is currently bound in three volumes, the first two comprising respectively Genesis and Exodus, while the third covers the rest of the Pentateuch. It was undoubtedly intended as a model for scribes. It contains the *Diqdukei Ha-Teamim* of Aaron b. Asher and note is taken of the presence of extraordinary *tagim*, or ornamental strokes on letters, as well as of certain peculiarly shaped letters.

The significance of the codex lies in the fact that it constitutes a seven hundred year old superb example of the Sephardi scribal art which, as the colophon asserts and the notes abundantly testify, was "carefully corrected according to the model called the Hilleli" at a time when that codex still resided in Toledo, the same place of execution of the present manuscript.

NOTES

1. *Aristeas to Philocrates*, ed. M. Hadas (1951), §§ 176–177, 179, p. 169.

2. *Ibid.* § 310, p. 221.

3. D. J. Wiseman, *Iraq*, XVII (1955), 3–13; M. Howard, *ibid.*, 14–20; A. Leo Oppenheim, *Ancient Mesopotamia* (1964), 23, 242.

4. Wiseman, *op. cit.*, p. 11.

5. *Epigrams*, XIV, 186, 188, cited by J. Finegan, *Light from the Ancient Past* (1959), 369; cf. C. C. McCown *Biblical Archaeologist Reader* I (1961) 254.

6. McCown, *ibid.*

7. J. Černý, *Paper and Books in Ancient Egypt*, (Inaugural Lecture, University College, London), 1947, 10.

8. T. P. Ma'aser. II:4 (49^d); Kilaim I:1 (27^a); T. B. Shabb. 156^a; Men. 70^a.

9. M. Shabb. XII : 5; Tos. Sotah XV:1 (ed. Zuck. p. 321, 1. 6); T. P. Ma'aser Sheni IV:6 (55^b); Mid Lam. Rab. I, ed. Buber, p. 26^b.

10. M. Kelim XXIV: 7.

11. On the *Pinax* in rabbinic literature, see S. Lieberman, *Hellenism in Jewish Palestine* (1962), 87, 203–217.

12. *Ibid.* 204f.

13. On the use of the codex among Christians, see C. C. McCown, *BA*, VI (1943), 21–31; revised, *BAR*, I (1961), 251–261; P. Katz, *JTS*, XLVI (1945), 63–65; B. M. Metzger, *BA*, X (1947), 26–44: D. Diringer *The Hand-Produced Book* (1953), 161–166; C. H. Roberts, *Proceedings of the British Academy* XL (1954), 169–204; *Cambridge History of the Bible*, I (1970), 48–66; E. Würthwein, *The Text of the O. T.* (trans. P. R. Ackroyd, 1957), 7–8; F. Kenyon, *Our Bible and the Ancient Manuscripts* (revised, A. W. Adams, 1958), 41–43; J. Finegan, *Light from the Ancient Past* (1959), 359–399.

14. For these statistics and those cited in the following paragraph, see the two works by Roberts cited in the previous note, pp. 183–186 and 56–57 respectively.

15. See McCown, *op. cit.*, 256.

16. Cf. T. P. Meg. III:1 (73^b).

17. Greek papyri rarely exceeded 35 ft. in length; see F. G. Kenyon, *Books and Readers in Ancient Greece and Rome* (2d. ed. 1951), 53f. The great leather Isaiah scroll from Qumran is about 24 ft. long.

18. Cf. T. B. B.B. 13^b: M. Sofer III:1, 5, 6, ed. Higger, pp. 122, 124, 125.

19. On these matters, see *Studies in Jewish Bibliography, History and Literature in Honor of I. Edward Kiev*, ed. Ch. Berlin (1971), 407–413, esp. 407–409.

20. The term *mishaf*, a loan-word from Arab. *Mushaf*, is first found in the *Halakhoth Gedoloth* (Hilkh. Megillah), ed. Venice, 1548, p. 80, col. a; cf. *Halakhoth Pesukoth*, ed. A. L. Schlossberg, 1886, p. 11, but the entire section is missing in the MS. edited by S. Sassoon, Jerusalem 1950 (v. p. 6, n. 8). The codex is termed שׁוּיִם in some colophons cited by A. Harakavy and H. L. Strack, *Catalog der Hebräischan Biblihandschriften der Kaiserlichen Offentilichen Bibliothek in St. Petersburg*, 1875, 227, no. 4; 229 (top), contrast no. 6, 1.3.

21. Cited by Roberts, *PBA* (*op. cit.*), 199 and fn. 1.

22. See E. F. Sutcliffe, *Biblica*, XXIX (1948), 195–204, esp, 198, 201, 203.

23. See C. Van Puyvelde in *Dictionnaire de la Bible* (suppl. 1957), V. col. 794.

24. See W. Hallo, *IEJ*, 12 (1962), 13–26; *JAOS*, 83 (1963), 167–76; *idem*, 88 (1968), 71–89; D. J. Wiseman, *Cambridge History of the Bible*, I, 39–40.

25. See G. H. Putnam, *Authors and Their Public in Ancient Times* (1894), 133–134; E. A. Parsons, *The Alexandrian Library*, (1952), 8, 109, 169, 219, 224.

26. On this subject, see *Encyclopaedia Judaica*, Vol. IV, cols. 832–836.

27. *Aristeas* §30, *op. cit.*, p. 111.

28. *Contra Apion* I:6, 8 ed. H. St. J. Thackeray, pp. 175, 181.

29. T. P. Ta'an. IV:2 (68^a); Sifrei Debarim § 356, ed. Friedmann 148^b, ed. Finkelstein p. 423; Aboth d. R. Nathan, XLVI^b end, ed. Schechter, p. 65^a; M. Sofer, VI:4, ed. Higger, p. 169.

30. M. Mo'ed Qatan III:4; T. P. Sanh. II:6 (20^c).

31. T. P. Sheq. IV:3 (48^a); B. Sheq. 4^b; Kethub 106^a.

32. B. Pes. 112^a.

33. B. Keth, 19^b.

34. On this subject, see M. H. Goshen-Gottstein, *Biblica*, 48 (1967), 243–290.

35. See H. J. Zimmels, *Ashkenazim and Sepharadim* (1958), 138; cf. *The Sephardi Heritage*, ed. R. D. Barnett, I (1971), 325–326, 345–346.

36. *Teshuboth Talmidei Menahem Le-Dunash* ed. S. G. Stern (1870), 67–68.

37. *Sefer Ha-Riqmah*, ed. M. Wilensky, (1930), 15f.

38. Glosses to Maimonides' Code, *Hilkhoth Sefer Torah*, VIII:2–4.

39. See Zimmels, *op. cit.*, p. 148.

40. *The Massoreth Ha-Massoreth*, ed. C. D. Ginsburg (1867, reprinted 1968), 93.

41. P. E. Kahle, *The Cairo Geniza* (2nd ed., 1959), 139–140.

42. *Sefer Yuhasin*, ed. Filipowski, 2nd ed. A. H. Freimann (1925), reprinted 1963), 220.

43. The date given in the editions of the *Sefer Yuhassin* corresponds to 1196. However, the correct year is 1197 as shown in H. Graetz, *History* (Hebrew ed.) Vol. IV (1871), 251, n. 1 and A. Neubauer in *Studia Biblica et Ecclesiastica* III (1891), 23 and n. 3. The Chronicle of Joseph b. Isaac Sambari (A. Neubauer, *Medieval Jewish Chronicles*, I [1887], 126), erroneously has 4959 AM. The date given in the printed editions of the *Minḥat Shai* to Gen. 1:15 is also a mistake.

44. *Sefer Ha-Mikhlal* (Venice, 1545), 93ª, 156ª, ed. Rittenberg (Lyck, 1862, reprint, Jerusalem, (1965/66). 71ª, 115ª; ed. W. Chomsky (1952), 20 § 6ᶜ; 166. §40P; *Sefer Ha-Shorashim*, ed. Jo. H. R. Biesenthal et F. Lebrecht (1847), 376, s.v. שום.

45. See his Commentary to Ps. 109:10; *Sefer Ha-Shorashim*, 149 s.v. דרש.

46. B. M. Oriental 2201 according to C. D. Ginsburg, *Introduction to the Massoretico-Critical Edition of the Hebrew Bible* (1897, reprint 1966), p. 669, No. 37.

47. Ibid., p. 775, No. 59.

48. *Ibid.*, p. 713, No. 48 = BM Oriental 2628.

49. See A. Berliner, *Hebräische Bibliographie*, XI. No. 64 (1871), 134, item 8.

50. Jacob Saphir, *Even Sappir*, 1 (1866), 15ᵇ; cf. A. Geiger, *Ozar Nechmad*, 11 (1875), 159; Z. Shereschevski, *Mizpeh*, I, 2 (1885), 18.

51. See the reference cited above, note 44. On Jacob b. Eleazar, see J. Schirman, *Ha-Shirah ha-Ivrith bi-Safarad u-be-Provence*, II, 1 (1961), 207–210.

52. See above, note 45.

53. *The Massoreth Ha-Massoreth*, *op. cit.*, 260.

54. The variants are often found in one and the same source. Thus, Menahem Ha-Meiri, *Kiryat Sefer* (1863), 8ª, had both הללייא and הללי; Kimhi uses הללי and הלאלי; MS. BM Add. 15252 cited by Ginsburg, *op. cit.*, 595, refers thrice to הלליה as well as to הללי. The Constantinople edition of the *Sefer Yuhasin*, 281, has הילליא; Kimhi's commentary to Ps. 109:10 inexplicably has הלולים.

55. See above note 53.

56. See A. Neubauer in *Studia*, *op. cit.*

57. *Op. cit.*

58. *Op. cit.*, note 43 above.

59. *Iggeroth Shir* (1885), 77–78.

60. *Ha-Carmel*, II, 21 (1842), 167–168.

61. See *Zion*, I (1840–41), 135–142; S. Pinsker, *Lickute Kadmoniot*, I (186), 32; A. Geiger, *Urschrift und Ubersetzungen der Bibel* etc., (1928), 485 (Hebrew ed., 1949, 319); H. Graetz, *History* (Hebrew ed.) III. 484–485; W. Wickes, *A Treatise on the Accentuation of the Twenty-one so-called Prose Books of the O. T.* (1887, reprinted 1970), 4 no. 8; M. Steinschneider, *Vorlesungen über die Kunde Hebräischen Handschriften*, 2d ed. 1937, 16 (Hebrew transl., 1965, 27)

62. *Geschichte des Karäerthums* (1862), 22, 138, n. 94.

63. Graetz, *op. cit.*

64. See S. Rubin, *Historia de riti hebraicl di Leon Modana Rabi* (Hebrew, 1867), 126; cf. *Ha-Mizpeh*, I (1886), 19.

65. See his note 40 to Levita's *Massoreth Ha-Massoreth*, *op. cit.*, 260.

66. *Op. cit.*

67. See his supplement, p. 40, to Graetz, *op. cit.* (Hebrew edition) IV. 250. A. Neubauer in *Studia*, *op. cit.* 23. n. 3, abandoned his earlier support of this theory.

68. See *Encyclopaedia of Islam*, III (1971), 389.

69. Cf. A. Neubauer, *Studia, op. cit.*
70. See Steinschneider, *op. cit.*, 6, n. 19 (Hebrew, 16, n. 19).
71. See *Minḥath Shai* to Gen. 1:15; J. Saphir, *op. cit.*, II 199; A. Merzbacher, *Ohel Avraham* (1888), MS. 156.
72. *Hastings Dictionary of the Bible*, IV, 728–9.
73. Ginsburg, *Introduction*, 432.
74. See, e.g., his note to 1 Kings 1:18.
75. Cf. J. Saphir, *op. cit.*, I, 15^b; II, 199, 200–213; A. Merzbacher, *op. cit.*, 15f.
76. *Commentary to Sefer Yeṣira*, Jerusalem, 1965, p. 77.
77. *Sefer Or Torah*, Berlin, 1745, *Passim*; cf. esp. p. 9^b.
78. For lists of the citations by Norzi of the Hilleli, see H. L. Strack, *Prolegomans Critica in Vetus Testamentum* (1873), 16–19, 114–115; J. Saphir, *op. cit.* II, 199. Norzi refers to a Ferrara copy העתק פיראדה (see his notes to Deut. 3:11; 28:68; 32:1; 33:29). Ch. B. Friedberg, *History of Hebrew Typography in Italy* (1956), 27 records a Torah with Haftaroth and Five Megilloth printed by Samuel Usque in 1555 under the title of העתק פיראדה. I have not been able to check whether this was indeed the source of Norzi's Hilleli citations, but it should be noted that he mentions a "Ferrara print" in his comment to Ex. 34:7.
79. See A. Neubauer, *Medieval Jewish Chronicles, op. cit.*
80. See H. L. Strack, *op. cit.*, 15–22.
81. See Ch. B. Friedberg, *op. cit.*, 93.
82. JTS Ms. 44^a (Accession number 01748), I am grateful to the librarian, Dr. M. Schmelzer, for his assistance in examining the codex as well as the notes of Mr. Lutzki thereon.
83. A. Neubauer, *Catalogue of the Hebrew Manuscripts in the Bodleian Library*, I (1886) 811, MS. No. 2331.
84. *Kiryath Sefer, op. cit.*, 8^b.
85. Comment to Amos 3:12.

Writing a Commentary on the Torah

The recent publication of the JPS Commentary, *blending the latest scholarship in history, archaeology, anthropology, and linguistic-textual research with the religious, ethical, and halakhic teachings of rabbinic sources, represents the newest link in the centuries-old Jewish tradition of writing Bible commentaries. So argues Professor Nahum M. Sarna in this illuminating essay, which both informs us as to the process by which the* JPS Commentary *came into being—from inception to publication, and which provides a suggestive aperçu of medieval trends of biblical exegesis. By demonstrating the rabbis' open-minded, even radical independence in exegesis, Sarna reinforces the historical-intellectual connection between the* JPS Commentary *and those which, through the ages, have preceded it.*

We express our deep gratitude to Dr. and Mrs. Sidney Peerless, immediate family of Rabbi Feinberg and long-time friends of the Judaic Studies Program, for their continued support of this lectureship and its publication.

Dr. Benny Kraut
Professor and Director
UC Judaic Studies Program

There are translations of the Bible and there are commentaries on it. The first is essentially a Christian enterprise; the second is characteristically Jewish. This dichotomy may sound strange, and may well be claimed to be unhistorical. After all, the early translations were made by Jews to serve the needs of Jewish communities. Nevertheless, it is also a fact that Jewish religious authorities generally frowned upon translations, resisted attempts to make them official, and even when they finally capitulated to the pressure of the non-Hebrew speaking

Jewish masses, they strictly circumscribed the public use of Bible translations in liturgical contexts, as we shall soon see.

There were, and are, several excellent reasons for this hostile rabbinic attitude—aside from the polemical purposes for which sectarian
and Christian theologians exploited translations. Next to the virus of
anti-Semitism, the universal acceptance of the one received Hebrew
text of the *Tanakh*—as the Hebrew Bible has come to be called among
Jews—has always been the great unifying agent in Jewish life. To give
recognition to a translation is to foster a divisive factor that is ultimately
destructive of that unity.

Furthermore, by uncompromising insistence on exclusive authority
for the Hebrew Bible, the Rabbis ensured the preservation of the
Hebrew language as the linguistic medium of Jewish intellectual creativity throughout the lands of the Jewish diaspora, even though
Hebrew ceased to be the language of everyday speech among all Jews.

Translations, particularly those adopted by ecclesiastical hierarchies,
tend to wield potent influence, frequently deleterious, over the hearts
and minds of their devotees. They often receive virtual, if not official,
canonicity. Either way, the phenomenon engenders an attitude that
encourages a fundamentalist, monolithic approach to the Scriptures,
one that is subversive of intellectual freedom, corrosive of tolerance,
and productive of doctrinal tyranny. Moreover, a translation of the Holy
Scriptures, however felicitously and elegantly executed, must perforce,
in the long run, be the enemy of truth. It is surely difficult enough to
transplant a piece of literature from its native cultural soil into another
milieu of quite a different character and composition. Can the fine
nuances of language, the deliberately introduced ambiguities, the
instinctive elements and distinctive qualities of style of a great national
opus of consummate artistry really be accurately conveyed and truth-
fully reproduced in another language? Can the cultural, linguistic, and
spiritual barriers really be overcome? These difficulties are compounded immeasurably by the large number of obscure Hebrew words,
phrases and grammatical forms that are scattered over the texts. The
truth is that despite the vast strides in our knowledge of the ancient
Semitic languages made over the past century, many passages in the
Hebrew Bible still remain imperfectly understood. In many instances,
therefore, translations are deceptive. They substitute simplicities or
speculative emendations for the obscurities, either of which can be
quite misleading.

No wonder the second century C.E. Palestinian sage Rabbi Judah declared that "He who translates a [biblical] verse literally is a falsifier, and he who amplifies it blasphemes and defames."[1] One might add that perhaps the most serious shortcoming inherent in all and any translation of the Hebrew Scriptures is the automatic fossilization of a single understanding of a text. Willy nilly, translation is interpretation, an exercise in exegesis; by virtue of this inescapable fact, it violates a cardinal principle of the rabbinic approach to the Bible. Traditionally, Jewish exposition of the Hebrew is firmly grounded in the conviction that embedded in the text is a multiplicity of meanings, the full richness of which cannot be expressed through a single body of doctrine or by any monolithic system that is logically self-consistent. The multiple sense of Scripture was always the lodestar of the Jewish interpreter.

"One thing God has spoken, two things have I heard," said the Psalmist.[2] And that is an understatement, for the school of Rabbi Ishmael cited Jeremiah 23:29: "Behold, My word is like fire—declares the Lord—and like a hammer that shatters rock." And they expounded it to mean that, "Just as a rock is shattered into numerous fragments (or, "generates innumerable sparks") so may a single verse convey a multiplicity of meanings."[3] Indeed, like a skillfully cut diamond, the brilliance and beauty of the Torah are enhanced by its "seventy facets."[4]

To be sure, Jewish popular pressure for vernacular translations of the Hebrew Scriptures was in itself highly commendable. It testified to an intense piety and passionate attachment to the heritage of Israel on the part of the ordinary, unlearned Jew to whom the ancient sources of his tradition were no longer intelligible in their Hebrew original. First, it was the Aramaic language, the lingua franca of the ancient Near East, that gradually encroached upon the native tongue. As early as the ninth and eighth centuries B.C.E., Aramaic was in use in the lands adjacent to the kingdoms of Israel and Judah—in the Syrian and Transjordanian regions. At least, it was employed for monumental inscriptions. Within Israel itself, the hundred years of warfare with the Aramean states in the north, and the intermingling of populations that inevitably occurs as national borders are violated back and forth with the waxing and waning of the fortunes of war—doubtless this situation greatly contributed to the incursions of the Aramaic language into Hebrew. Certainly, the most important factor in the spread of Aramaic was the massive transplanting of populations by the Assyrian kings Shalmaneser V and Sargon II following the destruction of the northern kingdom of Israel in 722–721 B.C.E. and the exile of much of its population. Aramaic-speaking peoples in sizable numbers were settled in the area. Of course, the successive deportations of the Judeans at the hands of the Babylonians in the years 597 B.C.E. and 587 B.C.E. provided the final and most powerful impetus for the Aramaization of the Jewish people. By the time of Ezra and the return of the exiles to Zion, Aramaic was the native tongue of large numbers of Jews.

A unique popular institution emerged to accommodate this unprecedented situation. The public reading of the Torah came to be accompanied by oral translation into Aramaic. Fearful that the latter might, in time, supplant the original, the religious authorities imposed certain judicious restrictions upon the practice. The *meturgeman,* as the interpreter was called, was not permitted to make use of an aide-memoir or even to look at the text of the Torah while translating. Nor might the official lector assist him in any way.[5] Further, when the *meturgeman* was present, the lector would read only one verse at a time, instead of the usual minimum of three verses.[6] In the course of time, the Aramaic translation—the Targum, as it came to be known—was officially accepted, was put into written form, and even became prescribed for study alongside the weekly Torah readings,[7] and this even long after Aramaic had ceased to be the spoken language of Jews.

Much less fortunate was the Jewish experience with the Greek translation of the Scriptures. The *Epistle of Aristeas,*[8] which purports to tell the history of the Septuagint, claims that the initiative for it came from Demetrius of Phalerum, historian and scholar at the great library of Alexandria, and that King Ptolemy Philadelphus (285–247) was its sponsor. We know, however, that this work was a clever piece of Hellenistic-Jewish propaganda and apologetics, and that in reality the Greek rendering of the Torah was meant to satisfy the needs of the enormous Greek-speaking Jewish community of Alexandria, Egypt, that had largely forgotten its Hebrew.

For a while, this translation was favored even by the Jewish religious leadership in Palestine. Rabbi Simeon ben Gamaliel (1st century C.E.) declared that investigation demonstrated that the Torah could be adequately translated only into Greek.[9] The Hellenistic Jewish philosopher Philo Judaeus of Alexandria (20 B.C.E.–50 C.E.) reported that the 8th day of the month of Teveth was an annual festival of thanksgiving to God for the gift of the Septuagint.[10] Later on, however, for several excellent reasons, that Greek translation fell from favor among Jews. *Megillat Ta'anit,* "The Scroll of Fasting," is a list of thirty-six days on which important events in Jewish history occured and on which it is forbidden to fast. It probably derives from about the time of the Bar Kokhba revolt (ca. 135 C.E.). An Appendix to it has a list of fast-days, among them "the eighth day of Tevet when the Torah was translated (literally, "written") into Greek in the days of King Ptolemy—and darkness descended on the world for three days." And Tractate Soferim adds that that day was as disastrous for Israel as the day when the golden calf was made, for the Torah cannot be adequately translated.[11]

Of course, Jews continued down the ages to translate the Tanakh into their particular vernacular. Often, they were pioneers in this enterprise. But, no one had any illusions about it. The translations were exercises that betrayed concessions to Jewish ignorance of Hebrew. They possessed no authority, and were not used liturgically—at least not until the period of Jewish emancipation in Europe. Not translation, but commentary became the standard universal mode of relating to the sacred texts. As Gershom Scholem has formulated it, "Commentary on Scripture became the characteristic expression of Jewish thinking about truth."[12] To put it another way, it was into commentary that Jews poured their intellectual energies. Commentary on Scripture became the main traditional vehicle for Jewish intellectual endeavor. How could it have been otherwise, seeing that the Hebrew Bible constituted the very protoplasm of Jewish existence, the matrix out of which emerged all subsequent development? To the delight of Jewish scholars, and especially of professors of biblical studies, there came a time when the Hebrew Bible could no longer be read, only studied. This state of affairs was the product of a specific historical circumstance. Following the sweeping victories of Alexander of Macedonia and the consequent Hellenization of the lands of the ancient Near East, the cultural environment that produced the Hebrew Bible was no longer familiar to the reader. Thereafter, the traditional metaphors of the biblical text ceased to be immediately intelligible. How, for instance, is one to relate to the Hebrew of Psalm 7:10, which literally tells us that the righteous God "examines hearts and kidneys?" If one does not know that in ancient Israelite psychology the heart was seen as the seat of the intellect and the kidneys the seat of the conscience, one might conclude that the psalmist conceives of God as a cardiologist and nephrologist, rather than One who probes the human mind and conscience to detect and react to hypocrisy, pretense, deception, duplicity, and similar unsavory human attributes. Without a commentary, one would not know this, and the sense of the text would be distorted. Of course, it may be claimed that a translation may equally convey the true intent of Hebrew idiom as does the new Jewish Publication Society version. This version renders the passage in question: "He who probes the mind and conscience is God the righteous," and it carries a footnote informing the reader of the literal meaning. But then that is commentary, and it raises at once the question as to the nature of a translation and the obligation of the translator. Is the rendering to be photographic or impressionistic? Should it seek to maintain a meticulous regard for verbal or phraseological equivalence or rather seek to convey the sense of the original? Is the prime consideration the genius and idiom of the receptor language or of the original? In each case, modern translations have opted for the alternative and have thereby transformed themselves into commentaries. As such, however, they are woefully defective for the interpretation has generally become monolithic. The translations violate the above cited cardinal rabbinic exegetical principal of the multiple sense of Scripture.

It goes without saying, that a Bible commentary means commentary on the Hebrew text, not on a translation. It should also be self-evident that commentary cannot be confined solely to elucidating the text by attempting to rescue the supposed "original meaning" of the writers through recourse to philological research and recovery of the contemporary cultural milieu in which the works were authored. This approach is without doubt indispensable. It is the *sine qua non* and starting point of any modern interpretive endeavor. But to believe that this alone is determinative is to commit what literary critics call the "intentional fallacy." Throughout the millennia Jewish interpretation of the Hebrew Bible was informed by the abiding consciousness that it was the major source for the national language, the font of all Jewish values, ideals and hopes, and the fountainhead of inspiration for the distinctive life-style of the Jew. These always were and still are matters of transcendent seriousness that demanded and demand, not surface reading, but deep study and comprehensive exposition. The unbelievably rich hermeneutical literature generally subsumed today under the rubric of *parshanut hamikra'* is characterized appropriately by infinitely variegated attitudes and approaches, and by an obstinately healthy refusal to absolutize any single stance. The intrinsically endless variety of interpretation, often internally contradictory and replete with antinomies has always confronted the literate Jew with a vast array of exegetical texts not one of which is authoritative but each of which commands attention and calls for concentration of thought and continuous study. The literature of biblical interpretation itself became an essential propaedeutic discipline for the cultivated Jew. This vast, inexhaustible store of exegetical material reinforced and enhanced the study of Tanakh as a religious obligation, a spiritual exercise, a mode of worship, and a moral training.

All this found concrete expression in what has become known in Hebrew as the *Miqra'ot Gedolot,* the "Rabbinic Bible." To my mind, this is one of the noblest expressions of rabbinic Judaism. What I mean is that the Hebrew text is surrounded by a sea of commentaries of diverse authorship, provenance, dating and exegetical approaches, often mutually incompatible and contradictory. They coexist within the confines of a single page, all accommodated within the framework of a single tradition.

The commentators themselves never entertained the notion that what they wrote was definitive. For instance, Rashi, according to the testimony of his grandson, the Rashbam (Rabbi Samuel ben Meir, ca. 1080/1085–1158), was quite clear about this. In the latter's commentary to Genesis 37:2 he explicitly relates that his grandfather told him that had he the time, he would have revised his commentaries to bring them into accord with "the innovative expositions of the text being made daily." Without doubt, Rashi was referring to the great grammatical, philological, and exegetical works of the Spanish Jews, a knowledge of which had begun to percolate into the communities of France and the Rhineland.

Moreover, the traditional commentators were sometimes none too gentle with each other. This same Rashbam relates to the dying patriarch Jacob's testament addressed to Judah in Genesis 49:9: "Judah is a lion's whelp; on prey, my son, you have grown." He comments: "Whoever interprets the verse as referring to the sale of Joseph is completely ignorant of both verse structure and the division of the cantillation signs." Interestingly, the interpretation that Rashbam rejects is to be found, *inter alia,* in such classical texts as Genesis Rabba 98:9 and the Pseudo-Jonathan Targum, as well as in his own grandfather's commentary. Nahmanides (1194–1270), in his exegesis of Genesis 9:18 remarks that the celebrated commentator "Rabbi Abraham [ibn Ezra, 1092–1167] has forsaken his path in the straightforward interpretation of Scripture, and has begun to prophesy lies." He also lashed out at Moses Maimonides (1135–1204) of whose explanations of Genesis 18:1 in his *Moreh Nevukhim* ("Guide for the Perplexed") II.42, he writes that "it is forbidden to listen to them, let alone believe them." In the same vein, he accuses Maimonides of "heaping foolishness upon foolishness"—so in his comment to Numbers 20:1.

It is an egregious error to believe that the traditional Jewish commentators regarded the exposition of the Tanakh as a self-contained, autonomous and closed field of intellectual endeavor. To the contrary, their free and practically untrammeled investigation of the Scriptures are replete with critical observations of a historical, textual, theological, and halakhic nature. They could interpret legal and ritual texts not in accord with halakhic rulings. Occasionally, they criticized the Sages of the Talmud for divesting the text of its plain meaning.

These scholars were people who were unquestionably committed to the halakhic authority of the rabbis in their rulings on matters of Jewish law in all its aspects. But they could question the exegesis by which such rulings were derived from the text. It is as though they held that the halakhah enjoys its own, autonomous existence and authority and that the scholars are free to investigate the text independently of dogmatic or traditional considerations. For instance, in expounding on Exodus 23:2, Rashi takes note of Mishnah Sanhedrin 1:6 and states: "There are interpretations of this verse by the sages of Israel, but the language of the text cannot accommodate them." Rashbam, in discussing the rabbinic exposition of Leviticus 7:18 as found in Mishnah Zevaḥim 2:2–4 and the *gemara* in Zevaḥim 29b, frankly asserts: "The Sages have wrested it (the verse) from its plain meaning." Samuel ben Hofni (d. 1030), Gaon (head of the academy) at Sura in Babylonia is cited by David Kimhi (1160?–1235?) in his comment to I Samuel 28:24 as follows: "Even though the words of the sages in the Talmud imply that the woman [i.e. the witch of Ein-dor] really did resurrect the dead Samuel, yet insofar as human reason rejects this they are unacceptable."

It will be remembered that Abrahm ibn Ezra tackles the problematic passage in Genesis 12:6, "The Canaanite was then in the land." First he cites Rashi's explanation: "Possibly Canaan seized the land of Israel from others." Then he seems to cast doubt on its validity, and cryptically adds: "If this is not so, I have a secret, and the prudent person will keep silent." The nature of this "secret" is not disclosed, but is left to the imagination of the reader. However, a supercommentary on Ibn Ezra by Joseph ben Eliezer Tov Elem (Bonfils; d. ca. 1335), called *Tsafenat Pa'aneaḥ*, clearly understood that Ibn Ezra meant that Genesis 12:6 is partly a textual gloss deriving from the post-Mosaic era. Further, he engages in a spirited theological defense of such a notion and implicitly denies it to be heretical. Basing himself on historical considerations, he concludes that "Moses did not write this word 'then' here, but Joshua or one of the other prophets wrote it." He adds the following rationalization: "Since we must believe in the words of tradition and prophecy, what difference does it make whether Moses or some other prophet wrote it, seeing that the words of all of them are truth and [given] by divine revelation (literally, 'prophecy')." No less a person than Rabbi Judah He-Hasid of Regensberg (1150–1217), the saintly mystic, ethicist, theologian, and halakhist, in his commentary to Deuteronomy 2:8 mentions that a certain verse is a post-exilic explanatory gloss inserted into the text of the Torah. Tanhum ben Joseph Yerushalmi (13th century), a rationalist biblical exegete and philologist, raises the possibility that some of the variant readings in Chronicles as opposed to parallel texts in Samuel-Kings, may well have originated with the errors of copyists.[13]

What is perhaps the most remarkable example of independent and radical exegesis is provided by the history of the exegesis on the prohibition of "seething a kid in its mother's milk," found in Exodus 23:19; 34:26, and Deuteronomy 14:21. These three verses constitute the scriptural source for the interdiction on cooking, eating, and deriving benefit from a mixture of meat and milk, as well as for the elaborate series of concomitant ordinances designed to safeguard the prohibition. Notwithstanding the authorities behind the traditional interpretation of those biblical texts, and the obvious centrality of the institution of *kashrut* in the everyday life of the Jew, there exists a wholly different pattern of exegesis of this biblical injunction in some medieval Jewish works.

Menahem ben Saruq[14] (910–970) noted that the prohibition of Exodus 23:19 and 34:26 is juxtaposed to the law of the first fruits. He surmised that there is a direct convection between the two. Accordingly, he took the Hebrew *gdiy* to mean "berries," and not "a kid," as it is usually understood. This eccentric explanation was taken up and expanded by another lexicographer, Menahem ben Solomon (first half, twelfth century), in his *Even Bohan*.[15] The "mother's milk" was interpreted to refer to the juice of the bud that contains the berry, and the entire injunction conveyed to him a proscription on bringing the first fruits to the priest before they are ripe.[16]

I register this selection of little known and generally ignored items, not because they typify medieval Jewish exegesis of the Bible: they do not. They do demonstrate, however, the open-mindedness, the latitude and the range of approaches that many commentators allowed themselves, particularities that have become ever more rare among traditional Jewish exegetes since the end of the Middle Ages. This brings me to the need for a new commentary geared to the English-speaking Jewish communities.

It is reported[17] that when the Prophetical division of the *Tanakh* was first translated into Aramaic by Jonathan ben Uzziel, the Land of Israel quaked over an area of four hundred square parasangs. No such violent reaction of Nature occurred when the new Jewish Publication Society translation of the Bible appeared a few years ago. Emboldened by this calm and obviously sympathetic and agreeable, if soundless, response, Chaim Potok and I approached the officers of the Jewish Publication Society with our proposal for the production of a new commentary. We pointed out that not translation but commentary was the traditional Jewish approach, and we drew attention to the phenomenon that in recent years most faith communities in the United States had published their own up-to-date commentaries. We Jews had none.

The work of J.H. Hertz on the Torah had been a bold educational enterprise for its day. It had successfully educated a couple of generations of Jews. But it had been composed to suit the needs of the immigrants from central and eastern Europe, and their first native-born generation in the English-speaking countries. The passage of more than a half century of fruitful research in many fields has rendered Hertz's scholarship and approach hopelessly out of date. Its apologetics are no longer appealing to the post World War II generation of Jews. Israel has since become the world's leading center of biblical studies and any modern commentary must take account of the considerable quantity of published research penned by highly competent scholars.

True, there is also the Soncino series of Bible commentaries, but in a very real sense it was obsolete even before its appearance in print. It was not executed by scholars trained in Bible and Semitics, and was apparently predicated on the presupposition that all productive scholarship came to an end early in this century. Rabbi W. Gunther Plaut's commentary on the Torah is a commendable production, but it is geared to the Reform Jewish community.

As I stated earlier, Chaim Potok and I presented the officers of The Jewish Publication Society with our proposal for a new commentary on the Bible for the entire English-speaking Jewish community. In their wisdom they realized that to do justice to the new JPS *Tanakh* translation, and to a venerable Jewish tradition, a commentary was sorely needed. The decisive step was taken in 1973.[18] In August of that year, the then JPS president, Jerome J. Shestak, met in Jerusalem with myself, Chaim Potok, Moshe Greenberg, Jonas Greenfield, and Yosef

Yerushalmi. After extensive discussions, we formulated guidelines for the project. Following this, I was appointed General Editor with Chaim Potok as Literary Editor. Jerome Shestak was to act as the liaison between the Society and those responsible for the Commentary.

Of course, it was understood from the beginning that the Commentary would stretch the resources of the JPS far beyond prudent limits. Hence, dedicated officers of the Society undertook to recruit patrons who would each contribute substantial sums to a special fund to be applied exclusively toward defraying the enormous expense that the production would entail.

The selection of the authors was the next step to be taken, and it proved to be no easy task. It was complicated by the very nature of the enterprise, which dictated certain obvious restrictions and criteria. It goes without saying that those who were to be assigned the commentaries on the various books had to be senior professional scholars, recognized authorities in the fields of biblical and ancient Near Eastern studies. They also needed to be thoroughly at home in rabbinic literature and in medieval Jewish exegesis. Another important qualification was the ability to write good, clear, readable English. The authors would have to know how to adapt the results of scholarly research to the needs of the lay reader, and would have to be able to resist the temptation to employ the kind of technical terminology that is so dear to academicians and specialists.

In the past, not many Jews entered the field of modern biblical studies, mainly for want of professional opportunity. This situation has been slowly changing. Today, there is a respectable cadre of young Jewish scholars of high caliber. But there is a dearth of senior scholars. Hence, the pool of potential authors for our Commentary series was severely limited. Two American Jewish professors and two Israeli scholars were recruited, aside from the present writer. Both Israeli scholars subsequently withdrew. We were fortunate to replace one of them with another professional American scholar of distinction, while this writer undertook to author two of the commentaries. The final line-up was: Sarna for Genesis and Exodus, Baruch Levine for Leviticus, Jacob Milgrom for Numbers and Jeffrey Tigay for Deuteronomy.

It had been decided previously to follow the format of the Hertz Pentateuch. That is, the Hebrew, and English translation would appear on a single page in parallel columns, with the commentary spread over the page underneath them. The new *Tanakh* translation, of course, would be the English text but the selection of a Hebrew text of the

Torah unexpectedly turned out to be a vexing problem. Because the entire volume was to be set by computer, it was necessary to find a good text with vowels and cantillation signs on the computer tape. We scoured the world for such a product but encountered repeated disappointment. We were informed that just such a program already existed in a European country at a distinguished academic institution. Its creation had been sponsored and financed by the government of that country. However, the person in charge turned out not to be possessed of the highest ethical standards. Sensing the possibility of self-enrichment, that person asked us to deposit quite a large sum of money in a private New York bank account so that, we were unabashedly told, a comfortable retirement for him could be assured. Of course, the Jewish Publication Society would have nothing to do with any such arrangement, and the search turned to Israel. There, a publishing firm possessed just the product that we were looking for. It transpired, however, that a fresh problem arose, not of ethics, but of expense. The firm demanded royalties on each volume to a degree that would have put it beyond the range of affordability for the average Jewish family, and would have doomed the Commentary to unprofitability from the start.

Further investigation yielded no results until we learned that back in Philadelphia itself, where the offices of the Jewish Publication Society have been housed for over a hundred years, there existed a very important research project on the Septuagint, being undertaken at the University of Pennsylvania. This involved the use of a computerized data base for research on the Greek Bible that required a parallel alignment of all elements of the Hebrew and Greek texts. What is known to scholars as the *Biblia Hebraica Stuttgartensia* was actually available on computer, at least in consonantal form without the vowels and cantillation signs. This is the latest revision of the famous *Biblia Hebraica* originally edited by Rudolf Kittel, which reproduced the Leningrad Codex (B 19A/L), the oldest dated manuscript of the complete Hebrew Bible. It contains a colophon to the effect that it was copied in 1008/1009 C.E. from a manuscript written by the distinguished Masorete Aaron ben Moses ben Asher who lived in the first half of the tenth century in Tiberias. This text would need to be vocalized and adapted in format to the weekly liturgical Torah readings, with their internal subdivisions (*'aliyot*) clearly noted. Another necessary adjustment would be the spacing of the Hebrew text to correspond to the arrangement of the recently completed translation of the Jewish Publication Society (*"The Tanakh"*). In this version thematic and literary units have been appropriately marked off by means of indentation, and poetic sections are graphically indicated. All these issues are relatively minor, technical matters that might be easily resolved by a competent programmer. The University of Pennsylvania project would, at last solve our problem of finding a computer-generated Hebrew text for our Commentary.

The holders of the copyright readily made *Biblia Hebraica Stuttgartensia* text available to us, and our own project could henceforth proceed smoothly. Or so we thought. However, to our dismay, receipt of the print-out of Genesis revealed numerous errors. The General Editor had to undertake the laborious task of checking every letter, vowel, diacritical point and cantillation sign. To guard as much as possible against inevitable human fallibility, a highly competent Orthodox Rabbi was hired to duplicate this inspection independently. The two sets of corrections were then collated, and a master-copy was produced and sent back to the programmer. Alas, the revised print-out uncovered fresh errors not previously present, and a further print-out was ordered. Finally, the process of correction was completed, and the commentary of Genesis was satisfactorily published.

The same inspection process has had to be repeated with each of the other four books of the Torah. Even this expensive and time-consuming system of checks and balances turned out not to be fool-proof. Inexplicably, an extra word mysteriously appeared in the text of Leviticus 23:18, which was not in the last corrected version of the Hebrew. Much to our embarrassment, the error appears in the first edition of the commentary on Leviticus. Three of the five volumes of the Commentary on the Torah have now appeared, and the fourth, which is that on Exodus, is due to be published in December 1990. The character and thrust of the series are available for all to see.

Our new JPS Commentary follows the traditional Jewish approach to the Hebrew Bible as a living organism that perpetually rejuvenates and transforms itself, so that what is time-bound becomes ever timely and what is timely becomes timeless. With deep reverence for the sanctity of the Scriptures, and with profound respect for the insights and teaching that twenty centuries of Jewish commentators have drawn from the texts, our new venture forges a fresh link in that unbroken chain of Jewish exegesis.

For the first time, the assured results of modern literary, archaeological, historical, sociological, anthropological, linguistic and textual research are systematically distilled and digested in non-technical language and presented to the intelligent Jewish public—together with heavy emphasis on the spiritual, ethical, and halakhic teachings of the rabbinic sources, all harmoniously interblended.

Permit me to conclude with a story, excerpted from a medieval Jewish fantasy written by Immanuel of Rome, who lived ca. 1265–1331. He was a friend of Dante and authored a Hebrew work called *Ha-Tofet Ve-ha'eden* (*Inferno and Paradise*), patterned after the famous Divine Comedy of his illustrious contemporary. In this work, he takes a tour of Hell and Heaven. Just as Dante had the great Virgil as his guide, so Immanuel of Rome had the biblical Daniel as his escort. When Immanuel ascends to heaven by what is clearly Jacob's ladder, he sees there King David sitting on his throne surrounded by all the great Jewish Bible commentators. They are discussing the interpretation of Ps. 68 which David had composed, but the meaning of which he himself had forgotten. This psalm, incidentally is the most difficult of all the 150 psalms that comprise the Book of Psalms. Each of the great Jewish commentators—Rashi, Ibn Ezra, Kimhi and so on—gives his interpretation, but none satisfies King David. Then Immanuel of Rome presents his own. King David enthusiastically confirms the correctness of the exposition, rises from his throne, and kisses Immanuel on his forehead. Buoyed by this experience, Immanuel then visits Hell. But there he becomes thoroughly alarmed and depressed at the sight of all those miserable wretches suffering excruciating tortures. He recalls his own sinful life, and wonders what fate will await him. The good Daniel, however, assures him that he has received divine pardon for all his numerous sins for the reason—and note this well—that he devoted his life to biblical studies.

Every commentary on the Bible is a child of its time. It can be none other. The emphases mirror and reflect its contemporary cultural, social, intellectual, and spiritual concerns and Zeitgeist. Hence, by definition, every commentary must embody that which is ephemeral side by side with that which is enduring. History will inexorably render its verdict on our enterprise. We trust that the enduring will outweigh the ephemeral.

NOTES

1. Kiddushin 49a; Tosefta Megillah 4:4, ed. Lieberman, pp. 364, 1223.
2. Ps. 62: 12; cf. Sanhedrin 34a.
3. *Ibid*.
4. Numbers Rabba, *Naso'* 13:15.
5. Tanḥuma *Va-yera'* 6: ed. Buber, p.87; cf. P. Megillah 4:1 (74d); Megillah 3:2a.

6. Mishnah Megillah 4:4.

7. Berakhot 8a; cf. Maimonides, *Hilkhot Tefillah* 13:25.

8. Edited and translated by M. Hadas, New York: Harper and Brothers, 1951.

9. P. Megillah 1:11 (70c).

10. Philo, *Vita Moses*, II:7.

11. Edition M. Higger, New York: Devei Rabbanan, 1937:1,7, pp. 100–102.

12. *The Messianic Idea in Judaism*, New York: Schocken Books, 1971:290.

13. See M. Z. Segal, *Parshanut Ha-Mikra'*, Jerusalem: Kiryat Sefer, 1952:93 for examples.

14. *Mahberet*, ed. H. Filipowsky, London: Hevrat Me'orerei Yeshenim, 1854:53.

15. W. Bacher, *Otsar Ha-Sifrut*, V (Cracow, 1896): 261–262.

16. Cf. Rashi to Deut. 14:22.

17. Megillah 3a.

18. See Jonathan D. Sarna, *JPS: The Americanization of Jewish Culture, 1888–1988*, Philadelphia: Jewish Publication Society, 1989:246–247.

PROPHETS

Naboth's Vineyard Revisited (1 Kings 21)*

King Ahab's unavailing attempt to acquire the vineyard[1] of a certain "Naboth the Jezreelite," and Queen Jezebel's infamous stratagem designed to ensure that her husband realize his desire, are narrated at length in 1 Kings 21. This text preserves several noteworthy and perplexing features that have not been fully elucidated.

It is clear from the start that even in paganized Northern Israel, the monarch had no power, in the present instance, simply to impose his will by force upon his subjects. He accepted the restraint of law. He offered to pay the full value of the property or even to exchange it for a superior parcel of land (vv. 1–3). Upon Naboth's refusal, he could only lie on his bed in a sullen mood, sulk, and reject food, but he could not confiscate the vineyard he so yearned to possess (v. 4).

This remarkable limitation upon crown rights[2] is of particular interest in light of the contrasting arbitrary authority and personal privileges that kings could assert and enjoy in Israel's neighboring states. Akkadian legal and other documents from Ugarit and elsewhere have shown that Samuel's denunciation of the institution of kingship, as recorded in 1 Sam 8:9–17, is an authentic reflection of the contemporary state of affairs in the region.[3] The prophet's assertion that the king would seize his subjects' "choice fields, vineyards, and olive groves" and dispose of them at will (8:14) is in striking opposition to the situation in which Ahab now finds himself.

The impotence of the Israelite king, from a legal point of view, explains the diabolical measures to which Jezebel feels she must resort. As a Phoenician princess, accustomed to a different, Near Eastern conception of tyrannical kingship, in which monarchs can indulge their whims and exercise absolute, arbitrary power, Jezebel evinces undisguised contempt for Israelite limitations on royal authority (1 Kgs 21:7). Nevertheless, she realizes that if she is to secure the coveted property for her husband, her scheme must scrupulously preserve the appearance of legality, even though the substance of justice can be disregarded.[4] So she lays on a veneer of legitimacy by cloaking injustice in the robes of law. Wielding corrupt royal influence, she issues a writ in the king's name, recruits unprincipled, servile judges, and suborns two malevolent false witnesses (vv. 8–10).[5] On her orders, Naboth is unjustly charged with two capital crimes, blasphemy and treason. Of course, the victim is found guilty on both counts, is summarily executed, and his property is expropriated by the king (vv. 11–16).

The two offenses, blasphemy and treason, are listed in the pentateuchal legislation. Exod 22:27 prescribes:

> You shall not revile God[6] nor put a curse upon a chieftain among your people.

While the Hebrew term *nāśî*,[7] here rendered "chieftain," is a designation for a tribal leader and reflects a premonarchic governmental administration, once the monarchy was established, its connotation of "ruler" would plainly be extended to include the king. The Covenant Code thus makes blasphemy and treason statutory offenses, but it specifies no penalty for infractions. However, Lev 24:15–16 is explicit regarding the punishment for blasphemy:

> And to the Israelite people, speak thus: Anyone who blasphemes his God shall bear his guilt; if he also pronounces the name LORD, he shall be put to death. The whole community shall stone him; stranger or citizen, if he has pronounced the Name, he shall be put to death.

Blasphemy appears to have been regarded everywhere as a capital offense, as a crime against public and social order, what in Roman law is termed *crimen publicum*.[8] The reason for this classification seems to have been the belief that the offense incurred the wrath of the insulted deity to the misfortune of the entire community. Hence the severity of the penalty and the involvement of the whole community in carrying out the punishment. The Middle Assyrian Laws, Tablet A 2, legislate that a woman who utters blasphemy "shall bear her liability; her husband, her sons, and her daughters shall not be touched."[9] The nature of the penalty is not specified, but as Driver points out, the explicit exclusion of her near relatives appears to be a revision of an earlier practice that seems to have entailed the punishment of the entire family. Some light on the lacuna in the Assyrian Laws is most likely shed by an inscription of Ashurbanipal (668–627 B.C.E.), which records the way in which two blasphemers were treated; their tongues were ripped out and they were skinned alive.[10]

As to the crime of reviling the king, no biblical legal text mentions the consequential punishment. However, since God and king are paired, implicitly in Exod 22:27[28] and explicitly here in 1 Kgs 21:10, 13 and in Isa 8:21 (in reverse order), it is reasonable to assume that this offense was understood to be on the same level of high crime as blasphemy. It too was taken to be a grave threat to the established social order, a crime against the state, an act of treason meriting capital punishment. Quite likely, this conception is reflected in the desire of Abishai, son of Zeruiah, to slay Shimei ben Gera for "outrageously insulting" King David, as told in 2 Sam 16:5–13, 1 Kgs 2:8–9.

Ahab's expropriation of the vineyard is, on the surface, a puzzling detail in the narrative. After all, Ahab and Jezebel felt compelled to comply, however reluctantly and perversely, with the demands and forms of Israelite law and tradition. Hence, it is certain that the king's taking possession of the property immediately following the pretended trial and judicial murder of Naboth was legally sanctioned in the circumstances. If this were not the case, the biblical historiographer, who displays such intense antipathy toward the house of Omri and especially toward Ahab and his pagan spouse,[11] would assuredly have added the illegality of the royal acquisition to the inventory of heinous sins they committed. Elijah's condemnation "Would you murder and take possession?" is a judgment on the criminal, immoral nature of the entire conspiracy, not just on the specific act of royal acquisition. It cannot be that Jezebel simply confiscated the vineyard extrajudicially,[12] something neither she nor Ahab dared to do in the first place. If in the end the king would still have to act arbitrarily and *ultra vires*, why go through the motions of a trumped-up indictment and spurious judicial proceedings? It is most probable then that the act was seen as juridically acceptable. The forfeiture must have been merited in accordance with existing, recognized procedure and tradition. It may therefore be assumed that some formal, symbolic ritual that validated and effectuated the transfer of title from Naboth to Ahab lies behind the repeated use of the term "take possession."[13] Jezebel instructs her husband to "go take possession of the vineyard." The text tells us that "Ahab set out for the vineyard of Naboth the Jezreelite to take possession of it" (vv. 15–16). Similarly, the divine directive to Elijah to confront the king stresses, "He is now in Naboth's vineyard; he has gone down there to take possession of it" (v. 18).

Jezebel's effort to create a fictional impression of legality, her careful attention to the proper judicial formalities, albeit in order to accomplish an immoral objective, raises a basic question. The queen undoubtedly knew full well that the crimes of which Naboth was to be accused would be punishable by his execution and the consequent confiscation of his property, so that Ahab's possession of it would be assured. But on what legal grounds did the vineyard become forfeit and devolve to the crown? This basic question exercised the medieval Jewish exegetes Rashi, David Qimhi, Gersonides, and Abrabanel. They all maintained that the "legal" justification for Ahab's final act was the existence of a law that the estate of a felon executed by royal degree escheated to the crown. This interpretation follows the majority view put forth in a debate among the tannaim of the second century C.E., as recorded in rabbinic sources,[14] although it is not clear whether the forfeiture was understood by these authorities to be a part of the penalty for the commission of high crime or a logical consequence of the punishment. The minority view held that Ahab received Naboth's estate by inheritance, since he was the deceased victim's first cousin and thus a rightful heir. This explanation is also cited by David Qimhi. What is of special significance is that the sages on both sides of the debate, as well as the medieval exegetes, took it for granted that Ahab obtained the property on the basis of some established juridical principle applicable in the particular circumstances.

It is hardly likely that the minority view presented above rests on anything more than an attempt to counter the claim of the majority and to find an alternative reason why Ahab could inherit the estate. But what is behind the majority view? Before dealing with this issue, we must note that a complicating factor appears in 2 Kgs 9:25–26.

In this text we are informed that when the rebel Jehu carries out his coup d'etat against Joram of Israel, the last of the Omrides, he has the body of the slain king dumped in "the field of Naboth the Jezreelite," and he cites a supposedly divine pronouncement, "I swear, I have taken note of the blood of Naboth and the blood of his sons yesterday. . . ." Surprisingly, the narrative of 1 Kings 21 makes no mention of Naboth's sons or of their execution.[15] The instructions sent by Jezebel to the judges contain not a word about them, nor are they referred to in the report of the fulfillment of her orders or in the announcement of the fulfillment to the queen, nor when she informs her husband, nor in the narration of the situation in v. 16. Indeed, had Jezebel really ordered the murder of the children, the narrator would surely have told of it as still one more example of the monstrous evil and the heinous crimes that characterized her reign. There would have been absolutely no reason to ignore or suppress the fact, and every reason to highlight it. The report of 2 Kgs 9:26 must derive from an independent, variant version of the Naboth affair.[16] At any rate, it is of interest that the above-mentioned rabbinic sources do not take the statement literally but treat it figuratively. That is, with the execution of Naboth the blood of his potential offspring was also shed, as it were, all of the generations now doomed never to be born.[17] Be that as it may, even if Naboth's children had been executed with him, we would still be without clear explanation for Ahab's lawful acquisition of the vineyard.

Although pentateuchal law features no such penalty as state forfeiture of a convicted criminal's property, the practice is attested over a long period of time and over a wide geographic and varied cultural area. In the Bible itself, Ezra (10:8) uses the threat of confiscation as a sanction to enforce obedience to an order to the returnees from the Babylonian exile. Moreover, the associated admonition that the offender shall be "excluded from the congregation" amounts to the Roman concept of civil death. It is hardly likely that this device was Ezra's innovation, even though it is not otherwise clearly mentioned in a biblical text. But we note that when David, in flight from Absalom, learned that Mephibosheth, grandson of the deceased Saul, had stayed in Jerusalem in hope of gaining the crown, he immediately decreed the confiscation of the traitor's lawful inheritance, and presented it to Ziba the informant (2 Sam 16:4).[18] These instances suggest that forfeiture of this kind was provided for in ancient Israelite customary law. Indeed, the strictures of Ezekiel (45:8, 46:18) against the confiscation of the people's land by "the prince" (Hebrew *nāśî'*), that is, by the king, in the prophet's idealized description of the restoration of Israel after the exile, indicate that such practices were not uncommon in the monarchy period. In extrabiblical sources, an Akkadian legal tablet from Alalakh from the reign of King Niqmepa, bearing the seal impression of his father, King Idrimi, and deriving from the fifteenth century B.C.E., records that a certain Arpa had become a criminal, a *bēl mašikti*, a term that has been shown to carry the implication of treason. He was executed for his crime, and his estate escheated to the palace.[19] In Attic law, the penalty for treason *(prodosia)* was death, followed by confiscation of the condemned's property and a declaration of dishonor and deprivation of civil rights *(atimia)*, which meant that his heirs too were disenfranchised.[20] This is what happened to the Athenian orator and politician Antiphon, who was executed in 411 B.C.E. after being convicted of high treason.[21] In ancient Rome, the property of a person convicted of a crime against the state *(crimen publicum)* became the property of the state *(res publica)*.[22] According to the Hanafi school of Islamic law, the blasphemer is disenfranchised, and all claims to property or inheritance are voided.[23] In England, the famous and perhaps most crucial provision of the Magna Carta extracted from King John in 1215, clause 39, decreed that "no freeman shall be taken or [and][24] imprisoned or disseised or exiled or in any way destroyed, . . . except by the lawful judgment of his peers or [and] by the law of the land.[25] It was aimed at preventing the arbitrary confiscation of property by the king; however, the law of the land did allow forfeiture of the property of a convicted criminal. English kings were still exercising this right in the seventeenth century.[26] The Statute of Treasons of 1352 specified that treason against the king entailed forfeiture of land and goods, and this law continued in force until the Forfeitures Abolition Act enacted in 1870, which abolished the whole law of escheat as a punishment for felony.[27]

The guiding principle that underlay the right of the state to impose forfeiture was the doctrine of "corruption of blood."[28] A convicted felon was deemed to be attainted; his blood was considered to be corrupt. The immediate consequence of this doctrine was the status of *civiliter mortuus*. In modern parlance, he became a "nonperson." "Civil death" operated retroactively and henceforth. It entailed automatic divestment of the rights of ownership. It extinguished the power to inherit, retain, and bequeath property. Descendants were thereby disinherited. Hence, the estate of the convicted felon, being now ownerless, belonged to the state.

The framers of the American Constitution took pains to nullify the doctrine of "corruption of blood." The second section of the second clause of Article III declared that "no attainder of treason shall work corruption of blood or forfeiture except during the life of the person attained." The legal implications of this clause have been explored several times in the courts, the most famous being the case of Avery v. Everett in the Court of Appeals of New York, October 2, 1888.[29]

The expression *corruption of blood* in the sense used in English law since feudal times has no counterpart in biblical Hebrew sources or in the cognate languages. But the concept, even if unarticulated, was implied in the recognized and accepted right of the monarch to take possession of the property of a felon convicted of blasphemy or treason, thereby disinheriting his heirs. Whether or not Naboth had heirs, Ahab was acting according to his legal rights in appropriating Naboth's vineyard following the unfortunate victim's condemnation on two capital charges, given the formal nature of the proceedings.

NOTES

* *Author's note:* I am indebted to attorneys Sheila Mondshein, David Mofenson, and Professor Alan Feld, as well as to Professor Marvin Fox, for their kind help.

1. 1 Kings 21 employs the word *kerem* ten times: vv. 1, 2 (2x), 6 (3x), 7, 15, 16, 18. However, 2 Kings 9 repeatedly designates the same property as *ḥelqah:* vv. 10, 21, 25, 26, 36, 37. A. Rofé (*The Prophetical Stories* [Jerusalem, 1988] 84) maintains that the object of Ahab's craving, according to 2 Kings 9, was "a plot—a field— not a vineyard" and that this is the original version of the story. Y. Zakovitch (in *The Bible from Within* [ed. M. Weiss; Jerusalem, 1984] 382) points out that Josephus' account also features "a field." However, it should be noted that while Josephus uses γρογείτων and γρῷν in *Ant.* 8.355–56 (Loeb edition, p. 762), γρῷ in 8.407 (Loeb, p. 790) and 9.118 (Loeb, p. 62) and γρὸν in 9.119 (Loeb, p. 64), he also uses, μπελῶνα "vineyard" in 9.359–60 (Loeb, p. 760). Zakovitch (p. 382 n. 9) observes that *śādeh* and *kerem* are frequently paired, as in Exod 22:4; Num 20:17, 21:22; and 1 Sam 8:14, and that occasionally the two are parallel, as in Prov 24:30; also cf. Lev 19:19 with Deut 22:9. N. Liphschitz and G. Biger (*Beit Mikra* [1993] 119–21), through analysis of archaeological evidence from the Valley of Jezreel, conclude that Naboth's property was an olive grove and not a vineyard. The phrase *kerem zayit* indeed appears in Judg 15:5, but the targum, LXX, Vulgate, and Syriac and thus David Qimḥi, all treat this compound as asyndeton; so NJPSV, "vineyard, [and] olive trees"; cf. *b. Ber.* 35a, b. *B. Meṣ.* 87b.

2. Cf. Deut 17:14 20; cf. Ezek 45:8–9, 46:18.

3. I. Mendelsohn, "Samuel's Denunciation of Kingship in the Light of the Akkadian Documents from Ugarit," *BASOR* 143 (1956) 17–22. J. A. Thompson (*The Bible and Archaeology* [Grand Rapids, Mich., 1975] 12) draws attention to Canaanite mythology. He contrasts Jezebel's legal maneuvers to the violent means by which a goddess obtains a coveted bow in a Ugaritic text, which he feels reflects the values of Canaanite society. The reference is undoubtedly to the Anat and Aqhat myth, on which see C. Gordon, *Ugaritic Literature* (Rome, 1949) 84–103; H. I. Ginsberg, "The Tale of Aqhat," in *ANET*, 149–55; T. H. Gaster, *Thespis* (Garden City, N.Y., 1961) 316–29.

4. The observation of E. W. Nicholson (*Deuteronomy and Tradition* [Philadelphia, 1967] 68), that "Jezebel had evidently no difficulty in having the unfortunate Naboth removed," needs modification.

5. This accords with Deut 17:6 and 19:15.

6. See on this clause *b. Sanh.* 66a-b; *Mekilta de Rabbi Ishmael*, section 19 (ed. M. Friedmann, p. 97; ed. Horovitz and Rabin, p. 317; ed. Lauterbach, p. 151). These sources understand the word *'ĕlōhîm* also to include a judge; see the targums, ad loc. This interpretation is probably based on the difference in style from the preceding and following verses, in which God, as the speaker, uses the first person.

7. On the meaning of this title, see M. Noth (*Das System der zwölf Stamme Israels* [Stuttgart, 1930] 151ff.; and his *Commentary on Exodus* [Philadelphia, 1962] 187ff.), who takes *nāśî'* to refer to the tribal spokesman at the amphictyony. J. van der Ploeg

("Les chefs du people d'Israëls ets leurs titres," *RB* 57 [1950] 40–61) rejects this understanding and takes the term as a secular title for a leader. E. Speiser ("Background and
Function of the Biblical *Nasi'*," *CBQ* 25 [1963] 111–17) takes it to mean simply a tribal
leader.

8. On the offense of blasphemy, see G. D. Nokes, *A History of the Crime of Blasphemy* (London, 1928); L. W. Levy, *Treason against God: A History of the Offense of
Blasphemy*, (New York, 1981). For the rabbinic understanding of the offense, see m.
Sanh. 7:5 and the gemara on it (pp. 55b, 60a), which lay down the precise conditions for
execution by lapidation. The name *YOSY* used there is a surrogate for the Tetragrammaton, and the numerical value of the consonants equals that of *'ĕlōhîm* "God".

9. G. R. Driver and John C. Miles, *The Assyrian Laws* (Oxford, 1935) 379, and the
discussion on p. 20; T. J. Meek, "The Middle Assyrian Laws," *ANET* 180. On Akk.
šillatu, see CAD Š/2 445–47; S. Paul, "Daniel 3:29: A Case Study of Neglected Blasphemy," *JNES* 42 (1983) 291–94.

10. E. F. Weidner, "Assyrische Beschreibungen des Kriegs-Reliefs Aššurbanâplis,"
AfO 8 (1932) 184.

11. On Omri, see 1 Kgs 16:25–26; cf. Mic 6:16; on Ahab, see 1 Kgs 16:29–33;
18:13, 18; 2 Kgs 8:15–18; 9:7–10; 10:10; 21:3; on Ahaziah, see 1 Kgs 22:52–54[51–
53]; on Jehoram, see 2 Kgs 3:1–3; 8:26–27; 9:22. As the text stands, Hos 1:4, "I will
soon punish the House of Jehu for the bloody deeds at Jezreel," seems to refer to the
massacre of the House of Ahab by Jehu (so Rashi, lbn Ezra). Y. Kaufmann (*Tolĕdôt Ha-
'Emûnâ Ha-Yisre'elit* [Jerusalem, 1976] 3.97–99 and n. 7) emends "Jehu" to "Jehoram." The LXX here reads "Judah" in place of "Jehu"; see the NJPSV, ad loc., footnotes.

12. Hugo Grotius (1583–1645), cited with approval by J. A. Montgomery (*A Critical and Exegetical Commentary on the Book of Kings* [Edinburgh, 1951] 332), explains
Ahab's act as exemplifying arbitrary royal power. J. Pedersen (*Israel: Its Life, and Culture* [London and Copenhagen, reprint 1959] 69) similarly regards Ahab's act as "the
arbitrariness of the despot" (cf. p. 125). R. de Vaux (*Ancient Israel: Its Life and Institutions* [New York, 1961] 55) likewise observes that Ahab's act may simply be an instance
of arbitrary confiscation. F. I. Andersen ("The Socio-Juridical Background of the
Naboth Incident," *JBL* 95 [1966] 46–47) notes that "interpreters have been at a loss to
discover any legal grounds for Ahab's subsequent seizure of Naboth's vineyard." Andersen rejects both the suggestion that it was an arbitrary act and the claim that the property
of certain criminals was forfeited to the crown. The first is indeed untenable, but the second can certainly be sustained.

13. This mode of legal acquisition is what is termed *hazaqah* in rabbinic parlance.
This was noted by B. Uffenheimer, *Ancient Prophecy in Israel* (Jerusalem, 1973) 223–24
[Heb.]. On *hazaqah*, see M. Elon, *Jewish Law: History Sources, Principles* (trans. from
Hebrew, B. Auerbach and M. J. Sykes; Philadelphia, 1994) 1.79–80, 297–98; 2.580–
87. In the Bible, Abraham's traversing the promised land, as told in Gen 13:17, is an
example of such a legal ritual; cf. *Tg. Ps-J.*, ad loc.; *y. Qidd.* 1:3 (60c); *t. Bab. Bat.*
2.11; *b. Bab. Bat.* 100a; *Gen. Rab.* 41:13; cf. Josh 24:3. According to E. R. Lacheman
("Note on Ruth 4:7–8" *JBL* 56 [1937] 53–56) it was the practice in Nuzi that, in order to
enhance the validity of a real property transfer, the owner would "lift up his own foot
from his property" and place the foot of the new owner on it. Some biblical passages
relating to Israel's acquisition of its promised land, such as Deut 11:24 and Josh 1:3–4,
may well be literary reflexes of this same symbolic gesture. See, however, J. M. Sasson,
Ruth (Baltimore, 1979) 141–48.

14. See *b. Sanh.* 48b, *t. Sanh.* 4.6. Maimonides (*Yad, Hilkhot Evel* 1:9) codifies the
law that the property of those executed by royal decree reverts to the crown. The same is
repeated by him in *Hilkhot Melakhim* 4:9. However, in 4:10, he stipulates that this

applies only when the royal actions are for purely idealistic reasons and are inspired by the noblest of causes. J. Weingreen ("The Case of the Daughters of Zelophehad," *VT* 16 [1996] 518–22) suggests that the protestation of innocence in Num 27:3 was a necessary part of the legal procedure and that it testifies to some ancient law, not recorded, about the property of a person convicted of treason.

15. C. F. Keil and F. Delitzsch (*Commentary on the Old Testament* [Grand Rapids, Mich.; reprint, 1980] 3.342) cite J. D. Michaelis and H. G. A. Ewald that the emission of the murder of Naboth's sons is "because it was so usual a thing that the historian might leave it out as a matter of course." This, of course, is nonsensical.

16. J. Gray (*I & II Kings: A Commentary* [Philadelphia, 1963], on 1 Kgs 21:13 (p. 392), citing the case of Achan (Josh 7:22ff.), explains that Naboth's family was executed with him in "punctilious observance of Semitic custom." He gives no source for this assertion. As to Josh 7:25, the text is quite unclear about the fate of Achan's family. The LXX omits the last two clauses, and the Syriac and Vulgate omit the last clause. Rabbinic sources display conflicting interpretations; see L. Ginzberg, *The Legends of the Jews* (Philadelphia, 1946) 6.176 n. 31. On 2 Kgs 9:26 (*I & II Kings*, 494), Gray notes that the "passage belonged to different sources." A similar judgment is made by J. M. Miller ("The Fall of the House of Ahab," *VT* 8 [1967] 307–24); by J. A. Soggin, (*A History of Ancient Israel* [Philadelphia, 1984] 207), who notes that "additions have been made to the narrative"; and by J. T. Walsh ("Naboth," *ABD* 4.978), who notes that there seem "to have been several versions of the Naboth story in circulation."

17. Cf. *m. Sanh.* 4:5 for a similar interpretation of the plural form of "blood" in Gen 4:10; and see the targums, ad loc.

18. 2 Sam 16:4. The king later relented somewhat and divided the estate between Mephibosheth and Ziba (2 Sam 19:30).

19. D. J. Wiseman (*The Alalakh Tablets* [British Institute of Archaeology at Ankara, 1953] 40, no. 17) translated lines 7–8 "Apra has turned against a private enemy. . . ." B. Landsberger ("Assyrische Königsliste und Dunkles Zeitalter," *JCS* 8 [1954] 60 n. 129) corrects the translation of *bēl mašikti* to *Verbrecher* "criminal." S. E. Loewenstamm ("Notes on the Alalakh Tablets," *IEJ* 6 [1956] 224–25) accepts Landsberger's rendering and shows that the crime referred to was rebellion against the king. J. J. Finkelstein ("Documents from the Practice of Law," *ANET*, 546) similarly renders the Akkadian phrase "committed treason."

20. See W. J. Woodhouse, "ATIMIA," *ERE* 2.192–94, esp. p. 193a; D. M. MacDowell. *The Law in Classical Athens* (Ithaca, N.Y., 1978) 255–56; cf. pp. 73–75.

21. Ibid., 176, 178.

22. A. Berger, *Encyclopedic Dictionary of Roman Law* (American Philosophical Society, Transactions n.s. 43, part 2; Philadelphia, 195) 661.

23. C. W. Ernst, "Blasphemy: Islamic Concept," *The Encyclopedia of Religion* (New York, 1987) 2.243.

24. On the ambiguity of *vel* here, see W. S. McKechnie, *Magana Carta* (2d rev. ed.; Glasgow, 1914) 381–82 and n. 3.

25. On clause 39, see ibid., 375–95; J. C. Holt, *Magna Carta* (2d ed.; Cambridge, 1992) 9, 277, 463.

26. Ibid., 331; W. Holdsworth, *A History of English Law* (5th ed.; London, 1942; reprint 1966) 67ff.

27. Ibid., 70–71.

28. On this doctrine, see ibid., 67ff.; *The Dictionary of English Law* (London, 1959) 174, 505; *The Guide to American Law* (St. Paul, Minn., 1984) 1.360–61, 3.320; *Encyclopaedia of the American Constitution* (New York, 1986) 1.80.

29. *Avery v. Everett,* 110 NY 317, 18 NE 148. For a different interpretation of 1 Kings 21, see Tsafrirah ben Barak in *Proceedings of the Ninth World Congress of Jewish Studies,* Division A (Jerusalem, 1986) 15–20 [Heb.].

The Abortive Insurrection in Zedekiah's Day (Jer. 27–29)

On the second of Adar in the seventh regnal year of Nebuchadnezzar, i.e. on the 15/16 March, 597 B.C.E., the city of Jerusalem surrendered to the Babylonian army after a brief siege. The short reign of Jehoiachin, son of Jehoiakim, came to an abrupt end, and Zedekiah, son of Josiah, was installed by Nebuchadnezzar on the throne of Judah as a vassal king.[1]

It was not long, however, before the anti-Babylonian party in Jerusalem gained the upper hand and plotted rebellion. Sometime in the last decade of the sixth century B.C.E., there took place a six-power regional conference, the aim of which was to plot coordinated rebellion against Nebuchadnezzar. This event is known to us solely from Jer. 27:2 ff. which relates that the envoys of the trans-Jordanian monarchies of Edom, Moab and the Ammonites, together with those from the Phoenician city-states of Tyre and Sidon, assembled in Jerusalem clearly for that purpose.[2]

Unfortunately, the date of this summit meeting is in dispute. In the first place, our received text of Jer. 27:1 assigns it to "the beginning of the reign of Jehoiakim", (בראשית ממלכת יהויקים;). This is clearly impossible in light of the mention of Zedekiah in vv. 3 and 12, of the explicit reference to the exile of Jehoiachin in vv. 16–22, and of the fact that Jer. 28:1 identifies "that self-same year" as "the beginning of the reign of Zedekiah". There can be no doubt, of course, that we must either substitute Zedekiah's name for that of Jehoiakim in Jer. 27:1 (as does the Syriac version) or (with the Greek) omit the line entirely. Either way, we have to explain the scribal error as an inadvertent carry-over from the superscription of Jer. 26:1.[3]

However, smoothing out this particular textual difficulty by no means settles the question of the date of the seditious conclave, since ממלכת בראשית itself requires definition and the problem is complicated by the date-line of Jer. 28:1, which identifies this formula with "the fourth year," without specifying of what.

THE ASSUMED DATING

It has been the well-nigh unanimous view of modern scholars that the diplomatic summit meeting took place in Jerusalem in the fourth year of Zedekiah's reign, i.e. 594/3 B.C.E.[4] This solution to the problem involves the adoption of the Greek text which omits entirely 27:1, deletes the reference to ממלכת בראשית in 28:1, and inverts the order of the words to read. . . וכו' לצדקיהו הרביעית בשנה.[5] Some would leave intact the received Hebrew text (other than emending Jehoiakim to Zedekiah in 27:1), but would interpret ממלכת בראשית in a general, rather than a literal, sense, meaning, "the early years."[6]

Support for a preferred fourth year dating has been sought in recent times in the Babylonian Chronicle which records in sequence the military campaigns of Nebuchadnezzar during the first eleven years of his reign (605–594 B.C.E.). This document reports that in Kislev and Tebet of his tenth year, i.e. Dec. 595–Jan. 594 B.C.E., Nebuchadnezzar did not campaign abroad but remained at home to suppress a revolt.[7] It has been assumed that the various vassal states in the west were encouraged by this uprising in the very heart of the kingdom to meet in Jerusalem some months later in order to plan their own rebellion on the periphery of the empire.[8]

All the foregoing arguments, however, are open to some very serious objections that cannot be overlooked and that have to be accounted for. Their effect is to make it extremely unlikely that the plot against Babylon did, in fact, take place in Zedekiah's fourth year.

THE TEXTUAL PROBLEM AND THE GREEK

In the first place, the caption to chapter 27 cannot be dismissed so easily. As has been frequently noted, there are excellent reasons for believing, and these will be adduced later, that chapter 27–29, like many other sections of the book,[9] once circulated as a separate pericope. As such, it is extremely unlikely that it would not have had its own superscription. Furthermore, that date-line "in that year" in Jer. 28:1 must refer back to some year already specified in the preceding chapter. To assume that the original title got lost, that 27:1 crept in solely by error as a duplication of 26:1 and that this, in turn, gave rise to a further erroneous insertion in 28:1, is to put an unnecessary strain on one's credulity.[10] On the other hand, to presume the flagrantly contradictory בראשית ממלכת and בשנה הרביעית in a single context to be the result of "harmonization"[11] is to presuppose the complete indifference of the editor or glossator to the unintelligibility and irrationality of the text he produced, a phenomenon for which some explanation ought to be given before it is accepted.[12]

There is no reason to believe that the Greek version of these particular disputed passages represents a superior text. Altogether, the relationship between the Greek translation of Jeremiah and our received Hebrew text is a very complicated one, since the former is shorter than the latter by about one eighth, the omissions including both single verses or parts thereof, as well as entire sections. It is by no means simplified by the Jeremiah fragments from Qumran which now prove that the Greek is not an abbreviated version of the proto-Masoretic text, but is based on a Hebrew *Vorlage,* and that we are dealing with two distinct redactional traditions of a Hebrew text.[13] The problem of chapters 27–29 is particularly thorny for the Greek treatment of 27:1 and 28:1 may itself be nothing more than a redactional attempt at harmonization. In general, it has been observed that the differences in chronological data between the Hebrew text and the various Greek versions chiefly appear in just those passages in which difficulties exist, and the Greek versions frequently constitute attempts to smooth out those disagreements.[14] On the other hand, it should be noted that the Lucianic recension of the Greek, as well as the Latin of Jerome and the Peshitta and Targum are all identical with our current Hebrew text of Jer. 28:1 with its inherent apparent contradiction.[15] As a matter of fact, recent studies have led to a positive re-evaluation of the chronological data supplied by the Lucianic recension, at least for the early monarchy period.[16]

"RESHIT MAMLEKHET"

As to the meaning of the formula בראשית ממלכת, it is widely accepted that this is the Hebrew equivalent of the Akkadian *reš šarruti* that usually signifies the accession year, i.e. the time that elapsed between the day the king acceded to the throne and his official coronation on the next civil New Year. This period was not counted in the numbering of his regnal years. Now it is perfectly true that the *reš šarruti* formula may occasionally be imprecisely used.[17] However, none can deny that the normal and overwhelming usage in Akkadian is very precise, and since the Hebrew equivalent is restricted to superscriptions in the Book of Jeremiah which is characterized by a relatively large number of chronological captions of otherwise invariable exactitude, it would be most strange if בראשית ממלכת constituted the sole exception. Would anyone seriously question the meaning of this formula were it not for the contradictory בשנה הרביעית? And if this phrase means that the events described took place in Zedekiah's fourth year, then in what way would our knowledge be enhanced by the addition of an ambiguous בראשית ממלכת; especially since well over a third of the king's reign would have already elapsed before then?

THE ORACLE AGAINST ELAM

Another argument that has been advanced in favor of the loose usage of this date formula is the oracle against Elam in Jer. 49:34 ff. The Babylonian Chronicle relates that in the ninth year of Nebuchadnezzar (596/5 B.C.E.) Elam advanced menacingly along the bank of the Tigris only to flee in panic at the appearance of the Babylonian army.[18] It is this event, it is claimed, that provides the historic background to the oracle of Jeremiah, and since Nebuchadnezzar's ninth year overlapped with Zedekiah's first and second regnal years, ראשית ממלכת cannot be the accession year.[19] However, the content of Jer. 49:34 ff cannot be reconciled with the Babylonian Chronicle, for the latter says absolutely nothing about the utter destruction of Elam and the exile of its people which are the themes of Jeremiah's prophecy. The precise historical background of that oracle still remains to be determined.

THE BABYLONIAN CHRONICLE

No more convincing is the argument that the insurrection being plotted in Jerusalem, supposedly in the fourth year of Zedekiah, was inspired by the rebellion in Babylon actually recorded in the Chronicle as having taken place in Dec. 595–Jan. 594 B.C.E.[20] It is difficult to understand why a local uprising that proved to be an immediate failure should have inspired other revolts in the west or should have generated false hopes for an early collapse of the Babylonian empire and the prompt return of the Judean exiles. On the contrary, the Babylonian Chronicle gives no indication of any other dissension in 595/4 B.C.E. or in the succeeding year. The revolt was speedily crushed and Nebuchadnezzar felt sufficiently secure to go to Syria in person and without the army in order to collect tribute, and he was able to return to Babylon before the end of his regnal year, i.e. all within the space of three months after the uprising.[21] This being the case, it is reasonable to assume that the swift suppression of the revolt in the capital would more likely have demoralized and discouraged the conspirators than have inspired their seditious activities.

THE PERICOPE CHAPTERS 27–29

No solution to the problem of Jer. 28:1 is possible without an examination of chapters 27–29 as a literary unit. As has been mentioned above, this section constitutes a distinct document within the Book of Jeremiah and there is good reason to believe that it must once have circulated separately.[22] Several independent, but complementary, lines of evidence abundantly demonstrate its pericopal nature.

We may cite the consistently exceptional spelling of the name of the king of Babylon as נבו(ו)כדנאצר[23] as opposed to נבו(ו)כדראצר throughout the rest of the book. Then there is the remarkable fact that the abbreviated form of the prophet's name ירמיה occurs here ten times,[24] but never again in the entire work, and the title הנביא is attached to the name quite disproportionately to its employment elsewhere.[25] The exiled king's name is extraordinarily given as יכ(ו)ניה[26] in contrast to the forms כניהו,[27] יכניהו[28] or יהויכין[29] otherwise used. There is a general predilection for the attenuation of the *-yahu* names[30] as is evidenced by גמריה,[31] שמעיה,[38] חלקיה,[32] חנניה,[33] מעשיה,[34] צדקיה,[35] צפניה,[36] קוליה,[37].

Equally decisive for the unity of the section is the subject matter. Each chapter is preoccupied with the same two interwoven themes that derive from a specific political situation. Jeremiah wages a bitter polemic against the activities of the prophets at home and in Babylon who predict a speedy return from exile,[39] and with all the emphasis at his command he seeks to refute the subversive notion that Babylon can be overthrown within the lifetime of the present generation.[40] By emphasizing the inevitability of a long exile he aims at discouraging rebellion.

That the events of chapters 27 and 28 occurred in close sequence is further made clear by the precise formula of 28:1 בשנה ההיא as by the fact that in his encounter with Hananiah b. Azzur, Jeremiah was still wearing the yoke that he had previously donned for the regional conclave reported in the preceding chapter.[41]

THE EPISTLES TO THE EXILES

What is the connection between chapter 29 and the preceding two? It shares with them the orthographic peculiarities, the onomastic idiosyncrasies and a thematic unity. The introductory ואלה (v.1) provides a further indication of contextual consecution.[42] But when did Jeremiah send his epistle to the Judean exiles? It must obviously have been some time between the planning of the revolt and the date set for its execution. The only specific chronological notation given is the parenthetic, "after King Jehoiachin etc. had left Jerusalem."[43] Unless this formula be intended to indicate "not long after,"[44] it is difficult to understand its function and its substitution for the usual dating according to regnal years or for a simple, imprecise, "in the days of Zedekiah."[45] This argument is reinforced by vv. 5 ff., 28, which imply a completely unsettled state of affairs among the exiles, far more in consonance with the first year of Zedekiah than with the fourth. This is in sharp contrast to their more stable social and economic conditions as reflected in the preaching of Ezekiel in the fifth and sixth years of the exile, just one and two years after the purported dating of chapters 27–29.[46]

But there are even more serious objections to assigning the epistle of chapter 29 to the fourth year.[47] Jer. 28:1 proves that the insurgents met in Jerusalem either a short while before the month of Ab or in that month, since the prophet was still wearing the yoke.[48] If we insist on 594/3, we are faced with the unavoidable conclusion that the delegation which carried Jeremiah's epistle warning against rebellion must have left for Babylon between Ab-Elul 593 B.C.E., otherwise the event would have fallen within the fifth year of Zedekiah.[49] This, in itself, is not impossible except for the report of another delegation from Judea to Nebuchadnezzar in the fourth year of the Judean king, as related in Jer. 51:59 ff.[50] That we are dealing with two distinct and separate commissions is evidenced by the different names of the emissaries involved.[51] On each occasion, Jeremiah used the opportunity to send a message to his exiled countrymen. But the two messages are mutually exclusive in content, the one in complete disharmony with the other. That of chapter 51:59 ff. is a doom prophecy predicting the destruction of Babylon. The epistle of chapter 29, with its emphasis on the futility of rebellion and the long duration of the exile, is its complete antithesis. Did Jeremiah send both messages within a single year? If that of chapter 51:59–64 followed the oracle of chapter 29, it would not only have vitiated its effect, but would actually have served to inflame the very revolutionary passions that Jeremiah tried so hard to quell. Moreover, we should be forced to postulate that the two delegations to Babylon bearing contradictory messages from the prophet were simultaneously dispatched or they could not, as we have seen, have gone forth in Zedekiah's fourth year. This is clearly an absurd and impossible situation.

The delegation of Jer. 51:59 ff. could, of course, have been the earlier of the two and could have set out for Babylon in Zedekiah's fourth year well before the revolutionary conclave might have gotten under way, although it would have had to reckon with Nebuchadnezzar's absence from Babylon campaigning in Hatti-land, presumably for a minimum of three months beginning in Kislev (Dec.) 594 B.C.E.[52] However, if it be assumed that the events of Jer. 27–28 also belong to the year 594/3, it becomes inexplicable that at any time in the course of those twelve months Jeremiah should have delivered himself of an oracle the content of which could only have served to reinforce the dangerously optimistic predictions of the false prophets operating both in Judea and Babylon.[53] The entire situation only makes sense if we assume a considerable lapse of time between the two messages of Jeremiah to the exiles, and if the words of Jer. 51:59 ff. were designed to bring a message of comfort to counteract the mood of hopelessness and despair that must have gripped the exiles once the failure of the revolt became apparent and it was realized that the activities of the prophets had been nothing but a snare and a delusion.

A RECONSTRUCTION OF THE EVENTS

The evidence would seem to be overwhelmingly against the simple assumption that the events described in Jer. 27–29 took place in the fourth year of Zedekiah's reign, i.e. in the course of 594/3 B.C.E. There is no good reason either to discard or to explain away the chronological notation [צדקיהו] בראשית ממלכת (Jer. 28:1) in favor of the apparently contradictory בשנה הרביעית. On the contrary, the beginning of Zedekiah's reign provides a far more satisfactory background to what took place than does the fourth year which creates insuperable difficulties.

The course of events may quite plausibly be reconstructed. Zedekiah came to the throne very soon after the 2nd of Adar, 597 B.C.E., the day when Jehoiachin was deposed, certainly not later than the first of

Nisan.[54] The six months that elapsed until his official enthronement in Tishri constitute the ראשית ממלכת, a phrase which is the equivalent of the Akkadian *reš šarruti*. Nebuchadnezzar must have returned home immediately after exacting the oath of fealty from Zedekiah.[55] This is confirmed both by the report in 2 Chr. 36:10 as well as by the Babylonian Chronicle which makes it clear that the king hurried back to his capital as quickly as possible after each foreign expedition.[56] He would certainly have had little reason to linger in Judea once he had appointed "a king of his own choice"[57] bound to him by oath of vassalage, a known pro-Babylonian and regarded as thoroughly trustworthy.

On the other hand, the fact that Zedekiah was regarded by the Judeans as a puppet of Babylon and was never accepted by them as the legitimate king diminished his authority. It was this more than anything else that accounted for the weak and vacillating rule that characterized his reign.[58] It would be just at the beginning—when he would still enjoy the confidence of the Babylonians, but before he would have had time to consolidate his power internally—that the anti-Babylonian party would find it most convenient to plot rebellion. Since he would certainly have lost his throne, and probably his life as well, had Jehoiachin returned, it must be assumed that Zedekiah was coerced into the insurrectionary conclave against his will and better judgment. The fact that he allowed Jeremiah to make use of his envoys to Babylon to discourage rebellion supports this presumption.[59]

If, now, we refer the events of Jer. 27–28 to the period between Nisan and Tishri 597 B.C.E., with the epistle of chapter 29 sent toward the end of this period, a satisfactory reconstruction not only becomes possible, but certain hitherto unexplained facts fall into place.

No acceptable interpretation has so far been adduced for the mysterious "two-year" limitation that the false prophets imposed on the exile with a precision that is quite unwonted in those quarters.[60] If it be noted, however, that the prophecy was made in the month of Ab 597 B.C.E.,[61] the revolt must have been planned for late in 595 B.C.E. In other words, the Jerusalemites and their allies in the west would really have been engaged in planning for the insurrection that actually took place in Babylon in Dec. 595 B.C.E., a record of which has been preserved in the Babylonian Chronicle. The seditious deliberations in Jerusalem were designed to coordinate the projected uprising in Babylon with a revolt in the west, timed for two years ahead. In this connection, the "universalism" of Hananiah b. Azzur, who included "all the nations" in his tidings of liberation from the yoke of Nebuchadnezzar, takes on new meaning.[62]

The reference would be to the international character of the revolt, to all those peoples whose representatives met in Jerusalem in the summer of 597 B.C.E.[63]

Jeremiah's epistle to the exiles certainly presupposes an awareness of some mutinous preparations on their part, spurred on by the local prophets in collusion with their counterparts back home. Jeremiah's strenuous opposition to Jewish participation, whether at home or in exile, as well as Nebuchadnezzar's swift suppression of the outbreak in Babylon, were probably the decisive factors in the abandonment of the Jerusalem plot altogether.[64] It was after this, in the year 594 B.C.E., in the fourth year of the Judean king, that a delegation again left Jerusalem for Babylon, perhaps this time headed by Zedekiah himself.[65] Its purpose must have been to reassure Nebuchadnezzar of the loyalty of Judah in the wake of the uprising. Jeremiah now took the opportunity to send a new message to the exiles who were thoroughly demoralized by the collapse of their naive hopes of return. This time the prophet emphasized the certainty of Babylon's ultimate collapse.

"THE FOURTH YEAR"

It now remains to examine the reference to "the fourth year" in Jer. 28:1. As we have demonstrated on historical and other grounds, it is this, and not ממלכת בראשית that is the crux. Stylistically, too, the phrase בשנה הרביעית is exceptional. Of the sixteen passages in which superscriptions with date-formulae occur in the Book of Jeremiah, nine conform to the pattern, "in the year X of Y (the king),"[66] three have "in the year X of his reign,"[67] the name of the ruling monarch having been previously mentioned, and four times we find the expression, "in the beginning of the reign of Y."[68] Only in 28:1 is such an undefined, isolated, *disjectum membrum* encountered.

The key to the solution of the crux lies in the omission of the expected phrase "of his reign" (ולמלכו) following the "fourth year" date formula (contrast Jer. 51:59). The reference need not at all be to the regnal years of Zedekiah, but to the fourth year in some other system of dating. Now it has been demonstrated elsewhere[69] that the sabbatical law of Deuteronomy 15 provided the immediate source of inspiration for the emancipation of slaves that took place late in 588 B.C.E. during Nebuchadnezzar's siege of Jerusalem.[70] The vocabulary and style of Jer. 34:8–22 have been drawn directly from Deuteronomy 15 which constituted the legal basis for the events that occurred in that year. This means that Tishri 588–Tishri 587 B.C.E. was a sabbatical year in Judah. It follows, then, that the previous sabbatical year fell in 595/4 B.C.E., so that the accession year of Zedekiah, which covered Nisan-Tishri 597 B.C.E., constituted the fourth year of the sabbatical cycle that had begun in Tishri 602 B.C.E. In other words, the chronological notation of Jer. 28:1 is no longer self-contradictory. The "beginning of the reign of Zedekiah" was, indeed, the "fourth year."[71]

There is one further aspect of the entire episode that can now be clarified in light of this solution, and that is the extraordinary confidence with which Hananiah b. Azzur predicted the imminent downfall of Babylon and the return of the exiles.[72] As has been pointed out above, that prophecy of a "two year" limitation on the exile was made in the month of Ab 597 B.C.E.[73] Two years from that date brings us to the last quarter of 595 B.C.E., to the time when the revolt in Babylon actually broke out. It will be noticed at once that this coincided with the advent of the sabbatical year 595–594 B.C.E., the "year of release," a date, the theoretical aptness of which was matched only by the ill-timed and impractical nature of the venture. Be this as it may, the date-line of Jer. 28:1 is not internally inconsistent and it also harmonizes well with the events described in chapter 34 and elsewhere. The relevant dates are as follows:

602–601 B.C.E.	(Tishri-Elul)	Sabbatical year.
597	(Nisan-Elul)	Zedekiah's accession year = fourth year of Sabbatical cycle. International conclave to plan rebellion.
	(Ab)	Hananiah b. Azzur's prediction of a two-year exile. First delegation to Babylon.
595–594		Sabbatical year.
	(Kislev-Tebet)	Revolt in Babylon.
594–593		Second delegation to Babylon.
588–587		Sabbatical year.
	(before Kislev 588)	Emancipation of slaves.

NOTES

1. The events are described in 2 Kgs. 24:8–17; 2 Chr. 36:9f. The precise dating is now fixed by the "Babylonian Chronicle"; see D. J. Wiseman, *Chronicles of the Chaldean Kings* etc. (London, 1956), 32–5, 48, 72–3. The literature on this subject is now legion. For an up-to-date review of the period in the light of the new material, see A. Malamat in *Jerusalem Through the Ages* (Hebrew) (Jerusalem, 1968), 27–48; *IEJ* 18 (1968) 137–56. The chronological and calendrical problems have recently been subjected to critical reexamination by K. S. Freedy and D. B. Redford, *JAOS* 90 (1970), 462–85.

2. The absence of Philistines from this list is due to their no longer having been a factor on the political-military scene at this time; see A. Malamat, *IEJ* 6 (1956), 251f.; 18 (1968), 141. J. Yoyotte, *VT* 1 (1951), 143 suggests a different explanation connected with Egypt's involvement in an African campaign. For the role of Tyre, see H. J. Katzenstein, *The History of Tyre* (Jerusalem, 1793), 315f.

3. Cf. M. H. Segal, *Mebo' HaMiqra'* (Jerusalem, 1955), §415, p. 351 n. 21; *Encyclopaedia Miqra'it*, iii, 882.

4. Even Y. Kaufmann, *Toledot Ha'Emunah HaYisre'elit* (Tel-Aviv, 1947), iii, 398, 401f. accepts the fourth year dating, and so does the *Encyclopaedia Miqra'it*, vi, 687. Surprisingly, A. B. Ehrlich, [*Randglossen zur hebraïschen. Bibel* (Leipzig, 1912), iv] has no comment on the textual problem. Exceptional is J. Yoyotte [op. cit.], who takes the "beginning of the reign" at its face value. H. G. May [*JNES* 4 (1945), 217 n. 4] believes "the fourth year" to be a scribal addition, on which, see C. F. Whitley, *VT* 14 (1964), 469. H. Schmidt [*ZAW* 39 (1921), 142] emends to "the seventh year", i.e. 591 B.C. M. Vogelstein [*Biblical Chronology* (Cincinnati, 1944), I, 16, 32 (Appendix F); *idem, Fertile Soil* (N.Y., 1957), 98f] unequivocally dates the events of Jer. 27–28 to the very beginning of Zedekiah's reign, although his emendation of 28:1 is hardly convincing. The same conclusion was arrived at on historical grounds by G. R. Driver [*Textus* 4 (1964), 83–7] who explains the text of Jer. 28:1 as the result of a mistaken solution to an original abbreviation בש'הר' (= בשנה הראשונה), on which see further below n. 71 and cf. NEB "translation", *ad loc.*

5. G (35: 1) καὶ ἐγένετῳ τῷ τετάρτῳ ῥέτει Σεδεκια Βασιλέως Ιονδα.

6. H. Tadmor in: H. G. Güterbock & Th. Jacobsen, eds., *Studies in Honor of Benno Landsberger* (Chicago, 1965), 352, n. 13.

7. Wiseman, op. cit., 36f., 72–3, = BM 21946. Rev. lines 21–4.

8. D. N. Freedman, *BA* 19 (1956), 58. This view has come to be widely accepted; so J. Bright, *A History of Israel*[2] (Philadelphia, 1972), 328 and n. 59; *idem, Jeremiah* (Anchor Bible) (N.Y., 1965), pp. L, 200f., 210; cf. J. P. Hyatt, *JBL* 75 (1956), 281; C. F. Whitley, op. cit., 469 n. 1.

9. Cf. Jer. 36.

10. Cf. Schmidt, op. cit., 139; P. Volz, *Der Prophet Jeremia* (Leipzig-Erlangen, 1922), 256, 259f.

11. *Ibid.*, 256; cf. Bright, *Jeremiah*, 200.

12. Note the very interesting observations on this problem of the eleventh-twelfth century Franco-Jewish commentator R. Joseph Qara to Jer. 28:1.

13. Cf. F. M. Cross *IEJ* 16 (1966), 82, 84f., 87, 92; and the important observations of E. Tov, *RB* 79 (1972), 189–99.

14. H. Tadmor in: *Encyclopaedia Miqra'it*, iv. 255; E. R. Thiele, *The Mysterious Numbers of the Hebrew Kings* (Grand Rapids, 1965), 197–9.

15. Anyone who examines F. Field, *Origenis Hexaplorum* (Hildesheim, 1964), II, 643, 646, to Jer. 27:1, 28:1, will see at once that our Hebrew text is well reflected in the ancient versions.

16. J. Maxwell Miller, *JBL* 86 (1967), 276–88; cf. Cross op. cit., 84, 88.

17. H. Tadmor, *JNES* 15 (1956), 227f. and n. 11; *idem, JCS* 12 (1958), 27ff.; in *Studies. . . B. Landsberger,* op. cit., p. 351f.; cf. his remarks in *Encyclopaedia Miqra'it*, iv, 258 n. 6 and 267–8. On the other hand, cf. R. de Vaux, *Ancient Israel* (London, 1961), 194; S. Mowinckel, *The Psalms in Israel's Worship* (Oxford, 1962), i, 128f.; A. Malamat, *IEJ* 18 (1968), 146. It is worth recording two precise usages of *reš šarruti* in Aramaic from the Persian period. Elephantine Papyrus 6:1–2 from 465 B.C. bears the superscription: *b 18 lkslw. . . šnt 21 r'š mlwkt' kzy 'rthšsš mlk' ytb bkrs'h*, "On the 18th Kislew. . . year 21 (i.e. of Xerxes), accession year when Artaxerxes sat on his throne" (A. Cowley, *Aramaic Papyri of the Fifth Century B.C.*. (Oxford, 1923), 16. Among the

fourth century B.C. documents from Dâliyah occurs the date formula: *b 20 l'dr šnt 2 r'š mlkwt (d)ryhwš mlk'.* . . . , "On the 20th Adar year 2, accession year of King Darius," identified as Darius III who succeeded Arses, slain in 335 B.C.E., his second year (F. M. Cross, *BA* 26 (1963), 113; *New Directions in Biblical Archaeology*, eds. D. N. Freedman and J. C. Greenfield (Garden City, NY., 1969), 44.

18. Wiseman, op. cit., 72–3, cf. 36, 48 = BM 21946, Rev. 11. 16–20. The text is indeed fragmentary, but the sense seems clear.

19. A. Malamat, *IEJ* 6 (1956), 254f.; cf. H. Tadmor, *JNES* 15 (1956), 230 and n. 27; note J. P. Hyatt's cautious observation in *JBL* 75 (1956), 283.

20. See above nn. 7–8. Driver, op. cit., 87 mistakenly dates the revolt to 596/5 B.C.

21. Wiseman, op. cit., 36f., 72–3, 11. 23f.

22. This has been widely acknowledged. See F. Giesebrecht, *Das Buch Jeremia* (Göttingen, 1894), 146f.; C. H. Cornhill, *Das Buch Jeremia* (Leipzig, 1905), 303f.; P. Volz, op. cit., 251f. A. Weiser, *Das Buch des Propheten Jeremia* (Göttingen, 1955), 244f.; W. Rudolph, *Jeremiah*[2] (Tübingen, 1958), 157f.; T. W. Overholt, *JAAR* 35 (1967), 241–9. The change from the use of the first person to third person in 28:5 is doubtless the result of Baruch's editorial activity.

23. 27:6, 8, 20; 28:3, 11, 14; 29:1, 3.

24. 27:1; 28:5, 6, 10[2], 11, 12[2], 15; 29:1. The fuller form occurs in 29:27, 29, 30. Cf. Dan. 9:2; Ezra 1:1.

25. 28:5, 6, 10, 11, 12, 15; 29:1, 29 as opposed to 23 times in the rest of the book.

26. 27:20; 28:4; 29:2.

27. 22:24; 28; 37:1.

28. 24:1.

29. 52:31. On the variant spellings, see J. Liver, *Toledot Bet David* (Jerusalem, 1959), 7 n. 15.

30. It should be noted that the full form alone appears in the Lachish inscriptions. H. Torczyner [*Te'udot Lakhish* (Jerusalem, 1940), 2f.] believes that the shortened form came into vogue in the exilic period under Aramaic influence. Note, however, the form ŠLMY, apparently shortened from Shelemiah or Shelemiahu, in a seventh/sixth century B.C.E. tomb [M. Dothan, *IEJ* 11 (1961), 174] and the form YŠ' YHW on a Hebrew seal from the same period [N. Avigad, *IEJ* 13 (1963), 324].

31. 29:3 contrast 36:10, 11, 12, 25.

32. 29:3 contrast 1:1.

33. 28:1, 5, 10, 11, 12, 13, 15[2], 17 (so 37:13) contrast 36:12.

34. 29:21, 25 (so 21:1; 37:3) contrast 35:4.

35. 27:12; 28:1; 29:3 (so 49:34). Otherwise, the fuller form appears throughout the book including 27:3.

36. 29:25, 29 (so 21:1; 52:24), contrast 37:3.

37. 29:21.

38. 29:31[2], 32, contrast 26:10; 36:12 and even 29:24.

39. 27:9f., 14–18; 28 *passim;* 29:1, 8f., 15, 21ff., 31.

40. 27:6ff., 22; 28:14; 29:5ff., 10, 28.

41. With 27:2, cf. 28:10. In 28:14 "these nations" is a clear reference to 27:3.

42. So noted by Rudolph, op. cit., 166; cf. *Shemot Rabba* 30:2 to Exod. 21:1.

43. 29:2. The same date-line is appended to the vision of chapter 24 and the two chapters are closely related as is shown by 29:17 which borrows the imagery of 24:2, 3, 8, and by 29:18 which is dependent on 24:9–10. In fact, 29:17 would be unintelligible without chapter 24 as a reference point. The connection between chapter 24 and the pericope 27–29 has been noted by several scholars; cf. F. Giesebrecht, op. cit., 113. G. A. Smith [*Jeremiah*, (N.Y., 1923), 238] regards chapter 24 as the prophet's earliest oracle

under Zedekiah, and Bright [*Jeremiah*, 193f.] sees no reason to question the correctness of the chronological notation.

44. Cf. *Bereshit Rabba*, 44:6 to Gen. 15:l; cf. Jer. 34:8 where qqqs can only mean "immediately after."

45. Cf. 3:6; 26:18; 35:1.

46. Cf. Ezek. 1:2; 3:15, 24f.; 8:1.

47. Giesebrecht, op. cit., 154; Cornill, op. cit., 315 and Rudolph, op. cit., 166, have recognized that chapter 29 must derive from the earliest part of Zedekiah's reign when the events of 597 B.C. were still fresh. In fact, several scholars, misled in regard to the "fourth year" problem of chapters 27–28, have actually made the events of chapter 29 earlier than those of the latter; thus, J. Skinner, *Prophecy and Religion* (Cambridge, 1922), 253; A. W. Streane, *Jeremiah* (Cambridge Bible) (1926), 173; R. Calkins, *Jeremiah the Prophet* (N. Y., 1930), 251 n. 6. The same is implicit in Rudolph, op. cit., 166 and A. C. Welch, *Jeremiah, His Time and His Work* (Oxford, 1955), 196.

48. 28:10, also presupposed by vv. 2, 4.

49. It is now generally accepted that the postdating and accession-year system was in operation in Judea at this time. This author accepts the thesis of a Tishri-Tishri calendar at this period, now convincingly argued by A. Malamat [*Jerusalem*, etc., op. cit., 41–47, esp. n. 20; *IEJ* 18 (1968), 137–56 esp. 146–50] since it provides a more satisfactory solution to a greater number of problems than the supposition of a Nisan-Nisan system; so Freedy and Redford, op. cit., 464f.

50. For the historicity of this report see Kaufmann op. cit., 415, 422; Bright, *Jeremiah*, 212; cf. Driver, op. cit., 85.

51. With 29:3 cf. 51:59. On the plenipotentiaries of Zedekiah and their political affiliations, see S. Yeivin, *Mehqarim BeToledot Yisra'el We'Arṣo* (Tel-Aviv, 1960), 250–93.

52. Wiseman, op. cit., 37, 74–5,1. 25. The text is broken, but it must be assumed that an absence from Babylon of about three months was involved.

53. This was correctly noted by Volz, op. cit., 438, who failed, however, to draw the more likely conclusion, namely, that far from casting doubt on the authenticity of Jer. 51:59–64, it rather proves that chap. 29 issued from a much earlier experience.

54. A. Malamat, *IEJ* 18 (1968), 144f.

55. The oath is referred to in 2 Chr. 36:13 and Ezek. 17:11–18; cf. Josephus, *Antiquities*, X. vii. 102. Although there is no explicit statement as to when it was exacted, it is reasonable to suppose that such was done by Nebuchadnezzar immediately on installing Zedekiah as his vassal, in accordance with the usual custom and especially since he was in a hurry to return home to Babylon, (see below, n. 56). On the nature of the oath, see M. Tsevat, *JBL* 78 (1959), 199–204; A. Malamat, op. cit., 145f., esp. n. 18. For the possibility that the change of name from Mattaniah to Zedekiah (2 Kgs. 24:17) may also be connected with the vassalage status, see A. M. Honeyman, *JBL* 67 (1948), 13–25; cf. also S. I. Feign, *Missitrei He'abar* (N.Y., 1943), 81, 202 n. 163 and now A. Malamat, in *Jerusalem*, op. cit., 36.

56. D. N. Freedman, op. cit., 57 n. 32; cf. A. Parrot, *Babylon and the O.T.* (London, 1958), 93.

57. BM 21946, Rev. 1. 13, *šarra ša libbi-šu ina lib-bi ip-te-qid*; Wiseman, op. cit., 72.

58. W. F. Albright, *BA* 5 (1942), 49–55.

59. Cf. Skinner, op. cit., 252–4; Volz, op. cit., 267. The phrasing of Jer. 27:3 that the envoys were "coming to Zedekiah" might suggest that the initiative for the conference did not come from the king himself. The same conclusion might be inferred from the fact that the prophets in Babylon did not address their complaints about Jeremiah's activities to the king, but to the high priest (Jer. 29:25).

60. Jer. 27:16, עתה מהרה is specified in 28:3, 11 (omitted in G.) to mean בעוד שנתים ימים.

61. 28:1. The accession year covered Nisan through Elul 597. The fifth month was thus Ab 597 and not 596 as Driver has it, op. cit., 87.

62. 28:11. With כל הגוים cf. 27:6,7.

63. 27:3,6,7.

64. Another factor may have been the unwillingness or inability of Egypt at this time to lend its support; cf. above n. 2.

65. So our received Hebrew text, Jer. 51:59 בלכתו את צדקיהו. The Greek (28:59) reads Σεδεκίον (= מאת).

66. 25: 1; 32:1; 36:1, 9; 39:1, 2; 42:7; 45:1; 46:2.

67. 1:2; 51:59; 42:4.

68. 26:1; 27:1; 28:1; 49:34.

69. See *Orient and Occident, Essays Presented to Cyrus H. Gordon,* ed. H. A. Hoffner (Neukirchen-Vlyn, 1973), 143–9.

70. The siege commenced on the tenth of Tebeth in the ninth year of Zedekiah (2 Kgs. 25:1; Jer. 52:4; Ezek. 24:1–2; cf. Jer. 39:1). This date corresponds to 15 Jan. 588 B.C.; see Thiele, op. cit., 168; A. Malamat, *IEJ* 18 (1968), 150.

71. This accords exactly with rabbinic tradition as found in the *Seder Olam* Ch. 25 (ed. B. Ratner, p. 113). Cf. Qimḥi's comment to Jer. 28:1, Driver's solution (see above, n. 4) creates a fresh contradiction between the "beginning of the reign", i.e. the accession year *(reš šarruti)* which covered Nisan through Elul 597, and the "first year" which covered Tishri 597 through Elul 596.

72. See above, n. 60.

73. See above, n. 61.

Zedekiah's Emancipation of Slaves and the Sabbatical Year

Cyrus H. Gordon was one of the first scholars in modern times to express the view that the institution of the sabbatical year may go back to pre-Israelite origins.[1] He pointed to the well established and widely diffused seven year cyclical pattern in the ancient Near East and noted that the narrative of Jer 34:12–16 attests to an attempted revival of the sabbatical obligations which had fallen into disuse.

Gordon's interpretations of some of the Ugaritic texts (e.g. *UT* 52) as having been connected with the inauguration of a new septennial cycle[2] have both won support[3] and encountered challenge.[4] Of greater importance to his thesis are recent studies in the institution known as the *mīšarum* which was practised in Mesopotamia in the old Babylonian period. J. J. Finkelstein has forcefully argued for the recurrent character of the *mīšarum,* if only for the reason that this economic reform, which involved the remission of debts and other obligations, must have occurred at predictable intervals, if economic chaos was to be avoided.[5]

The problem of the antiquity of the calculation of the sabbatical year in Israel is complicated by the silence of the sources. Lev 26:34f., 43 and 2 Chron 36:21 testify only to the neglect of the obligations of the sabbatical laws, not to the complete ignorance or abandonment of the septennial calculations. Since Jer 34 can be located in a historic context, it is worthwhile re-examining the relationship of the narrative there to the sabbatical institution.

JER 34

At some period during Nebuchadnezzar's siege of Jerusalem, King Zedekiah issued a proclamation of emancipation for male and female Hebrew slaves. The mass manumission, apparently initiated by the king and accepted with some reluctance,[6] was put into effect through a solemn covenant contracted within the Temple (Jer. 34:8–10, 15, 18–19).[7] However, during a temporary lifting of the siege, misinterpreted by the men of Jerusalem (Jer. 34:21–22), the former owners violated their commitments and pressed the liberated slaves back into their service (vv. 11, 16, 18).

THE HISTORICAL BACKGROUND

Although these events are not precisely dated by the Book of Jeremiah, the historical background can now be reconstructed with a goodly measure of confidence.[8]

Nebuchadnezzar began the siege of Jerusalem on the 10th of Teveth in the 9th year of King Zedekiah of Judea (2 Kings 25:1; Jer. 52:4; Ezek. 24:1–2; Jer. 39:1). This date may now be fixed as Jan. 15th, 588 B.C.E. It is clear that most of Judea had already fallen by the time the emancipation of the slaves took place; only the fortress towns of Lachish and Azekah still held out (Jer. 34:7). This fact presupposes that quite some time must have elapsed by then since the start of the siege. This would place the mass manumission of slaves toward the end of 588. It cannot be later than December of that year because soon after this, as will be seen, the slave owners found reason to reconsider their decision.

It is beyond doubt that what occasioned the rescission of the emancipation was the entry of an Egyptian relief force into Judea.[9] Nebuchadnezzar had no option but to raise the siege in order to deal with a serious threat to his flanks from the southwest. Jeremiah (34:21–22) specifically mentions the departure of the Babylonian army at this time. Elsewhere the prophet reports the Egyptian intervention and denounces it as false hope, predicts its defeat and foresees the Babylonian resumption of the siege (37:5–11). A further reference to Zedekiah's appeal to Egypt for military support is to be found in Ezekiel's denunciation of the king's violation of his oath of loyalty to Nebuchadnezzar (Ezek. 17:11–18).[10] He too scoffs at the Egyptian ability to aid Judea and, in another prophecy (29:1), this time dated to the 12th of Tebeth in the tenth year of Johoiachin's exile (= 7th Jan. 587), Ezekiel warns against reliance upon Egyptian help. This oracle comes almost exactly one year after Nebuchadnezzar had arrived at the walls of Jerusalem and its wording (vv. 6–7) strongly reflects the optimism that now pervaded the city.[11] It is thus certain that by Jan. 587 the Egyptian relief operation was imminent. Three months later, however, on the 7th of Nisan 587 (= 29th April), the same prophet could proclaim that the arm of Pharaoh had been broken (Ezek 30:20–21). The brief and ineffectual intervention of Pharaoh Hophra (Apries: 589–570) took place, therefore, between January and April 587, just about one year after the Babylonians had first invested Jerusalem.[12] It was sometime in the course of these few months that the sorry events which earned the fierce denunciation of Jeremiah occurred.

To sum up: Nebuchadnezzar invested Jerusalem from the middle of Jan. 588. Toward the end of that year an emancipation of Hebrew slaves, male and female, was effected within Jerusalem. This was rescinded, however, with the raising of the siege following the arrival of the Egyptian expeditionary force sent by Pharaoh Hophra to relieve the city early in 587.

If the historical circumstances surrounding these events are more or less clear, the actual nature of the social institutions involved and their legal basis are far from being so.

JER 34 AND DEUTERONOMY

A close examination of the vocabulary and style of Jer 34:8–22 leaves no room for doubt that the literary formulation of the episode there described has drawn its inspiration generally from the Book of Deuteronomy,[13] and specifically from ch.15 therein.

The opening declaration of the prophet which refers to the covenant at the time of the Exodus (v. 13) corresponds almost word for word to Deut 29:24. Indeed, the covenant at Sinai is a recurrent theme of the Deuteronomist (cf. 4:23; 5:2, 3; 9:9; 28:69; 29:11, 13, 21; 31:16). The description of Egypt as the "house of bondage" (Jer 34:13) is more frequent in D (5:6; 6:12; 7:8; 8:14; 13:6, 11) than in the rest of the Pentateuch (Ex 13:3, 14; 20:2). The expression "to do what is right in God's eyes" (Jer 34:15) is characteristically Deuteronomic (6:18; 12:25, 28; 13:19; 21:9) occurring elsewhere in the Pentateuch but once (Ex 15:26). Similarly, the phrase "transgressing my covenant" (Jer 34:18) occurs in the Torah only in Deut 17:2. The maledictions of D seem especially to have left their mark on this chapter for the threat of Israel becoming "a horror to all the kingdoms of the earth" (Jer 34:17) has its source in Deut 28:25. Likewise, Jer 34:18 was inspired by Deut 27:26, while the dire punishment of Jer 34:20 that the carcasses of those who transgressed the covenant would "become food for all the birds of the sky and the beasts of the earth," has been drawn directly from Deut. 28:26.

These many stylistic parallels reinforce the inescapable conclusions to be derived from a detailed comparison between the legal material of Jer 34 and Deut. 15. In the aggregate they exclude any possibility of the direct dependence of the events of Jer. 34 upon Ex. 21:1–11.[14] The evidence may be subsumed as follows:

(i) Jeremiah's characteristic phrase for manumission is *šillaḥ ḥofšî* (34:9, 10, 14, 16. cf. v. 10). This is precisely the term employed in Deut. 15:12, 13, 18. In Ex. 21, however, this formula is restricted to the release of a slave in compensation for the infliction of permanent bodily injury (Ex. 21:26f.), whereas the standard technical term for manumission is *yaṣa' (l)hofšî* (*ibid.*, vv. 2, 5; cf. 3, 4, 7, 11).

(ii) In Jer. 34:14 the previously discussed phrase is followed by *me'immak* which is the characteristic style of Deut. 15 (vv. 12, 13, 18).

(iii) The narrative refers to *haᶜibrî wᵉhaᶜibrîyāh* (Jer. 34:9) exactly corresponding to *haᶜibrî 'ow haᶜibrîyāh* of Deut. 15:12 and in contrast to Ex. 21:2 which provides only for the *ᶜebed ᶜibrî*.

(iv) Even though the prophet's citation of the law mentions only the male Hebrew slave (Jer. 34:14), vv. 9, 10, 11, 16 leave no doubt that the law in its operation made no discrimination between the sexes. This is the situation that exists in Deut. 15:12, 17. On the other hand, the legislation in Ex. 21:7–11 sharply differentiates between the fate of the male and female slave.

(v) The Hebrew slave is several times designated "brother" (Jer. 34:9, 14, 17[2]). This corresponds exactly to the formula of Deut. 15:12. In fact, the use of this appellation is one of the distinguishing features of D, where it appears more than twenty-five times in legal contexts.

(vi) Jeremiah's citation of the law begins with the phrase *miqqēṣ šebaᶜšānîm*[15] (Jer. 34:14). The same words head the chapter in D (15:1), in which the emancipation of slaves is dealt with and its only other occurrence is also in that book (31:10).

(vii) Jer. 34:14 expresses the means of enslavement by *'ašer yimmākēr lᵉkā* and Deut. 15:12 has *kî yimmākēr lᵉkā*. Ex. 21:2, on the other hand, has *kî tiqneh* regarding a male slave and *kî yimkōr iš 'et bittô* (v. 7) in respect of a female slave.

(viii) Both pentateuchal sources limit the term of service to six years. However, while the formulations of Jer. 34:14 and Deut. 15:12 coincide *(waʿabadᵉkā šēš šānîm)* the word order of Ex. 21:2 differs *(šēš šānîm yaʿabōd)*.

(ix) Both Jeremiah (34:13) and D (15:15) associate the emancipation of slaves with the redemption from Egypt, a connection that is wholly absent from Ex. 21.[16]

DEUT 15

The literary analysis as well as matters of substance demonstrate conclusively that the events that occurred in Jerusalem during the Babylonian siege, as detailed in Jer. 34:8–10, were grounded in D. This conclusion, however, raises serious problems of exegesis, for at first glance there would seem to be no way of reconciling the action of Zedekiah with the legal provisions of Deut. 15.

The relevant material of that chapter naturally divides into two parts. The first eleven verses deal with the remission of debts in the septennial release; the subsequent seven verses (12–18) restrict the service of the Hebrew slave, male and female, to six years. The two institutions would seem to be wholly unrelated. The cancellation of debts took place within the context of a fixed seven-year cycle of universal application. This interpretation is certainly assured by the initial formula *miqqēṣ šebaʿ šānîm* (v. 1), more closely defined as the "seventh year, the year of the release" *(šᵉmiṭṭāh* v. 9), as well as by the employment of the same expression and definition in Deut. 31:10 in a passage that unambiguously points to the fixed, cyclic and national nature of the institution referred to. On the other hand, the manumission of the slaves would seemingly have had to occur on an individual basis, since each bondman's six year period of service would naturally be completed at a different time.

In contrast to the apparently plain intent of Deut. 15:12–18, the action of Zedekiah took no account of the individual slave's term of service, but involved the general and simultaneous emancipation of Jerusalem's entire slave community. Appropriately, the royal edict is repeatedly designated *dᵉrôr* (vv. 8, 15, 17), a technical term that, to judge from its other biblical usages and ancient Near Eastern analogies,[17] is applicable only to an institution administered on a community-wide basis (Lev. 25:10; Is. 61:1–2; Ezek. 46:17). How is this to be reconciled with the indubitable fact that the legislation of Deut. 15 in its substance and literary formulation constituted the legal and theological foundation upon which rested the events that took place during the Babylonian siege of Jerusalem? This problem is exacerbated by another fact. Jeremiah himself acknowledges that Zedekiah's enactment was in fulfillment of, and in accord with, the provisions of the Sinaitic covenant, which earlier generations had honored more in the breach than in the observance (vv. 13–14). He cites directly from the original law code, the quotational form being confirmed by the introductory *le'môr* and by the presence of the 2nd. pers. sing.—*lᵉkā, wᵉcabadᵉkā, wᵉšillaḥtô*—in contrast to the use of the plural in the rest of his oration. Significant, because it is not in D, is the absence of the term *derôr* despite its prominence otherwise in the chapter. The question then remains as to the nature of Zedekiah's edict and its relationship to the legislation of Deut. 15.

THE RELEASE OF SLAVES AND THE SABBATICAL YEAR

In actual fact, no real contradiction between the Deuteronomist and Jer. 34 need be assumed, if the latter be understood to be reflecting an ancient interpretation of the intent of the former.

The phenomenon of debt-bondage in Israel is attested in several sources.[18] The institution is presupposed by Lev. 25:39, which must be understood in the light of the preceding legislation referring to the impoverished Israelite who is not to be subjected to usury (vv. 35f.).[19] Similarly, the sale into slavery of the thief who lacks the means to make restitution for his theft (Ex. 22:2) is nothing but a form of debt-bondage. That the seizure of the defaulting debtor by his creditor was indeed practised in life is clear from the narrative of 2 Kings 4:1 and from the fulminations of Amos (2:6; 8:6) and Deutero-Isaiah (50:1). In the time of Nehemiah people in financial straits were driven to press their sons and daughters into slavery (Neh. 5:5). The proverbial observation that "the borrower is the lender's slave" (Prov. 22:7) certainly reflected a sad reality of life, even if the enslavement of a debtor is not officially explicated in biblical legal texts. Although the sources do not say so outright, it is obvious that there must have been an inextricable connection between the remission of debts and the manumission of slaves.[20] Lev. 25:47–54 provides for the possible early redemption of an Israelite driven by poverty to sell himself to a resident alien. In 2 Kings 4:1–7 the peonage of the sons of the impoverished widow is ended after the miracle performed by Elisha enables her to pay off her creditors. Since the law codes, biblical and Mesopotamian,[21] limit the terms of bondage, they must have looked upon the service as simply a distraint of the debtor's person for the purposes of liquidating the debt.

It is difficult to believe that one who entered into slavery for debt should have had to continue in bondage beyond the cancellation of the original financial obligation. If, as is certain, insolvency constituted the prime cause of Hebrew slavery, then it is self-evident that the major portion of the slave population would automatically and simultaneously have gained its freedom with the general nullification of indebtedness.[22] For this reason, the juxtaposition of the septennial remission of debts and the manumission of slaves forms a perfectly natural and logical nexus. This is precisely the situation that exists in Deut. 15 and it is not surprising that Jeremiah should quote the legislation of Deut. 15:12 in connection with the mass liberation of slaves and that the entire pericope of Jer. 34 should be saturated with the language of that chapter.[23]

It is apparent, therefore, that in Zedekiah's day the provisions of Deut. 15:12 were interpreted in the context of the sabbatical year. The prescribed six year limit on debt-bondage was regarded as a maximum that would be reduced by the incidence of the sabbatical year.[24]

Evidence for the existence in ancient times of such a correlation between the *šemiṭṭah* and the manumission of slaves is provided by the Targum Pseudo-Jonathan to the Pentateuch.[25] This version has preserved traditions to this effect in its exegetical amplifications of its renderings of Ex. 21:7 and 22:2. In the former passage, the release of a slave-girl is differentiated from that of a bondman. "She shall not be freed as male slaves are" says the text, to which the Palestinian Targum adds ". . . in the year of the *šemiṭṭah*." The second passage legislates concerning the thief who, lacking the means to make restitution, must be sold into slavery. The Targum again specifies that the term of service lasts "until the *šemiṭṭah* year."

Now this exegesis of the Pseudo-Jonathan is in direct contradiction to the Tannaitic *halakhah*.[26] For this reason it must represent a much earlier legal stratum and reflect a tradition of great antiquity, one that is in direct line with that of Jer. 34 in its interpretation of the legislation of Deut. 15, namely, that the remission of debts in the sabbatical year automatically carries with it the freeing of slaves sold because of insolvency.

THE SABBATICAL YEAR 588–587 B.C.E.

It has been shown earlier that Zedekiah's proclamation of emancipation must have taken place late in the year 588 B.C.E. The most likely time would have been the Autumn New Year festival.[27] Lev. 25:8–10 indicates a Fall to Fall cycle for the sabbatical year. Deut. 31:10 provides for a septennial national assembly in the Fall in connection with the year of release. The national conclave held in Jerusalem in the time of Nehemiah took place in the seventh month (Neh 8:2; 9:1) and, significantly enough, the provisions of the covenant then drawn up included the fulfillment of the sabbatical year legislation requiring the fallowness of the land and the remission of debts (Neh 10:32). This last item was directly connected with the distraint of persons for reasons of insolvency (Neh 5:1–13).

It follows from the above that the year 588–587 would have been a sabbatical year in Judea. The Temple would then have fallen in a post-sabbatical year (586).[28] This fact exactly accords with rabbinic tradition.[29] The previous sabbatical year would have been 595–594. From the Babylonian Chronicle we now know that Zedekiah came to the throne soon after Nebuchadnezzar's capture of Jerusalem on 2nd Adar in his seventh regnal year, i.e., 15/16 March, 597.[30] His accession year covered Nisan-Tishri 597. This period was known in Akkadian as the *rēš šarrūti*[31] for which the Hebrew equivalent is *rēšît mamlākāh*[32] (Jer. 27:1; 28:1). The accession year of Zedekiah would then have fallen within the fourth year of the sabbatical cycle 595–594. This indeed provides a satisfactory explanation for the otherwise obscure superscription of Jer. 28:1 which equates the "beginning of the reign of Zedekiah" (*berēšît mamleket Ṣidkiyāhû*) with "the fourth year."[33]

In the light of the evidence here presented it seems clear that Gordon's original suggestion that Jer. 34 reflects the sabbatical legislation is correct. We now have a fixed date 588–587 B.C.E. as a base for the determination of some other sabbatical calculations.[34]

NOTES

1. C.H. Gordon, *Or* 22 (1953), 79–81.
2. *Ugaritic Literature* (1949), 4, 57.
3. Cf. J. Gray, *Archaeology and the Old Testament* (1962), 111.
4. J. C. de Moor, *Seasonal Pattern in the Ugaritic Myth of Ba'lu* (1971).
5. J. J. Finkelstein, *JCS* 15 (1961), 91–104; in *Studies in Honor of B. Landsberger* (1965), 233–46, esp. n. 38; *ANET* (Suppl., 1969), 526; on the need to re-evaluate the antiq-

uity of the sabbatical and Jubilee institutions, cf. M. Weinfeld, *Deuteronomy and the Deuteronomic School* (1972), 153, n. 1.

6. This is possibly hinted at in v. 10. *wayyišmᵉ'û*.

7. On this ratification of covenants by sacrifice, see M. Weinfeld, *op. cit.*, 102–04.

8. See E. R. Thiele, *The Mysterious Numbers of the Hebrew Kings* (1965), 167–9; A. Malamat in *Jerusalem Through the Ages* [Hebrew] (1968), 42–5; *IEJ*, 18 (1968), 137–56.

9. It should be noted that no formal abrogation of the covenant took place. Rather, it would seem that, with the raising of the siege, the need for manpower to work the neglected fields led many individual owners to pressure their erstwhile slaves back into their service. It is not unlikely in view of the prevailing conditions that many slaves required little persuasion. For a theological interpretation of Zedekiah's measure, see M. Kessler, *BZ* 15 (1971), 104–08.

10. See 2 Chron. 36:13; cf. Jos. *Ant.* x.7 (102). On vassal oaths of this type, see M. Tsevat, *JBL* 78 (1959), 199–204; A. Malamat, *IEJ op. cit.*, 145 n. 18; Jerusalem, *op. cit.*, 36 n. 17.

11. Lam. 4:17 most likely reflects this state of affairs.

12. For the importance of Ezekiel's anti-Egyptian prophecies as a historic source, see Malamat, Jerusalem, 42f.; *IEJ*, 152f. The relevant dates are also to be found in M. Greenberg, *Encyclopaedia Judaica*, 6, 1081f.

13. For an exhaustive listing of characteristically Deuteronomic phraseology, see Weinfeld, *op. cit.* 320–65, esp. 359–61.

14. The contrary thesis of A. F. Puuko, *BWAT* 13 (1913), 126–53, esp. 146f., has been effectively refuted by Y. Kaufmann, *Tôledôt Hā'Emûnāh Hayisre'ēlît* (1947), III, 437, esp. n. 39.

15. This is the text in all the ancient versions except G in which "seven" has been "corrected" to "six." The meaning of *miqqēṣ* here is not pertinent to the present discussion.

16. For the emphasis on the redemption from Egypt in D, cf. 5:15; 16:12; 24:18, 22 *et al.*; cf. Weinfeld, 326f.

17. On the *andurāru*, see G. R. Driver and J. C. Miles, *The Babylonian Laws*, I (1952), 224; II (1955), 207; J. Lewy, *Eretz-Israel*, 5 (1959) 21°–31°.

18. See I. Mendelsohn, *Slavery in the Ancient Near East* (1949), 14–19, 23–33; cf. E. E. Urbach, *Papers of the Institute of Jewish Studies London* (1964), 4.

19. A distinction must be made between a social phenomenon on the one hand and the acceptance or rejection of the same in the codified law on the other; cf. the remarks of M. Elon, *Freedom of the Debtor's Person in Jewish Law* [Hebrew] (1964), 2, n. 9.

20. This was noted by S. R. Driver, *Deuteronomy* (1902), 177–8; Mendelsohn, *op. cit.*, 147, n. 257; cf. also R.H. Pfeiffer, *Introduction to the O.T.* (1948), 222; R. de Vaux, *Ancient Israel* (1961), 83. A. Menes, *BZAW* 50 (1928), 79–80, also interpreted Deut. 15:12–18 as referring to the manumission of enslaved debtors and explained 31:10ff as presupposing the equality, i.e., the freedom, of all Israel following the sabbatical year. It is likely that Jer. 17:4 *wᵉšāmaṭṭāh. . . wᵉhaᶜabadtîkā* reflects the close connection between the *šemiṭṭah* and release from slavery.

21. Cf. Code of Hammurapi, § 117 on which see Driver & Miles, *op. cit.*, I, 217–221.

22. Thus, the *mîšarum* edict of Ammiṣaduqa makes clear provision for the automatic release of citizens in debt-servitude; see F. R. Kraus, *Ein Edikt des Königs Ammiṣaduqa von Babylon* (1958), 40, 41, § 18 (= *ANET*, 528, § 20). For the relation of this clause to CH § 117, see Kraus, 167–72.

23. The contention of W. Rudolph, Jeremiah (1947), 189, that the connection between Jer. 34 and Deut. 15 is "secondary" cannot possibly be maintained; cf. J. Bright, *Jeremiah* (1965), 223–4.

24. It is not necessary to assume with M. David, *OTS* 5 (1948), 63–79, that a socio-legal development took place whereby the original Deuteronomic individual manumission after six years yielded to a general one in a fixed year in the time of Jeremiah. In fact, the evidence seems to show that the reverse process took place, namely that the earlier interpretation of Deut. 15:12 which connected the "seventh year" with the sabbatical was later abandoned.

25. *Pseudo-Jonathan,* ed. M. Ginsburger (1903), 136, 138. On the remnants of the earlier *halākhāh* in this Targum, see B. J. Roberts, *The O. T. Text and Versions* (1951), 203f. and the literature there cited. It is remarkable that as late as the 12th century, the Jewish Bible commentator Joseph b. Isaac Bekhor Shor (of Orleans) explained the "seventh year" of Ex. 21:2 in terms of the *šᵉmiṭṭah* rather than the seventh year of service.

26. Cf. Mekilta d. R. Y., *Mishpaṭim* I, ed. H. S. Horovitz & I. A. Rabin (reprint of 1960), 249; Sifra, *Behar* II, 6, ed. A. H. Weiss (1862), 107b; Sifrei, *Re'eh*, § 111–12, ed. M. Friedmann (1864), 97[a-b]; P. Kid. 1:2; b Arak. 18[b]; Nid. 48[a].

27. It should be noted that the *mišarum* of Ammiṣaduqa formally took effect on Nisan 1st, the Babylonian New Year Festival (§ 3); cf. J. J. Finkelstein, *RA* 63 (1969), 49, 55; cf. S. Mowinckel, *The Psalms in Israel's Worship,* I (1962), 128f.

28. For the date 586, see Malamat, *op. cit.*; Thiele, *op. cit.*

29. b. Arak. 11b, Ta'an. 29b.

30. D. J. Wiseman, *Chronicles of the Chaldean Kings* etc. (1956), 32–35, 48, 72–73.

31. On the *rēš šarrūti,* see H. Tadmor, *JNES,* 15 (1956), 227 n. 11; *Encyclopaedia Miqrā'ît* 4, col. 258, n. 6 & cols. 267–8; in *Studies* in Honor of B. Landsberger (1968), 352 & n. 13; R. de Vaux, *op. cit.*, 194.

32. Cf. also Jer. 26:1; 49:34. In 27:1, MT "Jehoiakim" must certainly be corrected to "Zedekiah" (so Syriac) in the light of vv. 3, 12 and the reference to the exile in vv. 16–22; cf. also 28:1. In 49:34ff. the reference to Elam can have nothing to do with the Babylonian Chronicle's report of the defeat of an Elamite army (Wiseman, *op. cit.*, 72–73, cf. 36, 48) since that document says nothing about the utter destruction of Elam and the exile of its people which are the themes of Jeremiah's prophecy. Hence there is no reason to understand *bᵉrēšît malkût* other than the equivalent of *rēš šarrūti.*

33. On Jer. 28:1 see the present writer's study in *Hagut Ibrît b'Amerika* [Hebrew], ed. M. Zohori, *et al,* I (1972), 121–30.

34. The computation is complicated by the question as to whether the Jubilee year constituted a blank year or the first of the next sabbatical cycle. The lack of explicitness in the biblical formulation gave rise to a difference of opinion among the Tannaim; cf. b. R.H. 8[b]-9[a]; Ned. 61 [a]; Arak. 12[a-b], 32 [b].

Ezekiel 8:17: A Fresh Examination

The theological crisis in Judea occasioned by the destruction of the Temple in the year 587 B.C.E. left its indelible imprint upon the contemporary literature. The conflict between the popular belief in the inviolability of the House of God and the stark reality of the national catastrophe raised fundamental questions about the nature of God and divine justice. The books of Jeremiah, Ezekiel, and Habakkuk, in particular, bear repeated testimony to the pervasive urgency of the problem. Once the inevitability of the fall became an ineradicable conviction in the prophetic consciousness, the need for an explanation became no less imperious than if the disaster were already an accomplished fact.[1]

Naturally, the only satisfactory answer consistent with the national theology was that God himself, by the free exercise of his sovereign will, and for excellent reasons, had abandoned Zion. The physically destructive activities of the Babylonians merely gave concrete external expression to an already existing inner situation.

Nowhere is this prophetic rationalization more superbly illustrated than in the literary unit Ezekiel 8–11. With great clarity, and in logical sequence, these four chapters constitute a sort of telescoped, dramatic and symbolic presentation of the prophetic resolution of the theological crisis in all its aspects.

First, Ezekiel is transported to Jerusalem to witness, for himself, the "abominations" of the people. Here is the justification for the divine decision to abandon the Temple and Zion. Then comes the execution of the decision, the vision of the imaginary destruction which is, after all, just another way of emphasizing its God-forsaken state. This is confirmed all the more vividly through the description of the divine Presence withdrawing from the Temple in progressive stages. The vision culminates in the climactic declaration that God's glory had gone up from the midst of the city and was stationed on the mount to the east (11:23).

Now, within the framework of the vision the "abominations" recorded in ch. 8 are of great importance. They constitute the real core of the theodicy. But their importance lies less in their historic value than in the genres of sins they are meant to typify.[2] It is one of the outstanding characteristics of Ezekiel that he lays so much stress upon the ritual evils and that he constantly alternates sins of idolatry with violations of the socio-moral code.[3] Ch. 8 exemplifies this pattern, moving from ritual to the socio-moral plane in v. 17. In view of the unambiguous statement in v. 15, "you will yet see abominations even greater than the foregoing," it may be safely assumed that the presentation of sins is in ascending order of gravity. That is to say, what is described in v. 17 ought to be regarded as climactic.

That this is indeed the case may be confirmed by the fact that, although the people to be saved sigh and moan over "all the abominations," yet the socio-moral sin is the only one mentioned by God in ch. 9 in justification for his violent reprisals against the city (v. 9). Furthermore, we are explicitly told there that "the sin of the house of Israel and Judah is exceedingly great" (גדול במאד מאד). What was this sin? The indictment of the prophet leaves no room for doubt. It is bloodshed (or violence)[4] and the perversion of justice. Not a word is said about the foregoing ritual sins.

Accordingly, there is every reason to regard 8:17 והנם שלחים את־הזמורה אל־אפם, not as a reversion to the list of idolatrous practices, but as referring to a particularly blatant demonstration of the "violence" of the preceding clause.[5] In fact, וישבו להכעיסני, "they provoke me still more," actually implies that what follows is worst of all. Several additional arguments may be adduced in support of this conclusion.

In striking contrast to the Temple locale of all the other "abominations" in ch. 8, the particular outrage of v. 17 is more generalized, being committed "in the land."[6] Such a shift of scene would indicate an entirely different category of sin.

Ezekiel's theodicy and his impatience with human questioning of "the ways of the Lord" (18:25, 29; 33:17, 20) led him directly to insist upon the doctrine of retributive justice (3:17–21; 14:12–23; 18; 33:1–20). God metes out to man according to his deeds. No wonder that the phrase אני גם,[7] introducing the divine counter-measure, is so frequently used. If, then, in 8:18, which is the link between the "abominations" and the inevitable retribution, we are told that God says:

> I, too, will act in anger; my
> eye will not spare, neither will
> I have pity; and though they cry
> in my ears with a loud voice, I
> will not hear them,

we can assume that the sin of the previous verse involved an act of violence either deliberately provocative of God or performed in the heat of anger[8] without pity or mercy for the victims whose agonizing cries encountered but stony silence.

As if to dispel any lingering uncertainty as to the correctness of this interpretation, 8:18 is repeated in 9:10, again after a description of the sin of Israel and Judah as "violence," i.e., lawlessness and injustice. Noteworthy is the significant addition, דרכם בראשם נתתי "I requite their deeds upon their heads," that is, I deal with them measure for measure.[9]

This recognition of the point-counterpoint relationship of chaps. 8 and 9 leads us to a fresh examination of the celebrated crux of 8:17, והנם שלחים את־הזמורה אל־אפם. It should be obvious, by now, that none of the cultic explanations of the passage can possibly fit the context.[10] What is required is a rendering that will accord with the strange picture of the angelic demolition squad of chap. 9 and that is contrapuntal to it.

Fortunately, just such an explanation is at hand if we see in זמורה, not the word for "branch," but the well known Semitic root *d̠mr*.[11] This form appears in Arabic *d̠amir*, *d̠amîr*, "brave," and in Old South Arabic *md̠mr*, "strong." It achieved widespread popularity in the Semitic onomasticon. Witness OSA proper names *D̠mrmr*, *D̠mrkrb*, *D̠mr'l*; Phoenician *D̠mr* and *Zmr*; Ugaritic *d̠mrb'l* and *d̠mrhd*; the West-Semitic Mari names, *Zimrî-abum*, *Zimrî-erah̬* and *Zimrî-lim*; the North Israelite בעלזמר[12] and the biblical זמירה[13] (I Chr. 7:8), זמרי[14] (Num. 25:14, *et al.*) and, possibly, זמרן (Gen. 25:2; I Chr. 1:32).

Furthermore, the Semitic root *d̠mr*, in the form זמר, has been widely recognized as existing in several biblical Hebrew passages with the meaning "strength."[15] These are: Gen. 43:11 זמרת הארץ[16]; Exod. 15:2 (Isa. 12:2, Ps. 118:14) עזי וזמרת־יה[17]; 2 Sam. 23:1

נתן Job 35:10 [19]זמיר עריצים יענה Isa. 25:5 ;[18]נעים זמרות ישראל
זמרות בלילה.[20]

But it is, above all, in Ugaritic *dmr*[21] that the clue to the meaning of
Ezek. 8:17 lies. In several texts this vocable is parallel to *mhrm* "warriors,"[22] which itself parallels *ṣbim* "troops," and *ǵzrm* "heroes."[23] These
equations leave no room for doubt that Ugaritic *dmr* means, "strong
men," "troops," or the like.[24]

Accordingly, זמורה in our passage should be regarded as a derivation
of *dmr* meaning, "band of toughs." The reference would be to the manner by which the rich forcibly dispossessed the poor through the employment of hired thugs or "strong men." Such bands of freebooters and
opportunists have been known throughout history, and one is immediately reminded of Abimelech (Jud. 9:4f.), Jephthah (ibid. 11:3) and
David (I Sam. 22:2; 25:2ff.). In the prophetic age, Hosea (6:9) and Jeremiah (18:21f.) both mention the "troops" who attack and pillage the
innocent and even commit murder. Job (19:12) refers to the "troops" of
God who harass him at every turn.[25]

The זמורה, then, would comprise those "muscle-men" described
elsewhere individually as איש חמס (Ps. 18:49; 140:12), איש חמסים; (2
Sam. 22:49), and איש זרוע (Job 22:8). It must be obvious that in the
prophetic descriptions of the social decay that resulted from the ever-
sharpening contrast in the extremes of wealth and poverty the violent
injustices ascribed to the rapacious rich were actually carried out by
their hired henchmen.[26]

This interpretation of זמורה as a "band of strong men" fits in admira-
bly with the "violence" mentioned in the preceding clause of v. 17. It
also accords perfectly with Ezekiel's designation of Jerusalem as the
"city of blood" (22:2; 24:6, 9) and his repeated excoriation of bloodshed
and injustice in the city and the land.[27] At the same time, it explains the
strange nature of the imaginary punishment of the city in chap. 9, in
accordance with the doctrine of talion. The punitive band of six men,
each with his destructive weapon in his hand (9:1–2), corresponds
exactly to the form which the sin of violence took in the sending forth of
the זמורה on behalf of the exploiters of the poor.

It now remains to explain the phrase אל־אפם. We note at once that if
we take the noun in the sense of "anger" rather than "nose," it fits in
with להכעיסני in the same verse and בחמה in the following. The interchange of prepositions אל and ל is very frequent in biblical Hebrew,[28] so
that אל־אפם, if the text be authentic, would mean the same thing as
לאפם, namely, "in the execution of their anger." The expression is strik-

ingly parallel to Isa. 13:3 גם קראתי גבורי לאפי, "I have also summoned my mighty men to execute my anger."[29]

On the other hand, if the rabbinic tradition[30] be correct that the original text was אל־אפית[31] we may understand here the commonplace prepositional interchange of אל and על.[32] אל־אפי would then mean, "to
provoke me to anger," just as Jer. 32:31, על־אפי ועל־חמתי.[33]

Thus the entire phrase should be translated, "and they provoke me
still more, for see, they send out the strong men to execute their anger/to
anger me." The divine counter-action of 8:18–9:11 becomes readily
intelligible. God, in return, vents his anger by sending in punishment *his*
band of destructive angels.

NOTES

1. On the theological crisis, see J. Bright, A History of Israel (1959), pp. 311f.,
315ff.; Y. Kaufmann, Toledoth, III, 369–92; The Religion of Israel, ed. Greenberg
(1960), pp. 401–09; 426ff. The situation was not dissimilar from that confronting Christianity at the fall of Rome, on which see S. Dill, Roman Society in the Last Century of
the Western Empire (1958), pp. 59–73.

2. For the imaginary nature of chaps. 8–11 see Kaufmann, Toledoth, III, 499–505;
The Religion of Israel, ed. Greenberg, p. 430.

3. Cf. chaps. 6–7 (esp. 7:23); 16 (esp. 36, 38); 18 (esp. 5ff.); 22 (esp. 2–4, 6–7, 9,
12f., 25, 27, 29); 23 (esp. 37, 45, 49); 33 (esp. 25f.); 36 (esp. 16–18).

4. On the variants חמס/דמים in Ezek. 9:9, see the remarks of Kimchi and Minḥath
Shai, ad loc. Note, also, 7:23, in which both terms are used. On the general question of
synonymous variants in MT, see S. Talmon, Textus, I (1960), 144–84.

5. R. Gordis, JTS 37 (1936), 284–88; Kaufmann, Toledoth, III, 484, n.6; The Religion of Israel, ed. Greenberg, p. 429, n.8 have convincingly refuted the cultic explanation of the passage. L. Koehler, Lexicon (1948), p. 259, s.v. זמורה, has included the
baresma association, despite the overwhelming arguments against it brought by S. Spiegel, HTR 24 (1931), 298–301; JBL 54 (1935), 152–59. See further n. 10 below.

6. Spiegel, JBL 54 (1935), 157, n. 33.

7. Cf., 5:8, 11; 8:18; 9:10; 16:43; 20:15, 23, 25; 21:22; 24:9. See further note 9
below.

8. On this point, see further in connection with the interpretation of אל־אפם.

9. Cf., also, 11:21; 22:31; 36:19, and n.7 above.

10. See above, n.5. It should be noted that the cultic explanation is supported neither by the versions (on which see G. A. Cooke, Commentary, ICC [1937], ad loc.) nor
by the medieval Jewish commentaries (for a summary of which see E. Ben-Yehuda, Thesaurus, III, 1350, n.1). H. W. F. Saggs, JTS, N.S. II (1960), 318–29, who sees in the
phrase a reference to a ritual gesture connected with the sun-cult, has brought no effective arguments in favor of a ritual interpretation and has virtually ignored those against it.

11. C. Gordon, Ugaritic Manual (1955), 20.529. This root has been ignored both by
Charles-F. Jean, Dictionnaire des Inscriptions Sémitiques de L'Ouest (1954), and by his
reviser, J. Hoftijzer (1960).

12. Samaria Ostracon 12, 2–3.

13. Probably to be read זמריה; see M. Noth, Die Israelitischen Personennamen
(1928), p. 242, No. 438.

14. Ibid., p. 176 and n.3.

15. Koehler, Lexicon, p. 260, II זמרה, III זמר.

16. Ibid.; Tur-Sinai, Ha-Lashon veha-Sefer, I (1954), 51; Encyclopedia Biblica [Hebrew], II, 933.

17. Ben-Yehuda, op. cit., III, 1363f., n.6; T. H. Gaster, Expository Times 48 (1936–37), 45; U. Cassuto, Commentary to Exodus (1954), ad loc.; Koehler, op. cit.; F. M. Cross and D. N. Freedman, JNES 14 (1955), 243.

18. Freedman, ibid., note 6; Tur-Sinai, op. cit.; Commentary to Job [Hebrew] (1954), p. 297.

19. Tur-Sinai, ibid.

20. Ibid. I would also suggest Ps. 119:54 זמרות היו לי חקיך as another example, translating, "your statutes were a (source of) strength to me."

21. J. Aistleitner, Ignace Goldziher Memorial Volume, I (1948), 223; U. Cassuto, The Goddess Anath [Hebrew] (1953), p. 46; Gordon, op. cit.

22. Anat II (= VAB, β), lines 14–15, 28, 34–35.

23. Ibid., lines 21–22.

24. Since *ḏmr* in the Ugaritic texts is always singular, it would be regarded as a collective.

25. With the use of גדוד in these passages, cf. the inscription of Azitawadda of Adana I, 1.15 'šmi r'm b'l 'gddm. "evil men, gang-leaders."

26. Cf. Amos 2:6–7; 5:11–12; 8:4–6; Micah 2:8–9; 3:2–3,10; 6:10–12; 7:2–3. Incidentally, the prophets are describing what was known in India as "thuggee."

27. See n.3.

28. Cf. Num. 30:15 מיום אל־יום with Ps. 96:2 ליום מיום; 2 Sam. 18:4 אל־יד שער with Prov. 8:3 ליד שערים; 2 Kings 21:16 מפה לפה with Ezra 9:11 מפה אל־פה; Ps. 104:29 ואל־עפרם ישובון with 146:4 ישב לאדמתו; I Chr. 9:25 מעת אל־עת with Mishnaic מעת לעת (e.g., M. Giṭṭin III. 8).

29. Note the further analogy of v. 5 כלי זעמו with Ezek. 9:1 כלי משחתו, 2 מפצו כלי.

30. For a thorough elucidation of the rabbinic traditions about the "corrections of the Scribes," see S. Lieberman, Hellenism in Jewish Palestine (1962), pp. 28–37 esp. 33.

31. Symmachus, Aquila, Peshitta and Targum, all read אפם.

32. Cf. Ezek. 18:6 אל־ההרים with v. 15 על־ההרים.

33. With Ezek. 8:17 להכעיסני, cf. Jer. 32:30, מכעיסים 32 להכעיסני.

WRITINGS

Prolegomenon to an Edition
of the Psalms

Moses Buttenwieser[1] (1862–1939) was a product of German scholarship, having acquired his higher education at the Universities of Würzburg, Leipzig and Heidelberg. He came to the United States soon after receiving his doctorate from the latter institution in 1896, and was soon appointed to succeed the renowned Max L. Margolis as Professor of Biblical Exegesis at Hebrew Union College in Cincinnati, a position in which he served for thirty-seven years until his retirement in 1934. His earliest works were devoted to Apocalyptic literature,[2] but Biblical studies soon became his sole field of interest. His three major works in this area were *The Prophets of Israel* (New York, 1914), *The Book of Job* (London, 1922), and *the Commentary to the Psalms*. This latter was published in the year before his death and has long been out of print.

Buttenwieser stood at the parting of the ways in Psalms scholarship. In many respects he was the embodiment of the classic approach of the nineteenth century, that of the historical-chronological school, and he mainly represented, too, the prevailing text-critical side of exegesis. But he wrote at a time when this school was giving way to a completely new approach, and while in his *Commentary* he exhibited little consciousness of its existence, he nevertheless struck out on his own in several important and original ways in both Higher and Lower Criticism.

The first stage in Psalms exegesis had led an almost uninterrupted existence for nearly two millennia. It was dominated by the belief in Davidic authorship. "Belief" is perhaps too mild a term; "doctrine" would probably be more accurate. It is true that there are indications in rabbinic literature that the tradition claiming for David the entire Book of Psalms was but the crystallization of a trend which gradually displaced earlier and variant traditions.[3] But already in the second pre-Christian century the author of II Maccabees refers to "the books of David."[4] The rabbis of the Midrash did not shrink from comparing Mosaic composition of the Pentateuch with David's parentage of the five-book Psalter.[5] Indeed, they noted that David had actually chosen to commence his work with the same work that Moses had used in concluding his farewell address.[6]

The ascription of the Psalter to the shepherd king has its roots already in Biblical traditions. The Chronicler associated David with the establishment of the liturgical-musical tradition of the Temple.[7] The editorial colophon to the second book of Psalms clearly shows that the superscription *le-David* was very early understood as signifying authorship. The Greek translation did not hesitate to add Davidic titles to many psalms that are anonymous in our Hebrew text,[8] so that the number exceeds by far our seventy-three specifically labeled. How far this process went may be appreciated from the fact that the theory of Davidic authorship was unperturbed even by the presence of several other names in the superscriptions.[9] The Talmud was able to embrace them all under David's outstretched poetic wing:

David wrote the Book of Psalms
including in it the work of ten elders.[10]

Not only was Davidic authorship accepted uncritically, but so, too, were the titular notes purporting to describe the actual occasion of their composition.[11] Again, the Greek translation was able to identify still more psalms with incidents in the life of David.[12]

The tendency to claim Davidic authorship for the entire Psalter reaches its ultimate expression in the Psalms scroll from the caves of Qumran in which we are told that the king was responsible for the composition of no less than thirty-six hundred "psalms" *(tehillim)* and four hundred and fifty "Songs" *(Shir).*[13]

How all this colored the interpretation of the Book is obvious. The first task of the exegete was to determine the individual experiences in the life of David to which a particular psalm might correspond. Then, because David was at the same time a dynastic and national symbol and a Messianic figure, the individual becomes collectivized into a corporate personality, so that the composition is simultaneously expressive of Israel's fate and destiny, and embodies its national experiences and its aspirations for the future. The rabbis formulated this quite precisely when they remarked:

everything David said in his Book of Psalms
refers to himself, to all Israel, and to all times.[14]

The study and interpretation of Psalms was thus as much a matter of
historicizing the contents as it was an inspirational exercise, and rare
was the soul who departed from this exegetical tradition. It is true that
as early as the fifth century the Christian theologian of Antioch, Theodore of Mopsuestia, recognized that the titles and superscriptions were
secondary, and he even suggested that many psalms were composed as
late as the Maccabean period.[15] Much later, Moses ibn Chiqatella (died
ca. 1080), the Jewish Grammarian of Moslem Spain, defied accepted
belief by ascribing several psalms to the Babylonian exile.[16] But this
rationalistic approach was certainly exceptional. It was not until the
advent of Benedict Spinoza (who died in 1667) that the Second Temple
provenance of the Psalter was scientifically expounded.[17]

This view was slow to be accepted; but with the final abandonment
of the traditional approach to the Bible in the nineteenth century and
the rise of the critical-historical school of scholarship, the idea of
Davidic authorship of the Book of Psalms was almost completely discarded. The headings were no longer taken at their face value. It was
assumed to be axiomatic that the Psalms reflect the political and religious conditions of the time of their composition. If, then, they are "the
offspring of moods produced by definite historical circumstances,"[18] it
ought to be possible to identify those circumstances. It seemed to one
and all in the last century, and in the early part of this, that the post-
exilic period of Israel's history, especially the Maccabean era, was the
most likely candidate.

This conclusion, of course, had not been arrived at by objective
means. The chronological arrangement of the Pentateuchal documents
and their relationship to the prophets was vital to the attempt to reconstruct the history of the religion of Israel, which was the real goal of
scholarship. Within this scheme of things, there was little room for the
highly individualistic religion that the Psalms seem to mirror except in
the late stage of Israel's religious development.

Buttenwieser was an enthusiast of the Graf-Wellhausen school of
Biblical Higher Criticism. He was convinced that "the evolutionary process of Israel's religious life and thought" could be fairly accurately
reconstructed by treating the psalms as religious documents which still
reflect the period of their composition. Since to him there was "no
doubt that monotheism was unknown in Israel" prior to the advent of
the prophets,[19] the ninth and eighth centuries, more or less, could be

taken as the earliest starting point for Hebrew psalmography, though he did allow for even earlier exceptions. He regarded it as self-evident that the religious ideas of the psalms were influenced by prophetic teaching and that, consequently, stylistic and linguistic parallels between the two bodies of literature were to be explained thereby. This position, incidentally, was still thoroughly respectable until very recently.

It is not surprising that Buttenwieser, a devotee of Wellhausen and trained in Germany, should have held these views. The school of thought that Wellhausen had founded overawed and overshadowed for a good while all Biblical scholarship. The imposing structure, so painstakingly and laboriously put together, and buttressed by undoubted brilliance and prodigious scholarship, was as exciting as it was sophisticated. It took the scholarly world by storm and acquired an almost irresistible authority as a new orthodoxy. What is surprising, in fact, is Buttenwieser's relative independence and originality in the dating of the Psalms, despite his devotion to the System.

Wellhausen, himself, had clearly enunciated his own position. "It is not a question," he had written, "whether there be any post-exilic psalms, but rather, whether the Psalms contain any poems written before the exile."[20] B. Duhm had gone so far as to deny the existence of any pre-exilic psalms and had made Ps.137 the oldest! To him, only about a dozen or so were even pre-Maccabean and they all belonged to the Greek period. All others he assigned to the Maccabean period or later.[21] R. H. Kennett actually maintained that psalmography in Israel originated in the age of the Maccabees.[22] The Maccabean theory died a long, lingering death, as may be seen from the work of so recent a scholar as R. H. Pfeiffer.[23] It is refreshing, therefore, to find Buttenwieser not only vigorously and completely rejecting the theory, but actually espousing the belief that many of the psalms are pre-exilic and that one or two might even derive from the period of the Judges.[24]

Curiously, present-day Biblical scholarship almost unanimously concurs in the rejection of the Maccabean theory, though for different reasons. Buttenwieser had adduced both linguistic and historical arguments. He was sure that by the second half of the third century B.C.E. the Hebrew language had ceased to be a living tongue, had entered upon a stage of rigid decadence, and had given way to Aramaic. Compositions of such exalted Hebrew style could simply no longer be produced.[25] His historical argument bolstered the stylistic criterion. He assumed that the Psalms reflected national political conditions as well as religious developments. The "proper identification" of the historical background was necessary for the chronological sequence that was, in turn, vital to the reconstruction of religious history. Buttenwieser claimed to be able to establish this identification with great precision, and his conclusions simply precluded the Maccabean era. His favorite dating is the Persian period, four-fifths of the entire Psalter, according to him, deriving from this post-exilic, but pre-Hellenistic age.

It is highly instructive, at this point, to review briefly the opinions on the age of Israelite psalmography held by some outstanding representatives of recent trends in Biblical scholarship. S. Mowinckel, the foremost exponent of the Scandinavian "Myth and Ritual" School, states categorically that "by far the larger number of the extant psalms originates from the national Temple of Jerusalem, erected by Solomon. . . . Some of the psalms may derive from some North-Israelite sanctuary, such as Beth-el."[26] No less apodictic is the verdict of Y. Kaufmann, the dominant name in Israeli Biblical scholarship. To him, the "collections that eventually comprised the Book of Psalms are all pre-exilic. There is no psalm whose plain sense (as distinct from the Midrashic romancing of modern exegetes) requires a dating later than the exilic Psalm 137."[27] W. F. Albright, the doyen of American scholars, is more cautious, but still unmistakably bent in the same direction, He writes: "There is no reason to date any of the psalms after the fifth-fourth centuries B.C. and most of them are probably pre-exilic."[28]

This remarkable re-evaluation of the antiquity of the Psalms is not merely a natural concomitant of a more generally conservative approach to the Biblical materials that has increasingly characterized the field during the past quarter of a century. It is the cumulative effect of a fairly solid body of evidence that has slowly been building up over that period.

Kaufmann has carefully analysed the religious ideas of the Psalms in relation to the leading motifs of prophetic literature. He has noted that such dominant themes as national moral sin, the supremacy of morality over a ritual that has no intrinsic worth without it, clear eschatological judgment on the wicked, the basic technical terminology of prophetic eschatology such as the "day of the Lord," "in that day," "the end of days"—all these are missing from the Book of Psalms, which must, for this reason, be regarded is belonging to a literary domain completely independent of prophetic influence.

Kaufmann has further argued that if the Psalms were an exilic or post-exilic production, it would be passing strange that they contain no prayers for the ingathering of the exiles and no expression of the yearning for the restoration of the Davidic line. And as to the attempts to reconstruct the historical circumstances behind a psalm, Kaufmann can find no clear reference to events of the monarchy or post-monarchy period, and he regards it as significant that there are no proper-names later than Davidic-Solomonic times. Taking into account all these facts, there is only one way to explain the numerous and close parallels between the language of Biblical psalmody and that of the prophets. The latter must themselves have been under the influence of the former, rather than vice versa.[29]

This, of course, is the exact opposite of Buttenwieser's view, but it gives the death blow to the Maccabean theory and, as such, is in line with his own conclusions. The relationships with prophetic literature will be dealt with again in discussion of the work of Hermann Gunkel. For the present, we can supplement Kaufmann's internal analysis— even if it needs modification in many respects—by much external evidence.

The commanding and prestigious position which the Psalms held in the Hagiographa makes it virtually certain that it would have been the first of that Scriptural division to be translated into Greek. In fact, the Greek version, or part of it, may well have anticipated even the translation of some of the prophets, since liturgical considerations and needs certainly determined the process of translating the Hebrew Scriptures for the Jews of Alexandria, and none can deny that the Psalms played a dominant role in the liturgy of the synagogue in the Second Temple period. Certainly, by about the year 132 B.C.E. the grandson of Ben Sira had the Greek translation before him, so that the original composition of the individual psalms and the canonization of the entire book would have taken place before Maccabean times. It is, moreover, quite apparent that the Greek translators of the Psalms did not know the meaning of the technical Hebrew terms, a sure proof that by their time the living tradition had already been broken.

Whatever lingering hesitations about Maccabean psalms may have persisted, they have been finally laid to rest by the discovery of the sectarian Hebrew literature from the Dead Sea region. For the first time, we actually possess a second-century B.C.E. copy of the canonical Psalter. Despite its fragmentary nature, it is clear that the order and titles correspond to our received text.[30] In addition, the Thanksgiving Scroll, not much later than the Hasmonean period, made extensive use of the Book of Psalms. But these imitative hymns are themselves simply archaistic and no longer in classical Hebrew. They represent a later stage of linguistic, literary, and religious development than that of the Psalter.[31] Finally, the fragments of the Wisdom of Ben Sira in the original version, found at Masada in 1964, give us the Hebrew style of a highly educated Jew writing around the year 200 B.C.E. A comparison with the style of the Psalter once again yields a decisive verdict in favor of the greater antiquity of the latter.[32]

Buttenwieser, then, insofar as he vigorously rejected the Maccabean theory, anticipated in his conclusions, if not in his reasoning, the view that was to become dominant during the next two decades of Biblical scholarship. On the other hand, insofar as he concentrated upon a *zeit-geschichtliche* approach, attempting to establish a precise historical context for each psalm, he was stoutly resisting a trend that had already gathered momentum in his day and was soon to conquer the field.

Hermann Gunkel, in the first three decades of this century, had published a series of books and articles that completely undermined the methods and conclusions of the literary-analytical-historical school of Wellhausen; they were destined to revolutionize the interpretation and understanding of Biblical psalmody.[33] Gunkel, first of all, exposed the inadequacies of that school from a methodological point of view. He protested the insularity of Psalms scholarship, insisting that it must encompass not just the Psalter, but the entire genre of psalmody distributed throughout the Bible, as well as the corresponding literature of Egypt and Mesopotamia. Further, he maintained that since the Psalter has its source in the realm of living experience and is not just the aesthetic, literary expression of the free spirit, the ordinary canons of literary criticism applicable to *belles-lettres* are of little use for this Biblical book.

Gunkel perceived that the particular experience that calls forth the composition at the same time conditions its literary form. Content, form, and experience all interact and are interdependent, so that by a close examination of the first two we ought to be able to recover the proper setting of the composition in real life. He then proceeded to develop his famous *Gattungsforschung*, the generic classification of the religious poetry of Israel and the ancient Near East, based upon considerations of passages which share a commonality of theme, mood, and style, the latter being marked by recurrent use of a limited number of fixed patterns, and conventional modes of expression. In this way, Gunkel identified and isolated the individual literary units and was able to categorize them according to a relatively few major and minor types, each of which had its origin in a specific *Sitz-im-Leben*, a concrete situation in the religious life of the individual and the people. He believed that these types sprang from the cult and were initially transmitted orally by the priests. In the course of time, the poetic units came to be disengaged from their cultic settings to become independently developed "spiritual songs." This stage of growth began in the seventh century B.C.E. under the influence of the prophets.

It will be seen at once that attempts to place a psalm within a "time-historical" straitjacket loses all meaning within the context of the form-critical approach. Those songs that originated in the cult may be as old as the cult itself and as fresh as each recurrence of the specific situation for which their recitation may be suited. Those "spiritualized" poems that outgrew the cult, or that were composed in imitation of a cultic prototype, could use terminology that has assumed a purely figurative meaning. Either way, the thoroughly untrustworthy nature of the chronological approach is readily exposed.

Gunkel's primary interest had been in writing a history of Biblical literature, and his form-critical techniques constituted the tools of research. But is the history of Israelite psalmody coextensive with the history of the development of the various species? The successors of Gunkel, especially the Scandinavian scholars, became increasingly concerned with the cultic background, and there emerged a "cult-functional" school led by Sigmund Mowinckel that maintained that the Psalms, almost in their entirety, had their origin and permanent existence within the cult.[34] This approach criticized the idea of "spiritualized" psalms freed from formal, organized worship as being a manifestation of a bias that presumes an inverse relationship between genuine piety and cultic ties. Further, precisely by adopting Gunkel's own comprehensive approach, it is possible to see that the late psalms of Apocryphal and Qumran literature, undoubtedly dissociated from the cult, are not characterized by the earlier, fixed, formalized, literary conventions. The uniformity and formality of Biblical psalms prove their ritual purpose and ties. As to Gunkel's form-critical methods, while they are the starting point for all subsequent research, they contain certain weaknesses. By concentrating on externals and on formal aspects, Gunkel was accused of having overlooked important inner correspondences that would connect psalms of apparently diverse types.[35] His contention that the mixing of types within a single psalm is proof of an aging of the literature and the oblivion of its original setting in life, was strongly challenged. On the contrary, it was claimed that this mixing of types is already present in one of the earliest poetic documents of the Bible.[36]

The cult-functional interpretation of the Psalms as pursued by Mowinckel developed into a school of its own. It was admitted that the wisdom psalms[37] were indeed non-cultic in origin and purpose, but this was about all. For the rest, it was insisted that the psalms in Israel, as everywhere else in the Near East, had their source in the service of the cult. Therefore, the proper interpretation of each category of psalms isolated by form-critical methods demanded the precise identification of the specific act of ritual that stood behind it. This demand Mowinckel proceeded to satisfy, and he greatly extended, in so doing, both the variety of psalm-types and the number of individual psalms that can be subsumed under each type.

This conviction, that the psalms were inextricably tied to the cult, of course had some important higher critical implications. It made psalmography in Israel as old as the cult itself, and it affirmed the great antiquity of most of the Psalms, even as it thereby testified to the role of the individual early in the history of Israel's religion. In opposition to the axiom of the school of Wellhausen, it made the Psalms antedate the prophets; and contrary to Gunkel's view, it made the prophets imitate the psalmodic patterns and style of the cultic psalms of the individual. It was the prophets who were influenced by the public cults and not vice versa. Nevertheless, the cult-functional school looked upon the Israelite cult as having contained several primitive features in common with its Near Eastern contemporaries.

Mowinckel regarded many psalms as having been designed to neutralize the efficacy of magical spells. At first, he understood the frequently used word *áwen* as "sorcery" and the *po'ale áwen* as "sorcerers" who practised their baleful arts upon the worshiper.[38] Later, however, he admitted that this could not be consistently maintained and conceded that the "enemies" in the psalms who wrought *áwen* could often be simply the heathen who carried out evil intrigues and destructive activity.[39]

The tendency of Mowinckel to interpret the Psalms in terms of Near Eastern cultic analogues can be seen in his treatment of those classified as "royal." Gunkel had identified just ten such which mention or refer to the king.[40] Contrary to many of his contemporaries, Gunkel had contended that the royal personage who was the subject of the poem was a specific individual and not the community of Israel metaphorically described; that he was an Israelite king and not a foreigner; and that he was a pre-exilic monarch and not one of the Hasmoneans. These "royal psalms" had to be categorized by the specific occasion for which they were sung, namely, going forth to battle,[41] thanksgiving for a victorious return from a campaign,[42] nuptials,[43] the anniversary of the founding of the kingdom,[44] or the enthronement or annual royal festival.[45]

It is of interest to note that Buttenwieser had regarded only three of these ten as referring to a real king and, as such, pre-exilic.[46] In the others, mention of a royal personage is not to be taken literally. These psalms are post-exilic and relate to a "visionary" rather than to a genuine historical situation.[47] Mowinckel, on the other hand, fully accepted Gunkel's point of view, but went much further. He pointed to the various forms of "king ideology" that pervaded all Near Eastern religions. The king was the embodiment of the community and stood in a special relationship to the deity. He occupied a central role in the national cult. Accordingly, the "royal psalms" are certainly concerned with a real king, although they present an idealized portrait of him, not a realistic description. They issue from the celebrations in which the reigning monarch was the principal character. Foremost among these was, he conjectured, an annual commemoration and renewal of the king's annointment and enthronement ritual. Even when the king is not explicitly mentioned, a psalm may be classified as "royal," since the use of "we" or "I" may frequently be the king (or his liturgical representative) speaking as a corporate personality or on behalf of the community and as one through whom the community finds its self-expression. This concept, of course, vastly extends the scope of the limited category as first identified by Gunkel. As a matter of fact, Mowinckel thought that the "David" of the psalms' heading originally indicated a composition intended for the cultic use of the king who is referred to by a generic title.[48]

What really captured the imagination of the cult-functional school was Mowinckel's theory of an annual enthronement festival for YHWH. Actually, Gunkel had been the first to postulate such a celebration and he had isolated six psalms as having had their origin in this occasion.[49] All are characterized by the exclamatory "YHWH has become King!" Gunkel noted that ascription of kingship to a deity is found already in the Babylonian Creation epic which portrays the gods in assembly proclaiming "Marduk is king!" as they grant that divinity "kingship over the totality of the entire universe."[50] The Hebrew prophets used similar language about the God of Israel and frequently referred to His royalty.[51] At the same time, the Biblical sources make it clear that this kind of language must derive from the earthly coronation ceremony of a human monarch.[52]

Gunkel therefore maintained that these divine enthronement psalms are of a mixed type. They are patterned after the "royal psalms," but have been transformed in content into eschatalogical poetry under the influence of prophetic teaching. He found proof enough in their universal, cosmic sweep and their concept of the coming of a new world-order under the sovereignty of God. The impetus for the cultic celebration that lay behind these psalms was the desire to fashion a monotheistic,

Israelite, if adaptational, response to corresponding Babylonian festivals to which the Judeans had been exposed in the course of their experiences in the Exile.[53]

Mowinckel accepted the existence of this genre of psalms which Gunkel had isolated, together with the proposed *Sitz-im-Leben*, but he rejected the historical and eschatological explanation and he elaborated on the nature of the festival and its underlying complex of motifs. As a result, the class of "enthronement psalms" was expanded from the originally suggested six to about forty, a clear reflection of the outstanding importance which Mowinckel accorded the festival in the national religion.[54]

As a matter of fact, it was to him the chief festival in the liturgical calendar. It was part of the annual autumnal New Year celebration field in the Jerusalem Temple in conjunction with the "Feast of Tabernacles." He believed that the main event was a great festal procession, the victorious coronation entry of the Lord whose presence was symbolized by the Ark. The jubilant proclamation, *YHWH malakh*,[55] characteristic of the enthronement psalms, expressed the renewal of God's dominion over the world. It is thus to be understood, not in a durative or permansive sense as "YHWH reigns," but with an ingressive actual and contemporaneous signification, "YHWH has become King."[56] In addition, the festival expressed the themes of creation and judgment, as well as the historical aspect of the Kingdom of God, namely, divine intervention in history as illustrated through Israel's experiences. Other elements were the consecration of the Temple and the renewal of the Covenant with David. An important part of the celebrations was the symbolic, ritual, dramatic enactment of a creation myth in which God's conquest of the primeval forces of chaos is followed by His renewed appearance as King.

Mowinckel assumed that Israel had derived the conception of God as King from ancient Near Eastern religions mediated through the Canaanites. When Jerusalem, under David, became the official center of the worship of YHWH, the idea came to the fore in Israel. The Canaanite New Year festival was taken over, but was radically transformed in accordance with the spirit of the religion of Israel.

It was no wonder that Mowinckel extended the "enthronement" classification to embrace over a quarter of the Book of Psalms, all those that reflected in their contents any of the multiple themes that characterized the festival. It was also not surprising that he reversed Gunkel's psalms-prophets relationship. He insisted that if these psalms contain some of the conceptual ingredients of eschatology it is not because they are eschatological, but because the prophets drew upon the same cultic experience as do these psalms in developing their doctrine of the "end of time."

Mowinckel's insistence upon a cultic background to each individual psalm and the determined attempt to recover the underlying or accompanying praxis, generated an extremist school now known as "Myth and Ritual." Its methods and conclusions belong in reality to a discussion of the nature and history of Israelite religion rather than to a survey of Psalms research. But mention of it is relevant to the extent that the understanding of the "royal" and "enthronement" psalms is affected.

This school professes to discern a single, common pattern of cultic-mythic expression throughout the ancient Near East which involves, in brief, the victory in combat of a creator-god over his enemies, the forces of aridity and chaos. As a result, the creation of the world and the establishment of the divine kingdom ensues. This primeval struggle is really repeated annually in the death and resurrection of nature, i.e., in the loss and renewal of fertility. Hence, the cult constitutes a form of magic designed to ensure the annual renewal through the reenactment of these dramatic events. The king is the victor-god and he restores, by means of the potent cultic praxis, the creative powers of nature. This pattern is taken for granted as having existed in Israel, and some scholars, though not Mowinckel,[57] even went so far as to hypothesize a dying and rising god-king ideology in Jerusalem.[58]

Buttenwieser[59] took note of Gunkel's and Mowinckel's concepts of "royal" and "enthronement" psalms and expressed himself in no uncertain terms. He dismissed them as "a web of fancy, without basis in fact," and spoke of "the mythological rubbish" which these scholars had read into the texts. He questioned the value of the Near Eastern analogues, and he maintained that the use of "King" to describe God was so widespread as to have lost any formal, ideological meaning. He denied that *YHWH malakh* meant anything but "YHWH is King/reigns," and since he dated Psalm 68b to the time of Deborah, he could claim to show that the royal concept of God in Israel antedated and was, hence, independent of the establishment of Davidic kingship in Jerusalem.

These strictures, however dogmatically asserted by Buttenwieser, are not without validity. There has been built up over the years an impressive body of refutatory evidence which raises very serious questions which cannot be evaded.[60]

In the first place, the cultic *Sitz-im-Leben* of all or even most of the Psalms has not been really demonstrated. Similarities of structure, phraseology, and style between the Psalter and ancient Near Eastern poetic compositions indicate only that Israel shared a common literary heritage with her neighbors. They do not need to imply a common cultic background or, indeed, any such at all. The claim to the existence of cult-free, spiritualized psalms has not been factually invalidated and, any insistence to the contrary, must take cognizance of the complete absence of a recitative component in the provisions of the Priestly Code as well as the ascription of psalm authorship to Levites, but never to Aaronite priests. In fact, no adequate explanation has yet been offered as to why all reference to the cultic setting should have been excised from the superscriptions, or why, if there are apotropaic and purificatory psalms, the allusions thereto should be so veiled and not explicit. The question is all the more pertinent in view of the fact that the Akkadian psalms generally furnish the requisite, self-identifying, typological, and cult-functional information.

Furthermore, even if the Biblical psalms, or some of them, did have a cultic background, it could have been very different from that controlling its pagan counterparts, and even in the latter there was not necessarily uniformity. The king-ideology is an excellent case in point.[61] Nowhere in the Near East was kingship a purely secular institution. Some connection between the kingly office and the divine seems to have been a universal conception; but a glance at the evidence shows a wide variety of notions. In Mesopotamia there were basic differences between Babylon and Assyria. In neither place did the position of the king approximate that of the Egyptian monarch who was divinity incarnate, while among the Hittites the king was deified only at death. The evidence from the Syro-Canaanite sphere is too flimsy to permit definite conclusions or the reconstruction of any uniform pattern, and the position of the king is further complicated by political considerations. The area knew sovereign independence but rarely, and it must have been rather difficult for a vassal to claim divinity. At any rate, practically nothing is known of the cultic life of the immediate predecessors and neighbors of Israel.

As to the position of kingship in Israel, it must be remembered that the institution was of late emergence and that, too, only after a very hesitant beginning. The king was not the source of Justice, but was himself subject to the law and was chastised by the prophets for infringing the moral code. He was not the High Priest, though admittedly some kings did fulfil priestly functions. Sacral privileges, however, do not confer divine status. In short, it is methodologically unsound to explain the so-called "royal" psalms by Near Eastern analogues, and it is precarious to extend the "royal" category far beyond those psalms that actually mention the king.[62]

No less uncertain is the evidence for the annual enthronement celebrations. There is nothing in the Biblical sources to suggest the existence in Israel of a New Year festival, much less that such a one was a feature of the Fall harvest celebrations. The use of late rabbinic texts cited by Mowinckel in support of his thesis is a rather specious argument in itself. Actually, these very texts make it all the more difficult to understand why Scripture should have effaced any mention of the institution. Aside from this, there is the basic question as to whether the putative New Year motifs are indeed to be found in those psalms in which Mowinckel and his successors have located them. The fact of the matter is that in none of the "enthronement" psalms do all the allegedly characteristic components appear together. For instance, the theme of creation does not feature in Psalms 47, 97, 98, 99, and 149, even though God's Kingship is stressed. On the other hand, reference to creation is found in Psalms 95 and 96 but without any mention of a divine combat, while the idea of a divine warrior is clearly present in Psalms 97 and 98 but bereft of any notion of a primeval monster. Nowhere is it suggested that God's sovereignty commences with and derives its legitimacy from a victorious battle against such a foe.[63]

As for the dramatic rituals that supposedly accompanied the presumed enthronement festival, it requires explanation that just this element should have been omitted or expunged from the legislation regulating the festival rites as well as from the narratives that mention popular celebrations. It is surprising, to say the least, that the prophets did not include in their relentless fight against all forms of idolatry a denunciation of mythological features and the ritual presentation thereof, if ritual drama was practised in Israel.[64]

It should not be overlooked that the Biblical mythological material appears invariably in poetic texts and in extremely fragmentary form. The evidence is all against their having constituted living myths. It is hardly likely that such fugitive pieces are the stuff of a mimetic presentation in a ritual context. Even could it be shown that all the basic ingredients of a demonstrably ritual myth were present in a psalm and in proper sequence, it still would not prove a ritual function for that particular composition. We might well be faced with nothing more than a literary fossil, imitative or residual of a standardized pattern, now adrift from its original cultic moorings.[65] This possibility becomes all the more likely the clearer it becomes that Israel was a recent heir to a very advanced psalmodic tradition of hoary antiquity in the ancient Near East.

Nevertheless, after all has been said and done about modern developments in Psalms research, certain issues of a fundamental importance cannot be ignored. The validity of the form-critical approach as initiated and developed by Gunkel would seem to be incontestable and some explanation has to be found for the remarkable phenomenon that the psalms individually outlived their respective authors, influenced the prophetic style, and survived the corrosive effects of time, to be gathered into collections which achieved sufficiently wide diffusion to be ultimately turned into a canonized Book. What forces, other than the needs of cultic life, could have been at work in ancient Israel powerful enough to have ensured such developments?

The conviction that the psalms were tied to the cult has become strengthened in recent years through studies in the "history of tradition."[66] That the cult was the primary influence in the development of numerous specific and identifiable units of tradition, can hardly be doubted. That many of Israel's basic traditions are prominently manifested in the Psalms is also beyond question. This latter phenomenon would thus seem to be explained by the former. But whether a single autumnal New Year "enthronement festival" is supposed by Mowinckel, or an annual "covenant renewal" feast with its numerous constituent themes as propounded by Arthur Weiser,[67] or the complex autumn festival of H. J. Kraus,[68] is indeed *the* cultic *Sitz-im-Leben* for the majority of the psalms, is quite another matter. So little is known about the formal religious life of ancient Israel, that to attempt to compress all phenomena into one procrustean cultic bed is hazardous, to say the least.

The original inspiration for the form-critical and cult-functional approaches to the Psalms owed not a little, it will be remembered, to ancient Near Eastern analogies. There is no question but that this source will continue to enrich the field for a long time to come. Future research will tend, however, toward a more refined and less indiscriminate use of the Sumero-Akkadian material in its relation to the Hebrew psalms than has often been the case in the past. Not every parallel needs to be traced to direct borrowing, nor indeed to any borrowing at all. As has been already suggested, the similarities may often be reflexes of well established liturgical or literary patterns common to the entire Near East.[69] Sometimes one may even be dealing simply with the independent development of analogical cultural features. Furthermore, the evaluation of parallels is an uncertain business, for they might have been mediated through a third culture and have lost much of their significance in the process. They might also, even where directly borrowed, have played a major role in the parent culture, but an inconsequential one in that of the recipient. Finally, the limitation inherent in the tendency to compare a specific genre of Hebrew psalms with Sumero-Akkadian psalms in general is becoming increasingly recognized, and future work in this field will doubtless pay more careful attention to the individual types discernible within the generic classifications.[70]

Particularly important for Biblical studies, just because it derives from the very soil which Israel inhabited, would be the literature of the ancient Canaanites. The discovery toward the end of the last century, in the ruins of the ancient city of Akhetaton (Amarna), of the diplomatic archives of the department of state for foreign affairs of the Egyptian government in the 15th and 14th centuries B.C.E., opened new avenues for research into the evaluation of Biblical-Canaanite interrelationships. Those letters which derive from the rulers of the petty city-states of Syria and Palestine were written in Akkadian, but were liberally furnished with Canaanite glosses. Scholars were able to detect behind the epistolary style the use of poetic diction characteristic of religious hymnology. It was assumed, therefore, that in pre-Israelite times, Canaan possessed a psalms literature.[71] An obvious and intriguing question was its bearing upon the origins of Israelite psalmography. The unearthing of the incompatibly rich epigraphic finds from Ugarit-Ras Shamra on the North Syrian coast provided at last some source material and the tools for research.

Since the decipherment of the language of Ugarit in the thirties, a huge literature has come into being relating to Ugaritic-Biblical affinities. Because the initial finds were largely poetic, it is not surprising that it is the Hebrew poetic texts that have benefited most from research in this field.[72] Whatever will be decided in the future about the precise affiliations of Ugaritic within the Semitic family of languages, certain conclusions are beyond dispute.

Biblical and Ugaritic literatures represent two branches of a single and more diffused literary tradition. They share in common so many stylistic devices, set phrases, figures of speech and phraseological similarities, all of which appear with such frequency and consistency, as to rule out even the remotest possibility of coincidence. To take but one example: both employ the poetic principle of parallelism, and about sixty instances of the same fixed pairs of words in parallel relationship common to Hebrew and Ugaritic have so far been isolated. At the same time, the basic morphological dissimilarities between the two languages, in combination with chronological and geographic differences, preclude the likelihood of direct influence even though a historical connection between the two literatures is undoubted.

In respect to the Book of Psalms, it is clear that Ugaritic has served to illuminate the text in literally hundreds of passages and in a variety of ways that no future commentary can ignore. New features of Hebrew grammar and syntax, new meanings of existing roots, and entirely new vocables have been uncovered. The mythological metaphors have been elucidated and placed in context. A healthier respect for the received Hebrew consonantal text and a corresponding devaluation of the role of the ancient versions in textual criticism have ensued, even as Ugaritic studies have, at the same time, made for many an improved Hebrew reading.

The usefulness of Ugaritic in the exegesis of the Psalms has its definite limitations, however, and a caveat must be entered. Ugaritic has irrigated, with fruitful results, the study of the Psalms, but it must not be allowed to inundate it. Since we are not dealing with dependency through a vertical relationship and we are not at all certain about the channels of transmission, full allowance must be made for Israelite poetic originality and creativity even within the traditional patterns of Syro-Canaanite literary culture. It would be a most serious defect to overlook the fact that, so far, the Ugaritic finds have yielded neither hymns nor prayers, except in negligible fragments; and until we are in possession of such a body of liturgical compositions, we have no material available for the comparative study of Canaanite-Biblical hymnology, and no criteria for the kinds of form-critical and cult-functional studies which the abundant Mesopotamian sources permit.

If the early Ugaritic texts have had far-reaching repercussions for lexical and textual studies, the same may be said of the discoveries in the Judean Desert at the other end of the chronological spectrum. It has become increasingly recognized that, contrary to nineteenth-century scholarly prejudice, Palestinian Tannaitic and Amoraic Hebrew represents what was a living, vibrant language, the direct lineal descendant of the Biblical genre.[73] The Dead Sea Scrolls and the Masada finds have now supplied many missing links between these two stages of growth of the Hebrew language.

Mention has previously been made of the significance of the Qumran texts in helping to demolish the theory of the Maccabean origin of Psalms. The sectarian Psalter has further important consequences, for it reinforces our renewed respect for the antiquity of our received text, the history and constancy of which can now be traced back to the Maccabean era. At the same time, the sectarian and Masada texts, in conjunction with the undoubtedly post-exilic Biblical books and with Palestinian Rabbinic Hebrew, provide us with fresh and sound criteria for the determination of linguistic strata. An unusual concentration within a single psalm of linguistic phenomena which are otherwise characteristic of the Second Temple period would be indicative of late composition, or at least of late and extensive redactional activity. This type of study, as yet in its infancy, appears to have a promising future.[74]

This brings us back to Buttenwieser's work. That scholar had recognized the importance of linguistic layers, but did not have at his disposal the tools necessary for their isolation. In addition, and quite out of keeping with the tradition in which he had been raised, he was rather cautious in his approach to the text, which he subjected to careful and painstaking study. It is difficult today to accept his theory of the wholesale dislocation of verses, but his recognition of the precative use of the perfect verbal form was a real contribution to the understanding of the style of the Psalms.[75] His time-historical treatment, irrespective of the unacceptability of his conclusions, has not been invalidated or displaced entirely by the form-critical and cult-functional approaches. Modern commentators may rightly be repelled by the unscientific and extremist application of the method in the past, but they do not need to neglect it entirely. It seems inconceivable that great and historic events should not have evoked creative liturgical responses, or that some psalms, even if tied to the cult, should not betray the influence of important, innovative movements in Israel's intellectual and religious development. The fact that, for example, a national lament employs a certain conventional literary pattern, does not mean that an inspired poet would not compose such a lament in a specific set of circumstances which it might be possible to reconstruct.[76] Similarly, a strikingly new theological concept might well be traced to its historic setting even though the externals of style and form hew closely to well-documented stereotypes. Finally, Buttenwieser's appreciation of the Psalms as religious literature has much to commend itself, and the spiritual experience and theological concepts, as distinct from form and use, must be an integral part of all research.

In short, the ideal Psalms commentary of the future must explore all the avenues of research opened up during the past century and must represent a judicious synthesis of the assured conclusions of each.

NOTES

1. For biographical details, see *American Jewish Year Book*, VI, 5665 (1904–05), p. 72; XIV, 5704 (1943–44), p. 51; *Universal Jewish Encyclopedia* 11, *s.v.* For a scholarly evaluation, see H. M. Orlinsky, *JQR*, XLV (1955), pp. 402–406.

2. *Die hebäische Elias-Apokalypse*, Cincinnati, 1897; *Outline of Neo-Hebraic Apocalyptic Literature*, Cincinnati, 1901.

3. B. *Pesahhim*, 117ª; see B. Jacob, *ZAW*, XVI (1896), p. 162. f.; cf. H. M. Orlinsky, *Ancient Israel*, Ithaca, 1954, pp. 76 f.

4. II Macc. 2:13; but see the remarks *ad loc.* of S. Zeitlin in *The Second Book of Maccabees*, Dropsie College edition, New York, 1954.

5. *Midrash Tehillim* 1:2, ed. S. Buber, Vilna, 1891, p. 3. The reference is, of course, to the traditionally-marked book divisions after Psalms 41, 72, 89, and 106.

6. Ps. 1:1 *ashre*—Deut. 33:29 *ashre-kha*.

7. I Chron. 6:16 ff.; 25:1–7; II Chron. 29:25–30; cf. 23:18; Neh. 12:24.

8. Cf. the Greek to Pss. 33, 43, 71, 91, 93-99, 104, and 137(!).

9. E.g., Jeduthun (Pss. 39, 77), the Sons of Qorah (42, 44–49, 84 f., 87 f.), Asaph (50, 75–83), Solomon (72, 127), Heman and Ethan the Ezrahites (88, 89) and Moses (90).

10. B. *Baba Bathra* 14ᵇ, cf. 15ª. The number ten is obtained by Counting the Sons of Qorah as three (Exod. 6:24) and understanding the prepositional *lamed* before Solomon's name as denoting "about/concerning," not as *authorship* (cf. Greek to 72: 1). Ps. 139:16 was assigned to Adam (cf. Targ. Ps. 92: 1) and Ps. 110 to Melchizedek. Incidentally, Ethan was identified with Abraham (cf. Targ. Ps. 89:1).

11. Cf. the superscriptions to Pss. 3, 7, 18, 34, 51, 52, 54, 56, 57, 59, 60, 63, and 142.

12. Cf. Greek titles to Pss. 71, 97, 143, and 144.

13. J. A. Sanders, *The Psalms Scroll of Qumran Cave II (11 QPsᵃ)*, Oxford, 1965, col. XXVII, 4 f., 9 f., pp. 91 f.; *idem, The Dead Sea Psalms Scroll*, Ithaca, 1967, pp. 134–137.

14. *Midrash Tehillim* 18:1, ed. Buber, p. 135; cf. 4:1, p. 40; 24:3, p. 204.

15. See R. H. Pfeiffer, *Introduction to the O. T.*, New York, 1948, p. 43.

16. Cf. Ibn Ezra to Pss. 42, 47, 102, and 106.

17. R. H. M. Elwes, ed., *The Chief Works of Benedict Spinoza*, New York, 1955, 1, p. 147.

18. T. K. Cheyne in *Encyclopaedia Biblica*, III, Col. 3937.

19. See his *Prophets of Israel*, pp. xxi–xxii.

20. J. Wellhausen in *Sacred Books of the O. T.*, ed. P. Haupt, Leipzig-Baltimore, 1898, p. 163.

21. B. Duhm, *Die Psalmen*, Freiburg i.B., 1899, p. xix.

22. R. H. Kennett, *Old Testament Essays*, Cambridge, 1928, pp. 119–218.

23. *Op. cit.*, p. 628.

24. Commentary, *infra*, pp. 10–18.

25. M. Buttenwieser, *JBL*, XXXVI (1917), pp. 225–48; cf. Commentary, *infra*, p. 872. For a refutation of the Maccabean theory on canonical-historical grounds, see Fr. Baethgen, *Die Psalmen*³, Göttingen, 1904, pp. xiii ff.

26. S. Mowinckel, *The Psalms in Israel's Worship*, Oxford, 1962, II, p. 152.

27. Y. Kaufmann, *The Religion of Israel*, ed. M. Greenberg, Chicago, 1960, p. 311.

28. W. F. Albright, *CBQ*, XXV (1963), p. 3.

29. *Op. cit.*, pp. 309–311; *Toledoth Ha-Emunuth Ha-Yisre'elith*, Tel Aviv, 1947, II, pp. 646–727.

30. M. Burrows, *More Light on the Dead Sea Scrolls*, New York, 1958, p. 169 ff.; F. M. Cross, *The Ancient Library of Qumran*, New York, 1961, pp. 164 (n.2), 165.

31. H. H. Rowley, *The Zadokite Fragments and the Dead Sea Scrolls*, New York, 1952, p. 38 and nn. 3, 6; Cross, *op. cit.*, p. 166; Y. Yadin, *The Message of the Scrolls*, New York, 1957, p. 107; cf. also the observations of H. Gunkel on the style of the Apocryphal psalms, in *The Psalms: A Form-Critical Introduction*, translated by Th. M. Horner, Philadelphia, 1967, p. 23.

32. Y. Yadin, *The Ben Sira Scroll from Masada*, Jerusalem, 1965.

33. H. Gunkel, *Ausgewählte Psalmen*, Göttingen, 1904, 4th rev. ed. 1917; "Psalmen" in *Die Religion in Geschichte und Gegenwart*, IV (1913), cols. 1927–49; 2nd rev. ed. 1930, cols. 1609–27; *Die Psalmen*, Göttingen, 4th rev. ed. 1926; *Einleitung in die Psalmen: Die Gattungen der religösen Lyrik Israels* [completed by J. Begrich], Göttingen, 1933 (reissued 1966). In English, see *What Remains of the O. T.?* New York, 1928, pp. 57–149: "The Poetry of the Psalms," in *O. T. Essays*, ed. D. C. Simpson, London, 1927, pp. 118–142; and *The Psalms*, etc., n. 31.

34. S. Mowinckel, *Psalmenstudien*, I–IV, Oslo, 1921–24; *The Psalms in Israel's Worship*, translated by D. R. Ap-Thomas, 2 vols., Oxford, 1962.

35. *Ibid.*, I, pp. 29–35.

36. A Weiser, *ZAW*, LXXI (1959), p. 67 ff.

37. Pss. 1, 19[b], 34, 37, 49, 78, 105, 106, 111, 112, and 127; Mowinckel, *The Psalms*, II, p. 111; cf. p. 108 f.

38. E.g., Pss. 5:6; 6:9; 14:4; 28:3; 36:13; 53:5; *et al.*

39. *Op. cit.*, II, p. 250, Addit. Note xxviii.

40. Pss. 2, 18, 20, 21, 45, 72, 101, 110, 132, and 144:1–11.

41. Pss: 20; 144: 1–11.

42. Ps. 18.

43. Ps. 45.

44. Ps. 132.

45. Pss. 2, 21, 72, 101, and 110.

46. Pss. 20, 21, and 45.

47. Commentary, *infra*, pp. 377–82 on Ps. 132; pp. 453–65 on Ps. 18; pp. 779–86 on Ps. 72; pp. 791–794 on Ps. 2; pp. 794–96 on Ps. 110; p. 811 f. on Ps. 101; pp. 833–35 on Ps. 144:1–11.

48. *Op.cit.*, I, pp. 42–80.

49. Pss. 47, 93, 96 (partly), 97, 98, and 99.

50. *Enuma Elish*, iv:14, 28.

51. Cf. Isa. 24:23; 52:7; Ezek. 20:33; Obad. 21; Micah 4:7 (cf. 2:13); Zeph. 3:15; Zech. 14:9, 16 f.

52. For the formula "N has become king," see II Sam. 15:10; II Kings 9:13. For coronation ceremonies, cf. I Sam. 10:24 ff.; 11:15; II Sam. 15:10; I Kings 1; II Kings 9:13; 11:22 ff.; I Chron. 12:38 ff.; 29:22 ff.

53. H. Gunkel, *Einleitung*, § 3.1–7, pp. 94–100; see also Fleming James, *Thirty Psalmists*, ed. R. Lansing Hicks, New York, 1965, pp. 78–80.

54. *Op. cit.*, I, pp. 106–192; II, Addit. Note xxiv, pp. 243-248.

55. Pss. 47:8; 93:1; 96:10; and 97:1.

56. *Op. cit.*, II, Addit. Note vi, pp. 222–24.

57. *Op. cit.*, I, p. 99.

58. For the most important works on "Myth and Ritual" and "divine kingship," see H. D. Hummel in H. F. Hahn, *The O. T. in Modern Research*, 2nd ed. Philadelphia, 1966, pp. 277–280.

59. Commentary, *infra*, pp. 321–340.

60. Kaufmann, *The Religion*, etc., pp. 108–110; *Toledoth*, etc., I, pp. 580–83.

61. See above, n. 58.

62. M. Noth, *The Laws in the Pentateuch*, Philadelphia, 1967, pp. 145–78.

63. Kaufmann, *The Religion*, etc., pp. 117–120; *Toledoth*, etc., I, pp. 580–585; O. Eissfeldt, *ZAW*, XLVI (1928), pp. 81–105.

64. Kaufmann, *Toledoth*, etc., I, p. 582 f., 606.

65. Cf. Th. Gaster in *Interpreter's Dictionary of the Bible*, III, p. 485[a-b].

66. On this subject and its literature, see Hahn, *op. cit.*, pp. 130–137, 143 f., 287 f.

67. A. Weiser, *The Psalms*, Philadelphia, 1959, esp. pp. 11, 19–35.

68. H. J. Kraus, *Psalmen*, 2 vols., Neukirchen, 1960.

69. Cf. N. Sarna, *Fourth World Congress of Jewish Studies*, vol. I, Jerusalem, 1967, pp. 171–75.

70. Cf. E. R. Dalglish, *Psalm Fifty-One*, Leiden, 1962, esp. pp. xi, xiii, 249, 252 f.; W. H. Hallo, *JAOS*, LXXXVIII (1968), 71–89.

71. F. M. T. Böhl, *Theologisches Literaturblatt*, XXXV (1914), pp. 337–40; A. Jirku, *JBL*, LII (1933), pp. 108–120.

72. This subject has generated a huge literature. Among the works specifically devoted to Biblical-Ugaritic relationships that deal with Psalms are: H. L. Ginsberg, *The Ugaritic Texts* [Hebrew], Jerusalem, 1936; *idem*, *BA*, VIII (1945), pp. 42–58; J. H. Patton, *Canaanite Parallels in the Book of Psalms*, Baltimore, 1944; W. F. Albright, *CBQ*, VII (1945), pp. 5–31; J. Coppens, "Les parallèles du Psautier avec les textes de Ras Shamra-Ougarit," *Museon*, LIX (1946), pp. 113–42; M. Held, *Leshonenu* XVIII (1953), pp. 144–60; U. Cassuto, *The Goddess Anath* [Hebrew], Jerusalem, 1953, esp. pp. 9–41 and bibliography, p. 110; R. T. O'Callaghan, *VT*, IV (1954), pp. 164–76; S. Mowinckel, *VT*, V (1955), pp. 14 f., 22–26; S. Gevirtz, *Patterns of the Early Poetry of Israel*, Chicago, 1963. *The Ugaritic Handbook* by C. H. Gordon, Rome, 1965, is replete with such comparative material. No scholar can match the ingenuity and output of M. Dahood in the exploitation of the Ugaritic materials for Psalms research; so far, two volumes of *Psalms* (Anchor Bible), New York, 1966, 1968, have appeared.

73. M. H. Segal, *A Grammar of Mishnaic Hebrew*, Oxford, 1927, pp. 1–20; J. M. Grintz, *JBL*, LXXIX (1960), pp. 32–47; A. Bendavid, *Biblical Hebrew and Mishanic Hebrew* [Hebrew], Tel Aviv, 1967; cf. R. H. Gundry, *JBL*, LXXXIII (1964), pp .404–409.

74. A. Hurvitz, *The Identification of Post-exilic Psalms by Means of Linguistic Criteria* [Hebrew; unpublished], Hebrew University doctoral dissertation, 1966.

75. *Hebrew Union College Jubilee Volume*, 1925, pp. 89–111; Commentary, *infra*, pp. 11–25, 428 f.

76. Cf. N. M. Sarna in A. Altmann, ed., *Biblical and Other Studies*, Cambridge, 1963, pp. 29–46.

The Psalm Superscriptions
and the Guilds*

The Priestly Code makes no provision for any recitative or musical component in the official cult.[1] This fact takes on significance in light of the wealth of detail that, by contrast, characterizes its descriptions of the ritual. The omission is extraordinary in that the ritual word and the ritual act are two interconnected and inseparable elements in the ancient near eastern cults. A. Leo Oppenheim has described the situation as follows: "Prayers in Mesopotamian religious practice are always linked to concomitant rituals. . . . Ritual activities and accompanying prayers are of like importance and constitute the religious act."[2] The lacuna in the Priestly Code fits in with the all but total silence in the superscriptions of the psalms concerning the cultic settings or associations of the individual compositions. Here again, Oppenheim's remarks about Mesopotamian practice are pertinent: "These rituals are carefully described in a section at the end of the prayer which addresses either the praying person or the officiating priest; . . . to interpret the prayers without regard to the rituals in order to obtain insight into the religious concepts they may reflect distorts the testimony."[3] The fact that Akkadian psalms generally furnish the requisite, self-identifying, typological, and cult-functional information merely serves to emphasize the extraordinary nature of the silence of the biblical psalms about their connections with the cult.

These two reciprocal peculiarities, that of the Priestly Code on the one hand, and of the psalms on the other, are augmented by yet a third puzzling phenomenon. The individual psalms are ascribed exclusively to nonpriests. The superscriptions feature the names of Moses, David, Solomon, and various Levites, but never that of Aaron or Aaronite priests, although several psalms are attributed to the sons of Aaron's archenemy, Korah.[4]

All this harmonizes with the consistent postexilic traditions that clearly differentiate between the two institutions of sacrifice and psalmody, the former being attributed to Moses, the latter to David (2 *Chron.* 23:18).[5] It is as though these sources are fully aware that the cultic situation in Israel was extraordinary in that the ritual act and the ritual word appear to have individually distinct and differentiated histories.

The classical critical reconstruction of the history of worship in Israel is best illustrated by R. H. Pfeiffer, who maintained that the Pentateuch achieved its final edition about the year 400 B.C.E. Since it ignores the whole institution of temple singing, although the contemporary ritual is described in great detail, it proves that the regular, organized liturgy was still unknown in Jerusalem in 400 B.C.E. It was between 400 and 250 B.C.E. that the guilds of temple singers, according to Pfeiffer, "were organized and provided with their hymnals." The bulk of the psalter, in fact, "probably originated at this period."[6]

Y. Kaufmann, on the other hand, who by and large ascribed the composition of the psalms to the preexilic period, suggested a different explanation for the nonmention of any recitative or musical element in the cult of the Priestly Code. To him, the first Temple was "the temple of silence", a distinctive innovation of the priests who deliberately set about fashioning a nonpagan, nonmagical religion by disengaging the spoken ritual from the cultic act, downgrading the former in terms of relative importance.[7]

II

As attractive as Kaufmann's theory is, it fails to take into account several important aspects of the problem. It is well known that all literature in the ancient world waged a constant struggle for survival.[8] If the psalms had been wholly separated from the cult, it would be difficult to conceive of another ambience in ancient Israel powerful enough to have ensured the preservation of the individual compositions and to have encouraged their assemblage into large collections. Moreover, there is abundant evidence to prove that the spoken word and vocal and instrumental music could not have been entirely absent from temple service in the period before the exile, the general silence of the pentateuchal sources notwithstanding.

In the first place, it should be pointed out that even though *Deuteronomy* repeatedly refers to the chosen "place" almost exclusively in relation to sacrifice, yet it is also a peculiar characteristic of this book that it prescribes the recitation of prayers and other formulae in connection with certain ritual ceremonies, namely, the expiation of an unsolved murder of an unidentified victim (*Deut.* 21:1–9), the bringing of the first fruits (26:2–10) and of the third-year tithe (vv. 12–15).[9] Furthermore, even the Priestly Code itself makes provision for verbal confession accompanying the offerings (*Lev.* 5:5; 16:21).[10] It also prescribes a verbal admonition by the priest to a suspected adulteress (*Num.* 5:21–22) and an oral priestly blessing with a fixed formula (6:22–26). In another source, Hannah is engaged in prayer at the Temple of Shiloh when her family went there for an annual sacrifice (*I Sam.* 1:3, 10–15) and it is hard to believe that such a form of religious expression was unique to her. The prophet Samuel is reported to have prayed aloud as he offered up a burnt offering (*ibid.*, 7:9), and it is quite apparent from the book of *Amos* that songs and music went together with animal sacrifice and oblation as a fixed and regular constituent of the rituals practised in the temple at Bethel (*Amos* 5:21–23).[11] There is absolutely no reason to think that this mode of worship was exclusive to this place. On the contrary, in his dedicatory invocation which he recited before the altar in the Temple at Jerusalem, Solomon envisages the institution essentially as a place of "prayer and supplication," and he begins and concludes his address with sacrifices (*1 Kings* 8:5, 12–64).[12] Isaiah similarly portrays the Temple as a house of prayer, and he denounces equally the multiplicity of prayers and sacrifices (*Isa.* 1:13–15). His contemporary, King Hezekiah, must surely be reflecting the reality of the first Temple when he speaks of offering music at the house of the Lord all the days of his life (38:20). Such a sentiment would hardly have been acceptable had not instrumental music constituted a fixed part of the service. Again, if the prophet of the Babylonian exile designates the Temple at Jerusalem the "House of prayer" (56:7), this, too, must faithfully reflect preexilic actuality.[13] The same conclusion is to be drawn from another exilic document, one most likely of Levite origin, in which a "Song of Zion" is identified as a "song of the Lord" (*Ps.* 137:3f.).[14] Finally, and perhaps the most decisive argument of all, is the presence of a vast amount of psalmodic language embedded in the prophetic orations.[15] This phenomenon testifies to a deep-rooted, well-formulated, and long-established tradition of public psalmody, one that could only have had its roots in and been sustained by the cult.

The cumulative effect of all the foregoing evidence adduced from the Biblical sources is the intensification of the twin problems of the general silence of the pentateuchal sources about any recitative or musial accompaniment to the sacrifices and the absence of any information in the superscriptions to the psalms about the cultic *Sitz im Leben* of these compositions. The conclusions would seem to be inescapable, firstly, that in the eyes of the priests psalmody was indeed extrinsic to the sacrificial rites, as Kaufmann observed, and, secondly, that the origins, cultivation and preservation of the psalms must be sought outside of priestly circles, though not necessarily beyond a temple ambience.[16] This state of affairs, however, presupposes the existence of independent nonpriestly, musical guilds active within a temple complex. Can such an assertion be supported by the facts?

III

The only information that we have concerning temple singers and musicians derives from postexilic sources. As has already been mentioned, the Chronicler makes a sharp distinction between the institution of sacrifice, which he attributes to Moses, and that of psalmody, which he ascribes to David (2 *Chron.* 23:18). The same differentiation is made by the book of *Ezra* (3:2, 10), and the author of *Nehemiah* is likewise conscious of the fact that David had originally set up the musical guilds (*Neh.* 12:24, 45–46). The book of *Chronicles* purports to provide the historical background to this tradition. It describes how, when David moved the ark to Jerusalem thereby making the city the cultic center of Israel, he appointed Heman, Asaph, and Ethan, of the levitical clans of Kohath, Gershom, and Merari respectively, to take charge of the vocal music (1 *Chron.* 6:16–34). This story is amplified in 1 *Chron.* 15:16–24, and at the end of David's life there are supposedly no less than four thousand Levites whose responsibility it is to praise the Lord on musical instruments (23:5–6, 30). Further details of David's classification of the musicians are given in another passage (25:1–8), and no opportunity is lost by the Chronicler to emphasize the Davidic origin of the institution, whether the context deals with Solomon (2 *Chron.* 8:14), Jehoiada (23:18), Hezekiah (29:20, 25), or Josiah (35:15).

The obvious question is whether these traditions possess any historical kernel. Are they merely retrojections from the early second Temple into the first Temple? Admittedly, the genealogies of the biblical singers as recorded in the book of *Chronicles* leave much to be desired. They are often internally inconsistent, and they betray evidence of schematization and artificiality.[17] This, however, does not of itself discredit the claim of a preexilic origin for the guilds. In fact, a close examination of the various sources tends to support the basic proposition.

IV

Without doubt, the association of David with the institution of liturgical singing primarily arose from the fact that it was he who captured Jerusalem and who, by moving the ark there, transformed it into a great cultic center. There is no reason to doubt, and every reason to accept the authenticity of the traditions that stress David's ambition to build a temple (*2 Sam.* 7:2, 4 = *1 Chron.* 17:1, 4, *et al.*),[18] and if such be the case, why should he not have interested himself in the organization of its forms of worship? It is surely no accident that the biography of David depicts him as an accomplished harpist (*I Sam.* 16:16–23; 19:9), a composer of dirges (*2 Sam.* 1:17; 3:33) and hymns (22:1), and an inventor of musical instruments (*Amos* 6:5). This last-mentioned tradition is also prominent in the postexilic sources (*Neh.* 12:36; *1 Chron.* 23:5; *2 Chron.* 7:6, 29, 26f.).[19]

Postbiblical lore has, of course, credited David with the authorship of the book of *Psalms*, even though seventy-three only of its one hundred and fifty compositions actually have the title *le-dawid.*[20] It has been shown that this tradition is but the late crystallization of a trend that gradually displaced earlier and variant traditions.[21] But the antiquity of the tradition associating David with psalm authorship is apparent from the fact that no less than sixty-five of the seventy-three Davidic psalms are contained in the first two divisions of the book. These are universally agreed to constitute the earliest collection, and this conclusion is supported by the colophon, "The prayers of David son of Jesse are ended" (72:20), which demonstrates that the editor was oblivious of the existence of the other eighteen Davidic psalms. The paucity of Davidic ascriptions in the rest of the psalter despite the increasing tendency to associate David with the composition of that work, as is evidenced by the Greek translation[22] and the colophon to the *Psalms* scroll from Qumran,[23] proves that the canonical superscriptions were fossilized fairly early, and that scribes and editors did not feel free to add to them at will in the text tradition represented by the Masorah. An interesting case in point is provided by the *Chronicles* version of the removal of the ark to Jerusalem. At David's behest, the Levites, led by Asaph, chant *Pss.* 105,

96, 107, and 106 (*1 Chron.* 16). Nevertheless, none of these compositions appears in the canonical psalter with a Davidic or Asaphite ascription.[24] This is not to say, of course, that David is to be necessarily regarded as having been the author of all those psalms that bear the title *le-dawid*. It is to say that this ascription is very early and that it has its origin in an authentic tradition linking David with liturgical music.[25]

V

The question now arises as to whether the other names that appear in the superscriptions to psalms might not, in like manner, rest on ancient and genuine traditions. It is to be noted that Asaph, the Korahites, Heman and Ethan all appear as clan guilds[26] in the postexilic sources, and that neither these nor the psalter contains the name of a guild that does not appear in the other. Are all these sources interdependent?

The fact of the matter is that of all the clan guilds the Asaphites alone are recorded in the lists of those returning from the Babylonian exile (*Ezra* 2:41 = *Neh.* 7:44), and they alone participate in the ceremony marking the founding of the second Temple (*Ezra* 3:10). Not one of the others is even mentioned in *Ezra-Nehemiah*.[27] There would be no reason for the Chronicler to have invented Heman, Ethan, and the Korahites had they never existed and no ground for the book of *Ezra-Nehemiah* to have suppressed the fact of their existence had they indeed been active in the restoration period. This line of reasoning receives added impetus from recent archaeological finds, for the name *bny qrḥ* appears on an inscribed bowl from the Arad temple, showing that the clan bearing this name was active in preexilic times.[28] Incidentally, this conclusion is reinforced by evidence from the same site for the presence of the Kerosites in this period, a family of the Nethinim the existence of which is otherwise known from *Ezra* 2:44 (= *Neh.* 7:47) only and is not recorded in any preexilic source.[29] It may be added that if the levitical clan guilds, Asaph, Korah, Heman, and Ethan, be late inventions, it is strange that Books IV and V of *Psalms*, which by general consensus are the latest parts of the canonical psalter,[30] do not ascribe any compositions to them. Nor do the Greek and Qumran versions add any but Davidic superscriptions.

Furthermore, it can be demonstrated that the clan guild names attached to some of the psalms cannot be connected with the Chroniclestraditions, nor can the data of this work be a reflex of the psalms headings.

(a) Twelve psalms are attributed to Asaph[31] and eleven to the Korahites.[32] Clearly, there is little to choose between the two guilds in terms of their importance and roles in the history of psalmody as far as the evidence from the psalter is concerned. This picture, however, is in striking contrast to that reflected in the postexilic historiography. To the Chronicler, the Asaphites were by far the most prestigious of all the levitical clan guilds, and their association with the official cult is said to span the entire period from David to Josiah.[33] They participate in each of the great temple services and, as has already been noted, they are the sole remaining singers and musicians in the period of the restoration (*Ezra* 2:41; *Neh.* 7:44). The Korahites, on the other hand, are not mentioned among the levitical clans appointed by David to lead the recitative-musical side of the service. They play no role in any of the great national acts of public worship. Only once do they appear as participants in a cultic ceremony, and even then they share the honors with the Kohathites. This occurred in the days of King Jehoshaphat (873–849 B.C.E.) in connection with an Ammonite and Moabite attack at Eyn Gedi (*2 Chron.* 20:19).[34] Otherwise, the Chronicler depicts the Korahites as "guards of the threshold of the tabernacle" (*1 Chron,* 9:19), as "preparers of the wafers" (v. 31) and as "gate-keepers" (*1 Chron.* 26:1, 19).

(b) A similar discrepancy between the traditions of *Chronicles* and those of the book of *Psalms* emerges from an examination of the history of Heman. Only one psalm is associated with this name (*Ps.* 88), and this not exclusively so. Yet the postexilic historiographer accords Heman pride of place among the singers who are said to have officiated when David brought the ark to Jerusalem, and Asaph and Ethan acted as his assistants (*1 Chron.* 15:17, 19). Once the ark was in its resting place, Heman was appointed by David to lead the worship (6:18), and his precedence over Asaph is again demonstrated by his central position on that occasion, flanked as he was by Asaph on the right and Ethan on the left (vv. 24, 29). He bears the title "Heman the singer" (v. 18); he is connected with the Kohathites (*ibid.*), and is the grandson of none other than Samuel (*ibid.*). No less than twenty-one generations are listed back to Levi (vv. 18–23) in contrast with Asaph's fourteen (vv. 24–28) and, in addition, special mention is made of his fourteen sons and three daughters (*1 Chron.* 25:5). Moreover the Hemanites, like the Asaphites, took an active part in all the great occasions of public worship down to Josiah's time. Such is the Chronicler's picture; yet *Ezra-Nehemiah* ignores this guild and the psalter assigns it but a solitary composition!

There can be no doubt that in respect of Asaph, the Korahites, and Heman the data to be culled from the psalms superscriptions are totally at variance with the traditions of postexilic biblical historiography. Neither source is a reflex of the other. Each is independent of the other and both, as was shown above, contrast strongly with the realities of the restoration period as recorded in *Ezra-Nehemiah*. *Psalms* and *Chronicles* must both represent genuine preexilic, if irreconcilable traditions.

VI

The antiquity of organized liturgical music in Israel should not be regarded as in any way surprising in light of the documented history of the institution in the ancient near east. Sumerian musicological traditions can be traced back to as early as the middle of the third millenium B.C.E. From this time come the Early Dynastic lists of professions which include singers and musicians. By the Old Babylonian period this tradition was very highly developed.[35] Vocalists and instrumentalists, both male and female,[36] were a staple feature of Mesopotamian temple personnel.[37] In Egypt, likewise, singers and musicians of both sexes occupied an important place in the temple cult.[38] One wisdom text declares "singing, dancing and incense" to be the "food" of the god,[39] i.e., they constitute the proper forms of divine service. The Ugaritic texts have yielded several references to *šrm*, vocalist-instrumentalists, in lists of people grouped together according to guilds.[40] In some of these *khnm* and *qdšm*, the two main priestly classes, are also mentioned in addition to craftsmen,[41] while in one text *mṣlm*, cymbalists, also appear.[42] The existence of identifiable, organized groups of professional musicians as temple personnel at Ugarit is firmly established.[43]

One of the characteristics of the guilds in general was the familial pattern adopted for their organization. A member might be designated a "son" of a trade or profession,[44] or the members of the same calling might trace their descent back to a common ancestor.[45] The longevity of such traditions is astonishing. In mid-second millenium Babylon there were scribal families that claimed to trace their ancestry back ten or more centuries.[46] In Assyria, from *c.* 900 B.C.E. to the fall of Nineveh in 612 B.C.E., a single family monopolized the office of Head of the Royal Chancery.[47] There are recorded instances of artisans who claimed descent from one who lived at least seven hundred years earlier, and the onomastic evidence from the guild lists in the early Achaemenid period shows that skills could stay in the same family generation after generation.[48]

The foregoing evidence makes it difficult to understand why the notion of the antiquity of liturgical music in Israel should have encountered such scholarly resistance. Nor is it clear why the various clans of professional singers could not have followed the familial pattern common to the guilds of Mesopotamia. Already in the period of the united monarchy, we can discern the beginnings of the concentration of skills and of bureaucratic positions within individual families, when Solomon appointed as "scribes" the two sons of David's "scribe" (*1 Kings* 4:3; *2 Sam.* 20:25).[49] Unfortunately, the onomastic data in the Hebrew Bible is too meagre to permit the kind of reconstruction that is possible from the Mesopotamian sources, but we can follow the history of a few professional families from the period of Josiah to the destruction of Judea, and the results are most revealing.[50]

Members of the Shaphan family were active during the reigns of three Judean kings in succession. Thus, Shaphan "the scribe", as well as his son, Ahikam, served King Josiah (*2 Kings* 22:3, 12; *2 Chron.* 34:8, 20; *Jer.* 26:24). Another son, Gemariah, was a high official during the reign of King Jehoiakim (*Jer.* 36:10, 12, 25) as was also Gemariah's son, Micaiah (v. 11). Elasah, another Shaphanid, served King Zedekiah (29:3), while Ahikam's son, Gedaliah, became governor of Judea after the destruction (*2 Kings* 25:22; *Jer.* 39:14; 40:5 *et al.*). Another family whose bureaucratic service also spans the reigns of the last kings of Judah is that of Achbor son of Micaiah (*2 Kings* 22:12; *2 Chron.* 34:20) who served Josiah. His son Elnathan was ambassador to Egypt for King Jehoiakim (*Jer.* 26:22; 36:12, 25), and his grandson is most likely the "Coniah son of Elnathan" mentioned in the Lachish letters as performing similar service for King Zedekiah.[51] A third instance is that of Neriah, whose son, Baruch, was Jeremiah's amanuensis (*Jer.* 32:12 *et al.*) and whose other son, Seraiah, was part of the diplomatic entourage of Zedekiah on his visit to Babylon (51:59).

These few examples, fortuitously preserved in biblical literature, may safely be understood to be representative of the general pattern, especially in Judah where the unbroken stability of the Davidic dynasty over a period of half a millenium would have fostered and sustained the growth of professional families who traditionally derived their livelihood from service to the state. The concentration of skills within these families, transmitted from father to son(s), would have been a natural concomitant of their status.[52] There seems to be no reason at all why the same situation should not have obtained in the cult centers of Judah and Israel. Conforming to widespread near eastern practice, these institutions may be expected to have nourished professional guilds modeled after the family pattern. There is no reason for skepticism either as to the first temple antiquity of the liturgical musical clan guilds in Israel, or as to the basic genuineness of the traditions which associate these groups with the names of Asaph, Ethan, Heman, and the Korahites. These guilds were attached to temples which were the source of their income, but because of their specialized skills, they would also have been highly mobile. When one cult center was destroyed or declined, the professionals could migrate to another. The narratives about Micah the Levite in the days of the Judges (*Judges* 17) and about the migration of Levites from north to south in the days of Rehoboam (2 *Chron.* 11:13f.) provide excellent examples of this type of mobility.

VII

If we look upon the psalms collections as the repertoires of musical guilds that operated in the various cult centers throughout Judah and Israel, then we can explain how the individual compositions came to be preserved and we are able to account for many puzzling phenomena. The fact of the multiplicity of shrines in Judah and Israel throughout most of the monarchy period hardly needs documentation,[53] but it is worth recalling that several existed for hundreds of years, apparently enjoying great prestige. Dan,[54] Bethel,[55] Beer Sheba,[56] Geba,[57] and Gilgal[58] receive special mention in the sources. Gibeon[59] is of particular interest, because David is said to have assigned Heman and Jeduthun to act as liturgical singers there (1 *Chron.* 16:39–42). The surprising discovery of the Arad temple, not referred to in any biblical source, amply illustrates the ramified nature of this network of cultic institutions.[60] All these places may be assumed to have maintained a cadre of professional personnel and to have provided opportunities of employment for the clan guilds. It would have been at such places that psalms would have been composed, recited, preserved, collected, and transmitted from generation to generation within the local guild.

The migration of professionals from guild to guild and the absorption or displacement of one guild by another[61] supplies a plausible explanation for the duplication of individual psalms or units within the psalter[62] and for the occasional attribution of one psalm to two personages.[63] By the same token, the presence of the name of the same singer in different genealogical lists[64] need not necessarily always be the product of scribal confusion but may sometimes authentically reflect different historical situations, in which a member of one clan guild passed over to another and was incorporated within it. Moreover, the otherwise inexplicable presence within the book of *Psalms* of compositions of undoubted northern Israelite provenance now finds a natural explanation. Psalms like 77, 80, and 81 in which Israel is referred to as "Joseph" could not have originated in Judah. They belonged to the northern shrines and must have been brought south by the remnants of the temple personnel who fled from the destruction of their shrines by the Assyrians.[65] At this time, much of the archives and literature of the north was brought to Jerusalem and was in this way preserved from oblivion.[66]

The severance of tradition about the meaning of the technical terminology of the psalms is another problem that can find its solution through the well-founded assumption that guilds were the bearers and tradents of liturgical poetry. The Greek translation shows that the terms were already alien to the scholars who worked on it early in the second century B.C.E. In other words, even during second Temple times, when the chanting of psalms constituted the core of the worship, the musicological terminology was no longer intelligible. The reason for this loss of understanding is that the terms belonged to the era of the first Temple when the different collections of psalms were still the actual repertoires of the various temple guilds who may be assumed to have carefully guarded their professional techniques. A curious parallel to such a state of affairs derives, indeed, from the second Temple. Tannaitic literature has preserved a tradition about a certain Hygros b. Levi who was in charge of the temple singing and who earned the opprobrium of the sages for selfishly withholding his professional secrets from others.[67] At the other end of the chronological spectrum, Mesopotamian incantation and psalm literature provides us with another analogy, for the Akkadian scribes who inherited and copied the Sumerian texts were unable to understand the technical terms used therein.[68]

Another problem that can now be satisfactorily resolved is the discrepancy between the data that can be culled from the superscriptions to the psalms and that supplied by the book of *Chronicles*.[69] It is clear that the two sources reflect quite different perceptions of reality, the former having preserved the remnants of the guild repertoires, the latter the state of affairs in the Jerusalem cultus. If the Chronicler does not depict the Korahites as singers, it is because they did not function as such in Jerusalem. When the psalms headings disclose the importance of this guild in the composition and preservation of liturgical texts, they faithfully mirror the role of the Korahites in provincial shrines.[70]

VIII

It now remains to return to the problems with which this study opened, *viz.*, why the Priestly Code has nothing to say about any vocal-instrumental component of the cult, and why the superscriptions of the psalms carry no cult-functional information.

The resolution of these enigmas must be sought in the contrast between the primary role of sacrifice and the undoubtedly secondary nature of liturgical music in the Israelite cult. Sacrifice lay within the exclusive domain of the established priesthood; the singers were minor clerics. Even outside Israel, where the cultic role of singers and musicians was highly important, their social status was not correspondingly so. In Egypt, it appears that in the oldest epochs these functionaries were of low rank, and it was in late times only that their prestige increased.[71] In Mesopotamia, the overseer of the musicians could not compare in social status and power with the overseers of other specialized crafts.[72] In Israel, the separation of sacrifice from the vocal-musical side of the service, in emphasis of the nonmagical nature of the national religion,[73] meant that the singers would, merely in virtue of that fact, have assumed an inferior position in the temple hierarchy. The priestly texts are intended to be a manual of instruction for the levitical priesthood, and it should occasion no surprise that those aspects or forms of worship not entrusted to it should have been beyond their interest.[74]

As to the reason why the book of *Kings* ignores the singers, their lowly status in the first Temple and the additional fact that the main centers of psalmody were most likely the provincial shrines provide sufficient warrant.[75] But how to explain the absence from the superscriptions to the individual psalms of any information about an accompanying cultic act?

The possibility cannot be eliminated that such notices were once attached to the headings of individual compositions[76] and that in the course of time they fell out because they were rendered meaningless when the psalms came to be used for prayer independently of the temple service. However, the likelihood of this having happened is diminished by our inability to explain why, in the same circumstances, the information about the guilds and the technical musicological terminology was retained even though it, too, had become unintelligible. Accordingly, it will be prudent to assume that the psalms never did possess any such cult-functional notices.

In that case, when were the psalms recited? There is evidence to support the view that the times of the *tamid*, the regular daily burnt offering in early morning and late afternoon, were regarded as the most appropriate for intercession. The narrative in 2 *Chron.* 29:27 shows that the levitical choir burst into song as the early sacrificial rite began (cf. v. 20). Other passages in the same book indicate that this was the usual practice in the early second Temple (*1 Chron.* 16:40–42; 23:30–31), and Ben Sira's description of the temple service at the beginning of the second century B.C.E. specifies the same procedure (*Ben Sira* 50:11–19). There is no doubt that this coordination of the vocal-musical recitation with the regular offering was rooted in first Temple usage. This finds clear expression in *Ps.* 92:2–4:

> It is good to praise the LORD,
> to sing hymns to your name O Most High,
> To proclaim your steadfast love at daybreak,
> Your faithfulness each night
> With the ten-stringed harp,
> With voice and lyre together.

The morning and late afternoon temple services naturally became the times for individual prayer. The morning occasion is attested in the psalter in several passages:

> Hear my voice, O LORD, at daybreak;
> at daybreak I plead before you, and wait.
> (*Ps.* 5:4)

> But I will sing of your strength,
> extol each morning your faithfulness;
> for you have been my haven,
> a refuge in time of trouble.
> (*Ps.* 59:17)

> As for me, I cry out to you;
> each morning my prayer greets you.
> (*Ps.* 88:14)

On the other hand, it was at the time for the regular evening (meal-?) offering *(minḥah)* that Elijah chose to submit his prayer (*1 Kings* 18:29, 36). Daniel (9:3–19, 21) and Ezra (9:5) likewise selected the identical hour for the same purpose, and this would seem to reflect preexilic practice. One text, in particular, supports this and indicates that the custom of coordinating prayer with the evening temple service was well based:

> Take my prayer as an offering
> of incense,[77]
> my upraised hands as an

evening sacrifice.[78]
(*Ps.* 141:2)

This passage clearly belongs to a time when there was not only a close cultic connection between prayers and the late afternoon offerings but when prayer was itself achieving independent status. The psalm text, like all the preceding ones, does not mention animal sacrifice, although the burnt offering was prescribed for the evening as well as for the morning. The phrase used in each case is *minḥath ᶜerev*, "the evening (meal-) offering." It would appear that in the course of the monarchy period there were times when the animal sacrifices were suspended at the evening service.[79] Thus, the instructions of King Ahaz to the high priest concerning the use of his new "great altar," expressly distinguishes between the "morning burnt-offering" *(ᶜolah)* and the "evening (meal-) offering" *(minḥah)* (2 *Kings* 16:15). Similarly, Ezekiel mentions the morning sacrifice only and ignores completely that of the evening (*Ezek.* 46:13–15). In these circumstances, the evening service would comprise the incense-offering and the meal-offering, and it would be the smoke of the former that would be the signal for prayer. It cannot be accidental that in the great temple vision of Isaiah (ch. 6), the prophet observes the angels rhapsodizing God while the building kept filling with smoke (v. 4). This can be none other than the smoke of the incense,[80] since the visionary ritual takes place in the inner sanctuary which was the proper place for the altar of incense.[81] It must also be remembered that the incense had an expiatory function[82] that made it appropriate to the purposes of the ritual of *Isaiah* ch. 6.

This close association between the incense-offering and the prayers is of particular significance for the development of the Israelite liturgy in the cult places outside of Jerusalem. One of the intriguing questions relating to the religious history of Israel is the nature of the impact that the reformism of Hezekiah and of Josiah had on the type of worship carried on external to the Temple. Early in the eighth century B.C.E. widespread efforts were made under royal authority to restrict the practice of animal sacrifice.[83] The far-reaching and more thoroughgoing measures taken by Josiah about a hundred years later made the Temple in Jerusalem the exclusive cultic site.[84] The numerous cult centers that had existed for so long had clearly fulfilled a basic need for the individual and the community. What was the response to the centralizing measures of Hezekiah and Josiah? The fact that a precedent had already been set in the Jerusalem Temple for the possibility of a service without animal sacrifice but with incense offering, oblation, and psalmody, must have made the transition to new forms easier. It is possible, in fact, that archeology has supplied us with remarkable testimony to the reality of this development. If Aharoni's stratification and interpretation are correct, the temple at Arad remained in service for another hundred years after the altar of sacrifices had been removed in the time of Hezekiah, following two centuries in continuous use. In the subsequent intervening period there is evidence for the use of incense.[85] The proof is lacking, but it is reasonable to assume that prayer and psalmody became the core of the ritual.

A revealing narrative that supports the theory that incense and meal-offering developed independently of animal sacrifice is that of the eighty mourning men who set out for Jerusalem from Shechem, Shiloh, and Samaria. They carried with them "meal offering *(minhah)* and frankincense" *(Jer.* 41:5) even though the temple was known to be in ruins. Nothing is mentioned of animal sacrifice.[86] The most decisive text of all comes from the Elephantine papyri. Here we have a petition (dated 408 B.C.E.) on behalf of the Jews of Yeb to Bigvai, the Persian governor of Judea, for permission to rebuild the temple in that place. It states that in the past "meal offerings *[minhah]*, frankincense, and animal sacrifices *[ᶜalawah]*" had been conducted there and it requests their reinstatement. It reports that an earlier appeal to the civil and ecclesiastical authorities in Jerusalem had gone unanswered. What is of crucial importance is that the affirmative reply of the governor permits only meal offering *(minhatha)* and incense and that a further petition from the same source relating to this temple at Yeb emphatically excludes animal sacrifice. In other words, the priesthood in Jerusalem does not seem to have objected to this arrangement;[87] it already had a respectable history behind it.

It is worth noting that several texts from second Temple times, and beyond, have preserved mention of the practice of coordinating prayer with the incense-offering. Thus, it is related in the book of *Judith:* ". . . and the incense of the evening was now being offered at Jerusalem in the house of God and Judith cried unto the Lord with a loud voice. . . ." *(Judith* 9:1)[88] *The Testament of the Twelve Patriarchs* mentions "the archangels who minister and make propitiation to the Lord for all the sins of ignorance of the righteous, offering to the Lord sweet smelling savour, a reasonable and bloodless offering" (3:5–6).[89] A similar picture of angelic liturgy, which obviously is a reflex of terrestrial usage, comes from the *Book of Adam:* "And I beheld golden censers between your father and the chariot and all the angels with censers and frankincense came in haste to the incense-offering and blew upon it and the smoke of the incense veiled the firmaments. And the angels fell down and worshipped God, crying aloud and saying, JAEL, Holy One, have pardon, for he is thy image and the work of thy holy hands."[90]

Moving to the New Testament, we note a report that "the whole multitude of the people were praying outside at the hour of incense" (*Luke* 1:10). This close interplay of incense offering and prayer is explicitly and symbolically articulated in the book of *Revelation*, where "the golden bowls full of incense are the prayers of the saints" (5:8). A vision is described in which an "angel came and stood at the altar with a golden censer; and he was given much incense to mingle with the prayers of all the saints upon the golden altar before the throne; and the smoke of the incense rose with the prayers of the saints from the hand of the angel before God" (8: 3f).[91]

In rabbinic literature of postdestruction times, the memory of the meal-offering incense-prayer association was well preserved:

R. Yose said: "the afternoon (*minḥah*) prayer does not correspond to the *tamid* of eventide, but to the incense. How so? 'Let my prayer be as an offering of incense before you, my upraised hands as the evening meal-offering'" (*minḥah*) (*Ps.* 141:2).[92]

A midrashic text interprets *Mal.* 1:11 as follows: R. Samuel bar Naḥman said, "what is the pure meal-offering which in every place is fragrantly (*muqtar*) submitted for the name of the Holy One, blessed be He? It is the afternoon (*minḥah*) prayer. *Muqtar* means none other than the afternoon prayer, as it is said, etc." (*Ps.* 141:2).[93] Another midrash which expounds *Ps.* 141:2 recognizes prayer as a substitute for the now defunct incense offering: "Thus said David, 'My Lord, when the Temple existed we used to offer incense before you. Now that we have neither altar nor high priest, accept my prayer, etc.'"[94]

IX

A wealth of evidence of a varied nature, stretching from rabbinic times back through the second Temple and well into the monarchy period, demonstrates an interaction of the daily *tamid* ceremonies with prayer and psalmody. In the Jerusalem center itself, there were times when the constituents of the late afternoon service were the meal-offering, the incense-offering, and psalmody. As a result of the movement toward centralization of worship, the provincial shrines dropped the sacrificing of animals and in most cases also the meal-offerings. In these circumstances, psalmody would assume ever greater importance and become increasingly divorced from the sacrificial cult. It achieved independent status as an act of worship, a situation reflected in *Ps.* 141:2. The musical guilds attached to different cult centers would thereby gain increasing prestige. The repertoires of the guilds would be carefully collected and edited. As the provincial centers were progressively destroyed by successive invasions and by the sweeping reforms of Josiah, two forces would be set in motion which would interact to preserve the psalms literature. The movement of guild survivors southward to Jerusalem and their incorporation into the temple cult enriched the repertoires of the choirs and in this way ensured the survival of provincial and northern compositions. The various smaller collections that can be isolated within the psalter owe their origin to the historical processes here described, and just as the proverbs literature was edited by Hezekiah's literati (*Prov.* 25:1), so the psalms must have undergone similar treatment. At the same time, the closing down of the cult centers, whether by force of the deuteronomistic movement or by enemy action, obviously left in its wake a spiritual void that had to be filled. It is absurd to believe that the designation of Jerusalem as the exclusive cult center was either intended to, or could actually succeed in depriving all votaries of the national religion not within easy reach of Jerusalem of all form of self-expression. The one constituent of the cult that was independent of both edifice and priesthood was psalmody, and it must have filled the breach. In this way, the transition from a sacrificial, priest-controlled, cult to a democratized cultless religion was effected, and the people of Israel was enabled to overcome with relative ease the great crisis that the destruction of Jerusalem by the Babylonians was to create.

NOTES

* The research for this paper was done during a sabbatical leave supported by a fellowship from the ACLS.

1. Rabbinic sensitivity to this peculiarity is reflected in eisegetical attempts to find pentateuchal "sources" for the institution of liturgical song; cf. T.B. *ᶜArakhin* 11a; *Num. Rabbah* 6, 10.

2. A. Leo Oppenheim, *Ancient Mesopotamia*, 1964, p. 175.

3. *Ibid.* Cf. S. Mowinckel, *The Psalms in Israel's Worship*, translated by D. Ap-Thomas, 1962, i, p. 20: cf. W. W. Hallo, *Actes de la XVIIᵉ Rencontre Assyriologique Internationale*, 1969, pp. 116–134.

4. The consistent use of *beney* exclusively with Korah in the psalms superscription reflects the narrative of *Num.* 16; 26:1. The omission of a reference to Korah in *Ps.* 106: 17 may well be out of deference to the prestigious guild of Korahites.

5. Cf. also 2 *Chron.* 8:12–14.

6. R. H. Pfeiffer, *Introduction to the Old Testament*, 1948, pp. 624, 798, on which see the remarks of W. F. Albright, *JBL*, 61 (1942), p. 122.

7. Y. Kaufmann, *Toltdoth Ha-'emunah Ha-Yisre'elith*, ii, 1947, pp. 476–478; *The Religion of Israel*, translated and abridged by M. Greenberg, 1960, pp. 302–304.

8. For the situation in Greek literature, cf. M. I. Finley, *The World of Odysseus*, 1959, p. 9. For the underlying reasons, see the author's *Understanding Genesis*, 1970, pp. xviii–xix.

9. See M. Weinfeld, *Deuteronomy and the Deuteronomic School*, 1972, pp. 32, 42, 44, 213.

10. As noted by A. Rofé, *Kiryat Sefer*, 48 (1973), p. 86.

11. Pfeiffer's contention, *op. cit.* (*supra*, n. 6), p. 624, that Amos denounced liturgical music and song as such is simply untrue, nor is there any support for his assertion, p. 798, that the prophet found them to be "crude and noisy."

12. On Solomon's prayer, see Kaufmann, *op. cit.* (*supra*, n. 7), ii, pp. 361f., 367f.; Weinfeld, *op. cit.* (*supra*, n. 9), pp. 36, 195f. It should be noted that according to *1 Kings* 10:12 (= *2 Chron.* 9:11) Solomon makes provision for "harps and lyres for the singers," but it is not clear whether the latter performed in the Temple or in his palace: cf. *Ezek.* 40:44 where, however, the text and context are uncertain, as v. 45 and the Greek show.

13. The same notice is reflected in *Isa.* 60:6-7.

14. Cf. *2 Chron.* 29:27 in which the "song of the Lord" is musical prayer accompanying the sacrifice.

15. On this subject, see Kaufmann, *Toledoth* (*supra*, p. 295, n. 7), ii, pp. 646–727; iii, pp. 605–613.

16. Cf. M. Haran, *JBL*, 80 (1961), p. 158, n. 3.

17. The genealogies have been analyzed by J. Köberle, *Die Tempelsänger im alten Testament*, 1899; K. Möhlenbrink, *ZAW*, 52 (1934), pp. 184–231, esp. pp. 202f., 229–231; H. Gese, in *Abraham unser Vater. . . Festschrift Otto Michel* 1963, pp. 222–234 (drawn to my attention by Prof. M. J. Buss); J. Liver, *Chapters in the History of the Priests and Levites* [Hebrew], 1968, pp. 53–99, apart from the commentaries to *Chronicles*. For a rabbinic observation on the genealogies in the book of *Chronicles* in general, see *Lev. Rabba* (1, 3); *Ruth Rabbathi* (2,1).

18. Cf. *1 Kings* 5:17; 8:17f. = *2 Chron.* 6:7f.; *2 Kings* 21:7 = *2 Chron.* 33:7.

19. Rabbinic tradition would even make David a singer before his birth; cf. T.B. *Ber.* 10a.

20. *Mid. Tehillim* 1, 2, ed. S. Buber, 1893, p. 3; T. B. *Bava Bathra* 14b.

21. B. Jacob, *ZAW*, 16 (1896), pp. 162f. As B. S. Childs has shown, *JSS*, 16 (1971), pp. 137–150, the thirteen superscriptions containing historical references to David are the product of exegetical activity and not a reflection of independent historical tradition.

22. This adds the Davidic title to *Pss.* 33, 43, 71, 91, 93–99, 104, and even 137 (!). Note that *Acts* 4:25–26 cites the anonymous *Ps.* 2 as Davidic.

23. J. A. Sanders, *The Psalms Scroll of Qumran Cave II (II Ps^a)*, 1965, col. XXVII, 4f., 9f., pp. 91f.; *The Dead Sea Psalms Scroll*, 1967, pp. 134–137.

24. It is to be noted that the Greek assigns *Ps.* 96 to David, even though it adds a superscription with a reference to postexilic history.

25. The genuineness of the tradition associating David with the founding of psalmody in Israel has merited increasing scholarly support in recent years; cf. W. F. Albright in *Alexander Marx Jubilee Volume* [English Section], 1950, p. 66; *Archaeology, and the Religion of Israel*, 1969, pp. 121–125; *Yahweh and the Gods of Canaan*, 1968, pp. 250–253, 254 n. 134; R. de Vaux, *Ancient Israel*, 1961, pp. 382, 457; S. Mowinckel, *op. cit.* (*supra*, p. 295, n. 3), ii, pp. 80f.; R. North, *JBL*, 82 (1963), p. 374; 83 (1964), pp. 386f.; O. Eissfeldt, *Cambridge Ancient History*, 1965, ii, chap. XXXIV, fasc. 32, p. 49; H. H. Rowley, *Worship in Ancient Israel*, 1967, p. 206; I. Engnell, *A Rigid Scrutiny*, translated and edited by J. T. Willis, 1969, p. 74.

26. The use of the term "guild" in this study refers to the existence of recognizable cohesive groups of temple personnel. It should be noted that Jeduthun has been omitted

for the following reasons: (i) he is not mentioned in the lists of *1 Chron.* 6 and 15. (ii) He appears as a singer only where Ethan is omitted, *viz.*, *1 Chron.* 16:41, 42; 25:1, 3, 6; *2 Chron.* 5:12; 29:14; 31:15. (iii) No ancestry of his is given. (iv) Although the name appears with *lamed auctoris* in *Ps.* 39:1, it features in *Pss.* 62:1; 77:1, extraordinarily, with ͨ*al* (on which see Rashi and Ibn Ezra to 62:1). (v) His descendants are listed as gate-keepers, not as singers, in *1 Chron.* 16:38, 42.

27. *Neh.* 11:17 = *1 Chron.* 9:16 list a Levite (ͨAvda/Obadiah) of the fourth generation from Jeduthun, but he is not said to be a singer.

28. Y. Aharoni, *BA*, 31 (1968), p 11: *Qadmoniyyoth*, 1, 3 (1968), p. 102, who assigns the artifact to stratum VII, which he dates to the age of Hezekiah (715-687 B.C.E.), This, of course, throws into question the attempt of G. Wanke, *BZAW*, 97, 1966, pp. 23–31, to show that the Korahites were postexilic.

29. Y. Aharoni, *IEJ*, 16 (1966), pp. 5–6, fig. 2; B. A. Levine, *JBL*, 82 (1963), pp. 207–212: *IEJ* 19 (1969), pp. 49–51; *EJ*, 7, 552–554.

30. Whatever the date of the individual psalms contained in them, *IIQ Ps^a* clearly shows that Books IV and V were edited late (*The Psalms Scroll of Qumrân Cave II*, J. A. Sanders, 1965).

31. *Pss.* 50, 73–83.

32. *Pss.* 42, 44–49; 84, 85, 87, 88.

33. *1 Chron.* 6: 16f., 24, 15:3, 17f., 16:5f.; *2 Chron.* 5:12; 29:13; 35:15.

34. On this event, see J. Liver, *The Military History of the Land of Israel in Biblical Times* [Hebrew], 1964, pp. 198f.; Z. Ilan, *Beth Miqra*, 53 (2), 1973, pp. 205–211: J. Maxwell-Miller, *CBQ*, 32 (1970), pp. 58–68.

35. A. Draffkorn Kilmer, *Pr. Am. Ph. Soc.*, 115, 2 (1971), pp. 147–181: *RA*, 68 (1974), pp. 69–82.

36. On the question of female singers in Israel, see Liver, *op. cit.* (*supra*, n. 33) p. 53, n. 1, as opposed to W. Eichrodt, *Theology of the O.T.*, i, 1961, p. 131, n. 3.

37. B. Meissner, *Babylonien und Assyrien*, ii, 1925, pp. 67, 71. On the existence in general of organized guilds in old and neo-Babylonia as well as in Assyria, see Meissner, i, 1920, p. 231; A. T. Olmstead, *History of Assyria*, 1923, pp. 538, 559; I. Mendelsohn, *JAOS*, 60 (1940), pp. 68–72; A. Leo Oppenheim, *op. cit.* (*supra*, p. 295, n. 2), pp. 79–82. For the Achaemenid period, see D. B. Weisberg, *Guild Structure and Political Allegiance in Early Achaemenid Mesopotamia*, 1967.

38. S. Sauneron, *The Priests of Ancient Egypt*, 1960, pp. 67, 69.

39. *ANET*, p. 420; A. Erman, *The Ancient Egyptians* (1966), p. 235. The text derives from a copy made in the Twenty-first or Twenty-second dynasty (11th–8th cents. B.C.E.), but it goes back in origin several centuries.

40. *UT* 80:1:10; 113:66; 169 (= 1026):11; 300: rev. 9; 1039:2; 1024: rev. 10; 2011:17. It should be noted that Hebrew *šarim*, = Ug. *šrm* is used in *2 Sam.* 19:36; *1 Kings* 10:12 = *2 Chron.* 9:11; *Ps.* 68:26; *Eccles.* 2:8; *2 Chron.* 35:25. (On *Ezek.* 40:44 see above p. 296, n. 12). Otherwise, *mšrrm* is uniformly used in the postexilic literature.

41. *UT* 113: 66; 169:11.

42. *UT* 169: rev. 13.

43. *UT* 1107:4 refers to "singer(s) of Ashtoreth" (*šr ͭttrt*); 2011:37 mentions *šr ugrt* "singers of/at Ugarit." On the Ugaritic guilds, see C. H. Gordon in *The Aegean and the Near East*, ed. S. S. Weinberg, 1956, pp. 136–143; A. F. Rainey, *A Social Structure of Ugarit* [Hebrew], 1967, p. 72.

44. I. Mendelsohn, *JAOS*, 60 (1940), pp. 68–69. For a similar practice in Israel, cf. *Amos* 7:14; *2 Kings* 2:3, 5, 15 etc.; *Neh.* 3:8, 12, 15, 31 on which see *idem*, *BASOR*, 80 (1940), pp. 18f.; Z. W. Falk, *Hebrew Law in Biblical Times*, 1964, pp. 105f.; cf. J. S. Frick, *JBL*, 90 (1971), pp. 279–287. In the laws of Hammurabi, para. 188, *mâr ummânim*, lit. "son of an artisan," connotes a member of the guild; see G. R. Driver and J. C. Miles, *The Babylonian Laws*, ii, 1955, p. 246; Th. Meek in *ANET*, p. 174, n. 129.

On the Ugaritic lists see A. Alt, *Kleine Schriften*, iii (1959), pp. 198–213. For a thorough study of the professional use of "son" in Hebrew and throughout the ancient near east, as well as for a theory of its origin, see G. Brin, *Lešonénu*, 31 (1967), pp. 5–20, 85–96. A Hebrew seal found at Lachish appears to read *bn h'mn* (Y. Aharoni, *IEJ*, 18 (1968), p. 166) which would be the exact equivalent of Akk. *mâr ummânim*. (But see now his *Lachish*, 1975, p. 21).

45. W. G. Lambert, *Babylonian Wisdom Literature*, 1960, p. 14.

46. D. J. Wiseman in *The Cambridge History of the Bible*, i, ed. P. R. Ackroyd and C. F. Evans, 1970, p. 36.

47. *Ibid.*

48. Weisberg, *op. cit.* (*supra*, p. 297, n. 36), pp. 1, 78, 103.

49. Without doubt, Shisha *(šyš')* of *1 Kings* 4:3 is identical with Sheva *(šw')* (*Kethib šy'*) of *2 Sam.* 20:25, as Shavsha *(šwšh)* in *1 Chron.* 18:17 shows. *2 Sam.* 8:17 reads Seraiah *(Sryh)*.

50. See S. Yeivin, *Studies in the History of Israel and his* [sic] *Country*, [Hebrew], 1960, pp. 269–278; *Encyclopaedia Miqra'ith*, 6, cols. 547f.

51. Lachish 3:15. The reading of the name is virtually, but not entirely certain; see H. Torczyner, *The Lachish Ostraca* [Hebrew], 1940, pp. 76f.; W. F. Albright, *ANET*, p. 322.

52. Cf. the remarks of F. M. Cross, *Canaanite Myth and Hebrew Epic*, 1973, p. 208.

53. For a list and discussion of local shrines, see R. Brinker, *The Influence of Sanctuaries in Early Israel*, 1946, pp. 136–178; M. Haran, *Encyclopaedia Miqra'ithi*, vol. 5, cols. 322–328.

54. *Judges* 18:30; *Amos* 8:14.

55. *1 Kings* 12:28f.; *Amos* 4:6; 5:5: 7:13.

56. *2 Kings* 23:8; *Amos* 5:5; 8:14.

57. *2 Kings* 23:8.

58. *Hos.* 4:15, 9:15; 12:12; *Amos* 4:4, 5:5.

59. *1 Kings* 3:4–5; *1 Chron.* 21:29; *2 Chron.* 1:3, 13.

60. See above p. 297 nn. 28–29; Aharoni's discovery of the horned altar at Beer Sheba (*BA*, 37 [1974], pp. 1–6), which had been dismantled, apparently, during the reign of Hezekiah, should presage the unearthing of the temple there and shed further light on this phenomenon.

61. The guild of Ethan was perhaps absorbed or displaced by Jeduthun; see above, p. 352, n. 26.

62. *Ps.* 14 (Book I) = 53 (Book II); 31:2–4 (I) = 71:1–3 (II); 40: 14–18 (I) = 70 (II); 57:8–12 (II) = 108:2–6 (V); 60:7–14 (II) = 108:7–14 (V). It is worthy of note that there are no duplications within the same book of the psalter.

63. Thus, *Ps.* 39 is ascribed to both David and Jeduthun, *Ps.* 77 to both Jeduthun and Asaph, and *Ps.* 88 to both the Korahites and Heman.

64. E.g. Mattaniah belongs to Heman in *1 Chron.* 25:4 but to Asaph in *1 Chron.* 9:15; *Neh.* 11:17, 22; 12:35.

65. J. P. Peters, *The Psalms as Liturgies*, 1922, esp. pp. 9f., 17f., 210, 273, 275, discerned that many psalms could not have originated in Jerusalem. In particular, he regarded books II and III as Israelite and traced the Korah and Asaph collections to shrines of the Northern Kingdom. *Pss.* 42–49 were assigned to the temple at Dan. M. H. Segal, *Mevo' Ha-Miqra'* iii, 1955, p. 541, conjectures that the Korahites were originally singers in the Ephraimite temples who later migrated to Jerusalem. M. J. Buss, *JBL*, 82 (1963), pp. 382–392 not only confirmed the view that the psalms of Asaph and Korah are homogeneous collections, but also showed that they have distinctive characteristics and that the bearers of the Asaph traditions must be placed among preexilic and largely north Israelite Levites. Engnell, *op. cit.* (*supra*, p. 296, n. 25), pp. 79f., identifies Asaph,

Heman and Ethan, and especially the psalms of the Korahites, as north Israelite in origin. On the other hand, J. M. Miller, *CBQ*, 32 (1970), pp. 58–68 located the Korahites in southern Judah. Wanke, *op. cit.* (*supra*, p. 297, n. 28) has greatly overestimated the importance of the references to Zion in the Korahite psalms. My student Steven B. Kaplan, in an unpublished paper, has shown that the Asaphite psalms are even more homogeneous than had been previously noticed, and that they share in common numerous unusual linguistic, stylistic and contextual features.

66. Cf. the remarks of J. A. Montgomery, *The Book of Kings* (ICC), 1951, p. 44, on the migration of Israelite literati to Jerusalem. Archaeological evidence for a population movement from Israel to Judah after 722 B.C.E. is now available; see M. Broshi, *IEJ*, 24 (1974), pp. 21–26; E. Stern, *BA*, 38 (1975), pp. 35f.

67. M. *Sheq*, 5, 1; *Yoma* 3, 11.

68. Engnell, *op. cit.* (*supra*, p. 296, n. 25), pp. 93f.

69. See the analysis above, section V, pp. 285–86.

70. More than a hint of this situation is contained in 2 *Chron.* 20:19f., on which see above, p. 286, n. 33.

71. Sauneron, *op. cit.* (*supra*, p. 297, n. 37), p. 67.

72. Oppenheim, *op. cit.* (*supra*, p. 295, n. 2), p. 81.

73. See above, section I, pp. 281–82.

74. An analogous situation may perhaps exist in the Marseilles Tariff (*ANET*, p. 656). As M. Haran, *Encyclopaedia Miqra'ith*, 5, col. 883, has pointed out, the drink offering is ignored, since the inscription is concerned solely with payments to the priests.

75. No one would doubt the existence of Jeremiah on the grounds of his non-appearance in the book of *Kings*.

76. Cf. *Pss.* 92:1; 100:1. On the former and its title, see *JBL*, 81 (1962), pp. 155–168.

77. According to M. Haran, *VT*, 10 (1960), pp. 116f., *Keṭoreth* here refers to the meal-offering. The targum clearly took it as aromatic incense, and so did the Greek.

78. The raised hands as a symbol of prayer is widely diffused. See J. Ross, *HTR*, 63 (1970), p. 3. Akk. has *niš qātē* "prayer" and the verb *qāta nāšû* (W. Von Soden, *Akkadisches Handwörterbuch*, 1972, iii, pp. 762, 797); Ugar. texts have *ša ydk šmm (Krt A(lk)* 2, 75f.) and *nša (y)dh šmmh (ibid.*, col. 4, 167f.); the eighth cent. B.C.E. Aram. inscription of Zakir reads: *w'š' ydy 'l b'l š*[myn] (H. Donner and W. Röllig, *Kanaanäische und Aramäische Inschriften*, 1962, no, 202, A. 11), and Hebrew uses the verb *ns'* with both *yad* (*Ps.* 28:2; 134:2) and *kaf* (*Ps.* 63:5; 141:2; *Lam.* 2:19). G. Alon, *Studies in Jewish History* [Hebrew], i, 1967, pp. 181–184, has documented the prevalence of the custom of raising the hands in prayer during the period of the second Temple. See the writer's study of the chirotonic motif on the Lachish altar, in chapter 8 of Y. Aharoni's *Lachish*, 1975.

79. This was pointed out by M. Haran, *Encyclopaedia Miqra'ith*, 5, col. 29.

80. This was recognized by S. D. Luzzatto in his *Commentary to Isa.* 6:4 (Padua, 1867, p. 94) and has been noted also by de Vaux, *op. cit.*, p. 411 and M. Noth, *Exodus*, 1962, pp. 234f. One wonders whether the "cloud" that was filling the Temple, and that was the signal for Solomon to commence his dedicatory prayer (*1 Kings* 8:10–12), is not similarly to be identified with the smoke of the incense for which the same word '*anan* is used in both *Lev.* 16:13 and *Ezek.* 8:11. That the incense altar *of Exod.* 30 is not secondary, but an integral part of the inner temple ritual complex, has been effectively demonstrated by M. Haran, *Tarbiz* 26 (1957), pp. 115–125; *VT*, 10 (1960), pp. 113–129; *Yehezq'el Kaufmann Jubilee Volume* [Hebrew], 1960, p. 23, para r: pp. 40–42, para. 20.

81. *Exod.* 30:6, 36; 40:5, 26, 27; *Lev.* 4:7.

82. *Lev.* 16: 12f, *Num.* 17:11–13; cf. *Isa.* 6:7. As J. Milgrom, *JBL*, 90 (1971), p. 151, n. 14, has pointed out, the juxtaposition of the incense altar pericope (*Exod.* 30:1–

10) to that of the half-shekel (*ibid.*, vv. 11–16) is not accidental, since the latter, like the former, had an expiatory role; cf. T. B. *Yoma* 44a.

83. 2 *Kings* 18:3f.; 2 *Chron.* 30:14; 31:1. That the events recorded there are substantially correct, is clear from 2 *Kings* 18:22 = *Isa.* 36:7 = 2 *Chron.* 32:12.

84. 2 *Kings* 22–23; 2 *Chron.* 34–35.

85. See above, p. 297, n. 28. For a different view, see B. A. Levine, "Prolegomenon" to G. B. Gray, *Sacrifice in the Old Testament*, Ktav reprint, 1971, pp. xviii–xx. Decisive evidence may well be forthcoming when the temple at Beer Sheba is finally located, for the excavations to date show that the horned altar, now recovered, had been dismantled in Hezekiah's time; see Y. Aharoni, *BA*, 37 (1974), pp. 1–6; cf. *The Biblical Archaeology Review*, 1, 1 (1975), pp. 1, 8f., 15.

86. *Mal.* 1:11 probably mirrors the same cultic situation in that the prophet states that "in every place, *muqtar* and pure meal-offering *(minhah)*" are offered in God's honor. The *hapax legomenon muqtar* might, admittedly, be a generic term for aromatic sacrifice, but it is far more likely to mean simple "incense-offering" in light of the parallelism *qetoreth-minhah* in *Isa.* 1:13; *Ps.* 141:2 and the use of *minhah* exclusively in the sense of "produce" in priestly texts; cf. *Tanhuma*, ed. Buber, pp. 68f.; *Yalqut, Malachi*, para. 587.

87. A. Cowley, *Aramaic Papyri of the Fifth Century B.C.*, 1923, nos. 30, ll. 21, 25; 31, ll. 21, 24f.; 32, 1. 9; 33, ll. 10–11 explicitly excludes animal sacrifice, the crucial negative being confidently restored from the surviving 'aleph ([ל]א). See B. Porten, *Archives from Elephantine*, 1968, pp. 291f., 293, n. 29.

88. See the comments of Y. M. Grintz, *Sefer Yehudith*, 1957, pp. 139f.

89. R. H. Charles, *Pseudepigrapha*, 1913, p. 306.

90. *Ibid.*, p. 149, xxxiii, 4–5; K. von Tischendorf, *Apocalypses Apocryphae*, 1866, reprint 1966, p. 18, para. 33. On angelic liturgies, see J Strugnell, *VT Sup.* vii, 1960, pp. 318–345.

91. In *Acts* 3:1 mention is made of prayer offered in the Temple at the ninth hour; cf. 10:3, 30, Jos. *Ant.*, XIV, iv, 3 (Loeb ed., para. 65, pp. 480–481) describes the ninth hour as the hour of "sacred ceremonies at the altar." The references, of course, are to the *tamid* of the late afternoon *of Exod.* 29:38f.; *Num.* 28:3f., 8, and they correspond to the requirement of Mishnah, *Pesahim* 5, 1.

92. T. J. *Berakhoth* 4, 1 (7ᵃ).

93. *Tanhuma*, ed. Buber, p. 68f.; cf. *Yalqut Malachi*, para. 587.

94. *Mid. Pss*, ed. Buber, p. 531; cf. *Tosafoth* to T. B. *Ber.* 26b s. v. *ad.* It is an interesting coincidence that the recitation of T. B. *Kerithoth* 6a, dealing with the composition of the incense, is immediately followed by M. *Tamid* 7, 4, listing the psalm for each day, in the closing liturgy of the sabbath additional service.

Legal Terminology in Psalm 3:8

THE PROBLEM

Psalm 3 is a petition recited in the first person by an individual who must certainly be the king of Israel or the commander-in-chief of the army. Verses 6–7 show the occasion to be the eve of battle. The army of Israel finds itself outnumbered by far and encircled by the enemy (v. 2). The military situation appears to be desperate; there is demoralization in the camp, and forebodings of disaster are heard on all sides (v. 3). However, the psalmist knows that in the last resort the fortunes of war rest in God's hands (v. 4). His unshakable faith saves him from despondency. He is certain that God will answer his prayer and deliver his people (vv. 5–7). Emboldened, the psalmist exhorts God as follows:

> Rise, O LORD!
> Deliver me, O my God!
> For You slap all my enemies in the face;
> You break the teeth of the wicked.[1]

Initially, this verse looks beguilingly simple. Nevertheless, it presents problems:

1. The invocation hardly seems to match the reality of the grim situation. Anyone surrounded by an overwhelming mass of enemy troops, and in danger of being annihilated, would surely pray for something far more drastic and decisive than that the foe receive a slap on the cheek and some broken teeth!

2. Superficially, the breaking of the teeth might be seen as the consequence of the slap on the cheek.[2] However, in none of the other four biblical occurrences of slapping the cheek is any such connection even hinted at. Is there, then, another explanation for the association of the two?

3. The Hebrew phrase used for breaking the teeth would seem to be quite straightforward, requiring no further elaboration or clarification. Nevertheless, it is unique in the Hebrew Bible, other verbs being used to describe this action: the *Hiphil* of נפל is found in Exod 21:7, and הרס in Ps 58:7. Why, then, did the psalmist employ שבר?

The phrase "to smite the cheek" occurs in four biblical contexts:

(*a*) In 1 Kgs 22:24 (= 2 Chr 18:23) we read:

Zedekiah son of Chenaanah stepped up and struck Micaiah on the cheek.

This incident takes place "at the entrance of the gate of Samaria" (v. 10) in the presence of the kings of Judah and Israel and four hundred prophets (v. 6).

(*b*) Mic 4:14 discloses:

They strike the ruler of Israel
On the cheek with a staff.

This fragment of an oracle dealing with a siege of Jerusalem most likely refers to a real historical circumstance, and describes the action of the Assyrian commander.

(*c*) Job 16:10 laments:

They open wide their mouths at me;
Reviling me, they strike my cheeks;
They inflame themselves against me.

Here it is uncertain whether Job complains of an actual assault upon his person or uses metaphoric language.

(*d*) Finally, Lam 3:30 recommends:

Let him offer his cheek to the smiter;
Let him be surfeited with mockery.

The various contexts make it absolutely clear, beyond the peradventure of a doubt, that to be struck on the cheek was an intolerable insult, a deep humiliation, not a mere slight to be soon forgotten.[3] Obviously, the psalmist, in employing that phrase in his invocation has in mind a secondary, figurative sense. He is beseeching God to inflict a humiliating, crushing defeat on the enemy.

SMITING THE CHEEK IN IMPRECATIONS AND INCANTATIONS

This biblical understanding of the serious nature of a slap on the cheek reflects the universal attitude of the peoples of the ancient Near East, which can be documented over a wide area for a long period of time. I shall first examine the phenomenon in magical and imprecatory texts, for if a curse against one's enemies includes striking the cheek, then it is a sure index of the severity with which it was viewed.

In the composition generally known today as the "Descent of Ištar into the Netherworld," we read that the goddess Ereškigal, mistress of the abode of the dead, curses Asušunamir, a eunuch. She says to him, "I will curse you with a great curse *[lū-zir-ka iz-ra rabâ]*," which she promptly does, as follows:

> The food of the gutters of the city shall be your food;
> The sewers of the city shall be your drink;
> The shadow of the wall shall be your station;
> The threshold shall be your habitation;
> The besotted and the thirsty shall smite your cheek
> *[šak-ru ù ṣam-mu-ú li-im-ḫaṣ li-it-ki].*[4]

The identical curse is found once again on the lips of the ailing Enkidu in the Gilgameš Epic. Conscious of his impending death, he curses the harlot lass who had been hired to decoy him and teach him the arts of civilized living. Decreeing what he describes as a never-ending fate, he says:

> I will curse you with a great curse. . . .
> The besotted and the thirsty shall smite your cheek.[5]

In the Akkadian *Maqlû* texts, the incantation series composed for priests who specialized in magic, we find among the conventional repertoire of curses that the magician recites,

I strike your cheek, I tear out your tongue
a-maḫ-ḫaṣ li-it-ki a-šal-la-pa lišan-ki.[6]

Another instance of this action occurs in the Babylonian text on the New Year ritual, which details ceremonies performed in the Esagila. This includes a ritual in which the *urigallu* priest strips the king of all the insignia of royalty and then humiliates him by slapping his face. After this the monarch enters the innermost sanctuary, and in the presence of the image of the god Bel he makes a "negative confession" for the past year. Among the sins he disavows is smiting on the cheek a subordinate who has the status of *kidinnu.*[7]

Moving from Mesopotamia and Akkadian to North Syria and the Aramaic language, we find at Sfira the treaty between Barga'yah, king of KTK, and Matti''el, a king of Arpad, deriving from ca. 750 B.C.E. This treaty concludes with fearful curses to be heaped upon the violator, one of them being that his wives will be struck on the face.[8]

SMITING THE CHEEK IN LEGAL TEXTS

If this strikingly humiliating action has been incorporated into the ancient Near Eastern inventory of curses and magical incantations, then we should expect it to turn up in legal documents that relate to the offense of assault and battery. We are not disappointed; the evidence is at hand.

As early as ca. 1850 B.C.E. the laws of Ešnunna, the Amorite city-state east of the Tigris (now Tell Asmar), treat the slap on the face as an actionable assault, along with biting off the nose and knocking out an eye and a tooth:

A slap in the face—he shall weigh out 10 shekels of silver.
me-ḫe-eṣ le-tim 10 šiqil kaspam išaqqal[9]

A court document from the Old Babylonian period (eighteenth century B.C.E.) is a record of a trial for assault and battery of an Amorite infantry man, Bir-ilišu. He was accused of striking the cheek of Apil-ilišu son of Aḫušina. The defendant denied the charge, but balked at making a disclaimer under oath. He was fined three and one-half shekels of silver.[10]

Hammurabi's laws similarly feature the slap in the face, and treat it very severely in no less than four paragraphs.[11] The penalty for this particular offense varies according to the social standing of the assailant and victim. Paragraphs 202–3 are revealing, particularly in the contrasting penalties:

> If an *awilum* strikes the cheek of an *awilum* who is his superior, he shall be beaten sixty times in the assembly with an oxtail. If a *mar awilum* has struck the cheek of his equal, he shall pay one mineh [i.e., sixty shekels] of silver.[12]

Nearly two thousand years after Hammurabi, striking on the cheek is again featured as an actionable offense, this time in tannaitic sources. *Mishnah Baba Qamma* 8:6 prescribes a penalty of two hundred zuz (= one hundred shekels) for it and double that amount if the aggressor uses the back of his hand.[13] This ruling is expanded in *Tosephta Baba Qamma* 9:31:

> If one struck someone with the back of his hand. . . he must pay four hundred zuz, not because it is a painful blow but because it is a humiliating blow.[14]

The Tosephta does not specifically mention the face as the object of the smack but from its citation of Ps 3:8 as a proof text, it is clear that such is understood.

In modern times, Abraham Shapira (1870–1965), head watchman of Petah Tikvah and a keen student of the ways and customs of the Bedouin, once observed the trial of two members of a tribe. One had been accused of stabbing someone with a sword, the other of having smacked someone on the face. The presiding sheikh dealt leniently with the stabber but severely with the other one. In explaining his verdict, he stated: "The striking of the cheek is a graver offense than stabbing with a sword, for the latter enhances the dignity of a man, while striking him on the cheek humiliates him."[15]

THE LEGAL SITZ-IM-LEBEN

From all the foregoing, one may conclude that in choosing his phraseology, the psalmist of Ps 3:8 has carefully drawn on the conventional language of incantation and imprecation or on legal terminology.[16] We can only decide which after examining the second sentence of the couplet.

As in the preceding clause, we are dealing with a figure of speech, not with the primary meaning. Rashi takes note of this by glossing "teeth" by "might" (גבורתם). David Kimhi further explicates the underlying imagery. He says that the reference is to "those whose intention it is to tear him to pieces." By employing the verb טרף, Kimhi shows his understanding of the enemy being compared to a ravenous, ravaging beast (cf. also Ps 124:6, Zech 9:7), and he cites Job 29:17:

> I broke the jaws of the wrongdoer,
> And I wrested prey from his teeth.

I might also add Ps 58:7:

> O God, smash [הרס] their teeth in their mouth;
> shatter the fangs of lions, O LORD.

To break the teeth is to render impotent, ineffective, powerless to do harm.

All this is clear and uncomplicated, except that, as noted above, Ps 3:8 is the only text in the Hebrew Bible in which the phrase שבר שנים occurs. Does the uniqueness have any significance? In a recent article, Jo Ann Hacket and John Huehnergard pointed out that the exact Akkadian equivalent of this Hebrew term appears in a thirteenth-century B.C.E. legal document from the vicinity of ancient Emar (modern Meskeneh, about 100 km east-southeast of Aleppo).[17] The document in question is a will, and it contains a penalty clause, as it were, for anyone who would contest its legality. The specific phrase is:

> If they contest, this tablet will break their teeth.
> *šumma iraggumū ṭuppu annû šinntāīšunu ušabbar*

This tablet thus establishes a definite legal as well as incantatory context for the phrase. In other words, both clauses of Ps 3:8 under discussion can be documented as legal terminology.

We can go even further than this in elucidating the jurisprudential setting. The laws of Ešnunna (§42) and Hammurabi both exhibit a sequence of legal topics; for example, in the Hammurabi law code, injury through assault to the eye (§§198–99) is discussed first, then injury to the teeth (§§200–201), immediately followed by the cases of the striking of the face (§§202– 5).[18] The likelihood of an Israelite psalmist having been directly influenced by Ešnunna's or Hammurabi's laws is, of course, utterly remote. But it is certainly within the realm of possibility, indeed of probability, that some Israelite legal text, not preserved, featured the same two laws juxtaposed as in these two collections. It is elementary that the legal corpora of the Torah represent only a small part of a much larger body of common law, perhaps orally transmitted, that was current in ancient Israel.

An analogy to the above may be drawn from *lex talionis*. This "eye for an eye" formula is featured three times, once in each of the legal corpora of the Torah (Exod 21:22–25, Lev 24:17–22, Deut 19:18–19, 21). A careful analysis of their surrounding contexts and of the relation of the legal formulation to the specific topic to which each is attached leaves no doubt that the *lex talionis* once circulated quite independently of its present pericopes as a discrete fossilized, general statement of legal policy.[19] Whatever its original intent, the standardized formula came to express an abstract legal concept, the law of equivalence. In the same way, I would suggest that the two clauses of Ps 3:8 go back to some ancient juristic compilation. They then came to be used abstractly and figuratively in literary texts to connote the infliction of humiliation and reduction to impotence. Such a development should occasion no surprise, for the judicial system was not detached from the life of the community; justice was carried on at the city gate, in public, so that legal terminology easily penetrated everyday speech.

Having mentioned the *lex talionis,* it is appropriate to round out this paper with a brief mention of the well-known passage in Matt 5:38–39 (cf. Luke 6:29):

> You have heard that it was said, "An eye for an eye and a tooth for a tooth." But I say unto you, Do not resist one who is evil. But if one strikes you on the right cheek, turn to him the other also.

I shall not relate to the problem that Jesus is here referring to private injury and that he must surely have known that, in his day certainly, the Pharisaic interpretation of the *lex talionis* rejected the literal application and required monetary compensation. Rather, I am struck by the juxtaposition of a blow to the eye, tooth, and cheek in that order as in the laws of Ešnunna and in Hammurabi.[20] Jesus cites all three as examples of "evil," which would make no sense unless "striking the cheek" was taken to be an offense of the utmost severity. Is the sequence pure coincidence or does it, perhaps, reflect some fossilized legal formulation?

NOTES

1. Translations of biblical texts follow the rendering of NJPSV. For the present purposes, it is of no consequence whether or not the verbs הכית and שברת are precatives, as claimed by M. Buttenwieser, *The Psalms Chronologically Treated* (Chicago, 1938; repr. New York, 1969) 396, 400; see also pp. 18–25.

2. So C. A. Briggs and E. G. Briggs, *A Critical and Exegetical Commentary on the Book of Psalms* (ICC: Edinburgh, 1906), 1:26.

3. So recognized by Rashi and Kimhi, who use the phrase מכת בזיון. E. Dhorme, *Le Livre de Job* (Paris, 1926) 213 (Engl. trans.: *A Commentary, on the Book of Job* [trans. H. Knight; London, 1967; repr. Nashville, 1984] 235), points out that "to strike the cheeks, to give a slap in the face, is the supreme outrage." Similarly, R. Yaron, *The Laws of Eshnunna* (Jerusalem, 1969) 191 n. 86, notes that it was "the insult *par excellence*."

4. *ANET* 108, rev. 23–28. On the stem *m-ḫ-ṣ*, see M. Held, "*mḫṣ* °*mḫš* in Ugaritic and Other Semitic Languages," *JAOS* 79 (1959) 169–76.

5. *ANET* 86, VII:iii:19–22. On the relationship between the Ištar and the Gilgameš passages, see J. H. Tigay, *The Evolution of the Gilamesh Epic* (Philadelphia, 1982) 128–29, 170–73.

6. G. Meier, *Die assyrische Beschwörungssammlung Maqlû* (AfO Beiheft 2; Berlin, 1937) 50, 8:101; cf. T. Abusch, *Babylonian Witchcraft Literature: Case Studies* (BJS 132; Atlanta, 1987) 90, 92.

7. *ANET* 334, line 425.

8. *KAI* 1:42, no. 222:A:41–42; *ANET* 660.

9. *ANET* 163, line 42; Yaron, *The Laws of Eshnunna*, 43.

10. *ANET* 545, no. 11.

11. *ANET* 175, §§202–5: G. R. Driver and J. C. Miles, *The Babylonian Laws* (Oxford, 1952), 1:409, cf. 412 n. 5.

12. On this penalty, see the remarks of J. J. Finkelstein. "Ammisaduqa's Edict and the Babylonian 'Law Codes.'" *JCS* 15 (1961) 98–99.

13. סטרו נותן לו מאתים זוז לאחר ידו נותן לו ארבע מאות זוז.

14. M. S. Zuckermandel (ed.), *Tosefta, Mischna und Boraitha* (repr. Jerusalem, 1938) 366: הכה באחר ידו... נותן ארבע מאות זוז ולא מפני שמכה של צער ה'א אלא
מפני שמכה של בזיון היא שנא' קומה י"י... כי הכית את כל אויבי לחי.

15. Cited in the Israeli daily *Maʿariv*, 10 June 1983.

16. Abusch, *Babylonian Witchcraft Literature*, 92, 97, 130, and esp. 131–47, draws attention to the interrelation of incantatory and legal language.

17. J. A. Hackett and J. Huehnergard, "On Breaking teeth," *HTR* 77 (1984) 259–75. I thank Marc Brettler for drawing this article to my attention.

18. *ANET* 163, 175.

19. See N. M. Sarna, *Exploring Exodus* (New York, 1986) 185–89.

20. See *ANET* 163, 175.

Psalm XIX and the Near Eastern Sun-God Literature

Psalm XIX contains two extraordinary features. It is unmistakably divided into two parts, vv. 2–7 (part A) being clearly differentiated from vv. 8ff. (part B) by theme, metric arrangement and style.[1] Moreover, in all of biblical literature this psalm constitutes the sole instance of the natural functions of an astral body being described in the language of mythological personification. The biblical exegete has to take account of these two peculiarities. He has to try to explain why the disparate elements were united into a single psalm.

O. Schroeder,[2] followed and developed by L. Dürr,[3] drew attention to the undoubted points of contact between the mythological imagery of our psalm and the Mesopotamian Šamaš literature. They further observed that in the Šamaš hymns, the sun-god is invariably portrayed as both the god of light and the god of justice, the two motifs intermingling and succeeding one another smoothly and naturally. Hence, by analogy, the lack of logical thought sequence between the two parts of Ps. XIX may be more apparent than real, for we may be dealing with a reflex of a liturgical pattern well established in the ancient Near East.

This paper, extracted from a monograph on the psalm,[4] will summarize the evidence already adduced and bring additional evidence to establish that the writer of Psalm XIXA was indeed influenced by the Near Eastern sun-god literature. This, however, is introductory to its main purpose which is to demonstrate that this same genre of literature has also left its impress on Ps. XIXB, the hymn to the Torah, and has infused it with its characteristic terminology.

i. The Psalm opens with a cosmic motif in which all the elements of nature rhapsodize their Maker.

Verse 2: השמים מספרים כבוד־אל ומעשה ידיו מגיד הרקיע

Both these themes are basic to the Near Eastern sun-god literature. The sun-god is the god of creation. Among the epithets of Šamaš in Babylonian sources is: "creator of heaven and earth" *(pa-ti-iq šamē u irṣitim);*[5] "creator of everything in heaven and earth" *(ba-nu-u napḫar kul-lat šamē u irṣiti).*[6] In Egyptian literature the god Re is described as: "creator of all things . . . maker of things which are."[7] He it is: "who made mankind and created the gods . . .";[8] "who made what is and created what exists";[9] who is the "maker of all mankind, Creator and maker of that is . . ."[10]

And as in our psalm, so in the Near Eastern religious literature, all creation rhapsodizes its maker, in this instance, the sun-god. In the famous Šamaš hymn we read:[11] "At your appearing the counsellor gods rejoice. All the Igigi gods exult in you."[12] "Šamaš, at your rising the gods of the land assemble. . ."[13] "The whole of mankind bows down to you."[14] Mesopotamian cylinder seals pictorially depict the other gods worshipping Šamaš.[15]

In Egyptian hymns to the god Re we find: "Thou art exalted by reason of thy wondrous works."[16] All creatures praise Re "from the highest heights of heaven to the uttermost parts of the earth and to the lowest depths of the sea."[17] "The stars which never rest sing hymns of praise unto thee and the stars which are imperishable glorify thee."[18]

ii. The sun is described as "a groom coming forth from his bridal chamber" והוא כחתן יצא מחפתו (v.6) and as "a hero joyfully running his course" ישיש כגבור לרוץ ארח.

It is well-known that in Mesopotamian mythology the god Šamaš is provided with a consort Aya who is frequently referred to by the epithet *kallatu,* "bride."[19] One evening-hymn mentions that, "Šamaš has betaken himself to his chamber."[20]

As to the title גבור, this corresponds exactly to the frequently used epithet of Šamaš "the hero" *(qar-ra-du/ quradu, eṭlum).*[21] In Egypt, too, the morning sun is adored as a conquering hero, the "valiant" one, who overthrows his enemies.[22] In fact, the appellation fits in with the well-nigh universal concept of the sun-god as a youthful hero and mighty warrior, the *sol invictus* who once each twenty-four hours defeats the forces of darkness and evil.

As to this hero joyfully running his course, numerous parallels likewise exist in Near Eastern literature. Suffice it to cite from an Egyptian hymn to Re: "Thou stridest over the heavens being glad at heart,"[23] "Thou passest over the heights of the heaven, thy heart swelleth with joy."[24]

It should be noted that whereas the course of the sun across the sky is frequently expressed mythologically in terms of a chariot ride or even a boat ride, yet neither simile was regarded as being incompatible with the figure of a runner,[25] as symbolized in our psalm: לרוץ ארח.

In Egyptian literature, the sun-god is "the great runner swift of step."[26] He is described as "Runner, Racer, Courser."[27] The famous seal cylinders[28] showing Šamaš stepping forth from his mountain home really represent a runner. A Hittite sun-hymn reads: "O Istanu, mighty King! Thou stridest through the four eternal corners."[29] The term ארח evidently refers to the ecliptic of the sun, known in Akkadian as *ḫarran Šamši*.[30] Interestingly, one of the epithets of Šamaš is: "He who traverses the way (*arḫat*) of heaven and earth" (*ri-du-u ar-ḫa-at šamf u irṣitim*).[31]

iii. Verse 7: מקצה השמים מוצאו ותקופתו על קצותם

The circuit of the sun in the skies is an obvious and frequently stressed theme in the sun-god literature.

The Šamaš hymn notes that, "regularly and without cease you traverse the heavens. Every day you pass over the broad earth."[32] An Egyptian hymn to Amon-Re eulogizes his "Rising in the Eastern horizon and going to rest in the Western horizon."[33] A hymn to Re likewise emphasizes: "Thou goest forth each day over heaven and earth."[34]

iv. Verse 7: ואין נסתר מחמתו

Whatever be the meaning of חמה here—be it heat, light, sight or sun—the reference is certainly to the all-pervasive effects of the sun's presence. This theme, too, is frequently emphasized in the sun-god literature. In the famous hymn of Akh-en-Aton we read: "Thy rays encompass the lands to the limit of all that thou hast made. As thou art Re thou reachest to the end of them."[35] In the Babylonian Šamaš hymn the same note is sounded: "Your fierce light fills the lands to their limits.[36] Šamaš, your glare reaches down to the abyss."[37] One is also reminded of the Babylonian proverb: "Where can a fox go out of the presence of Šamaš?" (*šelibu la-pa-an dŠamaš e-ki-a-am il-lak*).[38] A Hittite sun-hymn declares: "When Istanu (the sun) rises from the sky in the morning, thy light, Istanu, comes to all the upper and lower lands."[39]

These numerous, varied and striking parallels make abundantly clear that the author of Ps. XIXA was thoroughly familiar with the contemporary sun-god literature. Of course, he assimilated and transformed its motifs to make them conform to the spirit of the religion of Israel, so that the sun is not an independent deity, but one of God's creatures, and it is not the sun who is the object of praise, but God who is extolled by the works of His creation.

v. We are now in a position to discuss the second part of the psalm, the hymn in praise of God's Law.

Mention has already been made of the Mesopotamian association of the sun-god with righteousness and law. Such was the case throughout the ancient world.[40] *Šamaš* represented the principle of cosmic justice. He was the "judge of heaven and earth" (*dayyān šamě u irṣitim*);[41] "the judge of gods and men" (*šaipi-iṭ ili u a-wi-lu-tim*)[42] supervising the moral order, and he therefore sired "equity and truth" (*mešaru* and kettu). As the inspiration of legislation his name was invoked in the law codes.[43]

A Hittite hymn to the sun-god Istanu exclaims: "Thou establishest the custom and law of the lands"; "A just lord of government art thou."[44]

In the religion of Egypt Re, too, exemplified justice, He "judges the wicked from the just;"[45] "judges the weak and the injured;"[46] he is "maker of righteousness."[47]

In earlier times, he presided over the divine tribunal.[48] The goddess Maat, the embodiment of truth and justice, law and order, was the daughter and confidante of Re.[49]

A remarkable parallel to the association of the Torah (and its synonyms) with the natural light of the sun exists in an Egyptian hymn to Amon-Re which, after extolling the natural functions of the solar body, has the following passage: "Who maketh decrees for millions of millions of years; Whose ordinances stand fast and are not destroyed; Whose utterances are gracious; Whose statutes fail not in his appointed season; Who giveth duration of life and doubleth the years of those unto whom he hath a favour."[50] Note the four synonyms: decrees, ordinances, utterances, statutes and the epithets attached to them, as well as the final promise of reward, with which is to be compared עקב רב (v. 12).

vi. Equally remarkable is the fact that most, if not all, of the descriptions of the Torah in XIXB are to be found as attributes of the sun-god.[51]

(a) Verse 8: משיבת נפש

The generative, life-giving powers of the sun-god are frequently stressed in the Near Eastern literature. In Egypt, "He maketh mortals to live," "He made all men to live," "He giveth duration of life," "He is the god of life."[52] In Mesopotamia Šamaš is "The one who gives life" (*qāʾiš balāṭi*), "who revives the dead" (*muballiṭ mēti*).[53] In a Hittite hymn to the sun, the worshipper says: "Thou art life-giving."[54]

(b) Verse 8: עדות ה' נאמנה

We compare the corresponding Egyptian eulogy to the sun-god: "whose ordinances are permanent, whose ordinances stand fast and are not destroyed. . . whose statutes fail not. . ."[55]

(c-f) Verse 9: פקודי ה' ישרים משמחי־לב מצות ה' ברה מאירת עינים

This verse alone is an excellent demonstration of how the epithets of the Torah are saturated with the language of the sun-god literature.

(c) ישרים is reminiscent of one of the most popular Akkadian epithets of Šamaš—*muštešir*, "the one who directs aright." He is *bēl kit-ti u me-šari* "lord of truth and right,"[56] and it is not without interest that *mešaru*, the personification of right, was regarded as the offspring of Šamaš.

(d) משמחי־לב

The analogy between the "joy" of the sun ישיש כגבור (v. 6) and the "gladdening of the heart" which God's directives bring, משמחי־לב, is obvious.

In Egyptian literature, not only does the sun-god embark on his daily journey filled with joy, but he also brings joy to all the gods, and to the living and the dead.

In a hymn to Re we are told that "when thou risest in the horizon of heaven, a cry of joy goeth forth to thee from all people." "In every place every heart swelleth with joy at thy rising."[57]

Furthermore, the combination of משמחי־לב with ברה and מאירת עינים is worthy of special consideration.

The parallelism אור and שמח occurs in several biblical passages: Ps. XCVII:11 אור זרע לצדיק ולישרי־לב שמחה; Ps. CVII:42 יראו ישרים וישמחו; Ps CXIX:74 יראיך יראוני וישמחו; Prov. XIII: 9 אור צדיקים ישמח ונר רשעים ידעך.

H. L. Ginsberg[58] has pointed to the striking analogy between II AQHT II, 8–9 *bdne [l]pnm tšmḫ wʾl y ṣhl peʾt]* "Danel's face lights up, while above his forehead shines,"[59] and Ps. CIV:15 ויין ישמח לבב־אנוש להצהיל פנים משמן.

In a recent study of שמח, J. C. Greenfield[60] cites another Ugaritic passage in which *šmḫ* occurs in combination with the verb *nr*.[61] He shows that שמח in Ugaritic and Hebrew (occasionally in Aram., and Syr.) can mean "to glow."

(e) מצות ה' ברה

That we have here a transfer of epithets from the sun to the Torah is demonstrated by Song VI:10 ברה כחמה. That this latter phrase is a cli-ché, is proven now by an Ugaritic legal text[62] in which we have the phrase: *km. špš/dbrt. kmt./br. ṣtqšlm. . .* "just as the sun is bright/free, so Ṣitqu-salim is free. . ."[63] In the light of the evidence here adduced, we have to conclude that the choice and concatenation of verbs in v. 9, משמחי־לב, ברה, מאירת עינים is by no means fortuitous, but has, in fact, been conditioned by the consciousness of the comparison of the Torah to the sun.

In this connection, mention should be made of the highly plausible suggestion of N. H. Tur-Sinai[64] that the use of נזהר in v. 12 may have been influenced by the meaning "to shine, glow," which זהר can bear in Hebrew, Aramaic and Arabic.

(f) Verse 10: ירֵאת ה' טהורה עומדת לעד[65]

Here, again, the epithet טהורה is innocent enough. However, in combination with עומדת לעד some striking parallels exist in the sun-god literature.

A Mesopotamian hymn to Šamaš from the Neo-Babylonian Empire carries this line: "By thy pure word which is unchanging" *(i-na a-ma-ti-ka/ el-li-ti/ ša la šu-pi-e-lam).*[66]

The concept of the purity of the sun has given rise to a standard cliché in Akkadian legal documents from Ugarit:[67] *Kima il šapaš/šapši zakiti/zaka-at; kima šamši zaki/zaka.* The sun as a symbol of permanence and stability is likewise a familiar theme in biblical and Near Eastern literature. Ps. LXXII:5 ייראוך עם־שמש ולפני ירח דור דורים; Ps. LXXXIX:37 זרעו לעולם יהיה וכסאו כשמש נגדי. The Phoenician inscription from *Karatepe* III, 1. 19, refers to שמש עלם.[68]

Not only is the sun a figure of permanence, but his word too is eternal. The famous Mesopotamian Šamaš hymn has: "Your manifest utterance cannot be changed" *(šu-pu-u zik-ru-ka ul in-nen-ne-u);*[69] "whose utterance cannot be changed" *(šá lā in-nen-ne-u qi-bit pi-šú).*[70]

A Babylonian proverb echoes the same idea: "Like Šamaš, the king's word is sure, his command unequalled, and his utterance cannot be altered" *(Šarru ki-ma d[ša-maš a-mat-su ki-na-at] qi-bi-is-su ul iš-ša-na-an 'si-t pi-šu' [ul ut-tak-kar]).*[71] Egyptian hymns speak of Re: "whose utterances are permanent[72]. . . whose ordinances stand fast and are not destroyed."[73]

(g) Verse 10: משפטי־ה' אמת

Among prominent epithets of Šamaš in Akkadian literature is: "lord of truth" *(bēl kitti),* "The one of truth" *(ša ki-na-a-ti).*[74] In Egypt, the same title is given to Re who is "the Lord of truth", "living on truth."[75]

(h) Verse 11: הנחמדים מזהב ומפז רב

This is a familiar enough simile, especially in wisdom literature.[76] Yet one might wonder whether its employment here has not been occasioned by the sun literature, for one of the epithets of Re is the Golden Sun Disk,[77] and this god is quoted as saying of himself: "My skin is of pure gold."[78] An Egyptian "Universalist Hymn to the Sun," has this line: "Fine gold is not like the radiance of thee,"[79] a sentiment very close to that of our verse.

(i) Verse 11: ומתוקים מדבש ונפת צופים

The "sweetness" of God's word is not unparalleled in biblical literature.[80] The same comparison is to be found in Egyptian and Hittite sun-god texts. A hymn to Amon-Re calls the god "possessor of sweetness," and to him it is said, "The sweetness of thee is in the northern sky."[81] Even closer to our psalm verse is a Hittite hymn which declares "that the sun-god Istanu's message is sweet to everyone."[82]

vii. The question now arises as to whether it is possible to fix the date of the psalm. To ask the question in a different way, what circumstances would have evoked a hymn of adoration to the Torah which made use of the standard terminology of the sun-god literature, combined with a nature hymn that describes the circuit of the sun in mythological language? The formulation of the problem in this manner itself points to a solution.

(a) A panegyric of the type of Ps. XIXB could only reflect a concept of Torah as a crystallized, authoritative body of literature. This is not possible before the Deuteronomic Reform of Josiah.[83]

(b) Of all the Pentateuchal documents, Deuteronomy is the only one that, in fact, makes the Torah an object of national glorification (Deut. IV:6–8).

(c) Of all the Pentateuchal documents, Deuteronomy alone contains an explicit prohibition of astral worship (Deut. IV: 19; XVII:3).[84]

(d) The Deuteronomic Reform of Josiah, when the Torah became the focal point of the national religion, followed a period when the astral cult, especially sun-worship, achieved its maximum penetration of Judea. King Manasseh (*ca.* 687–642) had actually turned the Temple of Jerusalem into a national idolatrous shrine in which astral worship played a conspicuous role, and in which "sun-chariots" were prominently displayed.[85] A notable feature of the Josianic Reform was the destruction of just these sun-chariots (II Kings XXI:3, 5; XXIII:5, 11).

(e) The prophet Zephaniah, who belonged to this same period, also recorded the sin of astral worship (Zeph. I:5). Most remarkably, in chapter III, vv. 4, 5 and 17 he mentions the Torah and, in the spirit and language of our psalm, he compares the moral order that governs the world (משפט) to the natural order exemplified by the shining forth of the morning sun: בבקר בבקר משפטו יתן לאור... (Zeph. III:5). He even

uses the simile of a "joyful hero" to describe God: אלהיך בקרבך גבור
יושיע ישיש עליך בשמחה... ה' (Zeph. III:17).

(f) Jeremiah (VIII:2)[86] and Ezekiel (VIII:16)[87] also describe the astral cult and specifically the sun-worship practised in Jerusalem and the Temple.

(g) All these facts in combination confirm Dürr's conjecture[88] that our psalm belongs to the period of the Josianic Reform. In my opinion, Psalm XIX is an anti-pagan polemic, specifically, an anti-sun-god polemic, that has made use of the standard terminology of the Near Eastern sun-god literature to combat the sun-cult ideologically and to glorify God and his Torah.[89]

NOTES

1. See A. Szoerényi, *Psalmen u. kult im A. T.* (Budapest 1961), p. 139f.
2. O. Schroeder, *ZAW* 34 (1914), p. 69f.
3. L. Duerr, *Sellin-Festschrift* (Leipzig, 1927), p. 37–48.
4. It is hoped that this monograph will be published some time in 1966.
5. K. Tallqvist, *Akkadische Götterepitheta* (Leipzig, 1938), p. 156. This work is hereinafter abbreviated as Tallqvist.
6. *Ibid.*, p. 59
7. E. A. Wallis Budge, *The Book of the Dead* (New York, 1960), p. 109 (hereinafter cited as Budge).
8. J. A. Wilson in J. B. Pritchard, ed., *Ancient Near Eastern Texts* (Princeton, 1955), (= ANET), p. 365.
9. *Ibid.*, p. 366.
10. *Ibid.*, p. 367.
11. The translation used here is that of W. G. Lambert, *Babylonian Wisdom Literature* (Oxford, 1960), p. 121–138 (abbreviated al Lambert).
12. *Ibid.*, p. 127, 11.7–8.
13. *Ibid.*, p. 129, 1.47.
14. *Ibid.*, p. 1. 41.
15. H. Frankfort, *Cylinder Seals* (London, 1939), p. 101f.
16. Budge, p. 489.
17. *Ibid.*, p. 109.
18. *Ibid.*, p. 488. With this passage, cf. Ps. CXLVIII:1–4; Job XXXVIII:7. It should be noted that in the description of the glories of God's creation in Ben Sirah 4. 3, the heavens, firmament and the splendour of the sun are mentioned and the sun declares the wondrous works of God. In view of the great affinities between that chapter and Ps. XIXA one might wonder whether the latter did not originally contain a similar passage.
19. Schroeder, op. cit., p. 69f.; Tallqvist, p. 110f.; 168, 245, 455; D. O. Edzard, in H. W. Haussig, ed., *Wörterbuch der Mythologie* (Stuttgart), n. d. I. p. 126. The title, "bride of the house of the sun" (*klt bt špš*), appearing in an inventory from Ugarit (O. Eissfeldt, *JSS* 5 [1960], p. 33) may be connected with this myth. For the bridegroom compared to the sun in Indian mythology, see S. Thompson, *Motif Index of Folk Literature* (Bloomington, Indiana, 1957), vol. 5, Z 62.2.
20. *ANET*, p. 391. On this passage, see A. Jeremias, *Handbuch der Altorientalischen Geisikultur* (Leipzig, 1913), p. 250, who interprets it as a reference to Šamaš leaving each morning the house of his beloved Aya and returning thereto at night.

21. Schroeder, op. cit., p. 70; Tallqvist, p. 162f., 457; *idem, Der Assyrische Gott* (Helsingfors, 1932), p. 99 and n., p. 107, n. 3. For the pictorial representation of "the sun-god militant" on cylinder seals, see Frankfort, *Cylinder Seals*, p. 100f.

22. See *ANET*, p. 365, 367f.; Budge, p. 348, 488; A. Scharff, *Aegyptische Sonnenlieder* (Berlin, 1922), p. 32f., 37, 39, 41 etc. For the Egyptian concept, see H. Frankfort, *Kingship and the Gods* (Chicago, 1948), p. 157; *idem., Ancient Egyptian Religion* (New York, 1948), p. 16, 132.

23. Budge, p. 488; cf. T. G. Allen, *The Egyptian Book of the Dead* (Chicago, 1960), p. 86.

24. Budge, p. 348.

25. See the remarks of G. Pinches in *HDB* 4, p. 628[d]-629[a].

26. Budge, p. 162; cf. Allen, op. cit., p. 285, 11. 5f.

27. *ANET*, p. 368.

28. Frankfort, *Cylinder Seals*, p. 105–108.

29. H. G. Gueterbock, *JAOS* 78 (1958), p. 241.

30. A. Deimil, *Pantheon Babylonicum* (Rome, 1950), p. 184, No. 373; W. von Soden, *Akkadisches Hand-wörterbuch* (Weisbaden, 1962), p. 326f.

31. Tallqvist, p. 174.

32. Lambert, p. 127, 11. 27f.

33. *ANET*, p. 367.

34. Budge, p. 348.

35. *ANET*, p. 370.

36. Lambert, p. 127, 1.20.

37. *Ibid.*, p. 129, 1. 37.

38. *Ibid.*, p. 282.

39. Gueterbock, op. cit., p. 240.

40. The same association of light and justice is found in the figure of Nah Hunte in Elamite mythology; see F. Guirand in *Larousse Encyclopedia of Mythology* (New York, 1960), p. 72.

41. Tallqvist, p. 456–7; Frankfort, *Kingship and the Gods*, p. 150–157.

42. G. Dossin, *Syria* 32 (1955), p. 12, 11. 1ff.

43. B. Meissner, *Babylonien u. Assyrien* (Heidelberg, 1920–25), Vol. 1., p. 148f.; Vol. II, p. 2, 21, 47. See Hammurapi's Code in *ANET*, p. 164f., 178f. and Lipit Ishtar's, *ANET*, p. 161 (Epilogue). It should be noted that among the Greeks Apollo likewise was regarded as the source of criminal, civil and constitutional law. See W. K. C. Guthrie, *The Greeks and their Gods* (Boston, 1955), p. 183–187, 203; J. E. Harrison, *Epilegomena to the Study of Greek Religion* (Cambridge, 1921), p. 439.

44. Gueterbock, op. cit., p. 237.

45. *ANET*, p. 24.

46. *Ibid.*, p. 366.

47. *Ibid.*, p. 367.

48. Budge, p. 110; J. A. Wilson, *The Culture of Ancient Egypt* (Chicago, 1960), p. 119; Frankfort, *Ancient Egyptian Religion*, p. 15; *idem, Kingship and the Gods*, p. 157, 308.

49. Wilson, op. cit., p. 119; Frankfort, *Ancient Egyptian Religion*, p. 117; E. O. James, *Ancient Gods* (London, 1960), p. 200f.

50. Budge, p. 112f.

51. Interestingly, Abraham ibn Ezra in his comments to Ps. XIX:8ff. connected the epithets of the Torah with the sun.

52. Budge, p. 109, 112f., 348.

53. Tallqvist, p. 458f.

54. Gueterbock, op. cit., p. 239, according to the variant reading.

55. See note 50.

56. Tallqvist, p. 47, 104–6, cf. 456.
57. Budge, p. 347f.
58. *BASOR* 98 (1945), p. 15, n. 20.
59. *ANET*, p. 150.
60. *HUCA* 30 (1959), p. 141–151; cf. S. Morag, *Tarbiz* 33 (1964), p. 144.
61. CH. Virolleaud, *Le Palais Royal d'Ugarit* II (Paris, 1957), text 15.08, 11.6–11.
62. *Ibid.*, text 15.125, 11.2–4.
63. See W. F. Albright, *BASOR* 150 (1958), p. 37, n. 10; S. Loewenstamm, *Tarbiz* 28 (1958), p. 246.
64. *Halashon vehasefer* II (Jerusalem, 1950), p. 93; cf. the remark of G. Ostborn, *Tōrā in the O. T.* (Lund, 1945), p. 47, n. 4.
65. The widely accepted correction of יראת to אמרת (see K. Budde, *JBL* 40 [1921], p. 42) seems to be incontestable both on grounds of context and the parallels in Ps. CXIX:11, 38, 41 etc., cf., also Ps. XII:7.
66. S. Langdon, *Building Inscriptions of the Neo-Babylonian Empire* (Paris, 1905), p. 98, 11.23–25.
67. J. Nougayrol, *Le Palais Royal d'Ugarit III* (Paris, 1955), p. 57f., 66, 68, 70, 102, 110, 111.
68. *ANET*, p. 500; cf. 1.21.
69. Lambert, p. 129; 1.64.
70. *Ibid.*, p. 138, 1.199.
71. *Ibid.*, p. 234, 11.2–3.
72. Budge, p. 112f.
73. *Ibid.*, p. 498
74. Tallqvist, p. 47, 181, cf. 193.
75. Budge, p. 109f.; cf. *ANET*, p. 365, (1) 1. 8; p. 366, (VIII), 1.5.
76. Cf. Prov. III:14; VIII:10, 19; XVI:16; Job XXVIII:15, 16; cf. Ps. CXIX:72, 127.
77. Frankfort, *Kingship and the Gods*, p. 379, n. 9.
78. *Ibid.*, p. 46, cf. p. 135, 149.
79. *ANET*, p. 367.
80. Ezek. III: 3; Prov. XVI:24; Ps. CXIX:103; cf. Jer. XV:16.
81. *ANET*, p. 366.
82. Gueterbock, op. cit., p. 243. It may be of interest to mention that in Greek mythology Aristaeus, who taught men to keep bees, was the son of Apollo, the sun-god; see R. Graves, *The Greek Myths* (New York, 1955), § 82 I and note 6. See also Tur-Sinai, op. cit., p. 89, 92.
83. See M. Weinfeld, *Yehezkel Kaufmann Jubilee Volume* (Jerusalem, 1961), p. 89 (Hebrew).
84. It is a remarkable coincidence that the glorification of the Torah and the prohibition of sun-worship happen to appear within the same chapter in Deuteronomy.
85. On Manasseh's idolatry, see Y. Kaufmann, *Toldot ha'emunah Hayisre'elit* (Tel Aviv, 1942–56), I, p. 671, 673ff; II, p. 233ff; M. Haran, *IEJ* 13 (1963), p. 48ff; cf. N. Avigad, *ibid.*, p. 133ff.
86. Cf. Jer. VII:17f.; XIX:13; XXXII:29–34; XLIV:17ff. M. J. Dahood, *Revista Biblica* VIII (1960), p. 166–68 has sought to identify the practices referred to in these passages with the cult of the Canaanite sun-goddess Shapash.
87. Since the number twenty was associated with Šamaš it seems likely that the Greek "twenty" is here to be preferred to the Hebrew "twenty-five"; see B. Meissner, op. cit., II, p. 21; E. Dhorme, *Les Religions de Babylonie et d'Assyrie* (Paris, 1945), p. 60; A. Parrot, *Babylon and the O. T.* (London, 1958), p. 141. On the authenticity of Ezekiel's description, see T. H. Gaster, *Thespis* (New York, 1961), p. 47.
88. Op. cit., p. 48; cf. B. Bonkamp, *Die Psalmen* (Freiburg i. Br., 1949), p. 117f.

89. Additional evidence for the influence of the Assyrian sun-cult on Judea from the time of Manasseh is provided by the introduction of the two-winged sun-disk as the royal emblem of Judea; see D. Diringer, *BA* 12 (1949), p. 75; P. W. Lapp, *BASOR* 158 (1960), p. 22; cf. Y. Aharoni in *Oz Ledavid* (Jerusalem, 1964), p. 421–429, for a different view of the dating. I hope to deal fully with this problem in my forthcoming monograph on Ps. XIX. Regrettably, for various reasons, this projected monograph has not yet been completed.

Psalm 89: A Study in Inner Biblical Exegesis[1]

I. THE PROBLEM

Much scholarly attention has been focused upon two aspects of Psalm 89. It has long been accepted that it is a composite of originally disparate elements[2] and it is widely agreed that verses 20–38 constitute a version of Nathan's oracle to David promising eternity to the Davidic dynasty. Little notice has been given, however, to the techniques by which the psalmist welded together the individual parts into a cohesive unity. And while the problem of the interrelationships of the several recensions of the oracle has been thoroughly explored, it has generally been overlooked that Psalm 89 verses 20–38 actually constitute, not a recension of the original oracle, but an interpretation of it.

It is the purpose of this paper to attempt to rectify both these omissions. In the course of our researches, it is hoped at the same time that we may be able to draw some new conclusions about the date and exact historical circumstances that called forth the psalm in its completed form.

II. THE INTEGRATION OF DISPARATE ELEMENTS

The combination of originally unrelated elements into an integrated unit is a literary phenomenon familiar to us from the ancient world. The

classic example is the Gilgamesh epic of Babylon, many of its component parts having been formerly independent episodes borrowed from
Sumerian compositions,[3] while the twelfth tablet has been appended to
the epic even without any attempt at integration.[4]

A similar situation obtains in the Greek epic. Without entering into
the complicated "Homeric question," it may yet be noted that both the
Iliad and the Odyssey exemplify the same process of literary development.[5]

The identical tendency is not lacking in Biblical literature. This is
true of Psalm 19, in which an old nature hymn (verses 1–7) has been
combined with a Torah hymn (verses 8–15). Psalm 70 has been incorporated into Psalm 40 (verses 14–18), and Psalm 108 is a composition of
parts of Psalms 57 (verses 8–12) and 60 (verses 7–14).[6]

In these particular instances it is not always easy to distinguish the
principle by which integration has been effected. However, there is an
ever-growing recognition of the fact that many Biblical passages have
been placed in juxtaposition solely on the basis of association of ideas,
words, or phrases.[7]

III. THE PSALM AS A UNITY

A careful study of Psalm 89 provides overwhelming evidence to prove
that this same principle has been operative in the successful cohesion of
the disconnected elements into a harmonious whole.

The psalm seems to fall naturally into three divisions:

(i) a hymn, verses 2–3, 6–19,

(ii) an oracle, verses 4–5,[8] 20–38, and

(iii) a lament, verses 39ff.

Now it may be noted at once that verses 4–5 have been inserted
designedly after verses 2–3, on the basis of a midrash connecting
God's חסד and אמונה in His sovereignty over the universe with His חסד
and אמונה in His promise of eternal sovereignty to the Davidic line.
It will be further observed that תכן, יבנה, לדר ודר, עולם in verses 2–3
correspond to אכין, ובניתי, לדר ודור, עדעולם in verse 5.

It is as though the psalmist, at the very outset, wanted to make this
piece of exegesis perfectly clear and beyond the possibility of misunder-
standing. Having so done, he then proceeded to unite the hymn with
the oracle on the basis of the juxtaposition of no less than twelve key
words or phrases, as can be readily seen in Table I.

TABLE I

The Hymn	*The Oracle*
חסד 15, 3; חסדי 2,	וחסדי 34; חסדי 29; וחסדי 25,
ואמונת 9; אמונתך 6, 3, 2,	באמונתי 34; ואמונתי 25,
עולם 3, 2,	עולם 38; לעולם 37, 29; עד־עולם 5,
שמים 6, 3,	שמים 30,
תכן 3,	יכון 38, תכון: 22; אכין 5,
בשחק 7,	בשחק 38,
הים 10,	בים 26,
אויביך 11,	אויב 23,
בשמך 13,	ובשמי 25,
זרוע 14,	זרועי 22,
תרום קרננו 18; תרום ימינך 14,	תרום קרנו 25,
כסאך 15,	וכסאו 37, 30; כסאך 5,

The transition between the hymn and the oracle is deftly made through the national motif of verses 16–19 being subtly superimposed upon the cosmic, while the emphasis upon the moral basis of God's rule (verse 15) serves, in turn, to accentuate the sacrosanct, inviolable nature of the Divine Promise of the Davidic rule. Finally, מלכנו as the concluding word of the hymn carries over the idea of kingship which is central to the oracle.

The consummate skill with which the psalmist handled the several elements so that they became mutually interdependent will be specially appreciated from an examination of the lament. The twin themes of the hymn and the oracle, the morality of God's rule and the imprescriptible nature of His pledge, obviously encourage the psalmist to give utterance to his bitter complaint contrasting the stark reality of history with the promised ideal. But as a literary device, and to point up this contrast all the more effectively, he has made use in the lament of the key words of both the hymn and the oracle (see Table II).

Table II

The Hymn and Oracle (verses 2–38)	*The Lament* (verses 39ff.)
משחתיו 21,	משיחך 52, 39,
ובריתי 29; ברית 4, בריתי 35,	ברית 40
עבדי 21, 4,	עבדיך 51; עבדך 40,

הרימות ימין, 43	תרום ימינך, 14
	;תרום קרננו, 18
	תרום קרנו, 25
צריו, 43	צריו, 24
אויביו, 52 ;אויביך, 43	אויב, 11; ואויביך, 23
וכסאו, 45	כסאך, 5, 15
	וכסאו, 30, 37
חסדיך־־באמונתך, 50	חסדי ה'־־אמונתך, 2
	חסד־־אמונתך, 3
	ואמונתי וחסדי, 25
	וחסדי־־באמונתי, 34
	[Cf. חסד אמת, 15
	חסדי... נאמנת, 29]
נשבעת, 50	נשבעתי, 36 ,4

This repeated use of a large number of key words and phrases and the smooth transitions from one section to another constitute the techniques by which the psalmist harmoniously integrated the varied elements into a perfectly homogeneous poetic unit. The cohesive effect is heightened by fact that the pivotal words חסד and אמונה appear, each one, seven times. It is, moreover, probably no accident that ברית is used four times and its synonym שבועה three times, thus making a sevenfold mention of the covenant oath as well.[9]

All this unmistakably bears the stamp of a single creative editor-psalmist. He it is who must have composed the lament (verses 39ff.) and who has been responsible for having welded together the diverse parts that make up Psalm 89. It follows, then, that neither the hymn nor the oracular element can be dated later than the time of the composition of the lament. This problem and its implications will be dealt with hereafter. But its solution will not be possible unless the true nature of the oracular element is properly understood.

IV. THE ANTIQUITY OF EXEGESIS

We have already noted above that verses 4–5, originally belonging to the oracle, were inserted in the hymn as a kind of exegetical note. Indeed, we shall have occasion to show that the entire oracle is a reinterpretation of Nathan's original prophecy to David. Before proceeding directly to do so, however, it will not be out of place to say a few introductory words on the history of the exegetical system involved.

The phenomenon of exegesis and exposition of a text evolves from a peculiar attitude to the written or oral word. It involves the idea of authority and immutability and, ultimately, of sanctity.[10] This notion is found for the first time in Biblical literature in Deuteronomy 4:2:

לא תספו על־הדבר אשר אנכי מצוה אתכם ולא תגרעו ממנו.

"Ye shall not add unto the word which I command you, neither shall ye diminish from it." We meet it again at the close of the prophetic age when Zechariah quotes the "earlier prophets" (הנביאים הראשונים) as authoritative (Zechariah 1:4, 7:7). But it is now clear that this Biblical concept has its roots in the more ancient Near East and was wide-spread, in fact, throughout the ancient world.

It is already implicit in the epilogue to the early-nineteenth-century B.C.E. laws of Lipit-Ishtar, in which the monarch curses him "who will damage my handiwork. . . who will erase its inscription, who will write his own [name] upon it."[11] A century and a half later, Hammurapi exhorts his successors not to alter his laws and invokes elaborate impre-cations upon him who has not treated them as immutable, but who "has abolished the law which I enacted, has distorted my words, has altered my statutes, effaced my name inscribed [thereon] and has then inscribed his [own] name [in its place]."[12]

Paradoxically, this very idea of authority and immutability itself engenders change. The past is drawn upon to give sanction to the present, and the ancient words, precisely because they are invested with authority, are reinterpreted to make them applicable to the contempo-rary scene.

This is particularly true of religious literature. An excellent example is the great Babylonian creation epic, the *Enuma elish*, which was sol-emnly recited by the high priest on the fourth day of the New Year's fes-tival. It is well known that this epic, dated to the time of Hammurapi,[13] was motivated by theological and political considerations. It justified Marduk's ascendancy to a supreme position in the Babylonian pantheon and at the same time it supported Babylon's claim to political pre-emi-nence.[14] Now, it is of interest to note that in the Assyrian version of this epic, the name of the hero is Ashur, and his great temple is not the Esagila of Babylon but the metropolis bearing Ashur's name.[15] A strik-ing analogy to this situation may be found in the political and theological motivations that induced the Samaritans to change the authoritative text of the Pentateuch to justify the pre-eminence of Mount Gerizim.[16]

This tendency, outside of Israel, to regard a text as authoritative and then to reinterpret it, is not restricted to Babylonian times. Thus, as Edward Meyer has pointed out, from the third century B.C.E., demotic papyri are extant which constitute midrashim on obscure prophecies about Egypt's fate.[17] Similarly, the four-monarchy theory of Daniel is but a development of an originally Achaemenian Persian doctrine, itself subjected to varying exegesis in the ancient world.[18] The history of the sibylline oracles in general and of the Jewish use of them in particular is a case in point in the Hellenistic world.[19] At the same time, Virgil's Fourth Eclogue, written about the year 40 B.C.E., is a midrash on the oracles of the Sibyl of Cumae; and the early Church, in turn, reinterpreted the Fourth Eclogue as a prophetic allusion to the birth of Jesus.[20] Philo's special brand of exegesis is well known,[21] and the Dead Sea Scrolls furnish numerous examples of the use of the midrash method in adapting Scripture to their own purposes.[22] The authors of the New Testament freely reinterpreted the Jewish Bible, albeit in its Greek form,[23] as a prophecy of Christian truths,[24] a tradition earnestly pursued by the early Church Fathers.[25] In the light of all this, it is abundantly clear that the highly developed midrash system of the Rabbis was not a late innovation, but had a very long and varied history behind it.

Wilhelm Bacher has described Biblical exegesis as "the one indigenous science created and developed by Israel."[26] On the basis of the well-known passage in Ezra 7:10: "כי עזרא הכין לבבו לדרש את תורת ה'" he attributed its foundation to Ezra the Scribe. In so far as the emphasis is upon the word "science," Bacher is no doubt correct. Yet Rabbinic tradition regarded the oral law as being conterminous with the written law. It thus actually looks for the origins of Biblical exegesis within the period of the formation of the Scriptures themselves. This Rabbinic tradition, in a generalized sense, must be upheld; for it cannot be denied that the literature of the Bible was subjected to exegesis even in pre-Exilic times.[27] The ancient Near-Eastern tradition would support such a view a priori, and the Biblical evidence itself is conclusive. A few of the more outstanding examples will suffice.

It is universally recognized that Daniel 9:2, 24–27, is a midrash reinterpreting Jeremiah's seventy years of exile (Jeremiah 25:11–12, 29:10; compare Zechariah 1:12; 7:5). H. L. Ginsberg has recently drawn attention to the fact that Daniel chapters 10–12 also constitute a complete midrash, mainly on the Book of Isaiah.[28] Few dispute the fact that the Book of Chronicles is in large measure a midrashic reinterpretation of earlier works with a view to a paradigmatic reconstruction of the history of Israel.[29] These examples belong to the Exilic period. It is now possible, however, to trace back Biblical exegesis to a still earlier period, for Kaufmann has clearly demonstrated the existence in Israel of an ancient body of prophetic oracles upon which the literary prophets freely drew and which they adapted to their needs.[30]

V. EXEGESIS IN PSALM 89

Now a recognition of this early phenomenon of inner Biblical exegesis holds the key to the solution of one of the problems of our psalm. Much attention has been paid to the relationship between Psalm 89:20–38 and the recensions of Nathan's oracle to David found in II Samuel 7:4–17 and I Chronicles 17:3–15. Scholarly speculation has, in fact, encompassed the entire range of possibilities. One view regards the prose version as original and our psalm as a free poetic paraphrase of it.[31] Another insists that precisely the poetic form must be the oldest version of the oracle on which the prose recensions are dependent.[32] Yet a third school of thought suggests that there need be no question of literary interdependence since the authors of Samuel, Chronicles, and our psalm could well have had equal and independent access to a common source, long since lost, that contained the text of the original oracle.[33]

To the present writer, a close comparison between our psalm and the texts of the oracle in Samuel and Chronicles shows that we are not dealing here with any problem of literary dependence or text transmission. The several variations from the prose versions are highly significant and can easily be otherwise explained. As a matter of fact, they add up to a pattern of deliberate and original exegesis on the part of the psalmist, who has adapted an ancient oracle to a new situation.[34] The evidence is as follows:

(i) In both versions of the oracle, the occasion of the original utterance is David's Temple project. The same is true of the quotations of Nathan's prophecy in I Chronicles 22:6ff., especially verse 10, I Chronicles 28:1ff., especially verses 6–7, II Chronicles 6:5–9, and Psalm 132:11ff. Solomon, too, quotes from the oracle in his Temple dedicatory speech (I Kings 8:25). This consistency must reflect an authentic situation. But what do we find in our psalm? Here, alone, the Temple project element is entirely lacking. The verses II Samuel 7:10–13 (I Chronicles 17:9–12) find no echo whatsoever in Psalm 89. This exclusion cannot be accidental. It accords completely with the omission of any mention of the Temple in the lament, an omission which we shall have occasion to discuss again in a different connection.[35]

(ii) The verse II Samuel 7:10 (to which compare I Chronicles 17:9) contains a promise to the people of Israel of respite from their national enemies. This is in agreement with the state of affairs toward the close of David's long reign, but it is clearly at variance with the subsequent history of Judah. A comparison with Psalm 89:23–24 shows that the psalmist has, therefore, cleverly and pointedly changed the wording so as to restrict its import to David personally.

(iii) This change is all the more forcefully emphasized by an expansion in the psalm, not to be found in either version. Verse 26 reads:

ושמתי בים ידו ובנהרות ימינו.

This is an undoubted reference to the Davidic empire,[36] and it serves a further purpose as well. It is related to the occasion of the lament. The psalmist wishes to point up the contrast between the Davidic victories and the military humiliation of his own day.

(iv) This same tendency to oppose reality to the oracular promise is to be observed in yet another expansion original to our psalm. In II Samuel 7:14 (I Chronicles 17:13) we find:

אני אהיה־לו לאב והוא יהיה־לי לבן.

This cultic formula is also repeated, almost word for word, in the quotations in I Chronicles 22:10, 28:6. But Psalm 89:27–28 has:

הוא יקראני אבי אתה אלי וצור ישועתי: אף־אני בכור אתנהו
עליון למלכי־ארץ.

This is an interpretation of the oracle stressing the implications of God's function as the father and emphasizing the benefits which the בכור (not בן!) relationship is supposed to bestow.

(v) Furthermore, it cannot fail to be noticed that, whereas in all the quotations cited above the father-son relationship refers to God's obligations to the immediate offspring of David, our psalm has applied the sonship to David himself.

(vi) In the same vein, the psalmist has transferred the threatened punishment for sin from the son of David (II Samuel 7:14) to the Davidic dynasty as a whole (Psalm 89:31). David has become the dynastic symbol.[37]

(vii) Finally, our psalmist has reinterpreted Nathan's oracle in terms of a covenant between God and David, sealed by a solemn oath (ברית, שבועה verses 4, 35–36, 40, 50). However, in neither prose recension of the prophecy is ברית or שבועה mentioned. David, too, in his response to the oracle (II Samuel 7:18ff.; I Chronicles 17:16ff.) makes no mention of either term. The psalmist here has, for his own purposes, made use of a very early exegetical tradition in departing from the original language of the oracle. This is clear from the "last words of David," in which the old monarch says that God gave him an "eternal covenant" (ברית עולם, II Samuel 23:5). According to the chronicler (II Chronicles 13:5), King Abijah recalls to Jeroboam and to all Israel as something well known that God gave the kingdom to David "forever" (לעולם) with a "covenant of salt" (ברית מלח). The quotation in Psalm 132:11 also refers to the oracle in legal terms of ברית and שבועה, and Jeremiah (Jeremiah 33:17, 21) and Deutero-Isaiah (Isaiah 55:3) both have the same understanding of it.[38]

The explanation for all this lies in the fact that the author of the lament needed to adapt Nathan's oracle to his own immediate purposes. He had not the slightest interest in the original occasion of the oracle, the Temple project, and, as a matter of fact, as we shall see later, the omission of any mention of the Temple was necessary for the subject of the lament. Likewise, the problem of David's successor was quite irrelevant to his theme. His sole concern was with the Divine Pledge of perpetuity to the Davidic dynasty as such and with the glaring contrast between the promised ideal and the present reality. It is this exclusive interest that explains the expansions, selectivity, departures from, and changes of emphasis in the psalmist's citations from the text of the oracle. Psalm 89, verses 4–5, 20–38, accordingly, do not represent a different, independent recension of Nathan's oracle to David, and there is no question of deciding upon the relationship of the prose to a supposed poetic version. These verses constitute, rather, an exegetical adaptation of the oracle by the psalmist to fit a specific historic situation.

VI. THE DATE OF NATHAN'S ORACLE

This conclusion as to the nature of verses 4–5, 20–38, presupposes the anteriority of Nathan's oracle to the psalm. The evidence for this assumption, however, requires elucidation in view of the astonishing divergence of scholarly opinion that has been expressed.

From some comes a rather vague admission that the prophecy contains an ancient nucleus.[39] Others are certain that it is Davidic[40] or, at latest, Solomonic.[41] It has been dated pre-Deuteronomic[42] as well as post-Deuteronomic,[43] and more precisely, Josianic,[44] Exilic,[45] post-Exilic, and even as late as the fourth century B.C.E.[46]

Notwithstanding the complete lack of consensus, it would appear to the present writer that the facts are overwhelmingly in favor of a Davidic date.

(i) The entire oracle is devoted to the idea of the perpetuity of the Davidic line. Now such an oracle would certainly be nonsensical in post-Exilic times unless it be Messianic or eschatological. It is true that it has been widely so interpreted in medieval and modern times, but such an understanding is possible only if the numerous other factors, hereafter described, are ignored. Furthermore, the fact that Solomon applied the oracle to himself (I Kings 8:20; II Chronicles 6:10) proves that to the Biblical writers, at least, the prophecy was well rooted in history.

(ii) The oracle makes very clear the possibility of sin on the part of David's offspring and its inevitable punishment (II Samuel 7:14). Yet the reference is entirely individual. In not one of the different recensions or quotations of the oracle is there any mention of national sin or national punishment. Subsequent to the work of the eight-century prophets this omission would be very strange.

(iii) Still more strange is the lack of even a hint of the division of the kingdom, despite the fact that this could most conveniently be interpreted as the promised punishment. The prophecy must therefore derive, at the latest, from before the time of Solomon's death.

(iv) Several times the oracle is cited in support of the legitimacy of the Solomonic succession. Solomon himself invokes it in his Temple dedicatory speech and applies it specifically to himself (I Kings 8:20; II Chronicles 6:10). Yet his quotation agrees with all the versions of the prophecy in maintaining the anonymity of David's successor. This is explicable only on the assumption that the text of the oracle was fixed before the Solomonic succession.

(v) This conclusion is strengthened by yet another consideration. The chronicler finds himself in desperate need of legitimating the Solomonic succession.[47] To this end he omits from his narrative several inconvenient episodes leading up to it. The murder of David's first-born son, Amnon, by Absalom (II Samuel 13), the murder of Absalom by Joab after the former's abortive revolt (II Samuel 15–18), Adonijah's bid for the crown with considerable and important court support (I Kings 1:5–10), the swift and successful pro-Solomonic reaction headed by Nathan and Bath-Sheba in which the decisive event is Nathan's invocation of a promise by David to Bath-Sheba (I Kings 1:11–53), the subsequent murder of Adonijah (I Kings 2:25)—on all these decisive incidents which regulated Solomon's accession to the throne, the chronicler is significantly silent, for they interfere with his notion of Solomon's natural and divine right of succession. Now in view of this situation, it is passing strange that neither in I Chronicles 17 nor in the abbreviated quotation in II Chronicles 6:5–9 is the text of Nathan's oracle tampered with in order to identify the unnamed successor of David. This, once again, can be explained only on the supposition that the text of Nathan's oracle as it appears in I Chronicles 17 and II Samuel 7 from the mouth of Nathan was substantially fixed before Solomon's accession to the throne.

(vi) The chronicler's historiosophical purposes led him on other occasions to adapt the text of the prophecy to his needs. David is made to recite it to Solomon as though Nathan had actually named Solomon in it (I Chronicles 22:7–10). This is in glaring contrast to II Samuel 12:25, in which Nathan names Solomon ידידיה but makes no mention of his own oracle in reference to the newly-born son. Likewise, in David's address to the princes, he is made paraphrastically to quote Nathan's oracle as though Solomon had actually been named in it (I Chronicles 28:1–7). Yet, in the original citation in II Samuel 7, and I Chronicles 17 (compare also II Chronicles 6:5–9), Solomon's name is not to be found. The absence of identification of David's successor must be due to the fact that the oracle indeed preceded the designation of Solomon as David's successor and that II Samuel 7 and I Chronicles 17 were not reworked in the light of subsequent events.

(vii) Biblical literature is emphatic that David was called to the throne by divine designation (compare I Samuel 25:30, II Samuel 5:2). The oracle, too, stresses this point (II Samuel 7:8, I Chronicles 17:7; compare Psalm 89:20–21). But, significantly, there is no Divine Word recorded in Samuel or Kings on the election of Solomon. He attains the throne only by order of David's decision, based upon a promise he had once made to Bath-Sheba (I Kings 1:16ff.). Moreover, Nathan, who played no minor role in the palace intrigue, strangely, does not invoke his own oracle in support of Solomon's claim to the throne. In the light of the foregoing argument, this is conceivable only if the successor to David was not designated in the original oracle. In other words, Nathan's prophecy must antedate both David's death and the designation of Solomon as his successor.

(viii) We have previously taken note of a consistent tradition linking Nathan's oracle to David's Temple project. The validity of this tradition is enhanced by the fact that it harmonizes perfectly with yet another, equally consistent, Biblical tradition. Deuteronomy 12:9ff. makes the selection of a centralized place of worship dependent upon the attainment of peace and national security. The formula is significant:

והניח לכם מכל־איביכם מסביב וישבתם־בטח.

Solomon uses it in enlisting the aid of Hiram, King of Tyre, to build his Temple (I Kings 5:18–19) and it is repeated several times in the same connection (I Kings 8:56; I Chronicles 22:7–9, 28:3). This, as Wellhausen has pointed out,[48] is due to the fact that Israelite historiosophy envisaged this stage as being first fully realized in the times of David and Solomon. Accordingly, David's Temple project would be just the appropriate time for a prophecy such as that of Nathan. National security and peace having advanced to a point that allowed for the building of the Temple, an opportune occasion presented itself for a prophecy promising eternal stability to the Davidic dynasty.

(ix) Finally, the fact that the exclusive right of the Davidic line to kingship was never challenged in Judah proves conclusively that in the popular conception the legitimacy of the dynasty must have been based upon a Divine sanction of commitment to the descendants of David.

To sum up, the converging lines of evidence are overwhelmingly conclusive in proving that the Biblical tradition about the original prophecy of Nathan to David is an authentic document, contemporaneous with the events it describes. There is, accordingly, no chronological objection to our interpretation of the second element of Psalm 89 as being an exegetical adaptation of that prophecy.

VII. THE DATE AND BACKGROUND OF THE PSALM

It now remains to determine, if possible, the particular historical circumstances that stirred the author of the lament to put together the psalm in substantially its present form. We may, at the outset, emphatically and completely rule out the possibility that the Babylonian destruction of Jerusalem and the Temple and the subsequent Exile evoked the bitter complaints to be found in verses 39ff.[49] For one thing, the total absence of any mention of or reference to any of these cataclysmic events would be utterly inexplicable. For another, there is not the slightest suggestion of even a threat to Jerusalem or of a foreign yoke, no notion of a national sin, no hint of the dissolution of the monarchy, no prayer or hope for national and monarchical restoration. Anyone who compares this psalm with Psalms 79 or 137 will note immediately the striking contrast in historical background and treatment. There cannot be the slightest doubt that the lament must reflect some situation prior to the Babylonian invasion.

Now any attempt further to narrow down the historical circumstances that inspired the psalmist must take account of his exegetical treatment of Nathan's oracle, which, as we have shown, was adapted to the immediate purposes of the lament. It must explain why the Divine Promise of eternity for the Davidic line is there the exclusive theme and why David's Temple project, which evoked the oracle, is ignored. It has to make clear why, in turn, the lament refers only to some danger to the ruling dynasty, but passes over in silence Jerusalem, the Temple, and the people at large. We have to know why the sin mentioned in the original oracle only in reference to David's immediate successor is reinterpreted to apply to the royal descendants of David in general. Finally, we must understand the meaning of the repeated emphasis upon חסד, and the appeal to the inviolable nature of the ברית.

Bearing in mind all the foregoing, it is possible to reconstruct the nature of the events which produced the lament. This latter must reflect an invasion of Judea, but it must have been one that did not have as its primary goal the conquest of Jerusalem or the Temple. The real target was the reigning monarch, whom the invaders wished to depose and replace by an outsider, not of Davidic descent. In other words, the invasion constituted a mortal threat, not to the integrity of the kingdom, but to the Davidic dynasty. This alone explains the reiterated invocation of God's eternal covenant with the House of David.

At the same time, the psalmist did not have too high an opinion of the ruling king; in fact, he clearly regarded him as a sinful man who had forsaken God's law and had not walked in His judgments; who had violated the Divine Statutes and had not heeded God's precepts (verse 31f.). Very significantly, the psalmist does not mention the injustice of the situation he is lamenting. The monarch, through his personal unworthiness, would really have had no legal case were it not for the appeal to God's חסד, to the Divine "covenant-love," which promised the unbroken continuity of the Davidic line (verses 29, 34–37, 50).

From the language of the lament, it is possible to glean yet one more vital and illuminating detail. The invasion of Judea had inflicted a humiliating defeat upon the king (verses 40–45). True, he had emerged from it alive, but he was a young man and had now become prematurely aged (verse 46).[50]

Such an understanding of the historic situation alone makes the singularities of Psalm 89 intelligible. It also enables us to pinpoint the particular event. The only known threat to the Davidic dynasty in Judea is that recorded in Isaiah 7:5–6[51] when, in the year 735–34 B.C.E., an anti-Assyrian coalition led by Rezin of Damascus and Pekaḥ of Israel launched an invasion of Judea with the expressed purpose of deposing King Ahaz and of replacing him by an Aramean puppet, one ben Tab'el.[52] Ahaz was only twenty years old at the time (II Kings 16:2; II Chronicles 28:1), having just ascended the throne. That he suffered defeat and humiliation is related by the chronicler[53] (II Chronicles 28), and this dovetails very well into the circumstances presupposed by the lament. This invasion did not really bring with it a danger of destruction to Jerusalem or the Temple, only a threat to King Ahaz, scion of the House of David. His experience must indeed have shortened his days, for he died at the early age of thirty-six (II Kings 16:2; II Chronicles 28:1). That Ahaz was a sinful man, thoroughly deserving of God's chastisement, is clear from the Biblical evaluation of him (II Kings 16:2ff.; II Chronicles 28:1ff.; Isaiah 7:13ff.). The profound impact of the invasion and the consternation, bordering on panic, that ensued in Jerusalem can easily be imagined from the vivid account in Isaiah 7:1ff. and the more prosaic, detailed narratives in II Kings 15:37–16:5 and II Chronicles 28:5ff. A psalm such as ours would certainly have been written immediately after the humiliation of the king, when the final outcome of the Aramean-Israelite venture was still uncertain. In all probability the psalmist was a court poet, but totally out of sympathy with the pro-Assyrian policy of Ahaz and opposed to his religious perversions.

VIII. SUMMARY

Psalm 89, in its present form, is a unity of originally diverse elements. This unity has been skillfully constructed through the reiterated use of key words and phrases, combined with a subtle interweaving of motifs and themes. The second of the three natural divisions of the psalm constitutes an exegetical adaptation, not another recension, of Nathan's oracle about the House of David, and this oracle is certainly Davidic. The writer of the lament is the real author of our present psalm, which was inspired by the Aramean-Israelite invasion of Judea in 735–34 B.C.E., when an attempt was made to depose Ahaz and to replace him by a non-Davidic king.

POSTSCRIPT

My attention has been drawn to two relevant articles which have appeared too late to be referred to in the foregoing study.

J. M. Ward in *VT* II:321–339 (1961) has independently reinforced my own conclusions as to the integrity and unity of the psalm. He has not, however, sufficiently considered the possibility of a specific historic situation as the occasion of the psalm.

Gerald Cooke, *ZAW* 73:202–225 (1961) agrees that at least part of Nathan's prophecy stems "from near the time of David himself." He further states that there is no need to "assert the dependence of the midrashic author of II Sam. 7 upon Ps. 89." However, Cooke has failed to realize that the Psalm 89 version is itself a midrash on the original oracle of Nathan.

NOTES

1. I wish to thank my colleagues, Professor H. L. Ginsberg and Professor Gerson D. Cohen, for their helpful comments on this paper. They are not, of course, responsible for the opinions expressed.

2. Cf. Martin Luther's observation, "In psalmo 89 est maxime contrarietas," cited by H. J. Kraus, *Psalmen* (*Biblischer Kommentar* XV, Neukirchen, 1960), p. 615.

3. S. N. Kramer, *JAOS* 64:7ff. (1944), and his *History Begins at Sumer* (New York, 1959), pp. 182–199, esp. pp. 188f.; A. Heidel, *The Gilgamesh Epic* (Chicago, 1946), p. 13.

4. See. E. A. Speiser's remarks in *Ancient Near Eastern Texts Relating to the Old Testament*, ed. J. B. Pritchard (Princeton, 1950).

5. See Gilbert Murray, *The Rise of the Greek Epic* (New York, 1960), esp. the remarks of Moses Hadas, p. v.

6. The Greek has combined the Hebrew Psalms 9 and 10, as also 114 and 115, into single psalms, while Masoretic text Psalms 116 and 147 have been each broken down into two separate psalms.

7. See U. M. D. Cassuto, *Ha-Kinnūs Ha-'Olami Le-Mada^{c}ē Ha-Yahadūt*, I (Jerusalem, 1952), 165–169. Cassuto repeatedly drew attention to this phenomenon in his commentaries to Genesis and Exodus. L. J. Liebreich, *JQR* 46:259–277 (1956), 47:114–138 (1957), has made an exhaustive study of the principle of arrangement by key words in Isaiah. For the same in Ezekiel, see U. M. D. Cassuto, *Miscellanea Giovanni Mercati* (Vatican, 1946), I, 40–51. D. B. Macdonald, *The Hebrew Literary Genius* (Princeton, 1933), pp. 88f., describes the book of Amos as a "collection of fragmentary utterances arranged by a collector according to a purely mechanical principle." Franz Landsberger, "Poetic Units Within the Song of Songs," *JBL* 73:203–216 (1954), arrives at a similar conclusion about the arrangement of the poetic units of Canticles. Much the same point has previously been made by Cassuto, *Ha-Kinnūs*, p. 168, and subsequently by Otto Eissfeldt, *Einleitung in das alte Testament* (Tübingen, 1956), pp. 603f. M. H. Segal, *Mĕbō Ha-Mikra'* (Jerusalem, 1955), I, 12–13, explains the present order of the Minor Prophets by this principle of juxtaposition of key words. By the same token, the Song of Hannah (I Samuel 2:1–10) and the Prayer of Jonah (2:3–10) have both acquired their present positions. For סמיכות הפרשיות as a recognized technique in Rabbinic exegesis, see W. Bacher, *Die exegetische Terminologie der jüdischen Traditionsliteratur*, I (Leipzig, 1899), 142f.

8. That verses 4–5 undoubtedly belong to the oracle is proved by considerations of content and meter, on which see S. Mowinckel, *Psalmenstudien*, III (Kristiania, 1923), 35f., and Kraus, *Psalmen*.

9. For the significance and widespread use of the number seven in antiquity see J. and H. Lewy, *HUCA* 17:1–146 (1942–43), esp. p. 22, where reference is made to Assyro-Babylonian hymns and prayers which contain sevenfold mention of Enlil's name.

For a Biblical analogy with this latter, cf. The heptad of tetragrammata to be found in Psalm 92, designated "for the Sabbath day."

10. Cf. the remarks of Louis Ginzberg, *JE*, I, 403, "Allegorical Interpretation."

11. *Ancient Near Eastern Texts*, p. 160.

12. G. R. Driver and J. C. Miles, *The Babylonian Laws* (Oxford, 1952–55), I, 39; II, 101, 107. *Ancient Near Eastern Texts*, p. 61.

13. Speiser, *Ancient Near Eastern Texts*, p. 61.

14. A. Heidel, *The Babylonian Genesis* (Chicago, 1942), p. 5.

15. *Ibid.*, p. 1. This must constitute one of the earliest examples of the kind of תקון סופרים known to us from Rabbinic literature, on which see S. Lieberman, *Hellenism in Jewish Palestine* (New York, 1950), pp. 28–37.

16. On the question of the relationship of Masoretic text Deuteronomy 27:4 to the Samaritan, see Y. Kaufmann, *Sefer Yehoshuᶜa* (Jerusalem, 1959), pp. 129–132.

17. E. Meyer, *Kleine Schriften* (Halle, 1924), 67–91. Cf. also H. L. Ginsberg, *Encyclopaedia Biblica* [Hebrew], II (Jerusalem, 1958), 689. On ancient Egyptian prophecy, see Gunter Lanczkowski, *Altägyptischer Prophetismus* (Wiesbaden, 1960).

18. Ginsberg, *Encyclopaedia Biblica*, II, 689, and *Studies in Daniel* (New York, 1948), pp. 5ff., 63ff. On the latter, cf. the remarks of Y. Kaufmann, *Tōlĕdōt Ha-Emūnah Ha-Yisreelit* (Tel-Aviv, 1956), vol. IV (8), p. 424, n. 12.

19. E. Schürer, *A History of the Jewish People in the Time of Jesus Christ* (Edinburgh, 1890), div. II, vol. III, pp. 271–292.

20. J. B. Mayor, *Virgil's Messianic Eclogue* (London, 1907), pp. 87–138, believes that the sibylline original is itself influenced by Isaiah's prophecies. Against this view, however, see the detailed objections of Kaufmann, *Tōlĕdōt Ha-Emūnah Ha-Yisraelit*, vol. III (6), pp. 293–296.

21. On Philo's exegetical methods, see the literature cited by S. W. Baron, *A Social and Religious History of the Jews* (Philadelphia, 1952), vol. I. p. 389, n. 51.

22. See F. F. Bruce, *Biblical Exegesis in the Qumran Texts* (Grand Rapids, 1959).

23. W. Dittmar, *Vetus Testamentum in Novo* (Göttingen, 1903); H. B. Swete, *Introduction to the Old Testament in Greek* (Cambridge, 1902), pp. 381–405.

24. K. Fullerton, *Prophecy and Authority* (New York, 1919).

25. Swete, *Introduction to the Old Testament in Greek*, pp. 406–432.

26. *JE*, III, 162; so I. H. Weiss, *Dōr Dōr Ve- Dōrshav* (New York-Berlin, 1924), I, 52.

27. Cf. the observation of W. F. Albright, *From the Stone Age to Christianity* (New York, 1957), p. 296, n. 27, "There was undoubtedly much more exegesis of the Hebrew text in pre-Exilic times than we often realize." See also Weiss, *Dōr Dōr*, I, 51f.; M. H. Segal, *Parshanūt Ha-Mikra'* (Jerusalem, 1952), pp. 5–7; *Mĕbō'*, IV, 981–982, and especially the study of I. L. Seeligman, *Congress Volume* (Supplements to *VT* vol. I, Leiden, 1953), pp. 150–181.

28. Ginsberg, *Encyclopaedia Biblica*, II, 949–951.

29. The evaluation is not at all invalidated by recent, more positive appraisals of the chronicler's work; see, in particular, W. F. Albright, "The Judicial Reforms of Jehoshaphat," *Alexander Marx Jubilee Volume* (New York, 1950), I, 61–82, and J. Liver, *Sefer Biram* (Jerusalem, 1956), pp. 152–161.

30. Kaufmann, *Tōlĕdōt*, vol. III (6), pp. 1–55. See also the sources cited in note 27.

31. R. Duhm, *Die Psalmen* (Tübingen, 1899), p. 222; A. F. Kirkpatrick, *The Book of Psalms* (Cambridge, 1904), p. 530; Z. P. Chajes, [Hebrew] Commentary to Psalms (Kiev, 1908), p. 193; E. G. Briggs, *The Book of Psalms*, II (New York, 1917), 253; H. Gunkel, *Die Psalmen* (Göttingen, 1926), p. 392; E. A. Leslie, *The Psalms* (New York-Nashville, 1949); M. Simon, *Revue d'histoire et de philosophie religieuses*, 32:41–58 (1952); Segal, *Mĕbō'*, III, 563; *Sifrē Shĕmuel* (Jerusalem, 1956), p. 280; H. van den Bussche, *Le Texte de la prophétie de Nathan sur la dynastie Davidique* (Louvain, 1948), p. 6, n. 2, upholds

the primacy of the prose version, but maintains that both II Samuel 7 and I Chronicles 17 are dependent on an older text, with the Chronicles version nearer the original.

32. Mowinckel, *He That Cometh* (New York-Nashville, 1954), p. 100, n. 3; C. R. North, *The Old Testament Interpretation of History* (London, 1946), p. 99; R. H. Pfeiffer, *Introduction to the Old Testament* (New York, 1948), p. 371f; A. R. Johnson, *Sacral Kingship in Ancient Israel* (Cardiff, 1955), p. 23, n. 2; G. W. Ahlström, *Psalm 89* (Lund, 1959), p. 182, also doubts the priority of II Samuel 7.

33. J. L. McKenzie, *Theological Studies*, VIII (1947), 187–218. Cf. also the view of H. van den Bussche, cited in Note 31, and the remarks of Kraus, *Psalmen*, p. 622.

34. Segal, *Sifrē Shĕmuel*, is one of the few to observe that the psalmists have made free use of the oracle.

35. See below, Section VII.

36. This is so, even if, as A. R. Johnson, *Sacral Kingship*, p. 24, n. 2, points out, the phraseology is borrowed from mytho-cultic sources; see J. Pedersen, *Israel*, vol. III–IV (London-Copenhagen, 1959), pp. 655 and 724, n. 1.

37. A. Alt, *Kleine Schriften zur Geschichte des Volkes Israel*, II (Munich, 1953), 132f., points out the analogy with the covenant of God with Levi mentioned in Deuteromony 33:8ff., Jeremiah 33:21, Malachi 2:4ff., and Nehemiah 13:29. Cf. also the covenant with Phineas, Numbers 25:12f. The supreme importance of the dynastic symbolism probably explains why the theme of the shepherd origins of David, mentioned in II Samuel 7:8 and I Chronicles 17:7, irrelevant to the psalmist's purposes, has been replaced in Psalm 89:21 by the simple phrase מצאתי דוד עבדי.

38. For an analogous exegetical development, cf. Genesis 8:21f. with Jeremiah 33:20, 25. This proves, incidentally, that the terms ברית and שבועה need not always have cultic significance.

39. J. Hänel, in Rothstein-Hänel, *Das erste Buch der Chronik* (Leipzig, 1927), pp. 332ff.; McKenzie, *Theological Studies*, VIII, 208; J. Bright, *A History of Israel* (Philadelphia, 1959), p. 204 and n. 94.

40. A. Klostermann, *Die Bücher Samuelis und der Könige* (Nordlingen, 1887); C. Steuernagel, *Lehrbuch der Einleitung in das Alte Testament* (Tübingen, 1912), p. 325; M. Noth, *Die Gesetze in Pentateuch* (Halle, 1940), p. 12; cf. his *The History of Israel* (New York, 1958), p. 222; Kaufmann, *Tōlĕdōt*, II, 369; A. Bentzen, *Introduction to the Old Testament* (Copenhagen, 1959), I, 161.

41. Segal, *Sifrē Shĕmuel*, p. 276.

42. E. Sellin, *Introduction to the Old Testament* (London, 1923), p. 112, gives a date *ca.* 800 B.C.E. S. R. Driver, *An Introduction to the Literature of the Old Testament* (Edinburgh, 1913), p. 183, thinks it can hardly be later than 700, in the main.

43. P. Dhorme, *Les Livres de Samuel* (Paris, 1910), p. 362.

44. J. Wellhausen, *Die Composition des Hexateuchs* (Berlin, 1889), p. 257.

45. H. P. Smith, *The Books of Samuel* (New York, 1909), p. 297; cf. B. Stade, *Encyclopaedia Biblica* (New York, 1903), column 4278, who feels it may even be post-Exilic.

46. Pfeiffer, *Introduction to the Old Testament*, p. 371.

47. See on this and the following, Kaufmann, *Tōlĕdōt*, vol. IV (8) (1956), pp. 460-465.

48. J. Wellhausen, *Prolegomena to History of Ancient Israel* (New York, 1957), p. 19, n. 1. Cf. Kaufmann, *Tōlĕdōt*, vol. II (4), p. 396. This is true even through Deuteronomy 25:19, which uses the same formula, was interpreted in I Samuel 15:2ff. as referring to the time of Saul.

49. *Contra* Pfeiffer, *Introduction to the Old Testament*, p. 373, whose view has recently been upheld by J. Liver, *The House of David* [Hebrew] (Jerusalem, 1959), pp. 64 f., esp. n. 1. Even if his own view is mistaken, Liver's criticism of Kaufmann, *Tōlĕdōt*, vol. II (5), pp. 525–526, 663, n. 39, who sees in the lament a reference to Hezekiah, is correct. See also the criticism of this view by Segal, *Mbŏ'*, vol. III, p. 531, n. 23. Equally

objectionable are the views of Segal himself, *ibid.*, and Chajes, [Hebrew] Commentary to Psalms, p. 97, who refer to the death of Josiah, and of Briggs, *The Book of Psalms*, II, 250, who sees in the exile of Jehoiachin the occasion of the lament. Apart from other objections, in neither instance was any attempt made to place an outsider upon the throne of David.

50. This is only possible meaning of verse 46, "הקצרת ימי עלומיו," as may be seen from Psalm 102:24, where the speaker is the psalmist himself. Further, the preceding verses all imply that the king is still alive.

51. On Isaiah chapter 7, see H. L. Ginsberg, "Judah and Transjordan Steles from 734–582 B.C.E.," *Alexander Marx Jubilee Volume* (New York, 1950), pp. 347–368, esp. p. 348, n. 7, and his "Immanuel," *Tarbiz* 20:29–32 (1950). It is quite likely that the use of the expression בית דוד in Isaiah 7:2, 13, is intended to point up the threat to the dynasty. Note also Isaiah 9:1–6, the affirmation of the eternity of the Davidic House and cf. verse 6, "ועד עולם. . . אתה להכין, ממלכתו ועל דוד כסא על" with Psalm 89:5, 30, 37 and II Samuel 7:12–13, 16.

52. For the name ben Tab'el, see W. F. Albright, "The Son of Tabeel," *BASOR* 140:34f. (1955). It is not necessary to presume, with Albright, that the puppet was a son of Uzziah or Jotham. Noth, *The History of Israel*, p. 259, thinks he was probably an Aramean, and B. Mazar, "The House of Tobias," *Tarbiz* 12:122f. (1941); *Encyclopaedia Biblica* [Hebrew], II, 80, makes the interesting suggestion that the imposter may have been connected with the later distinguished Tobiad family.

53. For the general historicity of the Chronicles account, see the remark of J. Bright, *A History of Israel*, p. 256, n. 10.

The Psalm for the Sabbath Day (PS 92)

I. THE LEVITICAL PSALMS

As is well known, the Levitical choir in the second temple chanted each day of the week a chapter of the Psalter to accompany the libation of wine that followed the *tamid* offering.[1] According to rabbinic report, the seven selections were the Hebrew Psalms 24, 48, 82, 94, 81, 93, and 92.[2] The Greek Psalter, too, reflects this liturgical tradition in the additional superscriptions it had affixed to five of these seven.[3]

It is no longer possible to determine with certainty the origin of this temple custom. Graetz[4] assigned it to the declining years of the Second Commonwealth. He maintained that the content and message of the seven selected psalms were felt to be peculiarly appropriate to the depressing events of those times. Maarsen,[5] apparently quite independently of Graetz, similarly connected them with the deteriorating conditions of that period.

However, in the total absence of any source material on which to base this theory, it must be admitted that Cheyne's criticism of Graetz is very convincing.[6] He pointed out that the last years of Persian rule also constituted a gloomy chapter in Jewish history and could, as well, have supplied the motive for initiating the daily psalm readings. However, and this is even more decisive, the explanation of Graetz would make the completion of the Greek translation far too late. If, as is generally accepted, the Greek Psalter achieved its final form some time in the second century B.C.E.,[7] then the choice of the Levitical psalms must have been made at a still earlier period.

Liebreich[8] has pointed out that the seven psalms share a common association of ideas, words, and phrases. According to him, it is this phenomenon that accounts for the particular choice and the order of recitation in the temple service. In fact, says Liebreich, it is only in this way that it is possible to explain Ps 92 as the last of the series, for it serves as a sort of ideological climax to the preceding six with which it has some undoubted affinities. The order of the Levitical psalms thus follows a determined pattern.

This thesis has the merit of relieving the choice of psalms from dependency upon any specific set of historical circumstances. But it implies either that all seven were simultaneously chosen for their liturgical purpose or, if not, that Ps 92 was certainly the last of the selections. The fact of the matter is, however, that our received Hebrew text has a liturgical rubric for Ps 92 and for that alone. The possibility arises, therefore, that at the time of the final redaction of the Book of Psalms only Ps 92 was sung in the temple in connection with the *tamid* offering on the Sabbath, the recitation of the other six not yet having been instituted. To be sure, Graetz believed that these latter, too, once had their liturgical superscriptions in the Hebrew text; but attempts to explain the omission, either on deliberate or accidental grounds, have not proved convincing.[9] Furthermore, if all the seven psalms were selected at one and the same time, and if that selection antedated the final redaction of the Psalter, it would indeed be strange that the order of the latter was not made to conform to the temple liturgical practice, at least in respect of the three psalms belonging to the fourth book. Consequently, the likelihood is that the Levitical psalms became part of the *tamid* service after the Book of Psalms had achieved its present form. In that case, the lone rubric for Ps 92 is highly significant. It must be indicative of deliberate selection for the Sabbath day, prior to, and independent of, the other six.

II. THE SABBATH AND THE CULT

Now it would be most surprising if the earliest liturgy did not, in fact, comprise psalms written for, or selected for the Sabbath. For in biblical literature it is the day of God, *par excellence*. It was common to both the northern and southern kingdoms[10] and undoubtedly belongs to the most ancient institutions of Israel.[11] Of all the sacred days in the Hebrew calendar, it alone is ascribed to pre-Israelite times. Its great antiquity is attested to by its frequent association with the new moon festival[12] which, likewise, does not have its origin in the history of Israel. The great prominence which it achieved in the religious life of the people is illustrated by the fact that it is the only festival included in the Decalogue. We encounter it immediately after the exodus[13] and again during the desert sojournings.[14] It repeatedly heads the lists of sacred seasons,[15] and its injunctions are to be found no less than ten times in the Pentateuch.[16] For the individual, the Sabbath observance meant special and unique restrictions[17] and its profanation carried with it the penalty of death or excision.[18] For the community as a whole it was a joyous day of solemn assembly,[19] highlighted by sacrificial exercises,[20] and, apparently, by the changing of the temple royal guards.[21] Above all, in biblical theology, the Sabbath, "holy unto God,"[22] is the symbol of the covenant between God and Israel;[23] thus its neglect could be looked upon as one of the causes of the national disasters.[24] In view of this pre-eminence of the Sabbath in the religious and cultic life of Israel, as well as in the prophetic consciousness, it cannot be doubted that the choice of a psalm (or psalms) to accompany the Sabbath sacrifice must have preceded the selections for the weekday offerings. If then, the psalm for the Sabbath day, of all the seven Levitical psalms, is the only one with a superscription in the Hebrew Bible, it is precisely because it was chronologically the first of the series, the other six having been instituted at a later time and as a daily extension of the Sabbath practice.

III. THE LITURGICAL CHARACTER OF PS 92

Gunkel[25] and Mowinckel[26] classified Ps 92 among the individual thanksgiving hymns. Briggs,[27] on the other hand, observed that it was "eminently suited for worship whether in the temple or synagogue." Snaith[28] goes so far as to state that the psalm "was definitely written for the service of the Temple." There is much evidence to support this view. The mention of morning and evenings (vs. 3) suggests a connection with the daily sacrificial worship.[29] The opening exhortation strengthens the impression. The phrase טוב להודות לד' (vs. 2), with the mention of חסדך (vs. 3), is strongly reminiscent of the recurrent liturgical formula הודו לד' כי־טוב כי לעולם חסדו.[30] We are reminded of it in connection with the *todah* offering (Ps 100 4–5): הודו לו ברכו שמו. It finds an echo in Jeremiah's vision of the temple rebuilt (Jer 33 10–11): עוד ישמע במקום־הזה ...,קול אמרים הודו את־ד' צבאות כי־טוב ד' כי־לעולם חסדו מבאים תודה בית ד' and again in the Psalter in connection with sacrifice (Ps 54 8): בנדבה אזבחה־לך אודה שמך ד' כי־טוב. The Chronicler[31] thus finds it necessary to have the Levitical choir sing it to the accompaniment of instrumental music at Solomon's dedication of the temple. It was also, apparently part of the congregational service recited on the eve of battle.[32] It may be safely assumed then that vss. 2–3 are an invocation to worship in connection with sacrifice. If, in addition, we note the musical instructions in vs. 4, and if we compare them with those cited in other psalms undoubtedly produced in the temple service,[33] then our psalm becomes indisputably stamped as congregational and cultic.

IV. THE CHOICE OF THE PSALM

The foregoing conclusion naturally leads to consideration of the reason for choosing Ps 92 as the temple Sabbath hymn. Scholarly opinion is well-nigh unanimous that the rubric merely designates the occasion on which, in later times, the psalm was publicly recited, and that there is absolutely no connection between the content of the psalm and the Sabbath day.[34] But surely, whoever was responsible for introducing the hymn into the Sabbath liturgy obviously did find what was to him a satisfactory relationship. He must have discovered something in it that intimately corresponded to the dominant themes of the day for which it was selected. In the same way that Ps 30 was found to be eminently suited for a temple dedication, and Ps 100 appropriate to the *todah* offering, so the caption to Ps 92 must be regarded as descriptive as well as liturgical. It remains, therefore, to examine the contents of our psalm in the light of the biblical Sabbath.

V. THE CREATION MOTIF

The first great Sabbath theme in biblical literature is the mythic-cosmogonic. The Sabbath is the symbol of creation and of cessation from creation. It expresses human imitation of "the primordial gesture of the Lord"[35] when he transformed chaos into cosmos. This is three times explicitly stated in the Pentateuch[36] and is clearly presupposed, if not specifically mentioned, in the frequent polarity of six days of work and a seventh of rest.[37] Does this cosmic theme find expression in our psalm?

Let us begin with vs. 8. It has not been entirely overlooked that the syntactical construction ויציצו . . . בפרח points to a particular event that has taken place in the past.[38] This is the usual import of the infinitive with a preposition being followed by an imperfect consecutive.[39] What salvation does the psalmist have in mind? The commentaries variously refer, without a shred of supporting evidence, to the great events of the exodus,[40] the return from Babylon,[41] or the Maccabean victories.[42] In the opinion of this writer the reference is not historical but mythological, and it is this mythological background which provides one of the keys to the selection and suitability of Ps 92 for the Sabbath day. Behind the literary composition lurks the popular creation myth of the Hebrew Bible. This myth controls the imagery and influences the very language and style of the psalm.

The first clue is the striking parallel between vs. 10 and Ugaritic text III AB. A, 8 f. (Gordon 68:8 f.). This was pointed out long ago by Ginsberg[43] and has been frequently cited since;[44] but never in relation to vs. 8 or the problem of the psalm as a whole. It will be remembered that in the great struggle for dominion between Baal, god of fertility, and Yam, personification of watery chaos, the divine craftsman, *Ktr - w - Ḥss*, encourages Baal with these words: *ht . ibk / bᶜlm . ht . ibk . tmḫs . ht. tṣmt ṣrtk,*[45]

> Now thine enemy, O Baal,
> Now thine enemy wilt thou smite,
> Now wilt thou cut off thine adversary.

The resemblance to MT Ps 92 10 is undeniable, not only in verbal correspondence, but also syntactically:

כי הנה איביך ד' כי־הנה איביך יאבדו יתפרדו כל־פעל יאון,

> For, behold, thine enemies, O Lord,
> For, behold, thine enemies shall perish;
> All workers of iniquity shall be scattered.

The basic question is: is this biblical parallel nothing more than mere literary convention, or is there a more direct relationship with the context of the Ugaritic passage? In other words, is vs. 10 part of a more elaborate mythological background upon which the understanding of the psalm hinges? To find an answer to this question we shall have to analyze carefully the language of the psalm in the light of other biblical passages dealing with God's victory over His enemies. We note at once that one of the most common devices is to express the evil deeds and punishment of the historical wicked in terms of the mythical conflict of God with the rebellious forces of primeval chaos.[46] The most outstanding passages are these:

(i) *Isa 17 12–14.* The plunderers and bespoilers of Israel (vs. 14) are compared to noisy seas and turbulent mighty waters. Gunkel and Cassuto both recognized that the language is saturated with that characteristic of the Hebrew combat myth: מים רבים, מים כבירים ימים, מים כבירים, שאה, גער.

(ii) *Isa 27 1.* The sinful ones of the earth (26 21) are the historical objects of divine wrath who are designated by the very names of the mythological monsters, לויתן נחש ברח, לויתן נחש עקלתון, התנין אשר בים.

(iii) *Isa 51 9–10.* The prophet invokes God's mighty power for the redemption of Israel, demonstrated in days of old in victory over primeval monsters רהב, תנין, ים, תהום רבה. It is apparent from the context that the oppressor of Israel is meant.

(iv) *Hab 3 8–15.* God, in his fury, strides the earth thrashing the nations and smashing to pieces the head of the wicked to deliver his people. The mythological background is too well known to need stressing. The entire passage is replete with the key words of the combat myth.

(v) *Ps 74 13–15.* God's decisive defeat of his mythical, primeval enemies is invoked as an assurance of a like victory over the present historical enemies of Israel, mentioned in vss. 3, 10, 18.

(vi) *Job 38 8–11.* Here again, the defeat of the monster ים, cited as evidence of God's overwhelming power, is followed by mention of the impotence of the wicked (vss. 13, 15).

In the light of this well-established, consistent, and widespread exegetical tradition, we are entitled to conclude that the similarity of Ps 92 10 to the Ugaritic text cited above implies that the Hebrew verse, too, has its origin in the combat myth. To clinch the argument, we may cite the psalmist's use of יתפרדו. The scattering of the enemies is an element common to many of the biblical fragments of the myth. Practically identical with the idea expressed in our verse is Ps 89 11 : אתה דכאת כחלל רהב בזרוע עזך פזרת אויביך. The same notion is expressed in Ps 104 7: מן־גערתך ינוסון, which corresponds phraseologically and contextually to Isa 17 13: וגער בו ונס ממרחק. It is more than likely that the cultic cry of Num 10 35, קומה ד' ויפצו איביך וינסו משנאיך מפניך, expressing the same theme, has its origin in the language of the same ancient epic of the divine combat. All this, of course, is strongly reminiscent of Enûma Eliš IV: 106–109, which describes how, after the slaughter of Tiâmat by Marduk, the band of rebels was routed and dispersed.[47]

To sum up thus far: the events of the past referred to in vs. 8 are those described in vs. 10. The latter is an historicized, if fragmentary, version of the popular Israelite combat epic. Despite its disintegrated form, the verse has preserved the characteristic elements and even the terminology of the original.

This conclusion has now to be coordinated with another feature of the Israelite tradition. In the Ugaritic texts, no material has yet turned up showing any cosmogonic association with the struggle between Baal and Yam (or Lotan).[48] But in the corresponding Babylonian version the combat between Marduk and Tiâmat is basic to the creation of the world. Gunkel[49] effectively demonstrated, and the Canaanite material confirmed his conclusion, that it is the Mesopotamian story to which popular Israelite poetic tradition is closest in content if not in language. Building upon Gunkel's material, and having the Ugaritic epics to work with, Cassuto[50] established beyond a shadow of a doubt that a popular and independent epic existed in ancient Israel in which the struggle between God and the mutinous forces of primeval chaos was inextricably interwoven with the Hebrew ideas of creation. Several biblical passages most clearly illustrate this association:

(i) *Isa 51 9 ff.* It is to be noticed how the struggle with the forces of chaos took place in "days of old," ימי קדם. That the time of creation is meant is quite apparent from Ps 74 12 which also uses מקדם in the same context and is followed in vss. 16–17 by the divine ordination of day and night and the seasons of the year. Further, Prov 8 22, in the identical mythological reference, expressly defines קדם as the onset of the cosmogonic process.[51] Finally, Isa 51 13, which recalls the creation of the world, precedes another allusion to the combat myth to which, in turn, is juxtaposed a second recital of cosmogony.

(ii) *Jer 31 35.* Here again, the fixing of the heavenly luminaries is immediately associated with the "stirring-up of the sea." The phrase רגע הים ויהמו גליו is part of the standard vocabulary of the combat myth, occurring in the same connection in Isa 51 15 and Job 26 12. Moreover, the final phrase, ד' צבאות שמו, is to be found, significantly enough, also in Isa 51 15; Amos 4 13; and 5 8 (cf. 9 6), all of which are cosmogonic references.

(iii) *Pss 74 12–17;* (iv) *89 10–13;* (v) *93 1–4.* In each case we have the identical pattern of God's triumphant exploits at the time of creation described in the same stereotyped language.

(vi) *Ps 104.* The establishment of the cosmic order is described in vs. 5, followed at once by mention of the turbulent seas put to flight by

God's rebuke, גערתך. With vs. 7a is to be compared especially Isa 17 13, as well as Isa 50 2; Nah 1 4; Ps 18 16; Job 26 11, in all of which âðø occurs as part of the standard vocabulary. Similarly, vs. 9 is to be found, with but slight variation, in Jer 5 22 and Prov 8 29.

(vii) *Psalm 148.* Vs. 5 mentions creation by divine fiat. Then follows חק נתן ולא יעבר (vs. 6b). The phrase is a clear echo of the combat myth, for it corresponds to Jer 5 22, חק־עולם ולא יעברנהו; Ps 104 9, גבול שמת בל־יעברון; Prov 8 27, בחקו חוג על־פני תהום; Job 26 10, חק חג על־פני־מים. In each one of these instances the reference is explicitly to God's confining of the rebellious sea. The mutinous enemies, תנינים and תהמות, appear, in fact, in Ps 148 7. The very attenuated form of the myth in this psalm makes its connection with cosmogony all the more significant.

(viii) *Prov 8 22–29.* This is perhaps the most specific of all the passages in which combat and creation are expressly associated. At the very outset of the cosmogonic process (vss. 22–26, 29), God constrained תהום (27) and confined ים (29). These latter phrases have already been discussed above in connection with Ps 148.

The reiterated association of the establishment of the cosmic order with the outcome of the combat, expressed through the constant repetition of a commonly shared vocabulary and the employment of standard clichés,[52] constitute proof enough that these passages are drawn from an independent Israelite version of the myth. The fact that the prophets occasionally[53] use the combat myth without reference to creation does not in the least imply a dependence upon the Canaanite tradition. It is simply that by the natural process of artistic development the myth has undergone degeneration and its language become used as a mere literary convention. In some instances the very inextricability of the association of combat and cosmogony may itself be responsible for the absence of the one or the other, the missing element being tacitly assumed.

A case in point is Ps 33. The clear description of creation in vss. 6–9 has no direct reference to the struggle between God and his primeval enemies.[54] Yet it cannot escape notice that immediately following is the somewhat inconsequential assurance that God nullifies the counsel of the nations and renders ineffectual the plans of the peoples (vs. 10). The juxtaposition is understandable, however, if the creation narrative conjures up a mental association of a mythical combat, at once historicized in the conventional manner.

This brings us back to our original starting point. Ps 92 8 refers to a specific event that has taken place in the past, an event elucidated in vs. 10. The latter is an historicized excerpt of the popular Israelite creation-combat epic. To be sure, the myth is not explicitly articulated, and the creation motif appears in an attenuated form. Nevertheless, they both are more than presupposed within the body of the psalm. Even in their present literary transmutation the twin elements are thoroughly discernible. Witness the connection of vss. 5–6 with 8 and 10, the association of the greatness of God's works and deeds with the overthrow of His enemies. True, the phrase מה־גדלו מעשיך ד' (vs. 6) does not necessarily have to refer to the acts of creation. But if we turn to Ps 104, the great cosmogonic hymn, we find, significantly enough, that it opens with ד' אלהי גדלת מאד, followed immediately by a description of the works of creation, interspersed with citations from the combat myth (vss. 6 ff.). Again in the same psalm appears מה־רבו מעשיך ד' (vs. 24), which is but a stylistic variant of Ps 92 6 and which is succeeded by further references to cosmogony, again in explicit correlation with the combat myth. Accordingly, it would be highly unreasonable to assume that Ps 92 6 is not likewise to be interpreted as praise of God in his capacity of creator of the world. This being so, then vs. 5, too, must be construed in the same way. For מעשי ידיך there cannot be different from מעשיך of vs. 6, while פעלך is basically the same expression as is found in Ps 74 12 (פעל) and Prov 8 22 (מפעליו), in both passages specifically connected with the combat and creation.

Finally, mention must be made of vs. 9, which serves to heighten the effect of the combat background. This brief line has been variously discarded as an interpolation interrupting the connection of vss. 8 and 10,[55] or regarded as a necessary expression of the contrast between the absolute and eternally transcendent rule of God and the evanescence of the wicked.[56] However, a closer analysis shows that it is, in reality, introductory to vs. 10 and prefatory to the combat idea.

The Hebrew notion of God arousing or exalting himself is expressive of his activating the quality of retributive justice against his enemies. The synonyms most frequently employed in this connection are קום,[57] נשא,[58] or רום. The last is found several times in the Psalms:

(18 47–48);   ... וירום אלוהי ישעי: האל הנותן נקמות לי
(21 14);   רומה ד' בעזך[59]
(46 11);   ארום בגוים ארום בארץ
(108 6–7);   רומה על־שמים אלהים ... למען יחלצון ידידיך ...
(149 6–7)   רוממות אל בגרונם וחרב פיפיות בידם: לעשות
נקמה בגוים תוכחות[60] בלאמים.

Isaiah, too, uses the same verb in the identical sense three times within a few verses. Isa 33 9–10, . . . יתפרדו . . . מרום ואתה. In Isa 33 5, נשגב ד' כי שכן מרום מלא ציון משפט וצדקה, God's exaltation fills Zion with justice and righteousness. In vs. 10, the prophet employs all three synonyms for added emphasis in describing God's impending and decisive action against the enemies of Israel: אנשא עתה אקום יאמר ד' עתה ארומם עתה.[61] Accordingly, מרום in Ps 92 9 explains the destruction of the wicked, mentioned in vs. 8. It is because God exalts himself to exercise judgment upon his enemies that the latter perish in disorder.

The first of the themes of the biblical Sabbath, the motif of creation, finds its clear expression in Ps 92 and contributed towards its selection as a Sabbath hymn.[62]

VI. THE SOCIO-MORAL MOTIF

The rationale of the Sabbath, as it appears in the Book of the Covenant (Exod 23 12) and the Deuteronomic decalogue (Deut 5 14–15) is that beast, slave, and stranger alike may enjoy freedom from toil. It is not without significance that in the former source the institution of the Sabbath, weekly or septennial, follows a series of laws demanding humanity and justice for those elements of society most susceptible to exploitation.[63]

This socio-moral motif finds its reflection in the prophetic literature. Amos (8 4–6) associates the Sabbath of the hypocritical wealthy class with fraudulent business practices and the exploitation of the poor. From this one may gather that in the prophet's view the true Sabbath should be an expression of social morality. Isaiah is even more explicit. In the same breath he exhorts the people to keep justice and to do righteousness, to observe the Sabbath and to desist from evil (Isa 56 1–2).[64] Ezekiel, to whom the Sabbath is especially dear, combines its profanation with the sins of bloodshed, dishonoring of parents, oppression of the stranger, orphan, and widow (Ezek 22 6).

Now this socio-moral theme of the biblical Sabbath is, in reality, the natural concomitant of the cosmogonic. For creation means precisely the transformation of chaos into cosmos,[65] and the combat myth implies the victory of stability and order over the forces of destruction that would negate creation. That is why so frequently the Bible associates creation with divine righteousness and why human wickedness is seen as endangering the very cosmos itself.[66]

The idea of creation as an expression of God's righteousness is to be found in Ps 33. Love of justice is affirmed as being the special characteristic of God (vss. 4–5), and this is immediately exemplified in the acts of creation (vss. 6 ff.). In Ps 89 the order is reversed, but the concept is the same. The description of cosmogony (vss. 10–14) is at once followed by an affirmation of divine righteousness (vs. 15). Similarly, the idea that God firmly established the world on an immovable foundation (Ps 93 1) is closely allied to the notion of the permanent stability of God's throne of justice (vs. 2). Nor is it accidental that this latter idea is there followed by several references to the combat myth (vss. 3–4). Again, in Ps 96 10, all nature is exhorted to acclaim God's sovereign rule in founding the world and in judging the peoples with equity.[67] Deutero-Isaiah gives utterance to this selfsame concept most forcefully, as may be seen from the fact that the recitation of the classic combat myth (Isa 51 9–10) is preceded by no less than six expressions of God's justice or righteousness (vss. 1, 4–8). On the other hand, this motif is indicated negatively, but with identical force, in the description of human evildoers in terms of the mythical primeval enemies of God and the designation of socio-moral corruption as shaking the very foundations of the earth (Ps 82 2–5).[68]

This inextricable connection between God's creative works and His righteousness manifests itself in the structure of Ps 92 and constitutes its literary framework. For, after the liturgical introduction of vss. 1–4, the psalm proper opens with a reference to cosmogony (5 f.) and closes, appropriately enough, with a declaration of God's righteousness. It is precisely this association of human evil with the undoing of creation, and of both with the primeval combat, that makes the theme of the fortunes of the wicked and the righteous so appropriate to the Sabbath. Very subtly has this been interwoven with the cosmogonic in three ways: the mythical enemies of God have become historicized and the events of prehistory have become the pattern for history; the wicked with their destructive works are suggestively designated פעלי און (vs. 8) in contrast to, and in negation of, God's creative works, פעליך (vs. 5); finally, there is the correlation between the eternity (לעלם, 9) of God's retributive justice and the perpetuity (עדי־עד, 8) of the destruction of the wicked.

The second of the themes of the biblical Sabbath, the socio-moral motif, also finds its clear expression in Ps 92 and contributed towards its selection as a Sabbath hymn.

VII. THE HEPTAD OF TETRAGRAMMATA

Ps 92 employs the divine name YHWH exactly seven times.[69] In view of the widespread use of the heptad as a stylistic device, often of cultic significance,[70] in both biblical and extrabiblical sources, one is tempted to wonder whether the unusual heptad of tetragrammata was not an additional factor in making the psalm appropriate for the seventh day of the week. Attention has been drawn to the interesting fact that Ps 24, chosen for the first day of the week, mentions the divine name six times, a number reminiscent of the six days of creation alluded to there in vss. 1–2.[71] As a matter of fact, two other elements of the later synagogue Sabbath liturgy were characterized by the use of the heptad. The Amidah prayer contains seven benedictions[72] instead of the daily nineteen (originally eighteen); and Ps 29, added to the service,[73] contains the sevenfold repetition of the phrase ‫קול ה׳‬.

In the light of all this, the presence of the heptad of tetragrammata in Ps 92 might very well have been suggestive of the seventh day of the week and so have contributed further towards the selection of the psalm for the Sabbath liturgy.

VIII. SUMMARY

Ps 92, alone of the seven Levitical psalms for the days of the week, bears a liturgical superscription. This is on account of its being the first of the group to be selected, the others having been chosen after the close of the Hebrew Psalter. This psalm is a public liturgy. It was selected for the Sabbath reading because its contents were felt to correspond to the two dominant themes of the biblical Sabbath, the cosmogonic and the socio-moral. The former motif is to be found primarily in vss. 5–6, 8, 10, on the basis of Ugaritic text III AB.A, 8 f. (68:8 f.) and biblical parallels to the cosmogonic combat myth. The latter, the socio-moral, appears in the problem of the wicked and the righteous. The presence of a heptad of tetragrammata probably contributed further to the suitability of the psalm as a reading for the seventh day of the week.

NOTES

1. M. Tamid 7, 3–4. The account of Ben Sira 50 14–19 is very similar to that of the Mishnah. On Tamid as the oldest tractate, cf. L. Ginzberg, *Studies into the Origin of the Mishnah* [reprinted, with additions and corrections, from *JJLPH*, 1 (1919), pp. 33–44; 265–295]. Cf. on this subject Nachman Krochmal, *Moreh Nebukhei Ha-Zeman*, ed. S. Rawidowicz, p. 224, and the remarks of Ch. Albeck, *Mabo La-Mishnah*, p. 72. For a

detailed description of the daily temple service, cf. E. Schürer, *A History of the Jewish People in the Time of Jesus Christ*, II, i, pp. 291–96; S. Bialoblotzki, *Alei Ayin: The Salman Schocken Jubilee Volume*, pp. 25–74, esp. p. 59.

2. M. Tamid 7, 4; B. Rosh Hashanah 31a; Aboth d'Rabbi Nathan 1:1, ed. Schechter, p. 3 [J. Goldin, *The Fathers According to Rabbi Nathan*, pp. 11 f.]; Soferim, ed. Higger, 18, 2, pp. 311 f.; Shir Hashirim Rabba 4, 8. On Tamid 7, 4 as a baraitha, cf. S. L. Rapoport, *Bikkurei Ha-Ittim* (1831), p. 52; Ch. Albeck, *Untersuchungen über die Redaktion der Mishna*, p. 134; Ginzberg, *op. cit.*, p. 283. On the transference of these psalms from the temple to the synagogue liturgy, cf. P. Taanith 4:5; 68d; B. Arakhin 11b; Soferim 18:2.

3. Ps 24 (23) τῆς μιᾶς σαββάτων; 48 (47) δευτέρα σαββάτου; 94 (93) τετράδι σαββάτων; 93 (92) εἰς τὴν ἡμέραν τοῦ προσαββάτου; 92 (91) εἰς τὴν ἡμέραν τοῦ σαββάτου. H. Graetz, *MGWJ*, 27 (1878), p. 218, assumes that Pss 81, 82, also originally had liturgical superscriptions in the Greek. The Syriac has a rubric only for Ps 24. However, the superscriptions generally in this version are quite arbitrary and historically worthless; cf. A. Neubauer, *Studia Biblica et Ecclesiastica*, II, p. 9; W. Bloemendaal, *The Headings of the Psalms in the East Syrian Church*.

4. *Op. cit.*, pp. 217–22; *Kritischer Commentar zu den Psalmen*, pp. 55–56.

5. I. Maarsen, *We-Zoth LiYhudah: Dissertationes Hebraicae Ludovico Blau*, pp. 197–99.

6. T. K. Cheyne, *The Origin of the Psalter*, p. 83.

7. B. J. Roberts, *The O. T. Texts and Versions*, pp. 115 f.

8. L. J. Liebreich, *Eretz-Yisrael*, III, pp. 170–73.

9. Graetz (*Kritischer Commentar*, pp. 55 f., 78) believed that the superscription to the other daily psalms were purposely omitted from our Hebrew text. Neubauer (*op. cit.*, p. 4), finding this explanation unsatisfactory, laid the blame on a careless copyist. It is strange that neither one considered the third possibility.

10. II Kings 4 22–23; Hos 2 13.

11. Cf. H. Gunkel, *Schöpfung und Chaos in Urzeit und Endzeit*, pp. 13 f.; J. Pedersen, *Israel*, III–IV, pp. 290 f.; W. Eichrodt, *Theology of the O. T.*, I, p. 131, n. 4; R. de Vaux, *Ancient Israel*, pp. 475–83, esp. pp. 479 f.

12. II Kings 4 23; Isa 1 13; 66 23; Ezek 46 1, 3; Hos 2 13; Amos 8 5. Cf. J. Wellhausen, *Prolegomena to the History of Ancient Israel*, p. 112; Yehezkel Kaufmann, *The Religion of Israel*, p. 306, n. 6.

13. Exod 16 22–27.

14. Num 15 32–36.

15. Lev 23 3; Num 28 9–10; Neh 10 34; I Chron 23 31; II Chron 2 3; 8 13; 31 3.

16. Exod 20 8–11; 23 12; 31 13–17; 34 21; 35 2–3; Lev 19 3, 30; 23 3; 26 2; Deut 5 12–15.

17. Exod 16 25–26; 20 10; 23 12; 31 14–15; 34 21; 35 2–3; Lev 23 3; Num 15 32–33; Deut 5 14; Isa 58 13; Jer 17 21–27; Amos 8 5; Neh 10 32; 13 15–22.

18. Exod 31 14–15; 35 2; Num 15 36.

19. Isa 58 13; Hos 2 13.

20. Lev 24 8; Num 28 9–10; Isa 1 13; Ezek 45 1; 46 1–5, 12; Neh 10 34. For further evidence of the cultic aspect of the Sabbath, cf. Isa 66 23; I Chron 9 32; 23 31; II Chron 2 3; 8 13; 23 4–8; 31 3.

21. II Kings 11 5, 7. Cf. J. A. Montgomery, *The Book of Kings*, p. 419; de Vaux, *op. cit.*, p. 469.

22. Exod 16 23; 31 15; 35 2.

23. Exod 31 13, 17; Ezek 20 12, 20. Cf. Isa 56 4, 6, in which the Sabbath is associated with God's covenant.

24. Jer 17 21–27; Ezek 20 13 ff.; 22 26–31; 23 38; so Neh 13 17–18. Cf. Lev 26 34–35 for a similar notion concerning the profanation of the sabbatical year.

25. H. Gunkel and J. Begrich, *Einleitung in die Psalmen*, § 2, 54; § 7, 8.

26. S. Mowinckel, *Psalmenstudien*, I, pp. 161, 163; VI, p. 28.

27. C. A. Briggs, *The Book of Psalms*, II, p. 283.

28. N. H. Snaith, *Studies in the Psalter*, p. 73.

29. Cf. Pss 5 4; 134 1.

30. Pss 106 1; 107 1; 118 1, 29; 136 1.

31. II Chron 5 13.

32. II Chron 20 21.

33. Pss 33 2–3; 98 4–6; 150 3–4. Cf. A. Bentzen, *Introduction to the O. T.*, I, p. 150; H-J. Kraus, *Psalmen* (*BKAT*, xv), pp. 261, 677, 969.

34. Cf. S. R. Driver, *An Introduction to the Literature of the O. T.*[9], p. 370; O. Eissfeldt, *Einleitung in das Alte Testament*[2], p. 557; Kraus, *op. cit.*, p. 642. A vague association with the Sabbath was found by Mowinckel, *op. cit.*, I, pp. 160 f., 163, who felt that the joyful tone of the psalm was the sole determining factor in its choice; and by B. D. Eerdmans, *The Hebrew Book of Psalms*, p. 440, who thought that later scribes wanted to stimulate "devotion to Jahu." Franz Delitzsch, *Biblical Commentary on the Psalms*, III, pp. 25 f., interpreted the superscription eschatologically, relying upon rabbinic sources. For the latter, in addition to those cited in note 2, cf. B. Sanhedrin 97a, Seder Eliahu Rabba (ed. M. Friedmann), p. 7; Mekilta (ed. J. Z. Lauterbach, 1935), III, p. 199. This eschatological interpretation of the rubric of Ps 92 was no doubt prompted by the solution to the problem of evil and the glorious future awaiting the righteous as expressed in vss. 8–16. For the use of "Sabbath" as a symbolic description of the world-to-come in Jewish and Christian literature, cf. L. Ginzberg, *The Legends of the Jews*, V, p. 128, n. 140. On the other hand, Delitzsch, *op. cit.*, also interpreted vss. 5–6 as referring to God's revelatory role in creation and history. Cf. A. F. Kirkpatrick, *The Book of Psalms*, p. 559. This view, too, though less prominent, figures in rabbinic sources; cf. B. Rosh Hashanah 31a and targum to Ps 92 1. For the idea of Adam's authorship of the psalm, cf. Ginzberg, *op. cit.*, p. 112, n. 103.

35. M. Eliade, *Cosmos and History*, p. 123; cf. T. H. Gaster, *Thespis*, pp. 17–18.

36. Gen 2 1–3; Exod 20 11; 31 17.

37. Exod 23 12; 31 14–15; 34 21; 35 2; Lev 23 3; Deut 5 13–14.

38. Cf. Kirkpatrick, *op. cit.*, p. 560: "The tenses. . . do not merely express a general truth, but point to some particular event." Cf. Delitzsch, *op. cit.*, p. 28; F. Baethgen, *Die Psalmen*, p. 283.

39. So Lev 16 1; I Kings 18 18; Isa 38 9; Ezek 16 36; Ps 105 12 f.; Job 38 7, 9 ff.—all with preposition ב. For examples with other prepositions, cf. Gen 24 30; 39 18; Jos 8 24; Jer 9 12. Cf. S. R. Driver, *A Treatise on the Use of the Tenses in Hebrew*, § 118, p. 139; *Gesenius' Hebrew Grammar* (ed. Kautzsch-Cowley), § 114r.

40. Cf. E. J. Kissane, *The Book of Psalms*, II, pp. 110, 112.

41. Cf. T. Witton Davies, *The Psalms* (The Century Bible), II, p. 137.

42. Cf. B. Duhm, *Die Psalmen*, § 14 and p. 348; Briggs, *op. cit.*, I, pp. xc, xcii; II, p. 283.

43. H. L. Ginsberg, *Kitbei Ugarit*, p. 76, n. 8–9; *BA*, 8 (1945), pp. 54 f.

44. Cf. W. Baumgartner, "Ras Schamra u. das Alte Testament," *ThR*, 13 (1941), p. 8; U. Cassuto, *Tarbiz*, 14 (1943), p. 3; *Knesseth*, 8 (1943–44), pp. 136 f.; *The Goddess Anath* [Hebrew] (Jerusalem, 1953), p. 56.

45. A. S. Kapelrud, *Baal in the Ras Shamra Texts*, p. 104, points out that these words are not only a promise, but a real incantation to influence the battle in favor of Baal.

46. This phenomenon has been thoroughly dealt with, first by H. Gunkel, *op. cit.*, in the light of the Accadian cosmogonic literature, and subsequently, by U. Cassuto, *Knesseth* (1943–44), pp. 121–42, with reference to the Ugaritic epics. For the historicizing of this myth, cf. J. Pedersen, *op. cit.*, I, pp. 472 ff.; Gaster, *op. cit.*, pp. 40, 442–52; B. S. Childs, *Myth and Reality in the O. T.* (Studies in Biblical Theology, No. 27).

47. Cf. S. Langdon, *The Babylonian Epic of Creation*, p. 141; E. Speiser, *ANET*, p. 67; A. Heidel, *The Babylonian Genesis*, p. 31.

48. Cf. Childs, *op. cit.*, p. 37, n. 3; Kapelrud, *op. cit.*, p. 131, n. 2. For the relationship between Yam and Lotan, see *ibid.*, p. 102.

49. *Op. cit.* Cf. W. F. Albright, *From the Stone Age to Christianity*, p. 271.

50. In addition to those works cited in n. 44, cf. *From Adam to Noah* [Hebrew] (Jerusalem, 1953), pp. 20–33, 30–31; *Commentary on the Book of Exodus* (Jerusalem, 1953), pp. 119–25; *Encyclopedia Biblica* [Hebrew] (Jerusalem, 1954), II, pp. 343–46; see also, Y. Kaufmann, *op. cit.*, pp. 11, 62.

51. Cf. further the use of מקדם in Hab 1 12.

52. The same phenomena exist in two other relevant passages—Job 26 7–13; 38 4–11.

53. Isa 27 1; Nah 1 4; Hab 3 8.

54. But note the mention of ים, and תהומות in vs. 7.

55. T. Witton Davies, *op. cit.*, p. 138.

56. Kirkpatrick, Delitzsch, Briggs, Kissane.

57. Pss 3 8; 7 7, 9 20; 44 22; 74 22; 76 10; 82 8. Cf. Num 10 35.

58. Pss 94 2; 99 8.

59. Note the plaint and prayers against the enemies in vss. 9–13.

60. רוממות here means "declarations of God's retributive justice."

61. With Isa 33 10 cf. Ps 7 7—קומה, הנשא followed by ועורה אלי משפט צוית; vs. 8—למרום; vs. 9—ד' ידין עמים.

62. That the combat myth persisted well after biblical times may be proved by the references to it in apocryphal and apocalyptic literature; cf. Enoch 60 7–9; Pr of Mana 2–4, Apoc Bar 29 4, Ps Sol 2 25–27; IV Esd 6 49–52. For the NT references, cf. H. Wallace, *BA*, 11, 3 (1948), pp. 61–68; G. E. Wright, *Biblical Archaeology*, p. 3. For the numerous rabbinic references, cf. Ginzberg, *op. cit.*, I, pp. 14–15, 18; v, pp. 17–18, n. 50–52; pp. 26–27, n. 72–73. Accordingly, there can be no question but that even in late second temple times the combat myth was still understood in connection with creation and that this theme was thoroughly recognizable.

63. Cf. the comment of Abraham ibn Ezra to Exod 23 12.

64. Cf. Isaiah's similar conception of the ideal fast day, 58 2–7.

65. Cf. Isa 45 18 f. and the remarks of J. Pedersen, *op. cit.*, p. 472.

66. For the relationship between God's attributes of creativeness and of goodness, cf. I. Epstein, *The Faith of Judaism*, pp. 238 f. The association of divine creation with divine justice is a prominent theme of the Jewish New Year liturgy. Cf. היום הרת עולם היום יעמיד במשפט כל יצורי עולמים.

67. Reference should also be made to Ps 94 9 which, in the context of the psalm as a whole, expresses the idea that God's creativity and his attribute of justice are interconnected.

68. It is quite possible that the "darkness" of those who pervert justice in Ps 82 5 contains more than a hint of the darkness of primeval chaos. On this latter theme, cf. J. Pedersen, *op. cit.*, I–II, pp. 464 f., 473. A similar imagery existed in Egypt where the sun, the creator, daily defeated his enemy, darkness (symbolized by the snake Apophis), representing the powers of death and destruction; cf. H. Frankfort, *Ancient Egyptian Religion*, pp. 18, 51 f., 132 f.

69. So noted P. Berakoth 4:3 (8a), P. Taanith 2:2 (65c): ז' אזכרות שכתוב במזמור שיר ליום השבת. Cf. Yalkut, Psalms §§ 709, 843. Briggs, *op. cit.*, p. 286, regards the divine name in vs. 9 as a gloss, unnecessarily lengthening the line. H-J. Kraus, *op. cit.*, p. 641, would delete, *metris causa*, the tetragrammata of vss. 5, 9. For the justification of our present text, cf. Delitzsch, *op. cit.*, p. 26. Furthermore, comparison might be made with Assyro-Babylonian hymns and prayers which contain a sevenfold mention of Enlil's name. For the latter, cf. J. and H. Lewy, *HUCA*, 17 (1942–43), p. 22.

70. R. Gordis, *JBL*, 62 (1943), pp. 17–26; Cassuto, *From Adam to Noah*, pp. 5 ff.; N. M. Sarna, *JBL*, 76 (1957), pp. 20 f.; G. D. Cohen, *PAAJR*, 29 (1960–61), p. 87, n. 115, 116. Cf. the present author's study of Ps 89. Loewenstam, *Tarbiẓ* 31 (1962), pp. 228–235.

71. L. J. Liebreich, *op. cit.*, p. 171.

72. Varying reasons for the significance of seven here are given in rabbinic sources; cf. B. Berakoth 29a and those cited in n. 69, on which cf. L. Ginzberg, *A Commentary on the Palestinian Talmud* [Hebrew], III, p. 290.

73. On the place of Ps 29 in the synagogue liturgy, cf. S. Spiegel, *The Jews*[3], ed. L Finkelstein, pp. 861–63.

Epic Substratum in the Prose of Job *

I. INTRODUCTION

The relationship of the prologue to the epilogue of the Book of Job and of both to the poem has long been a subject of scholarly debate.[1] Wellhausen[2] maintained that the poet borrowed directly from a folk saga both the material and form for his own work. Duhm[3] even went so far as to suggest that the entire prose parts were excerpted from a *"Volksbuch"* and that these antedate the poem. On the other hand, Kautzsch[4] held that nothing more than the name of a righteous man called Job was borrowed from tradition. Most recently, Tur-Sinai[5] has upheld the view that the present narrative framework of Job is much later than the poem and has supplanted an earlier story lost by the time the poem was put into its final form.

　　Whether or not the prose and poetry of the book originally constituted a unity is outside the scope of this study. But it is certain that the prologue and epilogue belong to each other and are the work of a single author. The points of contact are too numerous and too basic to be fortuitous.[6] In both God refers to Job as עבדי איוב (1 8, 2 3 ‖ 42 7, 8); Job acts the role of intercessor (1 5 ‖ 42 8–10); he offers עולות to assuage God's anger (1 5 ‖ 42 8); the order of enumeration of his material possessions is the same in both instances (1 3 ‖ 42 12); the precise figures of Job's restored and doubled possessions given in the epilogue (42 12) presuppose a knowledge of the prologue (1 3); the three friends are mentioned in exactly the same order (2 11 ‖ 42 9) and without any reference to Elihu.

If the narrative framework is the product of a single hand, is it late or early? The patriarchal background of the story is detailed and consistent. Wealth is measured in terms of cattle and slaves[7] (1 3, 42 12, cf. Gen 12 16, 32 5). Religion is primitive, expressing itself in private sacrifice without central shrine or priesthood and with the early concept that the anger of God can be assuaged by sacrifice[8] (1 5, 42 8). Sabeans and Chaldeans are still marauding bands of nomads (1 15, 17). The קשיטה is still current (42 11), being mentioned elsewhere only in connection with Jacob (Gen 33 19; Josh 24 32). Job's longevity (42 16) is paralleled only in the patriarchal and pre-patriarchal periods and the closing description זקן ישבע ימים (42 17) is the same as that used of Abraham (Gen 25 8) and Isaac (Gen 25 29).

Notwithstanding the detailed consistency in the patriarchal setting and the fact that there is no satisfactory reason why the author should have invented it since it adds nothing to the understanding of the narrative, scholars were inclined neither to accept it as genuine nor to regard it as of any real value in determining the antiquity of the prologue and epilogue.[9] This skepticism was in no way dissipated by reference to Ezekiel's mention of Job (Ezek 14 14, 20) for, it was maintained, this implied only the existence of a personality named Job but not necessarily any knowledge of our particular story. Yet the discovery of the Ugaritic epics has greatly enhanced the significance of the Ezekiel passage which has had to be freshly evaluated. Spiegel,[10] in an important and masterly study, has demonstrated beyond all doubt not only that Ezekiel refers to an epic of Job well known to his contemporaries, but that this tale underlies our own narrative in the prologue and epilogue. As a matter of fact, Cassuto[11] had earlier postulated the existence of a poetic version of the story of Job upon which our prose section was based and, most recently, Gordon[12] has drawn attention to some points of contact between the Job narrative and the East Mediterranean epic.

The time would seem to be ripe for a thorough investigation of the stylistic, linguistic, and literary characteristics of the narrative framework in comparison with the available literary material from the East Mediterranean littoral. The results, it is believed, will effectively demonstrate that our prologue and epilogue contain a considerable amount of epic substratum and that our prose version would seem to be directly derived from an ancient epic of Job.

II. STYLE AND LANGUAGE

The prose style of the story conforms generally to that of the narrative portions of the Pentateuch. Yet this statement requires modification, for there has been increasing recognition of late that the supposed rigid differentiation between Biblical Hebrew prose and poetry is largely artificial and that much of what has hitherto been considered to be "pure prose" is, in fact, saturated with poeticisms.[13] This is true in particular of our prologue and epilogue, for within the compass of three short chapters are to be found numerous instances of assonance and alliteration, some cases of parallelism, a relatively large number of words and phrases peculiar to poetry, some unique expressions and some forms morphologically and syntactically unique or rare.

A. Assonance and Alliteration:

1 1	ארץ עוץ
1 4	עשו משתה בית איש . . . ושלחו לשלשת אחיתיהם . . . ולשתות
1 5	. . . המשתה וישלח . . . ויקדשם והשכים . . . והעלה עלות . . . וברכו
	אלהים בלבבם
1 6, 2 1	ויהי היום
	ויבאו בני האלהים להתיצב . . . ויבוא . . .
1 7, 2 2	השטן . . . משוט
1 8, 2 3	השטן השמת
1 10	פרץ בארץ
1 12	אליו אל תשלח
1 17	כשדים שמו שלשה ראשים ויפשטו
1 19	באה מעבר המדבר
	בארבע פנו תהבית
1 20	ויקם . . . ויקרע
2 4	אשר לאיש . . . נפשו
2 6	נפשו שמר
2 11	וישמעו שלשת רעי . . . כל הרעה
	לבוא לנוד לו ולנחמו
2 12	מרחוק . . . קולם . . . ויקרעו . . . ויזרקו ראשיהם השמימה
42 8	אשא . . . עשות
42 9	ויעשו כאשר . . . וישא
42 10	שב . . . שבות

B. Parallelism:

1 10	ומקנהו פרץ בארץ מעשה ידיו ברכת
1 7, 2 2	משוט בארץ ומתהלך בה
1 22	לא חטא איוב ולא נתן תפלה לאלהים
42 11	וינדו לו וינחמו אתו[6]

C. Poetic Words and Phrases:

1 21 is pure poetry. The phrase יצא מבטן occurs, outside of Job, only in Eccles 5 14.

1 22 תפלה, outside of Job, occurs only in Jer 23 13.

2 3 לבלעו; this figurative usage in the sense of "destroying, annihilating," is infrequent in prose texts. It is worth considering whether the specialized meaning is not a reflex of Canaanite mythology. The reference may well be to the particular method by which the god Mot disposes of his prey. In the Ugaritic texts we find repeated mention of Mot swallowing his victims:

lyrt bnpš bn ilm mt	Thou shalt indeed go down into the throat of the god Mot
bmh/mrt ydd il ġzr[14]	Yea into the gullet of Il's Beloved, the Hero!
al tqrb lbn ilm mt	Do not draw near the god Mot
al yᶜdbkm kimr bph	Lest he make you like a lamb in his mouth,
klli bṯbrnqnh ṯḥtan[15]	Like a kid in his jaws ye be crushed.
yᶜrb bᶜl bkbdh bph yrd[16]	So that Baal may enter his inwards, yea descend into his mouth.

2 4 seems to be some ancient proverb.

2 7 קדקד occurs elsewhere in prose only Deut 28 35, II Sam 14 25.

Yet a closer look will show that in reality both these passages are poetic; *qdqd* is common in Ugaritic.

2 11; 42 11 נוד; in the sense of "to show grief, sympathy" it is used only in poetry.

2 13 ישב לארץ. This is an entirely poetic usage; cf. Ugaritic *ytḫ lkḫt* "sits on a throne."[17]

2 13 כאב; the nominal form is restricted to poetry.

42 12 אחרית ראשית. This combination, with one exception,[18] is never used in narrative prose. אחרית corresponds to Ugaritic *uḫryt*[19] "latter end, destiny, lot."

D. Words and Expressions Unique to Job:

1 5 הקיפו; the *hiphil* of נקף in connection with time, occurs only here. The *qal* form is found only in Isa 29 1 חגים ינקפו, cf. Ugaritic *nqpt* || *šnt*[20] = yearly cycle.

1 10 שכת בעדו; in the sense of "giving protection" the phrase is unique.

2 8 להתגרד is a *hapax legomenon*.

42 10 שב שבות (*kethib* שבית) occurs only here with reference to individuals. As such it probably reflects a very ancient, rather than late extended, usage in view of the Ugaritic personal names *ṯbᶜm, ṯbᶜnt*, which Gordon[21] takes to mean, "the god N. has returned, i.e., pitied and favored."

E. Morphology:

42 13 שבענה. The versions, commentators, and grammarians have varied in their explanation of this *hapax legomenon*. All the versions except the Targum take it as a variant of שבעה "seven." This tradition is reflected in the pre-Christian Testament of Job[22] and is followed by Ibn Ezra,[23] Kimḥi,[24] and RaMBaN.[25] Among the moderns, Ewald[26] explains the form as an old feminine collective meaning a heptad, while Gesenius[27] dismisses it as "probably a scribal error" for שבעה. On the other hand, there is evidence for a talmudic interpretation as a dual form,[28] so the Targum[29] and Rashi.[30] Dhorme,[31] in particular, defends שבענה as an old Semitic dual in *-ân*[32] and claims that the number of daughters remained constant in contrast to the doubling of the sons because girls in the Orient were not considered important. This explanation fails to take account of the different social milieu which the story of Job implies and of the epic treatment which tends to exalt the female.[33] We are thus left without any convincing reason for the disparity between sons and daughters if שבענה be taken as a dual. Accordingly, we must reject this rendering and otherwise explain the form.

As a matter of fact שבענה בנים has its counterpart in a Ugaritic form in a context similar to ours and in which there is no doubt of the meaning as seven: *wld šbᶜny aṯt iṯrḫ*[34] "The wives I have wed have borne seven." *Šbᶜny* is here explained as *šbᶜ* "seven"+adverbial *-ny*.[35] Thus the unique form שבענה is a poetic archaism which in all probability belonged to the original language of the epic of Job.

F. Syntax:

1 4 שלשת אחיתיהם. This unusual construction of the *-t* form of the numeral with a feminine noun[36] may well represent an archaic usage in which שלשת was still a collective and abstract term meaning "group of three, triad," and could be used with either gender.[37]

III. LITERARY STRUCTURE

The element of repetition is one of the most inherently characteristic features of the epic style, intended as it is for an audience rather than a reading public.[38] This "epic law of iteration"[39] is fully operative in the prologue. A close examination reveals a consistent pattern of repetition of precisely the kind associated with the epic. Moreover, there is a skilfully constructed symmetrical scheme of the kind that could only come from an epic archetype.

A. The Celestial Council:

ויהי היום ויבאו בני האלהים להתיצב על ה׳ ויבוא גם השטן בתכם ...	2 1	ויהי היום ויבאו בני האלהים להתיצב על ה׳ ויבוא גם השטן בתוכם	1 6
ויאמר ה׳ אל השטן אי מזה תבא ויען השטן את ה׳ ויאמר משט כבארץ ומהתהלך בה	2	ויאמר ה׳ אל השטן מאין תבא ויען השטן את ה׳ ויאמר משוט כבארץ ומהתהלך בה	7
ויאמר ה׳ אל השטן השמת לבך אל עבדי איוב כי אין כמהו בארץ איש תם וישר ירא אלהים וסר מרע	3	ויאמר ה׳ אל השטן השמת לבך על עבדי איוב כי אין כמהו בארץ איש תם וישר ירא אלהים וסר מרע	8
אולם שלח נא ידך וגע אל עצמו ואל בשרו אם לא אל פניך יברכך	5	ואולם שלח נא ידך וגע בכל אשר לו אם לא על פניך יברכך	11
ויאמר ה׳ אל השטן הנו בידך אך את נפשו שמר	6	ויאמר ה׳ אל השטן הנה כל אשר לו בידך רק אליו אל תשלח ידך	12
ויצא השטן מאת פני ה׳	7	ויצא השטן מעם פני ה׳	

B. The Character of Job:

2 3	1 8	1 1
אין כמהו בארץ איש תם וישר ירא אלהים וסר מרע.	אין כמהו בארץ איש תם וישר ירא אלהים וסר מרע.	והיה האיש ההוא תם וישר וירא אלהים וסר מרע.
2 10		**1 22**
בכל זאת לא חטא איוב בשפתיו.		בכל זאת לא חטא איוב ולא נתן תפלה לאלהים.

C. The Misfortunes of Job (1 14–19):

The swift unfolding of the miseries that beset Job in successive stages is strongly reminiscent of the literary treatment of the series of misfortunes that befell King Keret.[40] But even more important than this for uncovering the epic archetype is the distinct structural pattern very similar to that underlying the Ten Plagues.[41] We have here a symmetrical scheme consisting of three series of two blows each, the first striking animal life, the second humans, followed by the climactic seventh.[42] Furthermore, each series is encased within a framework comprising a formulaic introduction and a concluding refrain.[43] Finally, the cause of each series is alternately human and divine. The following chart illustrates the literary structure of this section:

Series	*No.*			*Cause*
		ומלאך בא אל איוב ואמר		
1.	(i)	Plundering of oxen and asses		human
	(ii)	Killing of servants		
		ואמלטה רק אני לבדי להגיד לך		
		עוד זה מדבר וזה בא		
2.	(iii)	Destruction of sheep		divine
	(iv)	Killing of servants		
		ואמלטה וכו׳		
		עוד זה וכו׳		
3.	(v)	Raiding of camels		human
	(vi)	Killing of servants		
		ואמלטה וכו׳		
		עוד זה וכו׳		
Climax	(vii)	Job's sons and daughters killed		divine
		ואמלטה וכו׳		

IV. THE SIGNIFICANCE OF NUMBERS

The special status of certain numbers and their peculiar schematized usage is popular in biblical literature. The phenomenon is now recognized to be a typically Near Eastern literary device.[44] Especially frequent and significant is the climactic use of the numeral seven.[45] Something is repeated day after day for six days, the seventh heralding a climax and inaugurating some new event.

The Ugaritic epics attest numerous examples. Thus, for six days a fire rages in the palace of Baal and ceases abruptly on the seventh.[46] King Danel offers oblation to the gods for six days and on the seventh is visited by Baal.[47] The same king celebrates the birth of a son for six days and his guests depart on the seventh.[48] King Keret reaches his goal on the seventh day of his journey and invests Udm for seven days.[49]

In the light of this epic tradition the exploitation of the numeral seven in the three chapters of the narrative framework acquires special significance. The seven day and night silent mourning of Job and friends is suddenly and dramatically interrupted when Job opens his mouth to curse the day of his birth (2 13). His sons and daughters hold seven-day feasts (1 14). A succession of seven blows in all is hurled against Job.[50] The three friends are told to offer seven bulls and seven rams as a propitiatory sacrifice (42 8).[51] Perfectly consistent too, with the classic treatment and of great importance in uncovering the epic substratum underlying the prose narrative, are the seven sons and three daughters of Job (1 2, 42 13). The theme of seven sons is common enough in Ugaritic literature.[52] We may cite the instances of Keret,[53] of the god El,[54] and of the god Mot,[55] all of whom sired seven males. Most striking of all is the fact that Baal,[56] like Job, had seven sons and three daughters.[57]

V. MYTHOLOGY

The mythological elements as represented by the two assemblies of celestial beings (1 6; 2 1) are in perfect accord with the epic background. Although Cassuto[58] has made a convincing case for the traditional Jewish interpretation of בני אלים בני האלהים as implying nothing more than angels or heavenly host,[59] the monotheistic twist does not disguise its pagan origins.

Both the terminology employed and the concept of the assembly of the gods are well attested in the Northwest Semitic literary sphere.[60] In the Ugaritic epics we find *bn il* (2:33), "sons of El, i. e., the gods"; *dr bn il* (2:17, 34; 107:2), "the coterie of gods"; *dr il* (128:iii:19); *pḥr ilm*[61] (17:7), "the totality of the gods"; *pḥr bn ilm* (51:iii:14); *mpḥrt bn il* (2:7, 34; 107:3); *ʿdt ilm*[62] (128:ii:7, 11), "assembly of gods." Similarly, the tenth century Phoenician *Yḥmlk* inscription from Byblos (line 4) refers to מפחרת אל גבל, "the totality of the gods of Byblos."[63] So, too, the magical text from Arslan Tash[64] mentions (l. 11) וכל בן אלם. Without doubt, therefore, we are dealing here in Job with a reflex of early Near Eastern mythology which formed part of the repertoire of the classical epic.[65]

This conclusion is further strengthened by the employment of certain key words and phrases which are common to other accounts of the heavenly council scene found in the Hebrew Bible. The use of התיצב על (1 6, 2 1) for the convocation of the celestial beings and of the root יצא (1 12, 2 7) to introduce the action about to result from the termination of their deliberations is highly significant. Zechariah (6 5) employs both terms: . . . ארבע רוחות השמים יוצאות מהתיצב על as does the prophet Micaiah with the variant עמד for התיצב[66] in a similar context (I Kings 22 19): וכל צבא השמים עמד עליו followed by (vs. 22) צא, אצא, ויצא הרוח. It would thus appear that the choice of phraseology is not fortuitous but is part of an established literary tradition with a stereotyped terminology.[67]

The question now arises as to whether the heavenly scene was indeed part of the original epic of Job. It has been held that 1 13 has an ambiguous subject and hence logically and syntactically follows directly upon 1 5, thus eliminating the Satan episode.[68] It is further maintained that 42 11 implies that God and not Satan is the author of all the evil that befell Job. Accordingly, Spiegel believes that the epilogue preserves the older layers of the Job saga and that the Satan scene belongs to a later version grafted on to a fossilized original.

However attractive the theory, the evidence would not seem to be conclusive, for the difficulties are more apparent than real. The subject of בניו ובנותיו in 1 13 is in fact not in the least ambiguous, the LXX[69] notwithstanding. It is perfectly obvious from vs. 12, אליו, לו and from the four preceding verses (11, יברכך, לו; 10, בעדו, ביתו, לו, ידיו, מקנהו; 9, איוב; 8, איוב, etc.) that the subject is and could be none other than Job. Moreover, the second heavenly court scene is absolutely essential to explain and introduce Job's physical sufferings which, after all, constitute the climax of the story.

As to 42 11, one must agree with Alt[70] and Spiegel[71] that the verse is out of place in its present context and must logically belong to the prologue, probably following 1 22. But it does not really, if properly understood, contradict the Satan story. Satan himself is merely an agent. He has no power of independent action and cannot work without divine permission. In this sense God may correctly be described as the author of Job's troubles and, as a matter of fact, he actually so describes himself in rebuking Satan (2 3), ותסיתני בו לבלעו חנם. It is God who is recognized to be the architect of Job's misfortunes, albeit goaded on by Satan.[72]

The assemblies of celestial beings are an integral part of the saga of Job and constitute the mythological element inseparable from the ancient epic.

VI. JOB'S DAUGHTERS

The prominence of women in epic literature, particularly in that reflecting East Mediterranean society, is well known.[73] The sociology of the story of Job accurately mirrors the same epic background. The daughters[74] participate in the seven-day feasts of their brothers (1 4, 13) in much the same way as the *Ktrt* wine and dine with Danel the week long[75] and as Octavia is summoned by her father King Keret ostensibly to share in his banquet.[76]

The naming of Job's three girls (42 14) is in striking contrast to the anonymity of his sons, a situation exactly paralleled in the case of Baal's three daughters, Pdry, Ṭly, and Arṣy, and his seven unnamed sons. To be compared also is the general prominence of the role of Octavia and the high esteem in which Pġt, daughter of Danel, is held in the Ugaritic epics.

As to the names themselves, it is possible that two of the three, at least, are now to be re-explained on the basis of Ugaritic. Gordon has pointed out that ימימה may well correspond to the epithet of the beautiful Anath—*ymmt limm*[77]—and קציעה could well be *qṣ ͨt*,[78] a bow, referring to its shapeliness.

The emphasis on the outstanding beauty of the girls (42 15) is likewise characteristic of the epic treatment which tends to exalt feminine pulchritude.[79]

Finally, we are told, the girls received from their father an inheritance together with their brothers (42 15). According to Mosaic law[80] the daughter inherits only in the absence of sons. It is obvious that we are dealing here with quite a different social milieu and we are at once reminded of the situation in the Ugaritic epic in which Octavia shares her father's estate with her brothers.[81]

VII. SUMMARY AND CONCLUSION

The Hebrew prose, in vocabulary and style, is saturated with poeticisms and employs some unique forms explicable by reference to Ugaritic. The literary structure contains all the classic elements of repetition and schematization associated with that of the epic. The exploitation of numerals with special status conforms exactly to the epic pattern. The mythological motif and the sociological themes find close parallels in the Ugaritic literature. In the light of all this the detailed and consistent patriarchal setting must be regarded as genuine and as belonging to the original saga.[82] In brief, the considerable amount of epic substratum indicates that our present narrative framework is directly derived from an ancient Epic of Job.

NOTES

[*] While the present writer assumes full and sole responsibility for the material herewith presented and the opinions expressed, he wishes to take the opportunity of making grateful acknowledgment to Prof. Cyrus H. Gordon whose Ugaritic seminar originally inspired this study and whose guidance and instruction saved the writer from many of the pitfalls of ignorance.

1. For the history of the problem see K. Kautzsch, *Das sogenannte Volksbuch von Hiob* (1900), and more recently, S. Spiegel, "Noah, Danel, and Job," *Louis Ginzberg Jubilee Volume* (New York, 1945), pp. 305–7.

2. J. Wellhausen, *Jahrbücher für deutsche Theologie,* XVI (1871), 155.

3. B. Duhm, *Das Buck Hiob* (1897), p. vii.

4. *Op. cit.*

5. N. H. Tur-Sinai, ספר איוב (2nd ed., 1954), pp. 17 f.; cf. אנציקלופדיה מקראית, I, 242.

6. On the supposed contradictions between the two see below § V.

7. עבודה רבה occurs elsewhere, only in Gen 26 14.

8. Incidentally, the sacrifices in 42 8 correspond exactly to those of Balaam (Num 23 1, 14, 29).

9. Cf. S. R. Driver and G. B. Gray, *The Book of Job* (1921), I, lxvi–lxvii. Almost every one of the wide variety of dates given by modern scholars had already been anticipated in talmudic sources; see B. Baba Bathra, 15a-b; Y. Sotah, v. 8.

10. *Op. cit.* E. A. Speiser, "Ancient Mesopotamia," in *The Idea of History in the Ancient Near East* (ed. R. C. Dentan [1955]), p. 71, believes that "the Mesopotamian origin of the three heroes of Ezekiel is assured beyond all doubt." Cf., also *ibid.*, n. 98.

11. U. Cassuto, "שירת העלילה בישראל" in כנסת, VIII (1944), 142.

12. C. H. Gordon, "Homer and Bible," *HUCA*, XXVI (1955), §§ 49, 72, 139.

13. Cassuto, *op. cit.*; also מאדם עד נח (Jerusalem, 1953), pp. 142–43, where Cassuto draws attention to a similar phenomenon in the writings of the Greek Logographi. Cf. also Jacob M. Myers, *The Linguistic and Literary Form of the Book of Ruth* (Leiden, 1955), p. 2.

14. 67:1:6–8. In the light of this passage, 51:vii:47–48 *yqra mt bnpšh* "Mot calls from his throat," may be a *double entendre* implying both the act of speech and a portent of destruction. The celebrated Isa 25 8 may well mean that Mot shall be hoisted by his own petard! Attention should also be drawn to the use of בלע in connection with the fate of Korah and his confederates (Num 16 30–32); Cf. Prov 1 12.

15. 51:VIII:15–20.

16. 67:II:3–4

17. 49:I:30

18. Deut 11 12, if this indeed be prose.

19. 2 Aqht:VI:35; *v.* Gordon, *Ugaritic Manual* (= *UM;* Rome, 1955) § 20. 92.

20. 52:66–67; 75:II:45–46.

21. *UM,* § 20.2013.

22. This is implicit in chap. i.2.

23. נרן שבענה כנון בשנה אפרים יקח; cf. following note.

24. D. Kimḥi, *Mikhlol,* ed. Chomsky (1952), § 69g, describes the *nun* as pleonastic on the analogy of Hos 10 6 בשנה.

25. ואולי הנון הנוסף במלת שבענה מורה על הידיעה.

26. H. Ewald, *Lehrbuch der hebräischen Sprache* (1855), § 269c.

27. *Gesenius' Hebrew Grammar,* ed. Kautzsch-Cowley (Oxford, 1910), § 97c.

28. B. Baba Bathra 16b מפני מה לא נכפלו בנתיו של איוב clearly implies that the number of sons was doubled.

29. ארבסר.

30. הם פעמים שבע שתי שביעיות.

31. P. Dhorme, *Le Livre de Job* (Paris, 1926), *ad loc.*

32. Cf. R. Kittel (ed.), *Biblia Hebraica* (1945) *ad loc.*

33. For the evidence in full see below, § VI.

34. 52:64.

35. *UM,* § 11:3. This adverbial suffix *-ny,* which may be attached to adverbs and adjectives, may also account for Gen 42 36, כלנה, which has no feminine antecedent. On the other hand, כלנה in Prov 31 29 may refer to the preceding בנות. For the pattern *-ay > ah,* cf. שרי > שרה; so *šbᶜny* > שבענה.

36. Elsewhere, only Gen 7 13; I Sam 10 3; Ezek 7 2 *(kethib).*

37. See G. R. Driver, "Gender in Hebrew Numbers," *JJS,* I (1948), 90–104. Cf. the remarks of Cassuto, מנח עד אברהם (Jerusalem, 1953), pp. 61 f.

38. Cassuto has made the point that Hebrew prose is an extension of the Canaanite epic tradition and that therefore, whenever Hebrew prose exhibits repetition we are entitled to detect therein the influence of that tradition. See his "ספרות מקראית וספרות כנענית," in תרביץ, XIII (1942), 197–212; XIV (1943), 1–10; "העלילה בישראל שירת," pp. 121–42; האלה ענת (1953), pp. 34–36; מאדם עד נח, pp. 142–43.

39. C. R. North, "Pentateuchal Criticism," in *The Old Testament and Modern Study,* ed. H. H. Rowley (Oxford, 1951), p. 65.

40. Krt 14 ff.

41. Cassuto, פרוש על ספר שמות (Jerusalem, 1953), p. 61.

41a. Cf. the remarks of the MaLBIM to Job 1 13.

42. For parallels to this kind of literary artifice in Ugaritic literature see *UM,* p. 39, n. 1. and § 17.3, n. 2.

43. Cassuto, תרביץ, XIII (1942), p. 207, nn. 31–32; מאדם ועד נח, pp. 5 f.; האלה ענת, pp. 36, 84ᵇ, esp., nn. 1–2.

44. In addition to the literature cited in the previous note, see B. Jacob, "The Decalogue," *JQR*, XIV (1923), 159–60 for a suggestive explanation of the origin of the special status of the number seven, and L. Ginzberg, *The Legends of the Jews* (Philadelphia, 1925), V, 9, n. 21, for the significance of the number in Jewish legend.

45. 51:VI:24–33.

46. 2 Aqht:I:6–16.

47. 2 Aqht:II:30–40. From 124:21–25 it is clear that the *Rpum* too, hold a weeklong feast, though the broken state of the text obscures the nature of the seventh day climax.

48. Krt 106–109, 114–120, 194–211.

49. See above § III C.

50. Such a sacrifice is paralleled elsewhere only in connection with the Balaam story (Num 23 1, 14, 29). Ugaritic text 52:15 has reference to a sevenfold offering.

51. For seven sons as a biblical ideal, cf. I Sam 2 5; Jer. 15 9; Ruth 4 15.

52. 128:II:24.

53. 52:64.

54. 49:VI:7–9, [ ]*bn ilm mt/* [ ] *u*[ ]*šbᶜt ǵlmh/*[ ] *bn ilm mt*. Despite the badly preserved state of the text the parallelism makes it certain that Mot had seven sons. For a reference to Mot's first-born, cf. Job 18 13 בכור מות.

55. 67:V:8. Arvid S. Kapelrud, *Baal in the Ras Shamra Texts* (Copenhagen, 1952), p. 79, states that "no son of Baal is mentioned in the [Ugaritic] texts." Now while it is true that *ǵlm* itself is indefinite as regards the relationship of the seven lads to Baal, nevertheless the juxtaposition with the three daughters would indicate that sons are referred to. This view is strengthened by Krt 152–53, 298–99, where *ǵlm* is parallel to *wld*.

56. 'nt : I :22 ff.; III :3–4. Gordon, *The Moslem World*, XXXIII, No. 1 (1943), 50–51, has pointed out the parallel between the three daughters of Baal and the same of pre-Islamic Allah, the latter notion being derived from the North Syrian littoral of the Amarna age at the beginning of the 14th century B.C. It is worth adding that the triad of daughters is also an exceedingly common theme in Greek mythology as attested by the Gorgons, the Graeae, the Hesperides, the Charites, the Moirae, the Muses, the Furies, and possibly, the Horae.

57. Cassuto, "מעשה בני האלהים ובנות האדם," in *Essays Presented to J. H. Hertz* (London, 1942), pp. 35–44, esp., 37–38; מאדם עד נח, pp. 200–203; אינציקלופדייה מקראית, Vol. II, art. בני אלים; cf. also Vol. I, arts. אל and אלהים. For the specifically Israelitish aspects of this notion, see the remarks of Y. Kaufmann, תולדות האמונה הישראלית (Tel-Aviv, 1947), II, 422–23.

58. The term is found elsewhere in the Hebrew Bible in Gen 6 2, 4; Pss 29 1, 89 7; Job 38 7 (cf. 15 8, 25 2) and in Deut 32 8 according to the LXX version now confirmed, according to Patrick W. Skehan, by a Hebrew fragment of Deut 32 from Qumran (*BASOR*, No. 136 [1954], p. 12). Cf. also Dan 3 25, בר אלהין (cf. vs. 28 מלאכה). In Pss 103 20–21, 148 2 מלאכיו || צבאיו; I Kings 22 19 וכל צבא השמים is to be compared with Job 1 6, 2 1 בני האלהים. אלים as a synonym for angels is very common in the Dead Sea scrolls; see Yigael Yadin, מגילת מלחמת בני אור בבני חושך (Jerusalem, 1955), p. 210.

59. See Frank M. Cross, Jr., "The Council of Yahweh in Second Isaiah," *JNES*, XII (1953), 274 ff. Marvin H. Pope, *El in the Ugaritic Texts* (Leiden, 1955), pp. 48–49.

60. Cf. Akkadian *puḫur ilâni*.

61. Cf. Ps 82 1.

62. See T. H. Gaster, *JQR*, XXXVII (1946), 62, n. 27; *ibid.*, XXXVIII (1947), 289; *Thespis* (1950), p. 76, n. 6. W. F. Albright, *From the Stone Age to Christianity* (Baltimore, 1946), pp. 199, 226–27, and esp., p. 331, n. 26.

63. Gaster, *Orientalia*, XI (1942), 41–79.

64. Cf. the remarks of Gordon, *Ugaritic Literature* (Rome, 1949), p. 132, n. 3.

65. Cf. Zech 3 1 ‏השטן עמד על ימינו‎.

66. Cassuto, "‏שירת העלילה בישראל‎," pp. 121–442 has abundantly illustrated this phenomenon as a feature of the Hebrew epic.

67. Spiegel, *op. cit.*, pp. 323–25.

68. οι υιοι Ιωβ και αι θυγατερες αυτου

69. A. Alt, "Zur Vorgeschichte des Buches Hiob," *ZAW*, LV (1937), 265 ff.

70. *op. cit.*

71. It is to be noted that Satan is included among the ‏בני אלהים‎ just as Mot is described in the Ugaritic texts (49:II:13, 25, 31) as *bn ilm mt*. Cf. I Kings 22 22 where the ‏רוח שקר‎, is part of the heavenly host. In the Talmud, Satan is identified with the Angel of Death ‏אמר ר'ל הוא שטן הוא יצר הרע הוא מלאך המות‎ (Baba Bathra 16a).

72. Cf. most recently, Gordon, "Homer," § 72 ff.

73. For the significance of the triad of daughters see above, n. 56.

74. 2 Aqht:II:26–40.

75. 125:39 ff., 61 ff.

76. *UM,* § 20.789. Cf. *ibid.*, § 5.26 where it is pointed out that *ymmt* < *ybmt* under the influence of the following *m*. So Albright, *BASOR,* No. 70, p. 19, n. 6, and J. Obermann, *Ugaritic Mythology* (New Haven, 1948), p. 35.

77. *UM,* § 20.1706.

78. Gordon, "Homer," § 85.

79. Num 27 8.

80. 128:III:16.

81. It is not without significance in this respect that ‏איוב‎ is a fairly common West Semitic proper name possessed by a number of kings in the second millennium. See B. Maisler, ‏תרביץ‎, XIII (1942), 72.

The Mythological Background of Job 18*

In a recent issue of the *JBL*,[1] William A. Irwin drew attention to the mythological background of Job 18–19. In particular, he tried to demonstrate the familiarity of the great poet with the famous Babylonian composition dealing with the descent of Ishtar to the nether world. On this basis he sought to interpret Job 18 14 as an allusion to the imperious rule of Ereshkigal, queen of the "Land of No Return." Unfortunately, the precision of the parallel, as he pointed out, is marred by the presence of verbs in the feminine (ותצעדהו; vs. 15 תשכון) interrupting a series of masculine forms, and by the phrase מלך בלהות. If Ereshkigal is indeed referred to, we should expect מלכת ב׳ instead.

Professor Irwin rightly resisted the temptation to facile emendation in order to strengthen his case. I believe that the present text can be generally satisfactorily explained provided that the mythological horizon be broadened.

The first term to be elucidated is בלהות (vs. 14). Significantly, every usage of this term in the Hebrew Bible is in connection with a figure of destruction.[2] In Job 24 17 we find it together with צלמות, itself a characteristic of Sheol.[3] The latter is described in Job 10 21 f. as ארץ חשך וצלמות ארץ עפתה כמו אפל צלמות ולא סדרים ותפע כמו־אפל. Similarly, in 38 17 שערי צלמות parallels שערי מות. These verses are, of course, strongly reminiscent of the description of the nether world in the Babylonian poem as "the dark house," "wherein the dwellers are bereft of light," "where they see no light, residing in darkness."[4] Thus the conjunction of בלהות with צלמות argues strongly for the former as an epithet of Sheol. Furthermore, in Ezek 26 21 בלהות is used in immediate

association with such appellations of the nether world as בור and
ארץ תחתיות.

In the light of all this, and in the context of Job 18–19 which Irwin
has so clearly illuminated, מלך בלהות (18 14) can be none other than the
king of the nether world. However, it is just at this point that the Babylonian analogy breaks down, since we should expect a female ruler of the
infernal regions, rather than a king.

Yet, Irwin has himself pointed the way to a solution of this problem
by stressing the fact that in Job there is a fusion of both Babylonian and
Canaanite mythological motifs.[5] It is precisely to the latter sphere that
we can look for further help.

Let us now examine the phrase בכור מות in vs. 13. This has frequently been interpreted figuratively as "fatal disease," "the terrors of
death," "one doomed to death."[6] The targum understood it as "the angel
of death."[7] In conformity with the mythological background there is no
reason at all why בכור מות should not be translated, as Cassuto long ago
suggested, "the first-born of Môt," alluding to the Canaanite figure associated with disease, destruction, and aridity.[8] There are several instances
in the Hebrew Scriptures in which the term מות has acquired a specialized personified meaning analogous to its usage as a proper name in the
Ugaritic epics. Cassuto has pointed to some remarkable verbal correspondences in this respect.[9]

Now there is no doubt whatsoever that Môt was the ruler of the
Canaanite nether world. Several Ugaritic passages refer explicitly to Môt
sitting on his throne in the depths of the earth.[10] Similarly, Philo of Byblos observed that the Phoenician Môt was the counterpart of Pluto, the
chthonian deity of the Greeks.[11] Accordingly, one may identify מלך
בלהות, "king of the nether world," with מות of vs. 13. Môt's "first-
born" (בכור מות) would then, indeed, occupy the same position in
Canaan as did Namtar, the messenger *(mār šipri)* and son of Ereshkigal
in Babylonian mythology.[12] He would be a demon of evil fate, the grim
herald of Môt, assigned the function of driving the souls into Sheol.[13]

This identification of בכור מות puts the understanding of vs. 13 in a
new light. It, too, may well be a reflex of Canaanite mythology. Characteristic of Môt is his penchant for devouring his prey.[14] A useful piece of
advice is found in Ugaritic text 51:VIII:15–20:[15] *al/tqrb. lbn. ilm/ mt.
al. y'dbkm/ kimr. bph/ klli. btbrn/ qnh. thtan*—"Draw not nigh unto the
divine Môt, lest he make you like a lamb in his mouth, like a kid in his
jaws ye be crushed."

The picture of the nether world as a voracious monster with a huge gullet and gaping jaws is familiar enough in biblical literature.[16] Isa 5 14 speaks of Sheol as extending its throat (נפשה) and opening wide its mouth without limit. The identical phrase is used by Hab 2 5 with the additional simile, "insatiable as death" (והוא כמות ולא ישבע).

In one Ugaritic passage (67:I:19–20) Môt, apparently boasting of his prowess, says of himself: *bklat/ ydy ilḥm. hm.*—"With both my hands I shall eat them." This phrase is very similar to Job 18 13, יאכל בדי עורו יאכל בדיו בכור מות. As a matter of fact, the difficult בדי most likely means "with two hands" and בדיו, "with his two hands." It has long been recognized that the uniconsonantal *d*, "hand," appears fossilized in the combination *bd*, "with/in the hand," in Ugaritic.[17] In a Canaanite gloss in a letter of Biridiya of Megiddo, found at Tell el-Amrna, *ba-di-ú* appears for the Accadian, *ina qâtišu*, "in his hand."[18] The form is well attested in biblical Hebrew and other Semitic languages.[19] Vs. 13, therefore, might well be translated, "The first-born of Môt will devour his skin with two hands, yea with his two hands he will devour (him)."

Admittedly, to "devour skin" is not a natural phrase. But this difficulty remains whatever construction is put on בדי. Most probably the idea is that even the very skin will be greedily devoured, leaving not a trace of the victim behind. The notion would be very similar, *mutatis mutandis*, to that expressed in Mic 3 3. It is also not improbable that עור here is synecdoche for body, as was indeed understood by ibn Ǧanaḥ and Saadia.[20]

We now come to the thorny ותצעדהו (vs. 14) and תשכן (vs. 15). Were the usual masculine forms employed here, none would doubt that the subject of the verbs would be בכור מות[21] He, it is, like Namtar, who marches off the designated victim to Môt in the nether world and who spreads desolation over the earthly habitation of his prey.[22] How are we then, to explain the apparent substitution of the feminine for masculine in these verbs?

Before attempting to answer the question, it should be pointed out that at least one other such example is to be found in the language of Job, namely, in 20 9 ולא־עוד תשורנו מקומו. The obvious incompatibility of the undoubtedly masculine מקומו with a verb in the feminine has either led to the emendation ישורנו[23] or been explained by taking עין of vs. 9a to be the subject, and understanding מקומו as though במקומו were intended.[24] Against this, however, is the equivalent phrase in 7 10 and Ps 103 16 ולא־יכירנו עוד מקומו, so that in 20 9, too, מקומו cannot be other than the subject of תשורנו. The only solution to the problem must be to regard the three verbs תשכון ,ותצעדהו, and תשורנו as rare masculine forms with a *t*-preformative.

Now, as a matter of fact, just such a form is known to us from the language of the Amarna letters. In addition to the Canaanite preterite 3. m. s. form *yikšud* and the present 3. m. s. *yikašad* appear also *tikšud* and *tikašad*.[25] Thus, EA Nos. 71:4 f.; 86:3 f.: *ilu a-ma-na ilu ša šarri be-li-ka ti-di-nu bašta-ka i-na pa-ni šarri* ("Aman, the god of the king, thy lord, give thee strength in the presence of the king").

EA No. 143:27 f.: *a-na-ku ki-ma amêli ta-az-ra-ḫi sisē ša šarri* ("I am like a man who grooms (?) the horses of the king").

EA No. 323:22: *mâr ilu šamaš ša ti-ra-am ilu šamaš* ("The son of Šamaš whom Šamaš loves").

In the light of the existence of this phenomenon within the Canaanite linguistic sphere, we may look upon the three forms in Job as vestigial 3. m. s. *t*- preformative imperfects. Accordingly, in 18 14–15, the subject of ותצעדהו and תשכון is בכור מות of vs. 13.

In short, what Bildad is saying is that Môt, king of the nether world, sends his first-born as his emissary to slay the unrighteous one and to march him off to the infernal regions. The world of the wicked collapses about him and dissolves into oblivion.

NOTES

* I wish to thank Prof. H. L. Ginsberg for many valuable comments on this paper.
1. *JBL*, 81 (1962), pp. 217–29.
2. Isa 17 14; Ezek 26 21; 27 36; 28 19; Ps 73 19; Job 18 11, 14; 24 17; 27 20; 30 15.
3. On צלמות, see now D. Winton Thomas, *JSS*, 7 (1962), pp. 191–200.
4. "The Descent of Ishtar to the Nether World," 11. 4 ff. (*ANET*, p. 107). On the theme of darkness and Sheol, see J. Pedersen, *Israel*, I–II, pp. 464–66.
5. *Op. cit.*, p. 225.
6. N. H. Tur-Sinai, *The Book of Job*, ad loc.
7. The other versions offer little help. LXX renders simply, θάνατος; MS A, Theod. Symm., πρῶϊμος θάνατος; Vulg., *primogenita mors*.
8. U. Cassuto, *The Goddess Anath* [Hebrew], (Jerusalem, 1951), p. 49.
9. *Ibid.*, pp. 47–49; cf. p. 22.
10. Ugaritic Texts 51:VIII:7–14; 67:II:14–16.
11. Eusebius, *Praep. Ev.* xv. 38d.
12. V. K. Tallqvist, *Akkadische Götterepitheta*, (Helsinki, 1938), pp. 297, 307, 387 f.
13. Both Namtar and Môt would thus fulfill rôles analogous to that of Hermes "Psychopompos" on behalf of Hades. It should be noted that no mention of Môt's "first-born" has yet turned up in the Ugaritic texts. "First-born" as a divine epithet is very common. For the use of *bukru* in Mesopotamian mythology, see Tallqvist, *op. cit.*, p. 66. It is now certain that the fragmentary Ugaritic text 49:VI:7–9 cannot be cited in sup-

port of "seven sons of Môt." What I have written in *JBL*, 76 (1957), p. 21, n. 54, is hereby withdrawn.

14. On this theme, see Cassuto, *op. cit.*; Sarna, *JBL*, 76 (1957), p. 16, esp. n. 14.

15. Cf. 49:II:22–23; 67:II:3–4.

16. See Th. Gaster, *Thespis*², pp. 206 f.

17. C. H. Gordon, *Ugaritic Manual*, §§ 8.16; 20.450.

18. EA 245:35.

19. C. Rabin, *JTS*, 6 (1955), pp. 111–15.

20. Jonah ibn Ǧanaḥ, *Perush LeKitvei Ha-Kodesh*, ed. Rabinowicz, (Tel-Aviv, 1936), p. 253; Saadia's commentary to Job, *ad loc.*, ed. Bacher, in J. & H. Derenbourg, *Oeuvres complètes*, (Paris, 1899), v, p. 60. Ibn Ezra similarly understood עור in Job 2 4 as body. The same is to be found in David b. Abraham, *Kitāb Jāmi' Al-Alfāz*, ed. Skoss, (Philadelphia, 1945), II, p. 380. For "skin" *as pars pro toto*, cf. the English phrase, "to save one's skin."

21. B. Duhm, *Das Buch Hiob*, and G. B. Gray, *The Book of Job*, *ad loc.*, emend to יצעדהו.

22. With the use of שכן here, cf. its employment as a characteristic verb in descriptions of destruction in Isa 13 21; 34 11; Ezek 31 13; 32 4.

23. So Gray, *op. cit.*

24. Tur-Sinai, *op. cit.*

25. E. Ebeling, "Das Verbum der El-Amarna-Briefe," *Beiträge zur Assyriologic und semitischen Sprachwissenschaft*, (Leipzig, 1910), 8, pp. 46, 48, 51. E. Dhorme, *RB*, 10 (1913), p. 379. Cf., also, Z. S. Harris, *A Grammar of the Phoenician Language*, p. 65. The use of *t-* preformative with 3. m. pl. was established beyond doubt by W. L. Moran, *JCS*, 5 (1951), pp. 33–35.

Bibliography of the Published Writings of Nahum M. Sarna

BOOKS

1953   *A Syllabus of Biblical History.* Pittsburgh: College of Jewish Studies.

1966   *Understanding Genesis.* New York: Jewish Theological Seminary.

1973   *A New Translation of the Book of Psalms.* Philadelphia: The Jewish Publication Society.

1980   *The Book of Job.* Philadelphia: The Jewish Publication Society.

1982   *The Writings.* Philadelphia: The Jewish Publication Society.

1986   *Exploring Exodus.* New York: Shocken Books.

1989   *Commentary on Genesis.* Philadelphia: The Jewish Publication Society.

       From Ancient Israel to Modern Judaism: Intellect in Quest of Understanding. Essays in Honor of Marvin Fox. (With editors Jacob Neusner and Ernest S. Frerichs.) Atlanta, GA: Scholars Press.

1991   *Commentary on Exodus.* Philadelphia: The Jewish Publication Society.

1993   *Songs of the Heart. An Introduction to the Book of Psalms.* New York: Schocken. (Reissued in 1995 as *On the Book of Psalms. Exploring the Prayers of Ancient Israel.*)

1997   *Genesis: World of Myths & Patriarchs.* (With authors Ada Feyerick and Cyrus H. Gordon.) New York: New York University Press.

2000   *Studies in Biblical Interpretation.* Philadelphia: The Jewish Publication Society.

ARTICLES

1955 "Some Instances of Enclitic-*m* in Job." *JJS* 6, pp. 108–10.

   "Ethanium, Job 12 19." *JBL* 74, pp. 272–74.

1956 "A Crux Interpretum in Job 22 3." *JNES* 15, pp. 118–19.

1957 "Epic Substratum in the Prose of Job." *JBL* LXXVI, pp. 13–25.

1958 "The Biblical Period." L. Schwartz, ed., Study Guide to Great Ages and Ideas of the Jewish People. New York: Hadassah Education Department.

1959 "The Interchange of the Prepositions *beth* and *min* in Biblical Hebrew." *JBL* 78, pp. 310–16.

1961 "From Wellhausen to Kauffman." *Midstream*, pp. 64–74.

1962 "Yehezkel Kaufman and Biblical Scholarship." *Jewish Chronicle*, p.19.

   "The Psalm of the Sabbath Day (Psalm 92)." *JBL* LXXXI, pp.155–68.

1963 "The Library of the Jewish Theological Seminary." *Jewish Book Annual* 21, pp. 53–59.

   "Psalm 89: A Study in Inner Biblical Exegesis." A. Altmann, ed., *Biblical and Other Studies and Texts, I*. Cambridge, MA: Harvard University Press, pp. 29–46.

   "Ashkenazim"; "Sephardim"; *Encyclopedia International*. Grollier.

   "The Mythological Background of Job 18." *JBL* LXXXII, pp.315–18.

1964 "Ezkiel 8:17: A Fresh Examination." *HTR* 57, pp. 347–52.

1966 "Cultural Influences on Biblical Israel (Psalm 19)." *Hadassah Magazine* 47.7, pp. 9, 31–32.

1967 "Psalm XIX and the Near Eastern Sun-god Literature." *Proceedings of the Fourth World Congress of Jewish Studies*, pp. 171–75.

1969 "Prolegomenon." In *The Psalms*, M. Buttenweiser, trans. New York: Ktav, pp. xxiii–xxxviii.

1970 "The Bible and Judaic Studies." L.A. Jick, ed., *The Teaching of Judaica in America Universities*. New York: Ktav, pp. 35–42.

1971 "Hebrew and Bible Studies in Medieval Spain." R.D. Barnett, ed., *The Sephardi Heritage*. London: Vallentine and Mitchell, pp. 323–66.

   "Saphon." (Hebrew) *Encyclopedia Miqraith*. Jerusalem, VI, cols. 747–51.

   "An Obscure Chapter in Jeremiah in the Light of the Babylonian Chronicle and Rabbinic Tradition." (Hebrew) *Haguth Ivrith Be'Amerika*. Tel Aviv: Yavneh, pp. 121–30.

   "The Order of the Books." C. Berlin, ed., *Studies in Jewish Bibliography, History, and Literature*. New York: Ktav, pp. 407–13.

1972 "Bible." (Hebrew) *Encyclopedia Ivrith*. Jerusalem, XXIV, cols. 281–83, 286–89.

"Aaron."; "Aaronides."; "Abihu."; "Ablmelech."; "Abraham."; "Acrostics."; "Amraphel."; "Asenath."; "Bible."; "Bible Canon."; "Boaz."; "Dothan and Abiram."; "Delilah."; "Genesis."; "Gershom"; "Gideon."; "Hallelujah."; "Hur."; "Ichabod."; "Isaac."; "Jacob."; "Jael."; "Jephthah."; "Jochebed."; "Joseph."; "Nadab."; "Orpah."; "Patriarchs."; "Psalms."; and "Rebekah." *Encyclopedia Judaica.*

1973   "Zedekiah's Emancipation of Slaves and the Sabbatical Year." H.A. Hoffner, ed., *Orient and Occident*. Neukirchen: Neukirchener Verlag, pp. 144–49.

"Biblical Literature, section II."; and "O.T. Canon, Text, and Versions." *Encyclopedia Britannica*. Macropedia, II, pp. 881–95.

1974   "Introduction to the Early Spanish Penatateuch Manuscript (Toledo, 1241)." Jerusalem: Makor.

1975   "Abraham Geiger and Biblical Scholarship." J.J. Petuchowski, ed., *New Perspectives on Abraham Geiger*. New York: Ktav, pp.17–30.

"The Chirotonic Motif on the Lachish Altar." Y. Aharoni, ed., *Investigations at Lachish*. Tel Aviv, pp.44–46

"Concerning the Problem of the Ordering of Biblical Books."(Hebrew) *Shnaton, An Annual for Biblical and Near Easter Studies* I, pp. 197–203.

"Biblical Studies: Some Recent Publications." *Association for Jewish Studies Newsletter* 14, pp. 12–13.

1976   "Rehab." (Hebrew) *Encyclopedia Miqraith*. Jerusalem, VII, cols. 328–29.

1977   "Paganism and Biblical Judaism." S.M. Wagner and A.D. Breck, eds., *Great Confrontations in Jewish History*. Denver: University of Denver, pp. 3–20.

"Abraham in History." *BARev* 3.4, pp. 5–9.

1978   "Rachel." (Hebrew) *Encyclopedia Ivrith*. Jerusalem, XXX, cols. 980–81.

"The Abortive Insurrection in Zedekiah's Day (Jer. 27–29)." *Eretz-Israel* 14, pp.89*–96*.

1979   "The Divine Title *'abhir ya'ăqôbh'*." *Essays on the Occasion of the Seventieth Anniversary of the Dropsie University*. Philadelphia, pp. 389–96.

"The Psalm Superscriptions and the Guilds." S. Stein and R. Loewe, eds., *Studies in Jewish Religious and Intellectual History Presented to Alexander Altmann*. University of Alabama, pp. 281–300.

"The Biblical Sources for the History of the Monarchy." A. Malamat, ed., *World History of the Jewish People*. Jerusalem: Massada Press, IV.1, pp. 3–19.

1980   "The Last Legacy of Roland de Vaux." *BARev* 6.4, pp. 14–21.

1981   "The Anticipatory Use of Information as a Literary Feature of the Genesis Narratives." R.E. Friedman, ed., *The Creation of Sacred Literature*. Berkeley, CA: University of California Press, pp.76–82.

1982   "Šemeš" and "Tehillim." (Hebrew) Encyclopedia Miqraith. Jerusalem, VIII, cols. 182–89, 438–62.

"The Decalogue." N. Stampfer, ed., *The Solomon Goldman Lectures*. Chicago, III, pp. 1–9.

"Genesis Chapter 23: The Cave of Machpelah." *Hebrew Studies* 23, pp. 17–21.

"Unusual Aspects of Biblical Exegesis During the Middle Ages." A.A. Greenbaun and A.L. Ivery, eds., (Hebrew) *Thought and Action: Essays in Memory of Simon Rawidowicz*. Tel Aviv, pp. 35–42

1983   "The Modern Study of the Bible in the Framework of Jewish Studies." *Proceedings of the Eighth World Congress of Jewish Studies*. Jerusalem, pp. 19–27.

"Understanding Creation in Genesis." R.M. Frye, ed., *Is God a Creationist? The Religious Case Against Creation-Science*. New York, pp. 155–75.

1984   "The Ravishing of Dinah: A Commentary on Genesis, Chapter 34." A.M. Shapiro and B.I. Cohen, eds., *Studies in Jewish Education in Honor of Louis Newman*. New York: Ktav, pp. 143–56.

"Exegesis, Jewish." J.R. Strayer, ed., *Dictionary of the Middle Ages*. New York: Charles Scribner's Sons, IV, pp. 538–42.

1985   "Hebrew Language, Jewish Study of." J.R. Strayer, ed., *Dictionary of the Middle Ages*. New York: Charles Scribner's Sons, VI, pp.128–29

1987   "Authority and Interpretation of Scripture in Jewish Tradition." C. Thoma and M. Wyschogrod, eds., *Understanding Scripture*. New York: Paulist Press, pp. 9–20.

"Biblical Literature: Hebrew Scriptures." M. Eliade, ed., *The Encyclopedia of Religion*. New York: Macmillan Publishing Company, II, pp. 152–73.

"The Call of the Prophet: Jeremiah, Chapter 1." *Proceedings of the Institute for Distinguished Community Leaders. Benjamin S. Hornstein Program in Jewish Communal Service, Brandeis University, July 26–28, 1987*, pp. 11–15.

"Hebrew in the University." (Hebrew) *Hadoar* 66.38, pp. 17–19.

1988   "Jewish Bible Scholarship and Translations in the United States." (Together with J.D. Sarna.) E.S. Frerichs, ed., *The Bible and Bibles in America*. Atlanta, GA: Scholars Press, pp. 83–117.

"Ruminations of a Jewish Biblical Scholar." Bible Review 4/3 (June), pp. 4–5.

"Israel in Egypt: The Egyptian Sojourn and the Exodus." H. Shanks, ed., *Ancient Israel: A Short History*. Washington, DC: Biblical Archaeology Society, pp. 31–52.

1989   "Ancient Libraries and the Ordering of the Biblical Books." Library of Congress, Center for the Book.

"Genesis 21:33: A Study in the Development of a Biblical Text and its Rabbinic Transformation." J. Neusner, E.S. Frerichs and N.M. Sarna, eds., *From Ancient Israel to Modern Judaism. Intellect in Quest of Understanding. Essays in Honor of Marvin Fox*. Atlanta, GA: Scholars Press, pp. 69–75.

"The New JPS Torah Commentary." *Judaica Book News* 20/1 (Fall/Winter), pp. 10–13.

1990   "Writing a Commentary on the Torah." University of Cincinnati, Judaic Studies Program.

1992   "Legal Terminology in Psalm 3:8." M. Fishbane and E. Tov, eds., *Sha'arei Talmon: Studies in the Bible, Qumran, and the Ancient Near East Presented to Shemaryahu Talmon*. Winona Lake, IN: Eisenbrauns, pp. 175–81.

"Exodus, Book of." *Anchor Bible Dictionary*. New York: Doubleday, II, pp. 689–700.

1995   "Variant Scriptural Readings in Liturgical Texts." Z. Zevit, *et al*, eds., *Solving Riddles and Untying Knots, Biblical Epigraphic, and Semitic Studies in Honor of Jonas C. Greenfield*. Winona Lake, IN: Eisenbrauns, pp. 203–6.

1996   "Notes on the Use of the Definite Article in the Poetry of Job." M.V. Fox, *et al*, eds., *Text, Temples, and Traditions. A Tribute to Menahem Haran*. Winona Lake, IN: Eisenbrauns, pp. 279–84.

"Parashat Ki Tissa (Exodus 30.11–34.35)." S. Kelman and J.L. Grishaver, eds., *Learn Torah With . . .* Los Angeles: Alef Design Group, pp. 154–157.

1997   "Naboth's Vineyard Revisted (1 Kings 21)." M. Cogan, *et al*, eds., *Tehillah le-Moshe. Biblical and Judaic Studies in Honor of Moshe Greenberg*. Winona Lake, IN: Eisenbrauns, pp. 119–26.

1999   "Rashi the Commentator." *Lexington Theological Quarterly* 34/1 (Spring 1999), pp. 1–11.

BOOK REVIEWS

1956   *The Book of Kings, I*, by L.I. Honor, *Conservative Judaism* 10.2, pp. 54–56.

1960   *The Semites in Ancient History*, by S. Moscati, JBL 79, pp. 288–89.

1964   *The Message of Deutero-Isaiah*, by J. Morgenstern, Jewish Social Studies 26, pp. 42–43.

1966   *The Psalms Scroll of Qumran Cave 11 (11QPsª)*, by J.A. Sanders, *Conservative Judaism* 20.4, pp. 63–66.

       The Tradition of the Exodus in its Development, by S.E. Loewenstamm, *JBL* 85, pp. 244–46.

1967   *The Old Testament: An Introduction*, by O. Eissfeldt, Conservative Judaism 22.1, pp. 63–86.

1968   *The Laws in the Pentateuch*, by M. Noth, Jewish Social Studies, pp. 175–76.

       The Bible as Read and Preached in the Old Synagogue (vol 2), by J. Mann, *JBL* 87, pp. 100–106.

       E.L. Sukenik Memorial Volume: Eretz Israel, VIII, *JBL* 87, pp. 462–64.

1969   *The Macmillan Bible Atlas*, by Y. Aharoni and M. Avi-Yonah, *Conservative Judaism* 23.3, pp. 91–93.

1974   *Genizah Bible Fragments with Babylonian Massorah and Vocalization*, I. Yelvin (ed.), Association for Jewish Studies Newsletter No. 10 (January), p.10.

       Documents of Jewish Sectaries, by S. Schechter, Prolegomenon by J.A. Fitzmyer, 1970, JAOS 94, pp. 515–16.

1975   *Canaanite Myth and Hebrew Epic*, by F.M. Cross, *Int* 29, pp.75–78.

1976   *Theological Dictionary of the Old Testament*, I, G.J. Botterweck and H. Ringgren (eds.), Association for Jewish Studies Newsletter, No. 17 (June), pp. 17, 22.

       Linguistic Evidence in Dating Early Hebrew Poetry, by D.A. Robertson, *JBL* 95, pp. 126–29.

       The Targun to Job from Qumran Cave XI, by M. Sokoloff, *IEJ* 26, pp. 51–153.

1987   *Justice and Righteousness in Israel and the Nations*, by M. Weinfeld, JAOS 107 (1987), pp. 144–45.

1992   *Max L. Margolis: A Scholar's Scholar*, by L. Greenspoon, JQR 82, pp. 557–58.

1994   *Students of the Covenant. A History of Jewish Biblical Scholarship in North America*, by S. David Sperling, et al, Journal of Religion 74, pp. 120–121.

1993   *I Have Built You an Exalted House. Temple Building in the Light of Mesopotamian and Northwest Semitic Writing*, by Victor Hurowitz, Biblical Archaeology Review 19/6, pp. 10–72.

List of Biblical Passages Cited

Note: Books of the Bible are listed sequentially, not alphabetically, according to Jewish tradition (Law, Prophets, Writings). New Testament books and Apocrypha follow in alphabetical sequence (after 2 Chronicles).

Genesis, Book of, 14, 19–21
1:1, 211
1:1–5, 199
1:3–6, 19
1:5, 151
1:8, 151
1:21, 19
1:22, 19
1:28, 19
2:8, 110
3:1, 111
3:8, 134
4:20–22, 20
5:2, 19
6:5–9:17, 20
6:9, 71
8:22, 3
9:18, 211, 213, 214, 259
9:18 f., 212
9:20 ff., 212
9:20–27, 14
9:22, 211, 212, 213, 214
9:22–23
9:24, 212
10:4, 145
10:6, 213
11:1–9, 20

11:10–32, 214, 218
11:26, 214
11:27, 214
11:27–28, 214
11:28, 214
11:29, 147, 215, 216
11:30, 215
11:31, 214
12:1, 147
12:1–4, 24
12:5, 214
12:6, 70, 152, 222, 260
12:7, 222, 224
12:8, 224
12:10–20, 213
12:11–20, 72
12:16, 412
13, 215
13:4, 224
13:7, 152
13:10, 215
13:13, 215
13:18, 223, 224
14, 224
14:14, 154
14:22, 224
15:16, 14
15:16–18, 25

18, 216
18:1, 259
18:3, 213
18:4, 223
18:8, 223
18:24 f., 213
19, 14, 216,
19:5–8, 213
20, 213, 215
20:9, 215
20:11, 14
20:12, 215
21:32, 221
21:33, xvii, 70, 221–227
22:14, 152
22:20, 216
22:20–24, 216, 218
24, 216
24:10, 214, 216
24:15, 214
24:22, 216
24:24, 214
24:29–30, 217
24:35, 217
24:36, 217
24:43, 177
24:47, 214
24:53, 217

24:67, 146
25:2, 307
25:8, 412
25:15, 220n.21
25:25, 217
25:27, 217
25:28, 217
25:29, 412
26, 217
26:23–25, 225
26:25, 224
26:34–35, 217, 218
27, 217
27:29, 3
27:42–48, 218
27:46, 218
28:1–2, 218
28:5, 132
28:11, 150
28:12, 110
29–31, 217
29:5, 214
30:14, 3
31:53, 214
32:5, 412
33:19, 412
33:20, 224
34, 213
35, 213
35:4, 223
35:7, 224
35:8, 223
35:13, 132
35:22, 218
36:31 ff., 108
36:31–39, 153
36:33, 107
37:2, 132, 259
39, 213
43:11, 132, 307
46:1–4, 225
49:3 f., 218, 219
49:9, 259
49:10, 178
49:24, 3, 5, 7

Exodus, Book of
2:6, 73
4:22, 25
6:3, 146
9:10, 77
12:24, 149
13:3, 297
13:14, 297
14:8, 148
14:9, 148
15:2, 307
15:22, 149,
15:26, 297
18:1–12, 147
19:10, 106
19:12, 106
19:23, 106
20:2, 297
20:8–11, 22
20:15, 148
20:18, 148
21, 298, 299
21:1–11, 298
21:2, 298, 299
21:3, 298
21:4, 298
21:5, 298
21:6, 179
21:7, 298, 301, 358
21:7–11, 298
21:8 f., 105
21:11, 105, 298
21:20–21, 149
21:22–25, 363
21:26 f., 298
22:2, 300, 301
22:27, 272, 273
22:28, 132
23:2, 77, 260
23:12, 404, 17
23:19, 261
24:12, 239
25:29, 107
25:31, 144
28:4, 132
28:22, 105
28:41, 132

31:14–15, 18
31:18, 239
33:18–23, 150
33:21, 154
34:1, 239
34:4, 239
34:21, 17
34:26, 261
35:2, 22
35:2–3, 17

Leviticus, Book of
5:5, 337
7:18, 77, 260
8:11, 132
11:7, 3
13:4, 132
14:3, 105
16:6, 150
16:21, 337
20:23 f., 213
23:3, 16, 17
23:11, 95
23:18, 265
24:15–16, 272
24:17–22, 363
25:8–10, 302
25:10, 179, 299
25:35 f., 300
25:39, 300
25:47–54, 300
26:5, 3
26:34 f., 295
26:43, 295
27:3, 132

Numbers, Book of
1:14, 145
2:4, 145
5:21–22, 337
6:22–26, 337
10:35, 400
15:40, 245
20:1, 259
21:1–2, 107
21:1–3, 153
22:11, 132

22:28, 111
25:14, 307
26:13, 132
28:9–10, 20
31:22, 3
32:2, 148
32:5, 148

Deuteronomy, Book of, 32
1:2, 152
1:8, 25
2:8, 261
3:11, 153
4:2, 381
4:6–8, 371
4:13, 239
4:19, 371
4:23, 297
4:25–27, 32
5:2, 297
5:3, 297
5:6, 297
5:12–15, 22
5:14–15, 404
5:19, 239
6:1 f., 32
6:12, 297
6:18, 297
7:8, 297
8:14, 297
9:9, 297
9:9–11, 239
10:1, 239
10:3, 239
11:10–12, 25
11:30, 222
12, 32,
12:2–4, 223
12:9 ff., 387–388
12:25, 297
12:28, 297
13:6, 297
13:11, 297
13:19, 297
14:21, 261
14:23–25, 32
15, 289, 297, 299–300, 301

15:1, 298, 299
15:1–11, 299
15:8, 299
15:9, 299
15:12, 298, 299, 301,
15:12–18, 299,
15:13, 298
15:13–14, 300
15:14, 105
15:15, 299
15:17, 105, 298, 299
15:18, 298
15:20, 32
16, 32
16:18, 147
16:21, 223
17:2, 297
17:3, 371
17:8, 32
17:10, 32
17:18, 193
18:6, 32
19:18–19, 363
19:21, 363
21:1–9, 337
21:9, 297
24:16, 32
26:2, 32
26:2–10, 337
26:12–15, 337
27:26, 298
28:15–69, 32
28:25, 298
28:26, 298
28:35, 414
28:69, 297
29:11, 297
29:13, 297
29:21, 297
29:24, 297
31:10, 298, 299, 302
31:10–13, 30
31:11, 32
31:16, 297
31:22, 152
33:6, 146
34:1, 152

Joshua, Book of, 32
10:12, 108
10:13, 33
12:14, 153
21:36, 245
21:37, 245
24:26, 222–223
24:32, 412

Judges, Book of, 32
4:5, 223
5:22, 6
6:10–21, 223
8:2, 3
9:4 f., 308
9:6, 223
9:37, 70, 223
11:3, 308
14:5, 3
14:15, 106
14:17, 106
14:18, 106
17, 344

Samuel, Books of, 29–30,
32, 33, 47

1 Samuel, Book of
1:3, 337
1:10–15, 337
3:3, 179
3:20, 105
4:1, 105
7:9, 337
8–15, 30
8:9–17, 271
8:14, 271
9–31, 29
10:3, 223
12, 32
12:15, 106
13:1, 42
13:19, 3
16:16–23, 339
16–1, 30
17:2, 223
18:19, 106

19:9, 339
21:8, 7
22:2, 308
25:2 ff., 308
25:30, 387
28:24, 77, 260
31:13, 224

2 Samuel, Book of, 29
1:17, 339
1:18, 33
2–8, 30
3:33, 339
5:2, 387
5:6–11, 42
6, 42
6:2, 41
6:23, 106
7, 42, 387, 391
7:2, 339
7:4, 339
7:4–17, 383–384
7:8, 387
7:11–16, 41
7:14, 386
7:15, 46
7:23–24, 41
7:25, 41
8:16–18, 35
9–20, 32
9–24, 30
11–12, 77
12:25, 387
13, 386
14:25, 414
15–18, 386
16:4, 275
16:5–13, 273
20:23–26, 35
20:25, 343
21:8, 106
21:19, 106
22:1, 339
22:49, 308
23:1, 307–308
23:5, 385

Kings, Books of, 15, 29,
30–31, 32, 33–34, 47

1 Kings, Book of
1:5–10, 386
1:11–53, 386
1:16 ff., 387
1:20, 35
1–2, 32
1–11, 30
2:3, 32
2:8–9, 273
2:25, 386
2:28, 106
2:33, 41
2:45, 41
2:46, 35
3:1, 39
3:8, 41
3:9–12, 54
4:1–6, 35
4:3, 343
5:7, 42
5:9–14, 54
5:16–32, 42
5:18–19, 388
6, 35, 42
6:1, 40
7:12–51, 42
7:13–51, 35
8, 35, 42
8:5, 337
8:12–64, 337
8:16, 32, 41, 42
8:17–18, 42
8:20, 386
8:25, 41, 383
8:44, 32, 42
8:48, 32, 42
8:56, 388
9:5, 41
9:15–16, 39
11–34, 41
11:1–6, 54
11:13, 32
11:14–22, 39
11:26–28, 39

11:29–31, 45
11:29–39, 35
11:31–39, 32
11:32, 32
11:36, 32
11:40, 39
11:41, 33
12–17, 30
12:22–24, 35
12:26–33, 43
12:32–13:32, 35
13:33–34, 44
14:1–16, 45
14:1–18, 35
14:7–11, 32
14:13–16, 32
14:15–16, 44
14:19, 33
14:23–24, 223
14:25–26, 39
14:26–28, 35
14:29, 33
15:3 f., 38
15:7, 33
15:9–25, 37
15:10, 37
15:18, 35
15:23, 33
15:31, 33
16:1–6, 38
16:1–7, 45
16:12, 45
16:19, 43
16:20, 33, 34
16:23–28, 38
17–19, 35
17:2, 105
18:5, 3
18:29, 347
18:36, 347
21, 35, 38, 271–280
21:1–3, 271
21:4, 271
21:7, 272
21:8–10, 272
21:10, 273
21:11–16, 272

21:13, 273
21:15–16, 274
21:16, 275
21:17–24, 45
21:18, 274
22:1–51, 37
22:19, 419
22:22, 419
22:24, 358
22:39, 33
22:42, 37

2 Kings, Book of
1, 35
2–13, 35
2:23–24, 73
2:24, 74
3:2, 43
4:1, 300
4:1–7, 300
8:9, 239
9:1–10, 45
9:25–26, 274
9:26, 275,
10:29–31, 43
12:1–22, 37
12:2, 37
12:5–16, 35
12:19, 35
14:6, 32
14:14, 35
14:23–29, 38
15:1–7, 38
15:2, 38
15:5, 33
15:11, 34
15:15, 34
15:27–31, 38
15:37–16:5, 38
16:2, 390
16:2 ff., 390
16:2–19, 43
16:10–18, 35
16:15, 348
17, 44
17–18, 15
17:7–23, 32

17:23, 32
17:24, 16
18–25, 31
18:3–4, 44
18:3–6, 43
18:8, 39
18:13–20:19, 35
18:16, 35
19:26, 3
19:36–37, 39
20:1–11, 40
20:12–13, 39
20:20, 39
21:1–18, 38
21:2–15, 32
21:3, 371
21:5, 371
21:7, 32
21:10–16, 32
21:21, 43
22–23, 40
22:2, 43
22:3, 343
22:3–7, 35
22:3–23:24, 32
22:12, 343
22:15–20, 32
22:16 f., 32
22:20, 33
23:5, 371
23:8, 57
23:11, 371
23:26, 43
23:26 f., 32
23:27, 32
23:29, 40
24:3, 32
24:3 f., 43
24:13, 35
25:1, 296
25:9–18, 43
25:13–17, 35
25:19, 3
25:22, 343
25:27–30, 36

Isaiah, Book of
1:13, 20
1:13–15, 337
1:24, 3, 7
2:3–4, 27
5:14, 427
6, 348
6:4, 348
7:1 ff., 390
7:5–6, 389
7:13 ff., 390
7:14, 177, 187
8:21, 273
9, 176
9:5, 190–191
11:1, 108
12:2, 307
13:3, 309
17:12–14, 400
17:13, 400, 402
21:8, 154
22:8–11, 39
24, 108
24:5–6, 25
26 f., 108
26:21, 400
27:1, 400
29:1, 414
30, 108
30:8, 239
33:5, 404
33:9–10, 404
33:10, 404
34, 108
34:4, 239
34:7, 7
35:9, 4
36–39, 29
38, 40
38:20, 337
39:1–2, 39
40 ff., 108, 153
46:12, 7
49:26, 3, 7
50:1, 300
50:2, 402
51:1, 405

51:4–8, 405
51:9 ff., 401
51:9–10, 400, 405
51:13, 401
51:15, 401
55:3, 385
56:1–2, 404
56:7, 337
58:13, 19
60:16, 3
61:1–2, 299
66:23, 20

Jeremiah, Book of, 15
3:11, 16
4:16, 105
5:22, 402
7:11, 4
8:2, 372
8:16, 6
17:1, 239
18:21 f., 308
21:1, 36
23:13, 414
23:29, 68, 255
25:11–12, 382
26:1, 282, 283
26:22, 343
26:24, 343
27–29, 281–294
27:1, 281, 282, 283
27:2 ff., 281
27:3, 281, 41
27:6, 63
27:7, 63
27:12, 281,
27:16–22, 281
27:20, 26
28, 39
28:1, 281, 282, 283, 285,
286, 287, 289, 290,
302
28:5, 25, 33
28:6, 25
28:10, 25, 33, 41
28:11, 24, 25, 33, 62
28:12, 25, 33

28:14, 40, 41
28:15, 25, 33
29, 286–287
29:1, 24, 25, 39
29:2,
29:3, 31, 32, 35, 343
29:5 ff., 286
29:10, 382
29:21, 37
29:25, 36
29:28, 286
29:29, 25, 36
29:31, 39
30:3, 16
31:1–19, 16
31:26, 16
31:30, 16
31:35, 401
32:12, 343
32:31, 309
33:7, 16
33:10–11, 397
33:14, 16
33:17, 385
33:21, 385
33:24–26, 16
34, 290, 295–299, 301,
302
34:7, 296
34:8–10, 296, 299
34:8–22, 289, 297
34:9, 298
34:10, 298
34:11, 296, 298
34:12–16, 295
34:13, 297, 299
34:14, 298, 299
34:15, 296, 297
34:16, 296, 298
34:17, 298
34:18, 296, 297, 298
34:18–19, 296
34:20, 298
34:21–22, 296
36:2, 239
36:4, 239
36:10, 343

36:11, 343
36:12, 33, 38, 343
36:25, 343
37:3, 36
37:5–11, 296
39:1, 70, 296
39:14, 343
40:5, 343
41:5, 349
46:15, 7
47:3, 7
49:34 ff., 284
50:11, 7
51, 29
51:59, 289, 67, 343
51:59 ff., 286, 287
51:59–64, 287
52:4, 296

Ezekiel, Book of, 15
2:9, 239
3:17–21, 306
6:13, 11
7:22, 4
7:23, 4
8, 306
8–11, 305
8:15, 306
8:16, 372
8:17, xviii, 305–310
8:18, 307
8:18–9:11, 309
9:1–2, 308
9:9, 306
9:10, 307
11:23, 306
14:12–23, 306
14:14, 412
14:20, 412
16:33 ff., 16
17:11–18, 296
18, 306
18:10, 4
18:25, 306
18:29, 306
22:2, 308
22:6, 404

24:1–2, 296
24:6, 308
24:9, 308
26:21, 425
29:1, 296
29:6–7, 297
30:20–21, 297
33:1–20, 306
33:17, 306
33:20, 306
37:15–28, 16
40:17, 133
45:8, 275
46:13–15, 348
46:17, 299
46:18, 275

Hosea, Book of
2:13, 12, 19
4:1–3, 25
4:13–14, 223
6:9, 308
8:6, 6
10:14, 105

Joel, Book of, 108

Amos, Book of, 15
2:6, 300
4:13, 401
5:5, 225, 56, 58
5:8, 401
5:21–23, 337
6:5, 339
8:4–6, 404
8:5, 17
8:6, 300
8:14, 225
9:6, 401

Obadiah, Book of, 108

Micah, Book of, 108
3:3, 427
4:14, 358

Nahum, Book of, 59

Habakkuk, Book of
2:2, 239
2:5, 427
3:8–15, 400

Zephaniah, Book of, 108
1:5, 371
3:4, 371
3:5, 371
3:17, 371, 372

Zechariah, Book of
1:4, 381
1:12, 382
2:12, 105
3:8, 154
6:5, 419
7:5, 382
7:7, 381
8:22, 27
9:7, 362
14:9, 27

Malachi, Book of, xix
1:11, 21, 350
3:23, 70

Psalms
1, xv
2, 45, 47
3, 357
3:2, 357
3:3, 357
3:4, 357
3:5–7, 357
3:6, 358
3:6–7, 357
3:8, 357–364
3:10, 358
5:4, 347
7:7, 61
7:10, 257
17:8, 105
17:9, 4
18, 42, 47

18:16, 402
18:47–48, 403
18:49, 308
19, xv, xvi, 365–375
19:1, 178
19:1–7, 378
19:2–7, 365, 366–368
19:8 ff., 365, 368–371
19:8–15, 378
20, 41, 46
21, 45, 46
21:14, 403
22:13, 7
23:2, 178
24, 395, 406
24:1–2, 406
29, 406
30, 398
33, 402, 405
37:1, 20
40:8, 239
40:14–18, 378
42, 109
45, 43, 46
46:11, 403
47, 109, 326
48, 395
49:11, 3, 136
50:13, 7
51, 77
51:20 f., 109
54:8, 397
57:8–12, 378
58:7, 358, 362
59:17, 347
60:7–14, 378
62:12, 133
68, 266
68b, 324
68:31, 7
69:10, 154
70, 378
71, 12
72, 9, 45, 47
72:5, 370
72:20, 339
74:3, 400

74:10, 400
74:12, 401, 403
74:12–17, 401
74:13–15, 400
74:16–17, 401
74:18, 400
76:6, 7
77, 344
77:3, 107, 146
78:25, 7
78:51, 213
79, 388
80, 344
81, 345, 395
82:2–5, 405
85, 154
88, 341
88:14, 347
89, xvi, 9, 377–394
89:2–3, 378–380
89:4, 384
89:4–5, 378–380, 385
89:6–19, 378–380
89:9, 3
89:10–13, 401
89:10–14, 405
89:11, 400
89:15, 405.
89:20–21, 387
89:20–38, 377, 378–380,
383–385
89:26, 384
89:27–28, 384
89:29, 389
89:31, 384
89:31 f., 389
89:34–37, 389
89:35–36, 384
89:37, 370
89:39 ff., 378, 379–380,
388
89:40, 384
89:40–45, 389
89:46, 389
89:50, 384, 389
92, xv, 395–410
92:1–4, 405

92:2, 397–398
92:2–4, 347
92:3, 397–398
92:4, 398
92:5, 405
92:5–6, 403, 406
92:8, 398–399, 401, 402–
403, 405, 406
92:9, 403–404, 405
92:10, 23, 399–401, 403,
406
93, 395
93:1, 405
93:1–4, 401
93:2, 405
93:3–4, 405
94, 395
95, 326
96, 326, 340
96:10, 405
97, 326
97:11, 369
98, 326
99, 326
100, 398
100:4–5, 397
101, 45, 47
102, 109
103:16, 427
104, 401–402, 403
104:5, 401
104:6, 105
104:6 ff., 403
104:7, 400, 402
104:9, 402
104:15, 369
104:24, 403
105, 339
105:23, 213
105:27, 213
106, 109, 340
106:20, 5–6
106:22, 213
107, 340
107:42, 369
108, 378
108:6–7, 403

110, 176
118:14, 307
119:74, 369
120, 154
124:6, 362
132, 44, 47
132:2, 3
132:5, 3
132:11, 385
132:11 ff., 383
137, 154, 316, 317, 388
137:3 f., 337
137:4–6, 26
140:12, 308
141:2, 347–348, 350
144:1–11, 41, 47
148, 402
148:5, 402
148:6, 402
148:7, 402
149, 326
149:6–7, 403

Proverbs, Book of
3:3, 239
4:12, 145
7:3, 239
8:22, 401, 403
8:22–29, 402
8:27, 402
8:29, 402
13:9, 369
22:7, 300
25:1, 351

Job, Book of, xv
1:1, 413, 416
1:2, 418
1:3, 411, 412
1:4, 413, 415
1:5, 411, 412, 413, 414,
419
1:6, 413, 416, 418, 419
1:7, 413, 416
1:8, 411, 413, 416, 419
1:9, 419
1:10, 413, 414, 419

1:11, 416, 419
1:12, 413, 416, 419
1:13, 419
1:14, 418
1:14–19, 417
1:15, 412
1:17, 412, 413
1:19, 413
1:20, 413
1:21, 414
1:22, 413, 414, 416, 420
2:1, 413, 416, 418, 419
2:2, 413, 416
2:3, 411, 413, 414, 416, 420
2:4, 413, 414
2:5, 416
2:6, 413, 416
2:7, 414, 416, 419
2:8, 415
2:10, 416
2:11, 411, 413, 414
2:12, 413
2:13, 414, 418
7:10, 427
10:21 f., 425
16:10, 358
18, 425–429
18–19, 425, 426
18:13, 426, 427, 428
18:14, 425, 426, 427, 428
18:15, 425, 427, 428
19:12, 308
20:9, 427–428
22:8, 308
24:17, 425
26:10, 402
26:11, 402
26:12, 401
29:17, 362
38:8–11, 400
38:13, 400
38:15, 400
38:17, 425
42:7, 411
42:8, 411, 412, 413, 418
42:8–10, 411

42:9, 411, 413
42:10, 413, 415
42:11, 412, 413, 414, 419, 420
42:12, 411, 412, 414
42:13, 415, 418
42:14, 420
42:15, 420
42:16, 412
42:17, 412

Song of Songs
6:10, 369

Lamentations, Book of
1:15, 7
3:30, 358
4:18, 145

Ecclesiastes, Book of
1:5, 127
5:1, 144
5:14, 414
49:10, 56

Esther, Book of
9:7, 130

Daniel, Book of
9:2, 382
9:3–19, 347
9:21, 347
9:24–27, 382
10–12, 382
11:14, 4

Ezra, Book of
2:41, 340, 341
2:44, 340
3:2, 338
3:10, 338, 340
7:10, 382
9:5, 347
10:8, 275

Nehemiah, Book of
5:1–13, 302

5:5, 300
7:44, 340, 341
7:47, 340
8:2, 302
9:1, 302
10:32, 302
10:34, 20
11:14, 3
12:24, 338
12:36, 339
12:45–46, 338

Chronicles, Books of, xix, 29, 31, 34, 47

1 Chronicles, Book of
1:7, 145
1:32, 307
3:10–26, 45
4:38–41, 39
4:41–43, 39
5:1, 218
5:25–26, 46
6:16–34, 338
6:18, 341
6:18–23, 341
6:24, 341
6:24–28, 341
6:29, 341
7:8, 307
9:1, 34
9:19, 341
9:34, 341
10, 31
10–29, 29, 31
10:1–4, 46
10:2–14, 42
10:12, 224
11:1, 46
11:3, 46
11:4, 46
11:10, 46
12:24, 46
12:38, 46
15:16–24, 338
15:17, 341
15:19, 341

16, 340
16:39–42, 344
16:40–42, 347
17, 387
17:1, 339
17:3–15, 383–384
17:4, 339
17:7, 387
17:16, 46
20:5, 106
21–26, 46
22:6 ff., 383
22:7–9, 388
22:7–10, 387
22:10, 384
23:5, 339
23:5–6, 338
23:30, 338
23:30–31, 347
23:31, 20
25:1–8, 338
25:5, 341
26:1, 341
26:19, 341
27, 46
28–29:9, 46
28:1 ff., 383
28:1–7, 387
28:3, 388
28:6, 384
28:17, 107, 145
29:29, 34

2 Chronicles, Book of, 29
1–9, 31
2:3, 20

2:30, 39
6:5–9, 383, 387
6:10, 386
7:6, 339
7:26 f., 339
7:29, 339
8:13, 20
8:14, 338
9:29, 34
10–36, 31
11:13 f., 344
11:13–15, 46
12:2–9, 39
12:15, 34
13:2–20, 46
13:5, 385
13:7, 73
13:22, 34
16:11, 34
18:23, 358
20:19, 341
20:34, 34
23:18, 336, 338
24:27, 34
25:7, 46
25:26, 34
26:22, 34
27:7, 34
28, 390
28:1, 390
28:1 ff., 390
28:5 ff., 390
28:26, 34
29–31, 40
29:20, 338, 346
29:25, 338

29:27, 346
31:3, 20
32:28, 39
32:32, 34
34–35, 40
34:8, 343
34:20, 343
35:15, 338
35:20–21, 40
35:26, 34
36:8, 34
36:10, 288
36:21, 295
36:22 f., 45

Judith, Book of
9:1, 349

Luke, Book of
1:10, 350
6:29, 363

1 Maccabees, Book of
3:48, 240

Matthew, Book of
5:38–39, 363

Revelation, Book of
5:8, 350
8:3 f., 350

Song of Solomon, Book of
5, 176

Index

Abominations in Ezekiel 8:17, 305–306
Abrabavel, Isaac, 77, 274
Accuracy, of Spanish biblical texts, 103–104, 144, 244
Adler, Cyrus, 189, 191
Al-Balkhi, Hiwi, 151
Al-Fasi, David ben Abraham, 101
Albright, W.F., 5, 317
Alexander, Egypt, Museum Library in, 62–63, 63–64, 243
Alt, 5, 420
Amarna letters, 428
"American Judaism," 174
Anticipatory use of information, literary device, 211–219
Arab influence on Medieval Spain, 85–86
Arabic language, 85, 101–103
Aramaic language, 101–103, 255–256, 316
Asher, Aaron ben Moses ben, 248, 264
Asher, Judah ben, 87
Ashur, Assyria, library in, 59
Authority, 17, 234, 271–272, 325
Authorship of Psalms, 314, 339–340
'Azriel, R. Abraham ben, 94

Baal, 6, 399
Babylon, influence on Medieval Spain, 83–84
Bacher, Wilhelm, 382
Bag-Bag, Ben, 68
Barr, James, 224
Barth, J., 4

Beer-sheba, 222, 225, 344
Ben-Yehuda, 3
Berit, 231–232, 233
Bible
    multiplicity of meaning, 255
    ordering of books, 64–65
    translations and versions
        Dobson, 180
        JPS 1917 translation, 186–194
        JPS 1982 translation, 197–202
        King James Version, 176–177, 190
        Lesser translation, 175–180
        Samaritan Pentateuch, 169–170
        Septuagint, 169–170, 256
        Targum, 256, 415
Biblical law, 229–236
Biblical scholarship in America, the rise of, 182–185, 194–195
Biblical studies and Jüdishe Wissenschaft, 162, 163, 164, 183
Blasphemy, 272–273
Bonfils, Joseph ben Eliezer, 155
Book making, history of, 239–241
Books, "uncorrected," 243
Buddle, K., 4
Bull/bull-god, and divine title, 4–8
Buttenwieser, Moses, 313, 315, 319, 330

Canaan, Canaanites, 13–14, 14–15, 328
Cassuto, Umberto, 401, 412, 418, 426
Cheek, slapping of the, 357–361
Cheyne, T.K., 395

Chiasmus, literary device, 147
Chiquitilla, Isaac ben, 95
Christian, Christianity
    approach to Scriptures study, 69
    and Jewish biblical studies in America, 179–180
    King James version, 190
    translations, 253–254
    use of the codex, 240–241
Civil death, 276
Clan guilds, 340–342
Codex, 57–58, 240–241
Codex Hilleli, 244–248
Combat epic, and creation, 401, 403
Commentary, compared to translation, 253–258
Commentators, 260
Cooke, Gerald, 391
Corruption of blood, 276–277
Covenant, 23–24, 231–232, 233
Creation and Sabbath, 398–404
Cult-functional school, and Psalms, 320–321, 322, 327

David, and authorship of Psalms, 314, 339–340
David, as dynastic symbol, in the Bible, 41
David, Judah ben, 95
De Wette, Wilhelm M.L., 161
Dead Sea Scrolls, 382. *See also* Qumran
Decalogue
    comparison to Hittite treaties, 231–232
    moral ideals prior to, 229–230
    royal authority, 234
Delmedigo, Joseph Solomon, 155
Dhorme, 415
Divine freedom, 17–18
Divine title, 3–8, 224
dmr, Semitic root, 307–308
Dobson, Thomas, 180
Driver, S.R., 72
Duhm, B., 316, 411
Dürr, L., 365

'Eben Bohan (Solomon), 93–94

Egypt, archives and libraries in pre-Hellenistic, 61
Eichorn, Johann Gottfried, 161, 162
Eissfeldt, 5
Eleazer, Jacob ben, 245
Eleazer, R. Jonathon ben, 77
Elem, Joseph ben Eliezer Tov, 260
Ellipsis, literary device, 92, 104, 105, 146
Enthronement celebrations, 326, 327
Evil, 22, 233
Ewald, Heinrich, 415
Exegesis
    Franco-German, 93
    historical, 107–109
    inner-biblical, 69–70
    rabbinic, 68-69, 76-78, 148, 179
    textual, 103–107
    types of, 109–116, 142
"Eye for an eye," 363

Finkelstein, J.J., 295
Finley, M.I., 74
Forfeiture of property, 271–277
Form-critical school, and Psalms, 320, 327
Freedom, divine, 17–18
Fürst, J., 246

Gamaliel, Rabbi Simeon ben, 256
Gans, Eduard, 164
Gaon, Hai, 83, 101
Gattungsforschung (Gunkel), 319
Geiger, Abraham, 161–172
Geography of Israel, 13–14
Gersonides, 274
Gesenius, 415
Ginsberg, H.L., 369, 382, 399
Ginsburg, C.D., 246
God, conceptions of, 17–18
Gordon, Cyrus H., 295, 412
Graetz, Heinrich, 163, 246, 395
Greek translation
    of the Bible, 243 (*See also* Septuagint)
    of Psalms, 318, 339
Greenberg, Moshe, 201, 202, 262–263
Greenfield, Jonas C., 201, 202, 262–263, 369
Gunkel, Hermann, 5, 318, 319–323, 397, 401

Ha-Galili, R. Eliezer ben Yose, 104
Ha-Kohen, Rabbi Meir, 144, 244
Ha-Levi, Judah, 102
Ha-Meiri, Menahem, 246, 248
Hacket, Jo Ann, 362
Hanokh, R. Moses ben, 83
Hayyim, Jacob ben, 69
Hayyuj, Judah ben David, 88, 96, 97, 102, 143
He-Hasid, Rabbi Judah, 261
Hebrew language
    Arabic, 85–86, 101–103
    Aramaic, 101–103
    comparative studies, 101–103
    daily usage, 87, 143, 316
    Dead Sea Scrolls and Masada finds, 329
    difficulties in translations, 253–255
    expansion, 88–89
    inadequacy of biblical, 86–87
    teaching of, in America, 181
Herder, Johann Gottfried, 162
Hertz, J.H., 262
Herzfeld, Levi, 163
Hilleli manuscript, 244–248
History, in the Bible, 36–37
History of the Religion of Israel (Kaufmann), 167
Hittite treaties, and the Decalogue, 231–232
Hoffmann, G., 5
Hofni, Samuel ben, 77, 83, 104, 151, 260
Horwitz, Jonathan, 180, 181
Huehnergard, John, 362

ibn Bal'am, Judah ben Samuel, 3, 90, 98–99
ibn Baron, Isaac, 99, 102
Ibn Benveniste. *See* ibn Baron
ibn Chiquitilla, Moses, 87, 90, 98, 153–154, 315
ibn Danan, Sa'adiah ben Maimun, 91
ibn Daud, Abraham, 87, 143
ibn 'Ezra, Abraham ben Meir, 84, 88, 91, 99–101, 100, 139, 259, 260, 415
ibn 'Ezra, Moses, 99
ibn Gabirol, Solomon, 88, 91, 154
ibn Hagar, David, 99
ibn Janah, Jonah, 3–4, 84, 87, 88, 91, 96–97, 105, 151, 244

ibn Kafron, Ephraim, 95
ibn Kamnial, Abraham ben Meir, 99
ibn Labrat, Dunash, 83, 90, 94–95, 95, 100, 102
ibn Nagrela, Samuel, 91, 97–98
ibn Parchon, Solomon, 3–4, 87
ibn Quraish, Judah, 93, 101, 102
ibn Shaprut, Hisdai, 86
ibn al-Tabban, Levi, 90, 99
ibn Tamim, Dunash, 101
ibn Tibbon, Judah, 143
ibn Yashush, Isacc, 99
Iggeret ha-Shabbat (Ibn 'Ezra), 149, 151
Immanuel of Rome, 266
Incense-offering, 349–350
Integration of disparte elements, literary device, 377–378
Interfaith movement, and biblical studies, 195
International affairs, and the Monarchy, 39–40
Irwin, William A., 425
Ishmael, Rabbi, school of, 255
Israel, as God's people, in the Bible, 41
Israel, geography of, 13–14
Israel, Israel ben Isaac ben, 248

Jacob, Benno, 222
Jacobs, Joseph, 163
Jastrow, Marcus, 188
Jellinek, A., 246
Jerusalem and its Temple, as God's chosen place, in the Bible, 42
Jewish-Christian relations in America, 179–180, 192–193
Jewish Publication Society
    1917 translation of the Bible, 186–194
    1982 translation of the Bible, 197–202
    Commentary, 262–266
Jewish scholarship, in America and Israel, 194, 195–196, 202
Jewish studies in secular institutions, 197
Jewish Theological Seminary, 248
Jews, as biblical and Hebrew experts, 181–182
Jews, as biblical experts, 182
Jost, Isaac Marcus, 163

Judah, 16
Judah, Rabbi, 225, 255
"Judaism, American," 174
Jüdische Wissenschaft, 162, 163, 164, 183

Kabbalah, 115
Kallir, Eleazer, 144
Kapelrud, 5
Kara, Joseph, 134
Karaites, 93, 101, 148–149, 151–152
Kashrut, 261
Kaufmann, Yehezkel, 167, 317–318, 336,
    382–383
Kautzsch, 411
Kennett, R.H., 316
Kimhi, David, 72–73, 77, 222, 260, 274,
    361–362, 415
King ideology of Israel, 325
King James Version, 176–177, 190
King's authority and the Decalogue, 234,
    271–272
Kitab 'al-Istighna (Ibn Nagrela), 97
Kitab 'Al-Luma' (Ibn Janah), 97
Kitab 'Al-Mustalhaq (Ibn Janah), 97
Kitab 'al Muwazana (Ibn Baron), 102
Kitab 'al Tadhkir w'al-Ta'anith (Ibn Chiq-
    uitilla), 98
Kitab 'al-Usul (Ibn Janah), 97
Kittel, Rudolf, 264
Kohler, Kaufmann, 190
Kraus, H.J.
Kuzari (Ha-Levi), 102

Lakish, Resh, 225
Leeham, Rabbi Saul, 201
Leon, and Hilleli manuscript, 247
Lesser, Isaac, 175–180
Lesser translation, 175–180
Levine, Baruch, 263
Levita, Elijah, 104, 144, 244, 246
Libraries in the Ancient World
    Alexander, Egypt, 62–63, 63–64
    Ashur, Assyria, 59
    Egypt, pre-Hellenistic, 61
    Mari, Syria, 58–59
    Messenia, Greece, 62
    Nineveh, Assyria, 59–60, 62

Qumran (*See separate entry*)
    Ras Shamra-Urgarit, Syria, 61–62
    Ur, Sumeria, 58
Liebreich, 396
Loewe, R., 74
Luther, B., 5

Maarsen, 395
Maccabean theory, of Psalm authorship,
    316, 318
Mahberet (Menahem), 92–93, 94, 98
Maimonides, Moses, 75, 150, 259
Manumission, 296–302
Margolis, Max L., 189, 191
Mari, Syria, library in, 58–59
Meir, Samuel ben (RaShBam), 77, 151,
    211–212, 259, 260
Mendelssohn, Moses, 162, 176
Messenia, Greece, library in, 62
Meyer, Edward, 381–382
Milgrom, Jacob, 263
Miller, P.D., 5
Monarchy, history of in the Bible, 29–52
Monarchy authority, limitations on, 234,
    271–272, 325
Monotheism vs. polytheism, 15–17
Moser, Moses, 163
Moskoni, Judah Leon ben Moses, 154–155
Mowinckel, Sigmund, 6, 317, 320–324,
    326, 397
Music guilds and Psalms, 335–351
Music in ancient Near East, 342–344
Myth and ritual school, 317, 320
Mythology, 19–21, 418–420, 425–428

Naboth the Jezreelite, 271–272
Nahmanides (RaMBaN), 72, 74, 77, 259,
    350, 415
Nationhood, 24–26
Near Eastern religious literature, 15, 365–
    372
Nehemian, R., 70, 225
Neuman, Abraham, 191
New Year festivals, 323, 326, 327, 360, 377
Nineveh, library in, 59–60, 62
Norzi, Jedidiah Solomon, 104, 144, 244, 247
Numbers, literary device of, 418

Oppenheim, A. Leo, 335
Orlinsky, Harry, 197–198, 198–200

Paganism
rise of monotheism over, 13–28
transformation from, 71, 226, 323, 336, 372
Palestine, influence on Medieval Spain, 83–84
Paltoi, Semah ben, 83
Parallelism, 92
Parchment, as writing material, 63
Peshat, 75–76
Pfeiffer, R.H., 316, 336
Philipson, David, 189, 190
da Piera, Meshullam ben Solomon, 89
Plaut, Rabbi W. Gunther, 262
Pleonasm, literary device, 92
Polytheism vs. monotheism, 15–17
Pope, M., 5
Potok, Chaim, 201, 262
Property, forfeiture of convicted criminal's, 271–277
Prophecy and history, 45
Psalms, authorship, 314, 339–340
Psalms, enthronement and royal, 321, 322–324

Qumran, 55–56, 169, 314, 318, 329, 339

von Rad, Gehard, 219
Ras Shamra-Ugarit, Syria, library in, 61–62
Rashi, 77, 93, 127–138, 151, 259, 260, 274, 361, 415
Rebellion, Jer. 27-29, dating the plotted, 281–290
Reform Judaism, 194, 262
Repetition, literary device, 148, 380, 416
Rozenberg, Rabbi Martin, 201
Ryle, H.E., 72

Sa'adiah, 83, 93, 94, 100, 101, 104, 151
Sabbath
and creation, 398–404
and the cult, 396–397
socio-moral theme of, 404–405
Sabbatical year, 295–302

Sacrifices, animal, 348–349, 412
Samaritan Pentateuch, 169–170
Šamaš, and Psalm XIX, 365–372
Sambari, Joseph ben Isaac, 247
Sarna, Nahum M., 262
Saruq, Menahem ben, 84, 86–87, 90, 92–94, 94–95, 95, 102, 104, 261
Scholem, Gershom, 68, 257
Schroeder, O., 365
Scribes, scribal schools, 35, 242–243, 244
Scrolls, 55–56, 241–242
Sefer ha-Mafteah (Ibn al-Tabban), 99
Sefer ha-Melakhim (Ibn Hagar), 99
Sefer ha-Serufim (Ibn Yashush), 99
Sefer Yesirah, 84
Semetic language, comparative studies, 101–103
Semetic studies, 184–185
Septuagint, 169–170, 256
Shapira, Abraham, 361
Shapiro, Rabbi David, 201
Sheshet, Yehudi ben, 95
Shestak, Jerome J., 262–263
Shrines, 344
Sitz-im-Leben, 319, 323, 324, 338
Skinner, J., 4–5, 72
Slaves, Zedekiah's emancipation of, 295–302
Smiting the cheek, 357–361
Snaith, 397
Solomon, ben Menahem, 93, 261
Soncino series, 262
Sorcery, sorcerers, 321
Spanish biblical texts, accuracy of, 103–104, 144, 244
Speiser, E.A., 222
Spiegel, 412, 419, 420
Spinoza, Benedict, 152, 315
Steinschneider, Moritz, 163
Substitution, literary device, 105–106, 145–146
Sulzberger, 189
Sun-God literature, Near Eastern, and Psalm XIX, 365–372

Tajnis (Ibn Bal'am), 99
Talmud studies, in America, 194

Tam, Jacob ben Meir, 93
Targum, 256, 415
Teeth, breaking of, 357–361
Temple singers, 336, 338–339
Tetragrammata, heptad of, 406
Thanksgiving Scroll, 318
Theodore of Mopsuestia, 315
Tigay, Jeffrey, 263
Title, divine, 3–8, 224
Toledo, Spain, 244–245, 248
Tractatus Theologico-Politicus (Spinoza),
    152
Translation, compared to commentary,
    253–258
Transposition, literary device, 147
Treaty, or *berit,* and the Decalogue, 231–233
Trees, 70, 221–223
Tur-Sinai, N. H., 6, 370, 411

Ugaritic
    epics, 412
    language and Hebrew, 328–329
    text, and Psalm 92, 399
Universality, of monotheism, 26–28
Ur, Sumeria, library in, 58
Urschrift (Geiger), 168

Vawter, 6

Ward, J.M., 390–391
Weiser, Arthur, 327
Wellhausen, Julius, 316, 411
Wellhausen school of Biblical Higher Criti-
    cism, 315–316, 319
Wisdom of Ben Sira, 318
Wolf, Immanuel, 164
Women in epic literature, 415, 420–421

Yerushalmi, Tanhum ben Joseph, 261,
    262–263
YHWH, heptad of, 406
Yose, R., 350

Zacuto, Rabbi Abraham ben Samuel, 244–
    245
Zeitgeschichtliche approach, 319
Zenodotus, 55
Zionist movement, and biblical studies, 195
Zunz, Leopold, 162, 164